S0-BEP-653

CLASS

GOODYEAR

AUTOCOURSE

The World's Leading Grand Prix Annual

HAZLETON PUBLISHING

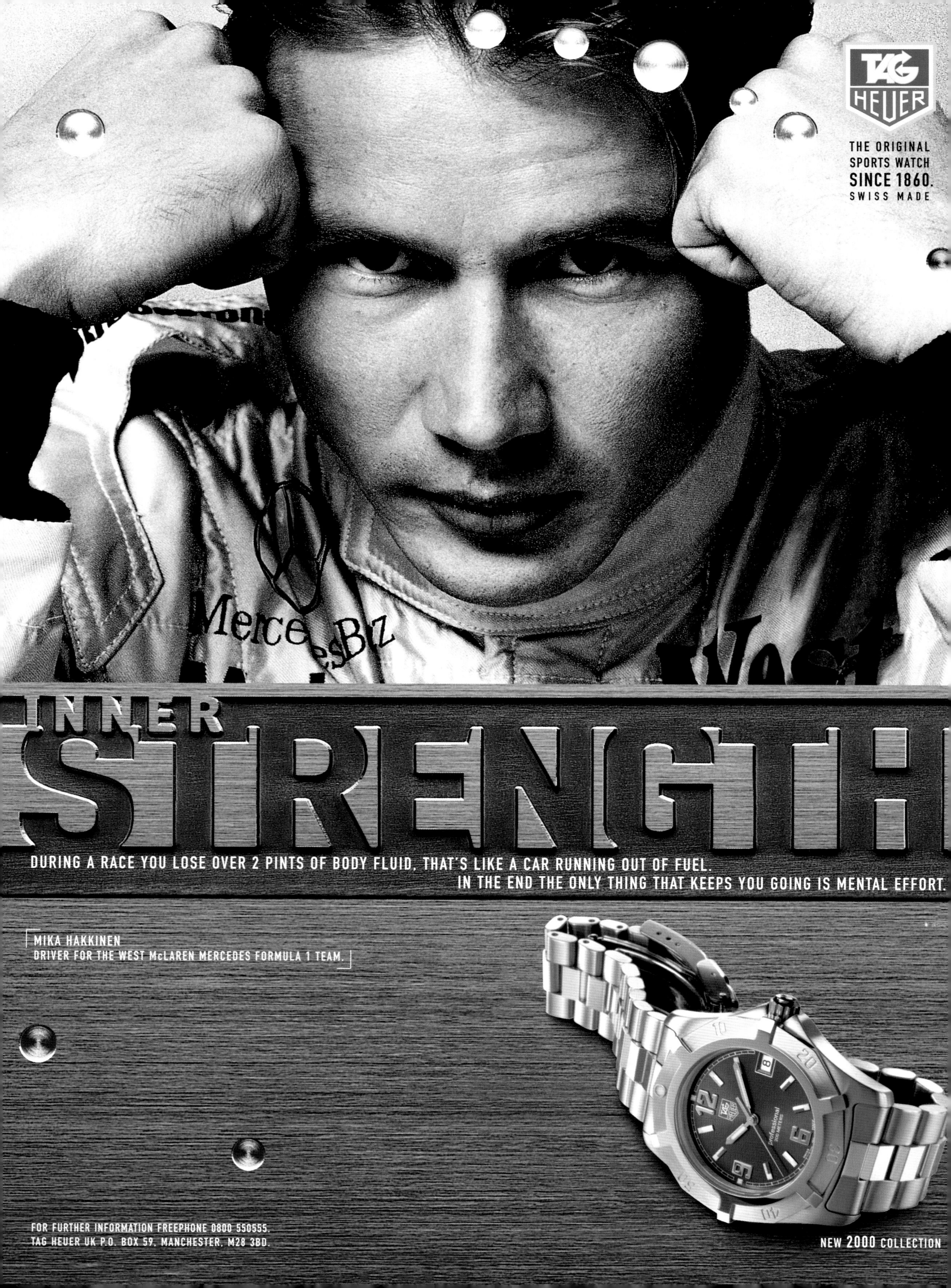

TAG HEUER

THE ORIGINAL
SPORTS WATCH
SINCE 1860.
SWISS MADE

INNER
STRENGTH

DURING A RACE YOU LOSE OVER 2 PINTS OF BODY FLUID, THAT'S LIKE A CAR RUNNING OUT OF FUEL.
IN THE END THE ONLY THING THAT KEEPS YOU GOING IS MENTAL EFFORT.

MIKA HAKKINEN
DRIVER FOR THE WEST McLAREN MERCEDES FORMULA 1 TEAM.

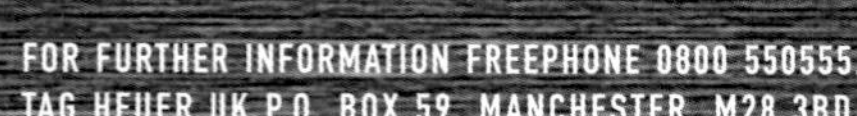

NEW 2000 COLLECTION

contents

AUTOCOURSE 1998-99
is published by Hazleton Publishing Ltd, 3 Richmond Hill, Richmond, Surrey TW10 6RE.

Colour reproduction by Barrett Berkeley Ltd, London.

Printed in England by Butler and Tanner Ltd, Frome, Somerset.

© Hazleton Publishing Ltd 1998. No part of this publication may be reproduced, stored in a retrieval system or transmitted, in any form or by any means, electronic, mechanical, photocopying, recording or otherwise, without prior permission in writing from Hazleton Publishing Ltd.

ISBN: 1-874557-43-8

DISTRIBUTORS

UNITED KINGDOM
Biblios Ltd
Star Road
Partridge Green
West Sussex RH13 8LD
Telephone: 01403 710971
Fax: 01403 711143

NORTH AMERICA
Motorbooks International
PO Box 1
729 Prospect Ave.
Osceola
Wisconsin 54020, USA
Telephone: (1) 715 294 3345
Fax: (1) 715 294 4448

AUSTRALIA
Technical Book and
Magazine Co. Pty
295 Swanston Street
Melbourne
Victoria 3000
Telephone: (03) 9663 3951
Fax: (03) 9663 2094

NEW ZEALAND
David Bateman Ltd
PO Box 100-242
North Shore Mail Centre
Auckland 1330
Telephone: (9) 415 7664
Fax: (9) 415 8892

SOUTH AFRICA
Motorbooks
341 Jan Smuts Avenue
Craighall Park
Johannesburg
Telephone: (011) 325 4458/60
Fax: (011) 325 4146

publisher
RICHARD POULTER

editor
ALAN HENRY

managing editor
PETER LOVERING

art editor
STEVE SMALL

production manager
STEVEN PALMER

publishing development manager
SIMON MAURICE

business development manager
SIMON SANDERSON

sales promotion
CLARE KRISTENSEN

production assistant
IMOGEN McINTYRE

results and statistics
DAVID HAYHOE
NICK HENRY

f1 illustrations
IAN HUTCHINSON
NICOLA FOX

chief contributing photographers
ALLSPORT
DIANA BURNETT
PAUL-HENRI CAHIER
PETER NYGAARD
MATTHIAS SCHNEIDER
NIGEL SNOWDON
SUTTON MOTORSPORT IMAGES
BRYN WILLIAMS

acknowledgements

The Editor of AUTOCOURSE wishes to thank the following for their assistance in compiling the 1998-99 edition: **Belgium:** Didier Coton; **France:** ACO, Fédération Française du Sport Automobile, FIA (Bernie Ecclestone, Max Mosley, Francesco Longanesi-Cattani, Alistair Watkins, Charlie Whiting and Herbie Blash), Mecachrome, Peugeot Sport (Jean-Claude Lefebvre), Prost F1 (Alain Prost, Sophie Sicot and Marie-Pierre Dupasquier); **Germany:** Formel 3 Vereinigung, Mercedes-Benz (Norbert Haug and Wolfgang Schattling); **Great Britain:** Gary Anderson, Arrows (Tom Walkinshaw, Daniele Audetto, Ann Bradshaw, Christine Goreham, Jackie Oliver and Mike Coughlan), *Autocar*, John Barnard, Martin Brundle, Colin Burr, Timothy Collings, Bob Constanduros, Cosworth Engineering, Steve Cropley, Edelman PR (Jean-Claude Torchia, Agnès Carlier, Graham Jones and Victoria Mizen), Kay Edge, John Fitzpatrick, Ford (Neil Ressler, Martin Whitaker, Ellen Kolby and Steve Madinca), Peter Foubister, Mike Greasley, Maurice Hamilton, Brian Hart and Jane Brace, Nick Henry, Ian Hutchinson, Ilmor Engineering (Mario Illien), Jordan Grand Prix (Eddie Jordan, Ian Phillips, Giselle Davies, Mike Gascoyne and Lindsay Haylett), McLaren International (Ron Dennis, Adrian Newey, Justine Blake, Anna Guerrier, Neil Oatley, Steve Nichols, Peter Stayner and Stuart Wingham), Chas Parker, Stan Piecha, Eric Silverman, Silverstone Circuits, Stewart Grand Prix (Jackie and Paul Stewart, Alan Jenkins and Cameron Kellaher), Simon Taylor, Tyrrell Racing Organisation (Craig Pollock, Harvey Postlethwaite and Rupert Manwaring), Murray Walker, Professor Sid Watkins, Williams Grand Prix Engineering (Jane Gorard, Patrick Head, James Robinson, Dickie Stanford, Lindsay Morle, Ffiona Welford and Frank Williams), Eoin Young; **Italy:** Benetton Formula (David Richards, Pat Symonds, Nick Wirth, David Warren, Andrea Ficarelli, Julia Horden and Luca Mazzoco), Commissione Sportiva Automobilistica Italiana, Scuderia Ferrari (Ross Brawn, Claudio Berro, Antonio Ghini, Stefania Bocci and Jean Todt), Minardi Team (Giancarlo Minardi and Silvia Frangipane), Giorgio Piola; **Japan:** Bridgestone (Hirohide Hamashima and Jane Parisi de Lima); **Switzerland:** Sauber (Gustav Busing and Peter Sauber); **USA:** CART, Daytona International Speedway; Goodyear (Stu Grant, Tony Shakespeare, Perry Bell and Dermot Bambridge); Indianapolis Motor Speedway, Indy Lights, NASCAR, Roger Penske.

photographs published in Autocourse 1998-99 have been contributed by:

Allsport UK/Michael Cooper/Stu Forster/Mike Hewitt/Clive Mason/Pascal Rondeau/Mark Thompson, *Allsport USA*/David Taylor, Gérard Berthoud, Bothwell Photographic, Michael C. Brown, Diana Burnett, Paul-Henri Cahier, Dave Cundy, Jon Eisberg, Steve Etherington/*EPI*, Lukas Gorys, *GP Photo*/Peter Nygaard, W.P. Johnson/*At Speed Photographic*, Nigel Kinrade, *LAT Photographic*, Pamela Lauesen/*FOSA*, *Minardi Team*/Ph. Colombo, John Overton, *Publiracing Agency*/Manfred Giet, Darren Price, Michael Roberts, Matthias Schneider, Simon Scott, *Shutterspeed Photografik*, *Sportsphoto/SIPA Press*, Nigel Snowdon, *Sporting Pictures (UK) Ltd*, *Sutton Motorsport Images*, Bryn Williams.

Dust-jacket photograph:
World Champion Mika Häkkinen
by Sutton Motorsport Images

Title page photograph:
Michael Schumacher
by Bryn Williams

MOËT
BRUT IMPÉRIAL
BRUT IMPÉRIAL
MOËT & CHANDON
CHAMPAGNE
BRUT
EPERNAY FRANCE
75cl
FONDE EN 1743

Sutton Motorsport Images

foreword

by Mika Häkkinen

EVER since I started competing in Formula 1 in 1991 I have seen a considerable number of race tracks and a wide variety of countries and international cities. Grand Prix motor racing is first and foremost a people business and all those involved sacrifice a huge part of their lives to be involved in the sport. That is why, on the occasion of my first World Championship, I want to thank everybody at the West McLaren Mercedes team – and all its partners – for the unstinting help and support they have offered me throughout my title battle.

I have been a member of the McLaren family ever since joining as test driver in 1993 and during that time I have seen the team consistently raising its levels of commitment and professionalism to the heights which have enabled us to compete successfully in this year's World Championship. I have a very strong relationship with everybody in the team from Ron Dennis down. Ron is a great leader as well as a friend and a man who cares deeply about the success of the company.

I also want to use this opportunity to thank the people immediately around me, including my wife Erja and my manager Keke Rosberg – who knows all about this World Championship business! – for their support, guidance and affection. I look forward to defending my World Championship in 1999 and I would like to think I may be back here writing the AUTOCOURSE foreword this time next year. Who can tell?

THE FLYING FINN

Former McLaren driver Jochen Mass stands at attention and gives a mock salute as Bernie Ecclestone cruises down the Hungaroring paddock in a chauffeur-driven limo. The tense battle for the World Championship between Michael Schumacher and Mika Häkkinen ensured that public interest in Formula 1 remained at an all-time high, and Ecclestone's massive investment in digital television looks set to reap huge dividends in the future.

...LET ME

BY any objective standards, the battle for the 1998 FIA Formula 1 World Championship was an outstandingly high quality contest, which lasted all the way to the final race of the year in Japan. Mika Häkkinen's early-season victories in Australia and Brazil at the wheel of the superbly engineered Bridgestone-shod McLaren MP4/13-Mercedes may have convinced many on the touchlines that the title contest would be little more than a formality, but the Anglo-German alliance was taking absolutely nothing for granted. Making hay while the sun shone early on in the season was certainly no luxury. In retrospect, it was a necessity.

The opposition may have taken two or three races to sort itself out, but once the Ferrari/Goodyear challenge gelled it provided Michael Schumacher with a base from which to launch a ferocious counter-attack against the Silver Arrows' initial domination.

Maranello's sporting director Jean Todt may have taken a risk stating that winning the World Championship was the only satisfactory outcome for the legendary Italian team, but it came close enough to survive with honour intact and Todt – nicknamed 'Napoleon' in some quarters – did not have to take a place in the executioner's tumbril.

Despite failing in its declared ambition, Ferrari could certainly reflect on a job well done in terms of consolidating its credibility as a consistently effective F1 force. In absolute terms the McLarens may have been quicker throughout the year, but speed is only part of the package. If Häkkinen had lost the championship it could have rightly been blamed on the fact that McLaren did not quite produce the bullet-proof mechanical reliability displayed by its key opposition.

Yet at the end of the day everything came right for the quiet, introspective 30-year-old Finn. Häkkinen was a shrewd operator who thoroughly deserved to win the World Championship. For the most part, not only did he drive beautifully, but he had the lucky knack of keeping clear of anything which might look vaguely like a pseudo-political controversy.

Even when McLaren was locked in a tense exchange of views with Ferrari over the legality of certain elements on its cars, Häkkinen seemed to remain personally insulated from the dispute. This had much to do with his considerable popularity within the F1 community. Not only has he been highly rated for some years, but the manner in which he fought back to fitness after that life-threatening accident during practice for the 1995 Australian Grand Prix has also been a source of additional respect and admiration.

The mutual sense of loyalty displayed by McLaren and Häkkinen has been a particularly attractive aspect of the aftermath of this near-tragedy. Mika has been the team's favourite son ever since, a reality which has made it slightly difficult for David Coulthard to penetrate the team's emotional heart, although not its technical and strategic soul.

For all that, Schumacher remains the driver of his generation, yet again displaying that fiery blend of precision and a dash of unpredictability which makes him such an audacious competitor. Sure enough, he made two key mistakes in colliding with David Coulthard's McLaren at Spa-Francorchamps and stalling on the line at Suzuka, but he basically did wonders with a car which was not quite as good as the McLaren. And for that he deserves bonus points.

With Coulthard's sole victory added to Häkkinen's eight wins, the McLaren-Mercedes combo won nine of the 16 races, leaving six to fall to Schumacher's Ferrari and a single, highly popular triumph in Belgium for Damon Hill and the Jordan-Mugen Honda squad.

Jordan's rise from early-season disarray to a level where it was a consistent and regular points-scorer sent an optimistic signal to aspirant teams still struggling to make their mark. Yet whether it is possible for constructors such as Jordan ever to match the competitive pitch of McLaren, Ferrari and – until this year – Williams remains a matter for conjecture.

It took McLaren four years to rebuild its winning base in partnership with Mercedes-Benz from a level where it was a top-six finisher, but no longer a regular contender for victory. The sort of massive effort McLaren and Mercedes have deployed is probably only available to Ferrari and Williams at the present time and the latter will have a chance to demonstrate its powers of recovery when it teams up with BMW, which is to be its engine supplier from the start of the 2000 season.

Certainly, McLaren's avowed intent when it embarked on its partnership with Mercedes was to rekindle the level of domination it enjoyed with Honda from 1988 to '91. It believes that 1999 will prove that it is back on that level.

The rule makers again sought to put a brake on F1 lap speeds in 1998, introducing a new breed of narrow-track car running on grooved tyres. It was effective as far as it went, although much of the on-paper speed reduction was cancelled out by the intensity of the tyre war between Bridgestone and Goodyear. Had it not been for these changes, however, it is clear that lap speeds would have spiralled dangerously out of control.

The popularity of international Grand Prix racing remained remarkable with Bernie Ecclestone making plans for the sport to be in pole position for the forthcoming digital television revolution, although his monopoly on F1 television rights has continued to attract the questioning – and certainly very protracted – scrutiny of EU competition commissioner Karel van Miert. His deliberations have yet to reach any concrete or formally published conclusion on these matters.

The 1998 season was good for Ecclestone and the competing teams because a new Concorde Agreement was finally approved, signed, sealed and delivered. Frank Williams and Ron Dennis had stood out against signing in 1997 because they considered the other competing teams had failed to understand precisely what intellectual property rights they were signing away. Eventually a new deal was formalised which should provide between $9 million and $23 million in annual television revenue for the 11 competing teams, which will become 12 when Honda's works operation joins in at the start of 2000.

The massive push for F1 success by Mercedes-Benz was not achieved at the expense of the German company's participation in other categories. The AMG Merc team dominated the FIA GT series, but the company's CART programme spearheaded by the factory Penskes was

GP Photo/Peter Nygaard

ENTERTAIN YOU!

a disappointment and the works Le Mans effort was downright embarrassing, with Porsche clinching the one sports car victory on the international calendar which really mattered.

The International F3000 series continued to be an excellent feeder formula, increasingly as a support event on European Grand Prix programmes. Juan Pablo Montoya took the title after a season-long battle with Nick Heidfeld, but in 1999 it will be '97 champion Ricardo Zonta, who this year proved himself an adept and capable GT competitor as well as an impressive McLaren test driver, who graduates to F1 with the new British American Racing organisation, which is set to rise like a phoenix from the ashes of the sadly defunct Tyrrell team.

In the USA the CART series continued to thrive with F1's most famous expat Alex Zanardi retaining the championship in Chip Ganassi's Reynard-Honda. His team-mate Jimmy Vasser took second place in the series, but the new star of the show was Dario Franchitti in Team Green's Reynard-Honda, the young Scot coming alive as a top contender as the season wore on. In 1999 Zanardi follows Jacques Villeneuve's tracks and heads for F1 with Williams. Will we see Franchitti doing the same in 2000?

Looking to the future, there seems little doubt that Formula 1 will continue to expand outside Europe despite continuing evidence of economic meltdown in the Far East. China and Malaysia have been included as provisional dates on the 1999 World Championship calendar. South Africa has allegedly been promised a fixture soon and a United States GP on a new road circuit at Indianapolis – symbolically using a small section of the famous oval – is hotly tipped to join the schedule, possibly as early as 2000.

With the tobacco companies continuing in their role as F1's most significant financial investors, Bernie Ecclestone and Max Mosley are clearly intending that the sport should seek new races in areas of the world where limitations on tobacco advertising are not as draconian and restrictive as they have become within the European Union.

On a purely pragmatic level, it is clear that Ecclestone, now 68 years old, is keen to realise some of the equity which he has built up over 25 years spent overseeing F1's commercial expansion. His decision to raise an estimated $1.5 billion by selling F1 bonds secured against future digital television rights tends to suggest that he is looking for fresh areas of business expansion which may yield to his magical, if autocratic, touch.

With a new Concorde Agreement in place, F1's commercial prosperity seems safely wrapped up for the foreseeable future. At a time when most people would be reaching for their slippers and bus pass, Bernie could now be aiming to conquer pastures new. How that might affect the future development of Formula 1 in the longer term is a matter of abiding fascination, if not a little concern.

Alan Henry
Tillingham, Essex
November 1998

Goodyear bowed off the Grand Prix stage at the end of the 1998 World Championship season with its reputation as Formula One racing's most successful ever tyre company enhanced and unchallenged. With a total of 368 Grand Prix victories achieved since Richie Ginther's Honda set the ball rolling with Goodyear's first F1 win at Mexico City in 1965, the company not only mastered the new grooved tyre regulations which were introduced in 1998 but played a central role in helping Michael Schumacher carry Ferrari's challenge for the title all the way to the final race in Japan.

Opposite page: The brilliance of Michael Schumacher aided in no small measure by the intensive development of Goodyear's programme took him to a breathtaking win in Hungary. His six victories for Ferrari in 1998 helped push Goodyear's number of Grand Prix wins to 368. An astonishing total which may never be surpassed.

Left: The Jordan crew with fuel and new Goodyear Eagles at the ready, wait to execute a pit stop.

When motor racing's governing body, the FIA, announced that grooved tyres would be introduced in 1998 as a means of keeping F1 lap times under control, Goodyear viewed this as a stimulating technical challenge even though the decision was taken to suspend its F1 participation at the end of that season. The introduction of grooved dry weather tyres was certainly something of a turning point in contemporary F1 history, bringing to an end the 27-year era of the 'slick' dry tyre which was originally pioneered by Goodyear in 1971 at the French Grand Prix when Jackie Stewart used them to win with his Tyrrell-Ford.

Making the best of the new regulations also called for some considerable technical ingenuity, balancing the need for tread stability against the requirement for as soft and competitive a tyre compound as would be needed to beat the competition.

While supplying the World Championship-winning slicks to Jacques Villeneuve and the Williams team throughout 1997, Goodyear also collaborated with Williams on the development of prototype grooved tyres in preparation for 1998 and these were tested on an on-going basis from as early as May 1997.

In August 1997 Goodyear's racing division was undergoing a major reorganisation in an effort to enhance its competitive product. Much work had gone into optimising rubber compounds for their slick tyres, but the introduction of the new rules generated fresh challenges and it took some time to match suitable compounds and constructions for the grooved tyres, which meant that Goodyear was at a slight disadvantage at the start of the 1998 season.

It soon became clear that Ferrari was emerging as Goodyear's number one runner in the battle against the McLaren-Mercedes team, which had defected to the rival tyre company after Goodyear's exit announcement at the end of 1997, and it was clear that a performance boost was required after the first two races of the year.

Lack of front-end grip was one of the issues highlighted by the drivers and plans were implemented to address this aspect. Goodyear pulled out all the stops to produce an all-new wider front tyre which was tested prior to the Argentine Grand Prix.

In parallel to this, Goodyear produced a new compound – in the original tyre sizes – which was tested at Barcelona prior to the South American races where Jordan team driver Damon Hill reported it offered more consistency and controllability. That compound went into the standard-sized front tyre for Brazil, but although Schumacher's Ferrari finished third in this second round of the championship it was clear that other developments, already in the pipeline, were needed.

The week after Brazil the new wider front tyre became available. Small batches of the new tyres were air freighted to tests at Mugello and Barcelona. Ferrari, Williams and Jordan gave it the thumbs-up and plans were made to produce the new tyre in time for the Argentine GP.

Above: Eagles set to fly. Another batch of tyres are checked and prepared before being tested to the limit in the Grand Prix arena.

Below: Damon Hill scored Jordan's first ever Grand Prix win in the Belgian Grand Prix at Spa. The wet-weather Goodyears once again proved their mettle in atrocious weather conditions.

However, with only one new mould available the gamble was taken to build the new tyres with the softer (option) rubber compound. This strategic decision paid off handsomely when Schumacher took the Ferrari to its first win of the season, beating both McLaren-Mercedes cars in a straight fight.

Now the challenge for Goodyear was to develop a further improved construction rear tyre which would complement the new wider front tyre. After the Spanish Grand Prix there was another key test session at Magny-Cours where Goodyear came up with a better rear tyre which was available for Monaco. Unfortunately at that race Michael got involved in an unfortunate collision with one of the Benettons and finished out of the points, but Eddie Irvine salvaged some consolation with third place.

'While we were still improving our dry tyres and widening the compound range throughout the summer', said Goodyear UK Racing Manager Tony Shakespeare, 'we were still continuing an intensive programme to improve our wet weather tyres.

'After the British Grand Prix at Silverstone we implemented a wet-weather tyre programme for which the Ferrari test track at Fiorano was specially flooded for a very valuable test which gave us data to produce a revised intermediate which, although not used until the Belgian Grand Prix, was a big step forward over the previous one. Michael was in a league of his own on this rubber and the comparison between the tyre's performance in similar conditions at Silverstone and Spa was quite dramatic.'

Supported and encouraged particularly by Ferrari, Goodyear's tyre development programme continued with remarkable intensity right through to the end of the season, a fact which the opposition had found difficult to believe in what promised to be Akron's final season in F1.

Although Schumacher went into the final race of the season four points behind Mika Hakkinen, he qualified on pole position for the Japanese Grand Prix at Suzuka where there seemed every prospect that he might clinch Ferrari's first Drivers' Championship for 19 years. Unfortunately he stalled at the start with the result that he was sent to the back of the grid for the restart, despite which he sliced through the field to hold third place before going out with a puncture caused by running over debris from an earlier accident.

Nevertheless, Goodyear drivers took six of the top ten places in the Drivers' Championship with Michael Schumacher second, Eddie Irvine fourth, Jacques Villeneuve fifth, Damon Hill sixth, Heinz-Harald Frentzen seventh and Ralf Schumacher tenth. Goodyear teams also took four of the top six places in the Constructors' Championship with Ferrari second, Williams third, Jordan fourth and Sauber sixth.

Above: Eddie Irvine played a significant role in supporting Michael Schumacher in his challenge.

'All of us at Goodyear have very mixed emotions this afternoon,' said Perry Bell, Goodyear's Operations Manager Formula One Racing, at the conclusion of the Suzuka race. 'We are disappointed at the result and sad that this is our last race, but we are immensely proud of what we have achieved over the last 34 years, and in particular, what we have achieved this year.

'I don't think there was ever a more exciting and demanding season than this, in Goodyear's 34-year history. At the beginning of the season some people had already written us off but our hard work, along with that of our teams, has proved those sceptics were very wrong.'

Stu Grant, Goodyear's General Manager, Racing Worldwide, summed up the season by saying: 'We were committed to finish the 1998 season and the company's retirement from F1 competition on a "high" and we certainly have. "We" includes everyone who designed, developed, built, inspected, shipped, mounted, inflated, took the temperature of, or otherwise touched a Goodyear F1 tyre this season.

'This includes our associates in Akron, the company's F1 European group based in Wolverhampton, England, as well as our research and chemical R&D associates who worked hand in hand with race tyre development to formulate the most competitive race tyre compounds possible.

'We are pleased and proud to have been associated this year with teams such as Ferrari, Williams, Jordan, Sauber and Tyrrell and, previously, with many other fine teams participating in F1.'

Ferrari Chairman Luca di Montezemolo also offered these words of appreciation: 'I think it is a great shame that Goodyear has left F1, not just from a professional viewpoint, but also from the view of human relations. We have achieved a great deal in our technical partnership together over so many years.'

GOODYEAR
#1 in Racing

The Race Leaders

Goldline Bearings Ltd

The suppliers of high quality bearings for high performance cars

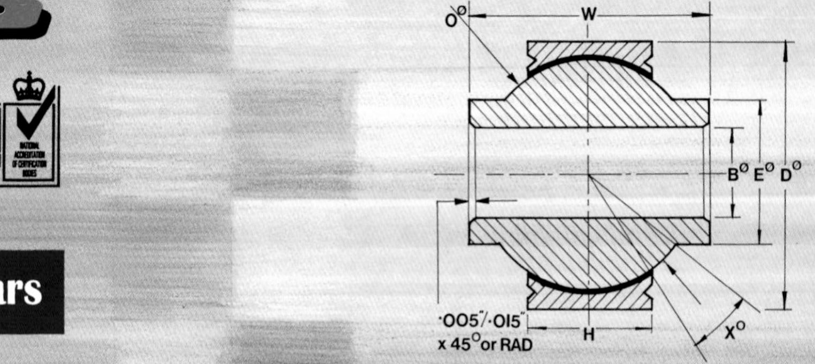

The Goldline F1 generation of self-lubricating plain bearings have been developed in conjunction with Formula 1 designers to keep friction to a minimum value. The bearings incorporate the AMPEP XL * liner/ counterface system, which exceeds the MIL-B-81820 performance requirements, with the added value of low breakout torque. By the use of exotic bearing materials, designers can reduce weight by up to 45% over a conventional joint plus increase the life by a factor of up to x8 for .004" backlash value over a normal X1 bearing.

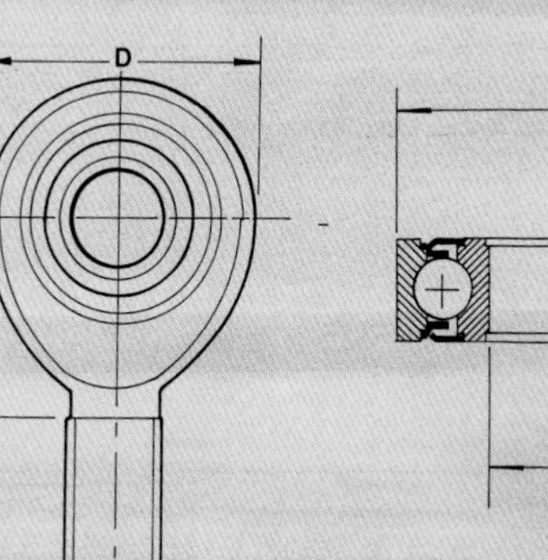

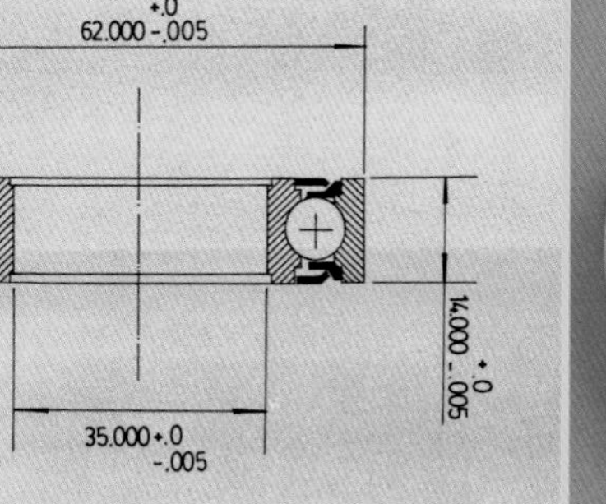

* SKF Trade Mark

The Goldline F1 C107FFTY5 clutch bearing has an aerospace pedigree and is manufactured in the UK by the Barden Corporation. It incorporates P4S running accuracy with 11 ceramic balls and a phenolic high strength riveted cage. The bearing will tolerate speeds in excess of 19,000 rpm and a temperature range in excess of 170 degrees centigrade.

Goldline Bearings Ltd

CONTACT: Mike Jones,
Ryan Currier
Stafford Park 17,
Telford TF3 3BN, England.
Tel No. 01952 292401
Fax No. 01952 292403

U.S.A. DISTRIBUTOR:
CONTACT: Bob Long,
Truechoice Inc
4180 Weaver Court,
Hilliard, Ohio 43026
Tel No. 001 614 8763483
Fax No. 001 614 8769292

Proven Quality and Performance is our commitment to excellence

24 Hour Delivery
Worldwide Export Service

top ten drivers

Chosen by the Editor, taking into account their racing performances and the equipment at their disposal

photography by

michael schumacher

Date of birth: 3 January 1969

Team: Scuderia Ferrari Marlboro

Grand Prix starts in 1998: 16

World Championship placing: 2nd

Wins: 6; Poles: 3; Points: 86

UNQUESTIONABLY he remains the outstanding driver of the post-Senna F1 generation. Throughout 1998 Michael continued to display an iron resolve and that remarkable ability to capitalise on any advantage, no matter how slender it might appear to be from the touchlines. His inspirational qualities have also been a crucial factor in underpinning the Ferrari team's self-belief that it could actually win a World Championship crown for the first time since its last, almost overlooked, constructors' title in 1983.

The wins were fantastic, sometimes achieved with an almost chilling ruthlessness which was awesome to behold. The advent of Goodyear's revised wider front tyre put the Ferrari F300 on the pace from the third round in Buenos Aires and Schumacher picked off both McLaren-Mercs in the opening stages of the race. Yet the manner in which he dealt with Coulthard, forcing his way ahead with two wheels on the grass, perhaps suggested that even more Messianic zeal than ever before was fuelling his mental motive power.

At the time, even for a man who marches alone to his own beat, the virulent media criticism in the wake of his collision with Jacques Villeneuve in the 1997 European Grand Prix seemed to make a firm impression on Schumacher. Yet by the start of the new season he was totally refreshed, ready to begin climbing the mountain again on Ferrari's behalf. It was a long slog, but with the McLaren challenge wobbling ominously in the middle of the year he pressed home his bid with fine wins in Canada and France followed by a somewhat fortuitous and highly controversial success at Silverstone.

Yet Schumacher's single most impressive performance came at the Hungaroring, where Ferrari switched from a two- to a three-stop schedule some way into the race, strategically wrong-footing McLaren and winning superbly. Two races later Maranello's technical reliability allowed him to head Eddie Irvine home in an emotional Ferrari 1-2 at Monza, although this was a day when the McLarens were again the class of the field only to be hobbled by technical failure.

As expected, from time to time Schumacher paid the price for his unyielding pace. At Monaco he came off second best in a wheel-banging match with Alexander Wurz, while at Montreal he not only declined responsibility for pushing Heinz-Harald Frentzen off the road but also ranted at Damon Hill for weaving at him on the straight. A case of the pot calling the kettle black, perhaps?

When he plunged into the back of David Coulthard's McLaren at Spa his pit lane outburst against the Scot showed an unattractive side to his personality, fuelled though it may have been by sheer fright. It proved that even the ice-cool Michael is not immune from the huge stresses involved in fulfilling the role of Ferrari's number one flag carrier.

MIKA Häkkinen was an absolute revelation throughout what must be regarded as the year when his and the McLaren team's mutual trust and confidence finally paid off. There have been very few such closely bonded partnerships in recent F1 history; even the chemistry between McLaren and the dictatorial Ayrton Senna never seemed as strong as the alliance which has grown between Häkkinen and McLaren, particularly with team chief Ron Dennis.

More than any other single driver in McLaren history, Mika was Dennis's protégé. Ever since his manager Keke Rosberg coaxed him into signing a testing contract with McLaren in 1993, rather than a race contract with Ligier, the reticent Finn with the equable temperament has occupied a special place in the team's affections. And in 1998 he finally had the equipment to deliver in relentless and uncompromising style.

Watching Häkkinen at speed in the steely silver and grey McLaren MP4/13-Mercedes was to witness a driver totally at one with his machinery. If he was slightly fortunate to have won his maiden Grand Prix victory at Jerez at the tail-end of the 1997 season, no such criticisms could be laid at his door this year. From the moment he took pole position at Melbourne and accelerated into the lead at the first corner, Mika was a man on a mission.

After Coulthard gave him back the lead following the misunderstanding which led to his unintentional pit stop in the Australian Grand Prix, Häkkinen needed no favours again. He blew David away at Interlagos and Spain to set the tone of a season in which he quickly and consistently gained the upper hand over his Scottish team-mate. He won in Monaco in brilliant style, free from David's challenge after an engine failure intervened, and was only shaded by the Scot at three of the 16 rounds – Buenos Aires, Imola and Canada.

Mika made mistakes at Silverstone (but not before he'd proved that Michael Schumacher doesn't have a monopoly when it comes to wet-weather genius) and at Magny-Cours, where he was frustrated by Eddie Irvine's presence between himself and race leader Schumacher. McLaren finger trouble cost him possible wins at the Hungaroring and Monza, where his performance in driving the final handful of laps to finish fourth with only rear brakes operative was rightly acclaimed as heroic.

One reason for Häkkinen's success at McLaren is his natural air of deference when he is out of the cockpit. Strapped inside his car it becomes a different story. Many observers judged his close-fought victory over Michael Schumacher at the Nürburgring to be a defining moment for the McLaren driver. Mika saw it differently. In his mind it was merely a public demonstration of what he always knew he could achieve. If anything, he handled the pressure even better than his key rival.

Date of birth: 28 September 1968

Team: West McLaren Mercedes

Grand Prix starts in 1998: 16

World Championship placing: 1st

Wins: 8; Poles: 9; Points: 100

2

mika häkkinen

jacques villeneuve

3

Date of birth: 9 April 1971

Team: Winfield Williams

Grand Prix starts in 1998: 16

World Championship placing: 5th

Wins: 0; Poles: 0; Points: 21

THE problem with assessing Villeneuve's potential over his first two seasons in F1 inevitably revolved round the fact that he was driving a Williams-Renault. Was the guy a great driver? Or just a competent operator enjoying a magic-carpet ride to stardom in the best car on the grid?

The 1998 season provided the answer to such conundrums. The Williams FW20 wasn't the fastest car in the F1 business, but Jacques did his best to lift it a notch or two beyond its obvious performance potential. He never quite managed to win a Grand Prix, but his third places in Germany and Hungary allied to his brilliantly opportunistic vault onto the front row at Monza served to keep him in play.

Starting the year as reigning World Champion, the season was always going to be a disappointment for Jacques as he knew from the outset that he would have to grapple with customer Mecachrome V10 engines which now lacked the sharp edge of Renault works development. Not until Hockenheim did he finally manage to get on the rostrum, posting a strong third place behind the McLaren-Mercedes duo and revelling in the Williams FW20's seeming preference for high-speed corners.

In the closing stages of the race there came a moment when it looked as though Jacques might actually be able to challenge for victory, but a differential problem slowed him over the last few laps and he settled for third. He produced the same result at the Hungaroring, then spun off after briefly taking the lead at Spa and finally excelled by planting himself on the front row of the grid alongside Schumacher's Ferrari at Monza. He spun off in the race, paying the inevitable penalty for running a precariously low-downforce set-up.

By Patrick Head's admission, Jacques developed a taste for much more conventional chassis set-ups in 1998 than had previously been the case. Williams wanted him to stay on for 1999 and beyond but the attraction of driving for the all-new British American Racing outfit run by his friend Craig Pollock proved irresistible. If he'd got to suffer another season with Supertec (née Mecachrome) engines he judged that BAR's new Reynard-built challenger would be a better bet than a Williams. Career decisions don't come much more audacious than that.

BEING paid lots of money to play second fiddle to Michael Schumacher may not be everybody's idea of the dream F1 scenario, but Eddie Irvine again managed splendidly when it came to juggling the conflicting pressures of such a demanding role. While maintaining his reputation as the perfect F1 team player, the Ulsterman also did a good job sustaining an image as a driver who deserves a number one seat in his own right elsewhere in the fullness of time.

Irvine was incredibly consistent. Starting the season with a fourth place in Melbourne, he failed to score in Brazil, after which he was only once out of the top four right through until Hockenheim. His drive at Magny-Cours, where he ran quickly enough to defend Schumacher from Häkkinen's advances while allowing his team leader to build up a commanding victory margin, may have attracted a degree of criticism from the opposition, but that overlooked the fact that this was precisely what he was being paid to do. Similarly, when he relinquished third place to Schumacher in the closing stages of the Austrian GP he was simply fulfilling a pre-arranged role.

Yet Irvine was no cipher. When Schumacher was railing against Coulthard for causing the celebrated Ferrari/McLaren collision at Spa, Eddie boldly stood up for the Scot, shrugging aside any suggestions that David would have even considered pulling an unethical move. In that respect, Ferrari's number two prides himself on being a scrupulous operator. When accused in print of weaving on the straight at Barcelona while defending his place from Giancarlo Fisichella's Benetton, he sought out the offending scribe and put him straight. 'I never, ever weave,' he insisted. 'I just hate that sort of thing.'

By the same token, he would have no truck with driving obstructively at the Nürburgring and keeping Häkkinen's McLaren back in third place for a lap longer than he felt he legitimately could. More than ever, Irvine consolidated a reputation as a man who honourably fulfilled his supportive role as Ferrari's second driver absolutely to the letter without ever once looking as though he was a subservient slave being forced to do the dirty work. It was a clever balancing act.

Date of birth: 10 November 1965

Team: Scuderia Ferrari Marlboro

Grand Prix starts in 1998: 16

World Championship placing: 4th

Wins: 0; Poles: 0; Points: 47

4

eddie irvine

david coulthard

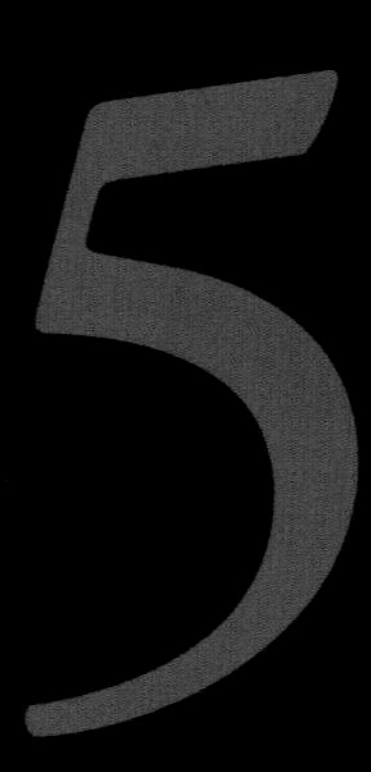

Date of birth: 27 March 1971

Team: West McLaren Mercedes

Grand Prix starts in 1998: 16

World Championship placing: 3rd

Wins: 1; Poles: 3; Points: 56

A SINGLE win ranged against the eight achieved by Mika Häkkinen in no way accurately reflects the pleasant Scottish driver's rightful position in the F1 order of things. Yet no matter how one wishes to present it, the season delivered less by far than David Coulthard had hoped for. By the end of the year Häkkinen had firmly consolidated his role as McLaren number one and only at Buenos Aires, Imola and Montreal could David lay claim to being a seriously quicker contender than the Finn.

It was always going to be a difficult challenge for Coulthard. No matter how McLaren explain it, he was psychologically disadvantaged in the early races. Starting the year with memories of having to help Häkkinen to his first victory at Jerez in 1997, he then found himself obliged to give up the lead to Mika at Melbourne in adherence to a pre-race pact.

Coulthard drove well for most of the time, although he was still prone to the occasional unforced error in practice and qualifying. It was just that Häkkinen generally drove better. Standing his ground when Schumacher came barging past to take an early lead in Argentina may have sent the right message to the Ferrari driver, but it worked against David on a day when Häkkinen was happy to settle for second on a circuit he dislikes. Sixth place was poor recompense.

David drove superbly at Imola to win the San Marino Grand Prix, was outclassed in Spain and was coming back at Mika in the opening stages at Monaco before engine failure intervened. He should certainly have won in Canada, where an incorrectly assembled Ilmor throttle mechanism fell apart as he was pulling away from Schumacher's Ferrari, and repeated glitches with the refuelling equipment at Magny-Cours must have left Coulthard wondering what he had done to upset the gods.

At Silverstone he flew off the road in heavy rain and in Austria he staged a great comeback drive to second place behind Häkkinen after being savaged by the Arrows team on the opening lap. By the time of the German GP at Hockenheim mathematics dictated that he would have to play second fiddle to Häkkinen's title ambitions.

After fielding Michael Schumacher's outburst at Spa with measured firmness, the final bitter disappointment for Coulthard came at Monza where he was given the green light to go for a win only for his hopes to be thwarted when another Mercedes V10 went up in smoke. For F1's most dignified gentleman, the 1998 season will be one to forget as quickly as possible.

THERE is a Peter Pan type quality about Jean Alesi which makes him such an irrepressibly optimistic personality. Yet even though by the end of the season his career total of 151 Grands Prix had yielded only a single Ferrari victory at Montreal back in 1995, the Frenchman is still as committed and determined as ever.

Thus it remained throughout the 1998 season although his first year with the Sauber-Petronas squad netted him just four helpings of World Championship points. Even his critics agreed that he deserved more. At Silverstone Jean made a sensational start to run fourth, losing only fractionally on Häkkinen, Schumacher and Coulthard during the opening phase of the race. But he failed to finish. In Austria he qualified on the front row of the grid alongside Giancarlo Fisichella's Benetton only to tangle with the Italian, eliminating them both from the contest.

On the positive side he posted a strong fifth place in Buenos Aires and drove superbly in the pouring rain to finish third behind the Jordans of Hill and Ralf Schumacher at Spa. He then finished fifth at Monza, a worthy enough result but one which Jean believed should have been even better on a circuit where he regularly goes well.

For most of the season Alesi qualified around the tenth-place mark, which was seldom high enough to allow him to get on terms with the leading bunch from the outset. Yet he was measured and constructive in his comments about the Sauber chassis and its Ferrari engine, feeling that, at best, they were knocking on the door of sustained success.

Many people felt that the Alesi/Sauber partnership could hardly expect to produce much in the way of long-term promise. Yet Jean proved to be a key motivating factor all season long. To some extent Sauber and Johnny Herbert had run the course of their partnership by the end of the season. Both needed a fresh challenge once their relationship went stale. Jean Alesi at least provided a brisk antidote to that unfortunate state of affairs.

Date of birth: 11 June 1964

Team: Red Bull Sauber Petronas

Grand Prix starts in 1998: 16

World Championship placing: 11th

Wins: 0; Poles: 0; Points: 9

6

jean alesi

damon hill

7

Date of birth: 17 September 1960

Team: B&H Jordan Mugen Honda

Grand Prix starts in 1998: 16

World Championship placing: 6th

Wins: 1; Poles: 0; Points: 20

THERE were times early in 1998 when Damon Hill looked as though he had lost the plot. Having made the switch to Jordan after a bleak season with the Arrows-Yamaha squad, it seemed as though the 1996 World Champion might again be in the wrong place at the wrong time. Could it be that he had missed the Jordan team's fleeting moment in the sun with Peugeot engines during 1997?

Watching Hill wrestle his way through the opening races of the year was akin to intruding on a very personal moment of private grief. Everybody knew how well Damon had performed in the past, but his assured confidence now seemed shattered. The car was dismal and, more worryingly, testing promise never quite translated itself into hard race results. He looked increasingly isolated, haunted and withdrawn. When he finished eighth at Monaco, two laps down and only just ahead of Shinji Nakano's Minardi, the Hill/Jordan partnership had plumbed rock bottom.

Yet Damon would soon remind the doubters that he only needed a sniff of something promising and his morale would start to soar. At Montreal he managed to run in the top three before the Jordan wilted and was so delighted at the performance boost that he was almost unaware of Michael Schumacher's verbal barbs to the media after they had been involved in a brief wheel-to-wheel tussle.

A silly spin in front of his home crowd at Silverstone meant that Hill had to watch Ralf Schumacher storm to a superb sixth place and post the team's first point of the season. But, thereafter, with a much improved car and extra power from the Mugen Honda V10, Damon simply flew to fourth places at Hockenheim and the Hungaroring.

Finally, at Spa-Francorchamps, Hill deployed his superb wet-weather car control to score the Jordan team's first victory. He had been bettered in the appalling conditions only by Michael Schumacher, whose Ferrari had benefited from a more suitable chassis set-up for the torrential rain. To those who remember Hill's win at Suzuka in 1994, it came as no real surprise.

WHEN Ralf Schumacher finally informed Eddie Jordan that he would be leaving at the end of the 1998 season, after only his second year in F1, he made a promise that he would win the team its first Grand Prix before he took his leave. That, more than any short-term frustration with the circumstances of the day, was why the young German driver felt so disappointed at having to settle for second place behind Damon Hill in the Belgian Grand Prix.

From the start of the season Ralf went through a process of readjustment at the wheel of the Mugen Honda-engined Jordan 198. He'd tended towards over-driving during his F1 freshman season and now had also to come to terms with developing a new car and engine package. In Melbourne he lasted a single lap before retiring after a collision. At Interlagos he departed the race on the second corner, where he spun off. Not until Imola did he manage to post a finish and his first championship point did not arrive until Silverstone.

Yet if Ralf projected a somewhat surly countenance during his first season in F1, by the middle of 1998 he was maturing fast. His handshake seemed firmer, his eye contact more positive. The boy was growing up and a slightly understated air of diffidence replaced the rather brash streak which had characterised his personality in 1997.

By the end of the year he was driving really well and taking full advantage of any imaginative strategies the team might offer him. In Austria he refused to be intimidated by the presence of his elder brother in his mirrors and held off the Ferrari for a couple of laps, making it clear that blood was not thicker than water on this particular occasion.

At Spa, an early first stop at which he changed from intermediates to full wets saw him emerge third behind brother Michael and team-mate Hill after the rest of the leading group had made their own stops. At Monza he wound up a strong third, which gave him his second visit to the podium in as many races. On home ground at the Nürburgring he was running fifth in the closing stages when a brake disc bell failed.

Next season Ralf Schumacher has a golden opportunity to stamp his own identity on the Williams team ahead of his highly rated rival Alex Zanardi. It could be a much-closer-run thing than observers anticipate. Jordan insiders, who also had experience with the Italian back in 1991, believe that Williams may have struck a rich seam of talent with its new driver pairing.

Date of birth: 30 June 1975

Team: B&H Jordan Mugen Honda

Grand Prix starts in 1998: 16

World Championship placing: 10th

Wins: 0; Poles: 0; Points: 14

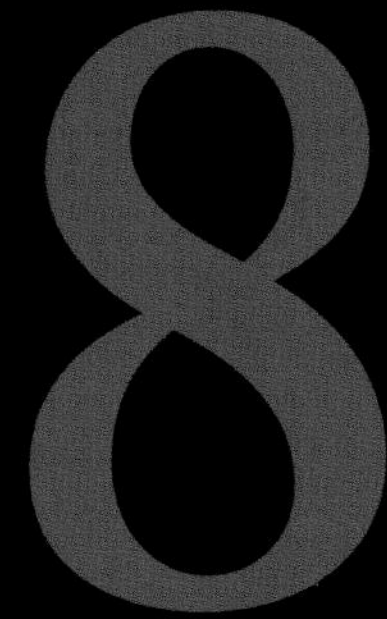

ralf schumacher

giancarlo fisichella

9

Date of birth: 14 January 1973

Team: Mild Seven Benetton Playlife

Grand Prix starts in 1998: 16

World Championship placing: 9th

Wins: 0; Poles: 1; Points: 16

THE pleasant Italian driver started the season with high hopes, but his resilience was sorely tested as Benetton's B198 failed to sustain its initially promising performance during the second half of the season, due in part to Bridgestone's perhaps understandable decision to make McLaren's tyre requirements an overwhelming priority.

There is a body of opinion which suggests that Fisichella is a stylish and very quick driver but somehow lacks that ultimate racer's edge, something which hampers him when it comes to uninhibited wheel-to-wheel dicing. This may be a harsh judgement. In the opening stages at Monaco he certainly looked every inch a potential winner, expertly withstanding pressure from Michael Schumacher's Ferrari as he led the chase of the McLarens. Coulthard's retirement gave him the opportunity of a clear run through to second place, which he duly achieved despite a spin from which a lesser driver might not have recovered so confidently.

At Montreal he finished second again, this time to Schumacher's Ferrari. Michael ran a two-stop strategy and had to make an additional visit to the pit lane for a ten-second stop-go penalty. Even so, he commandingly beat Fisichella into second place, the Italian running a one-stop strategy and also hobbled by slight gearchange problems towards the finish.

Giancarlo also demonstrated his mettle when he refused to give ground to Eddie Irvine's Ferrari as they diced for fourth place in the Spanish Grand Prix. It may have been a racing accident, but the young Benetton driver certainly indicated that he was not a soft touch, even though he collected a fine for failing to avert what officialdom regarded as an avoidable accident.

After those two impressive performances, Fisichella would only feature as a points-scorer on two more occasions. He finished fifth at Silverstone and then a slightly disappointed sixth in the Luxembourg GP at the Nürburgring, forced into a slight error on oil dropped by another car as he was running fifth ahead of Frentzen's Williams.

Yet it cannot be disputed that Fisichella, and indeed Alexander Wurz, both brought more to the Benetton party than can simply be measured in terms of results. After two seasons with Gerhard Berger and Jean Alesi, the team was lacking edge and motivation. The young Italian helped rekindle a mood of enthusiasm and a strong sense of purpose. The technical package may not have gelled as the team hoped, but having Fisichella on the books was a tonic. In that respect he was certainly a

PRIOR to leaving the team, Benetton Chief Executive David Richards judged his 1998 drivers as two very different individuals who reached similar results by separate routes. Perhaps unsurprisingly, they had contrasting personalities: whereas Fisichella was more of an extrovert with a taste for late-night discos, his team-mate Alexander Wurz was a quieter and slightly more introspective character.

Yet there were occasions in 1998 when the lanky Austrian drove with an assurance and a confidence which belied the fact that he had made his F1 debut as Gerhard Berger's stand-in only as recently as the 1997 Canadian Grand Prix.

Like Fisichella, Wurz was no soft touch. He proved this in dramatic style at Monaco, where he was prepared to bang wheels with Schumacher with such measured competitiveness that not even the highly motivated Ferrari ace could find fault with his tactics. Later, pressing hard after a refuelling stop, Wurz lost control at around 170 mph in the tunnel and emerged into the sunlight minus his Benetton's front wheels. He walked away from the wreckage outwardly unperturbed.

This cheerful insouciance was demonstrated yet again in Montreal when his car was pitched into the air in a first-corner collision and somersaulted into the gravel trap. Even before the Benetton had landed Alex was on the radio to the pits enquiring about the spare B198's availability. He duly took it over for the restart and kept out of further trouble to finish the restarted race in fourth place.

Wurz finished fourth on no fewer than five occasions up to and including the British Grand Prix, after which he got bogged down in a disappointing rut. Frustrated by the lack of availability of Bridgestone's wider front tyre, Wurz began to show signs of over-driving. Yet the team kept faith with him. He and Fisichella had been signed on long contracts so that they would not be apprehensive about pressing hard and having a go. Wurz certainly did that and more. Whether he can craft that obvious potential into achieving more consistent results as he matures remains the key question.

Date of birth: 15 February 1974

Team: Mild Seven Benetton Playlife

Grand Prix starts in 1998: 16

World Championship placing: 7th=

Wins: 0; Poles: 0; Points: 17

10

alexander wurz

mika salo

KNOCKING on the door of the Top Ten were both Mika Salo and Toranosuke Takagi, yet the fact that both had intermittently competitive, and often unreliable, machinery at their disposal made it difficult accurately to judge their real status. Salo's run to fourth place at Monaco was certainly impressive, coming a year after he finished fifth there for Tyrrell. The Finn has talent enough, but needs a competitive car before his career becomes time-expired. By the same token Pedro Diniz produced some flashes of genuine promise to back up his own personal contention that it is time to judge him on talent alone and not just the size of his sponsorship cheque. Next year he will be measured against Jean Alesi at Sauber, which will certainly be interesting.

Johnny Herbert may merit a return to the AUTOCOURSE Top Ten next year when he joins the Stewart-Ford team. This season his personal relationship with the Sauber squad simply ran out of steam. The resilient Englishman never actually drove badly, yet circumstances combined to ensure that he made virtually no impression. The same can be said of the Prost-Peugeot drivers. Olivier Panis's driving seems to lack something of its old sharpness and Jarno Trulli, while undeniably promising, never got a decent run all season.

In the present Stewart line-up, Rubens Barrichello proved that he could withstand considerable pressure with a fine drive to fifth place ahead of Jacques Villeneuve at Barcelona. Sadly, this was the only seriously upbeat performance by the Stewart-Fords and for most of the time the dignified, maturing Brazilian could do no more than survive in the midfield ruck. His team-mates Jan Magnussen and Jos Verstappen proved little more than cannon-fodder. The team suggested their biggest problems were a tendency to over-drive. Critics said that Magnussen in particular had been pummelled into a state of psychological ruin by the over-intense manner in which he was tutored by Jackie Stewart. Either way, both were disappointments.

The most spectacular absentee from this year's Top Ten is probably Heinz-Harald Frentzen. Even Williams concedes that the German driver has considerable natural skill. Perhaps the team could not unlock it. In 1999 Jordan will be hoping it can.

heinz-harald frentzen

THE REALISATION OF A DREAM

THE STORY OF THE CREATION OF BRITISH AMERICAN RACING

There will be a bright, fresh force in Formula One from 1999: British American Racing. The name is brand new, but it conceals a wealth of experience which lies behind this ambitious new project.

British American Racing is the realisation of a dream, a project put together by a dedicated group for whom success in motor racing is a tradition.

A year after the new team outlined its ambitions at a high-profile launch in London, Managing Director Craig Pollock has a brand new purpose-built factory, two star drivers, a hand-picked staff that grows daily, many months of sleepless nights behind him – and quite a few more to come as teams knuckle down to get ready for the opening race of the 1999 F1 season at Melbourne in March.

It's all systems go – and Pollock expects British American Racing to be a contender from the start, though he is taking a realistic view. After all, no Formula One team has won its maiden race since Jody Scheckter triumphed for Wolf in Argentina. And that was 21 years ago.

"I believe we will evolve gradually," he says, "but I certainly don't think we will start off at the back. We are aiming to be competitive from day one and we have the benefit of a former World Champion driver on our side. If Jacques Villeneuve can get into that area then his racing ability might carry us to victory. I know what it takes to be successful. We are willing to work round the clock, seven days a week, to ensure a bright future for British American Racing and we expect the same commitment from the entire team. At the same time, I want us all to have some fun along the way. We want to be as open and accessible as we intend to be successful."

Pollock admits that he is looking forward with great excitement to British American Racing's first Grand Prix, an occasion that will conclude a chain of events which began around the breakfast table at his Indianapolis residence in 1994. Joining him that morning were renowned volume race car manufacturer Adrian Reynard, plus business partner, Rick Gorne, and Tom Moser, then marketing manager for Player's, now head of global sponsorships for British American Tobacco.

"We were running Jacques in the Player's-sponsored Indycar team," says Pollock, "and the gist of our conversation was, 'Wouldn't it be something if we could move this into Formula One some day?' We were dreaming aloud that morning."

But now that dream has substance.

Pollock admits that he could have chosen simpler things to do with his time than creating a new Formula One team, but taking the easy option is not his style.

Born in 1956 in Falkirk, Scotland, Pollock graduated from Glasgow University with a degree in sports and biology. That led him into work as a physical education teacher and ski instructor before he moved into the world of business for two years. When he returned to his roots as director of sports at a private school in Switzerland, one of his most promising skiing pupils was Jacques Villeneuve, son of the late Ferrari hero Gilles.

Jacques picked up his father's racing thread in 1988, and since 1993 his interests have been managed by Pollock, whose successful sports management company's clients include the Ayrton Senna Foundation and Scot, Dario Franchitti, currently the hottest property in America's premier Champ Car series.

Despite his myriad business successes, Pollock says that he could not resist the challenge of adding an F1 team to his portfolio.

"It's true, I probably don't actually need to do this," he says, "but really I see it as the next step in the challenge. It was a dream which has turned into reality. I have always enjoyed building up projects and I just have to look at it as another business."

He talks calmly about the new deal, as though it were no more of a challenge than sauntering down to the newsagent to pick up the morning paper.

Right: Rick Gorne, Craig Pollock and Adrian Reynard

Centre right: The Supertec engine which will power British American Racing's 1999 challenger.

Far right: Craig Pollock on the grid at Monaco.

REAM THAT TURNED INTO A REALITY"

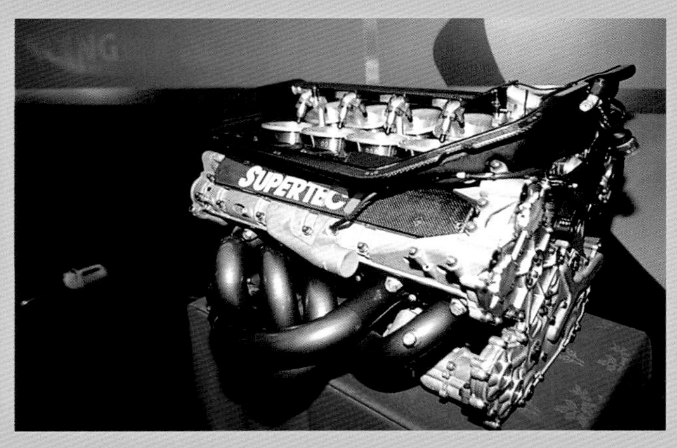

Right: Adrian Reynard has enjoyed huge success in racing worldwide. His cars have been winners across the globe. Now he faces his biggest challenge, to produce a Grand Prix car to compete with those from championship-winning teams such as McLaren, Ferrari and Williams.

Middle: The striking, new corporate livery of British American Racing was unveiled in July 1998

Far right: Reynard with chief designer Malcolm Oastler, the man charged with creating British American Racing's challenger.

Below: The team's new factory at Brackley, near Silverstone.

"It would have been easier to do other things," he admits, "but the fact that F1 is a multi-million dollar industry makes it more attractive to a businessman. Grand Prix racing is a small and exclusive club and it is a great challenge to establish yourself as one of only 11 or 12 members."

But it is not an easy challenge. History is littered with stories of teams whose ambitions exceeded their means. The list is long and, in some cases, inglorious: Andrea Moda, Forti, Pacific, Simtek, Life, EuroBrun, Rial, AGS...all have been and gone in the recent past, and some of them barely - if ever - even made it onto the grid during their short Formula One lives.

Only two of the new teams launched in the Nineties are extant today: Jordan and Stewart. And team figurehead Jackie Stewart is the first to admit that, even for a man with three World Championships under his belt and some of the most envied contacts in the business, seeing a nascent Formula One team through to its first race is a massive undertaking – and it can be even tougher to maintain an even keel once you are up and running.

Stewart has survived its first two seasons intact. When it made its F1 debut at Melbourne in 1997, it was not the only newcomer in the paddock...but it was the only one still running by the time the second race came around a couple of weeks later.

Most failed F1 projects are powered by dreams rather than hard cash, but British American Racing is a product of both.

Main sponsor, British American Tobacco is familiar in motor racing circles. Its impressive brand portfolio includes Gold Leaf, which pioneered major Formula One sponsorship with Lotus in the Sixties, as well as John Player Special, whose celebrated black and gold logos were synonymous with Team Lotus successes in the Seventies and Eighties.

No one is saying exactly how much has been invested in this project but the figure is believed to be in the region of £250 million for the first five years. Even by Formula One's elevated standards, this is a very big deal.

But not only does British American Racing have proven management expertise and a solid financial platform; it also has some of the most respected technical partners in the racing business.

The British American Racing chassis is being developed and built by Reynard Racing Cars, which has won its first race in every professional motor racing category it has entered – and those include Formula Three, F3000 and Indycar racing. Reynard has worked on F1 projects before – the most recent example evolved into Benetton's 1992 Grand Prix contender, a car which Michael Schumacher took to second place on its debut in Spain.

Reynard has recently moved into a brand new 135,000 sq ft factory in Brackley, near Silverstone, and this has been purpose-built for the British American Racing F1 programme. Company founder Dr Adrian Reynard has moved gradually up the motor racing ladder and has always harboured Formula One ambitions, albeit with strict conditions attached. "I have always said that Reynard would be interested in entering Formula One if the circumstances were correct," he says. "In British American Racing we know we have partners who share the same passion for winning that we do. On that basis we have committed 100 per cent to this project."

The chief designer is Malcolm Oastler, an Australian former racer who crafted the Formula 3000 chassis which won its first race in 1988 and the Indy racer which pulled off the same feat in 1994.

Oastler's chassis will be powered by the new Supertec Sport V10, which derives from the famous Renault engine that powered Nigel Mansell, Alain Prost, Michael Schumacher, Damon Hill and Villeneuve to five world titles in six years between 1992 and 1997.

Villeneuve, of course, will also be an integral part of British American Racing's Formula One challenge. The French-Canadian had seen enough potential in the project to sign up by the summer. And that

A BRAND NEW, PURPOSE-BUILT FACTORY HAS BEEN BUILT FOR THE FORMULA ONE PROGRAMME

meant walking away from Williams, the most successful F1 team of the Nineties.

But the 27-year-old insists it was not a difficult decision. He won the 1995 Indycar title driving a Reynard chassis – a season which included victory in the Indianapolis 500 – and he has every confidence that he will be able to challenge for championship success again in the near future. "I know from experience that Adrian and his people can produce a very competitive package," he says, "and I am very comfortable with the Supertec engine. Most importantly, I am happy to be back with Craig and Adrian in what is shaping up to be the team of the future. We share the same philosophy of racing."

Villeneuve will be joined by the promising 22-year-old Brazilian, Ricardo Zonta. Highly rated by both Jordan and McLaren, for whom he has tested F1 cars in the past, Zonta won the SudAm F3 title in 1995, was FIA Formula 3000 champion in 1997 and, during the season just past, he has been the outstanding driver in the all-conquering AMG Mercedes GT team. Four wins and a string of pole positions led him to yet another championship title. "I could wish for no more than to join a new team which intends to start winning as soon as possible," he says.

To an outsider, British American Racing's arrival in F1 looks to have been fairly smooth. Certainly, it has been facilitated by the acquisition, in December 1997, of the long-established and highly-respected Tyrrell team, a deal which guaranteed that the bold newcomer would have an entry – as well as rights to prize money and TV dividends. This, says Pollock, was much simpler than starting from scratch. The FIA, the sport's governing body, has recently acquiesced to a change of name: in 1999, the cars will be known as British American Racing-Supertecs.

"If things look to have gone smoothly from our side it's simply because we have applied a very businesslike approach to the way we have gone about everything," says Pollock. "It has not been 100 per cent without dramas along the way, but the hiccoughs we have come across tend to have been thrown up in front of us by the Formula One system, such as the procedure for changing the name. We have had a few hurdles but we have overcome them as we have gone along.

"The most difficult thing in reality is getting the key personnel in all the right positions. Without all of them it wouldn't matter that we had Jacques Villeneuve, Reynard, Supertec or whoever – you have to look at the broader picture."

And there are other leading industry figures behind the scenes, too. Villeneuve will be liaising again with race engineer Jock Clear, for instance. The two have worked together since Villeneuve switched from Indycars to F1 in 1996 – and they have experience of what it takes to win a world title.

And then there is Dutch-born, Australian-bred Willem Toet – a keen competitor in his own right and, more crucially, the former head of aerodynamic research at Ferrari.

"You can't come in to Formula One by trying to copy any existing models," adds Pollock. "We have studied what has happened to some new F1 teams in the past and we have tried to attain a higher level of professionalism for a newcomer. You can't re-invent the wheel, but you can try to do things so that they work best for all concerned at every level of the organisation."

By way of preparation British American Racing has already been working as a unit at the racetrack. A research and development team was established in the summer of 1998 and former Williams test star Jean-Christophe Boullion was snapped up to work with a hybrid chassis, featuring one of this year's Tyrrell chassis and one of next year's engines.

"The first time a British American Racing-built car ran it was slightly low-key," says Pollock, "because it was a Tyrrell chassis in Tyrrell colours, though the guts of the car were all British American Racing."

It was a proud day for all, but for Pollock the best is yet to come.

"I guess the true test of my feelings will only be when we get to the first race in Melbourne," he says, "and I can't wait to get going."

Above: A hint of things to come. The bold and vibrant colours announce a fresh face in Formula One.

Right: Craig Pollock on the grid with the Tyrrell in Canada.

Far right: British American Racing's drivers for the 1999 season will be French-Canadian Jacques Villeneuve and Brazilian Ricardo Zonta.

Craig Pollock
British American Racing
Adria

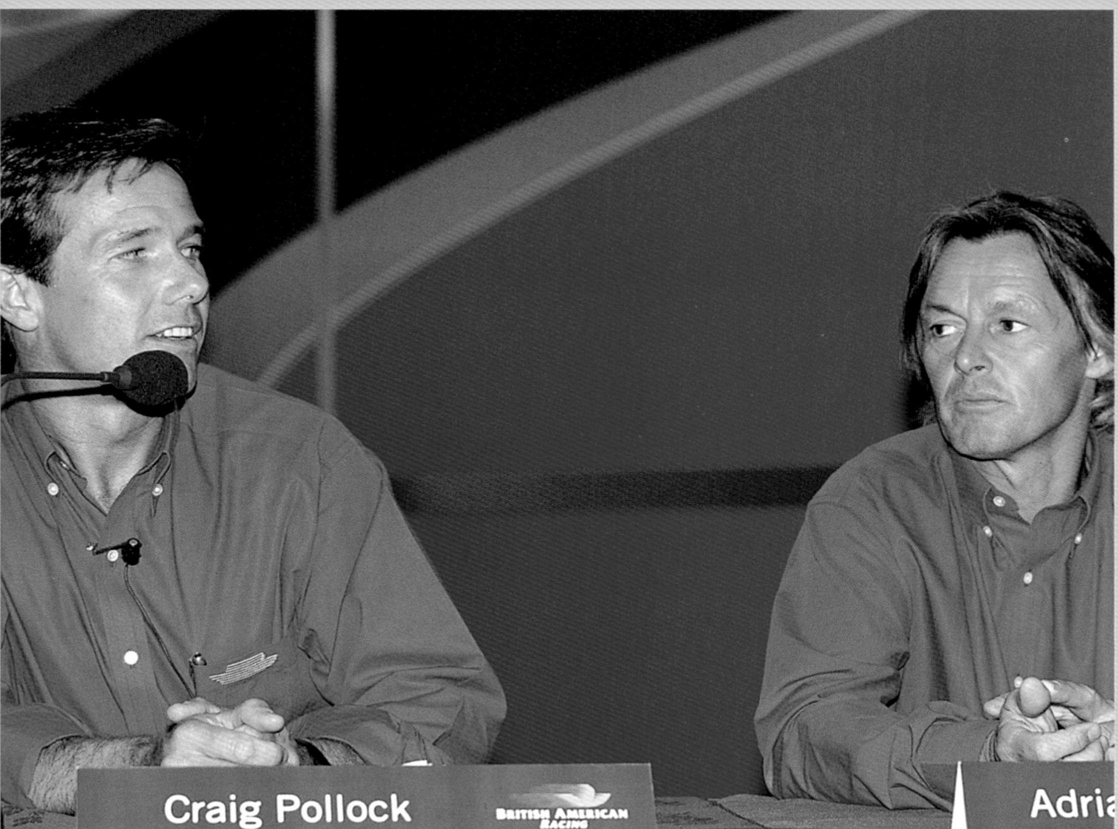

Right: Craig Pollock and Adrian Reynard answer questions from the motor sport press at the launch of British American Racing.

Below: The team is growing week by week as an exciting challenge is taking shape.

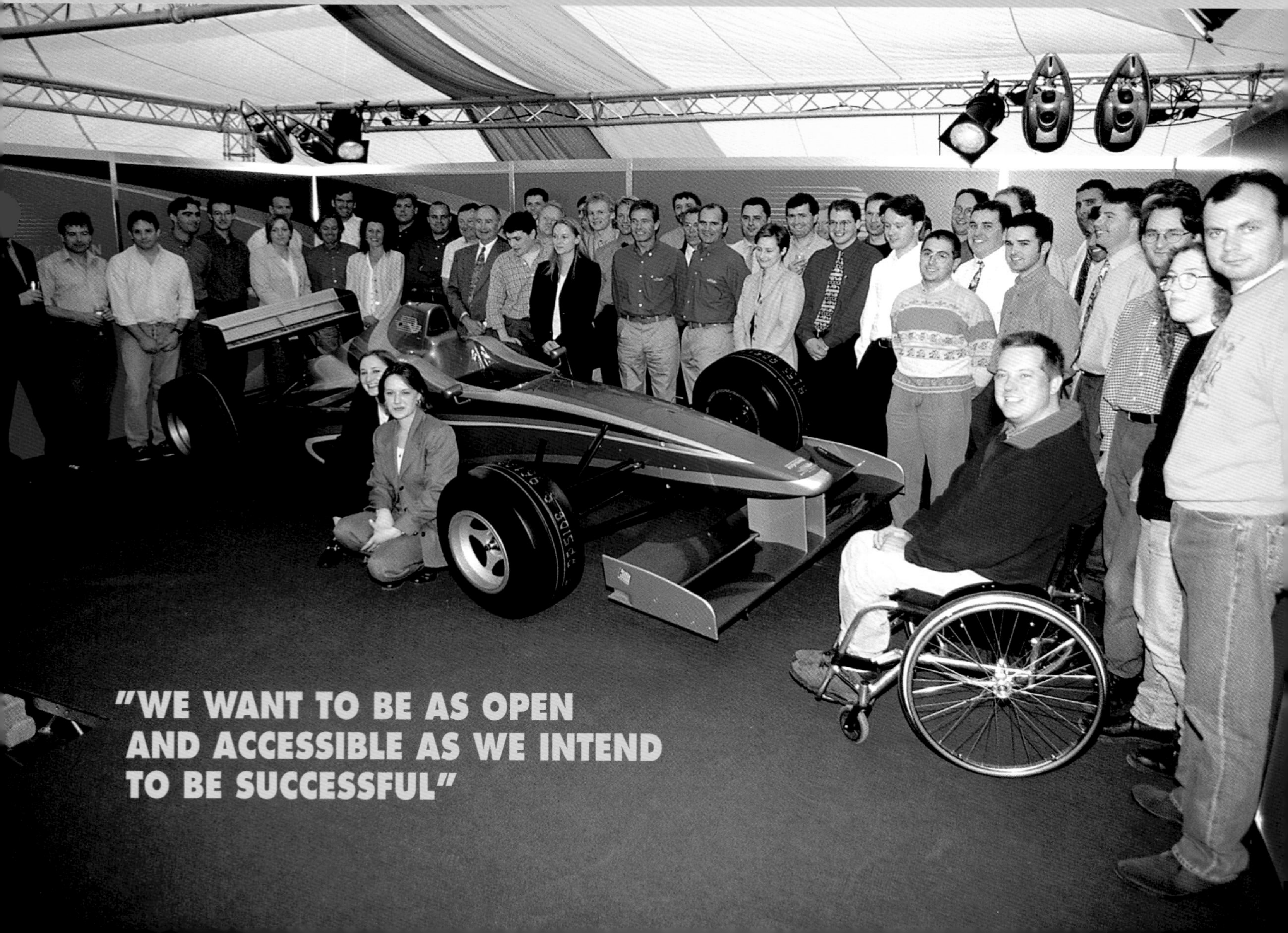
"WE WANT TO BE AS OPEN
AND ACCESSIBLE AS WE INTEND
TO BE SUCCESSFUL"

NICE GUYS CAN BE WINNERS

by Adam Cooper

Matthias Schneider

ONE way or another, 1998 was a pretty memorable year for Mika Pauli Häkkinen. In May, he married Erja, his girlfriend of three years. In September he turned 30, reminding us that he was no longer the fresh-faced youth who'd stepped straight from British F3 to a Lotus seat in 1991. And between March and November he scored eight GP victories on his way to securing the World Championship crown – achieving an ambition he'd first voiced as a teenage kart racer in his native Finland.

Few begrudged Häkkinen his success. It was a victory for an all-round nice guy, a man with no enemies in the paddock. McLaren clearly gave him a car which was in a class of its own for most of the season, but Mika had to wait a long, long time for such a silver-lined opportunity to come his way; in recent years only Nigel Mansell has spent more seasons in F1 before winning the title.

He finally claimed the honours just nine days short of the third anniversary of the accident which so nearly took his life. At one point on that Friday afternoon in Adelaide in 1995, it seemed that Mika was beyond help, the random victim of a puncture which sent his car careering into the barrier. Only the instant, skilled intervention of Prof. Sid Watkins and his Australian colleagues kept the Finn alive. Yet he was ready to race the following March, and in the overall scheme of things the potential catastrophe proved to be barely a blip on Häkkinen's career path. Through the difficult years the natural talent was never in doubt, and when everything finally fell into place for Mika this season he took full advantage.

Even before the launch of the MP4/13, we knew that the package of Adrian Newey, improved Mercedes V10 and Bridgestone tyres would be the one to beat in 1998. The last part of the success equation, out-running their own team-mate, was up to the drivers. Mika did not disappoint. He seized the initiative from David Coulthard early in the year, and effectively turned the previously confident Scot into a frustrated and at times humiliated number two.

Of more importance than the impressive statistics is the way Mika won. When you've grown used to battling for the minor placings, keeping a season-long title campaign on the road is no easy matter, even with a brilliant car underneath you. It may have been new to him, but Mika put barely a foot wrong, and racing at the front all the time helped to sharpen his skills.

'It's a great situation,' he explained before the Suzuka finale. 'But sometimes a very difficult situation, because it becomes very critical. Second is nothing any more. I remember a couple of years back, if I had been second or third in a race, I would have said "fantastic!" To get pole position, I would have jumped through the roof. But now it's normal. You don't get 100 per cent used to it, but you get so hungry, you want to win so much. Which is human nature. It's OK, as long as you keep your feet on the ground.'

In addition to his increasing domination of Coulthard – team orders formalised the situation in the later races – he responded superbly when Michael Schumacher and Ferrari turned the screw. His victory in the penultimate race at the Nürburgring is rightly cited as his most crucial drive, but no less impressive was his

As Mika closed in on the World Championship armchair fans around the globe became familiar with the sight of his wife Erja anxiously following his progress in the McLaren pit garage, and she was in the spotlight again when he finally clinched the title at Suzuka, three years after the accident in Australia that nearly claimed his life.

Below: When McLaren came up with a car that had an edge on the rest Mika made the most of his long-awaited opportunity, handling the pressures of being the clear title favourite who had everything to lose with remarkable aplomb.

Sutton Motorsport Images

feisty performance in the opening laps in Austria, where he had Michael snapping at his heels. The German cracked first.

Not that Mika was immune from mistakes, but somehow the good fortune which had eluded him over the years was now on his side. He clanged the barrier during his virtuoso performance in Monaco, but escaped unscathed. He spun in frustration while trying to pass Eddie Irvine at Magny-Cours, but gathered it up and continued on to third. He spun off in the atrocious conditions at Silverstone, and needed every ounce of that natural car control to steer himself back onto the track, and keep his engine running. He salvaged second place.

The same skills came into play when brake problems sent him into the gravel trap at Monza, and again he navigated himself away from potential disaster. Three points were saved. The only time he really let himself down was at Spa, where he tried to muscle it out through La Source with his chief rival, and spun into the path of a hapless Johnny Herbert.

'The fact is that he knew before the start that he was on tyres that he had no chance with,' says his manager and mentor Keke Rosberg. 'He didn't get the tyres that he wanted – somebody overruled him – and he was absolutely furious. In a way spinning in the first corner relieved us from a lot of pain, because he would have lost that race in a big way . . .'

Having shaped Häkkinen's career since he left FF1600 at the end of 1987, Rosberg understandably took much pleasure from the season. He is one of an élite group of close confidants who never lost faith in Mika through the years of frustration, and supported him through the trauma of the Adelaide accident and the months that followed. That period brought Mika closer to Ron Dennis, Mansour Ojjeh and Norbert Haug, and cemented a unique emotional bond between team and driver – something that Coulthard can do nothing about.

Not that emotion appears to play a large part in the Häkkinen success story, at least in public. One of Mika's great strengths is his ability to remain calm, and he refused to allow the pressure of Schumacher's charge up the points table to get to him. Those close to him talk of an incredible mental strength, an invaluable ability to concentrate and shut out anything which is of no importance to the job at hand. Considering that when he first arrived on the scene he was regarded as something of an absent-minded joker, who always needed someone to look after the day-to-day details of his life (in truth he still does), it's quite a turnaround.

Mika's character has contributed to an incredible synergy between himself and McLaren.

'As a team we're often criticised for being cold,' says Dennis. 'The reality is we're not cold. It's very much the opposite. But we are disciplined, and the environment in which we function as a team deliberately tries to remove – up to the point that the race is decided – all emotion. It can be detrimental to the performance of the driver or the team.

'It's easy to grasp that if you're angry or excessively hot, then your judgement when making a decision is not going to be as good as if you're cool and calm. I think Mika's grown that philosophy over the years, and utilised it to control how he approaches his racing. Mika has his emotions, and his thoughts, in control. Whatever is written has absolutely no effect on him. He stays cool, calm and keeps himself in that position. That best typifies his development as a racing driver. This year he has shown that he can drive in a very sensible manner; I think he's matured in a very disciplined and focused way.

'He's really not lacking in any areas. What weaknesses he had have been dealt with by himself, by his own determination. Even though they no longer exist, I don't wish to point them out. They're things of the past; we all get better.'

In public Mika regularly stresses the value of team-work. It's easy to dismiss as programmed 'Ronspeak', but it comes from the heart.

'Mika is a team worker,' explains wife Erja. 'He's not a guy who says that I did it, or this is mine. It's never that way. If you talk privately to Mika, his family is important, his parents, his friends in Finland. Everybody's part of it. For him it's very important that everybody in the team works together, that they understand him and he understands everybody else. I think that is his strength. He's not egocentric. People might think so, because he seems a bit closed.'

There's no doubt that Erja has made her own contribution to Mika's development. An articulate, strong-willed character, during 1998 she emerged from the shadows of Mika's carefully structured private life to inadvertently become the highest-profile 'other half' in the pit lane. She agrees that he's changed in the post-Adelaide years.

'Like everybody when you get older you understand things better. You understand good things, you understand bad things. In my case I've known Mika three and a half years. It's quite special because I'd known him half a year when he had his accident, and that was quite traumatic. But I think in this period Mika has learned a lot, not only about his job, and everything to do with it, but also about life.

'We still talk about it sometimes. There's nothing negative about it. You can say that when there's a bad thing, there's always something good about it. He's learned a lot of good things and it gave him a sort of forced stop to think about things, think about life, think about this job, think about his family and friends. He could calm down and think about everything, and that makes you stronger. That is the keyword for everything; it has really built him up stronger.'

This is the paradox of the Adelaide legacy. On the one hand it's an awful experience which any racing driver would naturally want to banish from his mind, yet on the other it seems to have ultimately benefited Mika, made him into a better driver – and perhaps a better human being.

'You can't go through life and suffer those sort of experiences without them sitting in your mind somewhere,' says Dennis. 'I think his ability to handle those thoughts is as much attributable to where he was born as anything else. I think Scandinavians have got a unique ability to lock things out of their mind and get on with life; different countries and different cultures do have a direct bearing on the thought processes of people.'

And yet it would be too simplistic to say that Adelaide is the only factor in Häkkinen's development, for he's learned a great deal more from the years of disappointment. Before this season started I asked him what was the lowest point of his spell at McLaren. The answer was revealing.

'It's silly to say, but probably when the decision was taken that I had to be a test driver in 1993. That was the time when I had difficulties to look in the mirror and say, "This is it. I'm a test driver." That was probably the lowest moment of my career in McLaren. But then that year I had time to think how I have to try, what I have to do, and get my concentration for the future. And it worked out really well. So it was the lowest time, and at the same time it gave me a lot, made me much stronger.'

Remember the ban for causing the 1994 Hockenheim first-lap crash? Both McLarens running round at the back at a damp Nürburgring in '95? The collision with Coulthard at Estoril the following year? David beating Mika to McLaren's first 'comeback' win in '97? All are events which have clearly helped to shape the man who experienced them. A few days before his victory in Japan, he expanded on his personal philosophy.

'After all, to be a good winner, you have to be a good loser. You have to learn to lose, and face your mistakes, or the mistakes of the team. You have to learn to take the pain. When you learn to do that, then winning is much better . . .'

Erja's description of how Mika recovers from setbacks is intriguing.

'When there's a disappointment there's a disappointment, but Mika has a very special way to handle it. It sometimes takes half an hour. He doesn't want to share it with anybody, he doesn't want to speak to anybody. He fights it inside himself, and he tries to understand why he's disappointed, what happened, and make the analysis inside himself. And when it's done, it's back to normal. It is incredible. Even I am surprised when I see it . . .'

'He doesn't allow himself to get mentally low at all,' says Rosberg. 'At the end of the day he led the championship from the first race to the last race, so you can't really say he was ever hurting bad. Of course, things were very critical at Nürburgring after the bad qualifying, with the points the way they were. Personally for me that was the worst part of the season, I was very, very nervous about that. But once he won that race, then after everything was easy.'

On the face of it Häkkinen is a simple, straightforward guy, with no evident hang-ups or secrets to hide. And yet he seems somehow far more enigmatic than any of his peers. After eight years in the F1 paddock we may know the smiling face, hunched shoulders and casual flick of the floppy fringe, but do we really know what makes the guy tick? Erja agrees that there are two Mikas, and only close friends are allowed to see the off-duty version.

'That is true,' she nods, 'I can confirm it. Mika has a very good way of seeing things. You have to have your private life, and you have to respect certain things and keep them for yourself. There's no reason to spread out everything about yourself in public. Because that is part of the inner strength, the strength that you have inside yourself. The results talk for you, but not what is inside of you. That's a sort of protection, and that's why he's so strong mentally . . .'

Somehow I think we've yet to see the best of Mika Häkkinen.

Silverstone™

SILVERSTONE powered through its 50th anniversary in 1998 and is all set for the 1999 season, better equipped than at any time in its glorious past. And, judging by the BRDC's bold plans, the home of the British Grand Prix will advance yet further at the millennium.

What started out as an extremely basic circuit laid out on the perimeter roads and runways of an abandoned World War Two airfield is now the world's leading circuit, offering no fewer than six different circuit layouts plus a rally stage. On top of this the BRDC plan to add a visitor centre that will help to turn Silverstone into a seven-days-a-week leisure facility. Those pioneer racers of the late 1940s wouldn't recognise the place...

The highlight of every season at Silverstone is the British Grand Prix in July, and this has already attracted a record level of interest for 1999. However, Silverstone also hosts rounds of three other World Championships, with a round of the FIA GT Championship, a round of the FIA Formula 3000 Championship and a round of the FIA World Rally Championship when the Network Q Rally of Great Britain drops in to use

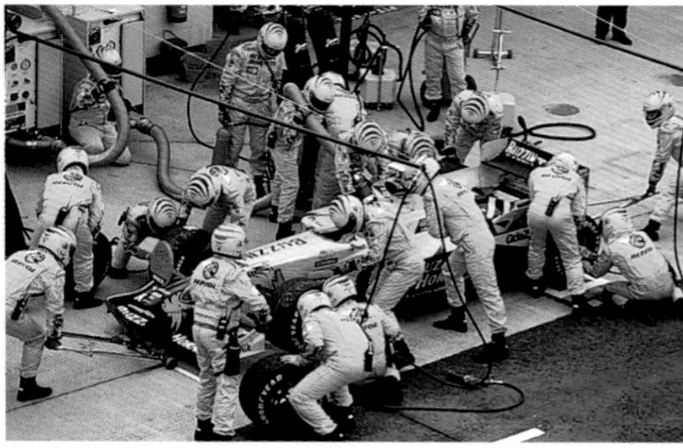

Silverstone's rally stage. No other circuit in the world can claim such a spread of major international events. Add to this the Spring Trophy meeting, at which the best of the world's young Formula 3 drivers do battle in their hope of attracting the attention of the team managers who could help them continue their ascent towards Formula 1, the two visits of the ultra-competitive British Touring Car Championship and the annual Historic Festival in July, and it's easy to see why Silverstone's race fans are the luckiest in the world.

Indeed, while their viewing facilities are constantly being improved with the expansion of Silverstone's very own radio and television stations and the installation of numerous large screens positioned around the circuit, they needn't remain on the outside, wondering what it's like to drive a car in anger, for the Silverstone Driving Centre offers a host of opportunities for them to have a go themselves. This has something for everybody, with indoor and outdoor karting, four-wheel drive off-road driving, skid-control cars, plus racing and rallying schools, with the world-famous Jim Russell Racing School now joining the Driving Centre to take pupils as far as they want to go, with their own championships for both single-seaters and saloons. There are also outlying schools at Croft and Donington Park.

Exciting new plans are in place to take Silverstone into the next millennium, with a bypass around the village of Silverstone finally having been given government approval. This will certainly improve access, with a monorail planned for transporting visitors from the car parks to the track. Further than that, virtual reality technology is set to be harnessed in a visitor centre-cum-museum using holograms to bring to life the great figures of the past. These are just a few of the ideas that will make Silverstone an even better sporting facility and represent the circuit management's policy of constant improvement for a venue that never stops looking ahead.

Silverstone – The Only Racing Choice

Silverstone, The Home of British Motor Racing and host to one of the most famous Formula 1 races in the world, the RAC British Grand Prix, offers you a whole range of motor sport action.

The support and commitment of the British Racing Drivers' Club, which owns Silverstone Circuits, means that all profits are ploughed back into British motor sport and into Silverstone, ensuring it continues to rank as one of Europe's premier motor sport venues.

See some of the best of the season's racing at the following events:

Silverstone RallySprint, Spring Trophy, Auto Trader British Touring Car Championship, British Empire Trophy, SuperBike International, RAC British Grand Prix, Coys International Historic Festival and Network Q Rally of Great Britain.

Silverstone also offers you the chance to get behind the wheel and see for yourself what it's really like to be a racing driver at a choice of 3 locations – Croft Circuit, North Yorkshire; Donington Park, Derbyshire or Silverstone Circuit, Northamptonshire.

Driving activities start at £95. Choose from Single Seaters, Race Saloons, 4x4's, Rally, Road Skills or the state-of-the-art Lotus Elise sports car.

Alternatively, start your racing career with Silverstone Driving Centre's Race Tuition Programme.

Call **01327 850107** for a free Driving Centre brochure or **01327 857273** for race meeting bookings and circuit information, or visit our website:
http://www.silverstone-circuit.co.uk

TYRRELL: THE END OF AN ERA

by Maurice Hamilton

Ken Tyrrell *(left)* was no longer a part of the F1 scene in 1998, after thirty years as a Grand Prix entrant. His team enjoyed its greatest successes in the days when flat caps were still *de rigueur* in the paddock *(right)*, the combination of Jackie Stewart and the familiar blue Tyrrell *(below)* dominating the sport in the early Seventies.

THE F1 paddock was a strange place in 1998. For the first time in 30 years, you could walk the length of it and not be berated by Ken Tyrrell for some misdemeanour, real or imagined.

That's not the criticism it sounds. In a business increasingly bound up in its own importance, Ken Tyrrell was a breath of fresh air, a total enthusiast whose love of the sport and impish sense of humour often brought a sense of proportion to affairs which were being treated with more seriousness than they frequently deserved. Ken knew how to laugh. Boy, could he laugh.

In fact, it wasn't a laugh at all. It was a very loud cackle – often delivered about an inch from your face. He was like that from the moment he arrived in F1 in 1968. Unfortunately, the cheerful guffaw was noticeably absent when Ken spoke officially for the last time as head of the Tyrrell Racing Organisation, the team which had been the emotional core of his life for longer than he cared to remember.

The occasion was indeed a sad one even if the team's new owners, British American Racing, did their best not to present it that way. On Friday, 28 November 1997, Ken had sold the team through choice. He and his son Bob could no longer find sufficient sponsorship as Formula 1 headed towards the millennium and even greater expense – beyond anything Tyrrell might have imagined when he started out with Jackie Stewart three decades before.

Formula 1 has never been cheap, of course. In the summer of 1967, Tyrrell travelled to Zandvoort to witness a powerful debut by the Ford DFV, an engine which was due to dominate Grand Prix racing for the next 15 years. Showing great foresight, if very little else, Tyrrell placed an order immediately even though he didn't have the £7500 asking price. Neither did he have a car, a driver or, indeed, any firm plans to move up to Formula 1. But he knew this was what he wanted to do. Moreover, he intended to go Grand Prix racing within six months! Life was so different then . . .

Stewart, who was racing with Ken in Formula 2 following their successful association in F3, said he would want £20,000 if he was to leave BRM and join the Tyrrell F1 team. Tyrrell agreed. His first move was to borrow the £20,000 from Walter Hayes, then the director of motor sport at Ford. Together, Stewart and Tyrrell persuaded Dunlop to invest £80,000 in a battle with Firestone and Goodyear. Ken returned the £20,000 to Hayes and went racing for a season with the remaining £60,000. Easy as that.

They used a chassis manufactured by the French aerospace company, Matra, and simply bolted the Ford V8 on the back of it. Then Stewart briefly led the first race of the 1968 season in South Africa. It went on from there.

They won their first race in Holland and, by the end of the season, Stewart was in a three-way fight for the championship. He lost out to Graham Hill at the final race in Mexico. Not bad for a team in its first season.

In 1969, Stewart won the drivers' title. The constructors' championship went to Matra thanks to Tyrrell's efforts and those of the works team which used the Matra-Simca V12. This, in fact, would prove to be a sticking point which, indirectly, would lead to Tyrrell becoming a chassis manufacturer in his own right.

Matra's parent company, Chrysler, indicated that it would be politically correct for Tyrrell to use the Simca V12. If not, then, 'malheureusement', there could be no Matra chassis for the 'rosbif' team. A quick test with the screaming V12 confirmed Stewart's and Tyrrell's worst fears: it sounded great but was no match for the smaller, lighter and more torquey Ford DFV V8. Even though it meant abandoning such an excellent chassis, Tyrrell felt he had no option. For 1970, therefore, we had the unusual predicament of the reigning World Champions going into a new season without a car!

Enter March Engineering and the slick-tongued Max Mosley, then a director of this new and very ambitious enterprise. Keen to make an impression in its first season, March happily sold a chassis to Tyrrell. Within a handful of races, Stewart knew the car was a dog, even though he managed to wring a victory out of the boxy blue machine in the Spanish Grand Prix. The message was that if

Photos left and above: LAT Photographic

Far left: Few episodes in Ken Tyrrell's long involvement in F1 were more unpleasant than the controversy surrounding alleged technical infringements in 1984.

The team enjoyed a brief revival after Ken took a chance on a youthful Jean Alesi *(below)*, but before long the Frenchman had moved on to Ferrari.

Tyrrell wanted full control of his team's destiny then he would have to design and build his own chassis.

By today's exacting standards, the methods employed would be considered antediluvian. In 1970, it was a major effort, one which Tyrrell and his designer, Derek Gardner, managed to keep a complete secret. The result, Tyrrell-Ford 001, was a simple but beautifully crafted piece of kit which belied the fact that it had been designed in the spare room of Gardner's home in Warwickshire, the mock-up constructed in his garage. It had cost £22,500 to make, a considerable sum when compared with the £7000 asking price for a March.

With this car and its derivatives, Tyrrell and Stewart (with help from François Cevert, the number two) carried off two championships and 16 victories before Jackie stopped at the end of 1973, his retirement coloured terribly by the death of Cevert during practice for what should have been Stewart's last race.

Despite the sad ending, it would turn out to be the finish of a golden era which would never be matched. In the years that followed, Tyrrell won just seven races, the last being at Detroit in 1983.

The decline was very slow to start with but picked up pace in the mid-Eighties when Tyrrell was one of the last to bow to the inevitable and make a switch to turbocharged engines. With the absence of results came a fall in financial backing, each succeeding year making Tyrrell less and less attractive. There were seasons when the cars carried no sponsorship identification at all. It seemed the team was not moving with the times, as reflected in the unfortunate sobriquet 'Dad's Army'. If nothing else, the intense loyalty displayed by the mechanics reflected the affection in which Tyrrell was held.

There was an upsurge with the arrival of Harvey Postlethwaite in 1989. Fresh from Ferrari, the English designer knew exactly what was needed to bring Tyrrell into line with the Nineties. It took a while to raise the funds to go even half-way towards the necessary technical upgrade at the Tyrrell headquarters in Ockham, Surrey. But the product was a neat and nimble car (powered once more by the Ford V8) which suddenly came to life when Jean Alesi was given his F1 debut midway through the season.

Alesi's 18-month sojourn would mark Tyrrell's last hurrah. When the French-Sicilian left to join Ferrari, and Postlethwaite subsequently moved on, the decline continued. Not even a return by Postlethwaite, coupled with his upgrade within the management structure, would bring about the desperately needed improvement. It was too late for that.

Tyrrell argued that nothing had really changed in Formula 1.

'It's no different,' he said. '£80,000 was an enormous amount of money in 1968 and it's the same now when looking for sponsorship.'

Nevertheless, a continuing shortage of funds would accelerate a downward spiral which would be reflected in the absence of decent engines and, as a result, quick drivers. With annual budgets edging closer to nine-figure sums, Ken Tyrrell felt the time had come to sell to BAR, which would use the team as the basis of its assault on F1 in 1999. It was, as he pointed out, his decision. But, in truth, he had no alternative. The moment had passed for a company which was still located in the same former woodyard where it had started more than 30 years before.

'I think what's happened is the way of the world, just one of the realities of Formula 1,' says Postlethwaite. 'I think we put together quite a good operation at Tyrrell but, over the last few years, the team was like a swan trying to take off. Every now and then it would get airborne, only to crash back into the water. You just can't keep going on like that.

'If there was a turning point, then it was when Jean Alesi left the team. It's clear these days that if you haven't got the driver, then forget it. You need to put together a good enough package to attract an emerging young star. So if you ask: "When was the last time Tyrrell had a driver of any class in the car?" the answer is Alesi.

'The fact of the matter is that the team in its existing form simply wasn't going to make it into the next millennium without some sort of absolutely enormous shake-up, take-over or whatever. There's no room for sentiment, I'm afraid. If the ghost of Tyrrell travels on to BAR, then so be it. Perhaps it's for the best.'

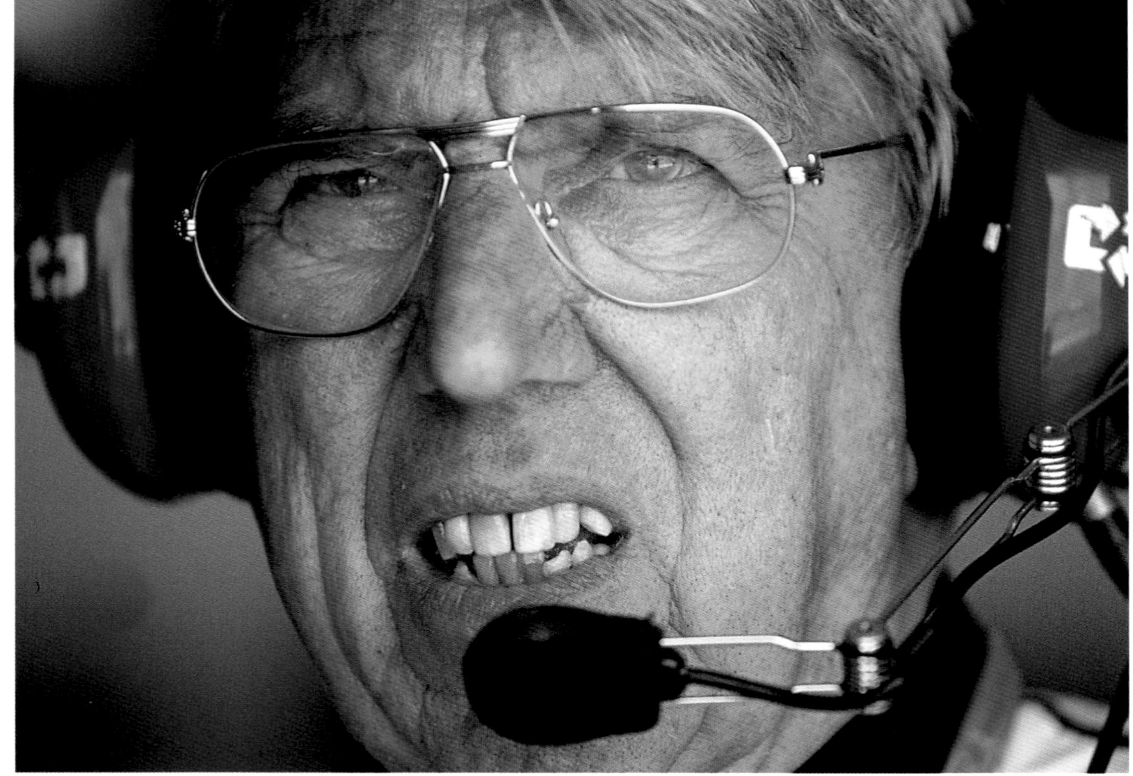

Photos: LAT Photographic

COSWORTH *Racing*

COSWORTH AND FORD PROVIDE MARRIAGE OF IDEALS

ADVERTISEMENT FEATURE

GRAND PRIX
Roll of Honour
Ford Cosworth Winners

1967 – 4 wins

Dutch GP	Jim Clark
British GP	Jim Clark
United States GP	Jim Clark
Mexican GP	Jim Clark

1968 – 11 wins

South African GP	Jim Clark
Spanish GP	Graham Hill
Monaco GP	Graham Hill
Belgian GP	Bruce McLaren
Dutch GP	Jackie Stewart
British GP	Jo Siffert
German GP	Jackie Stewart
Italian GP	Denny Hulme
Canadian GP	Denny Hulme
United States GP	Jackie Stewart
Mexican GP	Graham Hill

1969 – 11 wins

South African GP	Jackie Stewart
Spanish GP	Jackie Stewart
Monaco GP	Graham Hill
Dutch GP	Jackie Stewart
French GP	Jackie Stewart
British GP	Jackie Stewart
German GP	Jacky Ickx
Italian GP	Jackie Stewart
Canadian GP	Jacky Ickx
United States GP	Jochen Rindt
Mexican GP	Denny Hulme

1970 – 8 wins

South African GP	Jack Brabham
Spanish GP	Jackie Stewart
Monaco GP	Jochen Rindt
Dutch GP	Jochen Rindt
French GP	Jochen Rindt
British GP	Jochen Rindt
German GP	Jochen Rindt
United States GP	Emerson Fittipaldi

1971 – 7 wins

Spanish GP	Jackie Stewart
Monaco GP	Jackie Stewart
French GP	Jackie Stewart
British GP	Jackie Stewart
German GP	Jackie Stewart
Canadian GP	Jackie Stewart
United States GP	François Cevert

1972 – 10 wins

Argentine GP	Jackie Stewart
South African GP	Denny Hulme
Spanish GP	Emerson Fittipaldi
Belgian GP	Emerson Fittipaldi
French GP	Jackie Stewart
British GP	Emerson Fittipaldi
Austrian GP	Emerson Fittipaldi
Italian GP	Emerson Fittipaldi
Canadian GP	Jackie Stewart
United States GP	Jackie Stewart

1973 – 15 wins

Argentine GP	Emerson Fittipaldi
Brazilian GP	Emerson Fittipaldi
South African GP	Jackie Stewart
Spanish GP	Emerson Fittipaldi
Belgian GP	Jackie Stewart
Monaco GP	Jackie Stewart
Swedish GP	Denny Hulme
French GP	Ronnie Peterson
British GP	Peter Revson
Dutch GP	Jackie Stewart
German GP	Jackie Stewart
Austrian GP	Ronnie Peterson
Italian GP	Ronnie Peterson
Canadian GP	Peter Revson
United States GP	Ronnie Peterson

ADVERTISEMENT FEATURE

ONE of motorsport's most enduring and deep-rooted partnerships became even closer in 1998 with the purchase by Ford of Cosworth Racing, cementing a bond between the two companies which has extended back over 35 years to the virtual dawn of Ford's European competition programme.

Ironically, the close nature of the Cosworth/Ford partnership over almost four decades has been perceived by many outsiders as a marriage in all but name for many years. The two companies have indeed become so synonymous that some people believe that Ford has owned Cosworth for years.

In fact, the car maker had always been a willing suitor, but it was not until the summer of 1998 that it finally took the Northampton-based competition engine specialists to the altar, purchasing Cosworth Racing from the German Audi company, which had acquired the entire Cosworth group from its previous owners, Vickers, earlier in the year.

By the time Ford finally became Cosworth Racing's new owners some 31 years had passed since the Ford Cosworth DFV F1 engine had put the genius of the company's founder, Keith Duckworth, on very public view.

On its maiden outing, the DFV-powered Lotus 49 driven by the legendary Jim Clark scored an historic victory in the 1967 Dutch Grand Prix at Zandvoort, ushering in an era which would see the compact, lightweight and highly efficient V8 engine win no fewer than 155 World Championship Grands Prix over the following 16 years. When Cosworth manufactured this engine it successfully rewrote the parameters of overall Formula One car performance and integrated design concepts.

That great tradition is sustained to this day by the Ford Zetec-R V10 Formula One engine which is supplied to the Stewart-Ford Grand Prix team. In addition, the Italian Minardi organisation has enjoyed a separate commercial arrangement for the supply of a customer-specification engine in 1998 and will benefit from a much closer relationship with Cosworth for next season's FIA Formula One World Championship programme.

In addition to the F1 projects, Cosworth Racing will also provide the engines for the Ford Mondeos contesting the 1999 British Touring Car Championship which will be prepared by Prodrive at Banbury.

Cosworth Racing still occupies broadly the same site at St James Mill Road, Northampton, that has been its home since Keith Duckworth first moved the company there from north London in 1964, five years after he and Mike Costin originally founded it. It would put Northampton on the map as a centre of excellence in the fast-moving motorsports industry and has since become one of the biggest employers in the area.

There has always been a pragmatic edge to Cosworth's motor racing involvement which stretches back to Keith Duckworth's own personal philosophy when he directed the firm's fortunes. Apart from being an intuitive engineer, Duckworth was a firm believer that race engine designs should be as simple and uncomplicated as possible.

Keith Duckworth had worked from 1957-58 as transmission development engineer with Lotus before establishing his own business. The very first Ford design to which Cosworth contributed any technical input was the 1963 Cortina GT, using an inlet manifold and camshaft design which emerged from the Edmonton-based specialists.

Yet even by this stage Cosworth had used Ford engines as the basis of their racing units, most notably in the 1.1-litre Formula Junior category which came to an end in 1963. The engines were then reworked for the new 1-litre Formula Three which took over as the training ground for future Grand Prix stars with the MAE (Modified Anglia Engine) that would be developed into a winning unit which was enduringly successful right

Photo left: Eric Bryce, Scottish Borders Council Museum and Gallery Service

Opposite page: Top: Keith Duckworth and Walter Hayes pose behind the legendary Ford Cosworth DFV engine which rewrote the Grand Prix history books. *Bottom:* Jim Clark chats with Colin Chapman and Lotus chief mechanic Dick Scammell – now managing director of Cosworth Racing – before a race.

Top: The latest Ford Cosworth F1 engine is unveiled at the launch of the new Stewart prior to the start of the 1998 season. *Inset:* More than thirty years earlier Duckworth, Chapman, Clark and Hill begin the adventure at the 1967 Dutch Grand Prix.

Cosworth's racing success has come in many arenas. The Lotus Cortinas thrilled crowds in the mid-Sixties *(left)* while the Ford Mondeo *(above)* is a leading contender in the BTCC.

1974 – 12 wins

Argentine GP	Denny Hulme
Brazilian GP	Emerson Fittipaldi
South African GP	Carlos Reutemann
Belgian GP	Emerson Fittipaldi
Monaco GP	Ronnie Peterson
Swedish GP	Jody Scheckter
French GP	Ronnie Peterson
British GP	Jody Scheckter
Austrian GP	Carlos Reutemann
Italian GP	Ronnie Peterson
Canadian GP	Emerson Fittipaldi
United States GP	Carlos Reutemann

1975 – 8 wins

Argentine GP	Emerson Fittipaldi
Brazilian GP	Carlos Pace
South African GP	Jody Scheckter
Spanish GP	Jochen Mass
Dutch GP	James Hunt
British GP	Emerson Fittipaldi
German GP	Carlos Reutemann
Austrian GP	Vittorio Brambilla

1976 – 10 wins

Spanish GP	James Hunt
Swedish GP	Jody Scheckter
French GP	James Hunt
German GP	James Hunt
Austrian GP	John Watson
Dutch GP	James Hunt
Italian GP	Ronnie Peterson
Canadian GP	James Hunt
United States GP	James Hunt
Japanese GP	Mario Andretti

1977 – 12 wins

Argentine GP	Jody Scheckter
US GP West	Mario Andretti
Spanish GP	Mario Andretti
Monaco GP	Jody Scheckter
Belgian GP	Gunnar Nilsson
French GP	Mario Andretti
British GP	James Hunt
Austrian GP	Alan Jones
Italian GP	Mario Andretti
United States GP	James Hunt
Canadian GP	Jody Scheckter
Japanese GP	James Hunt

1978 – 9 wins

Argentine GP	Mario Andretti
South African GP	Ronnie Peterson
Monaco GP	Patrick Depailler
Belgian GP	Mario Andretti
Spanish GP	Mario Andretti
French GP	Mario Andretti
German GP	Mario Andretti
Austrian GP	Ronnie Peterson
Dutch GP	Mario Andretti

1979 – 8 wins

Argentine GP	Jacques Laffite
Brazilian GP	Jacques Laffite
Spanish GP	Patrick Depailler
British GP	Clay Regazzoni
German GP	Alan Jones
Austrian GP	Alan Jones
Dutch GP	Alan Jones
Canadian GP	Alan Jones

1980 – 11 wins

Argentine GP	Alan Jones
US GP West	Nelson Piquet
Belgian GP	Didier Pironi
Monaco GP	Carlos Reutemann
French GP	Alan Jones
British GP	Alan Jones
German GP	Jacques Laffite
Dutch GP	Nelson Piquet
Italian GP	Nelson Piquet
Canadian GP	Alan Jones
United States GP	Alan Jones

through to the end of the 1970 season when the formula was superseded.

Duckworth was one of the very first designers to appreciate that although an engine may be sufficiently powerful to fulfil its intended purpose, its potential can only be fully realised if it can be integrated with the chassis. This was also one of Lotus founder Colin Chapman's abiding principles and it was therefore no surprise when the DFV-engined Lotus 49 was regarded as such a spectacular trend-setter back in 1967.

The spark which produced the glittering partnership between Ford and Cosworth was initially kindled by Walter Hayes, a former Fleet Street journalist who joined Ford in 1962 at a time of great expansion of the company's ambitions. It was believed, correctly as it turned out, that the new Cortina saloon would transform the company's image.

In his new role as director of public affairs, Hayes immediately decided that the Cortina would be the ideal vehicle with which to take Ford into motor racing. Hayes knew very well that Cosworth had amassed much experience developing those production Ford engines for racing purposes, so when Coventry Climax withdrew from F1 at the end of 1965 it seemed an opportune moment for Ford to fill the breach with a totally new Grand Prix engine.

Cosworth initially built the DFV for Ford to supply on an exclusive basis to Team Lotus. However, when it became clear that the V8 would effectively render all other F1 units obsolete, Walter Hayes had a word with Colin Chapman and he most generously agreed to relinquish his exclusivity agreement in the wider interests of the sport.

The DFV package had also included the development of a four-cylinder Formula Two engine which became the highly successful 1.6-litre FVA four-cylinder that dominated motor racing's second division single-seater class from 1967 to 1971.

The Lotus 49 just failed to carry Clark to the 1967 World Championship, but in 1968 Graham Hill took the first Ford Cosworth DFV-propelled World Championship at the wheel of one of Chapman's cars. From then on only Ferrari would seriously stem the DFV tide when Niki Lauda won World Championships in 1975 and 1977 and Jody Scheckter in 1979.

Duckworth could be a controversial character and was always steadfast in his belief that turbocharged F1 engines did not strictly conform with the rules. Yet this purist streak did not stand in the way of Cosworth's engineering versatility. In 1986 the company produced a 120-degree turbocharged V6 engine for Ford which would be used by both the Beatrice Lola and Benetton teams. It was extremely compact for ease of installation in the chassis, but due to changing technical rules never quite realised its full potential.

Cosworth's outstanding versatility was also underscored by the development of the superb Ford Sierra high-performance saloon car. Dubbed the 'Sierra Cosworth', this was one of the very first super-performance saloon cars developed on a relatively modest budget.

This Sierra was also highly significant in that it was the first Ford road car to carry the Cosworth nomenclature. Powered by a 200 bhp-plus four-cylinder turbocharged engine, it went on sale in 1986, 5500 examples of the original large-winged two-door saloon being produced, followed by a variety of other models.

This in turn led to an even higher performance RS500 version of the Sierra Cosworth which enjoyed a string of successes in both racing and rallying. In 1988 a four-wheel-drive version of the Sierra Cosworth became available, by which time the company had become an extremely profitable organisation with huge commitments and obligations. It could no longer be run as a small operation in the manner originated by Keith Duckworth and Mike Costin.

Keith famously remarked: 'Over the years we've been doing things with a standard of reliability which is totally non-human. I'm one of those people who would rather do a few things well than what I see at the other extreme, in other companies, of making an average mess of doing a lot of things. It takes an enormous effort to get the last little things right.'

In terms of his commitment to engineering perfection he was absolutely right, of course. But to protect the future of Cosworth and its employees, in 1980 Keith sold out to United Engineering Industries, a Manchester-based engineering firm. As 85 per cent shareholder he naturally received the lion's share of the asking price, which was in the region of six million pounds.

Yet the manner in which Cosworth operated was relatively unchanging, as far as its customers were concerned. For the next decade the company would pass to Carlton Communications, to Vickers, and then to Audi before Cosworth Racing was hived off separately and sold to Ford.

Cosworth Racing's premises remain within the complex first occupied more than 30 years ago, although it no longer includes all the buildings on the site. It was, however, judged of considerable importance that Cosworth Racing retain the machine shop and associated facilities which have been expanded considerably as part of the wider group's competition business over the past few years.

In addition, the racing dynamometers have been retained, in contrast to the separate test beds for the road car engine programmes, which were kept by Audi.

In the longer term the Cosworth Racing operation will be relocated to a state-of-the-art, high-technology, purpose-built headquarters to cope with the anticipated growth and expansion of the company's business. This new base will remain within the Northampton catchment area

Opposite page: Colin Chapman with Walter Hayes, who brought Ford into Grand Prix racing.

Top: Graham Hill wins in Mexico City in 1968 to give the Ford Cosworth DFV its first World Championship. Emerson Fittipaldi *(inset)* and Jackie Stewart *(above)* extended the engine's dominance into the Seventies. Such was the brilliance of the DFV's design it remained competitive into the early Eighties. Michele Alboreto's victory in Detroit in 1983 brought the tally of victories to 155.

The breathtaking Sierra Cosworth road car *(above left)* soon bred competition versions including the successful rally machine *(above right)*.

Right: The turbocharged Lola-Ford of 1986 proved Cosworth's versatility.

1981 – 8 wins	
US GP West	Alan Jones
Brazilian GP	Carlos Reutemann
Argentine GP	Nelson Piquet
San Marino GP	Nelson Piquet
Belgian GP	Carlos Reutemann
British GP	John Watson
German GP	Nelson Piquet
Caesars Palace GP	Alan Jones
1982 – 8 wins	
US GP West	Niki Lauda
Belgian GP	John Watson
Monaco GP	Riccardo Patrese
Detroit GP	John Watson
British GP	Niki Lauda
Austrian GP	Elio de Angelis
Swiss GP	Keke Rosberg
Caesars Palace GP	Michele Alboreto
1983 – 3 wins	
US GP West	John Watson
Monaco GP	Keke Rosberg
Detroit GP	Michele Alboreto
1989 – 1 win	
Japanese GP	Alessandro Nannini
1990 – 2 wins	
Japanese GP	Nelson Piquet
Australian GP	Nelson Piquet
1991 – 1 win	
Canadian GP	Nelson Piquet
1992 – 1 win	
Belgian GP	Michael Schumacher
1993 – 6 wins	
Brazilian GP	Ayrton Senna
European GP	Ayrton Senna
Monaco GP	Ayrton Senna
Portuguese GP	Michael Schumacher
Japanese GP	Ayrton Senna
Australian GP	Ayrton Senna
1994 – 8 wins	
Brazilian GP	Michael Schumacher
Pacific GP	Michael Schumacher
San Marino GP	Michael Schumacher
Monaco GP	Michael Schumacher
Canadian GP	Michael Schumacher
French GP	Michael Schumacher
Hungarian GP	Michael Schumacher
European GP	Michael Schumacher

in order to retain the unique blend of skills offered by the current employees.

Cosworth Racing has a workforce of around 550 in Northampton plus another 50 or so in the United States, rebuilding engines for the CART series.

Cosworth Racing has retained every facility which it has had at its disposal in the past, except for the foundry at Worcester, which is now owned by Audi. This is useful for producing low-volume castings for cylinder heads and blocks, and although it has not been retained by Cosworth Racing arrangements have been concluded to continue using it in the short term while the company considers other options.

From the standpoint of motorsport tradition, the purchase of Cosworth Racing by Ford also continues the trend which saw Ford create a dynamic and youthful image with the various high-performance road cars which have carried Cosworth identification over the past three decades.

That purchase was finalised in order to secure the long-term future of its key motorsport programmes, including F1, CART and touring cars. These can now be conducted in a confidential and exclusive environment and this is almost certain to allow a smoother and more integrated approach to Ford's execution of these crucially important global motorsport programmes.

In recent years, Ford engineers have been working in conjunction with Cosworth personnel in order to facilitate various technological developments for production vehicles, and this move is therefore seen as consolidating an already vibrantly successful partnership.

Martin Whitaker, director of Ford's European motorsports programme, explained the rationale behind the company's acquisition of Cosworth Racing.

'We have been working closely and successfully with Cosworth for more than three decades and feel we are in a position to build on that,' he said. 'Our engineers have been working increasingly closely with those at Cosworth in recent years and we can now develop that relationship within the context of our global product engineering programmes.'

On a wider front, Ford will now use the Cosworth Racing facility to bring in-house development programmes for its other motorsport activities.

There are no plans to vary the Ford F1 programme. Stewart Grand Prix has an exclusive deal for works-supported engines which lasts through to the end of the 2000 racing season.

Cosworth's much-respected reputation has been founded on nearly 40 years of success in top-level motorsport around the world. Ford-Cosworth engines have powered cars to victory in 174 Grands Prix, 12 Indianapolis 500s and countless other international and national races and rallies.

The planned new 1999 Ford V10 engine will mark another milestone in the complex process of integrating the design and development of both F1 car and chassis to the sophisticated levels increasingly demanded by the rigours of Grand Prix competition.

Cosworth Racing's technology has been accelerated as a result of Ford's purchase. 'The relationship between the two companies has become even closer,' says Bernard Ferguson, sales and commercial director.

'There are a lot of facilities which Ford have for computer modelling, for example, and chassis solutions which can be harnessed to make the most of any F1 involvement. The air of confidentiality, which inevitably remained in place between Cosworth Racing and Ford, has now been dismantled and there is a free flow of information between us.'

Cosworth Racing was one of four divisions within the Cosworth group prior to its acquisition by Ford. The company believes that its commitment to excellent engineering standards, combined with the specialist understanding of the Ford Motor Company, will sustain its vibrantly successful and enterprising culture in the future under the control of its sympathetic new owner.

'The acquisition by Ford is the best thing that has happened to Cosworth Racing for many years,' said Dick Scammell, managing director of Cosworth Racing. 'After the initial takeover uncertainty, Ford has invigorated the organisation and provided us with many fresh opportunities for the future.'

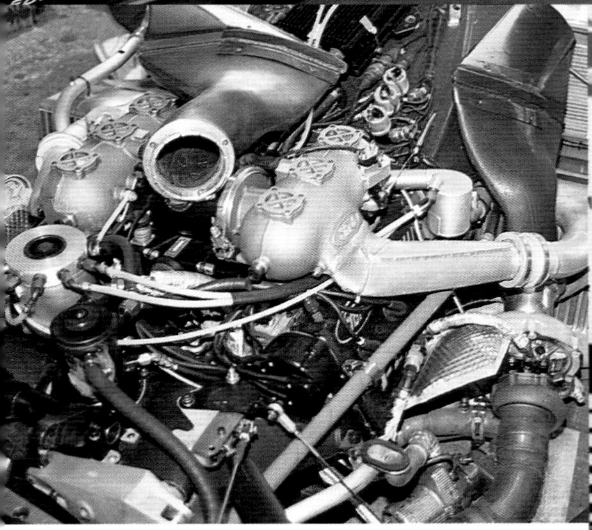

Opposite page: New World Champion Alan Jones *(top)* holds the winner's trophy aloft, United States Grand Prix, 1980.

Left: Cosworth, Ford and Stewart – in partnership until at least the year 2000.

Top: Tyrrell has been a loyal partner of Cosworth in Formula 1 for much of the past thirty years.

Top right: The Ford Zetec-R V8 which Michael Schumacher *(centre)* used to win the 1994 World Championship with Benetton-Ford *(right)*.

The Ford turbo *(above)* showed considerable promise in 1987, but its competition life was cut short by the governing body's decision to ban forced-induction engines. Cosworth soon returned to the winner's circle when the new naturally aspirated HB engine proved successful between 1989 and '93. Nelson Piquet *(below)* took a typically well-judged win for Benetton in Australia in 1990.

COSWORTH *Racing*

The team to lead Cosworth Racing into the Millennium

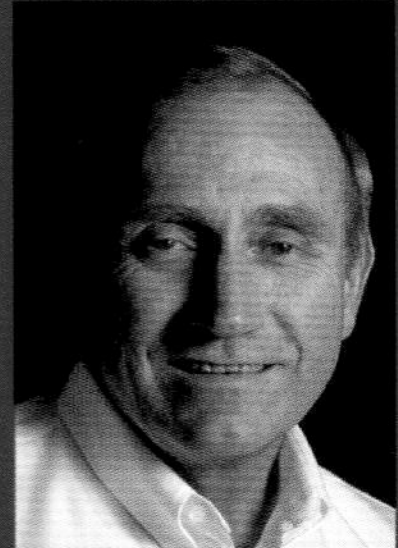

Neil Ressler
Vice-President of Advanced Vehicle Technology & Chairman, Cosworth Racing

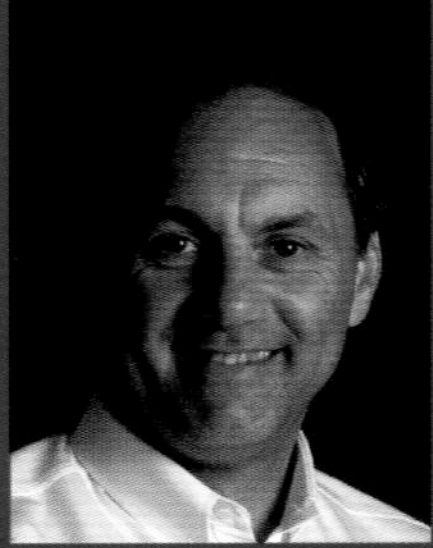

Dan Davis
Director,
Worldwide Motorsport

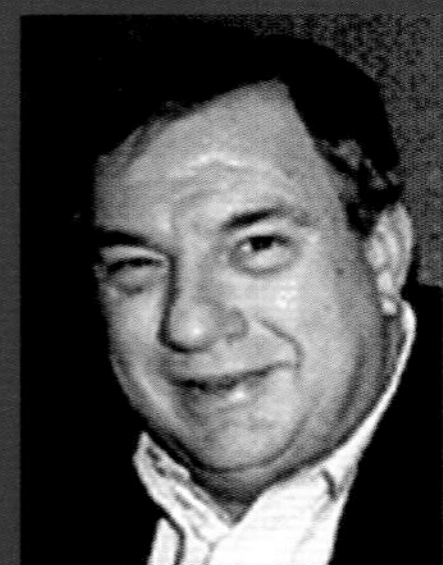

John Valentine
Chief Engineer, Ford Motorsport
Technology Department

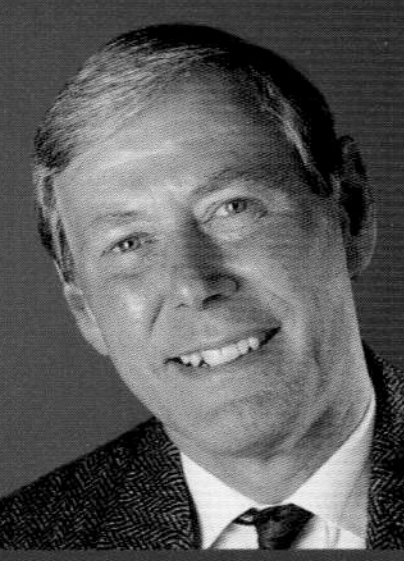

Dick Scammell
Managing Director

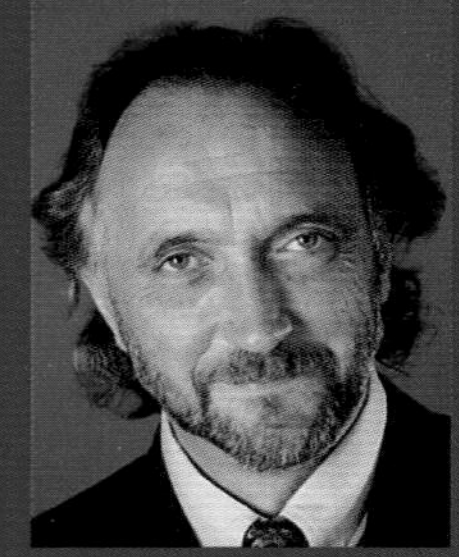

Bernard Ferguson
Sales & Commercial Director

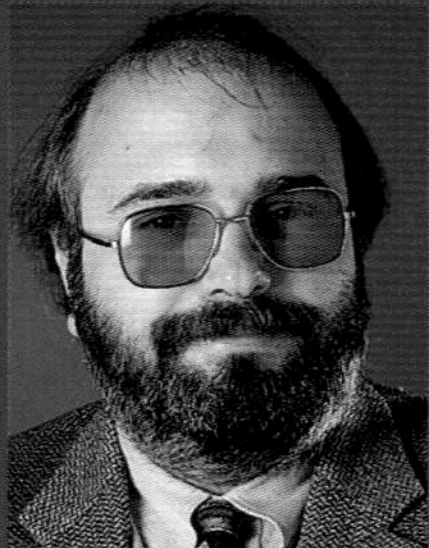

Nick Hayes
F1 Programme Director

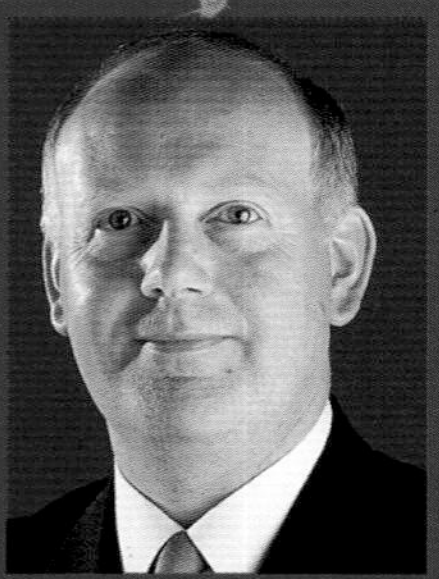

Graeme Hughes
Finance Director

Ford

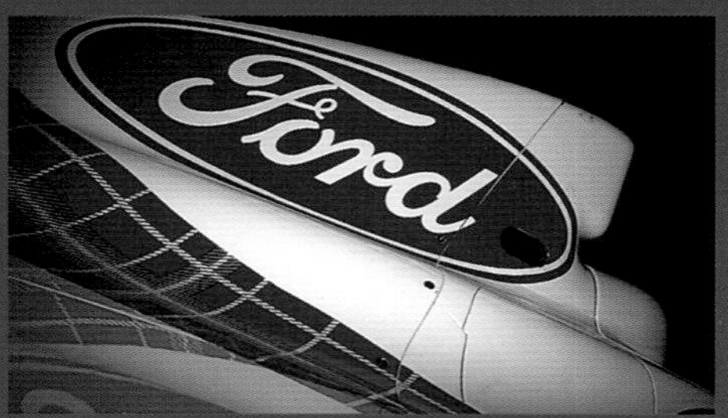

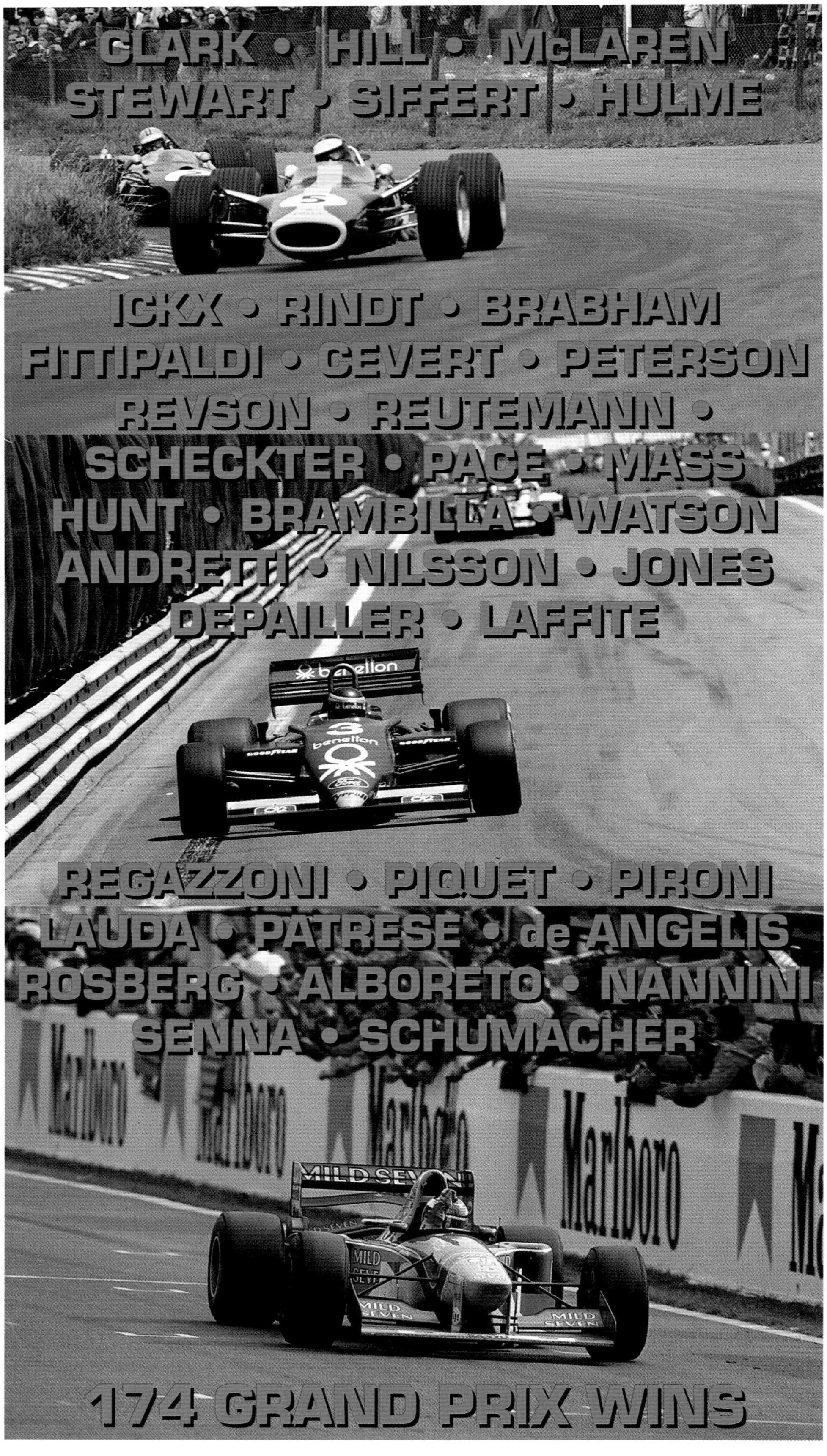
CLARK • HILL • McLAREN
STEWART • SIFFERT • HULME
ICKX • RINDT • BRABHAM
FITTIPALDI • CEVERT • PETERSON
REVSON • REUTEMANN •
SCHECKTER • PACE • MASS
HUNT • BRAMBILLA • WATSON
ANDRETTI • NILSSON • JONES
DEPAILLER • LAFFITE
REGAZZONI • PIQUET • PIRONI
LAUDA • PATRESE • de ANGELIS
ROSBERG • ALBORETO • NANNINI
SENNA • SCHUMACHER
174 GRAND PRIX WINS

COSWORTH Racing

ADVERTISEMENT FEATURE

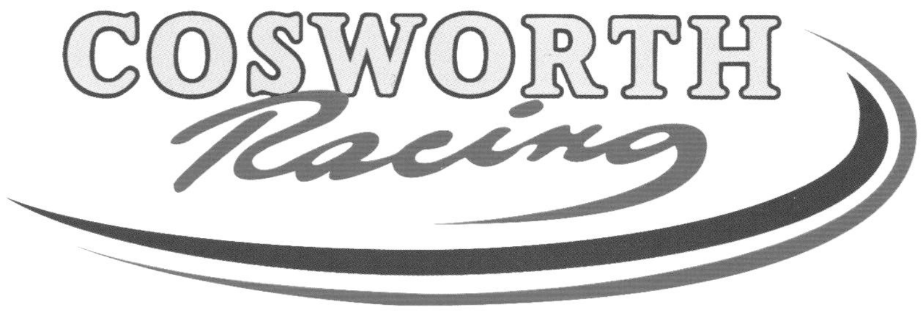

FORMULA 1 REVIEW

CONTRIBUTORS

Bob Constanduros • Maurice Hamilton • Alan Henry

F1 ILLUSTRATIONS

Ian Hutchinson

A 3.2 litre, 24 valve, in-line six cylinder engine producing 321bhp. 100bhp per litre in a car 70kg lighter than the BMW M3. 17 inch wheels and a bodyshell stiff enough to handle the extreme cornering forces of a race track. Brakes that bite hard and fast at operating temperatures of up to 750°C and that can take you from 60-0mph in under 2.8 seconds. Simple statistics

Model featured BMW M Coupé priced at £40,595 on the road. Price correct at time of going to press. BMW Information: P.O. Box 161, Croydon, Surrey CR9 1QB;

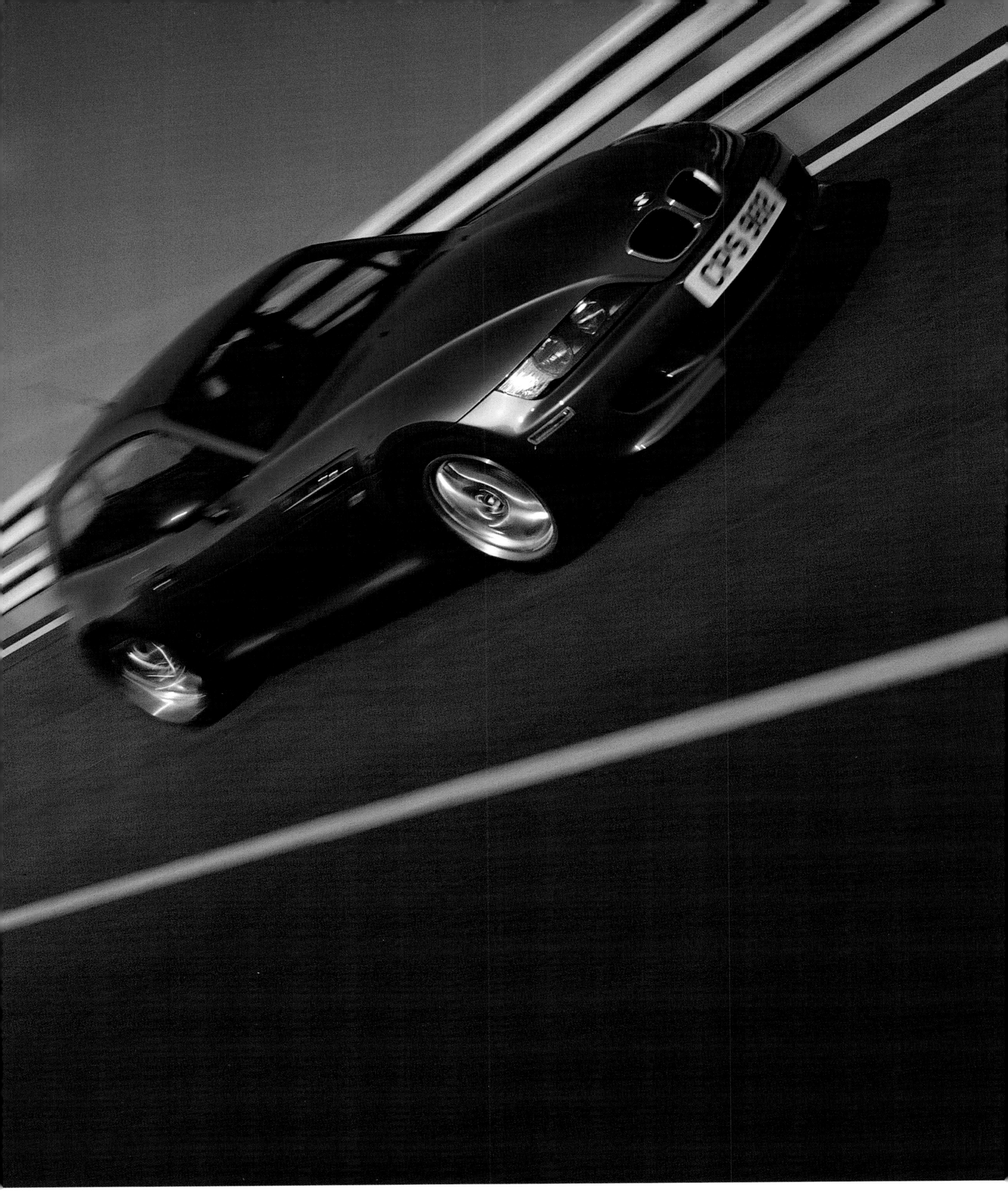

will tell you that the new BMW M Coupé is a car built for circuits that are a lot more testing than the M25. But if you ever want to test its impressive handling abilities to the full, then you will require around £40,000 and a note of the other three numbers at the top of the opposite page.

0800 325600; www.bmw.co.uk

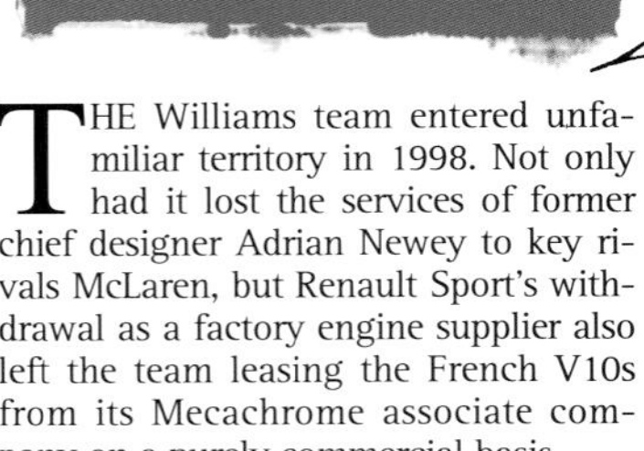

Diana Burnett

Nigel Snowdon

JACQUES VILLENEUVE

HEINZ-HARALD FRENTZEN

THE Williams team entered unfamiliar territory in 1998. Not only had it lost the services of former chief designer Adrian Newey to key rivals McLaren, but Renault Sport's withdrawal as a factory engine supplier also left the team leasing the French V10s from its Mecachrome associate company on a purely commercial basis.

Technical director Patrick Head started the year guardedly confident about the work done on the new FW20 by Gavin Fisher, Newey's successor as chief designer, and chief aerodynamicist Geoff Willis. The new Williams retained the transverse gearbox used on the 1997 car – in contrast to most rivals, who had opted for a longitudinal transmission to produce the best rear-end aerodynamic package.

'Adrian is a very capable engineer and I'm sure he and McLaren will produce a very good car this year,' he acknowledged. 'So if we are seriously challenged or beaten by them, I won't take the view that we can never beat them, because this engineering group is much earlier on in its learning cycle.'

The Williams management also hoped that its exhaustive programme of development work with a test car prepared to the new narrow-track regulations, and running on Goodyear's new grooved tyres, would give the team a flying start to 1998. But although from the touchlines the FW20s, now carrying the garish colour scheme of Rothmans' Winfield brand, looked promising in their initial tests, it quickly became clear that an easing of Goodyear tyre development and some incipient problems with the chassis would combine to make this the most disappointing Williams season in a decade.

Despite that initial promise, Head reflects that he quickly concluded the team was in trouble. 'I think it was plain, pretty early on, that we hadn't made any significant progress with the narrow-track rules,' he said. 'The FW20, in truth, did not show itself to be a significantly improved car over the narrow-track FW19B test chassis, which was pretty disappointing.

'So that's really been the story of the year. We've been playing catch-up. We sorted out some of the major initial problems: weight distribution and inadequate aerodynamic performance. But some of the other problems were too embedded, too inherent in the car.'

Head believed that the FW20's competitive position had been damaged by the relative lack of development on the engine front. 'You could see at circuits like Monza that the level of wing we've had to run in order to get competitive straightline speeds means we've had to run very little downforce, and that certainly hasn't helped,' he explained.

That said, Patrick admitted that the standard of service Williams has received from Mecachrome has been absolutely excellent. However, the internal architecture of the Renault RS9 engine was such that Mecachrome's development programme aimed at uprating the power output was seriously inhibited.

'It was not that they were not trying,' he continues. 'But the changes to that architecture were so big that it was something that would have been impossible to plan, initiate and introduce within the period of a racing season.'

As far as Goodyear was concerned, the Akron tyre giant initially stumbled on tyre development and this compromised the efforts of its contracted teams from the start of the new regulations. Of course the tyre maker was entering its final season of F1 competition and its decision to withdraw was not to be reversed even in the face of the most vigorous lobbying from teams like Williams and Ferrari, its most successful long-term partners.

'I think the biggest disappointment was the lack of effort they put into the narrow-track, grooved-tread development work in 1997,' says Head trenchantly. 'They had a great opportunity to make progress there, and they didn't use it. Although they had put some of the changes in place to pull back on that development by the end of '97, we didn't see the benefit of those efforts until '98.

'I don't think they quite realised what trouble they were in until Melbourne this year and then they went into overdrive to catch up. In fairness, their new programme to improve constructions and produce tougher compounds was already in place by then. I would also say that Goodyear's ability to go to a test, choose a new compound or construction, then have it manufactured, inspected, tested and

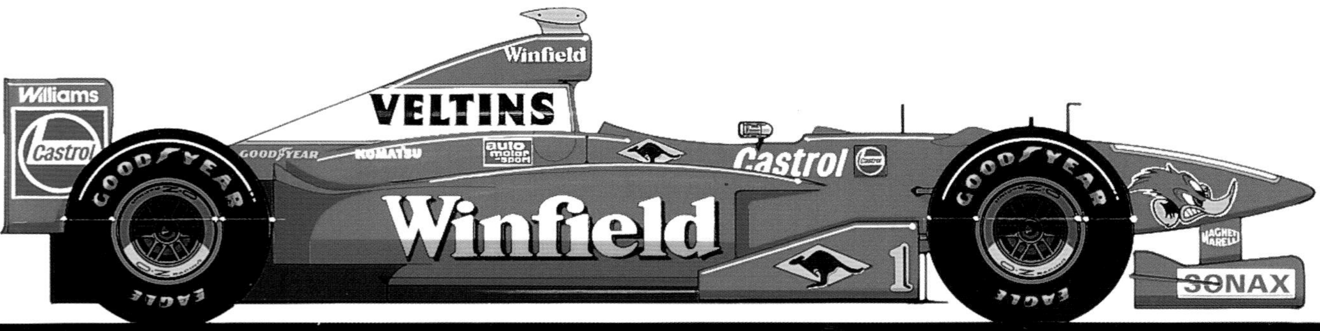

WILLIAMS FW20-MECACHROME

Sponsors: Winfield, Automotive Products, Castrol, Champion, Goodyear, Komatsu, Magneti Marelli, Petrobras, Andersen Consulting, *Auto Motor Und Sport*, Falke, Sonax, *The European*, Universal Studios, Veltins

Team principal: Frank Williams **Technical director:** Patrick Head **Team manager:** Dickie Stanford **Chief mechanic:** Carl Gaden

ENGINE **Type:** Mecachrome GC37/01 **No. of cylinders/vee angle:** V10 (71°) **Sparking plugs:** Champion **Electronics:** Williams/Magneti Marelli **Fuel:** Petrobras **Oil:** Castrol

TRANSMISSION **Gearbox:** Williams six-speed transverse semi-automatic **Driveshafts:** Williams **Clutch:** AP (hand-operated)

CHASSIS **Front suspension:** double wishbones, pushrod, torsion bar **Rear suspension:** double wishbones, pushrod, coil-spring/damper **Suspension dampers:** Williams/Penske
Wheel diameter: front: 13 in. rear: 13 in. **Wheel rim widths:** front: 12.5 in. rear: 13.7 in. **Wheels:** OZ **Tyres:** Goodyear **Brake pads:** Carbone Industrie
Brake discs: Carbone Industrie **Brake calipers:** AP **Steering:** Williams (power-assisted) **Radiators:** Secan/IMI **Fuel tanks:** ATL **Instruments:** Williams

DIMENSIONS **Wheelbase:** 114.7 in./2914 mm **Track:** front: 57.5 in./1460 mm rear: 55.1 in./1400 mm **Fuel capacity:** 27.5 gallons/125 litres

Diana Burnett

Diana Burnett

Diana Burnett

For Patrick Head, team manager Dickie Stanford, Frank Williams and everyone else at Grove it was a season to forget, with the team unable to match the pace of its key rivals.

Below: Heinz-Harald Frentzen's second season with Williams was even more disheartening than his first, and in 1999 he will attempt to revive his career at Jordan.

Reigning World Champion Jacques Villeneuve *(bottom)* was powerless to defend his title but enhanced his reputation with a number of gritty performances.

safety-approved *and* have it at a Grand Prix two weeks later in the requisite quantities was something that I don't think Bridgestone can match.

'At Melbourne and Brazil, the performance between the Ferrari and ourselves was very close. Then the introduction of the wide front tyre, introduced in Argentina, enabled Ferrari to make a step forward but we, if anything, took a step back because the wide front was actually a detriment to us. But they needed to do that because we were both so far away behind McLaren, but it took us quite a time to respond to get the best out of those new tyres.'

Jacques Villeneuve continued to lead the team as reigning World Champion, again partnered by Heinz-Harald Frentzen. In many ways the 1998 season looked likely to be a period of transition for the Williams driver line-up as, even before the first race, the official announcement of Craig Pollock's new British American Racing team had been made.

Although the issue was played down, from the word go there was a strong suspicion that Villeneuve would be unable to resist the temptation of moving to Pollock's team in 1999. Not that this affected Jacques's determination behind the wheel, but when the news of the anticipated split was made public over the Austrian Grand Prix weekend it was clear that Williams and Head would be facing the prospect of replacing both their drivers for next season as the decision to drop Frentzen had by then virtually been taken.

Nevertheless, the German opened the year with a third and a fifth in Melbourne and Brazil. Neither he nor Villeneuve scored in Argentina, but the FW20s took fourth and fifth at Imola, although well off the McLaren/Ferrari pace. Frentzen was unlucky at Monaco, where he was pushed off by Eddie Irvine's Ferrari, then again at Montreal, where Michael Schumacher's carelessness exiting the pit lane saw him shoved off at the first corner just as he was taking third place.

Frentzen unquestionably could drive well, it was just that he often spent too much time fiddling with the car's set-up during qualifying sessions rather than knuckling down and trying to get the best out of what he'd worked on during the free practice sessions.

Villeneuve scored the team's best results with third in Germany and

Bryn Williams

Bryn Williams

Jacques Villeneuve glowers at the camera during practice for the French Grand Prix. Disappointment with the FW20's lack of competitiveness was presumably a factor in his decision to join the new British American Racing team for 1999.

Bottom left: Heinz-Harald Frentzen ran well at Monaco until he was helped into a barrier by Eddie Irvine's Ferrari.

Steve Etherington/EPI

Diana Burnett

Hungary, but blotted his copybook by spinning off in the lead at Spa and then again at Monza while heading for a place in the top six. Generally, though, the Canadian got his head down and never gave up.

'Jacques was always very positive, always battling and fought hard,' said Patrick. 'I think there were quite a few races when he went off the track, but then again he's always been trying to make the car do more than it's actually capable of. He's never given up but, in the rain, well, it's not that he *can't* go quickly in the wet. But when you look at Silverstone and then Spa, somehow you don't feel confident that it's not going to end in grief, in a barrier somewhere.

'Ironically, on car set-up he's very conventional now, although he'd never admit it. He is now running a set-up which is more to my liking and I don't think you've seen so many reports in the press that we've been arguing over the set-up!

'As far as Heinz-Harald is concerned, his two years at Williams have been as much a disappointment for him as for us. Whatever is missing in the Heinz-Harald/Williams mix might well be unlocked at Jordan. The one thing that quickly becomes clear if you work with him is that there is no lack of skill there, merely the application of it.'

If there is one area from which Williams can gain some consolation it is the FW20's mechanical reliability. The cars may not have been quick enough, but they did not have a mechanical breakdown attributable to Williams all season. In fact, Frentzen's engine failure in Austria was the only occasion one of the team's cars failed to finish due to a technical problem. Apart from a couple of races where the team had to radio Frentzen to watch his brake wear rate, the red cars from Grove displayed near-bullet-proof reliability.

Right at the end of the season the team made a big technical push at Suzuka, where the cars appeared with a longer wheelbase, revised diffuser and high, McLaren-style barge boards. Frentzen and Villeneuve were happier with their handling and finished 5-6.

Everyone at Williams hopes that this impressive mechanical record will be sustained into the era of its partnership with BMW which starts in 2000. 'Meanwhile, there endeth a rather sorry saga,' shrugged Patrick. 'A season which all of us at Williams will be happy to put behind us as quickly as possible.'

Alan Henry

Sales
The largest selection of new and used Ferrari in the UK.

Other Makes
All top marques stocked with the facility to source any make or model as required.

Service & Parts
The most comprehensively equipped facilities in the UK for any age of Ferrari.

MARANELLO
SALES LTD

SALES SERVICE PARTS BODY REPAIRS FINANCE

Maranello Sales Ltd. Tower Garage, The By Pass (A30), Egham, Surrey TW20 0AX Telephone 01784 436431
Web Site: http://www.racecar.co.uk/maranello_sales

An Inchcape Company

Nigel Snowdon

Nigel Snowdon

MICHAEL SCHUMACHER

EDDIE IRVINE

Ferrari President Luca di Montezemolo *(below left)* has seen the company regain its position among the élite of Grand Prix racing since returning to Maranello in 1992, but the World Championship remains tantalisingly out of reach.

Diana Burnett

FERRARI'S F300 was a logical evolution of the previous year's car although technical director Ross Brawn admitted that under the new regulations basic elements in the design, such as the centre of gravity, were even more critical. The cockpit on the new car had been moved back slightly by about 10 cm to facilitate the use of shorter side pods while still conforming to the more exacting lateral impact tests and lowering the centre of gravity, a change also assisted by a slightly wider fuel tank and lower engine position.

New rules requiring the footwells to accept a 30 cm cubed template at scrutineering had obviously reduced the space available for suspension components. Ferrari also switched to a longitudinal gearbox to transmit the power from its outstandingly reliable V10 developed by Paolo Martinelli's engine group. Rory Byrne remained as chief designer working closely with Brawn while Aldo Costa was design office manager and Giorgio Ascanelli also continued to play a key role.

This was a hugely important season for Maranello. The team's sporting director Jean Todt opened the year by saying that anything less than winning the World Championship simply wasn't acceptable. The Frenchman had been in charge of Ferrari's F1 fortunes since the summer of 1993 and now, five years down the road, the level of expectancy was running on over-boost.

For the third straight season the driver line-up remained unchanged. Michael Schumacher now looked set to stay with the team through to the end of his F1 career and Eddie Irvine continued in his role as dedicated number two. Every other ambition was subjugated to the overwhelming priority of making Michael and Ferrari World Champions.

It was therefore something of a body-blow when Ferrari's season started on a bad note with Schumacher suffering an early engine failure at Melbourne. 'He had problems right from the start of the race,' recalls Brawn, 'so we knew it wasn't as bad as it looked. Goodyear was also fully aware of the need to improve, which they did dramatically during the early part of the year. I was very impressed; they were a sleeping giant which certainly woke up.'

From the start of the season it seemed as though Ferrari had been wrong-footed in the biggest possible way by the McLaren/Mercedes/Bridgestone alliance. Goodyear had been slow off the mark developing tyres for the new grooved regulations and their new wider front cover – which would prove crucial in boosting Ferrari's fortunes – was also later than hoped for, but Akron was worried that it did not have a rear cover which matched it.

The week after the Brazilian Grand Prix, where Schumacher's Ferrari struggled not to be lapped by the winning McLarens, the new wider mould became available at Akron. Prior to the Buenos Aires race tyres

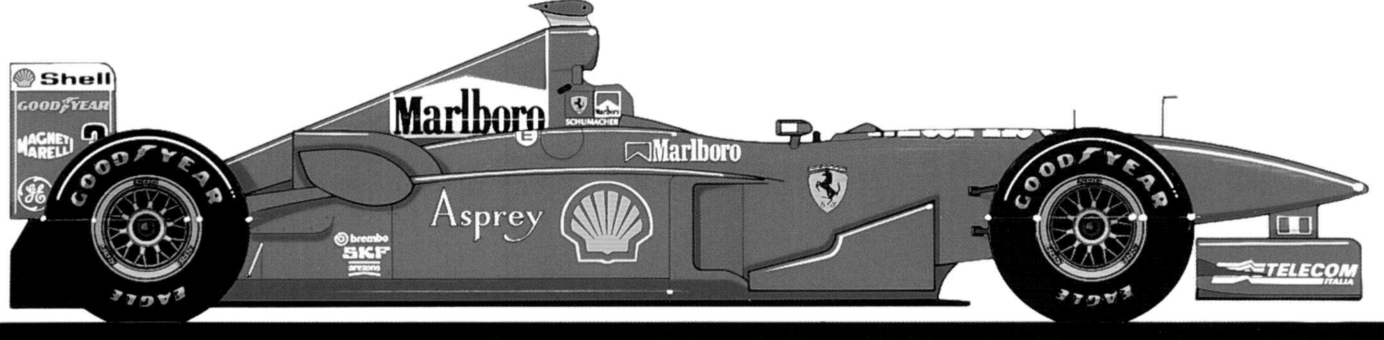

FERRARI F300

Sponsors: Marlboro, Shell, Asprey, Telecom Italia

Team principal: Jean Todt **Technical director:** Ross Brawn **Team manager:** Stefano Domenicali **Chief mechanic:** Nigel Stepney

ENGINE **Type:** Ferrari 047 **No. of cylinders/vee angle:** V10 (75°) **Electronics:** Magneti Marelli **Fuel:** Shell **Oil:** Shell

TRANSMISSION **Gearbox:** Ferrari seven-speed longitudinal semi-automatic **Driveshafts:** Ferrari **Clutch:** Sachs/AP (hand-operated)

CHASSIS **Front suspension:** double wishbones, pushrod **Rear suspension:** double wishbones, pushrod **Suspension dampers:** Sachs **Wheel diameter:** front: 13 in. rear: 13in.
Wheels: BBS **Tyres:** Goodyear **Brake pads:** Carbone Industrie **Brake discs:** Carbone Industrie **Brake calipers:** Brembo **Steering:** Ferrari (power-assisted)
Radiators: Secan **Fuel tanks:** ATL **Battery:** Magneti Marelli **Instruments:** Magneti Marelli

DIMENSIONS **Formula weight:** 1322.8 lb/600 kg including driver

Diana Burnett

Diana Burnett

Nigel Snowdon

There was greater continuity at Ferrari in 1998, with *(left to right)* Ross Brawn, Jean Todt and Rory Byrne once again playing a prominent part in the Italian team's quest for the title.

Below and bottom right: Still a doughty competitor, Eddie Irvine was a model of consistency, finishing in the top four in 11 of the 16 races, and reinforced his image as the ideal number two.

Michael Schumacher paid the price for his unwavering aggression at Monaco *(bottom left)*, where he failed to add to his points tally after a clash with Alexander Wurz's Benetton.

Bryn Williams

Nigel Snowdon

Diana Burnett

Nigel Snowdon

Left: Michael Schumacher produced a string of electrifying laps in mid-race to humble the opposition in Hungary.

Ferrari's superb 1-2 at Magny-Cours *(below left)* was a triumph for team-work, Eddie Irvine bottling up the frustrated McLaren drivers behind him in the opening laps while Schumacher made his escape. The pair also scored maximum points on home ground at Monza *(right)* after both McLarens hit trouble, Michael taking his sixth win of the season.

Below right: The Ferrari mechanics follow their drivers' progress on a pit garage monitor during qualifying at Hockenheim.

Diana Burnett

were airfreighted to Mugello for Ferrari to evaluate. The green light was given for production, but with only one mould available the gamble was taken to build the first batch of tyres to the softer (option) specification for Argentina. It worked perfectly with Schumacher posting a decisive win, beating both McLaren-Mercs on an even playing field.

Once Goodyear got into the swing of the season, so Ferrari could exploit its mechanical reliability to great advantage. That win in Buenos Aires was followed by second place at Imola and third in Spain. Then came Monaco and one of the season's biggest disappointments. Michael qualified fourth and found himself scrapping with the Benettons during the first part of the race.

By then it seemed as though it was worth his taking every risk available, such was his status as a rank outsider in the championship battle. As things developed, he would have been better advised settling for a third or fourth at Monaco, scoring crucial extra points, rather than attempting to sit it out at the Loews hairpin with the similarly determined Alexander Wurz. Michael brushed the wall and lost much time having a rear suspension link replaced. He finished tenth, a crucially disappointing result as things turned out.

Monaco was followed by three more decisive wins at Montreal, Magny-Cours and Silverstone. All were controversial. In Canada Michael pushed Frentzen's Williams off at the first corner, carelessly but possibly not deliberately, while in France McLaren was left crying 'foul' after an aborted start gave Michael a second chance after a poor getaway from the grid first time round. Second time he made no mistakes and won easily while Irvine finished second, having fended off the McLarens in the opening phase of the race.

Silverstone saw Häkkinen give the German a rare wet-weather driving lesson, but the Ferrari driver emerged triumphant after Mika spun even despite the inevitable controversy surrounding the ten-second stop-go penalty which Michael took after passing the chequered flag to win the race.

By this stage in the year Ferrari was coming under close scrutiny from McLaren, who believed their rivals were using some sort of asymmetric braking system, similar to that which the Mercedes-backed team removed from their cars in Brazil following objections from Ferrari. This was in addition to suspicions that Ferrari was using an engine mapping system which effectively duplicated the effects of the now-banned traction control devices, although this was less of an issue since most teams in the F1 field were attempting to develop these systems behind the scenes.

The controversy was defused without the need for an intrusive protest, but cynical eyebrows were raised again when Michael was well off the pace in qualifying at Hockenheim, lining up ninth and finishing fifth. The fact that he had spent Friday wrestling with the revised longer-wheelbase car and that a spin and an engine failure combined to guarantee him just two flying laps in the regular-spec car prior to qualifying on Saturday afternoon seemed rather to be overlooked.

Unquestionably Hungary was Schumacher's finest race of the season where a combination of fine pit-wall strategy and Michael's committed genius at the wheel ensured McLaren went down to an embarrassing defeat. Then came Spa and Schumacher's crucial stumble: over-wound and overwrought at the sight of Coulthard's McLaren ahead of him in a ball of spray, he made a momentary misjudgement. It could have cost him the title.

Monza brought with it a slice of good fortune with the faster McLarens hitting trouble, allowing Schumacher and Irvine to post another 1-2 for Maranello. But at the Nürburgring, Ferrari found its Goodyear tyre choice insufficiently soft for the job. 'It was a bit of a contrast to 1997 when we dreaded hot races,' Brawn reflected. 'This year's compounds have generally been very good in high temperatures, but we were too hard at Nürburgring and couldn't get the grip.'

After a further five weeks of intensive testing, Schumacher qualified on pole for the final race at Suzuka only to stall the Ferrari at the second restart. This episode gave rise to rumours from within the Italian team that Michael may have let his engine revs drop to a level so low that there was insufficient hydraulic pressure available to select first gear.

This suggestion was firmly dismissed by Brawn, who stated that a failure in the clutch mechanism engaged the drive even though the clutch was apparently disengaged. 'There is no way that could have occurred through driver error,' he said.

Brawn would continue to be highly impressed with Michael's complete dedication at the wheel and the manner in which he again motivated the entire Ferrari team around his efforts. Quite how long the German ace can sustain this sort of dynamism remains to be seen.

For his part, Irvine drove extremely well for much of the season. Fourth in Melbourne, he had a frustrating drive to eighth in Brazil, then was only once out of the top three all the way through to Austria, the blot on this run of success coming only when he collided with Giancarlo Fisichella's Benetton at Barcelona. He would also have finished third in Austria had it not been for the need to allow Michael through in the closing stages, aiding his quest for World Championship points.

Irvine also had those splendid second places in France and Italy, followed by another in Japan, plus his first-ever front-row qualifying position at the Nürburgring to console him for the fact that he had yet to win a Grand Prix.

On the technical side, much work went into developing the V10 engine's reliability. 'This was much improved because of the good quality-control system we instigated after the troubles of the 1996 season,' said Brawn. 'We subsequently hand-picked a lot of highly qualified key personnel from both within Fiat and other areas of Ferrari. We also ran lots of miles to iron out the bugs.'

The Ferrari had a triple spring/damper suspension set-up at the front with a third spring being used from time to time on the rear suspension. By the time the team was preparing for Suzuka the F300 was on its third rear floor/diffuser and its sixth front wing set-up, and the switch to a longer wheelbase was not, claimed Brawn, a big difference for the F300.

'It helped make the cars a little more stable riding the kerbs,' he reflected. 'That is something the McLaren does well and highlights our shortcomings in that area. But we're working on it!'

Alan Henry

Nigel Snowdon

Diana Burnett

GIANCARLO FISICHELLA

ALEXANDER WURZ

BENETTON sprung a last-minute surprise in December 1997 when its new B198 challenger was unveiled on Bridgestone tyres – a week after Giancarlo Fisichella and Alexander Wurz completed a four-day test at Jerez on rival Goodyear rubber.

The team's new chief executive David Richards ultimately concluded that there was little chance of persuading Goodyear to change its mind about withdrawing from F1 at the end of the season, despite the fact that Benetton's deal with them went through to the end of 1999.

Following McLaren into the Bridgestone fold looked a shrewd move at a time when the Goodyear runners were all acutely worried about how their tyre supplier's decision to quit F1 at the end of the '98 season would affect the performance of their products. Yet after a promising start, Benetton's effort rather fizzled out during the second half of the season. In fending off the Goodyear resurgence, Bridgestone tailored its tyre configuration to suit McLaren's requirements and Benetton, like most others who used the Japanese rubber, was left behind.

It was also a year which ended with a large question mark hanging over the Benetton family's long-term plans for the team. Almost exactly 12 months after Richards was welcomed into the fold as successor to the colourful Flavio Briatore, the British motor sport entrepreneur resigned and left after the Benettons declined to endorse his strategy for the team's future direction. It seemed a shame that the seasoned and experienced engineering base would not continue to be complemented by an equally experienced manager. His position was taken by Rocco Benetton, youngest son of the knitwear group's co-founder Luciano.

The new Benetton B198 was powered by the Mecachrome – formerly Renault – V10 engine, badged 'Playlife' in deference to one of Benetton's associated companies, and was the second of the team's F1 designs to be completed by Nick Wirth. The car had a longitudinal six-speed gearbox in order to take full advantage of the latest narrow-track technical regulations and two-pedal control, and was equipped with a hand-operated clutch.

It also featured distinctive side aerofoils – 'water wings' as the Benetton insiders call them – ahead of the radiator air intakes, enabling short side pods to be employed while still maintaining conformity with the side-impact rules. This configuration was judged to be an advantage aerodynamically, and in terms of centre of gravity height and rule conformity.

'The effect of the rules was quite fundamental,' reflected technical director Pat Symonds. 'Most teams decided they were going to run an interim car but we made a conscious decision that this was not what we wanted to do. The grooved tyres that were available to test in the latter part of the 1997 season were not representative of what the '98 tyres would really be.

'So we felt it would be better to concentrate our efforts on understanding the challenge of the new regulations, and seeing how we might go about producing a better car. As a result, a lot of the studies were theoretical, which I believe was a good choice because the trend of this year in moving the wheelbase around all over the place trying to work out the right weight distribution was not something which we initially had to do.

'Our studies had shown us what weight distribution we wanted and, with the tyres we had right up until the introduction of the new wide front at Hungary, we couldn't get the weight far enough forward. So we had to follow the then-fashionable development of extending the wheelbase.'

The wider front Bridgestone offered the B198s a substantial performance boost, but the McLaren drivers felt it produced too abrupt a turn-in, so it was not brought to races towards the end of the year. The B198 was left with a handling imbalance as a result, which proved very frustrating in the second half of the season.

'I guess the possibility of our being the poor relation in the Bridgestone equation was in the back of my mind from the first lap I saw the McLaren MP4/13 do in testing at Barcelona,' noted Symonds wryly.

'We put a lot of work in to utilise the wide front tyre as best we could and have proved, time after time, that we get a very considerable perfor-

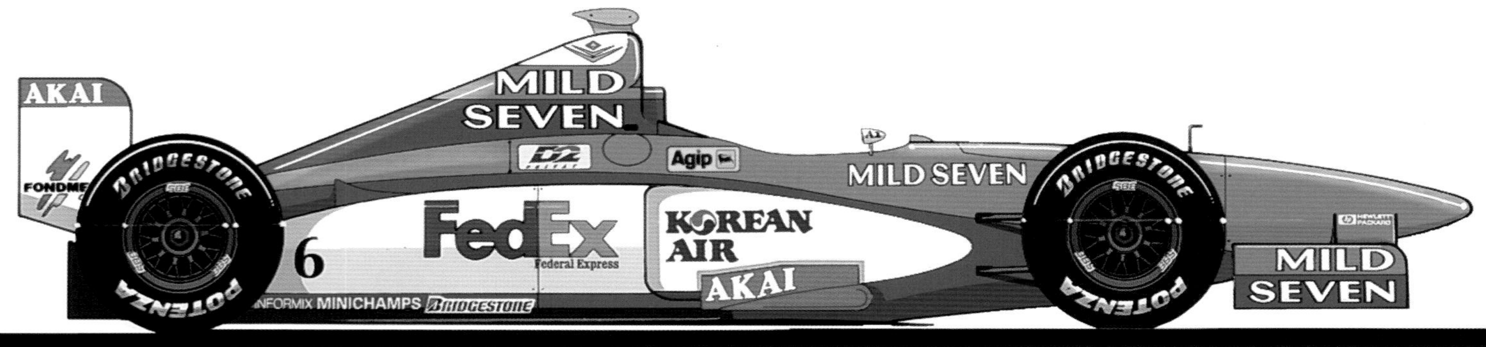

BENETTON B198-PLAYLIFE

Sponsors: Mild Seven, Agip, FedEx, Akai, Korean Air, D2

Team principals: Rocco Benetton, David Richards **Technical director:** Pat Symonds **Team manager:** Joan Villadelprat **Chief mechanic:** Michael Ainsley-Cowlishaw

ENGINE **Type:** Playlife **No. of cylinders/vee angle:** V10 (71°) **Sparking plugs:** Champion **Electronics:** Magneti Marelli **Fuel:** Agip **Oil:** Agip

TRANSMISSION **Gearbox:** Benetton six-speed longitudinal semi-automatic **Driveshafts:** Benetton **Clutch:** AP (hand-operated)

CHASSIS **Front suspension:** double carbon wishbones, pushrod, triple damper **Rear suspension:** double wishbones, pushrod, double damper **Suspension dampers:** Dynamic **Wheel diameter:** front: 13 in. rear: 13 in. **Wheel rim widths:** front: 12 in. rear: 13.7 in. **Wheels:** BBS **Tyres:** Bridgestone **Brake pads:** Carbone Industrie **Brake discs:** Carbone Industrie **Brake calipers:** Brembo **Steering:** Benetton (power-assisted) **Radiators:** Secan/Marston **Fuel tanks:** ATL **Battery:** Benetton **Instruments:** Benetton

DIMENSIONS **Wheelbase:** 114.2 in./2900 mm **Track:** front: 58.7 in./1490 mm rear: 55.3 in./1405 mm **Formula weight:** 1333.8 lb/605 kg including driver **Fuel capacity:** 27.5 gallons/125 litres

Photos: Diana Burnett

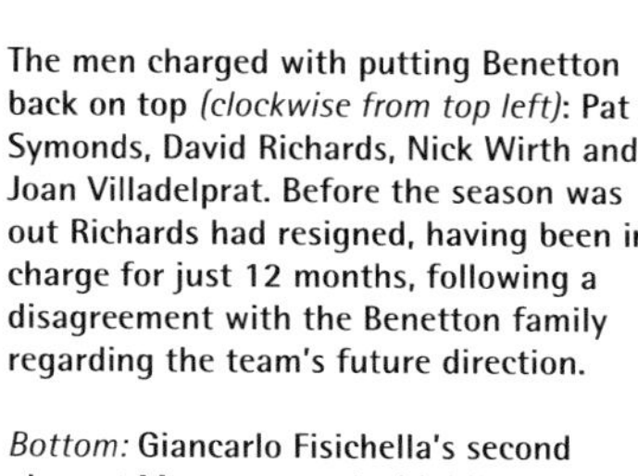

The men charged with putting Benetton back on top *(clockwise from top left)*: Pat Symonds, David Richards, Nick Wirth and Joan Villadelprat. Before the season was out Richards had resigned, having been in charge for just 12 months, following a disagreement with the Benetton family regarding the team's future direction.

Bottom: Giancarlo Fisichella's second place at Monaco was the highlight of the team's season, with the last seven races yielding just one point.

mance advantage from it. But we are not able to use it.'

On the driver front, there was a complete clear-out at the end of the 1997 season. The arrival of Fisichella and Wurz suffused everybody with enormous enthusiasm and optimism. Just as Jean Alesi and Gerhard Berger had sometimes seemed like soldiers suffering from battle fatigue, Giancarlo and Alex radiated a wide-eyed, get-up-and-at-'em enthusiasm. It was just the tonic Benetton needed.

'It is always something of a gamble having new drivers on the team, no matter how sure you might be about what they have to offer,' said Richards. 'There is no doubt that they both have the talent, and sometimes the sheer enthusiasm and commitment radiated by younger drivers has a beneficial effect. It rubbed off on everyone around them, inspiring everybody's efforts.'

The lanky Wurz opened the season with strong fourth places in both Brazil and Argentina, but it was Fisichella who tended to set the pace early on and Wurz only posted another fourth place in Spain after the Italian had been involved in a tangle with Eddie Irvine's Ferrari. But both Benetton drivers certainly looked potentially competitive runners.

At Monaco, both men displayed considerable mettle and resilience. Once David Coulthard's second-placed McLaren had retired with engine failure, the Italian fended off Michael Schumacher's Ferrari with expert precision for lap after lap. Despite a spin later in the race, Fisichella finished an impressive second to Mika Häkkinen's McLaren, a result he duplicated a fortnight later when he harnessed a one-stop strategy to great advantage at Montreal to finish second behind Schumacher's Ferrari.

Wurz also proved that he wasn't about to be intimidated by running in close company with Schumacher, sitting it out with the German as they rubbed wheels at the Loews hairpin, to the detriment of the Ferrari driver. The Austrian later crashed heavily exiting the tunnel, pushing too hard too soon with a heavy fuel load on cool tyres immediately after a routine pit stop. Wurz proved phlegmatic in the extreme as he walked away from this huge shunt, a quality we would see again in Canada when his Benetton somersaulted into the gravel trap at the first corner.

In general terms, both drivers proved pretty resilient to the B198's drop-off in performance. 'They are two extremely pleasant guys and very capable, hard-working drivers,' said Symonds. 'They started the season a little tentatively, perhaps, after which we spoke to them and said, "Go for it – we're not going to criticise you for having accidents," and I think you could see the immediate effect on Giancarlo.

'The drivers have stood up well to the disappointment of the last six races of the year. We have worked them hard and they have responded to the pressure well.'

Symonds agrees that criticism of Fisichella for not having got stuck in harder against Schumacher at Montreal is misplaced. 'I'm not sure that the car was as good there as it had been at some other races when we didn't get as good a result,' he said. 'We were not in a position to beat

Nigel Snowdon

When you need all the

PERFORMANCE

you can get

When you're spending £50 million in a season. When 220 mph still may not be enough. Whenever performance is everything, which spark plug do you choose? Champion. Over 340 Grand Prix wins. World Champion yet again in 1997, bringing the total to a remarkable 21 World Championships. Chosen by more Formula 1 teams than any other spark plug. And by you, if you care how your car performs.

Now part of Federal-Mogul

You can't beat a Champion

Bryn Williams

Former understudy Alexander Wurz demonstrated an ice-cool temperament and considerable tenacity as well as a promising turn of speed during a testing first full season in Formula 1.

Bottom: More than a dozen mechanics tend Giancarlo Fisichella's Benetton during a routine refuelling stop in Australia. The inclusion of two enthusiastic youngsters in the driver line-up gave the whole team a lift.

Michael there and he drove a very competitive race to finish second.

'I think there were some occasions where he was still a little bit over-awed, as he perhaps showed in Austria [where he qualified on pole, but let Häkkinen and Schumacher through at the start]. I am sure that is an attitude of mind. After Melbourne, for example, we told Alex that he had to prove his position in the F1 pecking order, and he did it. If there is a very slight criticism of Giancarlo it is that he could sometimes be a little more aggressive in the occasional race. But it is a minor niggle.'

During the course of the season Benetton has made a few aerodynamic changes to the B198, the most crucial being the introduction of a narrower-span front wing. 'This was first tried at Hockenheim,' said Symonds. 'It then disappeared again, because we initially couldn't make it work at higher downforce levels. But from Spa onwards it became the standard fitting for all downforce configurations. It was designed very much with the wide Bridgestone in mind, but we still got a benefit even with the narrow tyre.'

At Monza the B198 featured a new engine cover, rear bodywork and diffuser, which was a small, but worthwhile, improvement. There has also been considerable suspension development which has been quite clear-cut and beneficial. Quite a lot of work also went into braking systems, Benetton's lateral brake bias system being used only in testing. 'By the time we were ready to race it, the arguments were well under way,' said Symonds. 'In fact, they were over!'

Symonds mirrored Patrick Head's enthusiasm for the Mecachrome V10. 'I am sure that there are other engines, Mercedes and Ferrari perhaps, which have overtaken us in the power stakes,' he says. 'But I still think that the Mecachrome V10 is a good racing engine. If I could wish for something more from it, then I think, to be honest, it would be more for weight reduction than power increase. But it still does a very good job.'

Alan Henry

Diana Burnett

7 McLAREN 8

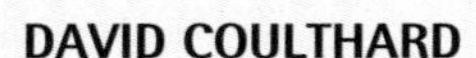

Nigel Snowdon

DAVID COULTHARD

Diana Burnett

MIKA HÄKKINEN

David Coulthard controls a slide at Monaco. The superbly liveried MP4/13 enjoyed a clear performance advantage for much of the year, and only a sequence of misfortunes prevented Coulthard and his team-mate Mika Häkkinen from adding to their tally of nine wins.

Below left: Ron Dennis and Norbert Haug ponder the long and winding road to the World Championship. It had been more difficult than many observers had anticipated, but in 1998 the McLaren-Mercedes alliance finally reached its goal.

Diana Burnett

THE 1997 season had seen McLaren win three Grands Prix in partnership with engine supplier Mercedes-Benz. This ended a drought of victories which had lasted for more than three years. But that was only part of the job which Ron Dennis and Mercedes motor sport manager Norbert Haug had vowed to complete when they formed the alliance in the summer of 1994.

In 1998 the aim was to win McLaren's first World Championship since Ayrton Senna claimed the title in a Honda-engined machine seven years before. To that end, the McLaren-Mercedes squad took two key decisions which were to represent the final crucial components in the jigsaw of success they had painstakingly assembled over the past three seasons. They hired former Williams chief designer Adrian Newey, and switched from Goodyear to Bridgestone tyres.

Newey had left Williams in the autumn of 1996 after a difference of opinion with Frank and Patrick Head over the terms of his contract. While the legal complications were worked out, Newey remained at home on 'gardening leave' until the following August before being free to join McLaren. He obviously could not work for his new employer during that time, but what he could do was clear his mind and start thinking in terms of what would be required from the new narrow-track, grooved-tyre F1 regulations which were to be implemented at the start of 1998.

By the time Newey joined McLaren the established design team had also been researching the challenge of the new rules. The former Williams engineer, whose proven forte had always been an ability to extract the maximum aerodynamic potential from any given situation, integrated quickly and well with long-serving chief designer Neil Oatley, aerodynamicist Henri Durand and their engineering teams.

Over the winter the McLaren design team reckoned it had expended more than 12,000 man hours attempting to claw back aerodynamic downforce lost to the new regulations. The new MP4/13 also had a completely revised Mercedes-Benz FO110G V10 engine, which weighed in at around five per cent lighter than its immediate predecessor.

McLaren had gambled to leave the build programme for the new car as late as possible, Newey reasoning that the team's serious development work for the new regulations had not really started until his arrival in August 1997. 'Williams and the others had been hard at it since February or March,' he said enigmatically, 'so we had a steep learning ramp to climb.'

The switch to Bridgestone tyres had cost the team a crucial extra week or so in terms of finalising the car's detailed suspension geometry, but this was judged well worth the effort. 'The

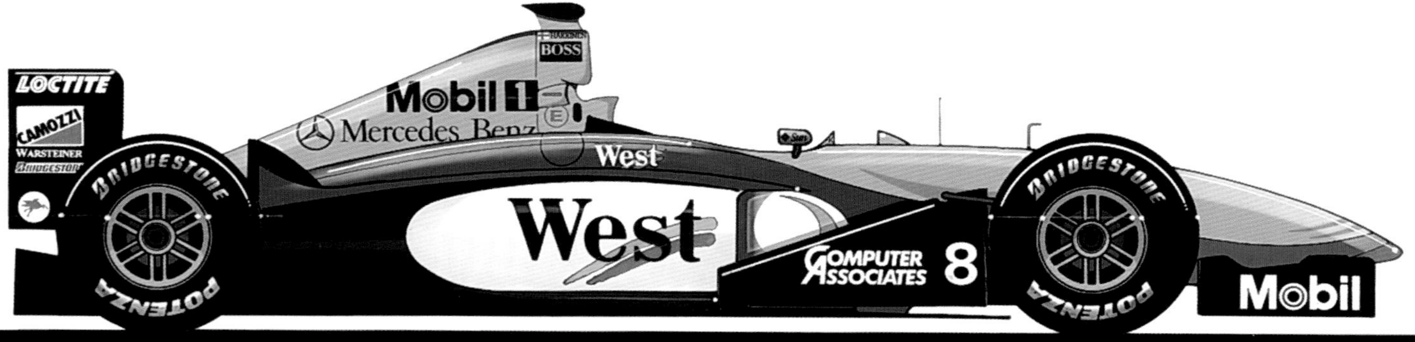

McLAREN MP4/13-MERCEDES

Sponsors: West, Mobil, Loctite, Camozzi, Computer Associates, Boss, Sun, Warsteiner, British Aerospace

Team principal: Ron Dennis **Technical director:** Adrian Newey **Team manager:** Dave Ryan **Chief mechanic:** Mike Negline

ENGINE **Type:** Mercedes-Benz FO110G **No. of cylinders/vee angle:** V10 (72°) **Sparking plugs:** NGK **Electronics:** TAG **Fuel:** Mobil **Oil:** Mobil

TRANSMISSION **Gearbox:** McLaren six-speed longitudinal semi-automatic **Driveshafts:** McLaren **Clutch:** AP (hand-operated)

CHASSIS **Front suspension:** double wishbones, pushrod **Rear suspension:** double wishbones, pushrod **Suspension dampers:** McLaren/Penske **Wheel diameter:** front: 13 in. rear: 13 in. **Wheels:** Enkei **Tyres:** Bridgestone **Brake pads:** Hitco **Brake discs:** Hitco **Brake calipers:** AP **Steering:** McLaren **Radiators:** Calsonic/IMI Marston **Fuel tanks:** ATL **Battery:** GS **Instruments:** TAG

DIMENSIONS **Formula weight:** 1322.8 lb/600 kg including driver

West
BRIDGESTONE
West
West
7
Mobil
1

MERCEDES E55 AMG FROM £60,540 ON THE ROAD (INCLUDES DELIVERY, NUMBER PLATES, FIRST REGISTRATION TAX, A FULL TANK OF FUEL AND, AT CUSTOMER REQUEST, 12 MONTHS ROAD FUND LICENCE).FOR DETAILS TELEPHONE 0171 536 3555 ext
www.mercedes-benz.co.uk

There are days

when the ocean reminds me of her

awesome hidden power.

In moments of tranquillity she charms me.

Then suddenly

very suddenly

she assumes a distinct and very definite existence.

From fathomless depths she produces that elemental sound.

That grumbling groan of pure, potential power.

As if for the first time,

I'm aware of the phenomenon that lurks beneath the surface.

All the while the current acquires a momentous velocity.

Each second adding to her speed

to her inevitable urge.

And I'm left captivated by her eternal energy.

E-class AMG

Diana Burnett

Diana Burnett

Formula 1 is no longer a cottage industry and a successful championship challenge is the product of the collective efforts of a small army of highly talented individuals. Neil Oatley *(near right)*, Paul Morgan of engine builder Ilmor *(far right)*, Adrian Newey, Mario Illien of Ilmor and team manager Dave Ryan *(below right)* all made substantial contributions to the McLaren-Mercedes partnership's triumph.

Bottom: His undoubted natural talent seemingly unlocked by his somewhat fortunate maiden victory at Jerez at the end of the previous season, Mika Häkkinen blossomed into an assured and authoritative race winner in 1998.

Diana Burnett

harder you use those tyres, the faster you go,' reported Mika Häkkinen. 'You can slide the car a lot and the rubber will sustain its grip. At last I can drive the car in the way I have always wanted to.'

The MP4/13 design retained the low-nose configuration used on the 1997 cars but the front suspension package was completely different. Inboard vertical dampers and torsion bars replaced the horizontally mounted coil-spring/dampers ahead of the cockpit on the MP4/12.

The new McLaren worked splendidly straight out of the box. In the opening race at Melbourne, Häkkinen and his team-mate David Coulthard lapped the field. The Scot adhered to a pre-race pact in which both drivers agreed that whoever got to the first corner in the lead should win the race. This involved David relinquishing his advantage after Mika had mistakenly come into the pits at the wrong time and the episode ignited a debate over whether such team tactics were permissible or not.

Since the flames of this controversy were largely fanned by the race promoter Ron Walker, who seemed to have a strangely misplaced sense of sympathy for anybody daft enough to wager money on the outcome of a Grand Prix, the issue soon died down. Among the F1 teams, at least.

In Brazil Ferrari indicated that it was not satisfied that the asymmetric braking system on the MP4/13 was legal. Given the fact that the FIA technical department had indicated they had no objections to the system when McLaren checked with them during the winter, it came as a surprise when the race stewards deemed it to contravene the regulations.

Paul-Henri Cahier

McLaren, diplomatically not wishing the World Championship to be blighted by a major row at this early stage, removed the system from both cars voluntarily. Häkkinen and Coulthard then went out and repeated their Melbourne 1-2, almost lapping Michael Schumacher's third-placed Ferrari in the process.

Yet this initial level of domination was not to be sustained. Goodyear's progress enabled Ferrari to defeat the McLarens in a straight fight in Buenos Aires, where Coulthard was pitched into a spin by the over-zealous Michael Schumacher while leading the early stages of the race.

Coulthard had the upper hand over Häkkinen in Buenos Aires, and again at Imola, where he posted his sole victory of the season. Apart from there and Montreal, however, Häkkinen was the dominant partner in this relationship. He out-qualified Coulthard 13–3 and usually looked the most convincing performer in a race situation. He was never lower than third on the grid and completed the season with nine poles, three second places and four third places in the starting line-up.

Coulthard posted one of his three pole positions in Montreal where, after Häkkinen stopped on the first lap with gearbox problems, he looked set to beat Schumacher's Ferrari only for the throttle mechanism on one bank of the Merc V10 to come adrift. It was finger trouble and extremely embarrassing. 'I just hope we don't look back and reflect this was where we lost the World

So big... We couldn't

RIDE WELL. RIDE SAFE. DRESS FOR PROTECTION. FOLLOW THE LAW. DON'T DRINK AND RIDE. PROPER MAINTENANCE IS ESSENTIAL.
Kawasaki Motors UK. Ltd. 1 Dukes Meadow, Bourne End, Bucks, SL8 5XF. Tel:01628 851000

We couldn't

For 1999 Kawasaki will be big, very big.

And we're going to offer you more... much more.

fit it all on one page

More choice, more value, more of what you've come to expect from us since Kawasaki started heads and wheels turning in the UK twenty five years ago.

First take a long look at a long, low bike, the New VN1500 Drifter. You won't go unnoticed on this 1940's styled cruiser or its equally striking cruisin' cousin the VN800 Drifter.

Drawing two lung-fulls of 1960's British influence is the new for '99 W650 twin, a triumph of tradition and technology.

And bringing biking bang up to date are the maxed-out ZX-6R and ZX-9R, both with new graphics and the Eddie Lawson styled ZRX1100. By way of a big finish, check out the stunning new ZR-7 representing the naked truth from Kawasaki.

For information on the whole range of Kawasaki products and services, call our Hotline on 0800 500 245, or visit your local franchised Kawasaki dealer and go 'biking big time in '99.

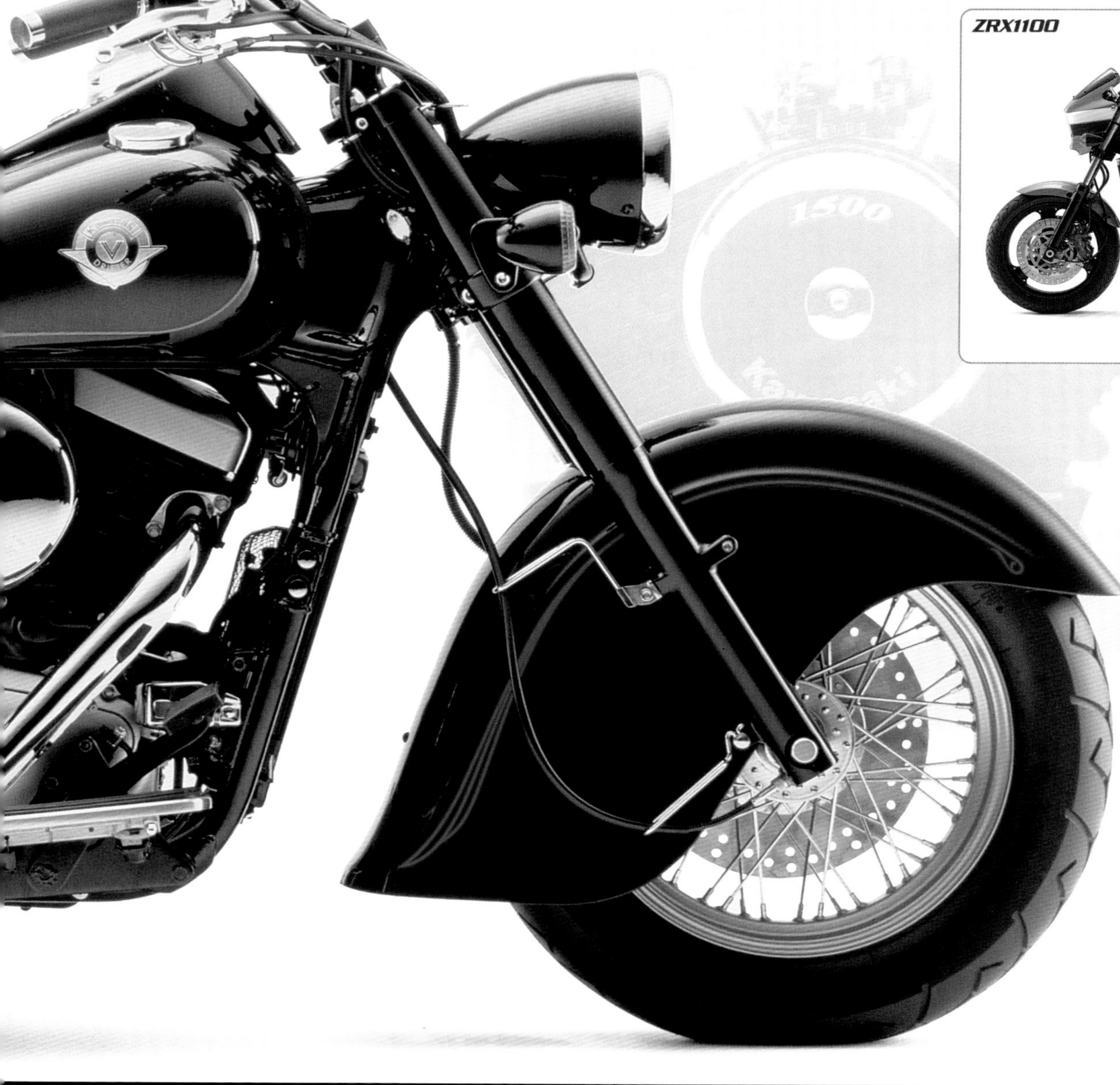

ZR-7

ZX-6R

ZX-9R

ZRX1100

W650

VN800 Drifter

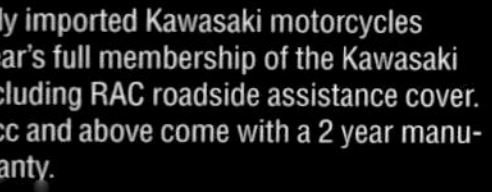
All new officially imported Kawasaki motorcycles come with a year's full membership of the Kawasaki Riders Club including RAC roadside assistance cover. Machines 250cc and above come with a 2 year manufacturer's warranty.

Kawasaki

Peter Nygaard/GP Photo

David Coulthard studies the timing screens in Austria. It was a bitterly disappointing season for the genial Scot, who was regularly out-qualified by his team-mate Mika Häkkinen and could manage only a single victory, but he bore his misfortunes with creditable stoicism.

Bottom: McLaren opened its campaign with a crushing 1-2 in Australia, where the silver and black cars lapped the rest of the field. Häkkinen took the win after Coulthard had surrendered the lead in accordance with the terms of a pre-race agreement and never looked back.

Championship,' said Ron Dennis thoughtfully after the race.

To be fair, this was a rare mechanical breakdown for the MP4/13. Häkkinen had already retired at Imola due to a rogue counterfeit gearbox bearing somehow finding its way into the build programme. It failed and the Finn retired from second place. Later there would be bottom-end failures of the Merc V10 at Monaco and Monza, both to Coulthard's car, and a preparation problem which caused a front anti-roll bar to work loose on Häkkinen's car at Budapest, intermittently jamming a pushrod which made the handling next to impossible. He faded from first to sixth as a result of this problem.

Arguably this was a race which McLaren should have won. The wrong fuel strategy prevented Coulthard, on a two-stop schedule, from getting ahead of Schumacher's Ferrari when it emerged from the last of its three stops. Häkkinen taking the restart at Spa on Bridgestone intermediates instead of full-wet tyres was also a questionable decision. Generally, though, McLaren's strategy was pretty good.

The McLaren-Mercedes squad tested relentlessly, which in practical terms meant they were hard at it most weeks when there was no Grand Prix. Test driver Ricardo Zonta was often employed to carry out some of the routine chores, but Häkkinen and Coulthard were generally very happy to do the bulk of the work as both were determined to play their part in sustaining the team's highly competitive edge.

One of the biggest disappointments came in the Italian Grand Prix where Häkkinen, who had been troubled by a handling imbalance on his first set of tyres, suffered a major front brake failure at 170 mph on his second set while closing on Schumacher's winning Ferrari. After recovering from the resultant high-speed spin he struggled home over the remaining seven laps to finish in fourth place, leaving him dead-heating on points with the Ferrari driver with two races still to run.

Häkkinen superbly turned that round at the Nürburgring, where he beat Schumacher in a straight fight to lead by four points going into the final race of the season. It was unbelievable to think that, twelve months earlier, the Finn had yet to win his first Grand Prix, but his spectacular level of success throughout 1998 was an endorsement of the mutual commitment which he and the McLaren team had shown each other ever since he'd signed up as test driver at the start of 1993.

For Coulthard, the season was a huge disappointment. He had driven better than his results suggested, but the way events had unfolded meant that he was perceived as a number two driver by everybody but his employers by the end of the season. McLaren was now back in the big time and it was Mika Häkkinen who had come out on top as its most convincing exponent.

Alan Henry

Nigel Snowdon

Diana Burnett

DAMON HILL

Nigel Snowdon

RALF SCHUMACHER

THIS will be looked upon as a memorable year for Jordan Grand Prix, a season which will make them both shiver and smile. On the one hand, Jordan finally won their first Grand Prix – and won it well. On the other, they went through hell to get there. But you would hardly expect anything else from a team which remains one of the most charismatic in the paddock thanks mainly to the influence of its colourful leader.

Eddie Jordan went into the new season with his usual brash optimism. He had no choice, really. His team had come close to winning a few races and he could hardly say second place would be satisfactory in 1998, particularly after signing Damon Hill to join Ralf Schumacher. The upward trend continued as Jordan hired no less an edifice than the Royal Albert Hall for the launch of his new car. Talk about 'Land of Hope and Glory'. On paper, this team had everything going for it.

Behind the scenes, there was a fair amount of turmoil. The anticipated teething troubles which came with a move from Peugeot to Mugen Honda engines had been exacerbated by serious problems with the electronics system. Instead of completing hundreds of miles of testing with an interim car (a 197 converted to accept the Mugen Honda V10) in November, the team had managed about ten laps – and hesitant ones at that.

As a result, an unavoidable decision to switch to TAG Electronics meant the early test schedule had to be torn up and thrown away. Apart from delaying the growth of the liaison between Jordan and Mugen Honda, the lack of running came at a crucial time.

The technical department, led by Gary Anderson, needed to learn about the effects of the revised regulations governing the dimensions of the cars and the introduction of grooves in the tyres. The problems meant there was no early feedback. Jordan-Mugen Honda were behind from the outset.

The initial tests with the 198 were reasonably encouraging. The new car was reliable but a lack of competitiveness began to show when major players such as McLaren and Ferrari got down to serious work. The painful reality was confirmed at the first race as Hill and Schumacher struggled to qualify on the edge of the top ten. The car wasn't working. The difficulty would be discovering the precise cause.

'The first thing was to actually accept that we had a problem,' says Trevor Foster, Jordan's race director. 'We couldn't be sure exactly where the difficulty lay. The Mugen Honda engine was a bit behind on development largely because of the time lost in October and November. We had been unable to sort the car for the same reason. Put all that together and there's the loss of pace. We could see flashes of promise but that was due more to reliability than anything else. We were getting maximum track time but we weren't actually getting maximum performance.

'We had to evaluate exactly where we were and pinpoint the problems. Then we had to put in some fairly major surgery. We looked at every area of the car. There wasn't one particular aspect which was giving trouble. We changed the mechanical specification [a 10 cm increase in wheelbase], we altered the aerodynamics, the engine was uprated and, at the same time, Goodyear picked up pace in response to Bridgestone. Since putting the car on the grid in Melbourne, we have made more than 70 changes, all in the name of performance.'

Monaco had proved to be the catalyst. After watching Hill and Schumacher fight with the Minardi drivers in a battle to avoid being the first cars lapped by the leaders, Eddie Jordan was galvanised into action. A two-hour meeting immediately after the race laid the foundations for reform which went beyond a thorough examination of the car. A proposed restructuring of the management system would include more responsibility for Foster and the employment of Mike Gascoyne, an aerodynamicist with Tyrrell, as chief designer. Gascoyne had Anderson's approval, unlike the proposed organisational changes.

In the meantime, a concentrated period in the wind tunnel saw Anderson introduce a package of modifications (shorter side pods, bigger barge boards, a new diffuser) which would contribute to a slow but sure rise in performance. The turnaround began at the British Grand Prix, a race which

JORDAN 198-MUGEN HONDA

Sponsors: Benson & Hedges, MasterCard, Repsol, Pearl

Team principal: Eddie Jordan **Technical director:** Gary Anderson **Chief designer:** Mike Gascoyne **Team manager:** Jim Vale **Chief mechanic:** Tim Edwards

ENGINE **Type:** Mugen Honda MF310C **No. of cylinders/vee angle:** V10 (70°) **Sparking plugs:** NGK **Electronics:** TAG **Fuel:** Repsol **Oil:** Elf

TRANSMISSION **Gearbox:** Jordan six-speed longitudinal semi-automatic **Driveshafts:** Jordan **Clutch:** AP/Sachs (hand-operated)

CHASSIS **Front suspension:** unequal-length double wishbones, pushrod-operated rockers **Rear suspension:** unequal-length double wishbones, pushrod-operated rockers **Suspension dampers:** Showa **Wheel diameter:** front: 13 in. rear: 13 in. **Wheel rim widths:** front: 12.5 in. rear: 14 in. **Wheels:** OZ **Tyres:** Goodyear **Brake pads:** Carbone Industrie **Brake discs:** Carbone Industrie **Brake calipers:** Brembo **Steering:** Jordan **Radiators:** Jordan/Secan **Fuel tanks:** Jordan/ATL **Battery:** Portalac **Instruments:** Jordan

DIMENSIONS **Track:** front: 58.3 in./1480 mm rear: 55.9 in./1420 mm **Gearbox weight:** 110.2 lb/50 kg **Chassis weight (tub):** 121.2 lb/55 kg **Formula weight:** 1322.8 lb/600 kg including driver **Fuel capacity:** 28.6 gallons/130 litres

Diana Burnett

Diana Burnett

It is a cruel irony that Gary Anderson *(far left)* should have decided to leave the team he had done so much to build up just as Eddie Jordan's unfailing optimism was about to be justified at last.

Below: Damon Hill drove faultlessly in dreadful conditions at Spa to give the team its long-overdue maiden victory.

Bottom: Eddie gives Ralf Schumacher a lecture during practice for the British Grand Prix. The young German responded as his employer would have wished, scoring the team's first point of the season after a fine performance.

Nigel Snowdon

Photos: Diana Burnett

Nigel Snowdon

Ralf Schumacher's expression at the post-race press conference at Spa makes plain his disappointment that he had been ordered not to challenge team-mate Damon Hill for the privilege of recording the team's first win.

The young German *(below)* was consistently impressive during the second half of the season, regularly figuring among the points-scorers, but he has decided to move to Williams for 1999.

was run in the rain. Previously, Hill and Schumacher had described the Jordan as almost undriveable in the wet. At Silverstone, the car was very competitive. Damon made a silly mistake but Ralf brought the team their first point of the season. There was to be no looking back from then on.

Jordan picked up points in the next five races but none would be more memorable than the maximum achieved at Spa as Hill and Schumacher not only gave Eddie Jordan his first win but also finished a very strong 1-2 on a day when more than half the field had fallen victim to the treacherous conditions. The cars had run like clockwork. Indeed, Jordan was the only team in the happy position of being able to load a pair of unmarked cars into the waiting transporters.

The pre-season hype had been justified. The only sadness was that Anderson had not been there to see it. After more than ten years with Jordan, the Ulsterman decided that it was time to move on. The irony was that he had become a victim of Jordan's growth which had been generated in part by the potential of his cars.

'The funding from Benson & Hedges in recent years allowed us to invest in equipment, a wind tunnel, R&D facilities and so on,' said Foster. 'We needed more staff to support that programme and it got to the point where we had 42 people directly responsible to the technical director. That's a huge management job and I think Gary found that aspect difficult. He's a very competent designer but it was a great, great shame that he was unable to adapt to the management role which had become necessary. We've had to grow and move away from a "hands on" style of doing things and try and maximise our resources. We managed them better and that had a significant effect on our results.'

The effect exerted by the drivers has been mixed. Hill seemed to suffer initially from the car's uncompetitiveness as he suddenly envisaged another season like the one he had just endured with Arrows. Apart from a high profile which pleased Benson & Hedges, the former World Champion had been employed (as a replacement for Giancarlo Fisichella) for the benefit of his experience. But the team had to give him a decent car in order to extract the maximum from their driver.

That moment came at Spa, Hill driving superbly all weekend. The same could be said for Schumacher as he shrugged off a reputation which had not been helped by some wild moments in the first half of the season.

'There was no question about Ralf's speed at the beginning of the year,' says Foster. 'But we had a problem with the car which wasn't helping his starting technique and that was compounded initially by the fact that we couldn't get people to accept that the car problem existed. Once we had addressed that, Ralf didn't look back. He has matured immensely and it's a great disappointment that he will not be here in 1999 when that maturity comes to fruition.'

Against all predictions, Hill and Schumacher worked extremely well together, the partnership being helped in turn by a productive co-operation between their respective engineers, Dino Toso and Sam Michael.

Despite problems which would have torn a lesser team apart, the mood within Jordan remained positive throughout a difficult first half of the season. It was a measure of their newsworthiness and a willingness to be open that Jordan continued to enjoy support from the media, even if the reports had, perforce, become less than flattering at times.

The pay-off came at Spa. There will scarcely be a more popular victory. Not only was Jordan better off but, arguably, Grand Prix racing was also a beneficiary of one of the fastest turnarounds in the history of Formula 1.

From having debated the best way to stop the Jordan name from sliding to the bottom of the constructors' championship, Jordan-Mugen Honda went into the final race fighting for third place. Not even Eddie Jordan would have believed that scenario had you run it past him at Monaco in May.

Spa ought to be the making of the team. Certainly, attitudes have changed, as witnessed by a refusal to take on a junior driver or one with a large bag of money to replace Schumacher in 1999. The growing-up process is showing signs of finally coming to an end – although, hopefully, not at the expense of a unique and cheerful personality.

Maurice Hamilton

Michael Roberts

Scania. The truck that got the Jordan Grand Prix team to the 1998 Belgian Grand Prix.
(Well done, boys. That was a nice one-two.)

Diana Burnett

OLIVIER PANIS

Diana Burnett

JARNO TRULLI

'WE knew it was going to be difficult, but not this difficult.' How many times did Alain Prost repeat that during 1998? The season was compromised by his car's poor weight distribution from the start, and only when the team ran a revised prototype AP01B chassis during the five-week gap between the Nürburgring and Suzuka was there a glimmer of hope.

In any event, Prost knew from the start it was going to be a holding year. A new factory at Guyancourt, 250 km to the north of the original base at Magny-Cours, new technical regulations and a new engine partner in Peugeot – plus a burgeoning workforce – meant that there were too many changes going on to expect the success which comes with stability. Peugeot's managing director, Frédéric Saint-Geours, pointed out that all the partners agreed it would be better to make all these changes at once and not to stagger them.

Then there was the question of the Prost AP01's gearbox. It was unreliable, too heavy, and with the weight in the wrong place, so whatever the engineers did to the car, it never really improved. Olivier Panis, his car 8 kg overweight, was 21st on the grid in Australia and only one place better in Hungary. Progress was slow. For Panis, a race winner at Monaco in 1996 and a podium finisher in 1997, a season-best result of ninth at that first race was simply devastating. Under the circumstances, Prost had to draw on all his professional experience to hold his team together.

The organisation underwent a massive transition during the year. 'When we started the gearbox project, we were just 60 people in total, so we were the smallest team in F1, smaller even than Minardi,' said Prost. 'We had to put our confidence in one guy to design the gearbox and it was difficult to supervise him day to day.'

The result was an overweight transmission which proved marginal in a number of areas. Modifications added weight and the positioning of the clutch on the back of the gearbox upset the handling of the car.

Prost's chief designer Loïc Bigois pointed out that it was costing them much horsepower, while Alain himself conceded: 'It was the worst feature on the car. Anything else would not have been too difficult to modify, but changing this took too much time.' The factory move also meant that component production was ceased for two months.

The Prost was also a short-wheelbase car which was too heavy in itself. 'We managed to reduce the weight quite quickly,' said Prost, 'but when everybody else is at least 20 kg under the weight limit, and can move their ballast about to best effect, it's a big disadvantage to be over that limit.'

When it came to personnel, the first place that Prost expanded was the drawing office. 'We have gone from ten to 30 people in that department,' he explained. Indeed, the whole workforce trebled from 60 to 180 in eight months. But in the early stages, trying desperately to integrate with Peugeot, it was hard to scrape together even two or three people to attend a meeting with their engine supplier.

'Then we worked on the car itself,' said Prost, 'on the suspension and the monocoque because the rigidity was not good at some circuits. With a narrow and short car you need to have everything perfect if it is to work well. I am still convinced that it can work well and that it is the way to go. But given the way the tyres have developed this year in F1, you have to go longer. There is no way you can have a short chassis.

'We worked very hard, but it did not make a big difference. We worked on aerodynamics, but every time we made quite a big step – which we could see in the wind tunnel and on the track – we just did not get the improvement in lap times. It was really frustrating.'

It was also expensive. At about the same time that Peugeot came up with a mid-season upgrade of its A16 engine, Prost had to make the decision whether to continue pouring money into this car or move on to the interim machine which he was desperate to run in the autumn.

He opted to make a fresh start, so the improvement from the 'version 4' Peugeot A16 engine was the team's only gain during the second half of the year.

The engine used by Jordan the pre-

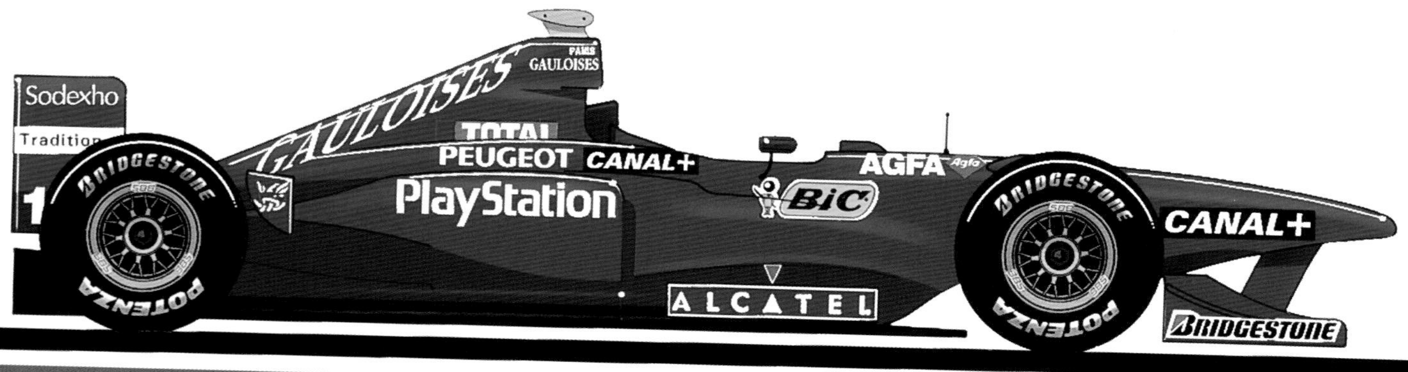

PROST AP01-PEUGEOT

Sponsors: Gauloises, Alcatel, Canal+, PlayStation, Bic

Team principal: Alain Prost **Technical director:** Bernard Dudot **Chief designer:** Loïc Bigois **Sporting director:** Cesare Fiorio **Chief mechanic:** Robert Dassaud

ENGINE **Type:** Peugeot A16 **No. of cylinders/vee angle:** V10 (72°) **Sparking plugs:** NGK **Fuel:** Total **Oil:** Total

TRANSMISSION **Gearbox:** Prost six-speed longitudinal semi-automatic **Driveshafts:** Prost **Clutch:** AP (hand-operated)

CHASSIS **Front suspension:** double wishbones, pushrod **Rear suspension:** double wishbones, pushrod **Wheels:** BBS **Tyres:** Bridgestone **Brake pads:** Carbone Industrie **Brake discs:** Carbone Industrie **Brake calipers:** Brembo/AP **Steering:** Prost **Radiators:** Secan **Fuel tanks:** ATL **Instruments:** Prost

DIMENSIONS **Wheelbase:** 110.0 in./2795 mm **Track:** front: 63.0 in./1600 mm rear: 63.0 in./1600 mm **Formula weight:** 1322.8 lb/600 kg including driver

Diana Burnett

Diana Burnett

Diana Burnett

It was a year of upheaval for the Prost team as it restructured in an effort to lay the foundations for greater competitiveness in the future. Technical director Bernard Dudot, sporting director Cesare Fiorio (who moved on to Minardi before the season's end) and Alain Prost himself have all known immense success in the past and will have few fond memories of 1998.

Weight distribution problems meant that all attempts to improve the AP01's handling were unavailing and in the circumstances drivers Jarno Trulli *(below)* and former race winner Olivier Panis *(bottom)* had little opportunity to shine.

Nigel Snowdon

vious season was known as the A14, but Jean-Pierre Boudy's V10 had changed little when it evolved into the A16 'version 2' for 1998. Explained Boudy: 'We adapted it for the Prost and it produced more power. It was basically the same engine we used for qualifying in 1997 but now we were using it for racing.

'The version 4 was lighter, and about two or three per cent more powerful. It revved higher and had improved combustion. There were a lot of changes inside the engine and we had also worked to reduce friction.' This engine was used for qualifying during the second half of the year, and made its race debut at Suzuka. Meanwhile the decision was made to take the interim AP01B with its new gearbox to Japan for Jarno Trulli, and this car was fitted with the latest version of the Peugeot V10, the smaller A18, in qualifying. Sadly, damage sustained in a warm-up crash prevented the Italian from driving it in the race.

Diana Burnett

While Boudy emphasised that the Peugeot team had worked tirelessly throughout, it was clear that the whole season represented an uphill struggle for all concerned and Prost could hardly blame the drivers for being demotivated.

'When we modified the car they could feel that they perhaps had more downforce and that they had better grip in some places,' said Prost, 'but they could not use it. In the wet, for instance, it was impossible to have a nice power oversteer because of the weight distribution.'

The team could have scored points in Melbourne and Montreal, but in the end they had to wait until the disastrous Belgian race before posting their first top-six finish. When testing went so well with the new interim chassis in October, the relief was almost tangible. Prost was finally on its way.

Bob Constanduros

The Digital Formula 1

Courtesy of Prost Grand Prix

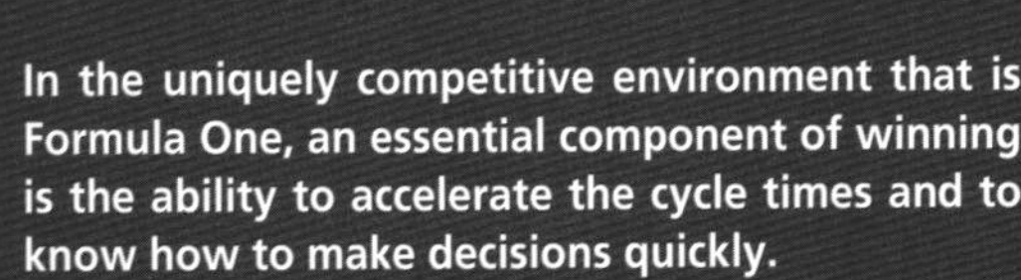

In the uniquely competitive environment that is Formula One, an essential component of winning is the ability to accelerate the cycle times and to know how to make decisions quickly.

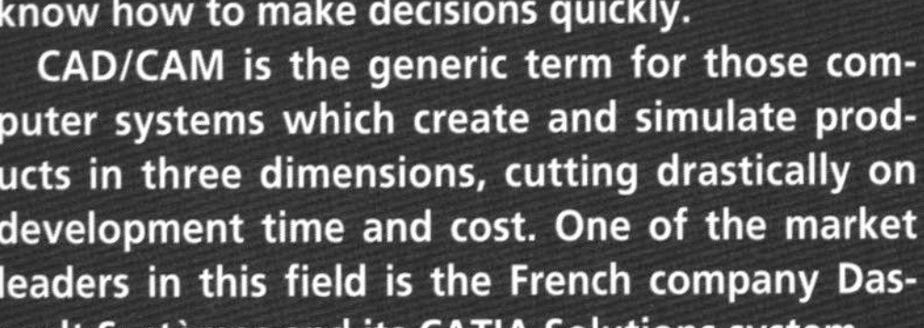

CAD/CAM is the generic term for those computer systems which create and simulate products in three dimensions, cutting drastically on development time and cost. One of the market leaders in this field is the French company Dassault Systèmes and its CATIA Solutions system.

Dassault Systèmes is a subsidiary of Dassault Aviation and it was in aeronautic design that CAD/CAM first came to be used. To begin with, CATIA was exclusively an in-house resource of Dassault Aviation, but CATIA was put on a more serious footing when, in 1981, Dassault Systèmes was created to develop the CATIA software. Its use quickly spread from the aircraft industry and today CATIA plays a crucial role in aerospace, consumer goods, shipbuilding, plant design, heavy machinery and the automotive industry and is widely used throughout the technological pinnacle of automotive design, Formula One. Computer giant IBM has a 'business partnership' with Dassault Systèmes for the CATIA system, and is licensed to sell it. Dassault Systèmes now boasts 117,000 CATIA seats at 12,000 customers.

Courtesy of Boeing Commercial Airplane

The entire life-cycle of the part from concept to operation, even including maintenance, can be simulated – all before making a single prototype. The design can thus be right before any expensive and time-consuming manufacture begins. Furthermore, an entire product – something as complex as an aircraft – can be designed and assembled in this virtual reality world. Boeing recently celebrated the completion of its first 100% digitally designed aircraft, the 777, featuring three million CATIA-designed parts. Had the information generated by this project been stored on conventional 3.5-inch diskettes, 2.3 billion of them would have been required! In the automotive world CATIA is used by Mercedes, BMW, Audi, Volkswagen, Chrysler, Honda, Fiat, Renault, Peugeot, Porsche, Mitsubishi, Volvo, Saab and Daewoo. With its Neon model, Chrysler set a record of 31 months from initial concept to production, largely thanks to CATIA.

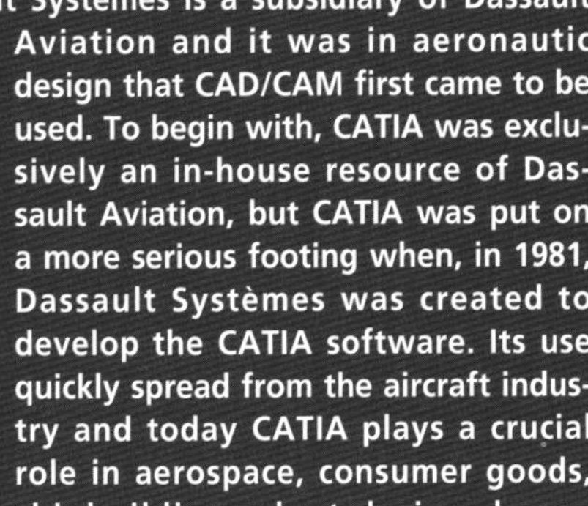

Courtesy of Daimler-Benz

Aside from the time and cost savings, there is also a great communication benefit. With the diversity of operations and skills in the design of a modern car, there is an inevitable tendency for the project to become somewhat abstract to those involved. Chrysler in particular has found that CATIA goes a long way to redressing this, allowing project members to understand the processes more fully and to monitor progress by using the 'CATIA television': simultaneous development in different areas thus becomes vastly easier.

With the speed of technological change in Formula One racing, the benefits of such a system are obvious. Ferrari, Sauber, Cosworth, Honda, Renault Sport, Peugeot Sport, Bridgestone and Prost all utilise it, the last-named enjoying a full technical partnership with Dassault Systèmes since 1997.

The Prost-Peugeot AP01 has been 100% digitally designed, with designer Loic Bigois noting that the car's all-new gearbox, involving the design and manufacture of three separate casings, took less than four months. 'In the past this would have taken us eight months,' he commented. The Peugeot V10 engine used by Prost for the first time in 1998 was itself digitally designed on CATIA – albeit separately from the car – and so the troublesome process for a designer of adapting to a new engine has been eased considerably.

But this is just the beginning. With Dassault Systèmes, Prost Grand Prix is looking to arrive at the point where not only will the 3000 parts making up an F1 car be CATIA-designed but all the information on the product life will also be visualised on one digital mock-up of the entire car. Bills of material, pricing, fabrication plans, production planning needs and machining information with automatically proposed tolerances will all be incorporated into this. CATIA will even design the machine tools required to make the components which it has simulated.

Bernard Dudot, Technical Director of Prost Grand Prix, comments: 'It will allow us to optimise our processes and we will be able to design our future cars quicker and earlier into the season. In the spiralling intensity of F1 development, the CATIA system should aid Prost Grand Prix in its aim of becoming one of the sport's elite super-teams.

Dassault Systèmes S.A. is a leading software developer for the CAD/CAM/CAE/PDM II market providing users with solutions for their product development needs.

CATIA-CADAM Solutions and Deneb Solutions enable total simulation of the creation of a product.

SolidWorks, a wholly owned subsidiary, offers design-oriented, software solutions based on Windows.

With Java-based CATWEB e-business tools, everyone can exploit engineering data over the web.

ENOVIA PDM II Solutions deliver a new multi-CAD collaborative and innovative environment for the virtual product and process modelling and management across the extended enterprise.

The company's customer base comprises over 12,000 CATIA-CADAM and 8500 SolidWorks customers and over 117,000 CATIA-CADAM and 22,600 SolidWorks seats.

www.dsweb.com
www.catia.ibm.com
www.enovia.com
www.deneb.com
www.solidworks.com
Formula 1 Coordination: jean-marc_galea@ds-fr.com

CATIA® Solutions and IBM Technologies, Champions in the Automotive Industry!

Visit us at:
www.dsweb.com
www.rs6000.ibm.com
www.catia.ibm.com

RS/6000

IntelliStation

CATIA® Solutions is developped by Dassault Systèmes and marketed worldwide by IBM/ETS
CATIA® is a registered trademark of Dassault Systèmes S.A. • IBM is a trademark of International Business Machines Corporation • Image computed with CATIA® Visualization Studio • Courtesy of Prost Grand Prix.

Diana Burnett

JEAN ALESI

Nigel Snowdon

JOHNNY HERBERT

'THE problem', said Sauber's technical director Leo Ress, 'is that we can't keep up the pace. It's something which happens a little every year: towards the middle of the season we drop back a little bit.' A point for Johnny Herbert at the first race of the season certainly augured well. Then Jean Alesi scored again in the Argentine and San Marino races. Subsequently, however, despite four seventh places shared between the two drivers, neither earned points again until Alesi mounted the third step of the rostrum in Belgium. That achievement doubled the team's points tally.

The year started with the signing of Alesi to join Herbert, thereby producing F1's most experienced pairing of the season. Ress, meanwhile, was somewhat nervous about the new regulations: 'You never know if you've got it right or not. It's all over if somebody has come up with a completely different solution, or a different concept. So, after the first test, we were quite delighted to see that we were not the odd ones out, that we were in line with everyone else.'

It started well for Herbert: fifth on the grid in Melbourne, then sixth in the race. 'But Jean had his problems in qualifying early on,' said Ress. 'He would push too hard and over-drive the car, and this car doesn't like that. You have to be very sensitive. It took him quite a while to get used to it because everything was new: the team and the car.' He was out-qualified by Herbert in five of the first six races, but wasn't headed thereafter until the final Grand Prix in Japan.

Ress doesn't mind admitting, 'We were a little bit afraid of Jean at the start. Everybody had told us a lot of stories about him, but he has developed quite well. He has confidence in the team and we have confidence in him. He races well and he's improved in qualifying recently by not trying too hard. We were surprised how well we've worked with him. He's become better and better, more and more relaxed.'

Ress was sorry that at the end of the year Herbert decided to head for Stewart in 1999. 'We're sad to see him go,' he admitted. 'Perhaps three years [with any team] is enough. He was very good at the start of the year, then he lost his way a bit and had some bad luck as well. Then he lost his motivation. It's a pity.'

Johnny himself has to agree, but explained further: 'I had to let Jean past in the race at Silverstone and then I had a similar thing in qualifying in Austria. I was quicker than him on wet tyres – we were sixth and seventh – but I never got a run on intermediates. It made me feel very low, especially when it happened two races in succession. I didn't feel I fitted in as much as I had before. I think my performance dropped off. I'm a bit annoyed with myself, but I just didn't have the right feeling.'

This, then, was a human relations thing, but Herbert also points out that there were mechanical problems as well. 'We had a lot of trouble with the gearbox at the beginning of the year,' he said. 'A lot of failures, but they did some software changes, worked on the shift, and it improved. But it took too long, maybe from race two or three through to race six or seven.'

Yet Johnny also praised what was a steady development programme initiated by the team, although he did note that Benetton and Jordan seemed to work faster. He would complain, as many drivers indeed did, of understeer. A longer-wheelbase chassis appeared at Magny-Cours as the intended cure. 'We had aerodynamic improvements at virtually every race,' said Ress. 'We had a new floor at Barcelona, another at Silverstone and yet another at Hockenheim. But maybe those steps were not big enough.

'On the other hand, we found it difficult to develop the car around the tyres. Very often we got the new tyre construction at 11 a.m. on the Friday of a race weekend. Of course, it was very good that Goodyear developed its tyres so quickly, but they were only able to test with Ferrari and Williams.

'It takes the engineers some time to adapt the cars to the tyres, and it takes the drivers time to get used to the tyres' stiffness and their behaviour. They have to feel confident in this respect, and sometimes they rather went round in circles so that by the Sunday morning warm-up they would end up with the same set-up that we had started with. It was just that the driver had got used to it.'

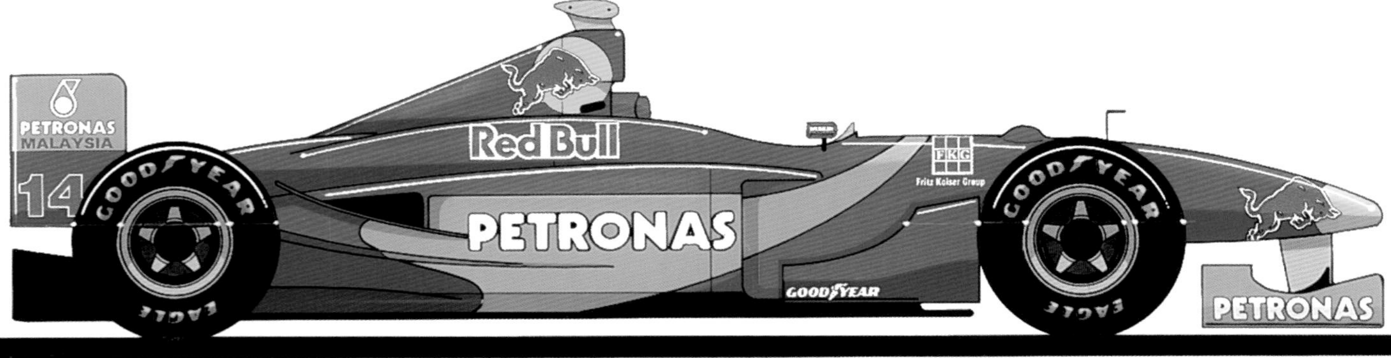

SAUBER C17-PETRONAS

Sponsors: Red Bull, Petronas

Team principal: Peter Sauber **Technical director:** Leo Ress **Team manager:** Beat Zehnder **Chief mechanic:** Ernst Keller

ENGINE **Type:** Petronas SPE01D **No. of cylinders/vee angle:** V10 (75°) **Sparking plugs:** Champion **Electronics:** Magneti Marelli **Fuel:** Shell **Oil:** Shell

TRANSMISSION **Gearbox:** Sauber six-speed longitudinal semi-automatic **Driveshafts:** Xtrac **Clutch:** Sachs

CHASSIS **Front suspension:** double wishbones, pushrod, inboard spring/damper unit **Rear suspension:** double wishbones, pushrod, inboard spring/damper unit

Suspension dampers: Sachs **Wheel diameter:** front: 13 in. rear: 13 in. **Wheel rim widths:** front: 12.5 in. rear: 13.7 in. **Wheels:** Speedline/OZ **Tyres:** Goodyear

Brake pads: Carbone Industrie/Hitco **Brake discs:** Carbone Industrie/Hitco **Brake calipers:** Brembo **Steering:** Sauber **Radiators:** Behr **Fuel tanks:** ATL

Instruments: Magneti Marelli

DIMENSIONS **Wheelbase:** 115.0 in./2920 mm **Track:** front: 57.9 in./1470 mm rear: 55.5 in./1410 mm **Gearbox weight:** 125.7 lb/57 kg **Chassis weight (tub):** 94.8 lb/43 kg

Formula weight: 1322.8 lb/600 kg including driver **Fuel capacity:** 30.3 gallons/138 litres

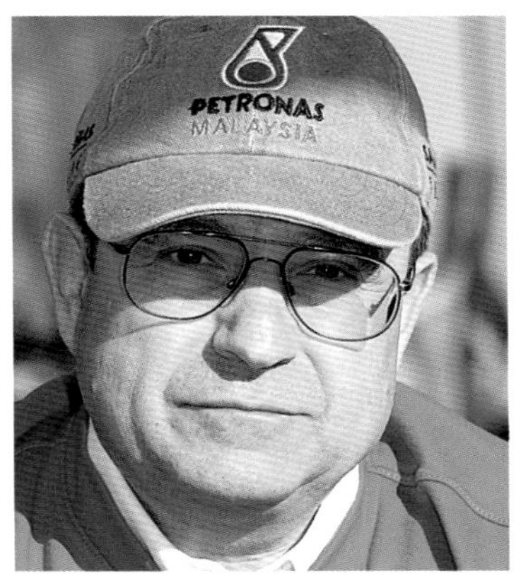

Diana Burnett

Diana Burnett

Diana Burnett

Although the C17 was respectably close to the pace at the start of the season, Peter Sauber, Leo Ress and team manager Beat Zehnder know that the Swiss constructor must introduce developments more speedily if that initial momentum is not to be lost once again next year.

The arrival of Jean Alesi *(below)* gave the team fresh impetus, and although he was never in a position to challenge for victory the Frenchman drove with characteristic heart and verve.

Bottom: Sauber made substantial changes to its Ferrari engines in an effort to maintain its place in the F1 pecking order.

Nigel Snowdon

After using an unmodified Ferrari 046 engine the previous season – badged Petronas, of course – the team decided to implement its own modifications this year with a revised bore and stroke, which in turn lowered the centre of gravity. This appeared for qualifying at Montreal and raced for the first time at Monza, finishing fifth in Alesi's hands. However, the need to work out their own engine mapping and fine tuning cost the team in terms of performance for several races, but Ress emphasised: 'Having the same engine two years running would drop us too far back.'

Like their rivals, the team continued to grow, adding some 60 people to reach 200 by the start of 1999. But Ress points out that 'you can't just count heads. The problem is to get experienced people in Switzerland. You have to count the heads by years of experience and that's what we have to look for.' Among those in the team were several imported names: Seamus Mullarkey joined from Jordan as head of aerodynamics, Andy Tilley was track co-ordinator, Rick Townend did the electronics and control systems while Tim Preston headed up the test team.

Lukas Gorys

Sauber knows where it is deficient and needs to improve. Herbert talks with affection about the team, emphasising that equipment and testing allocations are very fair. 'In some ways I'm disappointed I'm not staying,' he mused.

Bob Constanduros

Nigel Snowdon

PEDRO DINIZ

Diana Burnett

MIKA SALO

THE combination of a John Barnard-designed chassis and a Brian Hart-designed and developed engine seemed like a promising one for Arrows in its second year under the leadership of Tom Walkinshaw. For the first time since BRM disappeared in 1977 a British team had decided to go the Ferrari route and make the whole car itself.

Walkinshaw bought into Brian Hart's outfit, retaining the Harlow-based engine wizard, who already had his new V10 on the drawing board by the end of the 1997 season. Admittedly Damon Hill had left, but he had been replaced by the much-respected Mika Salo and the team could now begin to gel and settle down.

So it all looked promising until December, and then January, came and went without sight of the new car. 'I was mega-disappointed at the beginning of the year that the car was so late,' admitted Walkinshaw. 'We'd discussed it often enough that the priority was to get the car out in time during December. This was especially important when so many things [primarily the regulations] were new. You could only make progress if the car was going to be on time, but it wasn't, and that took three months to get out of the system.'

As far as Walkinshaw was concerned, that was the key to the team's frustrating season. 'You can't really complain about the drivers,' he insisted, 'because we didn't give them enough testing during the winter, so I think they've done a good job.'

The car eventually appeared on 17 February, although by then there had already been a delay in finalising the electronics specification. Two weeks later the A19 was in Melbourne for its first race, having scarcely turned a wheel in anger. It was therefore no surprise that the new car did not finish a race until the fourth round of the championship at Imola.

Initially the A19 was hamstrung by problems affecting both the engine and the gearbox, the latter being one of the two carbon fibre units to appear in F1 during 1998. While engine development was being stretched to the limit with resultant failures, the gearboxes were successfully sorted out by the time the team returned after the South American races to begin the European leg of the series. Only Salo's retirement in Hungary would be down to this problem in the later stages of the season.

Mika's ninth place at Imola was followed by a rash of engine problems which was caused by the hectic pace of development in trying to make up lost ground. Thankfully, Salo enjoyed mechanical reliability in his drive from eighth on the grid to fourth at Monaco – where his team-mate Pedro Diniz also finished sixth – to produce the team's best result of the year.

Perhaps surprisingly, the Finn was then involved in three incidents in the next four races, culminating in an unfortunate collision with Diniz at the second corner in Austria after the Arrows drivers had earned their best grid positions of the season.

By this stage, the Hart-designed V10 was beginning to produce light at the end of the tunnel. 'We did a lot of work on the cylinder head, valvegear, camshafts and inlets,' explained Walkinshaw, 'which gained us more and more revs. With the time we've had available I think we've made huge strides on that front and I think we can find a good bit more over the winter. I'm happy on the engine side.' By his own estimates, it had cost him £13 million at the very minimum.

The team began the year with the A-spec engine, the B-spec emerging at Barcelona, the C-spec at Silverstone and the D-spec appearing at Spa. But the Belgian race was truly disastrous for Arrows. Both D-spec engines broke before qualifying and then Salo crashed heavily exiting Eau Rouge. Finally, both cars were involved in the huge accident out of La Source on the opening lap. 'We wiped out the entire cupboard at Spa,' said Tom.

The drivers generally remained positive throughout. 'The car is good,' admitted Salo. 'Normally we had no problems setting it up and only twice during the whole year has it felt as though it was not my car – and then only for a day. It is just that it all came together about two months too late.'

Diniz, who contributed valuable sponsorship, again put in a succession of creditable performances. Twice he came close to improving on his per-

ARROWS A19

Sponsors: Danka, Zepter, Parmalat, Eagle Star, Quest, Brastemp, Diversey Lever

Team principal: Tom Walkinshaw **Technical director:** John Barnard **Team manager:** John Walton **Chief mechanic:** Les Jones

ENGINE **Type:** Arrows **No. of cylinders/vee angle:** V10 (72°) **Sparking plugs:** Champion **Electronics:** TAG **Fuel:** Elf **Oil:** Elf

TRANSMISSION **Gearbox:** Arrows six-speed longitudinal semi-automatic **Driveshafts:** Arrows **Clutch:** AP (hand-operated)

CHASSIS **Front suspension:** double wishbones, pushrod **Rear suspension:** double wishbones, pushrod **Suspension dampers:** Dynamic **Wheel diameter:** front: 13 in. rear: 13 in. **Wheel rim widths:** front: 12 in. rear: 13.7 in. **Wheels:** BBS **Tyres:** Bridgestone **Brake pads:** Carbone Industrie **Brake discs:** Carbone Industrie **Brake calipers:** AP/Arrows **Steering:** Arrows **Radiators:** Secan **Fuel tanks:** ATL **Battery:** FIAMM **Instruments:** Arrows

DIMENSIONS **Wheelbase:** 116.1 in./2950 mm **Track:** front: 70.9 in./1800 mm rear: 70.9 in./1800 mm **Formula weight:** 1322.8 lb/600 kg including driver **Fuel capacity:** 28.6 gallons/130 litres

Diana Burnett

Diana Burnett

Arrows boss Tom Walkinshaw and team manager John Walton remember to look on the bright side but it was another discouraging season for the Leafield squad, with the handsome black cars mired in midfield.

Below: Pedro Diniz proved once again that he deserves to be taken seriously as a Grand Prix driver but his team-mate Mika Salo seldom lived up to his star billing.

Bottom: Before the season was over highly regarded designer John Barnard *(right)* had decided that Arrows was not his cup of tea, leaving Walkinshaw to ponder his next move.

Nigel Snowdon

sonal best in qualifying and he again out-qualified his team-mate on several occasions. In addition to the point he scored in Monaco, the Brazilian survived the carnage in Belgium to finish fifth after a mature drive.

As the season drew to a close, Walkinshaw was able to reflect on what he had accomplished during the year. His designer, however, was by then on his way back to his own business, which he had kept running throughout.

'That was not the way the arrangement was supposed to have been,' said the Arrows chief. 'But I think the chassis was very good and in certain set-ups very efficient and very fast, but I think we needed to widen its window of performance. I think it has also suffered, along with other teams, from a tyre supplier which has developed its products around the McLarens. We have struggled more than most because the A19 is relatively light on tyres, so we've struggled to keep heat in them.

Bryn Williams

'I think next year will prove whether or not it was the right thing to do to build our own engine. The only [other] engine we could have got this year was a Cosworth rental deal, so I think, performance-wise, our decision has been vindicated.

'Next year will show even more of the benefits of making that decision, because we should start to get the benefit of a complete package then. It's been a hell of a lot of work, and one hell of an investment, but it should pay off in the long term.'

Bob Constanduros

Nigel Snowdon

RUBENS BARRICHELLO

Diana Burnett

JAN MAGNUSSEN

Lukas Gorys

JOS VERSTAPPEN

NEVER mind the first year. It's the second season which is the most difficult. Stewart-Ford spent 1998 digesting that piece of Formula 1 wisdom and doubtless agreeing with it.

Preparations for the debut season, tricky as they are, do not have the relentless distraction of racing worldwide on a fortnightly basis. It's hard enough to maintain the Grand Prix schedule and keep the current car competitive without having to think about the next one. But that's the grim reality which faced Stewart Grand Prix as they raced the SF1 and dealt with a strenuous first season. It was inevitable that the SF2 would suffer.

It was not until the fifth round in Spain that Rubens Barrichello qualified inside the top dozen, and he then backed that up with the team's first finish in the points. But despite this encouraging performance, the mixture of mediocrity and unreliability continued. Barrichello and Jan Magnussen would scrape together a few more points in Canada in June and that was the sum total for a team which had held the realistic belief that sixth place in the constructors' championship was possible. In the end, they were placed eighth out of 11; not the result either Stewart or Ford had expected.

In 1997, they had finished second at Monaco. Without detracting in the least from Barrichello's performance that day, it was a case of the Brazilian and the team making the most of their chances. But it was not an accurate indicator of form during a season wrecked by unreliability. On the other hand, without those retirements, Stewart-Ford were in line for a generous helping of points. There seemed no reason to doubt that anticipated technical development and messages from a steep learning curve would bring consistent results in 1998. That might have been the case but for one more painful lesson: the new car needed to be running long before the start of the season, something which Alan Jenkins, the technical director, had found difficult to achieve under the circumstances.

'Being late with the car had the biggest influence,' says Jenkins. 'But there was nothing else we could have done. It's easy to say we should have been earlier but there was only a handful of us in the team during the first year. We were racing, and racing reasonably well bearing in mind that we had brought in fairly substantial revisions to the SF1. We had done wind tunnel work for SF2 quite early on but, with the grooved tyres and other issues, the job of building a new car was too big for us to start any earlier than we did.'

Ford and Cosworth, meanwhile, were flat out on a new engine to replace the last Zetec-R to be built using the chain-driven cams which had been a considerable handicap during 1997. The latest V10 did not run for the first time until just before Christmas. So, even though the SF2 was launched in mid-January, it was a few more weeks before it was a serious runner. By which time, it was too late. Or, at least, too late for a team still struggling to find its feet.

'We were playing catch-up from then on,' says Jenkins. 'The other problem was that we didn't have the resources to catch up. When we finished in the points in Barcelona, we weren't too far off then. The longer wheelbase, which we introduced for the next race in Canada, made the car more predictable, gave the drivers more feel and generally made it easier to drive. But then it fell away from us a bit towards the end of the season.

'Reliability has been the biggest disappointment. We would have achieved a number of solid finishes in the top ten had we not let ourselves down with some problems, mainly to do with the gearbox. These have been put down to the fact that we introduced a carbon 'box but the early difficulties were software related, plus a few other things which tended to confuse the issue. We kept coming back to the fact that we hadn't done enough testing.'

Contrary to stories which had circulated in the media, Stewart have no complaint about their treatment at the hands of Bridgestone.

'They are in no way to blame,' says Jenkins. 'Bridgestone are working flat out to stay competitive and they've got a number one team. It's true that we

STEWART SF2-FORD

Sponsors: HSBC, MCI, Texaco Havoline, Lear, Hewlett Packard, Visteon

Team principals: Jackie and Paul Stewart **Technical director:** Alan Jenkins **Team manager:** Dave Stubbs **Chief mechanic:** Dave Redding

ENGINE **Type:** Ford Zetec-R **No. of cylinders/vee angle:** V10 (72°) **Sparking plugs:** Champion **Electronics:** PI/Visteon **Fuel:** Texaco **Oil:** Texaco

TRANSMISSION **Gearbox:** Stewart six-speed longitudinal semi-automatic **Driveshafts:** Xtrac

CHASSIS **Front suspension:** double wishbones, pushrod **Rear suspension:** double wishbones, pushrod **Suspension dampers:** Stewart/Penske **Wheels:** BBS **Tyres:** Bridgestone **Brake pads:** Carbone Industrie **Brake discs:** Carbone Industrie **Brake calipers:** AP **Steering:** Stewart **Radiators:** IMI, Secan **Fuel tanks:** ATL **Battery:** FIAMM **Instruments:** Visteon

DIMENSIONS **Formula weight:** 1322.8 lb/600 kg including driver

The competition is fierce.

Performance and reliability are key.

You need to take the lead and stay there.

©1998, MCI WORLDCOM, Inc. All Rights Reserved.

It's nice to be part of something so familiar.

MCI WorldCom is a proud sponsor of Stewart Grand Prix. Visit our site at www.mciracing.com

Diana Burnett

Diana Burnett

Diana Burnett

Paul and Jackie Stewart found their second season as F1 constructors far tougher than the first, with technical director Alan Jenkins and his colleagues unable to make up the ground that had been lost over the winter.

Jos Verstappen *(below left)* was brought into the team in place of the luckless Jan Magnussen and found favour with his positive approach.

Rubens Barrichello *(bottom)* gave the team its best result of the season with fifth place in Canada, but the SF2's persistent unreliability tended to mask his unquestioned talent.

Nigel Snowdon

were a bit upset – as were Prost and others – at one stage. We'd spent a lot of time testing at Monza only to come back for the race and find something different. We weren't beginning to suggest that Bridgestone should have brought a tyre to suit us; we were merely expressing disappointment at the way things had turned out as they followed the logical course of listening to McLaren's needs. Bridgestone work very closely with their teams. They're good guys and help as much as they can. But, at the end of the day, they're going for the championship.'

Whether or not Stewart-Ford get into that position remains to be seen. Certainly, Jenkins believes that Barrichello has it in him to become champion.

'I think Rubens is one of the best drivers around. I'm completely convinced of that,' says Jenkins. 'He's really on top of it now. He's mentally very strong, and physically too. You can see that in his condition at the end of a race. He's a much more complete driver now than he ever was. He was always quick and, given a chance, he could win races. We're all delighted that he's staying with us.'

There is genuine and obvious relief in that last statement, particularly after Barrichello showed signs of wanting to join Williams for 1999. His presence will bring continuity to a driver line-up which has been disturbed by the mid-season enforced departure of Magnussen, the irony being that he had just scored his one and only championship point in Canada.

'Jan remains a bit of a mystery,' says Jenkins. 'We all thought the world of him but sometimes it was difficult to know what was going on in his head in terms of commitment. It's true that we weren't really geared up to give him the attention he needed, like allowing him miles in the car and then having the time to stop and analyse it. The jury is still out on Jan. The ability is there and I hope he gets the chance to show it. But he needs to demonstrate to people that he really wants it.'

Magnussen was replaced after seven races by Jos Verstappen, formerly of Arrows and Tyrrell. On paper, the Dutchman fared little better than Magnussen as, on average, he qualified just a few places ahead of the Dane's usual position in the rear quarter of the grid.

'Bringing Jos in was the right thing to do for the team,' says Jenkins. 'He was not that much quicker than Jan but he was a lot clearer about where he wanted to go, a much more positive force in terms of involvement with everything from debriefs to tyre discussions.'

Johnny Herbert joins the team for 1999, bringing with him confidence, knowledge and a cheerful personality which will be ideally suited to a team with untapped potential but still lacking experience. The past two seasons have been very difficult for Stewart-Ford but, if the cumulative effect of the lessons learned and a move to impressive new premises can be properly harnessed, then Jackie Stewart's team is capable of delivering.

History has shown, however, that the third year is not much easier than the one before. F1 is a long, hard slog and, apart from starting off on the right foot at the beginning of the year, the team now needs to find the capacity mid-season to dig themselves out of the sort of trouble which made 1998 such a disappointment.

Maurice Hamilton

Jon Eisberg

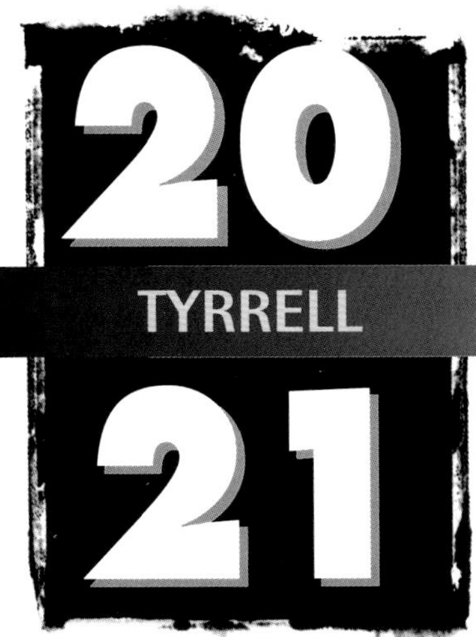

Nigel Snowdon

RICARDO ROSSET

Nigel Snowdon

TORANOSUKE TAKAGI

NOT to put too fine a point on it, working for the Tyrrell Racing Organisation in 1998 must have been like assisting at a wake. The team was in its death throes, waiting to drift into the hereafter following the buy-out at the beginning of the season by British American Racing. The new team was not due to come on stream until 1999, which left Tyrrell to struggle on as best it could.

The technical group, led by Dr Harvey Postlethwaite, and the loyal mechanics down at Ockham ought to get some sort of award for tolerance and fortitude under the most trying circumstances imaginable.

Not only had the BAR take-over prompted the departure of Ken Tyrrell after 30 years at the helm, but part of the reason for his going was a decision to employ Ricardo Rosset instead of keeping Jos Verstappen. With Mika Salo having moved to Arrows (not exactly a better option, as it would turn out), the Finn was replaced by Toranosuke Takagi, a novice whose lack of F1 experience was only marginally worse than that of Rosset.

Tyrrell reasoned that the 1998 car, with the help of an upgrade from the Ford V8 to the V10, was potentially a useful runner in the right hands. Quite how useful we'll never know but, indirectly, Takagi and Rosset proved the sub-text of Tyrrell's forecast to be correct when they could manage no more than a handful of finishes just inside the top ten. As crash-testers they were more than adept, Rosset in particular seemingly taking the view that gravel traps were there to be used.

In the face of an almost daily dumping of carbon fibre wreckage at the garage door, the team maintained a tactful silence (in public at least) and a sense of humour. Nevertheless, a fondness for Takagi was clearly evident thanks to considerable potential lurking beneath disappointing statistics which were a poor reflection on the team as a whole.

'I think the chassis was quite reasonable,' says Postlethwaite. 'We did a fair amount of development on it. Like everyone else, we shifted the weight distribution around to try and keep up with tyre development. We didn't need to do anything particularly drastic because we had decided at the beginning of the year to put quite a lot of the weight on the front wheels – which turned out to be a correct decision.'

Postlethwaite admits that the Ford V10 was not as bad as had been expected. Certainly, after the gutless V8 which was at least 50 bhp down in 1997, the customer V10 was reasonably powerful and certainly driveable.

'We've had some quite good speeds and I don't think we ever heard the drivers complain about driveability,' says Postlethwaite. 'It's been respectably reliable, apart from a slight glitch mid-season when an update caused a few problems, but also got us going again. We effectively had just the one development during the year so, by the end of the season, we were falling behind once again. But, overall, it was pretty good.'

So, the chassis and engine were reasonable, as was the budget (for once) and the team performed with its customary professionalism despite the destabilising influence created by the take-over. Postlethwaite pauses before identifying the main problem area.

'The difficulty has been that we had one driver who was learning and another who was . . . struggling. We tried to do everything we could for Ricardo. We gave him equal opportunities and quite a lot of testing but, for whatever reason, he found Formula 1 difficult.

'Tora went well in bursts. His qualifying performances were pretty good from time to time but he didn't do as well in the races as I would have hoped. He is definitely a talented driver. We could see that he was technically very good in the car. His lap times come through a very, very tidy and neat driving style. It was a couple of tenths here and a couple of tenths there, all of which put together a very nice lap time. It seems to be natural within him to do that. Having got his first year behind him and discovered the circuits, he has the potential to become a very good driver indeed.

'Having said all that, if we'd had Mika or Jos in the car then I am absolutely certain we would have scored five or six points. Look at Spa, for example. Tora was ahead of the guys who finished fourth and fifth – and he just drove off the road in a stupid accident. Also, an experienced driver would have

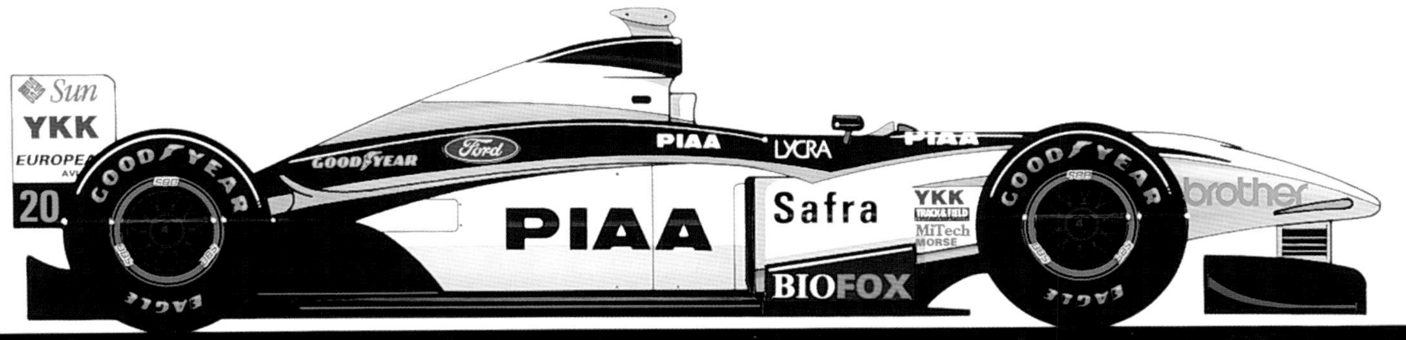

TYRRELL 026-FORD

Sponsors: PIAA, Morse, European Aviation, YKK, Brother, Safra, Lycra, Parametric, MiTech, Airwalk

Team principal: Craig Pollock **Technical director:** Harvey Postlethwaite **Team manager:** Steve Neilsen **Chief mechanic:** Paul Diggins

ENGINE **Type:** Ford Zetec-R **No. of cylinders/vee angle:** V10 (72°) **Sparking plugs:** Champion **Electronics:** PI Research

TRANSMISSION **Gearbox:** Tyrrell six-speed longitudinal semi-automatic **Driveshafts:** Tyrrell **Clutch:** AP (hand-operated)

CHASSIS **Front suspension:** double wishbones, pushrod, horizontal coil-spring/damper **Rear suspension:** double wishbones, pushrod, horizontal coil-spring/damper **Suspension dampers:** Koni **Wheel diameter:** front: 13 in. rear: 13 in. **Wheel rim widths:** front: 12 in. rear: 13.75 in. **Wheels:** BBS **Tyres:** Goodyear **Brake pads:** Hitco **Brake discs:** Hitco **Brake calipers:** AP **Steering:** Tyrrell **Radiators:** Tyrrell with Secan cores **Fuel tanks:** ATL **Battery:** Tyrrell **Instruments:** Tyrrell/PI Research

DIMENSIONS **Wheelbase:** 117.7 in./2990 mm **Track:** front: 70.9 in./1800 mm rear: 70.9 in./1800 mm **Gearbox weight:** 110.2 lb/50 kg **Chassis weight (tub):** 99.2 lb/45 kg **Formula weight:** 1322.8 lb/600 kg including driver **Fuel capacity:** 19.8 gallons/90 litres

Harvey Postlethwaite *(right)* took over the reins after Ken Tyrrell retired at the start of the season and ensured that the team was laid to rest with dignity.

Craig Pollock *(far right)*, guiding light of the team's new owners, British American Racing, had his sights set on 1999.

Below: Japanese novice Toranosuke Takagi showed flashes of promise that suggested he deserved another chance in Formula 1 in more favourable circumstances.

The hapless Ricardo Rosset *(bottom)* brought finance but precious little else to the Tyrrell cause.

Diana Burnett

Diana Burnett

Nigel snowdon

given us a benchmark. In a way, it was rather short-sighted of BAR not to have put a better driver in the car because, in the long term, they would have scored points and saved themselves money. But that was their choice and I'm sure they had their reasons.'

Driver choice was just one effect of the change of ownership which must have sapped the morale of team members, some of whom had been with Tyrrell since the start of his F1 campaign in 1968. It has been a mark of the company's professionalism that Tyrrell got through the final year in its present guise without becoming a phantom team going through the motions.

'As the year went on we obviously lost a number of key people,' says Postlethwaite. 'But most of them stuck with it and they've done an excellent job. The car has been reliable, and well turned out; the jobs have been done. It's a huge tribute to the unsung heroes in the background. I think I speak for everyone when I say we had the right to ask: "What the hell did we do to deserve this?" They could quite rightly have been expected to walk away from it but they didn't. They've done a super, super job. The morale has been fantastic, as good as it's ever been.

'There was this rather grandiose idea that since it was going to be Tyrrell's last year then "let's go out on a high note, chaps". It was never going to be like that. It was going to be a case of holding our heads up and coming out of this without it being a real disaster. We've managed that. It's not what anyone would have wanted but, under the circumstances, Tyrrell's been finally put to bed with, I'd like to think, a bit of dignity.'

Maurice Hamilton

Nigel Snowdon

EUROPEAN AVIATION

THE EUROPEAN FLEET

2 x 747-100 (leased to British Airways)
6 x Airbus A300
15 x Boeing 737 (13 leased to Sabena)
24 x BAC 1-11

Since commencing operations out of Bournemouth on 14th February 1994, European Aviation Air Charter has become one of the fastest-growing airlines providing a mix of VIP, ad hoc charters and inclusive tour and subcharter services.

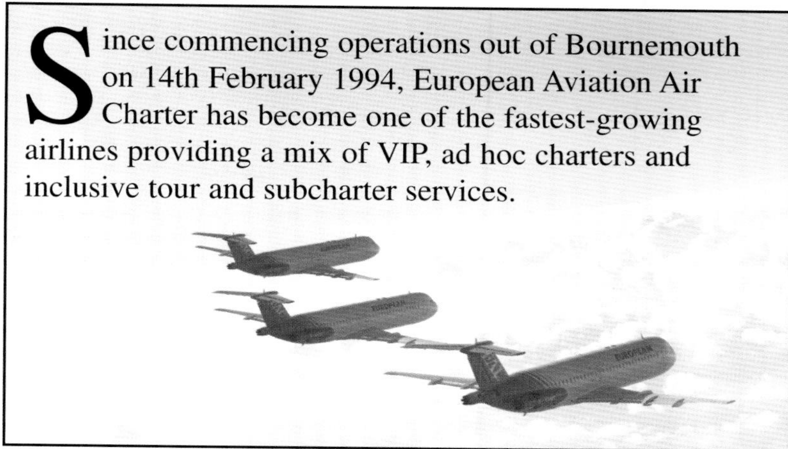

FIRST CLASS CHARTER

First for Comfort

The moment you enter our exclusive BAC 1-11 aircraft you will see luxury and comfort. Every first class seat has adjustable back recline and an extending leg support and foot rest with a very generous 47-inch seat pitch. The overall effect of space and quality is enhanced by pleasing colour schemes and subtle lighting.

First in In-flight Service

Our in-flight service will satisfy even the most demanding traveller: a champagne welcome, fine wines, cocktails, canapes, cream teas and gourmet four-course meals. Our cabin crew take pride in the standard of service they offer, are attentive but discreet and will ensure that all your guests enjoy every moment of their travel experience.

First in Europe

Our Rolls Royce-powered aircraft can fly to all major destinations in Europe. Flights will be scheduled to suit you – we will be there wherever and whenever you need us.

Tyrrell and EUROPEAN AVIATION

The European Aviation Group started sponsoring the Tyrrell Racing Organisation during the 1997 Formula One World Championship season by flying the team to all of the European race destinations on its VIP First aircraft. Its association with Tyrrell continued in '98.

"By flying VIP First, we were the envy of the paddock and welcomed European's continued support."

Rupert Manwaring
Commercial Director TRO

THE STRENGTH BEHIND THE AIRLINE

 FULL IN-HOUSE MAINTENANCE FACILITY JAR 145 APPROVED

FULL PARTS BACK-UP, NOT ONLY FOR OUR OWN FLEET BUT FOR VARIOUS AIRCRAFT TYPES

TRAINING CENTRE ...
BAC 1-11 Full flight simulator
L1011-100 Full flight simulator
L1011-200/500 Full flight simulator
Boeing 727-200 Full flight simulator

Head office: European House, Bournemouth International Airport, Christchurch, Dorset, BH23 6EA
Telephone: +44 (0) 1202 581111
Facsimile: +44 (0) 1202 578333
sita..BOHEACR

For further information about European Aviation, please contact...Terry Fox, Commercial Director

Nigel Snowdon

Diana Burnett

SHINJI NAKANO

ESTEBAN TUERO

'YOU need a fortune to stay last,' says Minardi's chief designer Gustav Brunner. 'If you don't spend a fortune then you fall off the back of the pack, and it's easy to do that. If you are two seconds behind, then you fall.'

Minardi very nearly did fall this year, despite that investment of a fortune and a season of re-organisation. If Brunner had not rejoined the team from Ferrari on 1 February he would not have found that the M198's anti-roll bars had far too much play in them, making the car virtually undriveable. The cure produced a gain of those vital two seconds per lap.

'My prediction before the start of the season was that we were always going to be last, with a gap to the team in front,' continues Brunner. 'But we haven't always been last. There have been races where we have beaten Tyrrell fair and square by being better on the day. So it has been more positive than I expected it to be.'

Brunner was part of the re-organisation set in motion by Gabriele Rumi, the Chairman of Fondmetal. Rumi became the major shareholder in the team and assumed the reins of the administrative side, allowing Giancarlo Minardi to do what he does best – race. Throughout the year the strengthening of the team continued. George Ryton joined from Prost, Gianfranco Fantuzzi as race engineer from Ferrari, Rupert Buchsteiner in a similar capacity from F3000 and Sauber's former composites chief, Herbert Ehrlinspiel, from Toyota.

The benefits brought by these men will become apparent next year, for even Brunner's arrival could not do much about the 1998 chassis. What was new had been produced by the four-strong design team, but with no chief or technical director to lead the way. Since they did not start until the middle of September 1997, it was something of a miracle that there was anything at all.

Having said that, Brunner recognised the rear wing and suspension uprights among other things. He'd designed them during his previous stint with the team in 1993! The continued presence of such components resulted in his starting his 1999 design within a month of rejoining the team. 'We have to renew everything,' he emphasised.

Apart from rectifying the anti-roll bar problem, the main change to the car during the year was aerodynamic with a strong contribution from Fondmetal's wind tunnel. This will be strengthened further with the help of Jean-Claude Migeot and his resident team in the future. But Minardi still managed to complete some 8000 km of testing during 1998, a record in itself, and by the end of the year they even had a small test team operated by former team manager Frédéric Dhainaut. In all, the team increased from 74 people at the beginning of the year to 110 by the early autumn.

Although Minardi and Cosworth had had their differences in the past, they joined forces once again for 1998 with the team using a V10 for the first time, the Ford Zetec-R JDM (for Minardi). This began the season in its M1 specification, pretty much as Stewart had used it at the end of the previous year although slightly modified to receive Minardi's Magneti Marelli electronic management system.

The M2 version appeared at Imola, basically comprising a modification to the oil system to improve performance by increasing the oil pressure. 'Not a huge change,' said Cosworth's Mark Parrish. However, the M3 was a much bigger evolution, a package which Stewart had tested at the end of 1997 as a further development of the P9. This involved a different firing order, crankshaft and camshaft in order to improve driveability and performance. It also produced a little more vibration, which was not popular with Nakano, who particularly noticed it. The M3 appeared in Canada.

Moreover, just to prove that development never finishes, the M4 was used for the final round of the series at Suzuka, featuring further improved driveability and mid-range power, at Minardi's request.

So how good was the engine? 'I think we were better than Arrows, probably better than Peugeot, and better than Honda at the beginning of the year,' suggests Parrish. 'Both our teams were pleased in terms of peak power and our reliability was good in pre-season test-

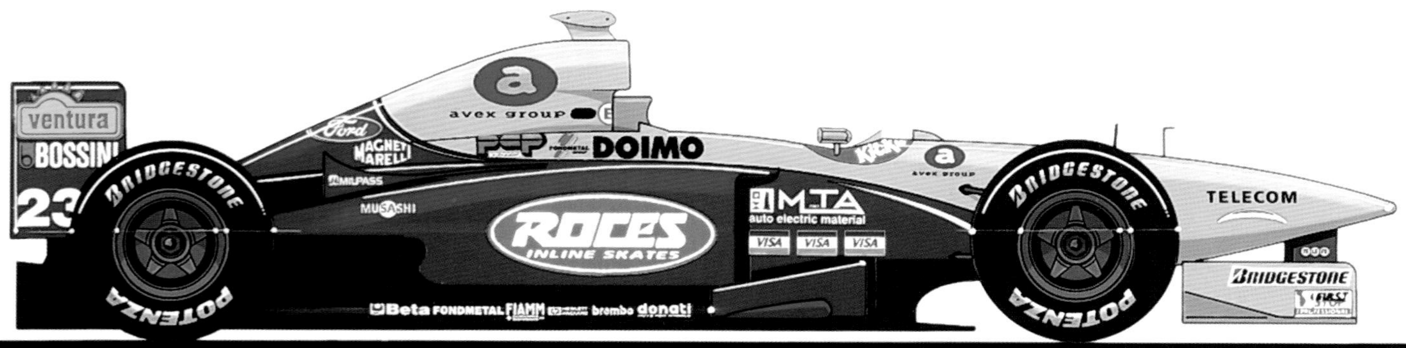

MINARDI M198-FORD

Sponsors: Fondmetal, Bridgestone, Ford, Magneti Marelli, Avex, Doimo, Roces, Telecom, VISA, Ventura, Musashi, Telefe

Team principal: Gabriele Rumi **Technical director:** Gustav Brunner **Team manager:** Giancarlo Minardi **Chief mechanic:** Gabriele Pagliarini

ENGINE **Type:** Ford Zetec-R **No. of cylinders/vee angle:** V10 (72°) **Sparking plugs:** Champion **Electronics:** Magneti Marelli **Fuel:** Elf **Oil:** Elf

TRANSMISSION **Gearbox:** Minardi six-speed longitudinal semi-automatic **Driveshafts:** Xtrac **Clutch:** AP (hand-operated)

CHASSIS **Front suspension:** double wishbones, pushrod with coaxial spring/damper and torsion bar **Rear suspension:** double wishbones, pushrod with coaxial spring/damper and torsion bar **Suspension dampers:** Dynamic **Wheel diameter:** front: 638 mm rear: 650 mm **Wheel rim widths:** front: 12.5 in. rear: 13.7 in. **Wheels:** Fondmetal **Tyres:** Bridgestone **Brake pads:** Carbone Industrie **Brake discs:** Carbone Industrie **Brake calipers:** Brembo **Steering:** Minardi **Fuel tanks:** ATL **Battery:** FIAMM **Instruments:** Magneti Marelli

DIMENSIONS **Wheelbase:** 116.1 in./2950 mm **Track:** front: 57.2 in./1452 mm rear: 55.9 in./1421 mm **Formula weight:** 1322.8 lb/600 kg including driver **Fuel capacity:** 32.3 gallons/147 litres

Diana Burnett

Diana Burnett

Diana Burnett

Minardi had undergone another shake-up, with Gabriele Rumi *(far left)* assuming overall control. As part of the re-organisation, Gustav Brunner *(bottom left)* returned to Faenza to work alongside Gabriele Tredozi *(middle left)*, while Giancarlo Minardi *(left)* was free to focus on the team's performance at the circuits.

Although the M198 *(below left)* was fitted with a V10 engine offering representative horsepower, some chassis components were scarcely state-of-the-art.

Esteban Tuero *(below)* and Shinji Nakano *(bottom)* performed as well as could be expected given their inexperience.

Photos: Nigel Snowdon/Diana Burnett

Photo: Courtesy Minardi/Ph. Colombo

ing. But then we had problems with Minardi in Australia and then at Imola – although not because of the new specification – and the low point was Magny-Cours, partially caused by the team's modifications. But we worked hard in a short space of time and it was soon OK again.' Reliability problems were evenly spread, Brunner agreed, explaining that electrical problems had been experienced by both cars.

Giancarlo Minardi is always fiercely proud of coaching young drivers and, once again, he took on a brace of youngsters. Japan's Shinji Nakano, who had a year's experience with Prost, was joined by 19-year-old Argentine novice Esteban Tuero. Their financial contributions kept the team going. Nakano, said Brunner, was better on circuits where precision was required; he was seventh in Canada, eighth at Silverstone in the wet and ninth at Monaco. As a late braker, braking stability was always important to him.

Yet it was Tuero who posted the team's highest qualifying position on his first outing in Australia where he lined up 17th. He would finish eighth at the San Marino Grand Prix, being more of a gutsy fast-circuit specialist, although Brunner noted that he needed to work on his fitness and concentration. 'But he's done better than expected,' he added.

However, this was a year of consolidation. Minardi was building for the future, not only on a personnel level, where the design team doubled, but also restructuring the headquarters with expanded offices and a 1000 square metre composite department. It is imperative to do so in today's F1 environment, even for the sport's perennial tail-end Charlies. Otherwise, as Brunner warned, you fall off the back.

Bob Constanduros

QUICK, QUICK,

SLOW

HOW FORMULA 1 HANDLES ITS ETERNAL DILEMMA

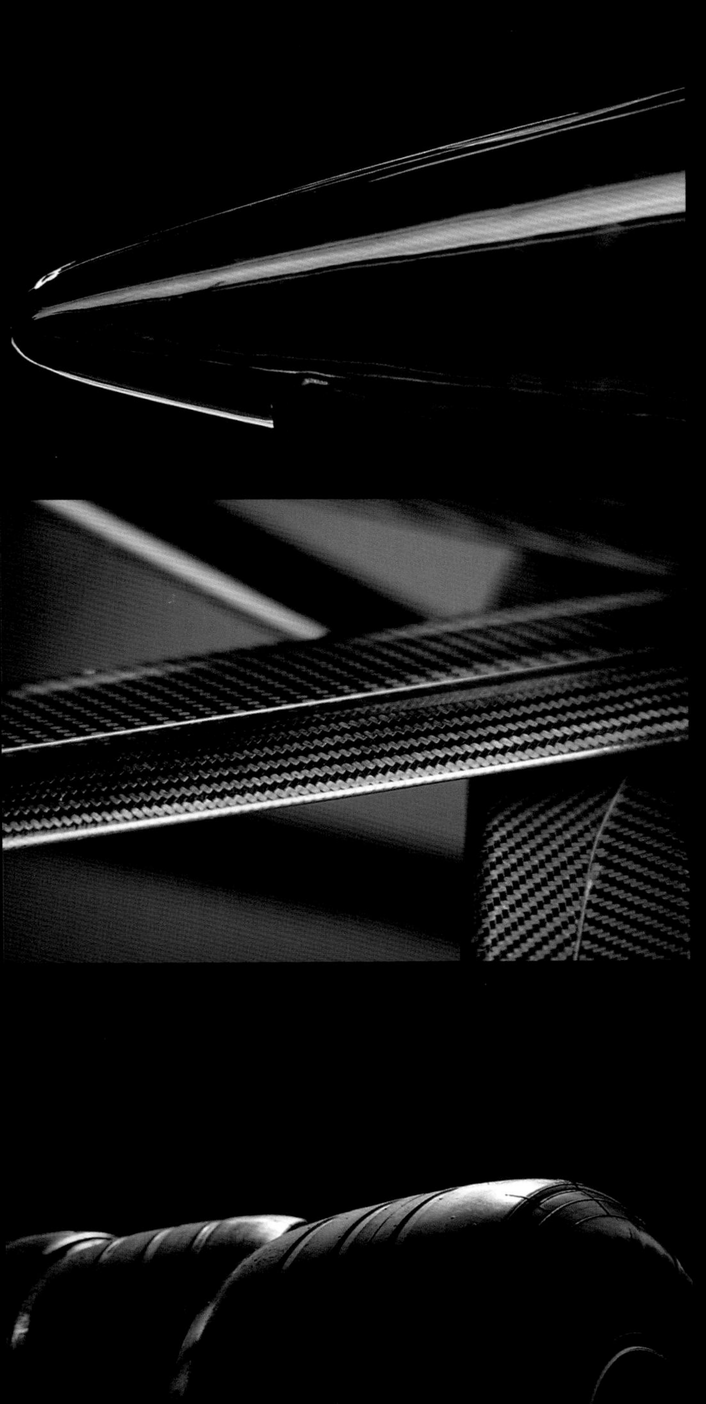

Photos: Paul-Henri Cahier

by Alan Henry

At cross purposes. While the Formula 1 teams continued to devote huge resources to areas such as aerodynamics and suspension in the never-ending quest for more speed, the governing body introduced grooved tyres in a bid to slow the cars down.

IT was just before 1.40 p.m. on Saturday, 31 October when Michael Schumacher made the point yet again. On the eve of the World Championship decider, the German driver took his Ferrari F300 round the 3.641-mile Suzuka circuit in 1m 36.293s to secure pole position for the Japanese Grand Prix.

The point at issue? Yet again a combination of technical ingenuity and frantic competitiveness had resulted in the 1998 breed of F1 car proving virtually as fast as its 1997 predecessor. Despite a whole raft of new regulations from the FIA designed to put the lid firmly on car performance.

Pole position for the 1997 race had fallen to Jacques Villeneuve's Williams FW19 on 1m 36.071s. The Canadian driver was at the wheel of a car fitted with slick tyres and with a wider track than Schumacher's 12 months later. Yet the momentum produced by a ferocious tyre war had meant that a switch to grooved rubber and a narrower overall car width had only lightly applied a brake to spiralling lap speeds.

'Twas ever thus. F1 history is littered with examples of the rule makers slowing the cars down only for the engineers to find fresh ways of making them quicker again. Possibly the most celebrated example of this came in 1988 in the final season of the 1.5-litre turbocharged engine regulations when the governing body limited the turbo-powered machines to 2.5-bar boost pressure, just 150 litres of fuel and a minimum weight limit higher than that applying to the 3.5-litre naturally aspirated cars which were being phased in that year.

'I promise you, gentlemen, in 1988 no way for the turbos,' predicted Jean-Marie Balestre, Max Mosley's predecessor as the FIA President, before the start of that year. Yet the McLaren-Honda turbos won a record 15 out of 16 races. Balestre's comments at the end of that remarkable season have not been preserved for posterity. But you get the gist of the problem.

So is this contest between the engineers and the rule makers destined to continue indefinitely? 'It's not an unhealthy situation,' said Williams technical director Patrick Head. 'The first narrow-track, grooved-tyre test cars in 1997 were six seconds a lap slower than the previous slick-tyred machines. Since then the tyre makers have made considerable progress, and then the cars are better as well. The speeds have at least been contained from increasing, anyway.

'I think with one tyre supplier, of course, in 1999 the FIA has an easier task if it thinks the cars are going too quickly again. They've only got to go along to Bridgestone, say, "Can you slow them down a bit?" and they just produce some harder compounds.

'I don't like tyre wars, really. I would rather we all had the same tyres.'

So what would Head say to those who argue that, if one follows that logic, perhaps F1 would be better if everybody had the same engines?

'I suppose if you are sitting on an engine advantage, you're going to say, "No, no, we must have all different engines,"' he grinned, 'and if you're sitting on an engine disadvantage I suppose you'd be saying, "No, let's have all the engines the same." But I suppose if the engines are different, you can get somebody to bankroll them. That's not going to be the case if they are all the same!'

Two days after the Japanese Grand Prix, Bridgestone hosted a preliminary test at Suzuka using prototype tyres developed for the 1999 F1 regulations which require four circumferential grooves on the front covers, one more than in 1998.

By the end of the first day David Coulthard's McLaren MP4/13 had posted a best time of 1m 41.296s – almost exactly six seconds away from the 1998 pole time. After just one more day's running he had trimmed another 1.5s off that initial yardstick.

Most F1 insiders believe this margin could be halved by the time the cars line up on the starting grid at Melbourne for the first round of the 1999 title chase.

Coulthard's initial impression was distinctly less than favourable, however. 'The car felt dangerous,' the Scot was quoted as saying. 'The tyres make very little difference to the straight-line speed, but give much less grip in the high-speed corners. This will ruin Formula 1.'

This was probably not a representative reflection of the real state of affairs. Coulthard was trying the new tyres barely 48 hours after finishing third in the Japanese Grand Prix. He was using them on the 1998 McLaren and not a chassis specifically designed for the four-groove fronts. Almost certainly, he had not given himself sufficient time to recalibrate his approach to the new technical situation.

However, it was also interesting to note that Hirohide Hamashima, Bridgestone Motorsport's technical director, considered that the new tyres – even on their first test – looked set to be much quicker than expected. However, Hamashima concluded: 'It is our judgement that when testing

Bryn Williams

Eddie Irvine searches for the limit of his Ferrari F300's cornering ability. Dramatic changes to the technical regulations intended to curb lap speeds had less effect than expected due to the intensity of the F1 tyre war.

resumes in December [1998] lap times on the new tyres will approximate to those seen on slick tyres during the 1996 season.'

This was the pre-tyre-war performance level which the FIA had indicated it wanted the cars' lap speeds to be pegged at.

Yet lingering concern remained. Was fiddling with tyre regulations really the best method of controlling lap times? It might seem satisfactory as we go into 1999 with a Bridgestone monopoly situation, but what happens if Michelin, for example, should decide to fill the gap vacated by Goodyear?

Surely draconian reductions in aerodynamic downforce might better enable the cars to run in closer company without being adversely affected by each other's turbulence?

Patrick Head continued: 'I don't think any progress has been made on that at all, because I don't think anybody – certainly not the FIA – has understood what the problem is.

'The fact of the matter is that a large part of this problem is the nature of the circuits. If you divide up every straight with chicanes, then even if you come out of that chicane a little faster [than the car in front] there is not a long enough distance to utilise that advantage.

'Equally, as well, I think the amount of wing the cars run is non-conducive to overtaking. When you are behind another car, the damage it does to you aerodynamically is so big that you can't get through the corner [cleanly] before the straight.

'The problem is that we are presented with a *fait accompli* by the FIA on these matters. Max Mosley decides. It's not something in which we play a part, really. We have to live with it.

'I have to say that just about everybody else says we shouldn't chop the tyres about. Leave us nice sticky tyres and take the wings off. But they won't try that.'

Veteran F1 designer Harvey Postlethwaite admits that it is perhaps inevitable that the present push-'n'-pull, they-make-the-cars-faster-and-we-slow-them-down situation continues to exist.

'Personally, I have for a long time thought that the rules we have are a total hotchpotch,' he said. 'And although they have just been rewritten in a more user-friendly way, I think the opportunity has been missed to rewrite them entirely.

'I think the rules should be written in a totally different form. What I have always wanted is a set of "box rules", by which I mean, at various points on the car you have complete freedom to do what you like within those boxes. If you want to limit performance you simply make the boxes smaller; be it the ones which contain the wheels and tyres, or be it the ones which contain the wings and bodywork, or whatever.

'I think there is scope to do something like that, although it would have to be very well thought out.'

As far as a wholesale reduction in downforce is concerned, Postlethwaite picks his words carefully. 'I have recently been involved in carrying out a proper mathematical study for Professor Watkins's FIA expert advisory group on the subject of overtaking in F1,' he said.

'While I am not in a position to discuss the findings in detail, I would agree that some sort of large downforce reduction is a good idea. There are also several things which need to be done in concert. I don't think it would be difficult to do, but doesn't that just amount to another tinkering job?

'Ironically, the simple way to make the cars go slower the FIA has in its hand, which is a limitation on the number of tyres you can use. It is ten sets at the moment, but what would happen if it was five sets for the weekend? That would certainly slow the cars down.

'The trouble is that the process by which all this happens is terribly unprofessional. I also don't believe that the governing body has access to sufficient information to be able to make properly framed rule changes. It needs more data and more information.'

Interestingly, this point was challenged by McLaren International managing director Martin Whitmarsh. 'It is often claimed by some of the engineers that the FIA is the rule maker,' he said. 'In fact the FIA technical working group frames future rules and the teams all have significant input into this.

'Yes, it is quite clear that the FIA often seeks to influence their deliberations, but I think if the teams sometimes took a more cohesive and long-term view towards the regulations this situation might improve. Sometimes they are only concerned with short-term issues, which is not necessarily the right way.'

It is believed that the report to the FIA expert working group concluded that a 50 per cent reduction in aerodynamic downforce, coupled with a ten per cent increase in drag and mechanical grip, would dramatically enhance the prospects of overtaking.

Sources close to the governing body suggest that it does not unreservedly accept these findings. Letting engine power rip and making the cars more difficult to drive is considered the best way forward.

'Controlling F1 speeds by reducing downforce was the method used for 30 years up until last season,' said Mosley, 'and it has proved completely unsuccessful. Putting grooves in the tyres did actually contain lap speeds for the first time ever. I believe that the best route for the future is to reduce grip and influence cornering speed without reducing engine power, so the cars will become more difficult to drive, which, in turn, will distinguish the best drivers from the less good.'

For the moment the FIA remains confident that, with Bridgestone as the sole tyre supplier in F1, it will have an easier job keeping lap speeds in check. They may be right. Moreover, there is speculation that the governing body may judge this the correct time to make F1 a single-tyre formula for good. In which case it should be able to exert more of an influence over lap speeds than ever before.

Bouncing back!

Top: John Cleland bounces over the kerbing in typical hard-charging style. The British Touring Car Championship takes no prisoners and every place is fought for tooth and nail.

Below: One up for the Vectra with both team drivers, Derek Warwick *(left)* and John Cleland, celebrating their success on the podium.

VAUXHALL came bouncing back in 1998 with John Cleland and Derek Warwick storming the winner's circle as the Vectra racers came on strong in the British Touring Car Championship. And their burgeoning competitiveness proved that Vauxhall and motor sport continue to go hand in hand.

One of the highlights of the year came in the third round, at Donington Park, when Cleland picked up a win in the sprint race and a third place in the feature event. The victory was his first in the British Touring Car Championship since he won the title for Vauxhall in 1995. The Scot's triumph came after he made a blinding start from third on the grid to outrun polesitter Rickard Rydell's Volvo and James Thompson's Honda. Although pressure was intense, Cleland edged away to win, sending Vauxhall's Triple Eight Engineering team wild with delight at its first victory and emphasising how far the Vectra has come since its launch at the start of the 1997 season. The victory also gave clear evidence that the Scottish veteran has nothing to fear from the young guns who are lining up to try and topple him.

Winning races is the most effective way of showing that one's car is the best, and there's no finer proving ground than the British Touring Car Championship, the most professional touring car series in the world with eight manufacturers entering works teams.

Not only is it professional, but it's ultra-competitive too and has become the main draw for British racing spectators and for the nation's armchair enthusiasts as well. Indeed, so good is the entertainment provided by some of the closest racing in any category in the world, whether you are watching from the spectator banking or from the other

side of the television, that you can often feel as though you are truly in the driving seat as the cars corner side by side or even nudge each other in the heat of the battle. No wonder the British Touring Car Championship has been such a success and is seen as a pinnacle of motor sport both at home and abroad.

With Triple Eight Race Engineering working continually to develop the racing Vectra, Cleland also won at the sixth round, again at Donington Park, this time scoring his victory in the feature event. Having run second in the wet sprint race until a collision with a rival slowed his progress, Cleland powered to the front in the feature race, battling long and hard with the Nissans of Anthony Reid and David Leslie, Yvan Muller's Audi and Nigel Mansell's Ford in extremely difficult conditions. Cleland kept his head while those around him lost theirs and spun off. It was touring car racing at its best. But, better still, it emphasised the seriousness of his title bid as he moved into second place overall.

Unfortunately, Cleland was forced to stand down for a round in August after being injured in a 120 mph impact at the start of the feature race at Snetterton, suffering heavy bruising and a broken rib after being T-boned and then careering into the banking. This was the first time Cleland had missed a British Touring Car race for ten years.

Warwick also made strong progress in the early part of the season, with third place in the Donington Park feature race won by team-mate Cleland his best result. Indeed, this marked Derek's first visit to a British Touring Car Championship podium.

However, when Cleland returned from injury for his home round at Knockhill, Warwick asserted his authority by winning the feature event. And what a race that was, as he started it by skidding on the rain-soaked surface and pushing none other than Cleland off the track... An instant call to pit for grooved tyres while the safety car was circulating to allow Cleland's wreck to be cleared proved to be inspired: Warwick powered into the lead as others pitted to change to grooved tyres as the rain worsened and won the race with ease.

To round out their year, Cleland and Warwick took a Vectra over to Australia for the annual 1000-kilometre race at Bathurst and finished fifth in this gruelling event after a stuck front wheel nut cost them four laps and a clear chance of victory.

All in all, it was a strong season for Vauxhall, and for 1999 French

VAUXHALL Sport

Above and left: **John Cleland, now a perennial in BTCC, brought Vauxhall back into the winner's circle in 1998.**

Opposite page: **Fans flock to the circuits not only to meet their idols such as Vauxhall Team drivers Derek Warwick and John Cleland, but to see exciting door-to-door action on the track enhanced by the excitement of pit stops.**

Right: **Making a splash was the new Astra Kit Car driven by Finn Jarmo Kytolehto.**

Kytolehto *(below right)* will surely be a leading contender for the British Rally Championship in 1999.

ace Yvan Muller, a multi-titled touring car racer with a year's experience of the championship and a soaring reputation, joins the team. Add to this the prowess of his team-mate Cleland and you can expect Vauxhall to improve yet further in the season ahead and make a serious bid for the title.

Rallying

VAUXHALL was also in the thick of things away from the circuits, with Finnish driver Jarmo Kytolehto starring in the works Vauxhall Astra Kit Car in the British Rally Championship, despite the car being brand new. At the start of the season so new was the latest-shape Astra that Kytolehto and the Vauxhall crew had to miss the Silverstone Rallysprint in February – an event that counted only for the manufacturers' championship – as the new car was waiting to be homologated.

The rally Astra arrived for the season-opening Vauxhall Rally of Wales with precious little testing. However, once it hit the stages, the Astra made marked progress which continued throughout the course of the season.

Considering that the Astra had been completed just two days before the Vauxhall Rally of Wales, Kytolehto did extremely well to run fifth overall before a holed radiator led to his retirement.

Kytolehto arrived at the second event, the Pirelli International Rally, with a good deal of useful testing under his belt. And it showed as he was third on the first leg of this double-header event held in the Kielder Forest, finishing just five seconds behind eventual champion Martin Rowe's Renault. Unfortunately, an outing into a ditch – the result of a brake failure caused by a rock splitting a brake pipe – on the second leg cost 15 minutes and left Kytolehto way down in the results. But a warning had been sounded to the opposition.

Intensive development continued between each championship round, with work being concentrated on refining the suspension geometry. The fruits of this work were obvious when Kytolehto was fourth on the first leg of the Scottish Rally and fifth on the second to be classified fourth overall. The Stena Line Ulster Rally was next and gave Kytolehto the chance to prove the Astra on a tarmac event. Sadly, he had a short run as the cambelt broke on the fourth stage when he was running fifth.

Proving how successful a development season it had been, Kytolehto was on course to finish the season in style on the high-speed Manx International Rally, running third until minor technical problems struck on the penultimate stage and dropped him to fourth at the finish. This left him sixth overall in the drivers' championship and Vauxhall fifth in the manufacturers' title race. However, the promise is there for all to see and the Astra will surely be one of the cars to beat in 1999 when Vauxhall will run a two-car programme for Kytolehto and British 1600 cc class champion Neil Wearden, who was given his first outing in the Network Q Rally of Great Britain in December.

Mark Blair *(left and below centre)* won the Vectra SRi Challenge and a drive in BTCC for 1999.

The Vauxhall Formula Junior championship was taken by Brazilian Antonio Pizzonia *(below far left and right)*.

Richard Lyons *(bottom right)* leads a gaggle of cars in a close-fought and highly competitive Vauxhall Formula Junior Championship.

Vectra SRis & Vauxhall Formula Junior

VAUXHALL'S own mini-touring car series for its Vectra SRi V6 racers was again a success in its second year, with a host of drivers looking to progress to touring cars lining up to take a crack at the big prize, a Vauxhall Vectra touring car for use in the BTCC Independents Cup.

Outwardly similar to their touring car counterparts, but running to a less highly developed specification to keep costs in check, the racing SRi V6s really look and sound the part. What's more, the racing was even closer than the British Touring Car Championship, as all cars were built to be equal in every respect.

It was clear from the opening round that the battle for outright honours, and that prize Vectra, was going to be between Simon Graves, Brazilian Flavio Figueiredo and Mark Blair. First, second and third that day at Thruxton, they were door-to-door all season.

Graves collected three further victories in the next five races, with his rivals picking up a win apiece. But he was not to triumph again until six rounds later, during which time Blair had won three times and Figueiredo twice. However, Graves was disqualified from the last two races and this opened the door for his rivals, with Blair lifting the title at the penultimate round.

Blair is working hard in preparation for driving his prize Vectra in next year's British Touring Car Championship, in which he will hope to emulate the success of former SRi V6 racer Mark Lemmer, who was a winner in the privateer class in last year's prize car.

Jason Yeomans was best of the rest, while Paula Sears proved that the Vectra SRi V6 Challenge is not a male preserve by finishing fifth overall, peaking with third at the final round.

The cars should be even better to drive in 1999 as Triple Eight Engineering's touring car know-how will be utilised to optimise the chassis, which will be fitted with new Hewland gearboxes, differentials and driveshafts.

Single-seaters remain an integral part of Vauxhall's agenda, with the Formula Vauxhall Junior series enjoying updated chassis and more powerful 16-valve engines. And it produced not only some excellent racing but also another champion who looks destined to go all the way, like Vauxhall Junior graduate Dario Franchitti, who was a regular Champ Car race winner in his second year of competing in America's premier category.

Brazilian Antonio Pizzonia started off as favourite, having been runner-up in 1997. But he was beaten in the first round by Richard Lyons and then again in the second, finishing behind Tomas Scheckter, younger son of 1979 Formula 1 World Champion Jody Scheckter. After that, however, he let loose with four wins.

Lyons won four of the next six races with Pizzonia picking up the other two, leaving the stage set for the final three rounds. But then another driver made life more complicated for the championship rivals by winning the next two races. This was Leighton Walker, who joined the series in mid-season. However, second place at Oulton Park was enough to give Pizzonia the title, before he rounded off the year with victory at Silverstone.

Walker's late charge saw him rocket to fourth overall behind Scheckter, outstripping the consistent Robert Bell and South African Johan Fourie, while Gary Paffett cleaned up in Class B as he raced to seventh overall.

For 1999, Formula Vauxhall Junior will be known as Formula Vauxhall, while the Formula Vauxhall Junior tag will live on as the new name for the current Class B category for year-old cars. And Formula Vauxhall will have an added attraction as there will be a test with a leading UK3000 team for the champion.

advertisement feature

GRANDS PRIX 1998

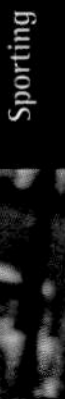
Sporting Pictures (UK) Ltd

AUSTRALIAN

grand prix

Paul-Henri Cahier

Pamela Lausen/FOSA

Left: The new season got off to a contentious start when David Coulthard surrendered the lead to team-mate Mika Häkkinen in accordance with the terms of a pre-race agreement.

The Finn went on to complete his second successive victory, but once again the podium festivities were overshadowed by controversy.

HÄKKINEN

COULTHARD

FRENTZEN

IRVINE

VILLENEUVE

HERBERT

CATCH us if you can. That was the tantalising message delivered by the McLaren-Mercedes team when the 1998 F1 World Championship kicked off with the Australian Grand Prix at Melbourne's Albert Park.

At the wheel of the new Bridgestone-shod McLaren MP4/13s, Mika Häkkinen and David Coulthard scored a decisive 1-2 success to start 1998 where they had finished off 1997 – right on top. Yet the after-taste of controversy which lingered at Jerez the previous November after Jacques Villeneuve had seemingly relinquished the race to the McLaren duo was uncomfortably revived in Melbourne when Coulthard handed the lead back to Häkkinen with only two laps left to run.

In last year's title finale at Jerez, Coulthard had been at the centre of attention after being instructed to let Häkkinen back ahead of him in the closing stages of the race. This time, the Scot was simply sticking to the terms of a pre-race strategy which the team had agreed to implement in the event of its demonstrating a measurable performance advantage over the opposition.

In these circumstances, Häkkinen and Coulthard abided by team instructions that whoever reached the first corner in the lead should take the win, assuming they had a clear-cut run at the front of the field without needing to fend off any outside opposition. Although Coulthard qualified second, he willingly agreed to the deal, believing that a track record of brilliant getaways stacked the odds strongly in his favour.

'Mika and I have learned a lot over the winter and are an awful lot closer together, and we agreed that whoever got to the first corner first, then we would not challenge the other,' said David. 'I think it was sensible under the circumstances as we had not done a full race distance prior to the race.

'I was very confident that I would beat Mika to the first corner, but Mika made the best start. They held us an awful long time on the grid, and I was distracted by the smoke beginning to come from my radiators. I think he deserved to win the race, no question about it. I could think about it clearly and did what I thought was the right thing to do.'

As events transpired, Häkkinen went on to dominate the race in flawless style, only losing the lead when a mix-up in the pits resulted in his coming in prematurely for his second refuelling stop with 22 of the race's 58 laps still to run. He was waved straight back into the race, returned to refuel four laps later and then resumed 33 seconds behind Coulthard.

The Scot duly made his second stop on lap 42, after which the two McLarens were left running in 1-2 formation 13.5s apart. Häkkinen then produced a stunning demonstration of driving, rattling off a sequence of quick laps to pull up onto Coulthard's gearbox as the Scot simultaneously eased his pace. With only two laps to go, Coulthard pulled over on the start/finish straight to honour his side of the agreement.

'What David did today was remarkable,' said Häkkinen after the race. 'I have been in F1 for many years and seen a great deal. It was really gentlemanly, unreal and fantastic.'

However, it was deeply questionable whether Coulthard should have been expected to abide by his agreement under these circumstances. Häkkinen's delay was nothing more nor less than a part of the natural ebb and flow of motor racing fortune. Correcting a 'discrepancy' for the second successive race not only made Coulthard appear over-anxious to please, but arguably also devalued the quality of Häkkinen's success.

By the end of last season, the McLaren-Mercedes were established as the fastest cars in the field and Melbourne was not a circuit on which Bridgestone tyres were expected to offer a significant performance advantage. The reality was that McLaren had got every variable – engine, chassis, tyres and aerodynamics – tuned to perfection, so much so that nobody else could get close.

Schumacher made a valiant effort to resist the prevailing tide on the opening lap. As Coulthard followed Häkkinen into the braking area for the second corner, Michael momentarily edged his Ferrari level with the Scot's McLaren, albeit on the outside line. For a fleeting split-second it looked as though he might wrong-foot Coulthard by running round the outside of him. But David simply took his legitimate line and Schumacher had no choice but to concede.

Further back, the Stewart-Ford team's painful weekend continued with Rubens Barrichello being left stranded on the grid with gearbox trouble. Jan Magnussen hardly lasted much longer. Midway round the second lap, hard on Ralf Schumacher's heels, he went for a gap inside the Jordan-Mugen Honda which wasn't quite there by the time he arrived.

The two cars spun off into the gravel for good with Tyrrell new boy Toranosuke Takagi also pirouetting into retirement.

The inevitable air of excitement and anticipation over the start of a new season was tempered at Albert Park by some concern that the outcome of the first round of the World Championship could be decided in the scrutineering bay long after the chequered flag had fallen on Sunday afternoon.

As the drivers grappled with significantly reduced levels of grip during Friday's intermittently wet free practice session, so pressure mounted for the governing body to ban the secondary braking system on the McLaren MP4/13s, which quickly emerged as pace-setters.

The McLaren system, which allowed the drivers to apply extra braking effort to the inside rear wheel for improved traction and stability during cornering, was first used by the team in 1997. It had been further developed over the winter, during which time McLaren was in regular communication with the FIA to ensure its conformity with the rules.

'We have been in constant touch with the FIA throughout the design and development of the car,' said Ron Dennis, 'and have consulted them on all aspects of its specification. The governing body is satisfied about its legality in every respect.'

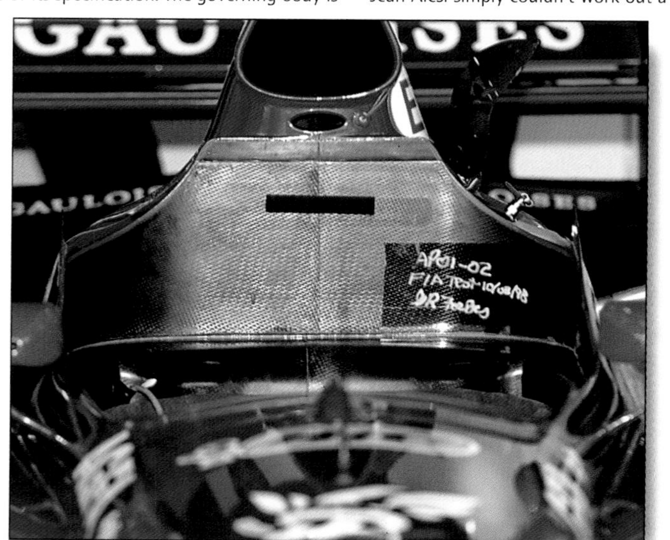

Sporting Pictures (UK) Ltd

However, before the start of practice, the Ferrari technical director Ross Brawn sent a memorandum to the FIA technical delegate Charlie Whiting claiming that the braking system employed on the McLaren was not, in his view, legal. The Italian team also sent copies of this memo to all the other competing teams.

On Friday morning Whiting had told the teams that he was satisfied that the McLaren braking system conformed to the regulations, but added that if they did not accept his opinion they could use their right to lodge a protest after the race. Ferrari then attempted to get the teams to countersign a letter objecting to the McLaren braking system. At least five agreed to do so, although the dissenters did not need to waste their time canvassing Williams for any support as they had been using a similar braking system.

Ferrari's critics suggested that the Italian team's attitude had primarily been motivated by the fact that it had been less successful in developing a similar system of its own. Ferrari sporting director Jean Todt vigorously denied that this was the case.

Whichever way this issue might be resolved, many team owners were left reflecting that the basic problem was that the F1 technical regulations are not sufficiently specific in terms of what is or is not permitted.

'It would be almost impossible to design a Grand Prix car using the rule book alone,' said Williams technical director Patrick Head. '[It has] to be supplemented by rule clarifications from the governing body, which inevitably makes it all something of a grey area.'

His opposite number at Arrows, John Barnard, agreed. 'What we really need is for somebody to go through the rule book and expand on each point,' he said.

Meanwhile, out on the circuit, the first signs showed that the grooved tyres and much reduced aerodynamic downforce had made the cars considerably less predictable to drive. In relatively cool conditions on Friday, even the lightest rain shower left competitors spinning in all directions as the harder tyre compounds proved more difficult to work up to operating temperature.

Nevertheless, Michael Schumacher remained in an extremely relaxed frame of mind after setting fastest time in Friday's lottery of a free practice session.

'We know we have done a good job on this car, and with a little bit of development we will be right there as a championship contender,' he remarked with some assurance.

However, this initial confidence was undermined significantly when it came to qualifying. Mika Häkkinen and David Coulthard simply blitzed the opposition to take first and second places on the grid in a quite remarkable McLaren-Mercedes *tour de force.*

Mika thus took the second pole position of his career despite admitting that he had had to abort a couple of quick laps, while David confessed to losing fractions of a second all round the circuit. 'On two corners round the back of the circuit in particular, I had a touch too much understeer,' he explained, 'and on the last two attempts I just couldn't quite get clean runs together.'

Third place on the grid fell to Schumacher, who admitted that to be best of the rest was probably as good as he could expect, even though he was annoyed to have been balked by Hill's Jordan late in the session. 'I am not unhappy, nor terribly happy,' he confessed. 'We have had to make some compromises with the car in the interests of reliability, but we hope to get those back within the next few races. We saw from the Barcelona tests just how quick the McLarens were, so their performance is no surprise.'

Williams were not alone in experiencing problems with heat build-up from the exhaust damaging their rear wings. Jacques Villeneuve trailed into the pits during Saturday morning free practice with a collapsed rear wing and then switched to the spare FW20 for qualifying as the team was still worried about potential overheating.

However, these problems had little impact on the Williams cars' overall competitive level. Villeneuve and Heinz-Harald Frentzen qualified fourth and sixth, losing time in particular during the third sector of the lap. With McLaren dictating the pace, Frank's lads were to spend the weekend in damage-limitation mode.

Johnny Herbert was pleased with fifth place in the Sauber C17, reporting that the new car felt nervous, but very quick. By contrast, Jean Alesi simply couldn't work out a decent balance and could not improve on 12th place.

In the Benetton camp, Giancarlo Fisichella found that the slight increase in ambient temperature during qualifying adversely affected the handling balance of his B198, leaving him battling excessive oversteer. He wound up seventh, four places ahead of Alexander Wurz, who spun off and then took over the race car set up for his team-mate.

Ferrari's Eddie Irvine had an engine problem which prevented him from achieving a trouble-free lap all session with the result that he lined up eighth fastest ahead of the Jordan-Mugen Hondas of Ralf Schumacher and Damon Hill.

Ralf just shrugged his shoulders and Damon was similarly resigned. 'We really have to make some improvements to be in the top six,' said the Englishman, 'but I still believe we can aim to come away from here with points, which would be a good start to the season.' As things transpired, this was an over-optimistic assessment.

However, the most enigmatic message came from Jordan's technical chief Gary Anderson. 'There have been a fair amount of negative comments recently and I think that with a more positive attitude and more fight, we could be up there in the top six,' he remarked trenchantly. What, one was left wondering, was he referring to?

Toranosuke Takagi did an excellent job to qualify 13th on his F1 debut with the Tyrrell-Ford, the Japanese driver lining up 0.1s ahead of Rubens Barrichello's Stewart-Ford. Both the Brazilian and his team-mate Jan Magnussen, whose race car was still being completed at the start of Friday's first free practice session, ran the gauntlet of seemingly endless transmission problems.

Barrichello needed a replacement gearbox prior to the qualifying session, but after this was installed his car suffered a hydraulic leak which meant it was extremely marginal whether the team would get him out in time to qualify at all. Magnussen was similarly afflicted, qualifying four places behind his colleague, just ahead of the second Tyrrell, driven by Ricardo Rosset.

Jarno Trulli lined up 15th for the Prost-Peugeot squad, although in reality the French team only got into the race at all by the skin of their teeth after the new AP01 chassis failed its side impact test no fewer than three times. In the event, the cars were cleared to run on the Thursday prior to the race when news came from the UK that it had successfully met the FIA's requirements.

Thereafter the new cars were stricken with reliability problems, most relating to the new ultra-narrow gearboxes, as well as lacking both balance and grip. Panis lined up 21st after losing his two best times following a spin in qualifying, abandoning his car in gear and paying the penalty.

Arrows drivers Mika Salo and Pedro Diniz had a similarly frustrating afternoon, lining up 16th and 20th. The team missed valuable set-up time in the Saturday morning free practice session after Salo's car developed a water leak and Diniz suffered hydraulic problems. In qualifying Salo then encountered a throttle problem and Diniz had a repeat glitch with the hydraulics, effectively wiping out their chances of a trouble-free run.

In 17th place Esteban Tuero did a respectable job on his F1 debut with the Minardi-Ford squad, easily outclassing team-mate Shinji Nakano, who had to use the spare M198 in qualifying after his race car suffered electronic problems.

Below left: **There were some anxious moments for the Prost team before their new AP01 chassis was allowed to compete.**

Right: **An impressive fifth fastest in qualifying, Johnny Herbert chalked up a point for Sauber.**

Below right: **Heinz-Harald Frentzen took a distant third for Williams but the FW20s were well off the pace of the dominant McLarens.**

'I had quite a bad start and lost several places,' said Ralf. 'The problem was I could not find my way into the centre [of the pack] so I had to stay on the outside, which was not a good thing to do. Then going into turn five I was touched by Magnussen. It was a racing incident; he did not do it on purpose. My mistake was to be so far back.'

Meanwhile, the two McLarens had completed the opening lap 1.5s apart with Häkkinen still ahead. Schumacher was third, but by lap three he had dropped 4.4s on Coulthard. On lap four he was 7.3s adrift, and as he crossed the start/finish line to complete lap five Schumacher's engine blew up spectacularly.

By this time Diniz had already swelled the list of retirements to five when his Arrows stopped with gearbox trouble after two laps, while Shinji Nakano's debut outing in the Minardi-Ford lasted only until lap nine when the Japanese driver retired with a driveshaft failure.

Schumacher was clearly not amused as he parked his crippled steed, almost throwing the detachable steering wheel away in frustration as he took his leave of the stricken car. It was hardly the opening shot he had been hoping for at the start of a crucial season in which Ferrari had pledged to take the championship, come what may.

Now Jacques Villeneuve took over third place some 17.8s behind Coulthard. He was being shadowed by the hard-working Giancarlo Fisichella's Benetton B198 and Johnny Herbert's Sauber C17, after which there was another gap back to Frentzen in sixth place. Eddie Irvine's Ferrari was seventh ahead of Damon Hill's Jordan and the Benetton of Alexander Wurz.

Fisichella had been obliged to take the spare B198 after cracking the steering rack bulkhead on his race car when he spun during the race morning warm-up. This change of machinery certainly didn't inhibit the gusto with which he snapped at Villeneuve's tail and, while many observers believed that his two-stop strategy should have enabled him to get ahead of the World Champion, Benetton team chief David Richards was quick to defend the young Italian. 'You've got to remember that Jacques is a pretty tenacious guy,' he noted.

Even at this early stage in the race, all that remained was to watch and marvel at the McLarens' superiority. The gap between Coulthard and Villeneuve was the key. On lap eight it was 24.1s, by lap ten it had expanded to 30.7s and on lap 18 it was out to 46.2s.

Elsewhere in the field, Minardi

Regulation changes for '98

The Australian Grand Prix provided the acid test for a veritable blizzard of revised F1 technical regulations aimed at enhancing the racing while at the same time reining in spiralling lap speeds.

Much had been made of the possibilities afforded by the new grooved tyres, wider chassis and narrower overall car width, which amounted to FIA President Max Mosley's personal manifesto, yet most chief designers remained sceptical that the status quo was likely to be affected. When rules change frequently, they say, this by definition favours the richer, better-sponsored teams who can deploy more research and development effort to coax the best out of the new rules.

'All the teams do all their testing, then turn up and run two days of practice, sorting themselves out on a grid in the order of their performance capability, so you might reasonably ask why should there be any overtaking in the race,' mused Patrick Head.

'Nevertheless, I believe that the relative deterioration of the tyres – which should be different from circuit to circuit – will produce quite a bit of overtaking.'

Yet the real concern among some teams was not the new type of tyres required, but whether or not they would be racing on a competitive brand. In the run-up to the season, Williams, Ferrari, Jordan, Sauber and Tyrrell had become increasingly concerned about the comparative effectiveness of Goodyear's products, the performance of which had frequently been bettered during testing by the Bridgestone-shod McLarens and Benettons. Testing had shown the Bridgestones retained their performance over longer periods. The Goodyears, although often slightly quicker at first, initially showed a tendency to lose grip after half a dozen or so laps.

Yet a combination of less aerodynamic downforce and reduced grip from the grooved tyres indicated that the season would start with lap times between three and five seconds slower than in 1997.

'The biggest difference compared with a normal car on slicks is just how much you can slide these grooved tyres,' said Häkkinen. 'But on Bridgestones, the harder you push them, the quicker you go.'

David Coulthard remained cautious, predicting that the performance between Bridgestone and Goodyear would vary from track to track, as it had the previous season. 'The difference is that in 1997, Bridgestone never really had a team capable of challenging seriously for a win,' he said. 'I think ourselves and Benetton will give them the opportunity to go out and get a win this year.'

A large part of the design work expended on the 1998 generation of F1 challengers was to comply with rigorously revised constructional requirements for the chassis.

The roll-over structures both in front of and behind the driver now had to sustain an impact of 7.5 tons, while the chassis was subjected to a much more severe side impact test. Because of this, the cars were expected to be safer in heavy accidents, even allowing for the fact that they might spin further.

In addition, the reduced width caused engineers to concentrate on developing more compact engines and very thin longitudinal gearboxes in order to maximise the airflow out of the side pods and over the aerodynamically crucial diffuser.

However, World Champion Jacques Villeneuve remained sceptical over precisely how the new rules would affect car performance. 'I don't think the racing will be any closer,' he said firmly. 'New regulations always spread the field out a little bit. It will be difficult to repeat last season when the qualifying performances were very close indeed.

'In fact, I expect it will be more difficult to overtake. With less grip we will rely more on downforce, so it will be more difficult to follow another car through the corner. It will also be possible for everybody to reach the limit of the cars' braking potential, so it will be harder again to outbrake another competitor.'

F1 SAFETY IMPROVEMENTS AT A GLANCE

Reduced car width (from 2000 mm in 1997 to 1800 mm in 1998)

Grooved tyres: three grooves in the front tyres, four in the rear. By adding more grooves in the future, cornering speeds can be further controlled

Minimum chassis width of 350 cm at front axle centre line to increase torsional stiffness of the chassis structure

Cockpit side protection now extends forward to level with the steering wheel

Chassis side impact structure moved forward and energy impact test increased

Mechanical fuel filler flap to provide additional protection against possible leakage

Larger mirrors

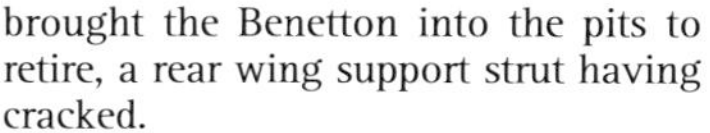

Michael Schumacher's hopes of opening his championship challenge with a win ended after just five laps with his Ferrari covered in oil following a dramatic engine failure.

Jacques Villeneuve *(below)* had to settle for fifth place after blocked radiator intakes forced him to moderate his normal aggression.

novice Esteban Tuero was having an uncomfortable education in the ways of F1 racing. Firstly he was called in on lap 12 for a ten-second stop-go penalty for jumping the start, but he managed to exceed the pit lane speed limit as he did so with the result that he was back for another penalty six laps later. Under the fraught circumstances, it must have been something of a relief when the 20-year-old's Grand Prix debut ended with an engine problem after 22 laps.

At the same time Fisichella became the first of the front-runners to make a routine refuelling stop, the Benetton driver dropping from fourth to ninth after being stationary for 8.3s. Then it was the turn of the McLarens. Häkkinen stopped on lap 24, allowing Coulthard through into the lead. David came in next time round and they resumed just over three seconds apart in their original order.

Villeneuve, pursuing a one-stop strategy like most Goodyear runners, hung on until lap 28 before coming in. Frentzen was by now up to fourth and when Jacques went into the pits the German driver really piled on the pressure, cutting his times by the best part of a second for several laps before making his sole stop on lap 33.

The net result of Frentzen's frenzied burst was to leave him third ahead of Fisichella and Irvine, with Villeneuve sixth ahead of Wurz and Herbert. The Italian moved ahead of the Williams driver on lap 39 but four laps later he brought the Benetton into the pits to retire, a rear wing support strut having cracked.

Pamela Lauesen/FOSA

Meanwhile, up at the front of the pack, it momentarily seemed as though the McLaren team's winning strategy was poised to unravel. On lap 36, Häkkinen unaccountably came into the pits, but accelerated straight back into the race, now in second place.

Four laps later the Finn returned to the pits to make his routine second stop at the appropriate moment, Coulthard duplicating his move two laps later. But the net result of this mess-up was to leave the Scot running 13.3s ahead of Häkkinen. The best laid plans of mice and men had gone straight out of the window. Or so it seemed at the time.

Just before his stop proper, Häkkinen had gone round in 1m 31.649s, the fastest lap of the race by a margin of 0.7s ahead of Coulthard – nobody else in the field proved capable of breaking the 1m 33s barrier, an index of just how complete the McLaren dominance was. With Coulthard now

Bryn Williams

ahead, there followed a discussion over the pit-to-car radio as to what should happen next.

David duly agreed that he would relinquish first place and let his lap times drift by a couple of seconds as compared with Häkkinen as the Finn caught up. Coming up to finish lap 56, Coulthard eased off on the start/finish straight to allow his team-mate to slip ahead. And that is how they finished.

Heading the also-rans in third place was Heinz-Harald Frentzen's Williams FW20 ahead of Eddie Irvine's Ferrari F300, both lapped by the victorious McLarens by the end of the race. The Williams driver found his choice of Goodyear tyre compound too hard for the conditions, but Irvine was quite content with the performance of his rubber.

'I don't think the gap between us and McLaren is as big as it looked today,' he said optimistically. 'We need to improve the driveability of our engine, but overall I was very happy with the car and think we can beat Williams and challenge McLaren with the improvements we have in the pipeline.'

Jacques Villeneuve's Williams finished fifth ahead of Johnny Herbert's Sauber, the World Champion bugged by dangerously high oil temperatures caused by blocked radiator intakes which meant he had to nurse the car carefully in the closing stages of the race. 'I am not used to being a victim,' shrugged Villeneuve.

Herbert was well satisfied with sixth place. 'With slightly better fortune we might have made the podium today,' he mused. 'I was able to stay with Jacques all through the race, but although I looked after my tyres very carefully in the early stages, I still had too much understeer.

'I made my pit stop early, but there was a problem with the refuelling rig which meant I couldn't get a full quota of fuel. That meant I had to conserve what I had for the rest of the race, by lifting off and rolling into the corners, but even so I nearly got Jacques right at the end.'

By contrast, Jean Alesi's debut outing for Sauber finished on a disappointing note when he retired from eighth place on lap 42 with engine failure.

'On the formation lap I had a problem selecting first gear,' he explained, 'so I pulled off the line in third, and at the proper start I did not get away very well either. During my race the car was understeering as it had in qualifying, so I could not push as hard as I wanted to. Then the engine began to lose power and broke altogether on lap 42.'

Wurz finished seventh, barely two seconds behind Villeneuve's fifth-placed Williams despite a two-stop strategy with the Benetton, while Damon Hill struggled home eighth after a distinctly inauspicious first outing at the wheel of the Jordan-Mugen Honda.

'The result today reflects more the fact that we did not qualify well, rather than that we had an average race,' said Hill. 'I want to go away and look at the telemetry data so that we can work on finding some more speed on the car, but I was encouraged by my performance toward the latter part of the race.

'I saw Wurz up ahead and pushed to catch up, but then went off, which made me cross with myself. It seems that the key to speed is to get angry, as after that I really picked up.'

In ninth place Olivier Panis's Prost-Peugeot completed the list of classified finishers, team-mate Jarno Trulli having climbed to seventh before being sidelined by gearbox troubles on lap 27.

As the other competitors reflected on their various misfortunes, Ron Dennis added that he expected the abrasive track surface at São Paulo's Interlagos circuit, venue for the second round of the title chase, to favour the MP4/13s even more than Melbourne. Coulthard and Häkkinen would play to the same rules in this second round of the championship, he explained, after which all bets were off.

Dennis might also have added that the reputed $2 million annual pay cheque which secured the services of the Williams team's former chief designer looked like something of a bargain on Sunday evening in Melbourne.

After all, who needs Schuey when you've got Newey?

Main photo: Paul-Henri Cahier

Lukas Gorys

DIARY

November 1997

British government offers Formula 1 ten years' grace before proposed EU tobacco ban affects the sport. Labour Party embarrassed when it is revealed that Bernie Ecclestone has made £1 million donation to its funds.

Ken Tyrrell sells his F1 team for reputed £18 million to British American Racing headed by Craig Pollock.

December 1997

Frank Williams, Patrick Head and Adrian Newey acquitted of manslaughter charges in connection with Ayrton Senna's fatal accident at Imola in 1994.

China and South Africa nominated as reserve races on 1998 Formula 1 calendar.

January 1998

Michelin decides against Grand Prix return in 1999.

EU competition commissioner Karel van Miert jeopardises Bernie Ecclestone's planned F1 stock exchange flotation with suggestions that his business infringes rules involving abuse of dominant positions.

Max Welti quits as Sauber F1 team manager.

February 1998

Road Atlanta makes bid for possible United States GP.

Damon Hill predicts that he will probably race for another three seasons in F1.

Bridgestone rejects accusations by Sauber's Jean Alesi that the Benetton team gave it Goodyear data before signing a deal to run on its tyres.

Main picture: **Under wraps. F1 cockpits contain a wealth of advanced technology, much of it a closely guarded secret.**

Below left: **The carefully packaged transmission and rear suspension of Gary Anderson's Jordan 198 was typical of the new breed of Grand Prix car.**

Below: **The one to beat. The Mercedes V10 started the season with a definite advantage over the rest.**

Lukas Gorys

Runners and riders

WILLIAMS-MECACHROME

Going into 1998 defending its record ninth constructors' championship title, Williams fielded the new FW20, its first F1 challenger of the post-Adrian Newey era. Designed by an engineering team led by Geoff Willis and Gavin Fisher, the new car remained powered by a Renault-built V10 engine, now badged Mecachrome and supplied on a commercial basis for an annual lease fee in the region of £13 million. Jacques Villeneuve and Heinz-Harald Frentzen remained on the driver strength supported by test drivers Juan Pablo Montoya and Max Wilson. The Williams was the only car of the new crop to retain a transverse gearbox.

FERRARI

New Ferrari F300 design from Rory Byrne and Ross Brawn carries responsibility for giving Maranello its first constructors' championship since 1983 and preferably its first drivers' title since 1979 as well. Enormous sense of expectancy surrounding new car, which originally broke cover just before Christmas and spent most of the run-up to the season testing at Mugello, well away from a head-to-head with other key players at Barcelona.

BENETTON-PLAYLIFE

Another potential top team which switched from Goodyear to Bridgestone tyres over the winter after the Akron-based tyre giant announced that it would withdraw from F1 at the end of 1998. Now under the ambitious management of Prodrive founder David Richards; chief designer Nick Wirth and technical director Pat Symonds opted for distinctive short side pods on the new B198 with additional side impact resistance afforded by aerodynamic deflectors alongside the cockpit. New driver line-up of Giancarlo Fisichella and Alexander Wurz using Mecachrome (*née* Renault) V10 engines badged with Benetton's 'Playlife' brand.

McLAREN-MERCEDES

Pre-season favourites, the latest 'Silver Arrows' were the first McLaren design to be co-ordinated by Adrian Newey. Carried type number MP4/13 – no superstition in this team – and powered by the latest Ilmor-built Mercedes FO110G V10-cylinder engine, which was around five per cent lighter than its immediate predecessor, developing around 770 bhp at 16,500 rpm with further improved driveability. The first top team to switch from Goodyear to Bridgestone tyres over the winter. Driver line-up of Mika Häkkinen and David Coulthard remained unchanged from previous season. Car also featured development of secondary braking system first used by the team in the middle of 1997.

JORDAN-MUGEN HONDA

Latest Gary Anderson-designed Jordan 198 powered by lighter, lower Mugen Honda V10 engine which replaced Peugeot power at the start of the new season. Ralf Schumacher joined in driver line-up by 1996 World Champion Damon Hill, who had quit Arrows after a single season.

PROST-PEUGEOT

Prost designer Loïc Bigois produced the all-new Peugeot-engined Prost AP01 with the benefit of former Renault Sport technical director Bernard Dudot also on the team strength to handle the team's interface with Peugeot Sport. Much pre-season gearbox trouble blighted shakedown efforts and further strain on the team's infrastructure caused by relocation of headquarters from Magny-Cours to Paris during the early months of the new season. Olivier Panis now partnered by Jarno Trulli in driver line-up.

SAUBER-PETRONAS

All-new Leo Ress-designed Sauber C17 again relying on Ferrari V10 power under 'Petronas' badging. With Jean Alesi joining Johnny Herbert at Hinwil, the Swiss team had a strong, experienced driver pairing but badly needed some solid results to match its obvious ambition.

ARROWS

Striking and lavishly engineered new John Barnard-designed Arrows A19 powered by Brian Hart-built V10 engine first unveiled in August 1997 and since re-engineered with revised pump and ancillary positions in deference to Barnard's design requirements. Impressively low engine cover for optimum airflow over rear wing, but car lacked pre-season testing and troubled by unreliability of carbon-fibre-cased gearbox. Mika Salo switched from Tyrrell to lead driver line-up alongside pay-driver Pedro Diniz.

STEWART-FORD

Neat Stewart SF2 designed by Alan Jenkins, fitted with the latest, lower and lighter Ford Zetec-R V10 engine, also transmitting its power through carbon-fibre-cased gearbox. Hoping for a steady upturn in fortunes in second season in F1, with Rubens Barrichello and Jan Magnussen retained as drivers and new test team scheduled to start operating from late spring.

TYRRELL-FORD

Ken Tyrrell sold his team to a consortium headed by Craig Pollock, business manager of Jacques Villeneuve, for a reputed £18 million. For Pollock, who had put together a $250 million, five-year package backed by British American Tobacco, acquiring Tyrrell was a trailer for an all-new Brackley-based F1 operation using Reynard-built chassis from the start of 1999. Customer Ford V10s powered the last Ripley-built Tyrrell, the type 026, to be driven by Toranosuke Takagi and Ricardo Rosset.

MINARDI-FORD

Switch from Hart to customer Ford Zetec-R V10 power for F1's perennial tail-enders, who had signed pay-drivers Shinji Nakano and Esteban Tuero to take the wheel this season. Nakano had learned the ropes with Prost in 1997, but Tuero had to complete 2000 km of pre-season testing in order to satisfy the FIA of his suitability for an F1 superlicence.

Team orders could be under threat

MOTOR racing's governing body signalled a crack-down on team orders just ten days after telling the Australian GP promoter Ron Walker that there was no question of taking sanctions against the McLaren team after David Coulthard had relinquished the race lead to Mika Häkkinen.

In the immediate aftermath of the race, Walker had written to FIA President Max Mosley and released a statement saying: 'It is not my place to discuss any punitive action, it is not my area of responsibility, but we have to seek clarification on this matter.

'It is not the right of team owners to decide who is going to win. I don't think you have heard the end yet. I think that Max Mosley will advise on this the moment he lands in London.'

The FIA's immediate response was to point out that team orders were, in effect, as old as the sport itself. Yet if McLaren nurtured any hopes of allowing Coulthard to square his account with Häkkinen in the second race of the season at Interlagos, the FIA World Council had other ideas.

It duly decreed that the stewards at all future Grands Prix would be informed that 'any acts prejudicial to the interests of any competition' should be penalised severely under the terms of the international sporting code.

'All we have done is drawn attention to provisions which have been in the rules for decades,' said Mosley, 'but everybody should remember that this is a drivers' contest, not just a team championship.'

Race distance: 58 laps, 191.117 miles/307.574 km

Race weather: Dry, warm and sunny

Pos.	Driver	Nat.	No.	Entrant	Car/Engine	Tyres	Laps	Time/Retirement	Speed (mph/km/h)
1	**Mika Häkkinen**	**SF**	**8**	**West McLaren Mercedes**	**McLaren MP4/13-Mercedes FO110G V10**	**B**	**58**	**1h 31m 45.996s**	**124.958/201.101**
2	**David Coulthard**	**GB**	**7**	**West McLaren Mercedes**	**McLaren MP4/13-Mercedes FO110G V10**	**B**	**58**	**1h 31m 46.698s**	**124.943/201.076**
3	**Heinz-Harald Frentzen**	**D**	**2**	**Winfield Williams**	**Williams FW20-Mecachrome GC37/01 V10**	**G**	**57**		
4	**Eddie Irvine**	**GB**	**4**	**Scuderia Ferrari Marlboro**	**Ferrari F300 047 V10**	**G**	**57**		
5	**Jacques Villeneuve**	**CDN**	**1**	**Winfield Williams**	**Williams FW20-Mecachrome GC37/01 V10**	**G**	**57**		
6	**Johnny Herbert**	**GB**	**15**	**Red Bull Sauber Petronas**	**Sauber C17-Petronas SPE01D V10**	**G**	**57**		
7	Alexander Wurz	A	6	Mild Seven Benetton Playlife	Benetton B198-Playlife V10	B	57		
8	Damon Hill	GB	9	B&H Jordan Mugen Honda	Jordan 198-Mugen Honda MF310C V10	G	57		
9	Olivier Panis	F	11	Gauloises Prost Peugeot	Prost AP01-Peugeot A16 V10	B	57		
	Giancarlo Fisichella	I	5	Mild Seven Benetton Playlife	Benetton B198-Playlife V10	B	43	Rear wing	
	Jean Alesi	F	14	Red Bull Sauber Petronas	Sauber C17-Petronas SPE01D V10	G	41	Engine	
	Jarno Trulli	I	12	Gauloises Prost Peugeot	Prost AP01-Peugeot A16 V10	B	26	Gearbox	
	Ricardo Rosset	BR	20	Tyrrell Ford	Tyrrell 026-Ford Zetec-R V10	G	25	Gearbox	
	Mika Salo	SF	17	Danka Zepter Arrows	Arrows A19 V10	B	23	Electrics	
	Esteban Tuero	RA	23	Fondmetal Minardi Ford	Minardi M198-Ford Zetec-R V10	B	22	Engine	
	Shinji Nakano	J	22	Fondmetal Minardi Ford	Minardi M198-Ford Zetec-R V10	B	8	Driveshaft	
	Michael Schumacher	D	3	Scuderia Ferrari Marlboro	Ferrari F300 047 V10	G	5	Engine	
	Pedro Diniz	BR	16	Danka Zepter Arrows	Arrows A19 V10	B	2	Gearbox	
	Ralf Schumacher	D	10	B&H Jordan Mugen Honda	Jordan 198-Mugen Honda MF310C V10	G	1	Collision	
	Jan Magnussen	DK	19	Stewart Ford	Stewart SF2-Ford Zetec-R V10	B	1	Collision	
	Toranosuke Takagi	J	21	Tyrrell Ford	Tyrrell 026-Ford Zetec-R V10	G	1	Collision	
	Rubens Barrichello	BR	18	Stewart Ford	Stewart SF2-Ford Zetec-R V10	B	0	Gearbox	

Fastest lap: Häkkinen, on lap 39, 1m 31.649s, 129.433 mph/208.303 km/h.

Lap record: Heinz-Harald Frentzen (F1 Williams FW19-Renault V10), 1m 30.585s, 130.929 mph/210.710 km/h (1997).

B – Bridgestone G – Goodyear

All results and data © FIA 1998

Grid order	1	2	3	4	5	6	7	8	9	10	11	12	13	14	15	16	17	18	19	20	21	22	23	24	25	26	27	28	29	30	31	32	33	34	35	36	37	38	39	40	41	42	43
8 HÄKKINEN	8	8	8	8	8	8	8	8	8	8	8	8	8	8	8	8	8	8	8	8	8	8	8	7	8	8	8	8	8	8	8	8	8	8	8	7	7	7	7	7	7	7	7
7 COULTHARD	7	7	7	7	7	7	7	7	7	7	7	7	7	7	7	7	7	7	7	7	7	7	7	8	7	7	7	7	7	7	7	7	7	7	7	8	8	8	8	8	8	8	8
3 M. SCHUMACHER	3	3	3	3	3	1	1	1	1	1	1	1	1	1	1	1	1	1	1	1	1	1	1	1	1	1	1	2	2	2	2	2	2	2	2	2	2	2	5	5	2	2	2
1 VILLENEUVE	1	1	1	1	1	5	5	5	5	5	5	5	5	5	5	5	5	5	5	5	5	15	15	15	15	15	2	4	4	4	4	4	5	5	5	5	5	5	2	2	4	4	4
15 HERBERT	5	5	5	5	5	15	15	15	15	15	15	15	15	15	15	15	15	15	15	15	15	2	2	2	2	2	4	14	5	5	5	5	4	4	4	4	4	4	4	4	5	1	1
2 FRENTZEN	15	15	15	15	15	2	2	2	2	2	2	2	2	2	2	2	2	2	2	2	2	4	4	4	4	4	14	5	1	1	1	1	1	1	1	1	1	1	1	1	1	15	15
5 FISICHELLA	2	2	2	2	2	4	4	4	4	4	4	4	4	4	4	4	4	4	4	4	4	12	12	12	12	12	5	1	15	15	15	15	6	6	6	15	15	15	15	15	15	5	5
4 IRVINE	4	4	4	4	4	9	9	9	9	9	9	9	9	9	9	9	9	9	6	12	12	14	14	14	14	14	15	15	6	6	6	6	15	15	15	9	9	9	14	14	14	6	6
10 R. SCHUMACHER	9	9	9	9	9	6	6	6	6	6	6	6	6	6	6	6	6	6	12	14	14	5	5	5	5	5	6	6	9	9	9	9	9	9	9	14	14	14	6	6	6	9	9
9 HILL	6	6	6	6	6	12	12	12	12	12	12	12	12	12	12	12	12	12	14	6	6	6	6	6	6	6	9	9	14	14	14	14	14	14	14	6	6	6	9	9	9	11	11
6 WURZ	12	12	12	12	12	17	17	17	17	17	17	17	17	17	17	17	17	17	17	17	17	17	17	9	9	9	11	11	11	11	11	11	11	11	11	11	11	11	11	11	11		
14 ALESI	14	17	17	17	17	14	14	14	14	14	14	14	14	14	14	14	14	14	9	9	9	9	9	11	11	11																	
21 TAKAGI	17	14	14	14	14	23	23	23	23	23	23	11	11	11	11	11	11	11	11	11	11	11	11	20	20																		
18 BARRICHELLO	10	23	23	23	23	20	20	20	20	20	11	20	20	20	20	20	20	20	20	20	20	23	20																				
12 TRULLI	19	20	20	20	20	11	11	11	11	11	20	23	23	23	23	23	23	23	23	23	23	20																					
17 SALO	21	11	11	11	11	22	22	22																																			
23 TUERO	23	22	22	22	22																																						
19 MAGNUSSEN	20	16																																									
20 ROSSET	11																																										
16 DINIZ	22																																										
11 PANIS	16																																										
22 NAKANO																																											

Pit stop

One lap behind leader

STARTING GRID

8 **HÄKKINEN** McLaren	7 **COULTHARD** McLaren
3 **M. SCHUMACHER** Ferrari	1 **VILLENEUVE** Williams
15 **HERBERT** Sauber	2 **FRENTZEN** Williams
5 **FISICHELLA** Benetton	4 **IRVINE** Ferrari
10 **R. SCHUMACHER** Jordan	9 **HILL** Jordan
6 **WURZ** Benetton	14 **ALESI** Sauber
21 **TAKAGI** Tyrrell	18 **BARRICHELLO** Stewart
12 **TRULLI** Prost	17 **SALO** Arrows
23 **TUERO** Minardi	19 **MAGNUSSEN** Stewart
20 **ROSSET** Tyrrell	16 **DINIZ** Arrows
11 **PANIS** Prost	22 **NAKANO** Minardi

47	48	49	50	51	52	53	54	55	56	57	58	●
7	7	7	7	7	7	7	7	7	8	8	8	1
8	8	8	8	8	8	8	8	8	7	7	7	2
2	2	2	2	2	2	2	2	2	2	2		3
4	4	4	4	4	4	4	4	4	4	4		4
1	1	1	1	1	1	1	1	1	1	1		5
15	15	15	15	15	15	15	15	15	15	15		6
6	6	6	6	6	6	6	6	6	6	6		
9	9	9	9	9	9	9	9	9	9	9		
11	11	11	11	11	11	11	11	11	11	11		

FOR THE RECORD

First Grand Prix start

Toranosuke Takagi

Esteban Tuero

TIME SHEETS

QUALIFYING

Weather: Bright and sunny

Pos.	Driver	Car	Laps	Time
1	Mika Häkkinen	McLaren-Mercedes	10	1m 30.010s
2	David Coulthard	McLaren-Mercedes	10	1m 30.053s
3	Michael Schumacher	Ferrari	11	1m 30.767s
4	Jacques Villeneuve	Williams-Mecachrome	12	1m 30.919s
5	Johnny Herbert	Sauber-Petronas	12	1m 31.384s
6	Heinz-Harald Frentzen	Williams-Mecachrome	12	1m 31.397s
7	Giancarlo Fisichella	Benetton-Playlife	12	1m 31.733s
8	Eddie Irvine	Ferrari	11	1m 31.767s
9	Ralf Schumacher	Jordan-Mugen Honda	11	1m 32.392s
10	Damon Hill	Jordan-Mugen Honda	12	1m 32.399s
11	Alexander Wurz	Benetton-Playlife	9	1m 32.726s
12	Jean Alesi	Sauber-Petronas	11	1m 33.240s
13	Toranosuke Takagi	Tyrrell-Ford	11	1m 33.291s
14	Rubens Barrichello	Stewart-Ford	8	1m 33.383s
15	Jarno Trulli	Prost-Peugeot	11	1m 33.739s
16	Mika Salo	Arrows	8	1m 33.927s
17	Esteban Tuero	Minardi-Ford	12	1m 34.646s
18	Jan Magnussen	Stewart-Ford	9	1m 34.906s
19	Ricardo Rosset	Tyrrell-Ford	11	1m 35.119s
20	Pedro Diniz	Arrows	7	1m 35.140s
21	Olivier Panis	Prost-Peugeot	12	1m 35.215s
22	Shinji Nakano	Minardi-Ford	12	1m 35.301s

FRIDAY FREE PRACTICE

Weather: Overcast, intermittent light rain

Pos.	Driver	Laps	Time
1	Michael Schumacher	15	1m 33.826s
2	Mika Häkkinen	12	1m 34.432s
3	Jacques Villeneuve	24	1m 35.023s
4	Alexander Wurz	21	1m 35.270s
5	David Coulthard	14	1m 35.409s
6	Ralf Schumacher	14	1m 35.708s
7	Johnny Herbert	10	1m 35.876s
8	Jean Alesi	9	1m 36.095s
9	Jarno Trulli	17	1m 36.231s
10	Heinz-Harald Frentzen	17	1m 36.741s
11	Mika Salo	16	1m 36.897s
12	Rubens Barrichello	12	1m 37.023s
13	Damon Hill	19	1m 37.102s
14	Olivier Panis	15	1m 37.102s
15	Ricardo Rosset	25	1m 37.144s
16	Jan Magnussen	8	1m 37.605s
17	Eddie Irvine	14	1m 37.891s
18	Pedro Diniz	8	1m 37.928s
19	Toranosuke Takagi	26	1m 38.817s
20	Giancarlo Fisichella	17	1m 38.860s
21	Shinji Nakano	8	1m 39.044s
22	Esteban Tuero	5	2m 16.609s

SATURDAY FREE PRACTICE

Weather: Overcast, becoming warmer

Pos.	Driver	Laps	Time
1	David Coulthard	24	1m 30.456s
2	Jacques Villeneuve	23	1m 31.178s
3	Michael Schumacher	33	1m 31.432s
4	Mika Häkkinen	25	1m 31.436s
5	Giancarlo Fisichella	28	1m 31.581s
6	Heinz-Harald Frentzen	30	1m 31.624s
7	Johnny Herbert	29	1m 31.870s
8	Eddie Irvine	25	1m 32.465s
9	Jean Alesi	26	1m 32.514s
10	Damon Hill	29	1m 32.518s
11	Ralf Schumacher	20	1m 32.667s
12	Alexander Wurz	12	1m 33.588s
13	Rubens Barrichello	23	1m 33.965s
14	Jan Magnussen	16	1m 34.543s
15	Toranosuke Takagi	17	1m 34.600s
16	Jarno Trulli	22	1m 34.837s
17	Ricardo Rosset	29	1m 35.010s
18	Shinji Nakano	25	1m 35.069s
19	Mika Salo	8	1m 35.539s
20	Esteban Tuero	33	1m 35.850s
21	Olivier Panis	14	1m 35.913s
22	Pedro Diniz	4	1m 36.351s

WARM-UP

Weather: Sunny and warm

Pos.	Driver	Laps	Time
1	Mika Häkkinen	12	1m 34.126s
2	David Coulthard	11	1m 34.257s
3	Michael Schumacher	12	1m 34.346s
4	Ralf Schumacher	15	1m 35.030s
5	Damon Hill	12	1m 35.033s
6	Johnny Herbert	12	1m 35.081s
7	Eddie Irvine	11	1m 35.192s
8	Giancarlo Fisichella	14	1m 35.215s
9	Jacques Villeneuve	12	1m 35.401s
10	Mika Salo	13	1m 35.411s
11	Heinz-Harald Frentzen	9	1m 35.497s
12	Esteban Tuero	10	1m 36.021s
13	Jean Alesi	11	1m 36.081s
14	Jan Magnussen	8	1m 36.160s
15	Jarno Trulli	15	1m 36.246s
16	Alexander Wurz	13	1m 36.257s
17	Rubens Barrichello	7	1m 36.690s
18	Pedro Diniz	9	1m 36.868s
19	Olivier Panis	11	1m 37.215s
20	Toranosuke Takagi	15	1m 37.482s
21	Shinji Nakano	12	1m 37.772s
22	Ricardo Rosset	11	1m 38.487s

RACE FASTEST LAPS

Weather: Dry, warm and sunny

Driver	Time	Lap
Mika Häkkinen	1m 31.649s	39
David Coulthard	1m 32.356s	24
Heinz-Harald Frentzen	1m 33.554s	33
Eddie Irvine	1m 33.790s	33
Damon Hill	1m 34.196s	55
Giancarlo Fisichella	1m 34.319s	40
Olivier Panis	1m 34.319s	55
Alexander Wurz	1m 34.738s	54
Jean Alesi	1m 34.878s	28
Jarno Trulli	1m 34.885s	25
Johnny Herbert	1m 35.624s	24
Jacques Villeneuve	1m 35.661s	53
Michael Schumacher	1m 35.774s	3
Mika Salo	1m 36.032s	18
Esteban Tuero	1m 36.475s	19
Ricardo Rosset	1m 38.116s	20
Shinji Nakano	1m 39.676s	3
Pedro Diniz	1m 39.916s	2
Ralf Schumacher	1m 50.966s	1
Jan Magnussen	1m 52.353s	1
Toranosuke Takagi	1m 53.124s	1

CHASSIS LOG BOOK

1	Villeneuve	Williams FW20/3
2	Frentzen	Williams FW20/2
	spare	Williams FW20/1
3	M. Schumacher	Ferrari F300/184
4	Irvine	Ferrari F300/181
	spare	Ferrari F300/183
5	Fisichella	Benetton B198/5
6	Wurz	Benetton B198/4
	spare	Benetton B198/3
7	Coulthard	McLaren MP4/13/3
8	Häkkinen	McLaren MP4/13/2
	spare	McLaren MP4/13/1
9	Hill	Jordan 198/4
10	R. Schumacher	Jordan 198/3
	spare	Jordan 198/1
11	Panis	Prost AP01/4
12	Trulli	Prost AP01/2
	spare	Prost AP01/3
14	Alesi	Sauber C17/3
15	Herbert	Sauber C17/1
	spare	Sauber C17/2
16	Diniz	Arrows A19/2
17	Salo	Arrows A19/3
	spare	Arrows A19/1
18	Barrichello	Stewart SF2/1
19	Magnussen	Stewart SF2/3
	spare	Stewart SF2/2
20	Rosset	Tyrrell 026/1
21	Takagi	Tyrrell 026/2
	spare	Tyrrell 026/3
22	Nakano	Minardi M198/1
23	Tuero	Minardi M198/3
	spare	Minardi M198/2

POINTS TABLES

Drivers

1	Mika Häkkinen	10
2	David Coulthard	6
3	Heinz-Harald Frentzen	4
4	Eddie Irvine	3
5	Jacques Villeneuve	2
6	Johnny Herbert	1

Constructors

1	McLaren	16
2	Williams	6
3	Ferrari	3
4	Sauber	1

BRAZILIAN grand prix

FIA WORLD CHAMPIONSHIP • ROUND 2

GP Photo/Peter Nygaard

Above: **Mika Häkkinen made a textbook start from pole position and remained in front to the chequered flag.**

Slip slidin' away. The Michael Schumacher/Ferrari/Goodyear combination struggled to match the pace of the Bridgestone-shod McLarens and the German was forced into a weekend of damage limitation.

HÄKKINEN

COULTHARD

M. SCHUMACHER

WURZ

FRENTZEN

FISICHELLA

Pascal Rondeau/Allsport

M. SCHUMACHER
HÄKKINEN
IRVINE
WURZ
ALESI
COULTHARD

MICHAEL Schumacher stopped the McLaren steamroller in its tracks with a dramatic victory in the Argentine Grand Prix at Buenos Aires which saw him not only elbow David Coulthard aside in unruly fashion during the opening phase of the race but also beat Mika Häkkinen fair and square in a sprint to the chequered flag.

It was a success which confirmed most pre-season predictions: give the Ferrari team leader an inch and he will take a mile. Having pushed Häkkinen's McLaren MP4/13-Mercedes off the front row of the starting grid, he then capitalised on Goodyear's latest, wider front tyre construction to maximum effect to post his first win of the '98 season.

Häkkinen's second place on a circuit he dislikes at least kept him comfortably in the lead of the Drivers' World Championship, but for Coulthard the race turned out to be a disaster. When the starting signal was given David accelerated cleanly into the lead from pole position with Häkkinen taking second place from Schumacher as the pack funnelled into the first long right-hander.

At the end of the opening lap the order was Coulthard, Häkkinen, Schumacher, then Heinz-Harald Frentzen's Williams FW20, Eddie Irvine in the other Ferrari F300, Jacques Villeneuve's Williams and Jean Alesi's Sauber C17.

However, any hopes that the McLarens might make an early break were dashed when Schumacher went ahead of Häkkinen to take second place midway round the second lap, Irvine emphasising the Ferrari threat by displacing Frentzen from fourth at almost the same point. The German driver's Williams had lost a front wing end plate on the formation lap and was suffering a dramatic handling imbalance as a result, making it difficult for him to sustain a consistent pace.

Now Schumacher was after Coulthard with a vengeance. On lap four David went slightly wide entering the slow right-hand hairpin at the end of the back straight, and the McLaren driver repeated this slight slip at the same point next time round.

Schumacher saw his opportunity, heaving his Ferrari's inside wheels up the kerb as he scrabbled round the corner. Coulthard tightened his line and the two cars collided, the silver McLaren-Mercedes being launched into a half-spin over the left-front wheel of its rival.

'I didn't feel obliged to lift off because I had the momentum,' said Schumacher, 'then David closed the door on me and we touched.' Coulthard resumed in sixth place, and that is where he finished despite being briefly rammed off the circuit by Jacques Villeneuve's Williams during their battle for the final championship point.

A detailed analysis of the situation inevitably cast another shadow of doubt over Coulthard's vulnerability under pressure. Braking hard for this hairpin, David found the downchange mechanism on his McLaren-Mercedes' gearbox 'balking' slightly.

This fault meant that the car was a fraction late in selecting the lower gear with the result that he ran a little wide from the apex of the right-hand corner. Sensing his opportunity, Schumacher pounced.

'It is unusual for drivers to collide on the exit to a corner,' said Coulthard quizzically. 'Usually it is on the entry and I was still a metre and a half ahead of Michael, so I just held my line. I think he was just expecting me to drive out of his way, or else he was just prepared to sit there and see what happened. I think Michael was being a bit aggressive, but I am thankful that at least I was driving a strong car.'

Schumacher retorted, 'David had run wide at that corner the lap before. I didn't want to slow my pace and lose time, so I went down the inside and then he shut the door.'

Meanwhile, lap three had seen Villeneuve nip ahead of Frentzen to take fifth place, which became fourth after Coulthard dropped down the order following his Ferrari-induced pirouette.

The race now settled down with Schumacher 6.4s ahead of Häkkinen by the end of lap six, an advantage which he expanded to 8.7s in another two laps and eased open to 12.5s by lap 15. The relatively cool track temperatures made McLaren's choice of the harder Bridgestone rubber a touch conservative, a factor which also helped Schumacher gain the upper hand at the front of the field.

Behind Irvine's third-placed Ferrari, Villeneuve, Alesi and Coulthard were soon running together in a tight train disputing fourth place, while Frentzen was seventh ahead of Alexander Wurz's Benetton, Damon Hill's Jordan and Giancarlo Fisichella's Benetton.

On lap 14 Pedro Diniz was posted as the race's first retirement, the Brazilian dropping from 19th place when his Arrows's gearbox failed. Three laps later it was the turn of Jan Magnussen's Stewart-Ford to bow out from 18th place with transmission problems.

'I got a reasonable start off the line, but there was so much traffic that I had to back off a bit after the start,' shrugged the Dane. 'I did make up a

The marked upturn in Ferrari's form brings a smile to the faces of Eddie Irvine and Michael Schumacher. Their confidence was to prove well founded.

Top: **Argy-bargy. The decisive moment of the race came on lap five, when Schumacher forced his way past David Coulthard's McLaren in typically uncompromising fashion.**

Paul-Henri Cahier

Sutton Motorsport Images

In the dark. Sauber's Johnny Herbert tries to get to the bottom of the problems that dogged him throughout practice and qualifying. He was eliminated from the race in a collision with Damon Hill.

Below left: Jean Alesi earned a couple of championship points for the Swiss team with fifth place despite one of the precarious-looking winglets fitted to his car being dislodged during a pit stop.

Below right: A new wider front tyre from Goodyear *(left)* helped Michael Schumacher to a place on the front row of the grid, in between the two McLarens.

few positions before I retired, but it's been a difficult weekend.'

Gearbox problems also sidelined Mika Salo's Arrows on lap 18, moments before Ralf Schumacher, who had made a bad start, spun his Jordan 198 up an escape road. The German was able to continue, but not before he had dropped from 13th to 19th. He then came in for his first stop (9.7s) and the team checked over the car while fresh tyres were fitted, but it was just as nervous after Ralf resumed the chase. He was running last when a rear top wishbone failed and the Jordan spun off for good five laps later.

On lap 27 Alesi made his first refuelling stop, dropping from sixth to tenth and losing his right-hand sidepod-mounted winglet, which was ripped off against the Arrows team's refuelling equipment in the adjacent pit as he accelerated back into the fray.

'On this circuit you pick up grip throughout the race,' explained Jean, 'so for sure it would have been better to have both wings on the car. But my pit stops were fantastic, especially after the second when my crew got me out ahead of Villeneuve and Coulthard.'

On lap 28 Schumacher made his first stop (9.5s) and dropped to second place some 11.1s behind Häkkinen. On the following lap Villeneuve, who was running a one-stop strategy, moved into third place when Irvine made his first stop. The World Champion remained there until lap 37 when he made a 12.4s stop to take on sufficient fuel to get through to the finish, resuming in eighth place, which soon became sixth.

Häkkinen now led from Schumacher, Irvine and Frentzen, who came in for his first stop at the end of lap 38 and exceeded the pit lane speed limit as he accelerated back into the race in 13th place after a long stop when his Williams's engine stalled. He would be back at the end of lap 43 to take his prescribed medicine in the form of a ten-second stop-go penalty.

While Alesi was going well for Sauber, Johnny Herbert's race – and indeed his South American tour as a whole – ended on a dismal note on lap 46. He'd chosen a one-stop strategy to make the best of his lowly grid position and admitted the C17 felt quite reasonable in the opening stages, but Damon Hill's Jordan hit his left-rear tyre while they were fighting for ninth place and, although he limped back to the pits, the car was too badly damaged to continue.

'I'm surprised Damon did that, given all his experience,' said Herbert. Hill, however, had a different viewpoint.

David Coulthard made no bones about it. He likes the Autodromo Oscar A. Galvez and, in qualifying, duly emerged from Mika Häkkinen's shadow to claim the sixth pole position of his career and his first since the 1995 Pacific GP when he was driving for Williams.

It was thus his first pole at the wheel of a McLaren-Mercedes and represented the high spot of his Argentine Grand Prix weekend. He had taken a total of five pole positions for Williams in '95, his first at Buenos Aires.

'To be on pole position means much more to me than just being five metres in front of anyone else on the grid,' he said. 'It is almost as good as winning a race, because in other situations it has been difficult to qualify well. On my final run I made a mistake and ran wide. I was trying to go faster, but just overcooked it. It was as simple as that.

'I think this circuit tends to suit my style a little more than Mika's, but I think the advantage is likely to swing back and forth between us over the next few races. Trouble is, Mika found more circuits which seemed to favour his style than I did through last year!'

For Michael Schumacher, splitting the McLarens in the starting line-up indicated that Goodyear's latest wider front tyre offered a considerable performance boost for his Ferrari F300. 'And it's not just that the tyres are better,' he explained. 'They also enable us to run a slightly different chassis set-up which is also a slight improvement in its own terms.'

Häkkinen was philosophical about lining up third fastest. 'Let's put it this way,' he said. 'I'm obviously not very pleased about it, because I didn't come here to be in third place. It's disappointing, but I am still extremely happy for David. He was able to get himself and the car adapted to the circuit very quickly and deserves to be on pole position.'

Eddie Irvine did an excellent job to qualify fourth, although he admitted to being very frustrated. 'I made a mistake on my fastest run, then there were yellow flags on another and Pedro Diniz held me up badly at one point,' he explained. 'My last run was very cautious as I had to make sure I got a good time and not take any risks. I think today I could have been up with Michael, or even quicker.'

Ralf Schumacher produced a splendid fifth-fastest time in the Jordan 198, although he was annoyed with himself after over-braking at the first corner. But he still had the satisfaction of beating the two Williams FW20s, which lined up sixth and seventh in the hands of Heinz-Harald Frentzen and Jacques Villeneuve.

Friday's free practice session essentially set the tone for the Williams team's disappointing weekend. Villeneuve's car spent much of the time standing forlornly in its pit lane garage, its gear selectors damaged after a wild pirouette across a gravel trap. Then Frentzen had a sudden lapse, slamming hard into the back of local driver Esteban Tuero's Minardi under braking for the hairpin before the pits. The two cars speared wildly off the circuit, the nose and front suspension of Frentzen's being quite badly damaged.

Small wonder that technical director Patrick Head didn't have much to say about this race, the last two editions of which the Williams team had won handsomely. On the strength of this evidence, the outside observer could have been forgiven for thinking that the Williams team was seriously struggling as the 1998 Grand Prix season took shape.

Yet it would have been premature to write off Williams as a potential winning force this early in the season. Going into the third round of the title chase, the team believed that the adoption of something as apparently straightforward as the latest, wider Goodyear front tyre could raise the competitive pitch of the Williams FW20 to dramatic effect. Well, almost.

'Everybody tends to forget that in the middle of last year, we had some dreadful races,' said Patrick Head, 'but we dusted ourselves down and got on top of the problems we encountered. As far as this year's car is concerned, you also have to remember that, as late as February, we did not have a front tyre available that did not shred itself after only a handful of laps.'

Alexander Wurz's Benetton wound up eighth fastest, the Austrian feeling cautiously optimistic about his prospects. By contrast, team-mate Giancarlo Fisichella was a touch disappointed not to have improved on tenth place. 'The car was not as good as it had been in free practice this morning,' he shrugged.

The two Benettons were split by Damon Hill's Jordan, which spun at the final hairpin on the British driver's last run. 'Basically, I am not overly excited by what I have done today,' he said crisply.

In 11th and 12th places, Jean Alesi and Johnny Herbert had their share of problems with the Sauber C17s. Alesi, who had initially been bugged by excessive understeer, now found himself hampered by too much oversteer.

Herbert had experienced a succession of brake problems from the start of the weekend, and eventually switched to the team's spare car after a brake master cylinder malfunction on his race car. 'My first run was generally OK, but on the second I lost all drive and coasted to a halt,' he shrugged with an air of exasperation.

'I ran back to the pits for my original chassis and went quicker still, but then the brake problem recurred and I spun on my final lap. It's been absolutely and totally frustrating and my grid position doesn't reflect our potential at all.'

Toranosuke Takagi's Tyrrell 026 qualified a fine 13th ahead of Rubens Barrichello's Stewart-Ford, the Brazilian finding that his car worked better on full tanks. Meanwhile Jan Magnussen spun on the first lap and had to take over the spare SF2 fitted with an earlier-spec engine than the Project 3 version which was installed in both race cars.

The eighth row of the grid was shared by the Prost AP01s of Olivier Panis and Jarno Trulli, the former doing his last run in a brand new spare chassis just to shake it down in case it was needed on race day while Trulli punctuated his efforts with a spin.

In the Arrows camp, Pedro Diniz had been fifth quickest when the track was wet at the start of Saturday free practice, but the Brazilian got lost on set-up when it dried for the crucial hour-long qualifying session and was unable to better 18th-fastest time. That put him one place behind team-mate Mika Salo, who complained of poor grip during qualifying and also lost time with repairs to his pit-to-car radio system.

Next came the three remaining customer Ford V10 runners – the Minardis of Shinji Nakano and Esteban Tuero, plus Ricardo Rosset's Tyrrell – which in itself made Magnussen's presence with a works Ford engine in last place seem a touch more embarrassing than the circumstances really were.

Paul-Henri Cahier

DIARY

San Francisco tipped to be the most likely venue for a US Grand Prix by the end of the century after Bernie Ecclestone has a meeting with the city's mayor Willie Brown at the Long Beach CART race.

Jos Verstappen has impressive first test outing in Benetton B198 in the rain at Silverstone.

Veteran NASCAR ace Tim Flock dies at 75.

Dario Franchitti's Team Green Reynard-Honda finishes second to Alex Zanardi's similar car at CART Long Beach Grand Prix.

Despite this impressive display of pyrotechnics, there were no fireworks from Ricardo Rosset, who was four laps down at the flag.

Below right: Esteban Tuero acknowledges the cheers of his home crowd. The Argentine youngster failed to finish after crashing heavily on lap 64.

'He opened the door, so I went to put my car down the inside and he just chopped across me,' he explained. 'I thought I had lost the nose because I felt a draught coming up through the car, but it was a hole, so I came in to change the nose cone.' He finished eighth which, as he admitted, 'is not much good to me'.

Häkkinen's McLaren was also on a one-stop strategy and stayed out in the lead until lap 42 before coming into the pits. Thereafter, the outcome of the race would hinge on whether or not Häkkinen could squeeze ahead of Michael when the Ferrari came in for its second stop at the end of lap 53. As things transpired, Mika failed to do so by the slender margin of 2.7s, having earlier been held up to the tune of four seconds in a single lap passing Frentzen's Williams.

'If I had chosen a two-stop strategy, I would have been able to push even harder,' mused Häkkinen after the race, 'and if I had been able to go quicker at the time of Michael's second pit stop I suppose I might have been able to stay ahead of him, although I believe he would still have overtaken me, probably quite easily.

'Considering that I had to start from third place on the grid, the one-stop strategy was the right choice and I don't think two stops would have made a big difference in the end.'

Meanwhile, in the Benetton camp, Wurz had been driving extremely well, his Bridgestone-shod B198 following a one-stop strategy with a long opening stint which kept him out until the end of lap 40, by which time he was running fourth. He lost only a single place and moved back up the leaderboard when Alesi made his second stop at the end of lap 50.

After Irvine came in at the end of lap 55, Wurz was in striking distance of the Ferrari. Getting past would clearly be quite another matter, but the young Austrian is made of strong stuff and wasn't put off in the slightest when Irvine chopped across him on lap 59 and the two cars made quite heavy contact.

The Benetton driver eventually elbowed his way past Irvine on lap 64 only to spin two laps later and drop back behind the Ferrari for the remainder of the race. 'I made a mistake,' shrugged Wurz, 'although after I collided with Irvine the car became a little more difficult to drive.'

Meanwhile, at the head of the field, Schumacher asserted his superiority after that final refuelling stop. From 4.8s ahead of Häkkinen on lap 56, he extended the gap to 9.0s on lap 60, and then 10.1s on lap 61, although it was back to 9.6s next time round after he had to lap Rubens Barrichello's Stewart-Ford.

Then a light rain shower brushed the circuit, and on lap 66 Schumacher took a slight detour over the gravel at the final hairpin before the pits, gently coaxing the car back onto the circuit with the minimum of delay. But by that point Häkkinen was beaten anyway, the World Championship points leader having effectively settled for second place, eventually crossing the line 22.8s behind the winning Ferrari.

After the race Michael explained that his car must have been slightly damaged by the collision with Coulthard as it seemed to be suffering from understeer in right-hand corners for the remainder of the event.

'I had to push really hard to be able to make the second pit stop without losing the lead and the boys did a great job under pressure to get me out quickly,' he admitted. 'Towards the end, it began to drizzle and I lost control where the track surface was shiny. I had seen people have trouble there in the warm-up so I did not even try and brake because I knew where the escape road was.'

Behind Irvine and Wurz, Alesi was delighted with fifth place while Coulthard admitted that sixth was about as good as he could have expected, given that his progress was punctuated by a collision with Villeneuve on lap 53. David had overtaken the Williams on an outside line going into the tight ess-bend behind the paddock, then found Jacques running into the side of him as he turned into the corner. As one might expect, there were two widely varying accounts of the accident, but Villeneuve was out on the spot with suspension damage.

Seventh place fell to Giancarlo Fisichella's Benetton after a race which had produced less than the Italian was hoping for. 'The car was good enough to finish in the points,' he said. 'Unfortunately I was tenth on the starting grid, too far back to score a good result. If I could have started two positions further forward I would have enjoyed as good a race as Alex, who did a fantastic job. My car was understeering too much with a full tank, but improved with less fuel.'

The dejected Hill was eighth ahead of Frentzen and Rubens Barrichello's Stewart, which might have been better placed had it not been for an unscheduled second pit stop to make minor repairs to some loose bodywork. Jarno Trulli's Prost survived to 11th ahead of Toranosuke Takagi's Tyrrell 026, Shinji Nakano's Minardi M198 and the other Tyrrell of Ricardo Rosset. Olivier Panis was classified 15th, but retired shortly before the finish when his Prost succumbed to engine problems.

Now it was back to Europe and the San Marino GP at Imola. How did Michael think his Ferrari would perform there? 'It is a different type of circuit, and I am sure we will improve the car,' he said thoughtfully. 'After Brazil, which was very bad for us, the tyre situation is now closer to what we would normally expect.

'I believe that Imola will give us an opportunity to do a good job and to be up there again.'

McLaren and Mercedes cement new five-year deal

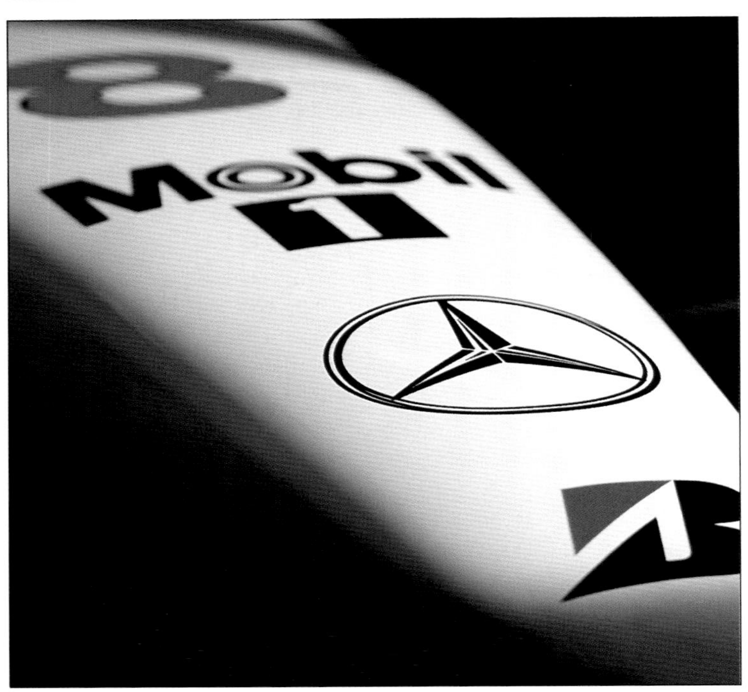

McLAREN-MERCEDES F1 cars were set to race on to the end of the 2002 season at least thanks to a new deal to extend the partnership between the companies which was signed in Stuttgart on the Monday prior to the Argentine Grand Prix.

This news, announced in Buenos Aires after qualifying, inevitably raised speculation that Michael Schumacher would quit Ferrari at the end of the 1998 season to lead the Silver Arrows line-up in '99.

The new five-year deal signed by TAG McLaren managing director Ron Dennis and Daimler Benz board member Jurgen Schrempp effectively superseded the current contract, which was due to expire at the end of 1999.

'The extension of our agreement not only furthers one of the best partnerships our company has ever had,' said Dennis, 'but it also allows the entire McLaren management to take key strategic decisions in respect of the group's long-term planning.'

His remarks were taken to refer to McLaren's lavish plans for a new state-of-the-art technology centre, at Mizens' Farm, near Woking, which is expected to come into operation at the end of 2000. In view of this undertaking, McLaren wanted an even longer-term commitment from its F1 engine partner to justify the reputed £20 million investment in this new facility.

However, Mercedes motor sport manager Norbert Haug did not rule out the possibility of supplying a second team, albeit with a secondary-specification engine – and only if McLaren agreed.

'We basically believe it is better to continue on this exclusive basis,' he said, 'because we think you cannot be partners with two teams trying to operate at the highest level. But should circumstances develop, it might be possible to consider an "A" and a "B" specification engine. But we cannot, and will not, supply two top teams.'

Sutton Motorsport Images

GRAN PREMIO MARLBORO DE ARGENTINA

10–12 APRIL 1998

BUENOS AIRES

Race distance: 72 laps, 190.418 miles/306.449 km

Race weather: Cool and overcast

Pos.	Driver	Nat.	No.	Entrant	Car/Engine	Tyres	Laps	Time/Retirement	Speed (mph/km/h)
1	Michael Schumacher	D	3	Scuderia Ferrari Marlboro	Ferrari F300 047 V10	G	72	1h 48m 36.175s	105.200/169.304
2	Mika Häkkinen	SF	8	West McLaren Mercedes	McLaren MP4/13-Mercedes FO110G V10	B	72	1h 48m 59.073s	104.832/168.711
3	Eddie Irvine	GB	4	Scuderia Ferrari Marlboro	Ferrari F300 047 V10	G	72	1h 49m 33.920s	104.276/167.817
4	Alexander Wurz	A	6	Mild Seven Benetton Playlife	Benetton B198-Playlife V10	B	72	1h 49m 44.309s	104.112/167.552
5	Jean Alesi	F	14	Red Bull Sauber Petronas	Sauber C17-Petronas SPE01D V10	G	72	1h 49m 54.461s	103.951/167.294
6	David Coulthard	GB	7	West McLaren Mercedes	McLaren MP4/13-Mercedes FO110G V10	B	72	1h 49m 55.926s	103.928/167.257
7	Giancarlo Fisichella	I	5	Mild Seven Benetton Playlife	Benetton B198-Playlife V10	B	72	1h 50m 04.612s	103.792/167.037
8	Damon Hill	GB	9	B&H Jordan Mugen Honda	Jordan 198-Mugen Honda MF310C V10	G	71		
9	Heinz-Harald Frentzen	D	2	Winfield Williams	Williams FW20-Mecachrome GC37/01 V10	G	71		
10	Rubens Barrichello	BR	18	Stewart Ford	Stewart SF2-Ford Zetec-R V10	B	70		
11	Jarno Trulli	I	12	Gauloises Prost Peugeot	Prost AP01-Peugeot A16 V10	B	70		
12	Toranosuke Takagi	J	21	Tyrrell Ford	Tyrrell 026-Ford Zetec-R V10	G	70		
13	Shinji Nakano	J	22	Fondmetal Minardi Ford	Minardi M198-Ford Zetec-R V10	B	69		
14	Ricardo Rosset	BR	20	Tyrrell Ford	Tyrrell 026-Ford Zetec-R V10	G	68		
15	Olivier Panis	F	11	Gauloises Prost Peugeot	Prost AP01-Peugeot A16 V10	B	65	Engine	
	Esteban Tuero	RA	23	Fondmetal Minardi Ford	Minardi M198-Ford Zetec-R V10	B	63	Accident	
	Jacques Villeneuve	CDN	1	Winfield Williams	Williams FW20-Mecachrome GC37/01 V10	G	52	Collision with Coulthard	
	Johnny Herbert	GB	15	Red Bull Sauber Petronas	Sauber C17-Petronas SPE01D V10	G	46	Collision with Hill/puncture	
	Ralf Schumacher	D	10	B&H Jordan Mugen Honda	Jordan 198-Mugen Honda MF310C V10	G	22	Spun off	
	Mika Salo	SF	17	Danka Zepter Arrows	Arrows A19 V10	B	18	Gearbox	
	Jan Magnussen	DK	19	Stewart Ford	Stewart SF2-Ford Zetec-R V10	B	17	Transmission	
	Pedro Diniz	BR	16	Danka Zepter Arrows	Arrows A19 V10	B	13	Gearbox	

Fastest lap: Wurz, on lap 39, 1m 28.179s, 108.043 mph/173.878 km/h.

Lap record: Gerhard Berger (F1 Benetton B197-Renault V10), 1m 27.981s, 108.286 mph/174.269 km/h (1997).

B – Bridgestone G – Goodyear

All results and data © FIA 1998

Grid order	1	2	3	4	5	6	7	8	9	10	11	12	13	14	15	16	17	18	19	20	21	22	23	24	25	26	27
7 COULTHARD	7	7	7	7	3	3	3	3	3	3	3	3	3	3	3	3	3	3	3	3	3	3	3	3	3	3	3
3 M. SCHUMACHER	8	3	3	3	8	8	8	8	8	8	8	8	8	8	8	8	8	8	8	8	8	8	8	8	8	8	8
8 HÄKKINEN	3	8	8	8	4	4	4	4	4	4	4	4	4	4	4	4	4	4	4	4	4	4	4	4	4	4	4
4 IRVINE	2	4	4	4	1	1	1	1	1	1	1	1	1	1	1	1	1	1	1	1	1	1	1	1	1	1	1
10 R. SCHUMACHER	4	2	1	1	14	14	14	14	14	14	14	14	14	14	14	14	14	14	14	14	14	14	14	14	14	14	7
2 FRENTZEN	1	1	2	14	7	7	7	7	7	7	7	7	7	7	7	7	7	7	7	7	7	7	7	7	7	7	14
1 VILLENEUVE	14	14	14	2	2	2	2	2	2	2	2	2	2	2	2	2	2	2	2	2	2	2	2	2	2	2	2
6 WURZ	6	6	6	6	6	6	6	6	6	6	6	6	6	6	6	6	6	6	6	6	6	6	6	6	6	6	6
9 HILL	9	9	9	9	9	9	9	9	9	9	9	9	9	9	9	9	9	9	9	9	9	9	9	9	9	9	5
5 FISICHELLA	5	5	5	5	5	5	5	5	5	5	5	5	5	5	5	5	5	5	5	5	5	5	5	5	5	5	9
14 ALESI	15	15	15	15	15	15	15	15	15	15	15	15	15	15	15	15	15	15	15	15	15	15	15	15	15	15	15
15 HERBERT	18	18	18	18	18	18	18	18	18	18	18	18	18	18	18	18	18	18	18	18	18	18	18	18	18	18	18
21 TAKAGI	10	10	10	10	10	10	10	10	10	10	10	10	10	10	10	10	10	11	11	11	11	11	11	11	11	11	11
18 BARRICHELLO	12	12	12	12	12	12	12	12	12	12	12	11	11	11	11	11	11	12	12	12	12	12	12	12	12	12	12
11 PANIS	21	21	21	21	21	21	21	21	21	11	11	12	12	12	12	12	12	21	21	21	21	21	21	21	21	21	21
12 TRULLI	11	11	11	11	11	11	11	11	11	21	21	21	21	21	21	21	21	17	23	23	23	23	23	23	23	23	23
17 SALO	17	17	17	17	17	17	17	17	17	17	17	17	17	17	17	17	17	23	22	22	22	22	22	22	22	22	22
16 DINIZ	16	16	16	16	16	19	19	19	19	19	19	19	19	19	19	19	23	22	20	20	20	10	20	20	20	20	20
22 NAKANO	23	23	19	19	19	16	16	16	16	16	16	16	16	23	23	23	22	10	10	10	10	20					
23 TUERO	19	19	23	23	23	23	23	23	23	23	23	23	23	22	22	22	19	20									
20 ROSSET	22	22	22	22	22	22	22	22	22	22	22	22	22	20	20	20	20										
19 MAGNUSSEN	20	20	20	20	20	20	20	20	20	20	20	20	20														

Grid order	28	29	30	31	32	33	34	35	36	37	38	39	40	41	42	43	44	45	46	47	48	49	50	51	52	53	54
7 COULTHARD	3	8	8	8	8	8	8	8	8	8	8	8	8	8	8	3	3	3	3	3	3	3	3	3	3	3	3
3 M. SCHUMACHER	8	3	3	3	3	3	3	3	3	3	3	3	3	3	3	8	8	8	8	8	8	8	8	8	8	8	8
8 HÄKKINEN	4	4	1	1	1	1	1	1	1	1	4	4	4	4	4	4	4	4	4	4	4	4	4	4	4	4	4
4 IRVINE	1	1	7	7	7	4	4	4	4	4	2	6	6	14	14	14	14	14	14	14	14	14	14	6	6	6	6
10 R. SCHUMACHER	7	7	4	4	4	2	2	2	2	2	6	14	14	6	6	6	6	6	6	6	6	6	6	14	14	14	14
2 FRENTZEN	2	2	2	2	2	6	6	6	6	6	14	15	1	1	1	1	1	1	1	1	1	1	1	1	1	5	5
1 VILLENEUVE	6	6	6	6	6	5	5	5	5	5	15	1	7	7	7	7	7	7	7	7	7	7	7	7	7	7	7
6 WURZ	5	5	5	5	5	15	15	14	14	14	1	7	5	5	5	5	5	5	5	5	5	5	5	5	5	11	11
9 HILL	9	15	15	15	15	14	14	15	15	15	7	5	18	15	15	15	15	15	15	11	11	11	11	11	11	9	9
5 FISICHELLA	15	14	14	14	14	7	7	7	7	7	5	18	15	11	11	9	9	9	9	9	9	9	9	9	9	2	2
14 ALESI	14	18	18	18	18	18	18	18	18	18	18	11	11	9	9	2	11	11	11	2	2	2	2	2	2	18	18
15 HERBERT	18	9	9	9	9	9	9	9	9	9	9	9	9	2	2	11	18	18	2	18	18	18	18	18	18	12	12
21 TAKAGI	11	11	11	11	11	11	11	11	11	11	11	2	2	18	18	18	2	2	18	12	12	12	12	12	12	21	21
18 BARRICHELLO	12	12	12	12	12	12	12	12	12	12	12	12	12	12	12	12	12	12	12	21	21	21	21	21	21	22	22
11 PANIS	21	21	21	21	21	21	21	21	21	21	21	21	21	21	21	21	21	21	21	22	22	22	22	22	22	23	23
12 TRULLI	23	23	23	23	23	23	23	23	22	22	22	22	22	22	22	22	22	22	22	23	23	23	23	23	23	20	20
17 SALO	22	22	22	22	22	22	22	22	23	23	23	23	23	23	23	23	23	23	23	20	20	20	20	20	20		
16 DINIZ	20	20	20	20	20	20	20	20	20	20	20	20	20	20	20	20	20	20	20								
22 NAKANO																											
23 TUERO																											
20 ROSSET																											
19 MAGNUSSEN																											

Pit stop

One lap behind leader

STARTING GRID

	7 **COULTHARD** McLaren
3 **M. SCHUMACHER** Ferrari	
	8 **HÄKKINEN** McLaren
4 **IRVINE** Ferrari	
	10 **R. SCHUMACHER** Jordan
2 **FRENTZEN** Williams	
	1 **VILLENEUVE** Williams
6 **WURZ** Benetton	
	9 **HILL** Jordan
5 **FISICHELLA** Benetton	
	14 **ALESI** Sauber
15 **HERBERT** Sauber	
	21 **TAKAGI** Tyrrell
18 **BARRICHELLO** Stewart	
	11 **PANIS** Prost
12 **TRULLI** Prost	
	17 **SALO** Arrows
16 **DINIZ** Arrows	
	22 **NAKANO** Minardi
23 **TUERO** Minardi	
	20 **ROSSET** Tyrrell
19 **MAGNUSSEN** Stewart	

8	59	60	61	62	63	64	65	66	67	68	69	70	71	72	●
3	3	3	3	3	3	3	3	3	3	3	3	3	3	3	1
8	8	8	8	8	8	8	8	8	8	8	8	8	8	8	2
4	4	4	4	4	4	6	6	4	4	4	4	4	4	4	3
6	6	6	6	6	6	4	4	6	6	6	6	6	6	6	4
4	14	14	14	14	14	14	14	14	14	14	14	14	14	14	5
5	5	5	5	5	5	5	5	7	7	7	7	7	7	7	6
7	7	7	7	7	7	7	7	5	5	5	5	5	5	5	
1	11	11	11	11	11	11	11	9	9	9	9	9	9		
9	9	9	9	9	9	9	9	2	2	2	2	2	2		
2	2	2	2	2	2	2	2	18	18	18	18	18			
8	18	18	18	18	18	18	18	12	12	12	12	12			
2	12	12	12	12	12	12	12	21	21	21	21	21			
1	21	21	21	21	21	21	21	22	22	22	22				
2	22	22	22	22	22	22	22	20	20	20					
3	23	23	23	23	23	20	20								
0	20	20	20	20	20										

TIME SHEETS

QUALIFYING

Weather: Cool and overcast

Pos.	Driver	Car	Laps	Time
1	David Coulthard	McLaren-Mercedes	12	1m 25.852s
2	Michael Schumacher	Ferrari	12	1m 26.251s
3	Mika Häkkinen	McLaren-Mercedes	12	1m 26.632s
4	Eddie Irvine	Ferrari	11	1m 26.780s
5	Ralf Schumacher	Jordan-Mugen Honda	12	1m 26.827s
6	Heinz-Harald Frentzen	Williams-Mecachrome	12	1m 26.876s
7	Jacques Villeneuve	Williams-Mecachrome	12	1m 26.941s
8	Alexander Wurz	Benetton-Playlife	12	1m 27.198s
9	Damon Hill	Jordan-Mugen Honda	12	1m 27.483s
10	Giancarlo Fisichella	Benetton-Playlife	12	1m 27.836s
11	Jean Alesi	Sauber-Petronas	11	1m 27.839s
12	Johnny Herbert	Sauber-Petronas	11	1m 28.016s
13	Toranosuke Takagi	Tyrrell-Ford	12	1m 28.811s
14	Rubens Barrichello	Stewart-Ford	12	1m 29.249s
15	Olivier Panis	Prost-Peugeot	12	1m 29.320s
16	Jarno Trulli	Prost-Peugeot	10	1m 29.352s
17	Mika Salo	Arrows	12	1m 29.617s
18	Pedro Diniz	Arrows	11	1m 30.022s
19	Shinji Nakano	Minardi-Ford	12	1m 30.054s
20	Esteban Tuero	Minardi-Ford	12	1m 30.158s
21	Ricardo Rosset	Tyrrell-Ford	12	1m 30.437s
22	Jan Magnussen	Stewart-Ford	11	1m 31.178s

FRIDAY FREE PRACTICE

Weather: Cool

Pos.	Driver	Laps	Time
1	David Coulthard	16	1m 28.130s
2	Michael Schumacher	22	1m 29.114s
3	Mika Häkkinen	15	1m 29.488s
4	Jacques Villeneuve	20	1m 29.610s
5	Eddie Irvine	29	1m 29.781s
6	Ralf Schumacher	24	1m 29.845s
7	Toranosuke Takagi	27	1m 30.054s
8	Heinz-Harald Frentzen	16	1m 30.317s
9	Damon Hill	35	1m 30.645s
10	Jean Alesi	14	1m 30.859s
11	Giancarlo Fisichella	22	1m 30.963s
12	Johnny Herbert	16	1m 31.081s
13	Olivier Panis	16	1m 31.297s
14	Jarno Trulli	24	1m 31.428s
15	Rubens Barrichello	20	1m 31.727s
16	Ricardo Rosset	25	1m 31.761s
17	Alexander Wurz	23	1m 31.850s
18	Mika Salo	22	1m 32.257s
19	Pedro Diniz	18	1m 32.660s
20	Shinji Nakano	19	1m 33.390s
21	Esteban Tuero	18	1m 33.731s
22	Jan Magnussen	18	1m 34.829s

SATURDAY FREE PRACTICE

Weather: Damp and overcast

Pos.	Driver	Laps	Time
1	Michael Schumacher	20	1m 27.737s
2	David Coulthard	19	1m 28.289s
3	Heinz-Harald Frentzen	30	1m 28.347s
4	Mika Häkkinen	24	1m 28.501s
5	Damon Hill	32	1m 28.701s
6	Eddie Irvine	30	1m 28.987s
7	Jean Alesi	30	1m 29.151s
8	Jacques Villeneuve	29	1m 29.614s
9	Ralf Schumacher	30	1m 29.633s
10	Giancarlo Fisichella	36	1m 29.781s
11	Alexander Wurz	16	1m 29.842s
12	Jarno Trulli	28	1m 30.402s
13	Rubens Barrichello	18	1m 30.432s
14	Olivier Panis	24	1m 30.722s
15	Johnny Herbert	19	1m 30.808s
16	Jan Magnussen	21	1m 31.283s
17	Pedro Diniz	28	1m 31.509s
18	Ricardo Rosset	26	1m 31.975s
19	Mika Salo	14	1m 32.563s
20	Esteban Tuero	28	1m 32.883s
21	Toranosuke Takagi	24	1m 33.299s
22	Shinji Nakano	21	1m 33.675s

WARM-UP

Weather: Cool and damp

Pos.	Driver	Laps	Time
1	Jean Alesi	13	1m 47.594s
2	Mika Häkkinen	12	1m 48.025s
3	Michael Schumacher	12	1m 48.501s
4	Giancarlo Fisichella	11	1m 49.030s
5	Eddie Irvine	12	1m 49.046s
6	Jacques Villeneuve	13	1m 49.224s
7	Mika Salo	13	1m 49.314s
8	David Coulthard	11	1m 49.435s
9	Rubens Barrichello	11	1m 49.568s
10	Olivier Panis	13	1m 49.673s
11	Alexander Wurz	11	1m 49.735s
12	Jarno Trulli	11	1m 50.607s
13	Toranosuke Takagi	11	1m 51.150s
14	Heinz-Harald Frentzen	10	1m 51.159s
15	Damon Hill	10	1m 51.240s
16	Jan Magnussen	12	1m 51.257s
17	Ralf Schumacher	12	1m 52.048s
18	Shinji Nakano	11	1m 52.483s
19	Esteban Tuero	8	1m 52.824s
20	Ricardo Rosset	11	1m 53.166s
21	Pedro Diniz	4	1m 53.294s
22	Johnny Herbert	3	9m 19.807s

RACE FASTEST LAPS

Weather: Cool and overcast

Driver	Time	Lap
Alexander Wurz	1m 28.179s	39
Mika Häkkinen	1m 28.261s	32
Michael Schumacher	1m 28.272s	23
David Coulthard	1m 28.468s	57
Giancarlo Fisichella	1m 28.507s	69
Eddie Irvine	1m 28.933s	27
Jean Alesi	1m 29.000s	44
Olivier Panis	1m 29.201s	57
Damon Hill	1m 29.310s	46
Heinz-Harald Frentzen	1m 29.592s	37
Jacques Villeneuve	1m 29.694s	35
Johnny Herbert	1m 29.857s	30
Rubens Barrichello	1m 30.408s	36
Jarno Trulli	1m 30.876s	25
Esteban Tuero	1m 30.992s	27
Toranosuke Takagi	1m 31.057s	41
Shinji Nakano	1m 31.168s	36
Ralf Schumacher	1m 31.541s	17
Mika Salo	1m 32.519s	12
Jan Magnussen	1m 32.808s	16
Ricardo Rosset	1m 33.091s	42
Pedro Diniz	1m 33.350s	8

CHASSIS LOG BOOK

1	Villeneuve	Williams FW20/3
2	Frentzen	Williams FW20/2
	spare	Williams FW20/1
3	M. Schumacher	Ferrari F300/184
4	Irvine	Ferrari F300/185
	spare	Ferrari F300/181
5	Fisichella	Benetton B198/5
6	Wurz	Benetton B198/4
	spare	Benetton B198/2
7	Coulthard	McLaren MP4/13/3
8	Häkkinen	McLaren MP4/13/4
	spare	McLaren MP4/13/1
9	Hill	Jordan 198/3
10	R. Schumacher	Jordan 198/4
	spare	Jordan 198/1
11	Panis	Prost AP01/2
12	Trulli	Prost AP01/3
	spare	Prost AP01/4
14	Alesi	Sauber C17/3
15	Herbert	Sauber C17/4
	spare	Sauber C17/2
16	Diniz	Arrows A19/2
17	Salo	Arrows A19/3
	spare	Arrows A19/1
18	Barrichello	Stewart SF2/1
19	Magnussen	Stewart SF2/3
	spare	Stewart SF2/2
20	Rosset	Tyrrell 026/1
21	Takagi	Tyrrell 026/2
	spare	Tyrrell 026/3
22	Nakano	Minardi M198/1
23	Tuero	Minardi M198/3
	spare	Minardi M198/2

POINTS TABLES

Drivers

1	Mika Häkkinen	26
2	Michael Schumacher	14
3	David Coulthard	13
4	Eddie Irvine	7
5 =	Heinz-Harald Frentzen	6
5 =	Alexander Wurz	6
7 =	Jacques Villeneuve	2
7 =	Jean Alesi	2
9 =	Johnny Herbert	1
9 =	Giancarlo Fisichella	1

Constructors

1	McLaren	39
2	Ferrari	21
3	Williams	8
4	Benetton	7
5	Sauber	3

FIA WORLD CHAMPIONSHIP • ROUND 4

SAN MARINO

grand prix

COULTHARD
M. SCHUMACHER
IRVINE
VILLENEUVE
FRENTZEN
ALESI

DIARY

The controversial side-pod-mounted winglets increasingly widely used on F1 cars in 1998, having been pioneered by Tyrrell the previous season, are banned by the FIA during the week immediately after the Imola race.

Stewart Grand Prix confirms that Jan Magnussen will continue to be retained on a race-by-race basis.

Nigel Mansell has his first test in a BTCC Ford Mondeo.

Jimmy Vasser's Reynard-Honda wins fourth round of FedEx Championship Series at Nazareth.

Eating dust. At the end of the opening lap, Michael Schumacher's be-winged Ferrari F300 is hot on the heels of the two McLaren-Mercedes, and the German was to inherit second place when Mika Häkkinen's MP4/13 retired after 17 laps.

Michael Roberts

DAVID Coulthard dramatically revived his World Championship prospects with a well-judged tactical victory over the Ferrari team in the San Marino Grand Prix, depriving a 100,000-plus crowd of fanatical enthusiasts of their first home-team victory since 1983 by the margin of just over four seconds.

With four of the season's 16 races completed, the Scot's long-awaited success meant that only six points covered Mika Häkkinen, who failed to finish, Coulthard and Michael Schumacher at the head of the title battle.

On the face of it, Coulthard seemed to be taking things very prudently, easing his pace in the closing stages of the race to conserve his McLaren MP4/13-Mercedes even though Schumacher's Ferrari F300 was closing dramatically in his wake. In reality, Coulthard's McLaren was suffering from a seriously overheating gearbox, the symptoms of a problem that had already eliminated his team-mate Häkkinen from second place only 17 laps into the 62-lap race.

It looked a little marginal, but Coulthard had the situation well under control and was able to pull out a quick lap whenever he needed to, subtly signalling that Schumacher could get so close but no further. By any standards it was an impressive success for the cool 27-year-old, who never looked seriously ruffled all afternoon.

Nevertheless, with Häkkinen's McLaren retiring early with the failure of a gearbox bearing which was subsequently identified as being a counterfeit component, there was a degree of concern in the McLaren camp that Coulthard's car might also be vulnerable. McLaren chief Ron Dennis could periodically be seen walking from his place on the pit wall to the back of the garage to check the electronic telemetry system which was monitoring Coulthard's problem, but the Scot was simply told to ease up and change gear as carefully as possible during the second half of the race. The team did not tell him specifically what was wrong.

'I wanted to run at a pace that wasn't too hard on the brakes or the engine, so I was just trying to maintain the gap to Michael,' he explained, unaware of the depth of his own car's technical problem.

'I was perfectly comfortable to let that gap be reduced, because I knew that I could have gone a little faster if necessary. I knew Mika had stopped, but I didn't ask why because I didn't want to be worrying about it for the rest of the race.'

Having qualified in pole position, Coulthard made full use of his advantage to accelerate cleanly into the lead as the pack headed towards the Tamburello chicane. As he did so, Häkkinen filled a supporting role by blocking the optimistic Schumacher out with a touch of weaving on the way to the first corner.

Further back in the pack, Alexander Wurz's Benetton B198 was slow off the mark, the Austrian's car abruptly slowing with apparent gear selection difficulties, and was rammed by Damon Hill's Jordan in the confusion. Both cars duly trailed into the pits for repairs at the end of the opening lap, Hill needing a new nose section and Wurz having a replacement steering wheel fitted as the gearchange problem seemed to be related to the fingertip paddle mechanism.

A little further round the opening lap Jan Magnussen's Stewart-Ford ran into the back of team-mate Rubens Barrichello's car with a hefty impact. The rear wing and floor of the Brazilian's SF2 were badly damaged and, although he tried to limp round for repairs, the car soon became undriveable and he spun off.

Magnussen also came in for a new nose section, the trio of troubled competitors resuming right at the back of the field. Sadly, Magnussen lasted only until lap eight when he retired with a third gear failure, rounding off a disastrous weekend for the increasingly beleaguered Stewart squad.

Meanwhile Coulthard comfortably led round to complete the opening lap just over a second ahead of Häkkinen, Michael Schumacher's Ferrari, Jacques Villeneuve's Williams FW20, Eddie Irvine's Ferrari and Heinz-Harald Frentzen's Williams.

The first phase of the race was distinctly processional and Coulthard had gradually pulled out a 3.3s advantage over his team-mate by the time ten laps had been completed. Schumacher was already moving clear of the rest of the pack, still led by Villeneuve, Irvine and Frentzen, who had been battling with excessive and dramatic oversteer ever since the start and was coming under increasing pressure from Giancarlo Fisichella's Benetton B198.

On lap 12 Johnny Herbert's Sauber C17 came trailing into the pits from 11th place. It had been an extremely frustrating afternoon for the English driver, who thought he had picked up a puncture in his right-rear tyre and misunderstood a radio message from his pit crew, who believed he had badly damaged the rear suspension.

'As a result, I got out of the cockpit, and by the time we realised that the problem was just a puncture it was too

Pit 1 0
32.72

IMOLA QUALIFYING

Prior to qualifying at Imola the pit lane pundits were divided into two distinct camps: those who believed that McLaren would have an easy time throughout the San Marino GP weekend, and those who reckoned Ferrari would give them the biggest fright of the season so far. In the event, neither prediction was quite on the button.

Rival teams jealously predicted that the Mercedes V10s were now nudging the 800 bhp mark, with around 30/40 bhp in hand over the closest opposition. With that in mind, you might have been forgiven for expecting Mika Häkkinen and David Coulthard to have the easiest rides of their careers.

Not so. The Schumacher factor meant that they had to pull every trick in the book to keep the Ferrari team leader corralled on the second row. In any case, more conservative opinion reckoned on 'just' 775 bhp for the Merc V10, a slender 10/15 bhp edge over the Italian engines.

Häkkinen, in particular, was visually astounding throughout practice and qualifying, his driving style a combination of Gilles Villeneuve and Ronnie Peterson rolled into one. A succession of brilliantly controlled opposite-lock slides punctuated lap after dazzling lap throughout free practice. Then came qualifying and Coulthard beat him to pole, the Scot posting the fastest time of the session despite complaining of excessive and obvious understeer.

'To be honest, yes, I'm disappointed not to have taken pole position,' said Häkkinen. 'My tyres went off through the last sector of the lap, which was where I was losing time. But generally the consistency of the Bridgestone tyres seems extremely impressive over long runs.'

The two McLaren drivers traded fastest times across the two days of practice and qualifying without anybody else getting a serious look-in. But Schumacher gave it his best shot, using the latest type 047D V10 engine he raced in Brazil and Argentina, high side-pod-mounted winglets and Goodyear's latest, slightly softer tyre compound in the wider front size.

Michael reckoned he could have picked up another two-tenths on his best lap had he not made a slight mistake at the final corner. 'We have a few things to change overnight,' he mused afterwards, 'which we will try in the race morning warm-up. Are the winglets better? The wind tunnel says so and sometimes you just have to trust your data.'

Eddie Irvine silenced his critics by qualifying fourth, although he was still 0.7s away from Schumacher. The Ferrari V10s certainly seemed to be close to the Ilmor-built Mercedes engines on power, if the speed-trap figures offered any guide. Häkkinen's McLaren-Merc registered the best straightline speed during qualifying with 185.66 mph, but Irvine was not far behind on 183.1 mph.

Eddie was delighted with his performance. 'It certainly relieves all the pressure here at home,' he grinned. 'This was the best time I could have done, as I was having problems in the first section of the lap. With both Ferraris on the second row, I hope we can certainly put pressure on the McLarens in the race.'

Behind the Ferraris, Alexander Wurz did a superb job to line up fifth fastest in his Benetton B198. 'I'm very happy with the feel of the car,' he said on what was his first visit to Imola. 'From such a position, I feel we can challenge for the podium.'

Williams arrived at the Autodromo Enzo e Dino Ferrari direct from a test session at Jerez and Jacques Villeneuve was moderately optimistic about the feel of the FW20. However, as usual, rear-end grip was the biggest problem and both he and team-mate Heinz-Harald Frentzen spent too much of the time battling their cars. 'I think we're both trying to over-drive it to go faster than it wants to,' said Jacques thoughtfully.

The Canadian took sixth place on the grid while Frentzen was eighth fastest behind an upbeat Damon Hill's Jordan 198, the Mugen Honda-engined cars now running to lengthened-wheelbase specification and fitted with a revised rear wing which improved their overall feel.

Hill was very satisfied. 'I'm happier with the car and it certainly feels more consistent,' he said after qualifying, 'and I can repeat lap times more precisely and make the right decisions on set-up. We may not have gone that far forward in terms of pure speed, but we have improved the car's consistency.'

Unfortunately Hill's engine broke on his final run, depriving him of any chance of further improvement. Ralf Schumacher, in the meantime, had a trip into the gravel trap on his last qualifying attempt and had to be content with ninth behind Frentzen.

Tenth place in front of his home crowd represented a big letdown for Benetton's Giancarlo Fisichella, the young Italian simply shrugging his shoulders with disappointment. 'The car's balance seems to have changed since the morning and I didn't have time to alter the set-up,' he explained.

In 11th place came Johnny Herbert in the faster Sauber C17. 'It was just a matter of staying committed this afternoon,' he said. 'The car felt as if it was weaving slightly on the straight, then going into the corners the initial turn-in was OK, but in mid-corner it went into understeer which snapped into oversteer on the exit. And if you use too much throttle, you just make the understeer worse.' In a couple of sentences he had effectively summed up the dilemma facing most of the Goodyear runners.

Jean Alesi was one place behind in 12th, for his part acutely disappointed with the handling of his Sauber. He lined up just ahead of Olivier Panis, who had to complete his first two runs in the spare Prost-Peugeot after his race car developed a gearbox fault during the morning free practice session. 'The team did a fantastic job to get my car ready,' said Olivier, 'but it was not enough to make up for the lost time. I think we should have been in the top ten.'

Mika Salo was next up, although his hopes of getting the best out of the new development engine in the Arrows A19 were dashed early on when his race car developed a gearbox problem. That meant the Finn had to switch to the team spare car, originally set up for Pedro Diniz, which was fitted with an earlier-specification engine. Under the circumstances, 14th in the grid order was a pretty respectable performance.

Diniz himself ended up 18th fastest, also suffering a gearbox failure in the morning session which lost him time while trying to find a decent chassis set-up. 'I also had too much oversteer during the qualifying session and could not improve on my placing,' he explained. 'It was a very disappointing session for me.'

Toranosuke Takagi performed creditably with the Tyrrell 026 to line up 15th ahead of Jarno Trulli's Prost-Peugeot, the Italian missing much of the morning free practice session due to gearbox problems. Trulli was quite satisfied, which is more than could be said for Rubens Barrichello, who could qualify his Stewart SF2-Ford only 17th fastest, plagued by excessive oversteer on the turn-in to the corners. He also lost time early in the session when part of the front torsion bar mechanism fell into the cockpit footwell, fouling the throttle pedal.

'To be honest, I felt like a passenger out there,' he admitted. 'The race can only get better.' Neither he nor his disappointed team-mate Jan Magnussen, who qualified in 20th place with a time almost one and a half seconds off the Brazilian's pace, could have imagined how far from the truth that prediction would turn out to be.

Behind Diniz, Esteban Tuero's Minardi M198 lined up 19th, two places ahead of team-mate Shinji Nakano, while Ricardo Rosset's Tyrrell completed the list of starters, the Brazilian being obliged to use the spare 026 to set his qualifying time after his race car had suffered an engine failure earlier in the session.

Ford to go it alone if VW buys Cosworth

FORD confirmed it would sever its relationship with Cosworth and develop its Formula 1 Zetec-R V10 alone if rival road car manufacturer Volkswagen ended up purchasing the Northampton-based engine specialist as part of a proposed multi-million-pound Rolls-Royce buy-out.

The battle between BMW and VW for control of Rolls-Royce seemed to be reaching its peak around the San Marino GP weekend and was one of the major talking points in the paddock at Imola. It was also being speculated that such a move could leave the path free for Cosworth to develop an F1 engine for Audi – with the possibility that Jackie Stewart might be tempted into using it when his current agreement with Ford comes up for renewal at the end of 2000.

Sources close to Ford confirmed that the company owns the intellectual rights to the Cosworth-built Zetec-R V10. 'The trucks would be backed up to the door and we would be loaded up,' said a Ford insider. 'No way would we deal with another car maker under these circumstances.'

However, it was understood that Audi has already built its own F1 engine, although any development programme would be in the long-to-medium term. Meanwhile, Jackie Stewart denied that he had been approached to run the engine.

'There have been some general inquiries,' he admitted, 'but nothing beyond that. We have our five-year programme in place with Ford and we remain very happy about their commitment.'

US sources suggested that Stewart's confidence over the strength of his Ford deal was certainly not misplaced. Although the company had meetings with Benetton's David Richards, Detroit insiders were hinting that Ford's senior management would be reluctant to collaborate with an F1 team which had a cigarette company as its title sponsor.

Elsewhere in the paddock, Mercedes personnel were vehemently denying rumours in the *Sunday Times* that a 'second string' F1 team using their engines could race as early as the 2000 season with the AMG organisation building the chassis.

'It is completely wrong,' said a Mercedes spokesman. 'We are really amazed that such stories can find their way into a paper like this. It is absolutely ridiculous. Our only priority at the moment is to win the World Championship in partnership with McLaren.'

Opposite: **Snug in the cockpit of his Arrows, Pedro Diniz contemplates the digital read-out on his steering wheel. Aesthetics will always take second place to aerodynamics in F1, but the John Barnard-designed A19 was proof that modern Grand Prix cars don't have to be ugly.**

late to continue,' he explained rather unconvincingly. 'My start wasn't particularly great, but what really spoiled things for me was when Hill and Wurz became involved with each other right in front of me.

'There was dirt and debris everywhere and I had to take avoiding action, which cost me momentum and places. I was bottled up behind Trulli's Prost when I first detected the puncture. That was the beginning of the end for a forgettable afternoon.'

With 15 laps run, Fisichella was getting really energetic in his pursuit of Frentzen's ill-handling Williams, darting around on the tail of the German's car and looking for any overtaking opportunity which might present itself. On lap 18 Fisichella got a little too close to the Williams going into the Villeneuve chicane, lost control and spun heavily into the wall. The Benetton was quite badly rumpled in the impact and, as if that wasn't enough for the team on its home turf, Wurz retired next time round with engine failure, having been lapped by the leaders following his earlier delay.

Meanwhile lap 17 had seen Häkkinen's demise, the World Championship leader coming into the pit lane and driving straight into the McLaren team garage, where he released his belts and vacated the cockpit without further ado. Now it was all down to Coulthard, who completed lap 20 some 14.8s ahead of Schumacher with Villeneuve running third ahead of Irvine.

On lap 21 Ralf Schumacher's Jordan 198 opened the first spate of refuelling stops, dropping from seventh to ninth. Next time round he was followed by Jean Alesi's Sauber and Jarno Trulli's Prost, which dropped from sixth and eighth respectively to seventh and tenth.

On lap 26 Coulthard came in, was serviced smoothly by the McLaren team and accelerated back into a comfortable lead ahead of Schumacher, who also stopped. Irvine continued running, taking third as Villeneuve pitted, the World Champion momentarily forgetting to press the button that released his fuel nozzle flap, which cost him a couple of extra seconds. He resumed running fourth.

Irvine and Frentzen stopped next time round, the Ferrari driver squeezing back into the fray three seconds ahead of Villeneuve, while, further back, Mika Salo's Arrows (which had already made one stop on lap 18) came in again – then had to return to the pits two laps later after it was discovered that the refuelling rig had not delivered its allotted load. This drama dropped the Finn back to 14th and last position.

With David Coulthard *(right)* in total command, the *tifosi* had to be content with second and third places for their beloved Ferraris.

Lukas Gorys

Trulli was running ninth when he retired with a throttle malfunction at the end of lap 34. 'After my first stop, with new tyres, my car did not feel so good,' explained the Italian. 'I was sliding around too much and then had a problem with the throttle pedal which caused me to stop. Overall, I didn't have a great deal of luck this weekend.'

On lap 40 Alesi made his second stop, dropping from fifth to sixth, and next time round Frentzen also came in from fifth, holding his position. On lap 44 Coulthard, Irvine and Villeneuve all stopped, allowing Schumacher to close to within a couple of seconds of the McLaren, but Michael came in for his second stop at the end of lap 46 before resuming 20.7s down.

During that final stint, Schumacher really piled on the pressure, slashing his lap times consistently to below the 1m 30s barrier. From 1.72s on lap 49 he trimmed Coulthard's advantage to 15.1s on lap 54 and then down to 11.1s by lap 58. But Coulthard was well in control and gently let out the rope, conserving his machinery to come home the winner by 4.55s at the end of 62 laps.

For his part, Michael Schumacher was philosophical, regarding second place as something of a bonus. 'I pushed right to the end, but I knew David was cruising,' he shrugged. 'The soft Goodyears were the perfect choice, but, to be honest, I would have finished third in normal circumstances.'

Nevertheless, with Eddie Irvine coming home in third, it was a fine day for Maranello as far as its constructors' championship tally was concerned. Even so, the Ulsterman freely admitted that he was under some pressure from Villeneuve in the closing stages as the Williams took the chequered flag only 2.8s behind.

'At the start Jacques beat me off the line and he was quite quick at first, but then I was able to catch him easily,' said Irvine. 'Later I thought he might catch me, but I knew he would not get past. My big problem again was with my back, which goes into spasm after about five laps. It was uncomfortable and distracting.'

Villeneuve added, 'Today saw the maximum I could get from my car. It was a case of qualifying laps from start to finish. I was pushing Irvine very hard, but both he and Michael seemed to have their cars working well and I just couldn't pressure them into a mistake.'

Frentzen at least managed to ensure that both Williams FW20s finished in the championship points, but he was another 22.8s behind Villeneuve and the last unlapped runner to go the distance. 'The set-up I tried this weekend was not the best,' he admitted. 'I had to deal with a lot of oversteer during the race, even though my tyres were fine.'

For Alesi, sixth was a worthwhile reward for a consistent performance from both driver and car, while Ralf Schumacher wound up two laps down in seventh place.

'I'm disappointed not to have finished in the points,' said the Jordan driver, 'but after my second pit stop I had a problem with loss of air-valve pressure which meant I was not able to go quicker.' For his part, Hill retired from eighth place in the closing stages of the race with a more serious loss of air-valve pressure afflicting his Mugen Honda V10.

Esteban Tuero drove a reliable race to take eighth place for Minardi ahead of the frustrated Salo, while Hill and Olivier Panis, who retired his Prost from seventh place with only five laps to go due to engine trouble, were the other classified finishers.

Pedro Diniz had been running in 15th place when engine maladies forced him into the pits on lap 18, while Shinji Nakano had completed 27 laps when he parked the other Minardi. Toranosuke Takagi had maintained his impressive qualifying form until his retirement on lap 40, but Ricardo Rosset was in last place when he dropped out after 48 laps.

There could be no disguising the McLaren team's delight in putting it across Ferrari in their Italian rivals' back yard. Yet it was clear from the exultant response from the fans that second and third was enough to put a smile on the nation's face and keep Maranello in play for the World Championship.

Even more gratifyingly, Ferrari President Luca di Montezemolo confirmed to the Italian media that he planned to open negotiations for Michael Schumacher to spend the rest of his active F1 career driving for the most famous team in the business. He also said it was his intention to retain Jean Todt's services as sporting director, irrespective of the outcome of the '98 title chase. If Luca managed to keep those two on the payroll, it would rank as possibly the biggest coup of his career.

Yet although Schumacher went home from Imola only six points away from the World Championship lead, he was a worried man. He knew that his Ferrari would improve over the races that followed. But he also knew McLaren would improve as well. By how much, he scarcely dared think.

LOCTITE
BOSS
Mobil 1
Mercedes-Benz
West
COMPUTER ASSOCIATES
Mobil

18° GRAN PREMIO DI SAN MARINO

24–26 APRIL 1998

IMOLA

Race distance: 62 laps, 189.782 miles/305.443 km

Race weather: Dry, warm and sunny

Pos.	Driver	Nat.	No.	Entrant	Car/Engine	Tyres	Laps	Time/Retirement	Speed (mph/km/h)
1	**David Coulthard**	**GB**	**7**	**West McLaren Mercedes**	**McLaren MP4/13-Mercedes FO110G V10**	**B**	**62**	**1h 34m 24.593s**	**120.619/194.117**
2	**Michael Schumacher**	**D**	**3**	**Scuderia Ferrari Marlboro**	**Ferrari F300 047 V10**	**G**	**62**	**1h 34m 29.147s**	**120.522/193.961**
3	**Eddie Irvine**	**GB**	**4**	**Scuderia Ferrari Marlboro**	**Ferrari F300 047 V10**	**G**	**62**	**1h 35m 16.368s**	**119.526/192.358**
4	**Jacques Villeneuve**	**CDN**	**1**	**Winfield Williams**	**Williams FW20-Mecachrome GC37/01 V10**	**G**	**62**	**1h 35m 19.183s**	**119.467/192.264**
5	**Heinz-Harald Frentzen**	**D**	**2**	**Winfield Williams**	**Williams FW20-Mecachrome GC37/01 V10**	**G**	**62**	**1h 35m 42.069s**	**118.990/191.497**
6	**Jean Alesi**	**F**	**14**	**Red Bull Sauber Petronas**	**Sauber C17-Petronas SPE01D V10**	**G**	**61**		
7	Ralf Schumacher	D	10	B&H Jordan Mugen Honda	Jordan 198-Mugen Honda MF310C V10	G	60		
8	Esteban Tuero	RA	23	Fondmetal Minardi Ford	Minardi M198-Ford Zetec-R V10	B	60		
9	Mika Salo	SF	17	Danka Zepter Arrows	Arrows A19 V10	B	60		
10	Damon Hill	GB	9	B&H Jordan Mugen Honda	Jordan 198-Mugen Honda MF310C V10	G	57	Engine	
11	Olivier Panis	F	11	Gauloises Prost Peugeot	Prost AP01-Peugeot A16 V10	B	56	Engine	
	Ricardo Rosset	BR	20	Tyrrell Ford	Tyrrell 026-Ford Zetec-R V10	G	48	Engine	
	Toranosuke Takagi	J	21	Tyrrell Ford	Tyrrell 026-Ford Zetec-R V10	G	40	Engine	
	Jarno Trulli	I	12	Gauloises Prost Peugeot	Prost AP01-Peugeot A16 V10	B	34	Throttle	
	Shinji Nakano	J	22	Fondmetal Minardi Ford	Minardi M198-Ford Zetec-R V10	B	27	Engine	
	Pedro Diniz	BR	16	Danka Zepter Arrows	Arrows A19 V10	B	18	Engine	
	Mika Häkkinen	SF	8	West McLaren Mercedes	McLaren MP4/13-Mercedes FO110G V10	B	17	Gearbox	
	Giancarlo Fisichella	I	5	Mild Seven Benetton Playlife	Benetton B198-Playlife V10	B	17	Accident	
	Alexander Wurz	A	6	Mild Seven Benetton Playlife	Benetton B198-Playlife V10	B	17	Engine	
	Johnny Herbert	GB	15	Red Bull Sauber Petronas	Sauber C17-Petronas SPE01D V10	G	12	Puncture	
	Jan Magnussen	DK	19	Stewart Ford	Stewart SF2-Ford Zetec-R V10	B	8	Gearbox	
	Rubens Barrichello	BR	18	Stewart Ford	Stewart SF2-Ford Zetec-R V10	B	0	Spun off	

Fastest lap: M. Schumacher, on lap 48, 1m 29.345s, 123.432 mph/198.645 km/h.

Lap record: Heinz-Harald Frentzen (F1 Williams FW19-Renault V10), 1m 25.531s, 128.936 mph/207.503 km/h (1997).

B – Bridgestone G – Goodyear

All results and data © FIA 1998

Grid order	1	2	3	4	5	6	7	8	9	10	11	12	13	14	15	16	17	18	19	20	21	22	23	24	25	26	27	28	29	30	31	32	33	34	35	36	37	38	39	40	41	42	43	44	45	46
7 COULTHARD	7	7	7	7	7	7	7	7	7	7	7	7	7	7	7	7	7	7	7	7	7	7	7	7	7	7	7	7	7	7	7	7	7	7	7	7	7	7	7	7	7	7	7	7	7	7
8 HÄKKINEN	8	8	8	8	8	8	8	8	8	8	8	8	8	8	8	8	3	3	3	3	3	3	3	3	3	3	3	3	3	3	3	3	3	3	3	3	3	3	3	3	3	3	3	3	3	3
3 M. SCHUMACHER	3	3	3	3	3	3	3	3	3	3	3	3	3	3	3	3	1	1	1	1	1	1	1	1	1	1	4	4	4	4	4	4	4	4	4	4	4	4	4	4	4	4	4	4	4	4
4 IRVINE	1	1	1	1	1	1	1	1	1	1	1	1	1	1	1	1	4	4	4	4	4	4	4	4	4	4	2	1	1	1	1	1	1	1	1	1	1	1	1	1	1	1	1	1	1	1
6 WURZ	4	4	4	4	4	4	4	4	4	4	4	4	4	4	4	4	8	2	2	2	2	2	2	2	2	2	1	14	14	14	14	14	14	14	14	14	14	14	14	14	2	2	2	2	2	2
1 VILLENEUVE	2	2	2	2	2	2	2	2	2	2	2	2	2	2	2	2	2	14	14	14	14	14	11	14	14	14	14	2	2	2	2	2	2	2	2	2	2	2	2	2	14	14	14	14	14	14
9 HILL	5	5	5	5	5	5	5	5	5	5	5	5	5	5	5	5	5	10	10	10	10	11	14	10	10	10	10	10	10	10	11	11	11	11	11	11	11	11	11	11	11	11	11	11	11	11
2 FRENTZEN	14	14	14	14	14	14	14	14	14	14	14	14	14	14	14	14	14	12	12	12	12	12	10	11	11	11	11	11	11	11	10	10	10	10	10	10	9	9	9	9	9	9	9	9	9	9
10 R. SCHUMACHER	10	10	10	10	10	10	10	10	10	10	10	10	10	10	10	10	10	17	11	11	11	10	9	9	12	12	12	12	12	12	12	12	12	9	9	9	10	10	10	10	10	10	10	10	10	10
5 FISICHELLA	12	12	12	12	12	12	12	12	12	12	12	12	12	12	12	12	12	11	21	21	9	9	12	12	17	17	17	9	9	9	9	9	9	12	21	21	21	21	21	21	23	23	23	23	23	23
15 HERBERT	15	15	15	15	15	15	15	15	15	15	15	17	17	17	17	17	17	21	9	9	17	17	17	17	9	9	9	21	21	21	21	21	21	21	23	23	23	23	23	23	17	17	17	17	17	17
14 ALESI	17	17	17	17	17	17	17	17	17	17	17	11	11	11	11	11	11	9	17	17	21	21	21	21	21	21	21	17	17	23	23	23	23	23	20	20	17	17	17	17	20	20	20	20	20	20
11 PANIS	11	11	11	11	11	11	11	11	11	11	11	15	21	21	21	21	21	23	23	23	23	23	23	23	23	23	23	23	23	20	20	20	20	20	17	17	20	20	20	20						
17 SALO	21	21	21	21	21	21	21	21	21	21	21	21	16	16	16	16	9	16	22	22	20	20	20	20	20	20	20	20	20	17	17	17	17	17												
21 TAKAGI	16	23	23	23	23	23	16	16	16	16	16	16	23	9	9	9	16	20	20	20	22	22	22	22	22	22	22																			
12 TRULLI	23	16	16	16	16	16	23	23	23	23	23	23	9	23	23	23	23	22																												
18 BARRICHELLO	9	20	20	20	20	20	20	20	20	20	20	20	20	20	20	20	20																													
16 DINIZ	20	22	22	22	22	22	22	22	22	22	9	9	22	22	22	22	22																													
23 TUERO	22	9	9	9	9	9	9	9	9	9	22	22	6	6	6	6	6																													
19 MAGNUSSEN	19	19	19	19	19	19	19	19	6	6	6	6																																		
22 NAKANO	6	6	6	6	6	6	6	6																																						
20 ROSSET																																														

Pit stop
One lap behind leader

STARTING GRID

7 **COULTHARD** McLaren	8 **HÄKKINEN** McLaren
3 **M. SCHUMACHER** Ferrari	4 **IRVINE** Ferrari
6 **WURZ** Benetton	1 **VILLENEUVE** Williams
9 **HILL** Jordan	2 **FRENTZEN** Williams
10 **R. SCHUMACHER** Jordan	5 **FISICHELLA** Benetton
15 **HERBERT** Sauber	14 **ALESI** Sauber
11 **PANIS** Prost	17 **SALO** Arrows
21 **TAKAGI** Tyrrell	12 **TRULLI** Prost
18 **BARRICHELLO** Stewart	16 **DINIZ** Arrows
23 **TUERO** Minardi	19 **MAGNUSSEN** Stewart
22 **NAKANO** Minardi	20 **ROSSET** Tyrrell

51	52	53	54	55	56	57	58	59	60	61	62	
7	7	7	7	7	7	7	7	7	7	7	7	1
3	3	3	3	3	3	3	3	3	3	3	3	2
4	4	4	4	4	4	4	4	4	4	4	4	3
1	1	1	1	1	1	1	1	1	1	1	1	4
2	2	2	2	2	2	2	2	2	2	2	2	5
14	14	14	14	14	14	14	14	14	14	14		6
11	11	11	11	11	11	9	10	10	10			
9	9	9	9	9	9	10	23	23	23			
10	10	10	10	10	10	23	17	17	17			
23	23	23	23	23	23	17						
17	17	17	17	17	17							

FOR THE RECORD

100th Grand Prix start

Mika Häkkinen

TIME SHEETS

QUALIFYING

Weather: Hot, dry and sunny

Pos.	Driver	Car	Laps	Time
1	David Coulthard	McLaren-Mercedes	11	1m 25.973s
2	Mika Häkkinen	McLaren-Mercedes	12	1m 26.075s
3	Michael Schumacher	Ferrari	11	1m 26.437s
4	Eddie Irvine	Ferrari	12	1m 27.169s
5	Alexander Wurz	Benetton-Playlife	11	1m 27.273s
6	Jacques Villeneuve	Williams-Mecachrome	12	1m 27.390s
7	Damon Hill	Jordan-Mugen Honda	11	1m 27.592s
8	Heinz-Harald Frentzen	Williams-Mecachrome	12	1m 27.645s
9	Ralf Schumacher	Jordan-Mugen Honda	11	1m 27.866s
10	Giancarlo Fisichella	Benetton-Playlife	12	1m 27.937s
11	Johnny Herbert	Sauber-Petronas	11	1m 28.111s
12	Jean Alesi	Sauber-Petronas	11	1m 28.191s
13	Olivier Panis	Prost-Peugeot	12	1m 28.270s
14	Mika Salo	Arrows	11	1m 28.798s
15	Toranosuke Takagi	Tyrrell-Ford	12	1m 29.073s
16	Jarno Trulli	Prost-Peugeot	11	1m 29.584s
17	Rubens Barrichello	Stewart-Ford	11	1m 29.641s
18	Pedro Diniz	Arrows	12	1m 29.932s
19	Esteban Tuero	Minardi-Ford	12	1m 30.649s
20	Jan Magnussen	Stewart-Ford	11	1m 31.017s
21	Shinji Nakano	Minardi-Ford	6	1m 31.255s
22	Ricardo Rosset	Tyrrell-Ford	12	1m 31.482s

FRIDAY FREE PRACTICE

Weather: Warm and sunny

Pos.	Driver	Laps	Time
1	Mika Häkkinen	27	1m 27.617s
2	David Coulthard	20	1m 27.940s
3	Michael Schumacher	28	1m 28.088s
4	Jacques Villeneuve	33	1m 28.644s
5	Ralf Schumacher	25	1m 28.891s
6	Giancarlo Fisichella	46	1m 28.963s
7	Eddie Irvine	35	1m 29.028s
8	Olivier Panis	35	1m 29.175s
9	Damon Hill	37	1m 29.246s
10	Heinz-Harald Frentzen	26	1m 29.470s
11	Jean Alesi	30	1m 29.516s
12	Mika Salo	28	1m 29.828s
13	Alexander Wurz	37	1m 29.864s
14	Toranosuke Takagi	39	1m 30.190s
15	Johnny Herbert	33	1m 30.223s
16	Pedro Diniz	20	1m 30.795s
17	Jarno Trulli	32	1m 30.804s
18	Rubens Barrichello	22	1m 30.849s
19	Esteban Tuero	32	1m 31.954s
20	Shinji Nakano	34	1m 32.052s
21	Jan Magnussen	17	1m 32.196s
22	Ricardo Rosset	23	1m 32.554s

SATURDAY FREE PRACTICE

Weather: Hot, dry and sunny

Pos.	Driver	Laps	Time
1	David Coulthard	29	1m 25.627s
2	Mika Häkkinen	26	1m 26.431s
3	Michael Schumacher	25	1m 27.056s
4	Damon Hill	35	1m 27.318s
5	Ralf Schumacher	30	1m 27.421s
6	Giancarlo Fisichella	35	1m 27.653s
7	Heinz-Harald Frentzen	28	1m 27.694s
8	Eddie Irvine	26	1m 27.751s
9	Olivier Panis	33	1m 27.854s
10	Jacques Villeneuve	26	1m 27.876s
11	Jean Alesi	26	1m 27.931s
12	Alexander Wurz	31	1m 27.959s
13	Mika Salo	16	1m 28.130s
14	Johnny Herbert	28	1m 28.291s
15	Rubens Barrichello	26	1m 28.712s
16	Toranosuke Takagi	22	1m 29.628s
17	Pedro Diniz	14	1m 29.954s
18	Jan Magnussen	27	1m 30.243s
19	Shinji Nakano	34	1m 30.349s
20	Esteban Tuero	13	1m 31.182s
21	Ricardo Rosset	28	1m 32.459s
22	Jarno Trulli	6	1m 43.882s

WARM-UP

Weather: Warm and sunny

Pos.	Driver	Laps	Time
1	David Coulthard	14	1m 28.085s
2	Mika Salo	13	1m 29.428s
3	Michael Schumacher	14	1m 29.434s
4	Mika Häkkinen	6	1m 29.525s
5	Giancarlo Fisichella	13	1m 29.891s
6	Eddie Irvine	12	1m 29.996s
7	Alexander Wurz	14	1m 30.216s
8	Damon Hill	14	1m 30.275s
9	Jacques Villeneuve	12	1m 30.330s
10	Olivier Panis	15	1m 30.423s
11	Jean Alesi	12	1m 30.449s
12	Heinz-Harald Frentzen	14	1m 30.492s
13	Jarno Trulli	12	1m 30.628s
14	Johnny Herbert	17	1m 30.662s
15	Shinji Nakano	14	1m 30.948s
16	Toranosuke Takagi	14	1m 30.991s
17	Ralf Schumacher	10	1m 31.321s
18	Esteban Tuero	12	1m 32.087s
19	Rubens Barrichello	13	1m 32.092s
20	Pedro Diniz	8	1m 32.345s
21	Ricardo Rosset	7	1m 33.303s
22	Jan Magnussen	8	1m 33.956s

RACE FASTEST LAPS

Weather: Dry, warm and sunny

Driver	Time	Lap
Michael Schumacher	1m 29.345s	48
David Coulthard	1m 29.497s	21
Jacques Villeneuve	1m 29.726s	55
Mika Häkkinen	1m 30.115s	15
Eddie Irvine	1m 30.206s	58
Heinz-Harald Frentzen	1m 30.283s	39
Jean Alesi	1m 30.391s	23
Olivier Panis	1m 30.481s	53
Damon Hill	1m 30.859s	53
Mika Salo	1m 31.267s	19
Alexander Wurz	1m 31.562s	14
Ralf Schumacher	1m 31.837s	20
Giancarlo Fisichella	1m 31.969s	15
Johnny Herbert	1m 32.215s	9
Jarno Trulli	1m 32.361s	9
Toranosuke Takagi	1m 32.430s	21
Pedro Diniz	1m 32.988s	11
Esteban Tuero	1m 33.443s	53
Shinji Nakano	1m 33.889s	21
Ricardo Rosset	1m 34.491s	9
Jan Magnussen	1m 35.069s	5

CHASSIS LOG BOOK

1	Villeneuve	Williams FW20/3
2	Frentzen	Williams FW20/4
	spare	Williams FW20/2
3	M. Schumacher	Ferrari F300/186
4	Irvine	Ferrari F300/185
	spare	Ferrari F300/184
5	Fisichella	Benetton B198/5
6	Wurz	Benetton B198/4
	spare	Benetton B198/1
7	Coulthard	McLaren MP4/13/3
8	Häkkinen	McLaren MP4/13/4
	spare	McLaren MP4/13/2
9	Hill	Jordan 198/3
10	R. Schumacher	Jordan 198/4
	spare	Jordan 198/1
11	Panis	Prost AP01/5
12	Trulli	Prost AP01/3
	spare	Prost AP01/2
14	Alesi	Sauber C17/3
15	Herbert	Sauber C17/4
	spare	Sauber C17/2
16	Diniz	Arrows A19/2
17	Salo	Arrows A19/3
	spare	Arrows A19/1
18	Barrichello	Stewart SF2/1
19	Magnussen	Stewart SF2/3
	spare	Stewart SF2/2
20	Rosset	Tyrrell 026/1
21	Takagi	Tyrrell 026/2
	spare	Tyrrell 026/3
22	Nakano	Minardi M198/4
23	Tuero	Minardi M198/3
	spare	Minardi M198/2

POINTS TABLES

Drivers

1	Mika Häkkinen	26
2	David Coulthard	23
3	Michael Schumacher	20
4	Eddie Irvine	11
5	Heinz-Harald Frentzen	8
6	Alexander Wurz	6
7	Jacques Villeneuve	5
8	Jean Alesi	3
9 =	Johnny Herbert	1
9 =	Giancarlo Fisichella	1

Constructors

1	McLaren	49
2	Ferrari	31
3	Williams	13
4	Benetton	7
5	Sauber	4

Following his disappointing non-finish at Imola, Mika Häkkinen scored a decisive victory in Spain, heading a crushing 1–2 for McLaren.
Photo: Paul-Henri Cahier

SPANISH *grand prix*

HÄKKINEN

COULTHARD

M. SCHUMACHER

WURZ

BARRICHELLO

VILLENEUVE

CATALUNYA QUALIFYING

David Coulthard again found himself obliged to settle for second-fastest time behind his McLaren-Mercedes team-mate Mika Häkkinen during first practice at Barcelona – a trend which continued through qualifying and the race – but his old sparring partner Damon Hill still rated him favourite to win the 1998 World Championship.

'Standing here now I would put money on David, who has looked stronger than Mika at Buenos Aires and Imola,' said Hill. 'I think he has an excellent chance of cracking it. Now he just has to keep his head and get on with it.

'It's fun to battle with your team-mate and certainly makes meal times together more interesting. I had a very healthy relationship with Jacques Villeneuve [at Williams in 1996].

'In those conditions you simply have to do a better job as a driver because, whatever you do with the car, the other guy knows the same information.'

Yet Coulthard was clearly going to have to rely on considerable guile and racecraft to outwit Häkkinen, who went into the race leading the title chase by three points. The Finn had generally been the quicker of the two McLaren drivers and was consistently driving with the uninhibited confidence of a man who knows his big opportunity has come.

Whatever the outcome, it was clear from the start that Barcelona would be an all-McLaren affair. The MP4/13s' precise handling qualities combined with the consistency of the Bridgestone tyres were particularly well suited to the characteristics of the Circuit de Catalunya, where long medium-speed turns mean that the cars are cornering for a large proportion of the lap.

'If your car is slightly off the pace here, it is not one-tenth of a second slower, more like a full second,' said Patrick Head. He spoke from first-hand experience. On this track where Jacques Villeneuve had won so commandingly 12 months earlier, both Williams FW20s were struggling to keep up.

The trend continued in Saturday qualifying where Häkkinen posted the fourth pole position of his career, and his third in 1998, by outrunning Coulthard's McLaren by 0.734s. The Finn had no problems to report, but David admitted that he did not quite have the confidence in the car to push as hard as he would have liked.

Häkkinen admitted that he was surprised about the track conditions he found at Barcelona. 'We tested here last week for four days, and every day it was different,' he said. 'It was pretty disastrous, in fact, to be quick one day and slow the next. The weather was changing so much that on one day we had a head wind, and on the same straight the next day it was a tail wind, so we were getting very confused.

'Today, however, although the wind has picked up since this morning, it hasn't produced any major change in the balance of the car. The circuit has been very quick all through today, even with the temperature having gone up for qualifying.'

Like Benetton's Giancarlo Fisichella, Coulthard had been fortunate to walk away unscathed from quite a heavy testing accident at the Circuit de Catalunya during the interval since the San Marino Grand Prix. Not that this had any influence on the Scot's qualifying performance.

'What Mika has been able to do this weekend, right from the word go, is to extract all the performance from his car,' said the Scot. 'I haven't had the confidence to attack the track. On every GP circuit you have to be able to hit the corners knowing what you want to do with the car.

'It's no good wondering what the car is going to do next, it's as simple as that. Of course, I would have preferred to have seen a smaller gap, so I shall work on the car tomorrow and hope to get to the finish.'

Michael Schumacher's Ferrari F300 wound up third, pipping Fisichella's Benetton B198 by barely one-tenth of a second. The German ace reckoned that was as much as he could do and expressed himself pretty satisfied with the car after adding a touch of additional downforce after his first run.

'We lost some time in the morning with an electrical fault,' said Michael, 'but it didn't hurt us as much as it might have done because we have done a lot of testing here and we knew what the car would be like. Obviously third place is the best we could have hoped for. It is less pleasant to see how big the gap is to the McLarens, but we have to live with it for the moment and hope for a better situation.'

Fisichella lined up just ahead of team-mate Alexander Wurz, both men being quite content with the progress they had made on car set-up over the two days of practice and qualifying, while Eddie Irvine completed the top six in the other Ferrari.

'I'm a bit disappointed as the car seemed better in the morning, and I thought I might have been on the second row, but maybe that was a little unrealistic,' he confessed. 'On my first run I had too much understeer, so we made some changes to the car, which did not work. As a result, on my final run I pushed a little too hard and made a couple of mistakes.'

Johnny Herbert was the fastest Sauber-Petronas runner in seventh place on the grid, the Englishman reporting that the C17 seemed at its best on his last run after he'd managed to dial out some lingering mid-corner oversteer. He passed up the chance of a possible fourth run, correctly judging that close challengers Rubens Barrichello and Jacques Villeneuve were not quite close enough. Instead, he preferred to save another set of tyres for the race.

Team-mate Jean Alesi finished the session a highly disappointed 14th, the Frenchman grappling with acute understeer. 'To do the times I was doing, I was having to run on new tyres and with fuel for only two quick laps,' he shrugged.

In the Jordan-Mugen Honda camp things were looking up. Damon Hill lined up eighth, Ralf Schumacher three places further back. The two men opted for the harder Goodyear compound in the hope that it would give them a strategic advantage during the race in terms of fewer pit stops. 'I am confident the car will be good in hot-weather race conditions, and I believe we will be in good shape tomorrow,' Hill predicted.

Barrichello was similarly upbeat about the performance of the latest P4 version of the Ford Zetec-R V10, lining up ninth ahead of Villeneuve. By contrast, everything went wrong for Jan Magnussen. On Saturday morning he had to stop early when a broken engine mounting stud was detected, then a fuel pressure problem during qualifying obliged him to take the spare Stewart SF2. Add to that the fact that he didn't have a crack with one of the new P4 engines and he did quite respectably to end up 18th.

The Williams motorhome was not a particularly happy place to be. Both FW20 drivers continued to struggle with unpredictable rear-end grip and Villeneuve actually aborted his third run in order to make minor set-up adjustments in an effort to improve the rear-end stability. When he went out again, he spun off, damaging the car's left-front corner and removing its wing. He qualified tenth. 'I just lost it – simple!' he shrugged.

Heinz-Harald Frentzen complained about broadly the same problem and was in 13th place on the grid, the two Williams drivers separated by Ralf Schumacher's Jordan and Olivier Panis in the best-placed Prost-Peugeot. It was a turn for the better for Panis, who had incurred a $2750 fine for speeding in the pit lane on Friday but was now using the Evo 2 version of the Peugeot A16 V10 to good effect, ending up four places ahead of team-mate Jarno Trulli.

It was clear that Arrows had paid quite a high price for missing the Barcelona test prior to this race, but the team had preferred to work on improving the A19's level of technical reliability back at base. Pedro Diniz had a trouble-free run to qualify 15th, but *de facto* team leader Mika Salo was two places further back after losing a lot of set-up time on Friday due to throttle problems. 'At least the car has become more reliable,' said the Finn by way of consolation.

Behind Magnussen the last two rows contained the Minardis of Esteban Tuero and Shinji Nakano, plus the lone Tyrrell 026 of Toranosuke Takagi, who capped off his worst F1 qualifying performance with a couple of spins. At least he did better than team-mate Ricardo Rosset, who missed the 107 per cent qualifying cut-off by less than one-tenth of a second.

Opposite: **Michael Schumacher's Ferrari is pushed back into its pit garage during practice. The Italian cars were fitted with a distinctive new exhaust system exiting through the top of the rear bodywork, but McLaren continued to enjoy a decisive performance advantage.**

THE McLaren-Mercedes steamroller continued its relentless advance towards the 1998 World Championship as Mika Häkkinen and David Coulthard left the opposition in the dust at the Circuit de Catalunya, lapping all but two of the other cars *en route* to their third 1-2 victory of the season in the Spanish Grand Prix. In their wake, only Ferrari's Michael Schumacher produced an even halfway convincing performance to take third place, sustaining lingering hopes that he might be able to turn the apparently unstoppable tide in the second half of the season.

It was a race in which it was necessary to scrutinise the also-rans in order to find much in the way of creative tactics or exuberant driving. Such was the margin of dominance produced by the McLarens that neither Häkkinen nor Coulthard seemed from the touchlines to be working particularly hard behind the wheel.

In Häkkinen's case that illusion was perhaps almost valid. 'The car was terrific,' he enthused after stepping down from the podium. 'Nothing is ever quite perfect, but I had no problems whatsoever.' Yet for Coulthard, who had hoped to follow up his victory at Imola with another win, the race was a little less convincing.

Throughout qualifying he had struggled slightly to feel totally confident with his car's handling, even spinning into a gravel trap during Saturday's free practice session. Sure enough, he qualified second alongside Häkkinen on the starting grid, but dropped away steadily from the start and never looked like challenging for the lead.

'My first set of tyres were not so good,' he explained, 'and I had made changes to the chassis set-up both after the morning warm-up and then again just before the start. The car's front end felt a little "pointy" from the start, but its handling got progressively better throughout the race and was at its best on the last set of tyres.'

The race took place in perfect conditions beneath a cloudless sky and with a temperature hovering around the 22-degree mark. There was a slight flap at the start of the final formation lap as Pedro Diniz's Arrows was left on the line with a flat battery, thence being pushed into the pits for a replacement to be fitted before joining the contest a lap down.

Meanwhile Häkkinen slipped cleanly into the lead as the pack accelerated towards the first corner with Coulthard fending off a challenge from Eddie Irvine, and Giancarlo Fisichella leading the chase from a slow-starting Michael Schumacher. Midway round the opening lap, Heinz-Harald Frentzen and Jean Alesi somehow contrived to tangle with each other, the Williams snapping into a quick spin, but continuing at the tail of the field.

'That incident with Frentzen on the first lap really ruined my race,' said Alesi later. 'He tried to come round the outside of me and we touched, but when you are in the pack like that everyone is trying everything that they can.'

Frentzen lost more time when he came into the pits at the end of the second lap to have a replacement nose section fitted to his Williams as a precautionary measure, resuming in 20th place.

By the end of the opening lap, Häkkinen was already 1.8s ahead of his team-mate. Second time round the Finn stretched his advantage to 3.0s, and he then increased it to 4.1s on lap three and 4.8s on lap four. Thereafter he pulled steadily clear at the rate of around 0.8s a lap for much of the opening phase of the race.

For the first 20 laps or so the Spanish Grand Prix developed – or failed to develop, depending on your viewpoint – into a routinely processional affair. From fifth place Schumacher's Ferrari chased Fisichella for all the German driver was worth, but could never get much closer than 1.5s.

Behind them Alexander Wurz ran in sixth place ahead of Rubens Barrichello, Jacques Villeneuve, Johnny Herbert's Sauber, Damon Hill's Jordan and the rest of the pack. By lap 16 Häkkinen was 13.2s ahead of Coulthard and a full 23.1s ahead of Schumacher in fifth place. Herbert was now pressing Villeneuve hard for eighth, but that was about it. We had to wait until lap 18, when Olivier Panis made his first 8.6s refuelling stop from 11th place, for a significant change of position, the Frenchman dropping back to 14th.

On lap 22 came the first retirements with Mika Salo and Diniz abandoning their Arrows A19s within yards of each other on the main straight due to engine failure, although the two cars were in fact running a lap apart due to Diniz's pre-start problems.

'I saw Mika's engine smoking and then I felt mine blow up,' said the Brazilian, while Salo confessed some degree of amusement over the incident. 'It was hard to try and look serious on

Marlboro
3
Shell
GOODYEAR
Marlboro
FIAT
Marlboro

HSBC
TEXACO
Havoline
18
Havoline
BRIDGESTONE
BRIDGESTONE

BENSON &
HEDGES
Jordan

Rubens Barrichello drove with great tenacity to keep Jacques Villeneuve behind him and was rewarded with fifth place, earning the troubled Stewart team's first points of the year.

It looked as though Damon Hill *(below left)* was set for another dispiriting season, with Jordan appearing to have lost its way after making impressive progress in 1997.

DIARY

Bernie Ecclestone confirms that an announcement about future plans for a possible US Grand Prix will be made by the end of the year.

Veteran Indy car driver Danny Ongais, 57, ends a racing comeback after crashing his G-Force-Aurora on the first lap of a test at Indianapolis Motor Speedway.

Juan Pablo Montoya wins Barcelona F3000 race, having qualified in pole position for the third round in succession.

Honda is rumoured to have commissioned the Italian Dallara organisation to carry out a wind tunnel research programme on its behalf with a view to its proposed F1 return as a chassis and engine constructor.

the walk back,' he admitted. Unsurprisingly, the Arrows team personnel failed to see the funny side of this episode.

On lap 22 Barrichello's Stewart made its first refuelling stop, dropping from seventh to eighth, allowing Villeneuve's Williams ahead. Herbert also brought the ninth-placed Sauber in, dropping only a single position when he resumed.

On lap 24 Villeneuve moved up to sixth place after Wurz brought his Benetton in for its first refuelling stop, the Austrian resuming in seventh, while next time round Irvine came in followed by Fisichella, which allowed Schumacher to surge by into third place. Irvine just squeezed back into the race ahead of his Italian rival, the pair now running fourth and fifth.

On lap 26 Häkkinen made his first refuelling stop, relinquishing the lead to Coulthard for just a single lap as David came in next time round and the Finn thus moved back in front. Lap 27 also saw Schumacher and Villeneuve heading for the pits, Michael resuming ahead of Irvine while the Canadian fell behind Wurz and Barrichello once again.

Schumacher was doing everything that could have been expected of him to finish the afternoon in third place, despite having got too much wheelspin at the start and dropped to fifth place by the end of the opening lap. Although that had allowed Irvine to take an immediate third place ahead of Fisichella, after his first refuelling stop Irvine had slowed his pace by three seconds in one lap under team orders, thereby allowing Schumacher to return to the circuit ahead, having made up two places.

Fisichella, who now found himself back in fifth place, then attempted to overtake Irvine round the outside of the first corner at the start of lap 29, the two cars colliding and spinning into retirement in the gravel trap.

Fisichella remonstrated energetically with Irvine as the two men walked away from their abandoned cars, but the stewards eventually decided that the fault lay with the Italian, who was fined $7500 for 'causing an avoidable accident'.

Irvine was characteristically direct about the episode. 'He just came down the outside and turned into me, taking the racing line despite the fact I was there,' he said. 'What did he expect me to do? Press a button and go into immediate helicopter mode?'

Fisichella clearly didn't think that was an explanation which warranted a great deal of credibility. 'I am very disappointed,' he admitted. 'I had already passed Irvine with most of the car and he should have let me through, but he kept on going and it resulted in a collision.

'At the beginning of the race the same thing occurred, but I was on the inside and I pulled back to let Eddie through as I knew it would end in an accident. Apart from the collision, after a few laps the car became difficult to drive with both understeer and oversteer, but I was in a strong position for third place.'

This little drama now left Wurz fourth from Barrichello and the ever-present Villeneuve while Herbert was seventh ahead of Hill. Villeneuve had been in the thick of the action from the outset, relentlessly tracking Barrichello's Stewart SF2, which was racing the latest P4 version of Ford's Zetec-R V10 for the first time.

Rubens was certainly not short on straightline speed, but Villeneuve believed the Williams was potentially quicker. When the Brazilian ducked in for his first refuelling stop, Jacques stayed out and piled on the pressure before coming in for his first stop five laps later.

He just failed to get back out ahead of the Brazilian, but felt his second set of tyres were excellent and had high hopes of being able to jump his rival at the second round of refuelling stops. Rubens came in from fifth place on lap 44, after which Villeneuve would have liked to stay out for a few more laps, but his fuel situation was such that he had to come in next time round.

With that in mind, he ran absolutely as hard as possible on his 'in' lap and reckoned this time he would be able to squeeze out ahead, only for the mechanics to have problems with the fuel filler cap. That lost him a crucial handful of seconds and meant that he was unable to reverse the status quo out on the circuit.

In the midst of this battle Schumacher's Ferrari had been signalled in to take a ten-second stop-go penalty at the end of lap 40, incurred for speeding in the pit lane during his first refuelling stop. That dropped him from third to fourth behind Wurz, while next time round Hill got extremely annoyed with what he saw as Frentzen's sloppy driving when the Williams driver accelerated straight out of the pits and, in his view, elbowed his Jordan onto the gravel.

'I was just going down to turn one when he came out of the pits and pushed me off the track,' fumed Damon, who had earlier lost eight seconds on the seventh-placed Herbert on the lap before his first refuelling stop. 'That was annoying, because I was up there possibly fighting for points and he was well behind, but in the end, of course, it did not matter as the engine failed.'

On laps 45 and 46, Häkkinen and Coulthard made their second refuelling stops, resuming their established 1-2 formation at the head of the pack. Wurz also made his second stop on lap 46, allowing Schumacher through, and when Michael came in for a second time two laps later he managed to get out ahead of the Benetton, where he stayed until the finish.

'I had some difficulty in pushing with the car, so I really couldn't battle with Michael,' said Wurz. 'Under the circumstances, fourth place was as good as it gets.'

Into fifth place came the superb Barrichello after a race in which he had made not a single slip despite the presence of Villeneuve virtually on his tail for the entire distance.

'This feels like a new beginning for me and the team,' said the delighted Rubens. 'It was a tough race, but I really enjoyed myself. The team did a terrific job, my pit stops were great and together we really deserved this result.'

Herbert was seventh ahead of Frentzen, who perked up superbly in the closing moments, slicing his way from 12th to eighth with some audacious overtaking, passing Ralf Schumacher, Alesi and Jarno Trulli with considerable zeal.

Yet at the end of the day, this race was about nobody but Mika Häkkinen and the McLaren-Mercedes team. 'My biggest problem today was keeping my concentration going,' said the Finn. His opposition simply longed for the chance to grapple with such a satisfying mental conundrum. Particularly if that meant running away from the field.

Benetton close to Mecachrome deal

BENETTON boss David Richards came to Spain on the verge of finalising a contract for the Italian team to continue using Mecachrome Renault V10s through to the end of the 1999 season. Richards had recently had a meeting with Renault Sport managing director Christian Contzen and received assurances that a development programme for the French V10 was in full swing.

'The only reason which would have stopped me from using the Mecachrome engines would have been if I couldn't have secured such assurances,' said Richards.

In fact, Benetton had been in something of a dilemma. With a certain impatience developing within some quarters of the Ford empire over the progress of the Stewart F1 team, discreet feelers were being put out to establish whether or not it would be possible for Benetton to use Ford engines again at some time in the near future.

Talk of a resumption of the Benetton-Ford alliance might on the face of it have seemed rather difficult to anticipate, for the US car maker had developed a strained relationship with the team during Flavio Briatore's time in the management hot seat. However, with David Richards in control, the prospects for a future partnership between Benetton and Ford would take a distinct turn for the better – as emphasised by the fact that, later in 1998, an agreement would be concluded for Richards's Prodrive operation to run the works Ford Mondeos in the following year's British Touring Car Championship.

Despite this, for the moment in F1 there was little either party could do to alter the status quo. Ford's exclusive arrangement for the supply of front-line works engines to the Stewart team remained in place to the end of the 2000 season. Richards and Benetton could do little more than mark time and take the safe option of continuing with the Renault-designed V10, the technical niceties of which they could hardly have known better.

Counterfeit component costs McLaren dear

A COUNTERFEIT gearbox bearing was the cause of Mika Häkkinen's retirement in the San Marino Grand Prix, the McLaren-Mercedes team revealed at Barcelona. He had been running in second place at the time.

Detailed examination of the MP4/13's transmission yielded this astonishing verdict a few days after the Finn was posted as the team's first mechanical retirement of the season in the fourth round of the title chase.

A subsequent check on the team's spares inventory revealed that several more such counterfeit components were in stock and that their packaging, ostensibly identical to that of the genuine article, had a slightly different colouration.

'We analysed the bearing and it didn' t have the correct properties,' said Ron Dennis. 'The manufacturer confirmed that it was a counterfeit bearing. Two or three steps down the supply line somebody has managed to put a very large number of counterfeits into the system.'

GRAN PREMIO MARLBORO DE ESPAÑA

8–10 MAY 1998

CATALUNYA

Race distance: 65 laps, 190.882 miles/307.196 km

Race weather: Hot, dry and sunny

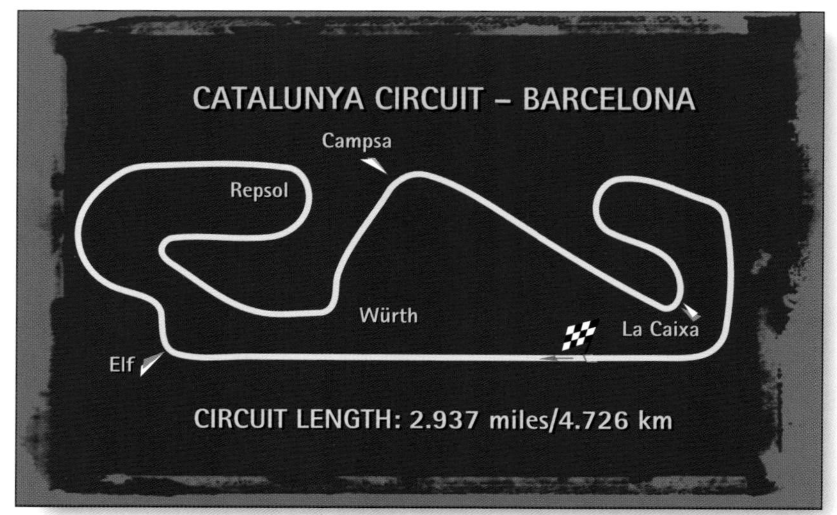

Pos.	Driver	Nat.	No.	Entrant	Car/Engine	Tyres	Laps	Time/Retirement	Speed (mph/km/h)
1	**Mika Häkkinen**	**SF**	**8**	**West McLaren Mercedes**	**McLaren MP4/13-Mercedes FO110G V10**	**B**	**65**	**1h 33m 37.621s**	**122.325/196.863**
2	**David Coulthard**	**GB**	**7**	**West McLaren Mercedes**	**McLaren MP4/13-Mercedes FO110G V10**	**B**	**65**	**1h 33m 47.060s**	**122.120/196.533**
3	**Michael Schumacher**	**D**	**3**	**Scuderia Ferrari Marlboro**	**Ferrari F300 047 V10**	**G**	**65**	**1h 34m 24.716s**	**121.308/195.227**
4	**Alexander Wurz**	**A**	**6**	**Mild Seven Benetton Playlife**	**Benetton B198-Playlife V10**	**B**	**65**	**1h 34m 40.159s**	**120.978/194.696**
5	**Rubens Barrichello**	**BR**	**18**	**Stewart Ford**	**Stewart SF2-Ford Zetec-R V10**	**B**	**64**		
6	**Jacques Villeneuve**	**CDN**	**1**	**Winfield Williams**	**Williams FW20-Mecachrome GC37/01 V10**	**G**	**64**		
7	Johnny Herbert	GB	15	Red Bull Sauber Petronas	Sauber C17-Petronas SPE01D V10	G	64		
8	Heinz-Harald Frentzen	D	2	Winfield Williams	Williams FW20-Mecachrome GC37/01 V10	G	63		
9	Jarno Trulli	I	12	Gauloises Prost Peugeot	Prost AP01-Peugeot A16 V10	B	63		
10	Jean Alesi	F	14	Red Bull Sauber Petronas	Sauber C17-Petronas SPE01D V10	G	63		
11	Ralf Schumacher	D	10	B&H Jordan Mugen Honda	Jordan 198-Mugen Honda MF310C V10	G	63		
12	Jan Magnussen	DK	19	Stewart Ford	Stewart SF2-Ford Zetec-R V10	B	63		
13	Toranosuke Takagi	J	21	Tyrrell Ford	Tyrrell 026-Ford Zetec-R V10	G	63		
14	Shinji Nakano	J	22	Fondmetal Minardi Ford	Minardi M198-Ford Zetec-R V10	B	63		
15	Esteban Tuero	RA	23	Fondmetal Minardi Ford	Minardi M198-Ford Zetec-R V10	B	63		
16	Olivier Panis	F	11	Gauloises Prost Peugeot	Prost AP01-Peugeot A16 V10	B	60	Engine	
	Damon Hill	GB	9	B&H Jordan Mugen Honda	Jordan 198-Mugen Honda MF310C V10	G	46	Engine	
	Eddie Irvine	GB	4	Scuderia Ferrari Marlboro	Ferrari F300 047 V10	G	28	Collision with Fisichella	
	Giancarlo Fisichella	I	5	Mild Seven Benetton Playlife	Benetton B198-Playlife V10	B	28	Collision with Irvine	
	Mika Salo	SF	17	Danka Zepter Arrows	Arrows A19 V10	B	21	Engine	
	Pedro Diniz	BR	16	Danka Zepter Arrows	Arrows A19 V10	B	20	Engine	
DNQ	Ricardo Rosset	BR	20	Tyrrell Ford	Tyrrell 026-Ford Zetec-R V10	G			

Fastest lap: Häkkinen, on lap 25, 1m 24.275s, 125.496 mph/201.967 km/h.

Lap record: Giancarlo Fisichella (F1 Jordan 197-Peugeot V10), 1m 22.242s, 128.919 mph/207.475 km/h (1997).

B – Bridgestone G – Goodyear

All results and data © FIA 1998

Grid order	1	2	3	4	5	6	7	8	9	10	11	12	13	14	15	16	17	18	19	20	21	22	23	24	25	26	27	28	29	30	31	32	33	34	35	36	37	38	39	40	41	42	43	44	45	46	47	48	49	5
8 HÄKKINEN	8	8	8	8	8	8	8	8	8	8	8	8	8	8	8	8	8	8	8	8	8	8	8	8	8	8	7	8	8	8	8	8	8	8	8	8	8	8	8	8	8	8	8	8	8	7	8	8	8	
7 COULTHARD	7	7	7	7	7	7	7	7	7	7	7	7	7	7	7	7	7	7	7	7	7	7	7	7	7	7	8	7	7	7	7	7	7	7	7	7	7	7	7	7	7	7	7	7	7	8	7	7	7	
3 M. SCHUMACHER	4	4	4	4	4	4	4	4	4	4	4	4	4	4	4	4	4	4	4	4	4	4	4	4	4	3	3	3	3	3	3	3	3	3	3	3	3	3	3	3	6	6	6	6	6	6	3	3	3	
5 FISICHELLA	5	5	5	5	5	5	5	5	5	5	5	5	5	5	5	5	5	5	5	5	5	5	5	5	3	4	4	4	6	6	6	6	6	6	6	6	6	6	6	6	3	3	3	3	3	3	6	6	6	
6 WURZ	3	3	3	3	3	3	3	3	3	3	3	3	3	3	3	3	3	3	3	3	3	3	3	3	5	5	5	5	18	18	18	18	18	18	18	18	18	18	18	18	18	18	18	1	1	18	18	18	18	1
4 IRVINE	6	6	6	6	6	6	6	6	6	6	6	6	6	6	6	6	6	6	6	6	6	6	6	1	1	1	1	6	1	1	1	1	1	1	1	1	1	1	1	1	1	1	1	18	18	1	1	1	1	
15 HERBERT	18	18	18	18	18	18	18	18	18	18	18	18	18	18	18	18	18	18	18	18	18	18	1	6	6	6	6	18	15	15	15	15	15	15	15	15	15	15	15	15	15	15	15	15	15	15	15	15	15	1
9 HILL	1	1	1	1	1	1	1	1	1	1	1	1	1	1	1	1	1	1	1	1	1	1	18	18	18	18	18	1	9	9	9	9	9	9	9	9	9	9	9	9	9	11	9	9	11	11	11	11	11	1
18 BARRICHELLO	15	15	15	15	15	15	15	15	15	15	15	15	15	15	15	15	15	15	15	15	15	15	12	15	15	15	15	15	11	11	11	11	11	11	11	11	11	11	11	11	11	9	11	11	9	9	12	12	12	1
1 VILLENEUVE	9	9	9	9	9	9	9	9	9	9	9	9	9	9	9	9	9	9	9	9	9	9	15	9	9	9	9	9	12	12	12	12	12	14	19	19	19	19	10	10	10	10	12	12	12	12	14	14	14	1
10 R. SCHUMACHER	12	11	11	11	11	11	11	11	11	11	11	11	11	11	11	11	11	11	12	12	12	12	9	12	11	11	11	11	14	14	14	14	14	19	10	10	10	10	19	19	19	19	14	14	14	14	10	10	10	1
11 PANIS	11	12	12	12	12	12	12	12	12	12	12	12	12	12	12	12	12	12	19	17	17	11	11	11	12	12	12	12	19	19	19	19	19	10	12	12	12	12	12	12	12	12	10	10	10	10	19	19	2	
2 FRENTZEN	19	19	19	19	19	19	19	19	19	19	19	19	19	19	19	19	19	19	17	11	11	14	14	14	19	19	19	19	10	10	10	10	10	12	14	14	14	14	14	14	14	14	19	19	19	19	2	2	19	1
14 ALESI	17	17	17	17	17	17	17	17	17	17	17	17	17	17	17	17	17	17	11	21	14	22	22	19	14	14	14	14	21	21	21	21	21	21	21	21	21	21	2	2	2	2	2	2	2	2	21	21	21	2
16 DINIZ	21	21	21	21	21	21	21	21	21	21	21	21	21	21	21	21	21	21	21	14	21	19	19	10	10	10	10	10	2	2	2	2	2	2	2	2	2	2	21	21	21	21	21	21	21	21	22	22	22	2
12 TRULLI	22	22	22	22	22	10	10	10	10	10	10	10	10	10	10	10	10	10	14	22	22	10	10	21	21	21	21	21	22	22	22	22	22	22	22	22	22	22	22	22	23	23	22	22	22	22	23	23	23	2
17 SALO	10	10	10	10	10	22	22	22	22	14	14	14	14	14	14	14	14	14	10	23	19	21	21	2	2	2	2	2	23	23	23	23	23	23	23	23	23	23	23	23	22	22	23	23	23	23				
19 MAGNUSSEN	23	23	23	23	23	23	14	14	14	22	22	22	22	22	22	22	22	22	22	2	23	2	2	22	22	22	22	22																						
23 TUERO	14	14	14	14	14	14	23	23	23	23	23	23	23	23	23	23	23	23	23	19	2	23	23	23	23	23	23	23																						
22 NAKANO	2	2	2	2	2	2	2	2	2	2	2	2	2	2	2	2	2	2	2	10	10																													
21 TAKAGI	16	16	16	16	16	16	16	16	16	16	16	16	16	16	16	16	16	16	16	16																														

Pit stop

One lap behind leader

STARTING GRID

8 **HÄKKINEN** McLaren	7 **COULTHARD** McLaren
3 **M. SCHUMACHER** Ferrari	5 **FISICHELLA** Benetton
6 **WURZ** Benetton	4 **IRVINE** Ferrari
15 **HERBERT** Sauber	9 **HILL** Jordan
18 **BARRICHELLO** Stewart	1 **VILLENEUVE** Williams
10 **R. SCHUMACHER** Jordan	11 **PANIS** Prost
2 **FRENTZEN** Williams	14 **ALESI** Sauber
16 **DINIZ*** Arrows	12 **TRULLI** Prost
17 **SALO** Arrows	19 **MAGNUSSEN** Stewart
23 **TUERO** Minardi	22 **NAKANO** Minardi
21 **TAKAGI** Tyrrell	

* started from pit lane

Did not qualify:

ROSSET (Tyrrell)

54	55	56	57	58	59	60	61	62	63	64	65	
8	8	8	8	8	8	8	8	8	8	8	8	1
7	7	7	7	7	7	7	7	7	7	7	7	2
3	3	3	3	3	3	3	3	3	3	3	3	3
6	6	6	6	6	6	6	6	6	6	6	6	4
18	18	18	18	18	18	18	18	18	18	18		5
1	1	1	1	1	1	1	1	1	1	1		6
15	15	15	15	15	15	15	15	15	15	15		
11	11	11	11	11	11	11	12	12	2			
12	12	12	12	12	12	12	14	2	12			
14	14	14	14	14	14	14	10	14	14			
10	10	10	10	10	10	10	2	10	10			
2	2	2	2	2	2	2	19	19	19			
19	19	19	19	19	19	19	21	21	21			
21	21	21	21	21	21	21	22	22	22			
22	22	22	22	22	22	22	23	23	23			
23	23	23	23	23	23	23						

TIME SHEETS

QUALIFYING

Weather: Sunny and hot

Pos.	Driver	Car	Laps	Time
1	Mika Häkkinen	McLaren-Mercedes	11	1m 20.262s
2	David Coulthard	McLaren-Mercedes	12	1m 20.996s
3	Michael Schumacher	Ferrari	11	1m 21.785s
4	Giancarlo Fisichella	Benetton-Playlife	11	1m 21.894s
5	Alexander Wurz	Benetton-Playlife	12	1m 21.965s
6	Eddie Irvine	Ferrari	12	1m 22.350s
7	Johnny Herbert	Sauber-Petronas	9	1m 22.794s
8	Damon Hill	Jordan-Mugen Honda	11	1m 22.835s
9	Rubens Barrichello	Stewart-Ford	12	1m 22.860s
10	Jacques Villeneuve	Williams-Mecachrome	10	1m 22.885s
11	Ralf Schumacher	Jordan-Mugen Honda	12	1m 22.927s
12	Olivier Panis	Prost-Peugeot	12	1m 22.963s
13	Heinz-Harald Frentzen	Williams-Mecachrome	11	1m 23.197s
14	Jean Alesi	Sauber-Petronas	11	1m 23.327s
15	Pedro Diniz	Arrows	12	1m 23.704s
16	Jarno Trulli	Prost-Peugeot	12	1m 23.748s
17	Mika Salo	Arrows	12	1m 23.887s
18	Jan Magnussen	Stewart-Ford	12	1m 24.112s
19	Esteban Tuero	Minardi-Ford	12	1m 24.265s
20	Shinji Nakano	Minardi-Ford	12	1m 24.538s
21	Toranosuke Takagi	Tyrrell-Ford	12	1m 24.722s
22	Ricardo Rosset	Tyrrell-Ford	12	1m 25.946s

107 per cent time: 1m 25.880s

FRIDAY FREE PRACTICE

Weather: Sunny and hot

Pos.	Driver	Laps	Time
1	Mika Häkkinen	17	1m 22.147s
2	David Coulthard	25	1m 22.965s
3	Johnny Herbert	43	1m 23.237s
4	Eddie Irvine	24	1m 23.421s
5	Michael Schumacher	20	1m 23.468s
6	Heinz-Harald Frentzen	29	1m 23.843s
7	Rubens Barrichello	25	1m 24.037s
8	Jacques Villeneuve	20	1m 24.198s
9	Jean Alesi	4	1m 24.257s
10	Olivier Panis	32	1m 24.272s
11	Giancarlo Fisichella	29	1m 24.286s
12	Alexander Wurz	20	1m 24.311s
13	Ralf Schumacher	36	1m 24.420s
14	Damon Hill	41	1m 24.888s
15	Jarno Trulli	38	1m 24.897s
16	Shinji Nakano	23	1m 25.280s
17	Toranosuke Takagi	19	1m 25.336s
18	Esteban Tuero	29	1m 25.525s
19	Pedro Diniz	28	1m 25.770s
20	Mika Salo	28	1m 26.285s
21	Ricardo Rosset	39	1m 26.371s
22	Jan Magnussen	15	1m 26.606s

SATURDAY FREE PRACTICE

Weather: Sunny and hot

Pos.	Driver	Laps	Time
1	Mika Häkkinen	22	1m 20.791s
2	David Coulthard	17	1m 21.223s
3	Giancarlo Fisichella	24	1m 22.102s
4	Alexander Wurz	27	1m 22.414s
5	Eddie Irvine	25	1m 22.497s
6	Rubens Barrichello	24	1m 22.673s
7	Michael Schumacher	16	1m 22.890s
8	Damon Hill	36	1m 22.974s
9	Johnny Herbert	36	1m 23.058s
10	Heinz-Harald Frentzen	26	1m 23.083s
11	Ralf Schumacher	29	1m 23.113s
12	Olivier Panis	24	1m 23.317s
13	Jean Alesi	27	1m 23.397s
14	Jacques Villeneuve	29	1m 23.483s
15	Toranosuke Takagi	35	1m 23.944s
16	Mika Salo	23	1m 24.096s
17	Esteban Tuero	32	1m 24.640s
18	Jarno Trulli	31	1m 24.680s
19	Pedro Diniz	22	1m 24.793s
20	Jan Magnussen	20	1m 24.862s
21	Shinji Nakano	28	1m 25.375s
22	Ricardo Rosset	26	1m 25.885s

WARM-UP

Weather: Sunny and hot

Pos.	Driver	Laps	Time
1	Mika Häkkinen	12	1m 22.460s
2	David Coulthard	13	1m 23.270s
3	Giancarlo Fisichella	15	1m 24.107s
4	Olivier Panis	14	1m 24.677s
5	Michael Schumacher	13	1m 24.852s
6	Eddie Irvine	14	1m 25.176s
7	Alexander Wurz	14	1m 25.382s
8	Heinz-Harald Frentzen	14	1m 25.536s
9	Jarno Trulli	14	1m 25.541s
10	Johnny Herbert	14	1m 25.630s
11	Rubens Barrichello	14	1m 25.702s
12	Ralf Schumacher	15	1m 25.925s
13	Esteban Tuero	12	1m 25.991s
14	Mika Salo	15	1m 26.087s
15	Pedro Diniz	12	1m 26.278s
16	Jacques Villeneuve	14	1m 26.370s
17	Jan Magnussen	12	1m 26.425s
18	Toranosuke Takagi	16	1m 26.452s
19	Jean Alesi	12	1m 26.698s
20	Damon Hill	14	1m 26.730s
21	Shinji Nakano	12	1m 27.226s

RACE FASTEST LAPS

Weather: Hot, dry and sunny

Driver	Time	Lap
Mika Häkkinen	1m 24.275s	25
Michael Schumacher	1m 24.625s	45
David Coulthard	1m 24.778s	61
Alexander Wurz	1m 25.343s	43
Jean Alesi	1m 25.668s	31
Eddie Irvine	1m 25.778s	20
Giancarlo Fisichella	1m 25.851s	18
Heinz-Harald Frentzen	1m 26.011s	3
Johnny Herbert	1m 26.354s	25
Jarno Trulli	1m 26.394s	25
Jacques Villeneuve	1m 26.407s	24
Damon Hill	1m 26.501s	37
Olivier Panis	1m 26.502s	57
Rubens Barrichello	1m 26.532s	23
Ralf Schumacher	1m 26.533s	40
Jan Magnussen	1m 27.203s	43
Esteban Tuero	1m 27.601s	45
Pedro Diniz	1m 27.638s	16
Mika Salo	1m 27.767s	22
Shinji Nakano	1m 27.767s	25
Toranosuke Takagi	1m 28.066s	34

CHASSIS LOG BOOK

1	Villeneuve	Williams FW20/5
2	Frentzen	Williams FW20/4
	spare	Williams FW20/3
3	M. Schumacher	Ferrari F300/186
4	Irvine	Ferrari F300/185
	spare	Ferrari F300/184
5	Fisichella	Benetton B198/6
6	Wurz	Benetton B198/4
	spare	Benetton B198/1
7	Coulthard	McLaren MP4/13/3
8	Häkkinen	McLaren MP4/13/4
	spare	McLaren MP4/13/5
9	Hill	Jordan 198/3
10	R. Schumacher	Jordan 198/4
	spare	Jordan 198/1
11	Panis	Prost AP01/5
12	Trulli	Prost AP01/3
	spare	Prost AP01/4
14	Alesi	Sauber C17/1
15	Herbert	Sauber C17/4
	spare	Sauber C17/2
16	Diniz	Arrows A19/2
17	Salo	Arrows A19/3
	spare	Arrows A19/1
18	Barrichello	Stewart SF2/1
19	Magnussen	Stewart SF2/2
	spare	Stewart SF2/3
20	Rosset	Tyrrell 026/1
21	Takagi	Tyrrell 026/2
	spare	Tyrrell 026/3
22	Nakano	Minardi M198/4
23	Tuero	Minardi M198/3
	spare	Minardi M198/2

POINTS TABLES

Drivers

1	Mika Häkkinen	36
2	David Coulthard	29
3	Michael Schumacher	24
4	Eddie Irvine	11
5	Alexander Wurz	9
6	Heinz-Harald Frentzen	8
7	Jacques Villeneuve	6
8	Jean Alesi	3
9	Rubens Barrichello	2
10 =	Johnny Herbert	1
10 =	Giancarlo Fisichella	1

Constructors

1	McLaren	65
2	Ferrari	35
3	Williams	14
4	Benetton	10
5	Sauber	4
6	Stewart	2

MONACO

grand prix

Paul-Henri Cahier

Practice and qualifying indicated that it was probably going to take more than a new-construction rear Goodyear, designed to improve slow-speed traction, to raise the standard of Ferrari's game to the McLaren level round Monaco.

Michael Schumacher certainly has a record as F1's great street-circuit specialist, but when he was forced to sit out the entire Saturday morning free practice session due to a broken driveshaft, it was valuable set-up time he never managed to claw back. Coming after a shunt into the tyre barriers outside the front door of the Hotel de Paris, it hardly helped Schumacher's composure.

Not that he was alone in contacting the scenery, of course. On Saturday morning both McLarens hit the wall, while qualifying saw Rubens Barrichello's Stewart and Eddie Irvine's Ferrari do the same. The Ulsterman would even have another shunt in the race morning action.

Monaco was certainly living up to its reputation as a high-wire act without a safety net, a uniquely challenging F1 environment in which to operate with an unforgiving track configuration. That historic corridor of steel guard rails certainly penalises established ace and bright-eyed novice alike with a dispassionate severity.

In 1997 Heinz-Harald Frentzen's Williams FW19 had bagged pole with a lap in 1m 18.216s and many tyre company insiders predicted that, even under the new narrow-track, grooved-tyre rules, this year's F1 generation would come very close to equalling that.

In the event, Mika Häkkinen sealed the fifth pole position of his career, and the fourth out of the six races so far in 1998, with a best lap of 1m 19.798s, out-gunning McLaren team-mate David Coulthard by 0.339s. The Finn explained that he had set his fastest time on his penultimate run, the main priority throughout the session being to find a trouble-free lap.

'My race engineers sent me out at the perfect time,' he reflected. 'The team worked hard to give me a competitive car capable of achieving this time, particularly after I touched the guard rail in the morning and damaged the suspension.'

For his part, Coulthard was disappointed not to have taken pole, having encountered problems getting a clear lap and also been forced to abort one of his runs after Ricardo Rosset spun at the exit of the swimming pool.

In the Benetton camp, Giancarlo Fisichella was well satisfied after posting third-fastest time. 'My target was always third place,' he said, praising the improved traction offered by the latest suspension set-up on his B198. Alexander Wurz lined up sixth, admitting that he was reasonably happy.

'I managed to reduce the time between myself and Giancarlo,' said the Austrian. 'Sixth place is OK and I am happy with the tyre choice, so things look good for tomorrow.'

In fourth place on the grid came Michael Schumacher on 1m 20.702s, a full second away from Häkkinen's pole-position McLaren. Michael had to use the spare Ferrari F300 for qualifying after his race machine suffered that driveshaft breakage during the morning's free practice session. Given the amount of time he had lost as a result, Michael was quite happy, although Rosset's spin also cost him time on his final lap.

Eddie Irvine crashed quite heavily on the approach to Rascasse, then switched to Schumacher's repaired race car to qualify seventh. The two Ferraris were split by Heinz-Harald Frentzen's fifth-placed Williams and Wurz's Benetton. The German was particularly happy with the chassis balance of his FW20 on this tight circuit, but his team-mate Jacques Villeneuve had a troubled time at Monaco from the start.

The reigning World Champion's free practice on Thursday ended on an uncomfortable note when he tangled with Rosset's Tyrrell at the swimming pool. The two cars slid together, intertwined, into the tyre barrier and Jacques made it quite clear that the Brazilian slow-coach should take more care when it came to looking in his mirrors.

On Saturday morning Jacques spun into the barrier at Ste Dévote, damaging the Williams's rear wing and suspension wishbones, and he had to be satisfied with 13th in the final line-up. Even so, he was not displeased with the feel of his car.

'The car handles better here than on most other tracks,' he admitted, 'it's just that this year we had a terrible qualifying session here. Even with a good start you cannot really overtake here unless you are at the front, so now it will be a matter of going through turn one and seeing who falls out.'

Mika Salo qualified the spare Arrows A19 a strong eighth, gearbox problems obliging him to switch from his race car. Despite the fact that the spare had originally been set up for team-mate Pedro Diniz, Salo did a good job and the Brazilian also performed respectably to post 12th-fastest time, despite being held up when Irvine crashed the Ferrari.

'We know we've got a good car,' said team chief Tom Walkinshaw, adding rather undiplomatically, 'we just need a proper engine now.'

Johnny Herbert squeezed his Sauber C17 into ninth place on the grid, frustrated after losing too much time with brake problems during the morning's free practice. He lined up two places ahead of team-mate Jean Alesi, the Frenchman grappling with what he regarded as excessive understeer as well as being one of many who lost time at the scene of Rosset's pirouette.

Jarno Trulli was happy with his Prost-Peugeot, qualifying tenth, but Olivier Panis's race chassis suffered an alternator failure which forced him to use the spare car, with which he struggled to qualify 18th.

In the Stewart-Ford camp, the first anniversary of the team's memorable second place in Monaco was celebrated in low-key mood after Rubens Barrichello spun at Rascasse, damaging his race chassis, which forced him to switch to the spare SF2. He ended the session 14th fastest, bugged by a troublesome rev limiter, but at least he was ahead of Jan Magnussen, who qualified the team's other car 17th.

Meanwhile, the Jordan team's fortunes went from bad to worse. Damon Hill crashed at the swimming pool a few laps into Thursday's practice session, then stopped with a seized gearbox in the afternoon shortly after Ralf Schumacher had rolled to a standstill with engine failure. Hill and Schumacher qualified 15th and 16th, reporting that the cars felt quite nicely balanced in the crucial hour-long battle for times, even though they had low levels of grip.

Like the sister car of team-mate Esteban Tuero, Shinji Nakano's Minardi suffered gearbox problems on Thursday, but the Japanese driver edged out the young Argentinian by a tenth of a second and two places for 19th slot on the grid, despite the fact that Tuero had F3 experience on this difficult track.

The two Minardis were split by Toranosuke Takagi's Tyrrell 026, the Japanese novice being the only member of the Ockham team to make the grid after Rosset wrote off his race car in Thursday's tangle with Villeneuve and failed to make the 107 per cent cut in the spare.

Mark Thompson/Allsport

Previous pages: **The streets of Monte Carlo present a testing examination and Mika Häkkinen confirmed the legitimacy of his claim to the World Championship crown with an assured victory.**

Mika Salo *(right)* **made the most of a rare opportunity to demonstrate his undoubted ability. Fifth in 1997 for Tyrrell, he went one better this time at the wheel of the underpowered Arrows.**

Below left: **The 1998 Concorde Agreement was signed at a ceremony presided over by Prince Albert of Monaco, bringing to an end the long-running dispute over the financial aspects of Grand Prix racing.**

MIKA Häkkinen's flawless drive to victory through the streets of Monaco was not simply another glittering entry in the fast-expanding McLaren-Mercedes record book, but many regarded it as possibly the decisive moment when the quietly spoken Finn made his break for the 1998 World Championship crown.

With his key rivals David Coulthard and Michael Schumacher both failing to increase their tally, Häkkinen ended the day 17 points ahead of his McLaren team-mate.

'I have competed here on seven occasions and have never before actually finished the race, although I did win one point in 1996,' said the delighted Finn. 'To win in Monaco is every driver's dream and to have achieved that today is something very special.'

In the closing stages Häkkinen had enough of an advantage to ease his pace and conserve the car. Earlier in the race he had tapped a barrier at the tight Rascasse hairpin before the pits and he was concerned lest his McLaren had suffered some suspension damage as a result.

In fact, he had no reason to worry and took the chequered flag 11.4s ahead of the impressive Giancarlo Fisichella, who drove his Benetton with great *élan*, despite a harmless spin, to beat Eddie Irvine's Ferrari into third place by almost half a minute.

Starting from pole position, Häkkinen just managed to squeeze Coulthard out on the crucial 300-metre sprint to Ste Dévote, the tricky off-camber right-hander which leads up the hill towards Casino Square. Thereafter he never looked back, trading fastest laps with his team-mate until Coulthard's engine blew up suddenly and comprehensively midway round the 18th lap.

'At the start, I tried to see if I could squeeze round the outside of Mika on the first corner, but I ran out of space and decided to drop back and assess the situation,' said Coulthard.

'I felt good physically and started to close on Mika again, deciding to try and put him under some pressure. But my engine blew without warning, and that was it, race over.'

The McLaren duo signalled its domination from the word go. Häkkinen was already 1.5s ahead at the end of the opening lap, but Fisichella's Benetton was running strongly in third place, protecting the Mercedes-engined cars from Michael Schumacher's fourth-placed Ferrari. Already the field had been depleted by one after Esteban Tuero's Minardi slid into the wall on the Massenet left-hander leading into Casino Square, less than half a minute after accelerating away from the grid.

DANKA
zepter

Williams snubs Briatore's new engine deal

REIGNING constructors' champion Williams publicly brushed aside plans for the flamboyant former Benetton team boss Flavio Briatore to take over as exclusive distributor for Mecachrome engines, which were to be supplied from the start of 1999 by a new company, Super Performance Competition Engineering.

Frank Williams made it quite clear that the formation of the new company had nothing to do with his existing agreement and did not affect his contract to use the Renault-based V10 engines through to the end of the 1999 season.

It was being speculated at Monaco that Briatore and Bernie Ecclestone now owned 40 per cent stakes in the new business with Mecachrome holding the remaining 20 per cent.

The engines to be used by Benetton and Williams in '99 would continue to be designed and developed by Renault Sport but would be distributed under the Supertec Sports brand name.

However, Williams made it clear that he wanted nothing to do with Briatore's company. In Monaco he issued a firm statement making the point that he had concluded his own deal with 'Renault's partner Mecachrome for the supply of engines'.

The statement went on to emphasise that 'This contract is for a fixed term of two years [until the end of 1999] and the name of the engine will continue to be known as Mecachrome.' Briatore wanted Williams and Benetton to tear up their existing deals and renegotiate fresh contracts with the new company, but Frank effectively dismissed these ideas as nonsense.

It was expected that the new British American Racing organisation would be the third Mecachrome/Supertec customer in 1999 with its Reynard-built F1 challenger, an assumption which eventually proved correct. Most F1 insiders judged that Briatore had become involved in this new project at Ecclestone's behest in an effort to even out possible future peaks and troughs in F1 engine supply.

The presence of Fisichella in third place was particularly beneficial for Coulthard who, on the second lap, straight-lined the harbour-front chicane. The Scot escaped penalty as he obviously gained no advantage from this misdemeanour, but had Schumacher been breathing down his neck it could have been a very different story.

By lap six Häkkinen was 2.7s ahead of Coulthard with Fisichella still under pressure from Schumacher, followed by Alexander Wurz and Heinz-Harald Frentzen, the Williams driver being hauled in by Eddie Irvine in the second Ferrari F300.

On lap ten Irvine tried to go for it at the Loews hairpin, gently tapping the Williams into the guard rail. It was just one of those unfortunate episodes bred by the follow-my-leader frustration which this circuit layout inevitably produces.

'Before the start I was worried that I would be stuck behind Frentzen as he was on soft tyres,' Irvine later explained. 'After the first few laps I could close on him and I had seen that he was weakest at the hairpin.

'I picked my moment and went down the inside. We made contact, but I was able to keep going. I was worried my car was damaged as we hit quite hard, but after the next couple of corners I realised that everything was all right.'

Needless to say, Frentzen was less than impressed with his colleague's move and was left with a long walk back to the pits during which he could cool down.

On lap 12 Rubens Barrichello's Stewart-Ford retired from 12th place ahead of Jacques Villeneuve's Williams after a rear suspension breakage. 'My times had been consistent and the car felt good,' reported the Brazilian. 'But all of a sudden, I felt something had broken at the rear of the car because it was jumping about and hitting the ground really hard. Maybe I'll go to the Casino tonight and my luck will change.'

Meanwhile Coulthard was gathering himself for a counter-attack against Häkkinen. The two McLaren drivers were extremely closely matched and set 12 fastest race laps between them between laps four and 12 as they battled for the initiative. Coulthard was coming back at Mika strongly when his engine expired spectacularly under braking for the chicane six laps later and he trickled into the escape road, where he abandoned his machine.

On lap 21 Häkkinen lapped Damon Hill's Jordan 198, which was running in 13th place just ahead of team-mate Ralf Schumacher. The Mugen Honda-engined cars were simply hopeless at Monaco, not only feeling unbalanced to drive but also bog slow. It was a state of affairs which seemed to be pushing the Silverstone-based team towards the brink of a major crisis.

The former World Champions were certainly falling like flies. Three laps after humiliating Hill, Häkkinen lapped reigning title holder Jacques Villeneuve's Williams FW20 going into Ste Dévote. On the same lap, Ralf Schumacher moved over to allow Fisichella and his brother Michael's Ferrari to lap his Jordan in the tunnel, but then lost control under braking, straight-lined the chicane and inadvertently overtook Hill as he did so. Shrewdly and quickly, Ralf slowed and waved Damon ahead again, thereby avoiding any penalty.

On lap 30 Michael Schumacher came in for a 7.4s refuelling stop. He retained third place, but now behind Wurz's Benetton B198 as Fisichella came in at the end of the following lap.

Just after Häkkinen made his sole refuelling stop at the end of lap 37, resuming with his lead intact, the Finn received a double bonus when Schumacher's Ferrari got involved in a vigorous barging match with Wurz's Benetton as they battled for second pace.

As they lapped a group of slower cars, Schumacher dived for the inside line under braking for the first-gear Loews hairpin, but Wurz had no intention of being intimidated into giving way, stayed with the Ferrari on the outside line and then cheekily repassed into the next right-hander.

Schumacher was clearly caught off-balance by his rival's audacity and barged back inside the Benetton to take second place as they accelerated out onto the waterfront. Unfortunately, as he did so, he hit Wurz quite hard, bending a left-rear suspension link on

Michael Schumacher attempts to scramble past the Benetton of Alexander Wurz at the Loews hairpin. The young Austrian refused to be intimidated and the pair collided when Schumacher tried his luck again a couple of corners further on.

Third fastest in qualifying, Giancarlo Fisichella *(below right)* survived a spin to take second place for Benetton at the flag after an impressively mature drive.

the Ferrari, which immediately forced him into the pits.

After a quick inspection, Schumacher's initial reaction was to climb out of the cockpit. However Ross Brawn, the team's technical director, instructed him to get back in immediately and refasten his belts while the mechanics worked methodically to repair the damage. Häkkinen had lapped him three times by the time the Ferrari driver accelerated back into the race, now firmly in last position and with very little hope of making up the ground he had lost.

Meanwhile Wurz came in for his refuelling stop at the end of lap 42, resuming in third place behind team-mate Fisichella, only to crash at high speed next time round through the tunnel. The Benetton team speculated that the accident might have been caused by damage sustained in the brush with Schumacher, or that the young Austrian may have just pushed too hard on cold tyres.

Either way, he was lucky to escape harm in his 170 mph impact against the barrier. Subsequent detailed examination revealed that the additional weight of the extra fuel load put into the car at the pit stop probably caused a suspension member, already damaged in the contact with Schumacher's Ferrari, finally to fail.

On lap 45 Irvine made his sole refuelling stop, retaining third place, while Ralf Schumacher retired his Jordan with broken suspension after hitting the barrier at Ste Dévote.

Meanwhile, Michael Schumacher was back in the chase. The relentless grind of Monaco imposes great technical strain on the cars and usually sees more than its fair share of mechanical casualties. With that in mind, Schumacher clearly hoped that perhaps a single championship point for sixth place might conceivably be within his grasp.

In fact, despite lapping consistently quickly on his return to the fray, Schumacher made little progress on the cars in front and finally settled for tenth, knocking his car's front wing off against Pedro Diniz's Arrows on the final lap after a spin at the chicane. By any standards, it was a deeply unconvincing display from the three-times Monaco winner.

'If we really fail to make more progress in terms of our competitive performance by the next race in Canada, our chances of winning the World Championship will have gone,' said Schumacher firmly.

'After the incident with Wurz, my car was damaged and I felt something was wrong at the rear, so I pitted. I

DIARY

Alain Prost calls for F1 refuelling ban, arguing that such a move would dramatically improve the quality of the racing.

New 1998 Concorde Agreement is finally signed at Monaco despite Swiss team owner Peter Sauber declining to append his signature.

Ron Dennis reassures David Coulthard by saying 'there is absolutely no doubt' he will be continuing with the McLaren-Mercedes team in 1999.

Despite talks with Ferrari, Alexander Wurz reaffirms that he will be staying with Benetton at least until the end of 1999.

Former F1 driver Eddie Cheever wins the Indy 500 at the wheel of his own team's Dallara-Aurora.

Photo below: Bryn Williams   Photo left: Publiracing Agency/Manfred Giet

Scooters often seem better suited to the narrow confines of the Principality than Grand Prix cars. Sporting an unfamiliar helmet, Monaco resident Jacques Villeneuve *(right)* prepares to negotiate the rush hour. Meanwhile Gerhard Berger *(below right)*, clearly enjoying his retirement from F1, offers a lift to fellow Ferrari hero Niki Lauda.

Bottom right: The Monaco balconies offer a variety of stunning views.

Opposite: Their teams' expectations inevitably differ, but the pressures are much the same. Pedro Diniz and David Coulthard prepare for trial by stopwatch.

Bryn Williams

GP Photo/Peter Nygaard

Bryn Williams

thought my race was over, but the mechanics managed to change the track rod and so I continued, but the car was not quite as good as before.

'Having lost three laps, there was not much more I could do. I had tried to pass Alex when he left the door open and we touched, but very lightly. It was just a normal race incident and I definitely do not blame him.'

Häkkinen, meanwhile, reeled off the remaining laps with all the disarming confidence of a man who knew his time had arrived. The silver McLaren MP4/13 seemed to shimmer between the barriers as if in some sort of freeze-frame slow motion. By any standards, it was the classic Monaco performance, making his progress through the tortuous streets appear slow compared with the rest, despite the fact that the timing screens recorded it as being appreciably quicker than that of anybody else on the circuit.

Häkkinen had set the fastest lap of the race as early as lap 29, after which he simply had to perform in survival mode, a task he successfully completed despite that brush with the barrier at Rascasse.

In the closing stages, the McLaren driver eased his pace to make sure of the most important victory of his career, slowing to the point that Fisichella's Benetton was only 11.47s behind at the chequered flag. It was nevertheless a great result for the young Italian.

'My target was to get onto the podium, but achieving second place is unbelievable,' he enthused. 'The race was very difficult at the beginning because Michael Schumacher was pushing very hard and I had some problems with the car. But after about 15 laps there was less understeer and I was able to pull away. Later I touched the inside barrier at Rascasse and spun, but Eddie [Irvine] was a long way behind me, so I was very lucky.'

The unexpected stars of the Monaco show were the two Arrows drivers. Mika Salo ran hard all the way, keeping Irvine in sight from eighth place in the opening sprint. He had got up to fifth by his sole refuelling stop on lap 41 and had moved into fourth, the last competitor not to be lapped, by the finish.

It was a fine effort which ranked with the Finn's non-stop run to fifth in the pouring rain for Tyrrell the previous year. But Mika was unimpressed. 'Without our qualifying problems, I think we might have finished on the rostrum,' he said. Diniz scrambled home in sixth despite that near-miss with Schumacher Senior on the last lap.

Separating the two Arrows A19s, Jacques Villeneuve climbed doggedly through from 13th on the grid to take fifth place at the chequered flag. Jacques had opted for the harder-compound Goodyears, but when he qualified so badly he chose to run a heavy fuel load from the start, staying out until lap 54 of the 78-lap race before making his sole pit stop.

The strategy worked quite well and Villeneuve made up a lot of places. It was just a shame that Irvine's intervention prevented Frentzen from showing what he could have done on the softer Goodyear compound from further up the grid.

The Sauber twins joined 'HH' in opting for the soft compound and the fast-starting Jean Alesi looked bang on course for a fine fifth place thanks to a two-stop strategy. Then he began to lose gears and his transmission failed shortly before the end. By contrast, Johnny Herbert had a disappointing race, boxed in for much of the distance behind Jarno Trulli's Prost. He wound up seventh.

Two laps down in eighth place, Damon Hill finished the day an extremely unhappy man. 'All weekend, nothing we have done has been good enough and it is quite tough to compete under those circumstances,' he said with masterly understatement and admirable self-control.

Eddie Jordan was quick to absolve his drivers of any blame for this unfortunate state of affairs. 'It was a pretty sorry end to a very, very difficult weekend,' he shrugged. 'The circuit here is unique, but there really are no excuses for our performance. I know we need to do a lot of thinking and decide how to eradicate our problems.

'There will have to be some changes because we need to become more competitive as soon as we can, although I am aware that there are no quick fixes. It is very difficult to be upbeat in circumstances like this, especially when everybody in the team puts their life and soul into it. But I am the team leader and I must try to give some encouragement, because everyone needs to be motivated again.'

Had they heard those words, Mika Häkkinen and the McLaren team would have been able to identify with the frustration and grief which inevitably attends those who are trying to climb the greasy pole to the pinnacle of F1 achievement. But now McLaren was back on top in one of its most familiar hunting grounds.

On the track which Alain Prost and Ayrton Senna had made their own in the past, now it had been Häkkinen's turn to post a memorable win for the famous Woking team. It was McLaren International's ninth victory through the streets of the pint-sized Principality.

Photo below: Mark Thompson/Allsport   Photo left: Michael Roberts

GRAND PRIX DE MONACO

21–24 MAY 1998

MONTE CARLO

Race distance: 78 laps, 163.186 miles/262.624 km

Race weather: Dry, hot and sunny

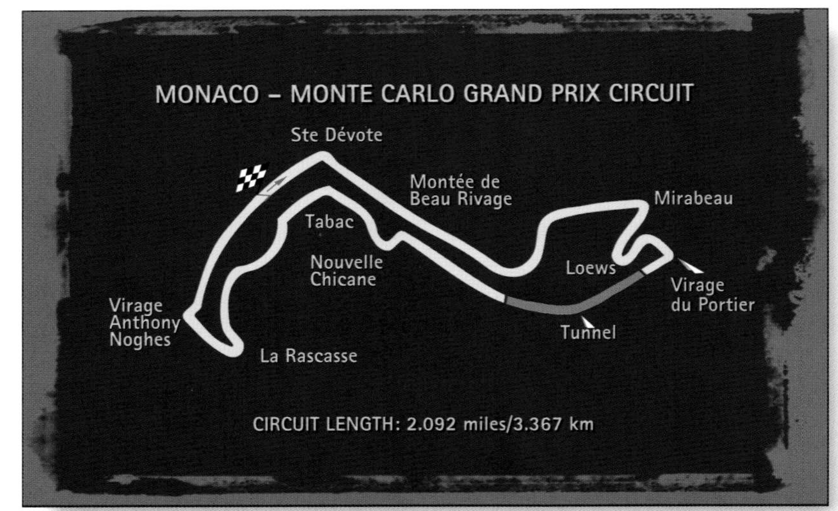

Pos.	Driver	Nat.	No.	Entrant	Car/Engine	Tyres	Laps	Time/Retirement	Speed (mph/km/h)
1	**Mika Häkkinen**	**SF**	**8**	**West McLaren Mercedes**	**McLaren MP4/13-Mercedes FO110G V10**	**B**	**78**	**1h 51m 23.595s**	**87.898/141.458**
2	**Giancarlo Fisichella**	**I**	**5**	**Mild Seven Benetton Playlife**	**Benetton B198-Playlife V10**	**B**	**78**	**1h 51m 35.070s**	**87.747/141.216**
3	**Eddie Irvine**	**GB**	**4**	**Scuderia Ferrari Marlboro**	**Ferrari F300 047 V10**	**G**	**78**	**1h 52m 04.973s**	**87.357/140.588**
4	**Mika Salo**	**SF**	**17**	**Danka Zepter Arrows**	**Arrows A19 V10**	**B**	**78**	**1h 52m 23.958s**	**87.111/140.192**
5	**Jacques Villeneuve**	**CDN**	**1**	**Winfield Williams**	**Williams FW20-Mecachrome GC37/01 V10**	**G**	**77**		
6	**Pedro Diniz**	**BR**	**16**	**Danka Zepter Arrows**	**Arrows A19 V10**	**B**	**77**		
7	Johnny Herbert	GB	15	Red Bull Sauber Petronas	Sauber C17-Petronas SPE01D V10	G	77		
8	Damon Hill	GB	9	B&H Jordan Mugen Honda	Jordan 198-Mugen Honda MF310C V10	G	76		
9	Shinji Nakano	J	22	Fondmetal Minardi Ford	Minardi M198-Ford Zetec-R V10	B	76		
10	Michael Schumacher	D	3	Scuderia Ferrari Marlboro	Ferrari F300 047 V10	G	76		
11	Toranosuke Takagi	J	21	Tyrrell Ford	Tyrrell 026-Ford Zetec-R V10	G	76		
12	Jean Alesi	F	14	Red Bull Sauber Petronas	Sauber C17-Petronas SPE01D V10	G	72	Gearbox	
	Jarno Trulli	I	12	Gauloises Prost Peugeot	Prost AP01-Peugeot A16 V10	B	56	Gearbox	
	Olivier Panis	F	11	Gauloises Prost Peugeot	Prost AP01-Peugeot A16 V10	B	49	Suspension	
	Ralf Schumacher	D	10	B&H Jordan Mugen Honda	Jordan 198-Mugen Honda MF310C V10	G	44	Collision damage	
	Alexander Wurz	A	6	Mild Seven Benetton Playlife	Benetton B198-Playlife V10	B	42	Accident	
	Jan Magnussen	DK	19	Stewart Ford	Stewart SF2-Ford Zetec-R V10	B	30	Suspension	
	David Coulthard	GB	7	West McLaren Mercedes	McLaren MP4/13-Mercedes FO110G V10	B	17	Engine	
	Rubens Barrichello	BR	18	Stewart Ford	Stewart SF2-Ford Zetec-R V10	B	11	Suspension	
	Heinz-Harald Frentzen	D	2	Winfield Williams	Williams FW20-Mecachrome GC37/01 V10	G	9	Collision with Irvine	
	Esteban Tuero	RA	23	Fondmetal Minardi Ford	Minardi M198-Ford Zetec-R V10	B	0	Accident	
DNQ	Ricardo Rosset	BR	20	Tyrrell Ford	Tyrrell 026-Ford Zetec-R V10	G			

Fastest lap: Häkkinen, on lap 29, 1m 22.948s, 90.801 mph/146.130 km/h (record).

Previous lap record: Michael Schumacher (F1 Ferrari F310B V10), 1m 53.315s, 66.447 mph/106.937 km/h (1997).

B – Bridgestone G – Goodyear

All results and data © FIA 1998

Grid order	1	2	3	4	5	6	7	8	9	10	11	12	13	14	15	16	17	18	19	20	21	22	23	24	25	26	27	28	29	30
8 HÄKKINEN	8	8	8	8	8	8	8	8	8	8	8	8	8	8	8	8	8	8	8	8	8	8	8	8	8	8	8	8	8	8
7 COULTHARD	7	7	7	7	7	7	7	7	7	7	7	7	7	7	7	7	7	5	5	5	5	5	5	5	5	5	5	5	5	5
5 FISICHELLA	5	5	5	5	5	5	5	5	5	5	5	5	5	5	5	5	5	3	3	3	3	3	3	3	3	3	3	3	3	6
3 M. SCHUMACHER	3	3	3	3	3	3	3	3	3	3	3	3	3	3	3	3	3	6	6	6	6	6	6	6	6	6	6	6	6	3
2 FRENTZEN	6	6	6	6	6	6	6	6	6	6	6	6	6	6	6	6	6	4	4	4	4	4	4	4	4	4	4	4	4	4
6 WURZ	2	2	2	2	2	2	2	2	2	4	4	4	4	4	4	4	4	17	17	17	17	17	17	17	17	17	17	17	17	17
4 IRVINE	4	4	4	4	4	4	4	4	4	17	17	17	17	17	17	17	17	14	14	14	14	14	14	14	14	14	14	14	14	14
17 SALO	17	17	17	17	17	17	17	17	17	14	14	14	14	14	14	14	14	12	12	12	12	12	12	12	12	12	12	12	12	12
15 HERBERT	14	14	14	14	14	14	14	14	14	12	12	12	12	12	12	12	12	15	15	15	15	15	15	15	15	15	15	15	15	15
12 TRULLI	12	12	12	12	12	12	12	12	12	15	15	15	15	15	15	15	15	16	16	16	16	16	16	16	16	16	16	16	16	16
14 ALESI	15	15	15	15	15	15	15	15	15	16	16	16	16	16	16	16	16	1	1	1	1	1	1	1	1	1	1	1	1	1
16 DINIZ	16	16	16	16	16	16	16	16	16	18	18	1	1	1	1	1	1	19	19	19	19	19	19	19	19	19	19	19	19	19
1 VILLENEUVE	18	18	18	18	18	18	18	18	18	1	1	19	19	19	19	19	19	9	9	9	9	9	9	9	9	9	9	9	9	9
18 BARRICHELLO	1	1	1	1	1	1	1	1	1	19	19	9	9	9	9	9	9	10	10	10	10	10	10	10	10	10	10	10	10	10
9 HILL	19	19	19	19	19	19	19	19	19	9	9	10	10	10	10	10	10	21	21	21	21	21	21	21	21	21	21	21	21	21
10 R. SCHUMACHER	9	9	9	9	9	9	9	9	9	10	10	21	21	21	21	21	21	22	22	22	22	22	22	22	22	22	22	22	22	22
19 MAGNUSSEN	10	10	10	10	10	10	10	10	10	21	21	11	11	11	11	22	22	11	11	11	11	11	11	11	11	11	11	11	11	11
11 PANIS	21	21	21	21	21	21	21	21	21	11	11	22	22	22	22	11	11													
22 NAKANO	11	11	11	11	11	11	11	11	11	22	22																			
21 TAKAGI	22	22	22	22	22	22	22	22	22																					
23 TUERO																														

Grid order	31	32	33	34	35	36	37	38	39	40	41	42	43	44	45	46	47	48	49	50	51	52	53	54	55	56	57	58	59
8 HÄKKINEN	8	8	8	8	8	8	8	8	8	8	8	8	8	8	8	8	8	8	8	8	8	8	8	8	8	8	8	8	8
7 COULTHARD	6	6	6	6	6	6	6	6	6	6	6	5	5	5	5	5	5	5	5	5	5	5	5	5	5	5	5	5	5
5 FISICHELLA	3	3	3	3	3	3	3	5	5	5	5	4	4	4	4	4	4	4	4	4	4	4	4	4	4	4	4	4	4
3 M. SCHUMACHER	5	5	5	5	5	5	5	4	4	4	4	6	14	14	14	14	14	14	14	14	14	14	14	14	17	17	17	17	17
2 FRENTZEN	4	4	4	4	4	4	4	17	17	17	17	14	17	17	17	17	17	17	17	17	17	17	17	17	14	14	14	14	14
6 WURZ	17	17	17	17	17	17	17	14	14	14	14	17	1	1	1	1	1	1	1	1	1	1	1	1	1	1	1	1	1
4 IRVINE	14	14	14	14	14	14	14	16	16	16	16	16	16	16	16	16	16	16	16	16	16	16	16	16	16	16	16	16	16
17 SALO	12	12	12	12	12	12	15	1	1	1	1	1	10	15	15	15	15	15	15	15	15	15	15	15	15	15	15	15	15
15 HERBERT	15	15	15	15	15	15	16	9	9	9	9	9	15	9	9	9	9	9	9	9	9	9	9	9	9	9	9	9	9
12 TRULLI	16	16	16	16	16	16	1	10	10	10	10	10	9	12	12	12	12	12	12	12	12	12	12	12	12	12	22	22	22
14 ALESI	1	1	1	1	1	1	9	15	15	15	15	15	12	10	22	22	22	22	22	22	22	22	22	22	22	22	21	21	21
16 DINIZ	9	9	9	9	9	9	10	12	12	12	12	12	22	22	21	21	21	21	21	21	21	21	21	21	21	21	3	3	3
1 VILLENEUVE	10	10	10	10	10	10	12	21	21	21	21	21	21	21	11	11	11	11	11	3	3	3	3	3	3	3			
18 BARRICHELLO	21	21	21	21	21	21	21	22	22	22	22	22	11	11	3	3	3	3	3										
9 HILL	22	22	22	22	22	22	22	11	11	11	11	11	3	3															
10 R. SCHUMACHER	11	11	11	11	11	11	11	3	3	3	3	3																	
19 MAGNUSSEN																													
11 PANIS																													
22 NAKANO																													
21 TAKAGI																													
23 TUERO																													

Pit stop

One lap behind leader

STARTING GRID

	8 **HÄKKINEN** McLaren
7 **COULTHARD** McLaren	
	5 **FISICHELLA** Benetton
3 **M. SCHUMACHER** Ferrari	
	2 **FRENTZEN** Williams
6 **WURZ** Benetton	
	4 **IRVINE** Ferrari
17 **SALO** Arrows	
	15 **HERBERT** Sauber
12 **TRULLI** Prost	
	14 **ALESI** Sauber
16 **DINIZ** Arrows	
	1 **VILLENEUVE** Williams
18 **BARRICHELLO** Stewart	
	9 **HILL** Jordan
10 **R. SCHUMACHER** Jordan	
	19 **MAGNUSSEN** Stewart
11 **PANIS** Prost	
	22 **NAKANO** Minardi
21 **TAKAGI** Tyrrell	
	23 **TUERO** Minardi

Did not qualify:

ROSSET (Tyrrell)

3	64	65	66	67	68	69	70	71	72	73	74	75	76	77	78	●
8	8	8	8	8	8	8	8	8	8	8	8	8	8	8	8	1
5	5	5	5	5	5	5	5	5	5	5	5	5	5	5	5	2
4	4	4	4	4	4	4	4	4	4	4	4	4	4	4	4	3
7	17	17	17	17	17	17	17	17	17	17	17	17	17	17	17	4
4	14	14	14	14	14	14	14	14	14	1	1	1	1	1		5
1	1	1	1	1	1	1	1	1	1	16	16	16	16	16		6
6	16	16	16	16	16	16	16	16	16	15	15	15	15	15		
5	15	15	15	15	15	15	15	15	15	9	9	9	9			
9	9	9	9	9	9	9	9	9	9	22	22	22	22			
2	22	22	22	22	22	22	22	22	22	3	3	3	3			
1	21	21	21	21	21	21	21	3	3	21	21	21	21			
3	3	3	3	3	3	3	3	21	21							

TIME SHEETS

QUALIFYING

Weather: Dry, hot and sunny

Pos.	Driver	Car	Laps	Time
1	Mika Häkkinen	McLaren-Mercedes	12	1m 19.798s
2	David Coulthard	McLaren-Mercedes	11	1m 20.137s
3	Giancarlo Fisichella	Benetton-Playlife	12	1m 20.368s
4	Michael Schumacher	Ferrari	11	1m 20.702s
5	Heinz-Harald Frentzen	Williams-Mecachrome	12	1m 20.729s
6	Alexander Wurz	Benetton-Playlife	12	1m 20.955s
7	Eddie Irvine	Ferrari	11	1m 21.712s
8	Mika Salo	Arrows	11	1m 22.144s
9	Johnny Herbert	Sauber-Petronas	11	1m 22.157s
10	Jarno Trulli	Prost-Peugeot	12	1m 22.238s
11	Jean Alesi	Sauber-Petronas	12	1m 22.257s
12	Pedro Diniz	Arrows	12	1m 22.355s
13	Jacques Villeneuve	Williams-Mecachrome	12	1m 22.468s
14	Rubens Barrichello	Stewart-Ford	11	1m 22.540s
15	Damon Hill	Jordan-Mugen Honda	12	1m 23.151s
16	Ralf Schumacher	Jordan-Mugen Honda	12	1m 23.263s
17	Jan Magnussen	Stewart-Ford	12	1m 23.411s
18	Olivier Panis	Prost-Peugeot	11	1m 23.536s
19	Shinji Nakano	Minardi-Ford	12	1m 23.957s
20	Toranosuke Takagi	Tyrrell-Ford	12	1m 24.024s
21	Esteban Tuero	Minardi-Ford	12	1m 24.031s
22	Ricardo Rosset	Tyrrell-Ford	9	1m 25.737s

107 per cent time: 1m 25.383s

THURSDAY FREE PRACTICE

Weather: Light overcast, warm

Pos.	Driver	Laps	Time
1	Mika Häkkinen	31	1m 21.937s
2	Giancarlo Fisichella	36	1m 22.205s
3	David Coulthard	29	1m 22.757s
4	Heinz-Harald Frentzen	42	1m 23.656s
5	Michael Schumacher	24	1m 23.685s
6	Eddie Irvine	43	1m 23.765s
7	Johnny Herbert	43	1m 23.914s
8	Alexander Wurz	40	1m 23.946s
9	Jacques Villeneuve	38	1m 24.081s
10	Jarno Trulli	32	1m 24.191s
11	Pedro Diniz	43	1m 24.735s
12	Jean Alesi	35	1m 24.901s
13	Olivier Panis	29	1m 25.119s
14	Mika Salo	41	1m 25.400s
15	Jan Magnussen	33	1m 25.836s
16	Rubens Barrichello	26	1m 25.863s
17	Damon Hill	22	1m 25.947s
18	Ricardo Rosset	47	1m 26.625s
19	Toranosuke Takagi	43	1m 26.761s
20	Ralf Schumacher	24	1m 27.160s
21	Esteban Tuero	22	1m 27.844s
22	Shinji Nakano	16	1m 28.652s

SATURDAY FREE PRACTICE

Weather: Mild and warm

Pos.	Driver	Laps	Time
1	Giancarlo Fisichella	29	1m 21.145s
2	David Coulthard	19	1m 22.091s
3	Mika Salo	22	1m 22.171s
4	Heinz-Harald Frentzen	31	1m 22.223s
5	Eddie Irvine	36	1m 22.314s
6	Alexander Wurz	29	1m 22.683s
7	Mika Häkkinen	21	1m 22.702s
8	Jarno Trulli	29	1m 22.830s
9	Rubens Barrichello	21	1m 23.100s
10	Jacques Villeneuve	28	1m 23.579s
11	Jean Alesi	20	1m 23.777s
12	Jan Magnussen	30	1m 23.823s
13	Esteban Tuero	23	1m 24.250s
14	Ralf Schumacher	32	1m 24.312s
15	Toranosuke Takagi	34	1m 24.456s
16	Damon Hill	37	1m 24.698s
17	Pedro Diniz	21	1m 24.759s
18	Johnny Herbert	17	1m 25.110s
19	Shinji Nakano	30	1m 25.512s
20	Ricardo Rosset	32	1m 25.615s
21	Olivier Panis	5	1m 29.010s
	Michael Schumacher	0	no time

WARM-UP

Weather: Sunny and warm

Pos.	Driver	Laps	Time
1	Mika Häkkinen	11	1m 23.878s
2	Michael Schumacher	12	1m 24.107s
3	David Coulthard	13	1m 24.199s
4	Alexander Wurz	14	1m 24.493s
5	Eddie Irvine	16	1m 24.611s
6	Mika Salo	14	1m 24.896s
7	Giancarlo Fisichella	12	1m 25.151s
8	Rubens Barrichello	16	1m 25.688s
9	Toranosuke Takagi	14	1m 25.861s
10	Jean Alesi	15	1m 25.887s
11	Heinz-Harald Frentzen	16	1m 25.920s
12	Ralf Schumacher	15	1m 26.348s
13	Shinji Nakano	12	1m 26.433s
14	Pedro Diniz	12	1m 26.650s
15	Jacques Villeneuve	12	1m 26.654s
16	Jan Magnussen	13	1m 27.012s
17	Johnny Herbert	13	1m 27.118s
18	Jarno Trulli	12	1m 27.173s
19	Damon Hill	13	1m 27.602s
20	Olivier Panis	6	1m 27.786s
21	Esteban Tuero	15	1m 28.287s

RACE FASTEST LAPS

Weather: Dry, hot and sunny

Driver	Time	Lap
Mika Häkkinen	1m 22.948s	29
David Coulthard	1m 22.955s	18
Michael Schumacher	1m 23.189s	64
Giancarlo Fisichella	1m 23.594s	26
Alexander Wurz	1m 23.970s	41
Jacques Villeneuve	1m 24.381s	70
Pedro Diniz	1m 24.456s	40
Eddie Irvine	1m 24.457s	29
Jean Alesi	1m 24.539s	51
Mika Salo	1m 24.582s	39
Olivier Panis	1m 24.874s	33
Johnny Herbert	1m 25.053s	66
Shinji Nakano	1m 26.054s	70
Damon Hill	1m 26.091s	69
Ralf Schumacher	1m 26.228s	24
Jarno Trulli	1m 26.501s	26
Toranosuke Takagi	1m 26.506s	59
Jan Magnussen	1m 26.637s	25
Heinz-Harald Frentzen	1m 26.777s	6
Rubens Barrichello	1m 27.719s	10

CHASSIS LOG BOOK

1	Villeneuve	Williams FW20/5
2	Frentzen	Williams FW20/4
	spare	Williams FW20/3
3	M. Schumacher	Ferrari F300/184
4	Irvine	Ferrari F300/185
	spare	Ferrari F300/181
5	Fisichella	Benetton B198/6
6	Wurz	Benetton B198/1
	spare	Benetton B198/4
7	Coulthard	McLaren MP4/13/3
8	Häkkinen	McLaren MP4/13/4
	spare	McLaren MP4/13/5
9	Hill	Jordan 198/3
10	R. Schumacher	Jordan 198/4
	spare	Jordan 198/1
11	Panis	Prost AP01/5
12	Trulli	Prost AP01/3
	spare	Prost AP01/2
14	Alesi	Sauber C17/3
15	Herbert	Sauber C17/4
	spare	Sauber C17/2
16	Diniz	Arrows A19/4
17	Salo	Arrows A19/3
	spare	Arrows A19/1
18	Barrichello	Stewart SF2/4
19	Magnussen	Stewart SF2/3
	spare	Stewart SF2/2
20	Rosset	Tyrrell 026/1
21	Takagi	Tyrrell 026/2
	spare	Tyrrell 026/3
22	Nakano	Minardi M198/4
23	Tuero	Minardi M198/3
	spare	Minardi M198/2

POINTS TABLES

Drivers

1	Mika Häkkinen	46
2	David Coulthard	29
3	Michael Schumacher	24
4	Eddie Irvine	15
5	Alexander Wurz	9
6 =	Heinz-Harald Frentzen	8
6 =	Jacques Villeneuve	8
8	Giancarlo Fisichella	7
9 =	Jean Alesi	3
9 =	Mika Salo	3
11	Rubens Barrichello	2
12 =	Johnny Herbert	1
12 =	Pedro Diniz	1

Constructors

1	McLaren	75
2	Ferrari	39
3 =	Williams	16
3 =	Benetton	16
5 =	Sauber	4
5 =	Arrows	4
7	Stewart	2

FIA WORLD CHAMPIONSHIP • ROUND 7

CANADIAN

grand prix

Paul-Henri Cahier

DIARY

Ford is shaken by news that Cosworth has been sold to Audi as part of the VW group's purchase of Rolls-Royce.

Mike Gascoyne tipped to leave Tyrrell to join Jordan as chief designer.

Alex Zanardi scores third CART win of the year in Detroit with Ganassi team Reynard-Honda.

Heinz-Harald Frentzen considers switch to CART for 1999.

Previous pages: Michael Schumacher made significant inroads into Mika Häkkinen's points advantage with victory in an incident-packed race.

Right: Jan Magnussen leads Stewart team-mate Rubens Barrichello. The first championship point of his F1 career was not enough to save the unfortunate Dane's place in the team.

Below: Craig Pollock, Adrian Reynard and Rick Gorne, key figures in the new British American Racing team, which would be joining the Grand Prix scene in 1999, were interested spectators in Montreal.

MONTREAL QUALIFYING

Even before Saturday qualifying at Montreal the news came through from Le Mans that both Mercedes had retired. The German team's high-profile return to the famous endurance event had been regarded as sufficiently important to keep Mercedes motor sport manager Norbert Haug away from the Canadian Grand Prix. Now it was down to McLaren to make up for this abject disappointment.

In Saturday morning's free practice session the two McLarens dead-heated for fastest time, but come official qualifying David Coulthard just managed to get the upper hand to clinch pole by less than one-tenth of a second.

Mika Häkkinen, who encountered traffic on his first two runs, eventually made some set-up changes for his final runs which didn't work to best effect. 'It was easier to drive, but not quicker,' he admitted.

Michael Schumacher qualified his Ferrari F300 third ahead of Giancarlo Fisichella's Benetton and an optimistic Ralf Schumacher's Jordan, leaving both Williams FW20s over a second shy of the front-running pace.

Sutton Motorsport Images

Obviously it was too much to hope that Jacques Villeneuve might celebrate the 20th anniversary of his father Gilles's maiden F1 victory in Montreal's first Grand Prix with a home-town win. Yet the heavily redesigned Williams was at least expected to allow him to produce his most convincing performance of the season so far.

Improvements included changes to the rear suspension geometry, repositioned exhaust pipes and revised aerodynamics. Prior to his home race Villeneuve tested this revised package at Monza, where he split the McLarens of Coulthard and Häkkinen. 'The car is now much better,' he said. 'We haven't quite found the limit yet because we are still doing work on the set-up. But it is getting better and represents a very positive step.'

Despite this, Villeneuve and team-mate Heinz-Harald Frentzen managed only sixth and seventh on the grid. Both were handicapped by Goodyear's softer 'option' tyre compound being a little too hard for the cool conditions, and the longer-wheelbase guise wasn't really expected to be ideal for this point-and-squirt circuit. Magny-Cours and Silverstone were thought likely to show it in a more favourable light.

On Friday Coulthard had had an off-track moment, then ripped his car's nose section off on one of the marker cones at the chicane before the pits, the Scot finishing the day fourth fastest behind Jean Alesi's Sauber.

Coulthard's incident came only minutes after Johnny Herbert's Sauber lost its front wing on the final corner before the pits, scattering debris all down the start/finish straight before he stopped the car just beyond the end of the pit lane. Since he had also lost a lot of time with brake system problems during the session, his 11th-fastest time was quite an achievement.

Like Williams, Ferrari was benefiting from a further revised Goodyear tyre compound which both teams hoped would enable them to make further inroads into the hitherto superior performance of McLaren's Bridgestone rubber.

Schumacher was satisfied with his third place, but Eddie Irvine spent most of Saturday morning in a gravel trap and then got lost on chassis set-up, qualifying eighth. Alongside Michael on the second row of the grid was an on-form Fisichella, who was really getting the best out of the Benetton B198 package, although team-mate Alexander Wurz was struggling with brake problems, qualifying 11th on the first anniversary of his F1 debut.

Using a revised Mugen Honda V10, worth perhaps another 20 bhp, the Jordan team at last looked as though it might be poised to turn the corner in qualifying. Ralf Schumacher lined up fifth, barely a second away from Coulthard's best.

'I had expected us to be between eighth and 12th,' said Ralf, 'so I am really happy about being fifth. The car suits this circuit much better than Monaco and the new Goodyear tyres and qualifying engine have made a big difference.'

For his part, Damon Hill was less effusive, qualifying a disappointing tenth. 'I had to fight the car today and want to compare the set-ups,' he said, 'because I basically found it difficult to get a good time out of it.'

Just ahead of Hill in the top ten came Alesi's Sauber C17, the Frenchman frustrated by excessive understeer. 'I lost my chance to improve on my last run when I pushed too hard and the understeer increased,' he said, 'but on the positive side the new engine [designated SPE02D] which we ran today is a lot better. It is stronger at the top end and driveability has improved.'

Clutch problems cost Herbert crucial track time on Saturday morning and that knocked on into qualifying, leaving him struggling slightly in 12th place. 'The middle section of the lap gave me the biggest problem, because the car was still moving around too much whenever I tried to push really hard,' he said later. 'I'm frustrated, because I know it could have been better here.'

In the Stewart-Ford camp, there was also a prevailing mood of acute disappointment. Rubens Barrichello found himself restricted to just eight laps thanks to a crank sensor malfunction, qualifying 13th, while Jan Magnussen had to use the spare SF2 after crashing quite heavily in the morning's free practice session and could not improve upon 20th-fastest time.

'I'm very disappointed,' said Rubens. 'I gave it my best, but things didn't go my way right from the start when I had trouble with my braking.' Magnussen complained of a lack of traction, but damage to his race chassis meant he would have to stick with the spare car for the race.

In 14th and 15th places came the Prost AP01s of Jarno Trulli and Olivier Panis, neither driver being able to develop adequate tyre temperatures despite the incorporation of some suspension revisions for this race. They just squeezed in ahead of Tora Takagi's Tyrrell 026, the Japanese driver using one of the new P10-spec Ford customer V10s for qualifying. Team-mate Ricardo Rosset made it into the race in 22nd and last position, a mere whisker behind Esteban Tuero's Minardi.

Sandwiching Shinji Nakano's 18th-placed Minardi were the Arrows A19s of Mika Salo and Pedro Diniz. There were no mechanical problems to speak of, but both drivers felt that the available Bridgestone tyre compound was too hard for their cars. 'I really hope the weather will get warmer for race day,' shrugged Salo, 'as this will suit our tyres better.'

MICHAEL Schumacher applied a gentle touch to the brakes of the McLaren-Mercedes advance for the second time this season at Montreal's Circuit Gilles Villeneuve when he scored his second consecutive victory for Ferrari in the Canadian Grand Prix. However, while his 1997 triumph had certainly been fortuitous, this latest success was downright controversial. The German driver survived not only two routine refuelling stops, but also an extra visit to the pit lane to take a ten-second stop-go penalty after pushing Williams driver Heinz-Harald Frentzen off the circuit as he was accelerating back into the race after his first visit to the pit lane.

One might have expected Schumacher to have adopted a low-key and somewhat apologetic approach after this incident, but that would be to misunderstand the man. No sooner had he descended from the rostrum than he launched a verbal assault on Damon Hill, accusing his old rival of attempting to force him off the track as he battled with the Jordan driver for second place on lap 38.

'You don't want to hear the words I thought at that moment,' said Schu-

Bryn Williams

macher, 'because that was purely dangerous. If someone wants to kill you, he can do it in a different way, because going down there [the straight before the pits] you are doing 180 mph and moving off-line three times is impossible.'

By contrast, Schumacher excused his part in the collision with Frentzen, remarking, 'If it was my fault, I apologise, but I just didn't see him at all.'

Frentzen viewed the incident in a very different light. 'He's the guy who is always complaining about people coming out of the pits and moving straight onto the racing line,' he fumed. 'I am really angry about what he did.'

Meanwhile David Coulthard's hopes of eroding the points advantage built up by his McLaren team-mate Mika Häkkinen at the head of the World Championship points table sustained another frustrating setback. This time both the Mercedes-engined cars retired with rare mechanical trouble, handing Schumacher a fast lane to his second victory of the season.

Schumacher, who beat Giancarlo Fisichella's Benetton into second place after a spirited showing by the young Italian star, returned from Canada splitting the McLaren drivers in the title stakes. After a race which for much of its distance seemed to have degenerated into a wholesale barging match, Schumacher now found himself 12 points behind Häkkinen, but five ahead of the luckless Coulthard.

It was certainly bad news for the Scot as this was a race at which he seemed to have the upper hand. He qualified on pole for the third time this season and led the pack into the first corner in dull, overcast but thankfully dry weather conditions.

Unfortunately, in the McLarens' wake, the race exploded into nerve-jangling chaos after Ralf Schumacher stalled his Jordan-Mugen Honda on the third row of the grid. Cars dodged in all directions to avoid the stationary machine, with the result that the second half of the field was well scrambled as it funnelled into the tight left-hander after the pits.

Alexander Wurz's Benetton apparently attempted to outbrake Jean Alesi's Sauber on the tight inside line, and clipped the front of the Swiss car as Alesi moved over to make room for Heinz-Harald Frentzen's Williams to take the racing line through the turn.

In a moment Wurz found himself launched into a spectacular series of somersaults, his car happily landing on its belly in the gravel trap on the outside of the corner. Alesi, his Sauber team-mate Johnny Herbert and the Prost of Jarno Trulli were also all involved and red flags were duly waved all round the circuit to bring the event to a premature halt.

As the race had not run more than two laps the grid lined up again to compete over the original 69-lap distance. For the restart, Alesi took the spare Sauber, Wurz the spare Benetton and Trulli the spare Prost. Herbert's Sauber was returned to the team garage, repaired and duly joined the restarted race from the pit lane.

This certainly was not Alesi's day for at the restart Ralf Schumacher hurtled past going into the first corner, spinning in the middle of the pack and again scattering cars in all directions. This time the mayhem ended with Trulli's spare Prost ending up perched over the back of Alesi's Sauber.

Ralf attributed his excursion to a clutch problem. 'On the first start I stalled the engine,' he confessed. 'At the second start I put the revs higher and that was too much for the clutch. There was a little drive to begin with, but at the first corner when I shifted down there was no more drive to the rear wheels, and no engine braking, so I spun.'

Even so, Alesi was not amused. 'At the start, the trick is to know when you have achieved enough,' he complained. 'Not to be greedy and try to pass too many people. There are some younger drivers who do not seem to understand this.

'Both times I made good starts, but at the first one I had Wurz's car rolling across the top of me, and at the second I had Trulli's sitting on top of me – after I had already lost my nose when Irvine moved across me!'

In the middle of all this, Häkkinen suddenly lost speed and he trailed slowly round at the tail of the field to retire at the end of the opening lap with gearbox trouble. Unfortunately for him, the F1 points leader was not given the chance to switch to the spare car as this time there was no red flag, the field simply forming up in an orderly queue behind the safety car while the track was cleared.

At the head of the crocodile was Coulthard, followed by Schumacher's

Paul-Henri Cahier

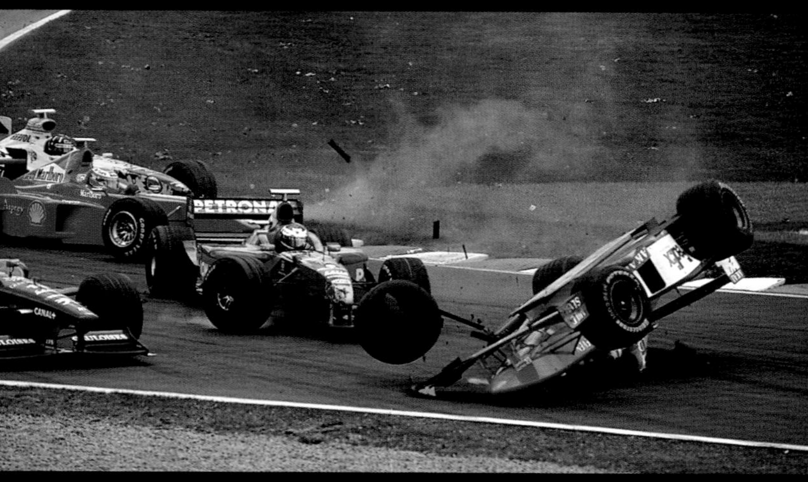

Crash sequence: Nigel Snowdon

Above left: Jacques Villeneuve locks a wheel as he brakes for the first corner at the first start, with his Williams team-mate Heinz-Harald Frentzen slotting in behind while the Sauber of Jean Alesi takes a tighter line.

Opposite: Alexander Wurz's Benetton is flipped into a terrifying barrel roll after tangling with the Sauber as the Austrian attempted to squeeze past Alesi on the inside, forcing the rest of the midfield bunch to take evasive action.

Above: Wurz is a helpless passenger as his car somersaults into the gravel trap on the outside of the turn, minus its front wheels. Mercifully, the Benetton ended its gyrations the right way up and he was able to walk away unhurt.

Below: Alesi was involved in another potentially disastrous incident at the restart, when the Prost of Jarno Trulli rode up on top of his Sauber and came to rest inches from the hapless Frenchman's head.

Photo left: Simon Scott   Top photo: Sporting Pictures (UK) Ltd

Benetton's Giancarlo Fisichella looked set for his first Grand Prix victory, but the Italian had no answer to Michael Schumacher's relentless counter-attack.

Ferrari, Fisichella and the Williams FW20s of Jacques Villeneuve and Heinz-Harald Frentzen. Irvine trailed into the pits at the end of the opening lap to have a deflated left-rear tyre replaced, but the safety car enabled him to catch up to the back of the bunch again so that even though he was in last place he was only 9.7s behind leader Coulthard by the time the pack was unleashed again at the end of lap five.

Coulthard was on a one-stop strategy and knew that he had simply to keep Schumacher under control in the opening stages to maximise his chances, for the Ferrari was clearly running a two-stop race. By the end of lap six the McLaren driver came through 0.6s ahead of his rival just as Rubens Barrichello's Stewart-Ford moved ahead of Frentzen to take fifth.

Coming down the long straight towards the pits chicane on the seventh lap, Schumacher made to move out of Coulthard's slipstream. Michael took a long look down the inside, but thought better of it and dropped back into line. Next time round the remarkable Barrichello moved ahead of Villeneuve for fourth place, the Brazilian showing signs of edging away from the Williams duo before squandering all his hard-won advantage by running wide at the old hairpin on lap 11, dropping back to seventh.

Schumacher continued to press Coulthard extremely hard, occasionally locking up his front tyres under hard braking as he worked away to provoke the Scot into a slight mistake. However, David was not about to be bullied into repeating the error that had cost him victory earlier in the season at Buenos Aires when Schumacher muscled his way past the McLaren and pitched the Scot into a spin.

After several laps Coulthard managed to stabilise his advantage over the pursuing Ferrari, but this was abruptly dissipated when the safety car was deployed for a second time between laps 14 and 17 after Arrows driver Pedro Diniz spun off and then resumed, scattering clods of earth and grass all round the circuit as he did so.

On lap 19 Coulthard suddenly slowed and the second McLaren trailed gently round to the pits to retire with an engine problem, eventually traced to a disconnected throttle mechanism controlling one bank of cylinders. Meanwhile Johnny Herbert retired the spare Sauber, having climbed through the field steadily after starting from the pit lane. He spun at the hairpin, perhaps frustrated by a slight problem with the gearbox downchange. Peter Sauber was not amused, given Alesi's fate on the opening lap.

Coulthard's retirement allowed Schumacher through into the lead, but at the end of lap 20, when it was signalled that the safety car was to be deployed for a third time to allow the Arrows of Mika Salo, which had crashed a lap earlier, to be removed, the German opportunistically ducked into the pits to make his first refuelling stop.

What happened next would have been vaguely amusing had it not been so potentially serious. As Schumacher emerged from the pits, Frentzen's Williams drew level on the outside racing line, but the Ferrari driver simply moved out to the right and pushed the FW20 off the circuit and into the gravel trap in an astonishing display of reckless driving.

Frentzen had momentarily moved into third place when his compatriot pulled this stunt. 'What makes it so irritating is that I had tons of fuel on board and could have stayed out late for my first stop,' said Frentzen. 'The car was feeling really quite good.'

Schumacher's pit stop had left Fisichella's Benetton leading from Villeneuve, but when the safety car was withdrawn at the end of lap 22 Jacques made an audacious attempt to pass the Italian as they went into the first corner and promptly lunged across the gravel trap which had claimed Frentzen. He just managed to get back on the track, only to be hit from behind by Esteban Tuero's Minardi, resulting in the local hero spending five laps in the pits having the Williams's rear wing replaced.

'The tyres were cold after the yellow,' shrugged Jacques, 'and I braked too late. But I got back on the track without losing too many positions, so it seemed to be OK until a Minardi ran into the back of me. It's very disappointing to have screwed up, because the car was good enough to have fought for a win. At the very least, I could have beaten Fisichella.'

The race now settled down with Fisichella leading by 2.6s from Schumacher, Damon Hill's Jordan third, and Jan Magnussen's Stewart-Ford, Shinji Nakano's Minardi and the Prost of Olivier Panis completing the top six, although the Japanese driver quickly began to lose ground.

After the stewards' due deliberation, Schumacher was called in for a ten-second stop-go penalty at the end of lap 35, resuming in third behind Hill. Three laps later, as he accelerated towards the final pits ess-bend, Schumacher pulled level with the Mugen

Williams protests Schumacher after wild race

Nigel Snowdon

FRANK Williams is not a man who readily lodges protests, but it was a measure of the British team owner's strong feelings about Michael Schumacher's performance at Montreal that Heinz-Harald Frentzen's entrant protested the Ferrari ace on three counts following his victory in the Canadian GP.

Even though Schumacher had served a ten-second stop-go penalty for pushing Frentzen off the circuit, Williams lodged his objection on three other grounds. Firstly, it was claimed that he overtook Jacques Villeneuve on the inside as the two cars were leaving their garages to take up their positions on the grid. Secondly, he made a practice start on each of the formation laps – forbidden by the rules – and thirdly he missed the last chicane when he overtook Hill's Jordan on lap 38.

'I was making a voice heard, rather than seeking redress,' said Williams, effectively confirming that he was making a symbolic stand against not only Schumacher's driving, but also perhaps the inconsistency of the penalties.

'I felt that Michael's behaviour was out of order on the Grand Prix track, and it's not the first time. I felt I wanted to protest his behaviour. I just wanted to put it on paper and get it to the stewards quickly.'

The Williams protest was rejected, but it certainly made a point. Whether Schumacher took it on board, of course, was another matter altogether.

Jon Eisberg

Honda-engined machine, only for Damon to weave at him in somewhat intimidating fashion.

Michael duly completed the overtaking manoeuvre, although to do so he had to drive behind the marker cones on that final corner, something which should technically have earned him another penalty. But the fact that he got away without any sanction in no way softened his vocal response to what he regarded as Hill's unacceptable tactics.

'I was so angry with that situation and I wonder why he didn't get a penalty for what he did,' fumed Schumacher. 'I know I cut the chicane, but I had almost lost my car avoiding that circumstance, and I was lucky even to get through the chicane anyway. It is impossible for such an experienced man to do such things. I can't handle that.'

On lap 39 Hill made his scheduled refuelling stop, which dropped the Jordan from third to sixth. Shortly afterwards he slowed up and he retired three laps later with electrical problems. 'It wouldn't rev and developed a misfire,' he shrugged.

Interestingly, Damon also praised Schumacher's relentless driving – before he heard about Michael's own outburst. 'It's just incredible when you race him,' said the Englishman. 'You can't even blink, he's that good.' Unfortunately Schumacher didn't feel moved to respond in like vein.

'We can take some comfort from the fact that we were not only up with the front-runners, but were making fairly respectable times and were competitive,' continued Hill. 'I was running beautifully on a one-stop strategy and it was the first time this year that I had been able to race for the top three positions. I was not going to let second or third place go that easily, so I enjoyed some racing with Michael!'

All this untoward drama had played firmly into the hands of those teams whose drivers had kept out of trouble. Hill's problems had allowed Panis to get through to third place with the Prost-Peugeot, but any hopes the Frenchman may have harboured of earning a place on the rostrum vanished on lap 40 when his engine seized and he spun off into the gravel.

On lap 44 Fisichella came in for his sole refuelling stop nursing a 17.8s lead over Schumacher's Ferrari. Knowing that he would have to bring the Italian car in for one more fuel stop, Michael now went to town in a big way, reeling off a succession of punishingly fast laps around the 1m 20s mark before coming in himself at the end of lap 50 for a quick 7.2s 'splash and dash'.

A lesser driver might have been flustered into an error under this sort of pressure, but Schumacher's 'in' and 'out' laps were so quick that they cost him only 16 seconds, with the result that he emerged 2.12s in front of the Benetton. It was all over bar the shouting and the Ferrari team leader steadily extended his advantage to 16.66s over the remaining 19 laps to the chequered flag.

Not that Fisichella was having an easy time, by any means.

'From the beginning the race for me was very difficult because our strategy was to do just one pit stop,' he explained. 'When Michael was behind me, about 20 laps after the start, the behaviour of the car was much better. Also, my lap times were quite good, even though I had been having a problem with third gear since the beginning of the race.'

Third place fell to Irvine, who had a busy afternoon battling through to snatch the final place on the podium by 3.6s from Wurz in the spare Benetton.

'I thought I had damaged the suspension [after the first-corner incident] because immediately after I was tapped up the rear the car felt strange to drive,' he explained. 'Something had sliced the tyre, probably someone's front wing end plate. The tyre went flat immediately and I thought it was the suspension which was damaged.

'I kept thinking, "Should I keep going?" because there were bits of tyre flying all over the place and I thought I might get into trouble for putting so much rubber on the track. The most important thing was that I did not lose a lap.

'I felt I was quicker than Wurz, but the two of us would sometimes drop back from whoever it was in the Minardi [Nakano] in front of us. It was a stalemate, but it worked out well and we did the two short stints at the end.'

Behind Wurz came the two Stewart-Fords of Barrichello and Magnussen, the latter chased home energetically by Nakano's Minardi, which was only just over a second behind the Dane at the chequered flag. Barrichello complained that his brakes were fading slightly in the closing stages, perhaps costing him a chance of third place, while Magnussen was understandably elated with his first World Championship point. Not that it would save his future with the team.

After posting his second victory of the season Schumacher was called to the stewards following a protest from the Williams team over the Frentzen incident (see sidebar). After lengthy deliberation no further sanction was applied to the winner. Nobody seemed unduly surprised.

GRAND PRIX PLAYER'S DU CANADA

5–7 JUNE 1998

MONTREAL

Race distance: 69 laps, 189.548 miles/305.049 km

Race weather: Cool and overcast

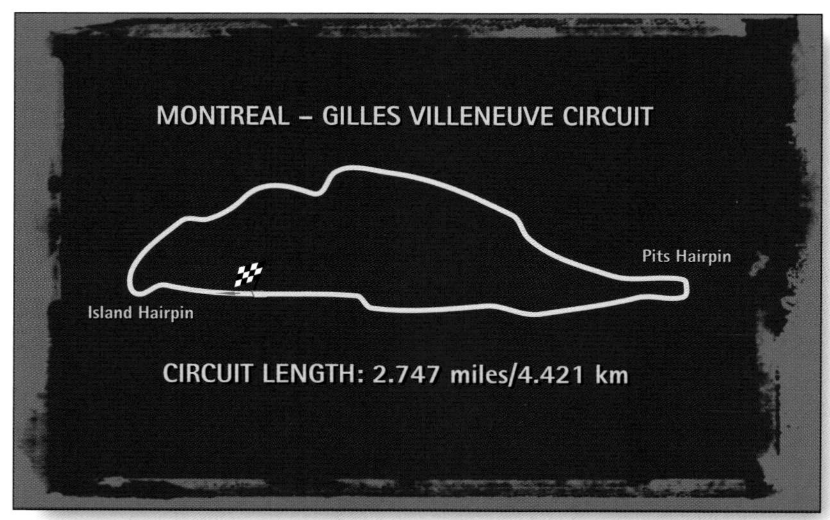

Pos.	Driver	Nat.	No.	Entrant	Car/Engine	Tyres	Laps	Time/Retirement	Speed (mph/km/h)
1	**Michael Schumacher**	**D**	**3**	**Scuderia Ferrari Marlboro**	**Ferrari F300 047 V10**	**G**	**69**	**1h 40m 57.355s**	**112.652/181.296**
2	**Giancarlo Fisichella**	**I**	**5**	**Mild Seven Benetton Playlife**	**Benetton B198-Playlife V10**	**B**	**69**	**1h 41m 14.017s**	**112.343/180.799**
3	**Eddie Irvine**	**GB**	**4**	**Scuderia Ferrari Marlboro**	**Ferrari F300 047 V10**	**G**	**69**	**1h 41m 57.414s**	**111.546/179.516**
4	**Alexander Wurz**	**A**	**6**	**Mild Seven Benetton Playlife**	**Benetton B198-Playlife V10**	**B**	**69**	**1h 42m 00.587s**	**111.488/179.423**
5	**Rubens Barrichello**	**BR**	**18**	**Stewart Ford**	**Stewart SF2-Ford Zetec-R V10**	**B**	**69**	**1h 42m 18.868s**	**111.156/178.889**
6	**Jan Magnussen**	**DK**	**19**	**Stewart Ford**	**Stewart SF2-Ford Zetec-R V10**	**B**	**68**		
7	Shinji Nakano	J	22	Fondmetal Minardi Ford	Minardi M198-Ford Zetec-R V10	B	68		
8	Ricardo Rosset	BR	20	Tyrrell Ford	Tyrrell 026-Ford Zetec-R V10	G	68		
9	Pedro Diniz	BR	16	Danka Zepter Arrows	Arrows A19 V10	B	68		
10	Jacques Villeneuve	CDN	1	Winfield Williams	Williams FW20-Mecachrome GC37/01 V10	G	63		
	Esteban Tuero	RA	23	Fondmetal Minardi Ford	Minardi M198-Ford Zetec-R V10	B	53	Electrics	
	Damon Hill	GB	9	B&H Jordan Mugen Honda	Jordan 198-Mugen Honda MF310C V10	G	42	Electrics	
	Olivier Panis	F	11	Gauloises Prost Peugeot	Prost AP01-Peugeot A16 V10	B	39	Engine	
	Heinz-Harald Frentzen	D	2	Winfield Williams	Williams FW20-Mecachrome GC37/01 V10	G	20	Accident	
	David Coulthard	GB	7	West McLaren Mercedes	McLaren MP4/13-Mercedes FO110G V10	B	18	Throttle	
	Johnny Herbert	GB	15	Red Bull Sauber Petronas	Sauber C17-Petronas SPE01D V10	G	18	Spun off	
	Mika Salo	SF	17	Danka Zepter Arrows	Arrows A19 V10	B	18	Accident	
	Mika Häkkinen	SF	8	West McLaren Mercedes	McLaren MP4/13-Mercedes FO110G V10	B	0	Gearbox	
	Ralf Schumacher	D	10	B&H Jordan Mugen Honda	Jordan 198-Mugen Honda MF310C V10	G	0	Clutch	
	Jean Alesi	F	14	Red Bull Sauber Petronas	Sauber C17-Petronas SPE01D V10	G	0	Collision	
	Jarno Trulli	I	12	Gauloises Prost Peugeot	Prost AP01-Peugeot A16 V10	B	0	Collision	
	Toranosuke Takagi	J	21	Tyrrell Ford	Tyrrell 026-Ford Zetec-R V10	G	0	Transmission	

Fastest lap: M. Schumacher, on lap 48, 1m 19.379s, 124.586 mph/200.501 km/h (record).

Previous lap record: David Coulthard (F1 McLaren MP4/12-Mercedes V10), 1m 19.635s, 124.185 mph/199.856 km/h (1997).

B – Bridgestone G – Goodyear

All results and data © FIA 1998

Grid order	1	2	3	4	5	6	7	8	9	10	11	12	13	14	15	16	17	18	19	20	21	22	23	24	25	26	27	28	29	30	31	32	33	34	35	36	37	38	39	40	41	42	43	44	45	46	47	48	49	50	51	52
7 COULTHARD	7	7	7	7	7	7	7	7	7	7	7	7	7	7	7	7	7	7	3	5	5	5	5	5	5	5	5	5	5	5	5	5	5	5	5	5	5	5	5	5	5	5	5	3	3	3	3	3	3	3	3	3
8 HÄKKINEN	3	3	3	3	3	3	3	3	3	3	3	3	3	3	3	3	3	3	5	1	1	1	3	3	3	3	3	3	3	3	3	3	3	3	9	9	9	3	3	3	3	3	3	5	5	5	5	5	5	5	5	5
3 M. SCHUMACHER	5	5	5	5	5	5	5	5	5	5	5	5	5	5	5	5	5	5	1	3	3	3	9	9	9	9	9	9	9	9	9	9	9	9	3	3	3	9	11	18	18	18	18	18	18	18	18	4	4	4	4	4
5 FISICHELLA	1	1	1	1	1	1	1	18	18	18	1	1	1	1	1	1	1	1	2	2	9	9	19	19	19	19	19	19	19	19	19	19	19	19	11	11	11	11	6	9	4	4	4	4	4	4	4	18	6	6	6	6
10 R. SCHUMACHER	2	2	2	2	2	18	18	1	1	1	2	2	2	2	2	2	2	2	18	18	19	19	22	11	11	11	11	11	11	11	11	11	11	11	6	6	6	6	18	6	6	6	6	6	6	6	6	6	18	18	18	18
1 VILLENEUVE	18	18	18	18	18	2	2	2	2	2	9	9	9	9	9	9	9	9	9	9	22	22	11	22	22	22	22	22	6	6	6	6	6	6	4	4	4	22	9	4	19	19	19	19	19	19	19	19	19	19	19	19
2 FRENTZEN	9	9	9	9	9	9	9	9	9	9	18	18	18	18	18	18	18	18	19	19	11	11	6	6	6	6	6	6	4	4	4	4	4	4	22	22	22	18	4	19	22	22	22	22	22	22	22	22	22	22	22	22
4 IRVINE	19	19	19	19	19	19	19	19	19	19	19	19	19	19	19	19	19	19	22	22	23	23	4	4	4	4	4	4	22	22	22	22	22	22	18	18	18	4	19	22	20	20	20	20	20	20	20	20	20	20	20	20
14 ALESI	16	16	16	16	16	16	16	16	16	16	16	16	15	15	15	15	15	15	11	11	6	6	18	18	18	18	18	18	18	18	18	18	18	18	19	19	19	19	22	20	9	23	23	23	23	23	23	23	23	23	23	23
9 HILL	20	20	20	20	20	20	20	20	20	20	20	15	20	20	22	22	22	22	23	23	4	4	20	20	20	20	20	20	20	20	20	20	20	20	20	20	20	20	20	23	23	16	16	16	16	16	16	16	16	16	16	16
6 WURZ	22	22	22	22	22	22	22	22	15	15	15	20	22	22	11	11	11	11	6	6	18	18	23	23	23	23	23	23	23	23	16	16	16	16	16	16	23	23	23	16	16	9	1	1	1	1	1	1	1	1	1	1
15 HERBERT	15	15	15	15	15	15	15	15	22	22	22	22	11	11	17	17	17	17	4	4	20	20	16	16	16	16	16	16	16	16	23	23	23	23	23	23	16	16	16	1	1	1										
18 BARRICHELLO	11	11	11	11	11	11	11	11	11	11	11	11	17	17	23	23	23	23	20	20	16	16	1	1	1	1	1	1	1	1	1	1	1	1	1	1	1	1	1													
12 TRULLI	17	17	17	17	17	17	17	17	17	17	17	17	23	23	6	6	6	6	16	16																																
11 PANIS	23	23	23	23	23	23	23	23	23	23	23	23	6	6	4	4	4	4																																		
21 TAKAGI	6	6	6	6	6	6	6	6	6	6	6	6	4	4	20	20	20	20																																		
17 SALO	4	4	4	4	4	4	4	4	4	4	4	4	16	16	16	16	16	16																																		
22 NAKANO																																																				
16 DINIZ																																																				
19 MAGNUSSEN																																																				
23 TUERO																																																				
20 ROSSET																																																				

Pit stop

One lap behind leader

STARTING GRID

	7 **COULTHARD** McLaren
8 **HÄKKINEN** McLaren	
	3 **M. SCHUMACHER** Ferrari
5 **FISICHELLA** Benetton	
	10 **R. SCHUMACHER** Jordan
1 **VILLENEUVE** Williams	
	2 **FRENTZEN** Williams
4 **IRVINE** Ferrari	
	14 **ALESI** Sauber
9 **HILL** Jordan	
	6 **WURZ** Benetton
15 **HERBERT*** Sauber	
	18 **BARRICHELLO** Stewart
12 **TRULLI** Prost	
	11 **PANIS** Prost
21 **TAKAGI** Tyrrell	
	17 **SALO** Arrows
22 **NAKANO** Minardi	
	16 **DINIZ** Arrows
19 **MAGNUSSEN** Stewart	
	23 **TUERO** Minardi
20 **ROSSET** Tyrrell	

* started from the pit lane

6	57	58	59	60	61	62	63	64	65	66	67	68	69	●
3	3	3	3	3	3	3	3	3	3	3	3	3	3	1
5	5	5	5	5	5	5	5	5	5	5	5	5	5	2
4	4	4	4	4	4	4	4	4	4	4	4	4	4	3
6	6	6	6	6	6	6	6	6	6	6	6	6	6	4
8	18	18	18	18	18	18	18	18	18	18	18	18	18	5
9	19	19	19	19	19	19	19	19	19	19	19	19		6
2	22	22	22	22	22	22	22	22	22	22	22	22		
0	20	20	20	20	20	20	20	20	20	20	20	20		
6	16	16	16	16	16	16	16	16	16	16	16	16		
1	1	1	1	1	1	1	1							

FOR THE RECORD

First Grand Prix point

Jan Magnussen

TIME SHEETS

QUALIFYING

Weather: Cool and overcast

Pos.	Driver	Car	Laps	Time
1	David Coulthard	McLaren-Mercedes	11	1m 18.213s
2	Mika Häkkinen	McLaren-Mercedes	11	1m 18.282s
3	Michael Schumacher	Ferrari	12	1m 18.497s
4	Giancarlo Fisichella	Benetton-Playlife	12	1m 18.826s
5	Ralf Schumacher	Jordan-Mugen Honda	12	1m 19.242s
6	Jacques Villeneuve	Williams-Mecachrome	12	1m 19.588s
7	Heinz-Harald Frentzen	Williams-Mecachrome	12	1m 19.614s
8	Eddie Irvine	Ferrari	12	1m 19.616s
9	Jean Alesi	Sauber-Petronas	12	1m 19.693s
10	Damon Hill	Jordan-Mugen Honda	12	1m 19.717s
11	Alexander Wurz	Benetton-Playlife	12	1m 19.765s
12	Johnny Herbert	Sauber-Petronas	12	1m 19.845s
13	Rubens Barrichello	Stewart-Ford	8	1m 19.953s
14	Jarno Trulli	Prost-Peugeot	11	1m 20.188s
15	Olivier Panis	Prost-Peugeot	11	1m 20.303s
16	Toranosuke Takagi	Tyrrell-Ford	12	1m 20.328s
17	Mika Salo	Arrows	12	1m 20.536s
18	Shinji Nakano	Minardi-Ford	12	1m 21.230s
19	Pedro Diniz	Arrows	12	1m 21.301s
20	Jan Magnussen	Stewart-Ford	11	1m 21.629s
21	Esteban Tuero	Minardi-Ford	12	1m 21.822s
22	Ricardo Rosset	Tyrrell-Ford	12	1m 21.824s

FRIDAY FREE PRACTICE

Weather: Sunny, light overcast

Pos.	Driver	Laps	Time
1	Mika Häkkinen	31	1m 19.613s
2	Michael Schumacher	41	1m 19.999s
3	Jean Alesi	45	1m 20.252s
4	David Coulthard	39	1m 20.316s
5	Giancarlo Fisichella	38	1m 20.480s
6	Heinz-Harald Frentzen	39	1m 20.622s
7	Eddie Irvine	50	1m 20.821s
8	Rubens Barrichello	32	1m 20.937s
9	Damon Hill	45	1m 21.069s
10	Olivier Panis	37	1m 21.191s
11	Johnny Herbert	31	1m 21.239s
12	Alexander Wurz	31	1m 21.274s
13	Jarno Trulli	41	1m 21.282s
14	Ralf Schumacher	41	1m 21.294s
15	Toranosuke Takagi	41	1m 21.370s
16	Jacques Villeneuve	26	1m 21.597s
17	Mika Salo	30	1m 21.962s
18	Pedro Diniz	31	1m 22.100s
19	Shinji Nakano	38	1m 22.137s
20	Esteban Tuero	51	1m 22.425s
21	Ricardo Rosset	27	1m 23.011s
22	Jan Magnussen	29	1m 23.146s

SATURDAY FREE PRACTICE

Weather: Cool and windy

Pos.	Driver	Laps	Time
1	Mika Häkkinen	30	1m 18.741s
2	David Coulthard	32	1m 18.741s
3	Michael Schumacher	31	1m 19.198s
4	Ralf Schumacher	23	1m 19.362s
5	Giancarlo Fisichella	27	1m 19.414s
6	Heinz-Harald Frentzen	28	1m 19.512s
7	Jean Alesi	33	1m 19.623s
8	Jacques Villeneuve	32	1m 19.898s
9	Eddie Irvine	23	1m 19.979s
10	Johnny Herbert	22	1m 19.990s
11	Mika Salo	32	1m 20.075s
12	Jarno Trulli	31	1m 20.170s
13	Damon Hill	31	1m 20.350s
14	Olivier Panis	29	1m 20.671s
15	Alexander Wurz	13	1m 20.956s
16	Rubens Barrichello	11	1m 21.196s
17	Pedro Diniz	24	1m 21.251s
18	Toranosuke Takagi	13	1m 21.281s
19	Shinji Nakano	30	1m 21.361s
20	Ricardo Rosset	25	1m 21.505s
21	Esteban Tuero	33	1m 21.700s
22	Jan Magnussen	9	1m 22.875s

WARM-UP

Weather: Damp, slowly drying

Pos.	Driver	Laps	Time
1	Heinz-Harald Frentzen	14	1m 21.940s
2	Mika Häkkinen	13	1m 22.065s
3	David Coulthard	13	1m 22.281s
4	Giancarlo Fisichella	11	1m 22.351s
5	Michael Schumacher	13	1m 22.360s
6	Johnny Herbert	16	1m 22.447s
7	Jacques Villeneuve	13	1m 22.822s
8	Jarno Trulli	16	1m 22.931s
9	Rubens Barrichello	14	1m 23.051s
10	Olivier Panis	13	1m 23.052s
11	Damon Hill	13	1m 23.086s
12	Mika Salo	15	1m 23.537s
13	Ralf Schumacher	16	1m 23.583s
14	Jean Alesi	14	1m 23.647s
15	Pedro Diniz	13	1m 23.801s
16	Alexander Wurz	12	1m 24.577s
17	Toranosuke Takagi	14	1m 24.774s
18	Shinji Nakano	12	1m 24.801s
19	Ricardo Rosset	12	1m 25.859s
20	Esteban Tuero	14	1m 26.042s
21	Jan Magnussen	10	1m 26.337s
22	Eddie Irvine	4	1m 30.685s

RACE FASTEST LAPS

Weather: Cool and overcast

Driver	Time	Lap
Michael Schumacher	1m 19.379s	48
David Coulthard	1m 20.852s	12
Giancarlo Fisichella	1m 20.942s	35
Jacques Villeneuve	1m 21.233s	61
Eddie Irvine	1m 21.327s	53
Olivier Panis	1m 21.669s	40
Alexander Wurz	1m 21.694s	66
Pedro Diniz	1m 21.814s	66
Damon Hill	1m 21.933s	26
Rubens Barrichello	1m 22.239s	44
Heinz-Harald Frentzen	1m 22.430s	13
Jan Magnussen	1m 22.867s	33
Shinji Nakano	1m 22.907s	67
Esteban Tuero	1m 22.939s	53
Ricardo Rosset	1m 23.418s	59
Johnny Herbert	1m 23.466s	10
Mika Salo	1m 24.451s	9

CHASSIS LOG BOOK

1	Villeneuve	Williams FW20/5
2	Frentzen	Williams FW20/4
	spare	Williams FW20/3
3	M. Schumacher	Ferrari F300/187
4	Irvine	Ferrari F300/185
	spare	Ferrari F300/186
5	Fisichella	Benetton B198/6
6	Wurz	Benetton B198/4
	spare	Benetton B198/5
7	Coulthard	McLaren MP4/13/3
8	Häkkinen	McLaren MP4/13/4
	spare	McLaren MP4/13/5
9	Hill	Jordan 198/3
10	R. Schumacher	Jordan 198/4
	spare	Jordan 198/1
11	Panis	Prost AP01/5
12	Trulli	Prost AP01/3
	spare	Prost AP01/2
14	Alesi	Sauber C17/3
15	Herbert	Sauber C17/4
	spare	Sauber C17/2
16	Diniz	Arrows A19/1
17	Salo	Arrows A19/3
	spare	Arrows A19/4
18	Barrichello	Stewart SF2/4
19	Magnussen	Stewart SF2/2
	spare	Stewart SF2/3
20	Rosset	Tyrrell 026/2
21	Takagi	Tyrrell 026/1
	spare	Tyrrell 026/3
22	Nakano	Minardi M198/4
23	Tuero	Minardi M198/3
	spare	Minardi M198/2

POINTS TABLES

Drivers

1	Mika Häkkinen	46
2	Michael Schumacher	34
3	David Coulthard	29
4	Eddie Irvine	19
5	Giancarlo Fisichella	13
6	Alexander Wurz	12
7 =	Heinz-Harald Frentzen	8
7 =	Jacques Villeneuve	8
9	Rubens Barrichello	4
10 =	Jean Alesi	3
10 =	Mika Salo	3
12 =	Johnny Herbert	1
12 =	Pedro Diniz	1
12 =	Jan Magnussen	1

Constructors

1	McLaren	75
2	Ferrari	53
3	Benetton	25
4	Williams	16
5	Stewart	5
6 =	Sauber	4
6 =	Arrows	4

Michael Roberts

FIA WORLD CHAMPIONSHIP • ROUND 8

FRENCH grand prix

M. SCHUMACHER
IRVINE
HÄKKINEN
VILLENEUVE
WURZ
COULTHARD

Mika Häkkinen took his fifth pole position of the season by a slender 0.23s from Michael Schumacher's Ferrari, the Italian car offering its Mercedes-engined rival a brisk challenge in France thanks, at least in part, to the advent of a further-revised-construction rear Goodyear tyre.

'I am happy with this result as we are now in a position to make a challenge,' said Schumacher. 'This is the closest the gap has been all season. From what we saw in testing last week, my car is very competitive in race trim, even if it lacks a few tenths for qualifying, as we have seen today. The championship could now be very open, as I think we can be this close for the rest of the season, thanks to improvements in aerodynamics and the tyres.'

Diana Burnett

David Coulthard was disappointed to have been pushed off the front row of the grid for the first time this season, reporting handling problems on the three slowest corners after claiming third place in the grid order. 'It was a bit of a disappointment,' he confessed, 'because I thought I could be in contention for pole, but in reality I wasn't. There was an instability in the rear end which meant I couldn't carry the speed on the entry to those corners. But in the chicanes and the faster turns, the car was OK.'

Eddie Irvine, fourth fastest in the second Ferrari, was also a little crestfallen not to have split the McLarens, explaining that he had some unlucky breaks with yellow flags during the course of the session.

On the inside of the third row sat Jacques Villeneuve's Williams FW20, the Canadian judging that it might have been possible to squeeze perhaps another tenth of a second out of the car as the conditions cooled slightly towards the end of the session. Heinz-Harald Frentzen's sister car had a precautionary engine change prior to qualifying; this lost him crucial time, after which he went the wrong way on set-up and could not better eighth fastest.

The new rear Goodyear also helped the Jordan-Mugen Hondas, which eventually qualified in sixth and seventh places, Ralf Schumacher fractionally ahead of Damon Hill. Eddie's two lads also benefited from the use of a revised qualifying engine. 'I am very happy,' said Ralf, 'as the car improved on each set of tyres we used.' Hill described the car as feeling 'really very good indeed', although he stopped shortly before the end of the session with a hydraulic failure.

By contrast, the Benetton B198s were both struggling for grip on this circuit, Giancarlo Fisichella and Alexander Wurz lining up in ninth and tenth places on the grid behind Frentzen. The team had experienced problems balancing the chassis to the drivers' tastes during testing and that problem carried over into official practice and qualifying. In addition, Fisichella stopped out on the circuit shortly before the end, but both he and Wurz seemed confident they could bid for a top-six finish come Sunday afternoon.

In the Sauber camp, the revised, longer-wheelbase C17 which had been tested the previous week did not make an appearance for the race. On Saturday morning both Jean Alesi and Johnny Herbert were frustrated by engine failures, after which the Frenchman was quite satisfied at qualifying 11th, two places ahead of his English team-mate.

'The handling feels even better than during the test,' said Herbert, 'but we're slower on the straights even though we are running the same aerodynamic package.'

In 14th and 15th places on the grid, Rubens Barrichello and Jos Verstappen were hardly delighted with their Stewart-Fords. Verstappen found that he needed to trim the size of his driving boots to allow them to fit comfortably into the footwell, but, taken as a whole, it wasn't quite ideal.

'I was reasonably happy with my best lap,' said Barrichello, 'and I have to thank the team for solving the brake problem I experienced yesterday and this morning. I think that's the best I could have done, although I fell short of my target of the top 12 or better.'

The Prost team may have derived a sliver of satisfaction from Jarno Trulli's 12th place on the grid, but Olivier Panis was 0.8s adrift, having switched to the spare AP01, which he preferred, only for a clutch failure to force him back into his unloved race chassis. He was 16th fastest overall. Despite stiffened rear suspension uprights and a stiffer front to the monocoque, the Prost was still way off the pace.

In 18th place, splitting the two Arrows of Pedro Diniz – who crashed quite heavily into a tyre barrier – and Mika Salo, came a surprisingly on-form Ricardo Rosset, who for once managed to get the Tyrrell 026 working properly following speculation that he might be replaced in the team. His best time put him 0.3s ahead of team-mate Toranosuke Takagi, who had to take the spare car, fitted with an earlier-spec Ford V10, after his race chassis suffered an engine failure. Takagi would line up in 20th place. 'Ricardo has proved he can do a very good job,' said team owner Craig Pollock. 'Maybe he needed a bit of a push.'

Rounding off the grid were the two Minardi-Fords of Shinji Nakano and Esteban Tuero, the Argentine driver having crashed on Saturday morning and been obliged to take the spare M198 for qualifying.

Paul-Henri Cahier

Previous pages: **Eddie Irvine backed up his championship-chasing team-mate Michael Schumacher in exemplary fashion with a gritty drive to second place.**

Left: **Dutchman Jos Verstappen made another attempt to relaunch his stuttering Grand Prix career, replacing the luckless Jan Magnussen at Stewart.**

Below left: **A worried-looking Ron Dennis seeks some advice from Frank Williams.**

Right: **Jarno Trulli corrects a slide in the Prost-Peugeot. Even at a circuit the team knows so well, the French cars remained hopelessly uncompetitive.**

IT was the first time that Ferrari had posted a 1-2 finish in a World Championship Grand Prix for almost eight years. Not since the volatile pairing of Alain Prost and Nigel Mansell had stormed home first and second in the 1990 Spanish GP at Jerez had the Prancing Horse monopolised the top two positions on the rostrum. This time a display of perfect teamwork saw Michael Schumacher dominate the French GP at Magny-Cours, followed by Eddie Irvine, the Ulsterman riding shotgun for most of the distance, protecting Schumacher's rear from the marauding McLaren-Mercedes of World Championship leader Mika Häkkinen and David Coulthard.

For Häkkinen, this was a definite setback for his title hopes, but not a terminal one. By contrast, Coulthard's championship aspirations were dealt another potentially crippling blow when a succession of refuelling hitches relegated him from what at one point looked like a strong second place to a distant sixth at the finish.

The race itself began on a controversial note. Jos Verstappen, who was making his F1 return at the wheel of a Stewart SF2-Ford in place of Jan Magnussen, stalled his car on the grid and officials attempted to abort the start. But it was too late.

The red starting lights went out a fraction of a second before the flashing orange lights indicating that the start procedure had been halted came on, and Mika Häkkinen's McLaren surged away into an immediate lead, followed by the rest of the pack. The field was signalled to a halt at the end of the opening lap, after which the Finn squandered his pole position advantage by making a poor getaway at the restart, allowing Schumacher and Irvine to take a commanding early lead.

The sequence of events which led to the restart had the conspiracy theorists out in force, displaying all the symptoms of acute paranoia. What had happened, they reasoned, was that the FIA officials had used Verstappen's dilemma as a pretext to stop the race and give the slow-starting Ferraris a second chance. All part of the FIA's grand plan to spoon-feed the Italian team the 1998 World Championship, you understand.

'Sometimes the playing field doesn't seem level, and this is one of those times,' noted McLaren's Ron Dennis after Schumacher and Irvine had firmly beaten his best-placed car, driven by Häkkinen, into third place.

In fact, this turned out to be an over-hasty reaction. A detailed reconstruction of events proved that the

ALCATEL
CANAL+
CANAL+
PlayStation
BIC
AGFA
ALCATEL
ALCATEL
12
CATIA
TOTAL
ALCATEL
ALCATEL

BUZZIN
HORNETS
GOODYEAR
DELPHI
PlayStation
HONDA
MUGEN 無限
HONDA
DAMON HILL

Last-minute adjustments for Damon Hill's Jordan on the starting grid. It was to be another disappointing race for the Silverstone-based team, Hill retiring with hydraulics trouble and Ralf Schumacher dropping down the order after a collision with Alexander Wurz.

button had been pressed to illuminate the orange lights before the front row cars had even moved. Häkkinen made the best start first time round, Schumacher at the restart.

'In fact, I wasn't relieved about the race being restarted,' said Schumacher, 'because I thought I had done a good start first time when I kept my position away from the line. Usually starting against the McLarens is difficult, and although we have definitely improved our starting procedure we are not yet where we want to be.

'So when I saw there was going to be a restart, I was worried that the same thing might happen to me that we saw in Canada, and I could lose a position again. But luckily both Eddie and I made fantastic starts; we jumped both McLarens, and that was one of the factors that won the race for us.'

By the end of the opening lap Michael was already 1.5s ahead of the pack, with Irvine, Häkkinen, Coulthard, Jacques Villeneuve's Williams, the Jordans of Ralf Schumacher and Damon Hill, Alexander Wurz's Benetton and Jean Alesi's Sauber heading the pursuit. Further back, Heinz-Harald Frentzen had made a particularly bad start in the other Williams, dropping from eighth on the grid to 12th first time round, while Johnny Herbert, who had taken the spare Sauber after his race car's clutch felt peculiar on the warm-up lap, had also made a poor getaway.

By lap three, Schumacher had 3.9s in hand over Irvine, who was subtly keeping the pace down, as evidenced by the fact that the Ferrari team leader went round in 1m 17.819s while Häkkinen, boxed in back in third, could only turn a 1m 19.036s.

Coulthard was jostling his team-mate in an effort to hurry things along, but lost a little ground on lap five when his McLaren ran wide at the Adelaide hairpin. By lap seven Schumacher was 8.1s ahead of the close-running threesome in second, third and fourth places, and there was a gap of six seconds from Coulthard back to Villeneuve and the two Jordans, another trio also running in close company.

At the end of lap 16 Ralf Schumacher made an early first pit stop, only to collide with Wurz's Benetton, which had just moved up into sixth place, as he accelerated back into the race. The net result of this little drama was for Schumacher to scuttle back into the pit lane for a replacement steering arm to be fitted, a task which dropped him to the very tail of the field.

This was the start of the rot for Jordan. On lap 17 Hill made his first stop, and he then came back to retire two laps later with a repeat of the hydraulic problems which had sidelined him at the end of Saturday qualifying. On the same lap Wurz made his first refuelling stop, dropping from sixth to tenth, while next time round his Benetton team-mate Giancarlo Fisichella also came in for a routine stop, dropping from seventh to 11th.

On lap 20 Häkkinen momentarily overtook Irvine for second place, only to spin on the tight right-hander in front of the pits, the McLaren snapping round in its own length and escaping contact with the guard rail by an uncomfortably slender margin. Next time round Mika ducked into the pits for an 8.8s first stop, picking up the chase again in sixth place.

For his part, Coulthard duly made his first stop on lap 22 but there was a major problem with the refuelling rig which meant that he resumed the race in sixth place after being stationary for 17.1s. Three more similarly frustrating stops on laps 55, 56 and 63 of the 71-lap race would follow, dropping him as low as eighth. Yet by piling on the pressure he retook sixth from Jean Alesi's Sauber on his last lap to claim the final championship point of the day, following Villeneuve's fourth-place Williams and the Benetton of Wurz across the line.

'It was real Keystone Cops stuff,' said Coulthard afterwards. 'It just went from bad to worse. To get a point is some consolation, but in a World Championship campaign it is just not good enough. I believe that I drove hard to get past Irvine and I was in second place when I made my first stop, and that's where I should have finished.

'The reason I didn't finish second is not because of something I've done wrong, but because of a problem with the car. Technical problems do happen from time to time, but, touch wood, I haven't made mistakes so far in throwing the car off the circuit. It will happen at some stage, but so far I think I've been disadvantaged through no fault of my own.

'I overtook Eddie for second place the lap the team called me in and I just presumed they knew I'd passed him. The strategy had been to put a lot of fuel in at that first stop so I could go longer on the second stint in order to pass him, which I already had.

'So I was not only sitting there taking on more fuel at the first stop, but I also had the refuelling problem. So that cock-up at the first stop meant that I went back into the race in fourth place [after the first round of stops had been completed]. Then I had three more stops because we couldn't get fuel into the car, so every time I had a bad stop it put me in the wrong place on the track in traffic.'

Not until the team got back to base the following week was the reason for the problem pinpointed precisely as being due to new components fitted within the hose connector assembly of the refuelling rigs.

'It is our belief that these components were not as tolerant as far as fitting onto the car adaptor was concerned,' explained Martin Whitmarsh, McLaren International's managing director. 'This prevented us from continuing with the refuelling process. They proved prone to jamming if they were offered up at a slight angle rather than absolutely in the right position.'

Häkkinen had no problems with his refuelling rig, to which Coulthard was switched for his third and fourth stops. In a test back at the factory it was found that the nozzle would not connect on Coulthard's car in about 30 per cent of the attempts and, after consultation with the FIA, reworked components would be fitted to the McLaren rigs for future events.

Lap 22 also saw Schumacher making a flawless 8.4s stop, which dropped him momentarily to second place behind Irvine. But the status quo was restored next time round when Irvine

Irvine considers his options

Michael Roberts

EDDIE Irvine finished the French Grand Prix poised to challenge David Coulthard for third place in the Drivers' World Championship stakes. Yet he also knew he was on the verge of a major career decision. Should he stay with Ferrari for 1999? Or look for a number one seat in his own right?

'I suppose it's good in a way [at Ferrari], because you are measuring yourself against the very best,' he admitted. 'You are always aiming to climb Mount Everest every day you get into the car, whereas if there was somebody else in the other car it would just be a gentle stroll up the Alps, wouldn't it?'

By the same token, Irvine was seriously considering what would be his best personal career path in the future. 'If Michael had broken down in France, I would have won,' he smiled, 'so it's a matter of deciding whether or not this is the best car available to me, or is there another car, or team, which is nearly as good.

'It's a difficult decision, because here at Ferrari we have a good car and a very good team. Strategy-wise, we're second to none, we really are. To improve on my situation here would be quite hard, but at the same time I'm always being compared to Michael, which is obviously not the easiest thing in the world.

'If you are running the team, everything goes your way. If you say something which is ignored because somebody in the team is more powerful – as Michael is here at Ferrari – then it's not good for your psyche. So if I joined another team where I could decisively beat my team-mate, going really well, it would raise my confidence and help me drive even better.

'So I've really got to sit down over the next month and seriously decide in which direction I've got to go.'

Irvine shrugged aside any notion that Schumacher might quit Ferrari at the end of the year in favour of a possible McLaren-Mercedes drive.

'Why would he leave?' he asked rhetorically. 'He doesn't want to win the World Championship for McLaren, he wants to do it at Ferrari. He hasn't spent three years here just for the money. The team do everything for him here. They couldn't go out of their way for him more and he's very happy here.

'My money is still on him to win the World Championship. Michael is a bit of a phenomenon, isn't he?'

Clive Mason/Allsport

DIARY

McLaren chief Ron Dennis denies that his team is contributing extra funds to Ferrari as part of the deal over the 1998 Concorde Agreement.

Rumours of a possible return to Paul Ricard for the French Grand Prix start circulating again.

CART star Alex Zanardi tipped to be in detailed talks with Williams as a possible candidate for 1999.

Lateral tyre grooves proposed as a possible means of further slowing F1 cars down in the future.

spin moments after he had found a y past Eddie Irvine's second-placed rrari ended Mika Häkkinen's hopes of tory but he recovered to collect four luable World Championship points.

ichael Schumacher and Eddie Irvine ebrate Ferrari's first 1-2 success since 90, a victory that owed as much to m tactics and opportunism as it did technical excellence.

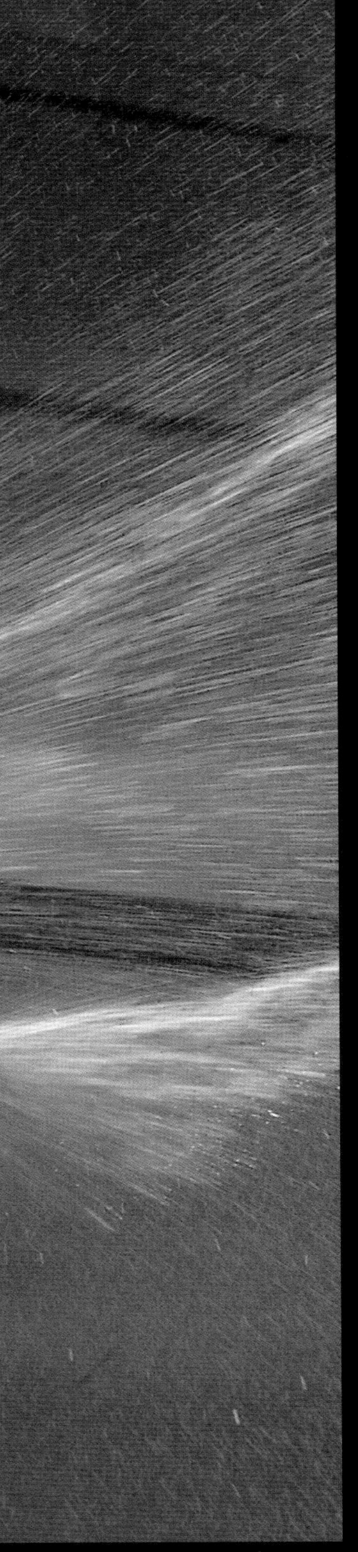

Diana Burnett

came in for an 8.5s stop, dropping back to third. Jean Alesi also brought his Sauber in for its first stop, dropping from fifth to eighth.

Meanwhile, Villeneuve moved briefly into second place ahead of Irvine before pitting on lap 24, dropping back to fifth in the queue. But the World Champion was pretty happy with the feel of his Williams FW20, and happier still after changing its first set of tyres, which for some reason produced a touch too much oversteer. From then on he was flat-out all the way into what turned out to be an eventual fourth place.

'I was pushing hard all the way through the race,' said Jacques, 'even when I was ten seconds behind David, as he wasn't really going any quicker than me. Today our car was actually pretty good on the high- and mid-speed corners; where we were lacking was coming out of the hairpins, but otherwise we had a strong race.'

By lap 30 Schumacher had opened a twenty-second advantage over Irvine while four laps later the Benetton pit erupted in chaos as Wurz pulled in for the second of his three planned stops just as Fisichella arrived for a replacement nose section following a brush with Alesi.

'On the first start I managed to get into sixth position,' said the frustrated Italian. 'Unfortunately the race was stopped and, at the second start, I ended up tenth. From that moment on everything went wrong. I damaged the nose and then lost time waiting to change it because the pits were busy with Alexander's stop. Apart from this, the car was very difficult to drive.' The two Benettons resumed in seventh and 12th.

The race for the leading positions, such as it was, had now settled down with Schumacher running steadily just over twenty seconds ahead of Irvine. Häkkinen was third ahead of Coulthard with a huge gap back to Villeneuve, Alesi, Wurz and Frentzen. The outcome of the race now depended on whether Häkkinen could effectively vault past Irvine to take second place at the final spate of refuelling stops, thereby giving himself a chance of closing the gap to Schumacher in the final sprint to the flag.

This crucial sequence of events began to unfold on lap 43 when Irvine made his second refuelling stop (9.6s), following which he resumed in fourth behind Häkkinen and Coulthard. Häkkinen ran through until lap 54 before making his second refuelling stop in 8.9s, but just missed getting out in front of Irvine.

Coulthard came in for his second stop on the following lap but more trouble with the refuelling mechanism meant that he was sent away to come in next time round for another try. After that, the luckless Scot found himself back in seventh place and he then came in again on lap 63 for a final frustrating visit.

Häkkinen piled on the pressure for all he was worth in the closing stages, but Irvine's Ferrari was quicker through the fast right-hander onto the long back straight, giving the Ulsterman a key edge. At the chequered flag he just managed to hang on to second place by 0.1s from the hard-trying McLaren driver.

Irvine was understandably elated. 'I did not try to push too hard at the start and tried to drive steadily,' he explained. 'Mika got close when I was held up by back-markers, but here it is easy to keep someone behind you.

'I knew he was going to have a go at the last corner, as I was entering slowly because my rear wheels were always locking up on the downchange. Luckily, the first time [he tried it], he made a mistake [the spin] and on the last lap I slid a bit wide. But we hung on.'

As for McLaren, the team felt that events had conspired to make a difficult race even less profitable than it might have been. Some observers suggested they had been defeated by precisely the sort of team-work that had brought such opprobrium onto their own heads in Melbourne. Was there one rule for Ferrari and another for everybody else? McLaren was certainly beginning to think so.

Others felt that an objective analysis of the events at Magny-Cours confirmed that the restart fiasco was just one of those unfortunate things.

Villeneuve finished fourth ahead of the lapped Wurz, while Coulthard struggled home in sixth with at least the race's fastest lap to his credit. The Saubers of Alesi and Herbert were next up, just out of the points. 'We were unlucky not to score today,' said Alesi, who was hit by Frentzen as they battled for sixth with three laps left to run.

'At one stage Fisichella hit the back of my car, but that just made me laugh because he was trying to pass where there was no possibility to do so. Later Frentzen hit me in the last corner. I thought I was going to score a point, but there was nothing I could do about Coulthard on the last lap. My car had been suddenly oversteering more, and when I stopped in *parc fermé* there was oil on the rear tyres. I think maybe there was a leak of some kind; possibly that brush with Frentzen caused some damage.'

Herbert was a disappointing 43 seconds behind his team-mate at the end. 'The car felt really good and my times were really consistent,' he said, 'but all through there was a hole at the bottom of the power curve and on my first stop the engine stalled as I hit the rev limiter coming into the pit road.'

Fisichella ended up a frustrated ninth, while the Stewart-Fords of Rubens Barrichello and Jos Verstappen took tenth and 12th places, sandwiching Olivier Panis's Prost-Peugeot. Barrichello reported that he was fighting the car for much of the race and failed really to get the best out of it, while Verstappen was happy to have finished his debut race for the team after that glitch which caused the race to be restarted.

For Panis, this was at least the end of a frustrating sequence of retirements, but Jarno Trulli had to make an unscheduled pit stop at the end of the second lap when he felt something jammed under his pedals. Later the Italian would spin off after picking up dirt on his tyres avoiding a pirouette by Herbert's Sauber.

The classified finishers were completed by the Arrows A19s of Mika Salo and Pedro Diniz, Frentzen, who retired with a bent track rod after his brush with Alesi on lap 67, Ralf Schumacher, who was three laps down at the chequered flag, and Shinji Nakano, whose Minardi stopped with engine trouble on lap 66.

Immediately after the race, Ferrari's success received personal praise from the company's high-profile President, Luca di Montezemolo. Having telephoned the Circuit de Nevers to personally congratulate his team on the result, he also confirmed that sporting director Jean Todt had renewed his contract to remain in his current role until the end of the 2001 season.

Todt's decision to stay on at Ferrari ensured a hitherto undreamed-of level of management stability within the most famous team in the F1 business. It was also destined to be a major factor in tempting Schumacher to sign a further long-term contract with the team beyond the end of the 1999 season.

'This is a dream result,' said Todt after the French event. 'Schumacher and Irvine had an incredible race and Eddie did a great job to keep the McLarens behind him.'

McLaren still privately believed that only the possibility of technical unreliability stood between them and the World Championship. For their part, Schumacher and Irvine left the Circuit de Nevers with a rather more clear-cut view. They were starting to think they had McLaren on the defensive.

GRAND PRIX MOBIL 1 DE FRANCE

26–28 JUNE 1998

NEVERS MAGNY-COURS

Race distance: 71 laps, 187.383 miles/301.564 km

Race weather: Dry, hot and sunny

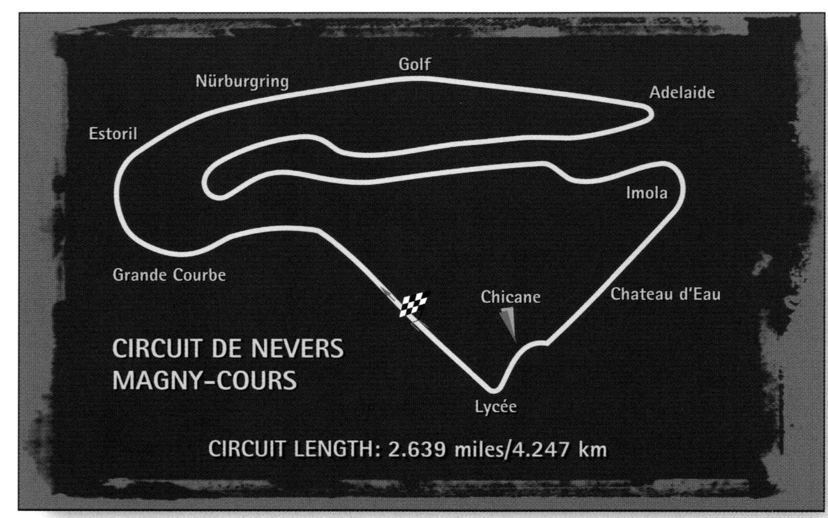

Pos.	Driver	Nat.	No.	Entrant	Car/Engine	Tyres	Laps	Time/Retirement	Speed (mph/km/h)
1	**Michael Schumacher**	**D**	**3**	**Scuderia Ferrari Marlboro**	**Ferrari F300 047 V10**	**G**	**71**	**1h 34m 45.026s**	**118.659/190.963**
2	**Eddie Irvine**	**GB**	**4**	**Scuderia Ferrari Marlboro**	**Ferrari F300 047 V10**	**G**	**71**	**1h 35m 04.601s**	**118.251/190.307**
3	**Mika Häkkinen**	**SF**	**8**	**West McLaren Mercedes**	**McLaren MP4/13-Mercedes FO110G V10**	**B**	**71**	**1h 35m 04.773s**	**118.248/190.302**
4	**Jacques Villeneuve**	**CDN**	**1**	**Winfield Williams**	**Williams FW20-Mecachrome GC37/01 V10**	**G**	**71**	**1h 35m 51.991s**	**117.277/188.739**
5	**Alexander Wurz**	**A**	**6**	**Mild Seven Benetton Playlife**	**Benetton B198-Playlife V10**	**B**	**70**		
6	**David Coulthard**	**GB**	**7**	**West McLaren Mercedes**	**McLaren MP4/13-Mercedes FO110G V10**	**B**	**70**		
7	Jean Alesi	F	14	Red Bull Sauber Petronas	Sauber C17-Petronas SPE01D V10	G	70		
8	Johnny Herbert	GB	15	Red Bull Sauber Petronas	Sauber C17-Petronas SPE01D V10	G	70		
9	Giancarlo Fisichella	I	5	Mild Seven Benetton Playlife	Benetton B198-Playlife V10	B	70		
10	Rubens Barrichello	BR	18	Stewart Ford	Stewart SF2-Ford Zetec-R V10	B	69		
11	Olivier Panis	F	11	Gauloises Prost Peugeot	Prost AP01-Peugeot A16 V10	B	69		
12	Jos Verstappen	NL	19	Stewart Ford	Stewart SF2-Ford Zetec-R V10	B	69		
13	Mika Salo	SF	17	Danka Zepter Arrows	Arrows A19 V10	B	69		
14	Pedro Diniz	BR	16	Danka Zepter Arrows	Arrows A19 V10	B	69		
15	Heinz-Harald Frentzen	D	2	Winfield Williams	Williams FW20-Mecachrome GC37/01 V10	G	68	Steering	
16	Ralf Schumacher	D	10	B&H Jordan Mugen Honda	Jordan 198-Mugen Honda MF310C V10	G	68		
17	Shinji Nakano	J	22	Fondmetal Minardi Ford	Minardi M198-Ford Zetec-R V10	B	65	Engine	
	Toranosuke Takagi	J	21	Tyrrell Ford	Tyrrell 026-Ford Zetec-R V10	G	60	Engine	
	Jarno Trulli	I	12	Gauloises Prost Peugeot	Prost AP01-Peugeot A16 V10	B	55	Spun off	
	Esteban Tuero	RA	23	Fondmetal Minardi Ford	Minardi M198-Ford Zetec-R V10	B	41	Hydraulics	
	Damon Hill	GB	9	B&H Jordan Mugen Honda	Jordan 198-Mugen Honda MF310C V10	G	19	Hydraulics	
	Ricardo Rosset	BR	20	Tyrrell Ford	Tyrrell 026-Ford Zetec-R V10	G	16	Engine	

Fastest lap: Coulthard, on lap 59, 1m 17.523s, 122.634 mph/197.360 km/h.

Lap record: Nigel Mansell (F1 Williams FW14B-Renault V10), 1m 17.070s, 123.355 mph/198.521 km/h (1992).

B – Bridgestone G – Goodyear

All results and data © FIA 1998

Grid order	1	2	3	4	5	6	7	8	9	10	11	12	13	14	15	16	17	18	19	20	21	22	23	24	25	26
8 HÄKKINEN	3	3	3	3	3	3	3	3	3	3	3	3	3	3	3	3	3	3	3	3	3	3	4	3	3	3
3 M. SCHUMACHER	4	4	4	4	4	4	4	4	4	4	4	4	4	4	4	4	4	4	4	4	4	4	3	1	4	4
7 COULTHARD	8	8	8	8	8	8	8	8	8	8	8	8	8	8	8	8	8	8	8	7	7	7	1	4	8	8
4 IRVINE	7	7	7	7	7	7	7	7	7	7	7	7	7	7	7	7	7	7	7	8	8	1	8	8	7	7
1 VILLENEUVE	1	1	1	1	1	1	1	1	1	1	1	1	1	1	1	1	1	1	1	1	1	14	14	7	1	1
10 R. SCHUMACHER	10	10	10	10	10	10	10	10	10	10	10	10	10	10	10	6	6	14	14	14	14	8	7	6	6	6
9 HILL	9	9	9	9	9	9	9	9	9	9	9	9	9	9	6	10	14	5	2	2	15	15	15	15	14	14
2 FRENTZEN	6	6	6	6	6	6	6	6	6	6	6	6	6	6	14	14	5	2	15	15	6	6	6	14	5	5
5 FISICHELLA	14	14	14	14	14	14	14	14	14	14	14	14	14	14	9	5	2	15	6	6	18	5	5	5	2	2
6 WURZ	5	5	5	5	5	5	5	5	5	5	5	5	5	5	5	2	15	6	18	18	5	18	2	2	11	11
14 ALESI	12	2	2	2	2	2	2	2	2	2	2	2	2	2	2	9	10	18	5	5	11	11	18	11	18	18
12 TRULLI	2	18	18	18	18	15	15	15	15	15	15	15	15	15	15	15	18	11	11	11	2	2	11	18	15	15
15 HERBERT	18	11	11	11	15	18	18	18	18	18	18	18	18	18	18	18	9	19	19	19	19	16	16	16	16	16
18 BARRICHELLO	11	15	15	15	11	11	11	11	11	11	11	11	11	11	11	11	11	9	9	16	16	17	17	17	17	17
19 VERSTAPPEN	15	19	19	19	19	19	19	19	19	19	19	19	19	19	19	19	19	16	16	17	17	21	21	21	21	21
11 PANIS	19	20	20	20	20	20	21	21	21	21	21	21	21	21	21	16	16	17	17	22	21	19	19	19	19	19
16 DINIZ	20	21	21	21	21	21	20	20	20	20	20	20	20	20	20	17	17	22	22	21	22	22	22	22	22	22
20 ROSSET	21	12	16	16	16	16	16	16	16	16	16	16	16	16	16	22	22	21	21	23	23	23	23	12	23	23
17 SALO	16	16	22	22	22	22	22	17	17	17	17	17	17	17	17	20	21	23	23	12	12	12	12	23	12	12
21 TAKAGI	22	22	17	17	17	17	17	22	22	22	22	22	22	22	22	21	23	10	12	10	10	10	10	10	10	10
22 NAKANO	17	17	23	23	23	23	23	23	23	23	23	23	23	23	23	23	12	12	10							
23 TUERO	23	23	12	12	12	12	12	12	12	12	12	12	12	12	12	12										

Grid order	27	28	29	30	31	32	33	34	35	36	37	38	39	40	41	42	43	44	45	46	47	48	49	50	51	52	53
8 HÄKKINEN	3	3	3	3	3	3	3	3	3	3	3	3	3	3	3	3	3	3	3	3	3	3	3	3	3	3	3
3 M. SCHUMACHER	4	4	4	4	4	4	4	4	4	4	4	4	4	4	4	4	4	8	8	8	8	8	8	8	8	8	8
7 COULTHARD	8	8	8	8	8	8	8	8	8	8	8	8	8	8	8	8	8	7	7	7	7	7	7	7	7	7	7
4 IRVINE	7	7	7	7	7	7	7	7	7	7	7	7	7	7	7	7	7	4	4	4	4	4	4	4	4	4	4
1 VILLENEUVE	1	1	1	1	1	1	1	1	1	1	1	1	1	1	1	1	1	1	1	1	1	1	1	1	1	1	1
10 R. SCHUMACHER	6	6	6	6	6	6	6	6	14	14	14	14	14	14	14	14	14	14	14	6	6	6	6	6	2	6	6
9 HILL	14	14	14	14	14	14	14	14	6	6	6	6	6	6	6	6	6	6	6	14	2	2	2	2	6	14	14
2 FRENTZEN	5	5	5	5	5	5	2	2	2	2	2	2	2	2	2	2	2	2	2	2	14	14	14	14	14	2	2
5 FISICHELLA	2	2	2	2	2	2	5	5	15	15	15	15	15	15	15	15	15	15	15	15	15	5	5	5	5	5	15
6 WURZ	11	11	11	18	18	18	18	18	18	18	18	18	18	18	18	18	18	18	18	18	5	15	15	15	15	15	5
14 ALESI	18	18	18	15	15	15	15	15	11	11	11	11	11	11	11	11	11	11	5	5	18	18	18	18	18	18	18
12 TRULLI	15	15	15	11	11	11	11	11	5	5	5	5	5	5	5	5	5	5	11	11	11	11	11	11	11	11	11
15 HERBERT	16	16	16	16	16	16	16	16	16	16	16	16	19	19	19	19	19	19	19	21	21	21	21	21	19	19	19
18 BARRICHELLO	17	17	17	17	21	21	21	21	19	19	19	19	16	21	21	21	21	21	21	19	19	19	19	19	21	17	17
19 VERSTAPPEN	21	21	21	21	17	19	19	19	21	17	17	17	21	17	17	17	17	17	17	17	17	17	17	17	17	16	16
11 PANIS	19	19	19	19	19	17	17	17	17	21	21	21	17	16	16	16	16	16	16	16	16	16	16	16	16	21	21
16 DINIZ	22	22	22	22	22	22	22	22	22	22	22	22	22	22	22	22	12	12	12	12	12	12	12	12	12	12	12
20 ROSSET	23	23	23	23	23	23	12	12	12	12	12	12	12	12	12	12	22	22	22	22	22	22	22	22	22	22	22
17 SALO	12	12	12	12	12	12	23	23	23	23	23	23	23	23	23	10	10	10	10	10	10	10	10	10	10	10	10
21 TAKAGI	10	10	10	10	10	10	10	10	10	10	10	10	10	10	10												
22 NAKANO																											
23 TUERO																											

Pit stop

One lap behind leader

STARTING GRID

	8 **HÄKKINEN** McLaren
3 **M. SCHUMACHER** Ferrari	
	7 **COULTHARD** McLaren
4 **IRVINE** Ferrari	
	1 **VILLENEUVE** Williams
10 **R. SCHUMACHER** Jordan	
	9 **HILL** Jordan
2 **FRENTZEN** Williams	
	5 **FISICHELLA** Benetton
6 **WURZ** Benetton	
	14 **ALESI** Sauber
12 **TRULLI** Prost	
	15 **HERBERT** Sauber
18 **BARRICHELLO** Stewart	
	19 **VERSTAPPEN** Stewart
11 **PANIS** Prost	
	16 **DINIZ** Arrows
20 **ROSSET** Tyrrell	
	17 **SALO** Arrows
21 **TAKAGI** Tyrrell	
	22 **NAKANO** Minardi
23 **TUERO** Minardi	

7	58	59	60	61	62	63	64	65	66	67	68	69	70	71	●
3	3	3	3	3	3	3	3	3	3	3	3	3	3	3	1
4	4	4	4	4	4	4	4	4	4	4	4	4	4	4	2
8	8	8	8	8	8	8	8	8	8	8	8	8	8	8	3
1	1	1	1	1	1	1	1	1	1	1	1	1	1	1	4
6	6	6	6	7	7	7	6	6	6	6	6	6	6		5
4	7	7	7	6	6	6	14	14	14	14	14	14	7		6
7	14	14	14	14	14	14	2	2	2	7	7	7	14		
2	2	2	2	2	2	2	7	7	7	2	2	15	15		
5	15	15	15	15	15	15	15	15	15	15	15	5	5		
5	5	5	5	5	5	5	5	5	5	5	5	18			
8	18	18	18	18	18	18	18	18	18	18	18	11			
1	11	11	11	11	11	11	11	11	11	11	11	19			
9	19	19	19	19	19	19	19	19	19	19	19	17			
7	17	17	17	17	17	17	17	17	17	17	17	16			
1	21	21	21	16	16	16	16	16	16	16	16				
6	16	16	16	22	22	22	22	22	10	10	10				
2	22	22	22	10	10	10	10	10							
0	10	10	10												

TIME SHEETS

QUALIFYING

Weather: Very warm, light overcast

Pos.	Driver	Car	Laps	Time
1	Mika Häkkinen	McLaren-Mercedes	12	1m 14.929s
2	Michael Schumacher	Ferrari	12	1m 15.159s
3	David Coulthard	McLaren-Mercedes	12	1m 15.333s
4	Eddie Irvine	Ferrari	12	1m 15.527s
5	Jacques Villeneuve	Williams-Mecachrome	12	1m 15.630s
6	Ralf Schumacher	Jordan-Mugen Honda	12	1m 15.925s
7	Damon Hill	Jordan-Mugen Honda	9	1m 16.245s
8	Heinz-Harald Frentzen	Williams-Mecachrome	12	1m 16.319s
9	Giancarlo Fisichella	Benetton-Playlife	12	1m 16.375s
10	Alexander Wurz	Benetton-Playlife	12	1m 16.460s
11	Jean Alesi	Sauber-Petronas	12	1m 16.627s
12	Jarno Trulli	Prost-Peugeot	12	1m 16.892s
13	Johnny Herbert	Sauber-Petronas	12	1m 16.977s
14	Rubens Barrichello	Stewart-Ford	12	1m 17.024s
15	Jos Verstappen	Stewart-Ford	11	1m 17.604s
16	Olivier Panis	Prost-Peugeot	11	1m 17.671s
17	Pedro Diniz	Arrows	8	1m 17.880s
18	Ricardo Rosset	Tyrrell-Ford	11	1m 17.908s
19	Mika Salo	Arrows	11	1m 17.970s
20	Toranosuke Takagi	Tyrrell-Ford	10	1m 18.221s
21	Shinji Nakano	Minardi-Ford	12	1m 18.273s
22	Esteban Tuero	Minardi-Ford	10	1m 19.146s

FRIDAY FREE PRACTICE

Weather: Cool and overcast

Pos.	Driver	Laps	Time
1	Mika Häkkinen	28	1m 16.515s
2	Eddie Irvine	33	1m 16.597s
3	David Coulthard	25	1m 16.707s
4	Heinz-Harald Frentzen	35	1m 17.026s
5	Michael Schumacher	35	1m 17.429s
6	Ralf Schumacher	35	1m 17.505s
7	Giancarlo Fisichella	30	1m 17.664s
8	Alexander Wurz	26	1m 17.706s
9	Damon Hill	40	1m 17.895s
10	Johnny Herbert	32	1m 17.977s
11	Jarno Trulli	38	1m 18.036s
12	Jean Alesi	22	1m 18.172s
13	Olivier Panis	26	1m 18.367s
14	Ricardo Rosset	34	1m 18.649s
15	Mika Salo	33	1m 18.656s
16	Rubens Barrichello	27	1m 18.703s
17	Jacques Villeneuve	18	1m 19.008s
18	Pedro Diniz	32	1m 19.023s
19	Toranosuke Takagi	46	1m 19.057s
20	Jos Verstappen	15	1m 20.286s
21	Shinji Nakano	20	1m 20.445s
22	Esteban Tuero	21	1m 20.871s

SATURDAY FREE PRACTICE

Weather: Sunny and hot

Pos.	Driver	Laps	Time
1	Mika Häkkinen	26	1m 15.613s
2	Michael Schumacher	17	1m 15.738s
3	Eddie Irvine	27	1m 15.870s
4	David Coulthard	17	1m 15.909s
5	Ralf Schumacher	35	1m 16.678s
6	Heinz-Harald Frentzen	31	1m 16.745s
7	Jacques Villeneuve	35	1m 16.782s
8	Giancarlo Fisichella	29	1m 17.106s
9	Alexander Wurz	19	1m 17.205s
10	Damon Hill	28	1m 17.426s
11	Jarno Trulli	26	1m 17.711s
12	Toranosuke Takagi	26	1m 17.847s
13	Johnny Herbert	26	1m 17.873s
14	Mika Salo	25	1m 18.075s
15	Rubens Barrichello	25	1m 18.170s
16	Pedro Diniz	28	1m 18.389s
17	Ricardo Rosset	24	1m 18.405s
18	Jos Verstappen	29	1m 18.451s
19	Olivier Panis	20	1m 18.706s
20	Jean Alesi	4	1m 18.893s
21	Shinji Nakano	28	1m 19.324s
22	Esteban Tuero	27	1m 19.475s

WARM-UP

Weather: Sunny and warm

Pos.	Driver	Laps	Time
1	David Coulthard	14	1m 16.483s
2	Mika Häkkinen	12	1m 16.718s
3	Michael Schumacher	14	1m 17.189s
4	Eddie Irvine	14	1m 17.628s
5	Jacques Villeneuve	14	1m 18.442s
6	Heinz-Harald Frentzen	17	1m 18.466s
7	Giancarlo Fisichella	11	1m 18.545s
8	Alexander Wurz	14	1m 18.607s
9	Jean Alesi	13	1m 18.611s
10	Olivier Panis	12	1m 18.729s
11	Ralf Schumacher	14	1m 18.790s
12	Damon Hill	11	1m 18.819s
13	Johnny Herbert	15	1m 19.092s
14	Rubens Barrichello	13	1m 19.097s
15	Jarno Trulli	18	1m 19.442s
16	Jos Verstappen	12	1m 19.641s
17	Mika Salo	13	1m 19.733s
18	Toranosuke Takagi	13	1m 19.788s
19	Shinji Nakano	17	1m 19.835s
20	Pedro Diniz	14	1m 20.240s
21	Esteban Tuero	16	1m 21.376s
22	Ricardo Rosset	13	1m 22.160s

RACE FASTEST LAPS

Weather: Dry, hot and sunny

Driver	Time	Lap
David Coulthard	1m 17.523s	59
Michael Schumacher	1m 17.770s	4
Mika Häkkinen	1m 18.493s	52
Jacques Villeneuve	1m 18.913s	42
Eddie Irvine	1m 18.956s	25
Ralf Schumacher	1m 19.052s	56
Heinz-Harald Frentzen	1m 19.229s	48
Giancarlo Fisichella	1m 19.307s	48
Alexander Wurz	1m 19.320s	36
Damon Hill	1m 19.490s	4
Jean Alesi	1m 19.660s	48
Johnny Herbert	1m 19.771s	51
Jarno Trulli	1m 19.869s	6
Olivier Panis	1m 19.953s	32
Toranosuke Takagi	1m 20.299s	37
Rubens Barrichello	1m 20.651s	43
Jos Verstappen	1m 20.849s	47
Mika Salo	1m 21.502s	61
Pedro Diniz	1m 21.765s	38
Shinji Nakano	1m 21.883s	42
Ricardo Rosset	1m 22.435s	3
Esteban Tuero	1m 22.761s	34

CHASSIS LOG BOOK

No.	Driver	Chassis
1	Villeneuve	Williams FW20/5
2	Frentzen	Williams FW20/4
	spare	Williams FW20/3
3	M. Schumacher	Ferrari F300/187
4	Irvine	Ferrari F300/185
	spare	Ferrari F300/186
5	Fisichella	Benetton B198/2
6	Wurz	Benetton B198/6
	spare	Benetton B198/4
7	Coulthard	McLaren MP4/13/3
8	Häkkinen	McLaren MP4/13/6
	spare	McLaren MP4/13/4
9	Hill	Jordan 198/3
10	R. Schumacher	Jordan 198/4
	spare	Jordan 198/5
11	Panis	Prost AP01/2
12	Trulli	Prost AP01/3
	spare	Prost AP01/5
14	Alesi	Sauber C17/3
15	Herbert	Sauber C17/2
	spare	Sauber C17/4
16	Diniz	Arrows A19/1
17	Salo	Arrows A19/5
	spare	Arrows A19/2
18	Barrichello	Stewart SF2/4
19	Verstappen	Stewart SF2/3
	spare	Stewart SF2/2
20	Rosset	Tyrrell 026/2
21	Takagi	Tyrrell 026/1
	spare	Tyrrell 026/3
22	Nakano	Minardi M198/4
23	Tuero	Minardi M198/5
	spare	Minardi M198/3

POINTS TABLES

Drivers

Pos.	Driver	Points
1	Mika Häkkinen	50
2	Michael Schumacher	44
3	David Coulthard	30
4	Eddie Irvine	25
5	Alexander Wurz	14
6	Giancarlo Fisichella	13
7	Jacques Villeneuve	11
8	Heinz-Harald Frentzen	8
9	Rubens Barrichello	4
10 =	Jean Alesi	3
10 =	Mika Salo	3
12 =	Johnny Herbert	1
12 =	Pedro Diniz	1
12 =	Jan Magnussen	1

Constructors

Pos.	Constructor	Points
1	McLaren	80
2	Ferrari	69
3	Benetton	27
4	Williams	19
5	Stewart	5
6 =	Sauber	4
6 =	Arrows	4

FIA WORLD CHAMPIONSHIP • ROUND 9

BRITISH

grand prix

M. SCHUMACHER
HÄKKINEN
IRVINE
WURZ
FISICHELLA
R. SCHUMACHER

Main picture: Michael Schumacher leaves a thick curtain of spray in his wake as he charges into Copse Corner. The Ferrari star made the most of his rivals' misfortunes to score a controversial win.

Left: Doubtless still somewhat bemused by the bizarre conclusion to the race, Mika Häkkinen and Michael Schumacher make their way to the podium.

IT was almost as if Bernie Ecclestone had written the script. You might have thought that on World Cup Final day the media – and particularly the television attention – would have been firmly focused on the match between France and Brazil in Paris on the Sunday evening. But no; Michael Schumacher, the Ferrari team and an incredible set of circumstances produced by the weather on a typically wet English summer's afternoon conspired to produce a bizarre and highly controversial British Grand Prix which easily eclipsed anything even the convoluted world of professional football could deliver.

About the only fact beyond dispute was that Michael Schumacher removed the British Grand Prix from the dwindling list of races he had never won. That said, almost every other element of the rain-soaked Silverstone event was surrounded by varying degrees of controversy and uncertainty.

Having emerged victorious from a remarkable high-speed battle with Mika Häkkinen's McLaren-Mercedes on a track surface intermittently assailed by torrential rain, Schumacher capped the day by bringing his Ferrari F300 into the pits to serve a ten-second stop-go penalty *after* he had actually taken the chequered flag. This was the climax to a sequence of events that ensured that the race ended enveloped in bad feeling and controversy which took a considerable time to subside.

The nub of the problem was that Schumacher had earlier allegedly lapped the Benetton of Alexander Wurz on lap 43 of the 60-lap race while the field was banked up behind the safety car, which had been deployed to slow the pace of the race during the height of the downpour.

This rule infringement resulted in the Ferrari team leader being handed a ten-second penalty, but the stewards decided that this should be added to his race time rather than bringing him into the pits for a more time-consuming delay. However, according to the rules, the sanction of adding ten seconds to the elapsed race time can only be applied if the race is within 12 laps of the finish, which in this case it clearly was not (see sidebar).

The FIA stewards also seemed at variance with their previous decisions in similar circumstances. In last year's Austrian Grand Prix, for example, Schumacher incurred a ten-second penalty but had to come into the pits to take it.

This was not the first time that Schumacher had been in trouble at Silverstone. In the 1994 British Grand Prix he was shown the black flag after overtaking Damon Hill's Williams on the parade lap, then disqualified for ignoring the warning signal. Ironically, the Benetton team for whom he was then driving used as their defence their belief that the ten seconds would be added to his overall time at the end of the race. This controversy set in train a sequence of events which would see Schumacher suspended from the Italian and Portuguese Grands Prix later in the season.

Yet this year Silverstone's weather produced conditions which looked from the outset as though they were going to play straight into Schumacher's hands. The warm-up took place on a soaking track surface and, even though the worst of the rain seemed to have passed by the time the cars lined up on the grid, the circuit remained extremely treacherous.

The Ferrari drivers in fact opted for a full-dry chassis set-up in conjunction with intermediate rubber – the preferred tyre choice for most Bridgestone and Goodyear runners alike – although the Stewart-Ford team took the unaccountable decision to start on dry-weather rubber. This was optimism of an unusual order under the circumstances.

Ferrari's pace when the track surface was very wet could be put down to the performance of the aquattro full-wet tyre, which was available in two compounds. Some Goodyear runners believed that it was not the best choice for the conditions, but others accepted the tyre company's view that it offered a longer transitional period of sustained performance as the track surface dried out. Certainly, it seemed to work well enough for Ferrari.

Meanwhile Benetton was taking a slightly more scientific approach with commercial director David Warren being sent aloft in chief executive David Richards's helicopter, which was flown in precisely the direction from which the prevailing weather was coming. The strategy worked perfectly: the 'flying eye' reported that more rain was on its way and the team's estimate as to when it would arrive proved accurate.

Häkkinen led the sprint for Copse from Schumacher's Ferrari and David Coulthard's McLaren with Jean Alesi's Sauber C17 making a simply stupendous getaway from eighth on the grid to slot into an immediate fourth. Mika duly slammed through at the end of the opening lap with 0.3s in hand over Michael, with Coulthard pressing hard and Alesi keeping up well. Already a slight gap was opening to the Williams FW20s of Jacques Villeneuve and Heinz-Harald Frentzen in fifth and sixth places.

Mika Häkkinen duly qualified his McLaren-Mercedes in pole position at Silverstone, but it was an uncomfortably close-run thing for the World Championship points leader. With only a minute of the hour-long Saturday afternoon session still to run, Michael Schumacher's Ferrari F300 was 0.001s inside the Finn's best time to the first timing split, and looked on course to grab the honours.

Then he locked a brake at the Abbey chicane. So near, yet so far; Michael aborted the lap and came straight into the pits, pragmatic as always. He would have to be satisfied with second-fastest time, half a second slower than his rival's best.

'It's all "if and whether" but it doesn't matter now,' he reflected. 'I had a very good first sector on that run and just locked the inside wheel at Abbey and ran wide, and in this moment I knew the time had gone.

'Even on my previous run I had run wide in that corner and still managed more or less a line to continue, so overall, yes, there were a couple of tenths [that I needed] to improve.'

For his part, Häkkinen was satisfied with his efforts and acknowledged that Bridgestone had done a terrific job producing another new tyre since he'd set the pace in the final pre-race Silverstone test. In qualifying he did three runs, then went out for a final tour round just in case somebody threatened unexpectedly.

'I was just waiting for information from the team, to know whether I should start pushing on that fourth set of tyres,' he explained, 'but in the end I was able to save them.' Häkkinen's best time came on his first run.

Behind Schumacher, Jacques Villeneuve brought a collective smile to the face of the Williams team by qualifying the further revised FW20 third, its best grid performance of the season. New, shorter side pods, some engine developments for qualifying and the car's proven preference for faster corners all worked to Villeneuve's advantage.

'The new bits have settled the car down and we gradually dialled out its oversteer by the last run,' said Jacques. 'This was the first time this season when we had a package that was strong enough to fight like that, so it's a great feeling.'

Yet if the fastest three qualifiers were upbeat about their prospects, David Coulthard finished the session feeling extremely disappointed. Fourth place on the grid, a full second slower than Häkkinen, was a painful note on which to start a weekend for which he'd harboured such high hopes. 'It felt heavy and sluggish,' he murmured. 'I was just completely up against a brick wall.'

Coulthard's abiding problem seemed to be a lack of rear-end stability and grip, perhaps a by-product of using the softer available Bridgestone compound for qualifying and the race. It was a shortcoming which bugged most of the Bridgestone runners, apart from Häkkinen, who was the only one to take the harder 'prime' tyre.

Eddie Irvine qualified a satisfied fifth, catching up time lost during the Saturday morning free practice session when he spun off the road. He thought he might have been able to push DC off the second row, but reflected that fifth place – on the 'geographical' outside of row three on the Silverstone grid – might offer him more of a possible advantage.

Alongside the second Ferrari was Heinz-Harald Frentzen's Williams. 'On my last run I felt I could beat Coulthard, but at Bridge Corner I made a slight mistake, was too quick and had to brake a little so I lost some time,' he explained. Apart from that he was pretty satisfied.

Damon Hill was slightly disappointed after being unable to improve on seventh-fastest time with the Jordan 198, despite slightly more power from the Mugen Honda V10 for qualifying. 'I think there was potential to do better,' said Hill, 'but I gave it everything I had and kept coming up with the same lap time.'

At least he had better fortune than team-mate Ralf Schumacher. The young German spun at Abbey and then had to take the spare 198, which was kitted out for Hill and had a touch too much oversteer for his taste.

He also had other problems. Having overtaken under yellow flags during the Saturday morning free practice session, Ralf was under notice that he would lose his fastest lap in qualifying. His car then failed the driver egress check – as did Olivier Panis with the Prost-Peugeot – with the result that his tenth-place qualifying time was also disallowed and he joined the Frenchman on the back row of the starting grid.

In the Sauber garage, meanwhile, there were plenty of smiles as Jean Alesi posted his best qualifying performance of the season to date with eighth-fastest time, just 0.003s ahead of team-mate Johnny Herbert, who was next up. Johnny reckoned the car felt better in race set-up than it did in practice trim, but Alesi was pretty content.

Tenth and 11th after Ralf Schumacher's demotion were the Benetton B198s of Giancarlo Fisichella and Alexander Wurz. Both drivers were very unhappy, complaining that, while the cars' handling balance seemed OK, there was a dire shortage of grip and the car did not respond to set-up changes.

'We're not getting the most out of the tyres,' reflected chief designer Nick Wirth, 'and we're working with Bridgestone to find out what we need to do to improve it. We seem to be having a problem on medium-to-high-speed corners and are around half a second slower than we were in the test last week.'

There was much optimism at Arrows surrounding the team's latest C-spec engine, which was rated a worthwhile improvement over its predecessor. Pedro Diniz and Mika Salo lined up 12th and 13th, although they were still bugged by lack of balance from the latest Bridgestone tyre specification.

'We had a few problems in the morning which were fixed for qualifying,' said Salo. 'I started to have some gearbox problems on the second run and jumped the gears a few times, which lost me a lot of time. In the end, I decided to stop the car on the circuit.'

In 14th place came Jarno Trulli's Prost, the Italian unable to work out a decent chassis balance despite alternating between his race car and the spare. Jos Verstappen and Rubens Barrichello were next up in the Stewart-Fords, both men grappling with frustrating mid-corner understeer produced by the latest Bridgestone rubber.

The Tyrrell duo should have been able to capitalise on the Bridgestone problems among the second division teams in order to move up the grid slightly, but Tora Takagi could manage no better than 17th (after the grid had been amended) with Ricardo Rosset 20th. They were separated by the Minardi drivers, who continued to struggle. Esteban Tuero had a clutch problem with his race chassis and took the spare in qualifying while Shinji Nakano was unhappy with his car's handling balance throughout.

Sutton Motorsport Images

A sodden Union Jack adds to the difficulties faced by Giancarlo Fisichella and Jos Verstappen as they contend with the ever-changing track conditions.

Below right: Ralf Schumacher chases the Ferrari of Eddie Irvine. Relegated to the back row of the grid after a technical misdemeanour, the German drove with great verve to give Jordan its first point of the season.

Below left: Johnny Herbert searches in vain for the missing fractions of a second beneath his Sauber C17.

With four laps completed, as the rain began to fall again, Häkkinen seemed to be gaining the upper hand, coming through 3.1s ahead of Schumacher. Eddie Irvine, having made a very bad start from fifth place on the grid to come round in tenth at the end of the opening lap, was by this time already up to eighth, overtaking Johnny Herbert's Sauber to take the position going into Copse at the start of lap four.

Midway round the fifth lap Coulthard neatly outbraked Schumacher's Ferrari to take second place at the Abbey chicane just as Frentzen moved ahead of Villeneuve. By lap seven the two McLaren-Mercs were firmly entrenched in the lead with ten seconds now separating Häkkinen from Schumacher's third-placed Ferrari.

Further back, while Damon Hill was running a solid seventh in his Jordan 198, his team-mate Ralf Schumacher was really making mincemeat of the midfield runners, having been consigned to the back row of the grid thanks to a technical infringement on Saturday. With seven laps completed he was already up to 12th place and charging hard with just the right blend of aggression and restraint.

On lap 14 Hill, who had earlier lost a place to Irvine's Ferrari, spun off and stalled his Jordan's engine at Brooklands. Damon walked away in a mood of acute frustration. 'I was hugely disappointed not to have performed as I had hoped,' he admitted. 'I feel very sad not to have given my fans a good result.'

By this stage in the proceedings light drizzle was fast turning to rain proper. On lap 16 Frentzen, by now back in sixth, spun off for good at Bridge. Three laps later Schumacher's Ferrari came in for its first refuelling stop, switching to another set of intermediates, and this dropped him to 41 seconds behind the leading McLaren.

On lap 21 Coulthard made his first stop, retaining second behind Häkkinen, but the McLaren team kept him on intermediates whereas Mika, who stopped two laps later, switched to full wets.

The weather was changing all the time by this point in the race. Although the conditions eventually looked as though they would play into Coulthard's hands, at the time his car was fitted with another set of intermediates he was certainly not terribly happy about it.

However, Ron Dennis explained: 'When David made his stop, the weather looked as if it was clearing, which resulted in the decision for him to get a set of intermediates. By the time Mika stopped, a few laps later,

igel Snowdon

Darren Price

Sutton Motorsport Images

DIARY

Ford confirms purchase of Cosworth Racing from new owners Audi.

CART champion Alex Zanardi now tipped to join Williams F1 squad for the 1999 season to replace Jacques Villeneuve, who recently announced his planned move to the new BAR team.

Eddie Irvine brands Damon Hill 'a sad old man' after accusing the Jordan driver of weaving in front of him during the early stages of the British GP.

Ron Dennis calls for the FIA to legalise traction control in F1 due to the difficulties of policing bans on such systems.

Alain Prost makes preliminary offer to Jean Alesi for 1999.

Both McLaren drivers left the track – and paid the price. David Coulthard *(far left)* pirouetted into retirement after 37 laps, while damage sustained during a lurid high-speed spin *(left)* probably cost Mika Häkkinen victory.

Below left: Eddie Irvine maintained his fine form, recovering from a poor start to claim third place at the flag.

the weather was getting worse, meaning he changed to wets.'

Meanwhile, on lap 23, Herbert had got his Sauber ahead of Alesi, the 1995 British GP winner running on a one-stop strategy in contrast to the Frenchman's two-stopper. Over the next few laps Jean began to get a little frustrated to the point that, on lap 27, Johnny spun into the gravel, just missing his team-mate, as he tried to wave the other Sauber ahead in response to instructions from the pit wall.

'The team began talking to me on the radio,' he explained, 'but it was impossible to hear what anybody was actually saying because of the interference.

'Going into Priory on the 27th lap, I started to wave him by, but it's difficult when you are racing in such conditions, trying to decipher a radio message and watching your mirrors. I spun off into the dirt, and as soon as I felt the marshals pushing me I knew it was over because outside assistance in such situations is illegal. I just drove round to the pits to retire.'

Meanwhile, Michael Schumacher was dropping steadily away from the McLarens on his intermediates and on lap 29 Coulthard closed to within 0.9s of Häkkinen at the head of the field. On lap 30 both Ricardo Rosset's Tyrrell and Esteban Tuero's Minardi spun off the road, while two laps later Ralf Schumacher's Jordan – now up to sixth – made its second stop, almost mowing down Williams technical director Patrick Head, who was crossing the pit lane at the time.

On lap 38 things began to go wrong for McLaren. As he lapped Giancarlo Fisichella's Benetton going into the Abbey chicane, Coulthard spun off into the gravel and out of the race. To say he was furious was an understatement as he wondered out loud why he'd been given intermediates at that first stop. But it had seemed like a good idea at the time.

On lap 39 Irvine, by now up to third, made his second stop, taking on full wets. Next time round both Häkkinen and Schumacher did the same, the main protagonists now separated by over half a minute. Häkkinen, who had driven with absolute precision and control in the treacherous conditions up to this point, looked as though he had victory in the bag.

Two laps later, however, with the rain absolutely tipping down, Häkkinen spun wildly at Bridge, careering across the grass and gravel trap, miraculously managing to keep things more or less under control and finding his way back to the circuit. But his right-hand front wing end plate was well mangled as a result of this little excursion, to say nothing of the McLaren's diffuser. Still, he had a 37-second cushion which should have seen him through.

Not so. On lap 43 the safety car was deployed as the rain came down in stair rods. At a stroke, Häkkinen's hard-won advantage evaporated. Moreover, at about the same time, Schumacher inadvertently blundered past Wurz's Benetton under a stationary yellow caution flag. This incident would exert a profound effect on the outcome of the race.

At the end of lap 49, the safety car came in and the pack was unleashed. Häkkinen judged his restart to perfection, leaping away as Schumacher lined up to pass Giancarlo Fisichella's Benetton – second in the traffic jam – under braking for Copse on the first 'green' lap.

At the end of lap 50, though, Schumacher was right on the tail of the McLaren as they slammed across the start/finish line. In reality, Mika was now a sitting duck, his car refusing to turn in properly with its damaged aerodynamics. Midway round lap 51 he just understeered off over the grass at Becketts and Michael was through. It was all over bar the shouting.

It also seemed as though Irvine might be a threat to the second-placed McLaren, but in the closing stages of the race the Ferrari driver eased back perceptibly.

'As I closed on Mika, I thought I could pass him,' he explained afterwards. 'I closed on the first part of the lap, but then lost downforce as I got behind him. After that, I seemed to lose grip and traction and the rear was stepping out. I was not sure why, so I decided to back off.'

Meanwhile, on lap 54, Alesi's Sauber stopped out on the circuit with a malfunction which caused the electrical system to lose its charge, all but shutting down the electro-hydraulic gearchange mechanism. Jean had experienced the first signs of this problem during the safety car period, but struggled on until six laps from the end when he had to call it a day. A pity, for he certainly deserved that fourth place.

At the front of the field, events began to unfold in chaotic fashion. Three laps from the finish, the Ferrari team was handed a handwritten document advising it that Schumacher was being subjected to a ten-second penalty. The Italian squad was uncertain which section of the rules was being applied at this point, but Michael was brought in for a stop-go penalty within the three-lap window allowed to teams after being advised of such a penalty.

Bryn Williams

Mobil
Mercedes-Benz
Mercedes-Benz

Full steam ahead. Until his McLaren suddenly swapped ends, Mika Häkkinen appeared to be on course for an assured victory in the most searching conditions imaginable.

Right: Having crossed the finish line in the pit lane, race winner Michael Schumacher serves his ten-second stop-go penalty under the supervision of the Ferrari mechanics.

This just happened to be on the last of the race's 60 laps, so we were treated to the somewhat bizarre sight of Schumacher's winning Ferrari passing the chequered flag in the pit lane – and then taking his penalty *after* he had won the race. It goes without saying that all hell broke loose afterwards. These events are examined in detail within the accompanying sidebar.

Häkkinen finished a worthy second, although brutally disappointed that the cards had fallen against him so unexpectedly. Behind Irvine, Wurz and Fisichella finished fourth and fifth for Benetton after steady runs which had seen both drivers keep out of trouble, the most important priority in such dire conditions.

Ralf Schumacher completed the top six after a truly terrific drive to score the Jordan team's first championship point of the season, while Jacques Villeneuve had a somewhat confused race which saw him wind up seventh after an unplanned extra tyre stop.

'Somehow my first set of tyres was useless,' shrugged the World Champion. 'I rooted the rears right away, so the car was oversteering a lot and it was difficult to keep pace with the cars in front. Then on the second set, the car was very neutral and balanced, so I could attack.

'Then it started raining again, but I wasn't having any problems with aquaplaning, so I came into the pits [on lap 39] and opted for intermediates again. Just at that moment, too much water fell and you couldn't even go down the straight. We caught it with our wrong decision!' As a result, he was back two laps later for full wets and lost too much time to have a hope of bagging any points.

With Shinji Nakano's Minardi and Toranosuke Takagi's Tyrrell being the only other cars running at the end, just nine of the 22 starters made it to the finish. Apart from Jos Verstappen, whose Stewart-Ford suffered engine failure, and Alesi, the non-finishers all succumbed to the slippery surface and pirouetted into retirement.

Beyond question, Schumacher had driven brilliantly on this occasion to win and, although Häkkinen had clearly got the upper hand in the opening stages, the Finn eventually made a key driving error which was as much the reason he failed to win as was losing his big lead when the safety car came out.

More worryingly, Michael had now moved to within two points of Häkkinen at the head of the Drivers' World Championship table. The title outcome looked balanced on a knife edge. It could go either way from here on in.

Why did they give that penalty in that manner?

Peter Nygaard/GP Photo

GIVEN the events at Silverstone, it would have been all too easy to claim once again that the FIA seemed to be giving Ferrari a tacit helping hand towards the World Championship. Yet such suggestions belonged to cynical minds who hadn't examined the hard facts correctly, according to FIA President Max Mosley.

With the restart controversy at Magny-Cours – where again a detailed analysis of the situation tended to quash the conspiracy theories – fresh in everyone's mind, Mosley rejected all allegations of partiality on the part of the governing body.

'Anyone who looks at all the races [this year] would realise that there is no conspiracy,' said Mosley. 'Take the Canadian Grand Prix, where the race was stopped and restarted. You could say that Schumacher was disadvantaged on this occasion as he was second at the first start and then third at the second. But it is just not the case.'

The McLaren team's appeal against the results at Silverstone centred on apparent ambiguities and inconsistencies in the sequence of events that took place as the race unfolded in connection with Schumacher's rule infringement.

Michael was running third on lap 43 when he lapped Wurz's sixth-placed Benetton under a stationary yellow flag. This incident took place at 3.15 p.m. and the safety car was deployed to slow the field in heavy rain only one minute later.

However, the stewards did not get round to deliberating on the matter until 3.39 p.m. and the Ferrari team timed their receipt of the decision that a 'time penalty' of ten seconds had been imposed at 3.46 p.m.

By this time there were only three laps to go before the end of the race and, in order to produce a symbolic compliance with the instruction, Schumacher came in to take his stop-go penalty on lap 60 just *after* taking the chequered flag.

'When the official handed us the document relating to the penalty, he was unable to tell us which rule it referred to,' said Jean Todt, Ferrari's sporting director. 'Because of this doubt we brought Michael in for a stop-go penalty in conformity with the regulation allowing you to make the stop within three laps of its notification.'

When the results were published it was clear that the organisers had simply added ten seconds to Schumacher's elapsed race time, giving him the win by 12 seconds. In fact, because the race was not into its final 12 laps by the time of the rule infringement (Article 57(e)), Schumacher should have been brought into the pits for a ten-second stop-go penalty, a punishment which would have cost him more of his advantage when the 'in' and 'out' laps are also taken into account.

McLaren's view was that this was unfair and amounted to preferential treatment of the Ferrari team. What they wanted to know was just why it took so long to advise Ferrari of the penalty in the first place – and why the penalty imposed on Schumacher was not displayed on the timing monitors (Article 57(a)).

This was an absolutely crucial omission as the rules say that the three laps of grace during which the ten-second stop-go penalty must be taken start only from the moment the message '10 sec stop-go penalty' alongside the driver's name appears on the screen (Article 59(b)).

With that in mind the stewards concluded that 'under the circumstances, the time penalty imposed [on Schumacher] cannot apply and is therefore rescinded.

'No alternative penalty is imposed [on Schumacher] in view of all the circumstances.' However, tacit acknowledgement that there had been an administrative error was made when the stewards refunded the McLaren protest fee. McLaren duly lodged an appeal which would be heard, in due course, by the FIA.

Sources close to the FIA conceded that the initial evidence pointed to the race stewards making a major error of judgement in applying the rules, excused in part by race control's preoccupation with monitoring the safety car's progress while slowing the field during the most dangerous period of heavy rain during the middle of the Grand Prix. Either way, it was hardly satisfactory.

THE RAC BRITISH GRAND PRIX

10–12 JULY 1998

SILVERSTONE

Race distance: 60 laps, 191.566 miles/308.296 km

Race weather: Dry at start, then heavy rain and windy

Pos.	Driver	Nat.	No.	Entrant	Car/Engine	Tyres	Laps	Time/Retirement	Speed (mph/km/h)
1	**Michael Schumacher**	**D**	**3**	**Scuderia Ferrari Marlboro**	**Ferrari F300 047 V10**	**G**	**60**	**1h 47m 02.450s**	**107.379/172.810**
2	**Mika Häkkinen**	**SF**	**8**	**West McLaren Mercedes**	**McLaren MP4/13-Mercedes FO110G V10**	**B**	**60**	**1h 47m 24.915s**	**107.004/172.207**
3	**Eddie Irvine**	**GB**	**4**	**Scuderia Ferrari Marlboro**	**Ferrari F300 047 V10**	**G**	**60**	**1h 47m 31.649s**	**106.893/172.028**
4	**Alexander Wurz**	**A**	**6**	**Mild Seven Benetton Playlife**	**Benetton B198-Playlife V10**	**B**	**59**		
5	**Giancarlo Fisichella**	**I**	**5**	**Mild Seven Benetton Playlife**	**Benetton B198-Playlife V10**	**B**	**59**		
6	**Ralf Schumacher**	**D**	**10**	**B&H Jordan Mugen Honda**	**Jordan 198-Mugen Honda MF310C V10**	**G**	**59**		
7	Jacques Villeneuve	CDN	1	Winfield Williams	Williams FW20-Mecachrome GC37/01 V10	G	59		
8	Shinji Nakano	J	22	Fondmetal Minardi Ford	Minardi M198-Ford Zetec-R V10	B	58		
9	Toranosuke Takagi	J	21	Tyrrell Ford	Tyrrell 026-Ford Zetec-R V10	G	56		
	Jean Alesi	F	14	Red Bull Sauber Petronas	Sauber C17-Petronas SPE01D V10	G	53	Electrics	
	Pedro Diniz	BR	16	Danka Zepter Arrows	Arrows A19 V10	B	45	Spun off	
	Olivier Panis	F	11	Gauloises Prost Peugeot	Prost AP01-Peugeot A16 V10	B	40	Spun off	
	Rubens Barrichello	BR	18	Stewart Ford	Stewart SF2-Ford Zetec-R V10	B	39	Spun off	
	Jos Verstappen	NL	19	Stewart Ford	Stewart SF2-Ford Zetec-R V10	B	38	Engine	
	David Coulthard	GB	7	West McLaren Mercedes	McLaren MP4/13-Mercedes FO110G V10	B	37	Spun off	
	Jarno Trulli	I	12	Gauloises Prost Peugeot	Prost AP01-Peugeot A16 V10	B	37	Spun off	
	Ricardo Rosset	BR	20	Tyrrell Ford	Tyrrell 026-Ford Zetec-R V10	G	29	Spun off	
	Esteban Tuero	RA	23	Fondmetal Minardi Ford	Minardi M198-Ford Zetec-R V10	B	29	Spun off	
	Johnny Herbert	GB	15	Red Bull Sauber Petronas	Sauber C17-Petronas SPE01D V10	G	27	Spun off	
	Mika Salo	SF	17	Danka Zepter Arrows	Arrows A19 V10	B	27	Spun off	
	Heinz-Harald Frentzen	D	2	Winfield Williams	Williams FW20-Mecachrome GC37/01 V10	G	15	Spun off	
	Damon Hill	GB	9	B&H Jordan Mugen Honda	Jordan 198-Mugen Honda MF310C V10	G	13	Spun off	

Fastest lap: M. Schumacher, on lap 12, 1m 35.704s, 120.139 mph/193.346 km/h.

Lap record: Michael Schumacher (F1 Ferrari F310B V10), 1m 24.475s, 136.109 mph/219.047 km/h (1997).

B – Bridgestone G – Goodyear

All results and data © FIA 1998

Grid order	1	2	3	4	5	6	7	8	9	10	11	12	13	14	15	16	17	18	19	20	21	22	23
8 HÄKKINEN	8	8	8	8	8	8	8	8	8	8	8	8	8	8	8	8	8	8	8	8	8	8	8
3 M. SCHUMACHER	3	3	3	3	7	7	7	7	7	7	7	7	7	7	7	7	7	7	7	7	7	7	7
1 VILLENEUVE	7	7	7	7	3	3	3	3	3	3	3	3	3	3	3	3	3	3	3	14	14	3	3
7 COULTHARD	14	14	14	14	14	14	14	14	14	14	14	14	14	14	14	14	14	14	14	4	4	14	15
4 IRVINE	1	1	1	1	2	2	2	2	2	2	2	4	4	4	4	4	4	4	4	3	3	4	4
2 FRENTZEN	2	2	2	2	1	1	1	4	4	4	4	2	2	2	2	1	1	1	15	15	15	15	14
9 HILL	9	9	9	9	9	9	9	1	1	1	1	1	1	1	1	15	15	15	1	10	10	10	10
14 ALESI	15	15	15	4	4	4	4	9	9	9	9	9	9	15	15	6	6	6	6	17	1	1	1
15 HERBERT	6	4	4	15	15	15	15	15	15	15	15	15	15	6	6	5	5	5	17	1	6	6	6
5 FISICHELLA	4	6	6	6	6	6	6	6	6	6	6	6	6	5	5	17	16	17	10	6	5	5	5
6 WURZ	5	5	5	5	5	5	5	5	5	5	5	5	5	17	17	16	17	16	5	5	17	17	17
16 DINIZ	17	17	17	17	10	10	10	10	10	10	10	10	10	16	16	10	10	10	16	16	16	16	16
17 SALO	16	16	10	10	17	17	17	17	17	17	17	17	17	10	10	21	11	11	11	11	11	11	11
12 TRULLI	10	10	16	16	16	16	16	16	16	16	16	16	16	21	21	11	21	21	21	21	22	22	22
19 VERSTAPPEN	12	12	21	21	21	21	21	21	21	21	21	21	21	11	11	20	20	20	22	22	12	12	19
18 BARRICHELLO	21	21	12	11	11	11	11	11	11	11	11	11	11	20	20	18	22	22	20	20	20	19	12
21 TAKAGI	19	11	11	20	20	20	20	20	20	20	20	20	20	19	19	19	12	12	12	12	19	20	20
23 TUERO	20	20	20	12	12	12	12	12	19	19	19	19	19	18	18	22	18	19	19	19	21	21	21
22 NAKANO	11	19	19	19	19	19	19	19	12	18	18	18	18	22	22	12	19	23	23	23	23	23	18
20 ROSSET	23	23	23	23	23	23	22	18	18	12	12	12	22	12	12	23	23	18	18	18	18	18	23
10 R. SCHUMACHER	22	22	22	22	22	22	18	22	22	22	22	22	12	23	23								
11 PANIS	18	18	18	18	18	18	23	23	23	23	23	23	23										

Grid order	24	25	26	27	28	29	30	31	32	33	34	35	36	37	38	39	40	41	42	43	44	45
8 HÄKKINEN	8	8	8	8	8	8	8	8	8	8	8	8	8	8	8	8	8	8	8	8	8	8
3 M. SCHUMACHER	7	7	7	7	7	7	7	7	7	7	7	7	7	7	3	3	3	3	3	3	3	3
1 VILLENEUVE	3	3	3	3	3	3	3	3	3	3	3	3	3	3	4	4	4	4	4	4	4	4
7 COULTHARD	4	4	4	4	4	4	4	4	4	4	4	4	4	4	14	14	14	5	14	14	14	14
4 IRVINE	15	15	15	14	14	14	14	14	14	14	14	14	14	14	1	5	5	14	5	5	5	5
2 FRENTZEN	14	14	14	10	10	10	10	10	10	10	10	1	1	1	5	6	6	6	6	6	6	6
9 HILL	10	10	10	1	1	1	1	1	1	1	1	10	5	5	6	1	1	1	10	10	10	10
14 ALESI	1	1	1	6	6	6	6	6	5	5	5	5	6	6	10	10	10	10	1	1	1	1
15 HERBERT	6	6	6	5	5	5	5	5	6	6	6	6	10	10	16	16	11	22	22	22	22	22
5 FISICHELLA	5	5	5	15	16	16	16	16	16	16	16	16	16	16	11	11	22	21	21	21	21	21
6 WURZ	17	17	17	17	11	11	11	11	11	11	11	11	11	11	19	18	21	16	16	16	16	16
16 DINIZ	16	16	16	16	22	22	19	19	19	19	19	19	19	19	18	22	16					
17 SALO	11	11	11	11	19	19	18	18	18	18	18	18	18	18	22	21						
12 TRULLI	22	22	22	22	18	18	22	22	22	22	22	22	22	22	21							
19 VERSTAPPEN	19	19	19	19	21	21	21	21	21	21	21	12	12	12								
18 BARRICHELLO	20	18	18	18	20	20	12	12	12	12	12	21	21	21								
21 TAKAGI	18	20	21	21	23	23																
23 TUERO	21	21	20	20	12	12																
22 NAKANO	23	23	23	23																		
20 ROSSET	12	12	12	12																		
10 R. SCHUMACHER																						
11 PANIS																						

Pit stop

One lap behind leader

STARTING GRID

8 **HÄKKINEN** McLaren	3 **M. SCHUMACHER** Ferrari
1 **VILLENEUVE** Williams	7 **COULTHARD** McLaren
4 **IRVINE** Ferrari	2 **FRENTZEN** Williams
9 **HILL** Jordan	14 **ALESI** Sauber
15 **HERBERT** Sauber	5 **FISICHELLA** Benetton
6 **WURZ** Benetton	16 **DINIZ** Arrows
17 **SALO** Arrows	12 **TRULLI** Prost
19 **VERSTAPPEN** Stewart	18 **BARRICHELLO** Stewart
21 **TAKAGI** Tyrrell	23 **TUERO** Minardi
22 **NAKANO** Minardi	20 **ROSSET** Tyrrell
10 **R. SCHUMACHER** Jordan	11 **PANIS** Prost

49	50	51	52	53	54	55	56	57	58	59	60	●
8	8	3	3	3	3	3	3	3	3	3	3	1
3	3	8	8	8	8	8	8	8	8	8	8	2
4	4	4	4	4	4	4	4	4	4	4	4	3
14	14	14	14	14	5	6	6	6	6	6		4
5	5	5	5	5	6	5	5	5	5	5		5
6	6	6	6	6	10	10	10	10	10	10		6
10	10	10	10	10	1	1	1	1	1	1		
1	1	1	1	1	22	22	22	22	22			
22	22	22	22	22	21	21	21					
21	21	21	21	21								

TIME SHEETS

QUALIFYING

Weather: Cool, dry and overcast

Pos.	Driver	Car	Laps	Time
1	Mika Häkkinen	McLaren-Mercedes	10	1m 23.271s
2	Michael Schumacher	Ferrari	11	1m 23.720s
3	Jacques Villeneuve	Williams-Mecachrome	12	1m 24.102s
4	David Coulthard	McLaren-Mercedes	12	1m 24.310s
5	Eddie Irvine	Ferrari	12	1m 24.436s
6	Heinz-Harald Frentzen	Williams-Mecachrome	12	1m 24.442s
7	Damon Hill	Jordan-Mugen Honda	12	1m 24.542s
8	Jean Alesi	Sauber-Petronas	12	1m 25.081s
9	Johnny Herbert	Sauber-Petronas	12	1m 25.084s
10	Ralf Schumacher	Jordan-Mugen Honda	12	*1m 25.461s
11	Giancarlo Fisichella	Benetton-Playlife	12	1m 25.654s
12	Alexander Wurz	Benetton-Playlife	12	1m 25.760s
13	Pedro Diniz	Arrows	12	1m 26.376s
14	Mika Salo	Arrows	12	1m 26.487s
15	Jarno Trulli	Prost-Peugeot	11	1m 26.808s
16	Olivier Panis	Prost-Peugeot	12	*1m 26.847s
17	Jos Verstappen	Stewart-Ford	12	1m 26.948s
18	Rubens Barrichello	Stewart-Ford	12	1m 26.990s
19	Toranosuke Takagi	Tyrrell-Ford	12	1m 27.061s
20	Esteban Tuero	Minardi-Ford	11	1m 28.051s
21	Shinji Nakano	Minardi-Ford	12	1m 28.123s
22	Ricardo Rosset	Tyrrell-Ford	12	1m 28.608s

* fastest time disallowed

FRIDAY FREE PRACTICE

Weather: Cool, dry, overcast

Pos.	Driver	Laps	Time
1	David Coulthard	36	1m 25.640s
2	Mika Häkkinen	25	1m 25.764s
3	Heinz-Harald Frentzen	31	1m 26.107s
4	Jacques Villeneuve	38	1m 26.114s
5	Eddie Irvine	18	1m 26.791s
6	Giancarlo Fisichella	32	1m 26.840s
7	Michael Schumacher	27	1m 26.884s
8	Alexander Wurz	32	1m 27.121s
9	Ralf Schumacher	30	1m 27.460s
10	Damon Hill	41	1m 27.667s
11	Johnny Herbert	25	1m 27.978s
12	Jean Alesi	27	1m 28.136s
13	Toranosuke Takagi	35	1m 28.258s
14	Rubens Barrichello	23	1m 28.339s
15	Jarno Trulli	40	1m 28.685s
16	Jos Verstappen	32	1m 28.983s
17	Olivier Panis	22	1m 29.193s
18	Mika Salo	32	1m 29.262s
19	Pedro Diniz	6	1m 29.375s
20	Ricardo Rosset	35	1m 29.664s
21	Shinji Nakano	36	1m 30.090s
22	Esteban Tuero	30	1m 30.266s

SATURDAY FREE PRACTICE

Weather: Cool and overcast

Pos.	Driver	Laps	Time
1	Mika Häkkinen	30	1m 23.639s
2	David Coulthard	24	1m 24.233s
3	Michael Schumacher	30	1m 24.260s
4	Ralf Schumacher	28	1m 24.496s
5	Damon Hill	29	1m 24.683s
6	Jacques Villeneuve	31	1m 24.791s
7	Eddie Irvine	27	1m 24.834s
8	Heinz-Harald Frentzen	27	1m 25.187s
9	Jean Alesi	27	1m 25.769s
10	Giancarlo Fisichella	17	1m 25.822s
11	Alexander Wurz	30	1m 25.904s
12	Johnny Herbert	31	1m 25.949s
13	Toranosuke Takagi	26	1m 26.521s
14	Olivier Panis	31	1m 26.881s
15	Pedro Diniz	27	1m 26.929s
16	Mika Salo	28	1m 26.947s
17	Jarno Trulli	27	1m 27.002s
18	Rubens Barrichello	31	1m 27.323s
19	Jos Verstappen	31	1m 27.690s
20	Esteban Tuero	29	1m 28.224s
21	Shinji Nakano	26	1m 28.317s
22	Ricardo Rosset	26	1m 28.650s

WARM-UP

Weather: Wet, cold and windy

Pos.	Driver	Laps	Time
1	David Coulthard	11	1m 37.910s
2	Mika Häkkinen	12	1m 37.921s
3	Giancarlo Fisichella	14	1m 39.802s
4	Eddie Irvine	14	1m 40.127s
5	Michael Schumacher	12	1m 40.296s
6	Alexander Wurz	13	1m 40.917s
7	Mika Salo	12	1m 41.582s
8	Heinz-Harald Frentzen	12	1m 41.620s
9	Olivier Panis	12	1m 41.762s
10	Pedro Diniz	11	1m 41.938s
11	Jacques Villeneuve	13	1m 42.133s
12	Jean Alesi	13	1m 42.369s
13	Shinji Nakano	15	1m 42.510s
14	Rubens Barrichello	12	1m 42.530s
15	Esteban Tuero	14	1m 42.779s
16	Johnny Herbert	13	1m 42.908s
17	Jos Verstappen	13	1m 43.305s
18	Ralf Schumacher	11	1m 43.738s
19	Damon Hill	10	1m 43.797s
20	Jarno Trulli	13	1m 44.526s
21	Toranosuke Takagi	11	1m 46.189s
22	Ricardo Rosset	9	1m 48.865s

RACE FASTEST LAPS

Weather: Dry at start, then heavy rain

Driver	Time	Lap
Michael Schumacher	1m 35.704s	12
Mika Häkkinen	1m 35.961s	2
David Coulthard	1m 36.120s	3
Eddie Irvine	1m 36.530s	12
Heinz-Harald Frentzen	1m 36.884s	2
Jacques Villeneuve	1m 37.199s	12
Jean Alesi	1m 37.202s	11
Damon Hill	1m 37.223s	12
Johnny Herbert	1m 37.343s	12
Ralf Schumacher	1m 37.389s	9
Pedro Diniz	1m 37.887s	10
Alexander Wurz	1m 37.982s	12
Mika Salo	1m 38.160s	9
Giancarlo Fisichella	1m 38.424s	9
Rubens Barrichello	1m 40.097s	11
Ricardo Rosset	1m 40.948s	10
Jos Verstappen	1m 41.114s	12
Toranosuke Takagi	1m 41.629s	4
Olivier Panis	1m 42.346s	11
Shinji Nakano	1m 43.755s	33
Jarno Trulli	1m 44.083s	29
Esteban Tuero	1m 44.700s	3

CHASSIS LOG BOOK

No.	Driver	Chassis
1	Villeneuve	Williams FW20/5
2	Frentzen	Williams FW20/4
	spare	Williams FW20/6
3	M. Schumacher	Ferrari F300/187
4	Irvine	Ferrari F300/185
	spare	Ferrari F300/186
5	Fisichella	Benetton B198/6
6	Wurz	Benetton B198/7
	spare	Benetton B198/4
7	Coulthard	McLaren MP4/13/3
8	Häkkinen	McLaren MP4/13/6
	spare	McLaren MP4/13/4
9	Hill	Jordan 198/3
10	R. Schumacher	Jordan 198/4
	spare	Jordan 198/5
11	Panis	Prost AP01/2
12	Trulli	Prost AP01/6
	spare	Prost AP01/5
14	Alesi	Sauber C17/2
15	Herbert	Sauber C17/4
	spare	Sauber C17/6
16	Diniz	Arrows A19/1
17	Salo	Arrows A19/5
	spare	Arrows A19/2
18	Barrichello	Stewart SF2/4
19	Verstappen	Stewart SF2/3
	spare	Stewart SF2/2
20	Rosset	Tyrrell 026/2
21	Takagi	Tyrrell 026/3
	spare	Tyrrell 026/4
22	Nakano	Minardi M198/4
23	Tuero	Minardi M198/5
	spare	Minardi M198/3

POINTS TABLES

Drivers

Pos.	Driver	Points
1	Mika Häkkinen	56
2	Michael Schumacher	54
3	David Coulthard	30
4	Eddie Irvine	29
5	Alexander Wurz	17
6	Giancarlo Fisichella	15
7	Jacques Villeneuve	11
8	Heinz-Harald Frentzen	8
9	Rubens Barrichello	4
10 =	Jean Alesi	3
10 =	Mika Salo	3
12 =	Johnny Herbert	1
12 =	Pedro Diniz	1
12 =	Jan Magnussen	1
12 =	Ralf Schumacher	1

Constructors

Pos.	Constructor	Points
1	McLaren	86
2	Ferrari	83
3	Benetton	32
4	Williams	19
5	Stewart	5
6 =	Sauber	4
6 =	Arrows	4
8	Jordan	1

AUSTRIAN grand prix

HÄKKINEN
COULTHARD
M. SCHUMACHER
IRVINE
R. SCHUMACHER
VILLENEUVE

Steve Etherington/EPI

Mika Häkkinen gets a well-deserved hug from his wife Erja after ending Michael Schumacher's recent run of success with his fifth win of the year.

Below left: Giancarlo Fisichella had snatched pole position with a perfectly timed run on a drying track surface right at the end of qualifying, but Häkkinen lost no time in putting the upstart in his place once the race was under way.

Bryn Williams

THE pendulum of F1 World Championship fortune at last swung dramatically in favour of the McLaren-Mercedes squad in the Austrian Grand Prix at the A1-Ring. After three straight wins by Michael Schumacher's Ferrari F300, Mika Häkkinen and David Coulthard shrugged aside Maranello's challenge to post another decisive 1-2 success which left Schumacher and Eddie Irvine trailing in third and fourth places.

It was Häkkinen's first victory since Monaco and, while the Finn achieved this latest win with the same deft confidence he had deployed through the streets of the Principality, he certainly had no easy ride. In the early stages he had to fight tooth and nail to keep the lead in the face of Schumacher's relentless challenge, a nail-biting confrontation which ended only when Michael slid into the gravel after 17 laps and had to rush into the pits for repairs.

In Häkkinen's wake, the Austrian Grand Prix was all about fight-backs. Coulthard stormed back from 19th to second after being mauled by both the Arrows A19s of Mika Salo and Pedro Diniz at the second corner of the race, while Schumacher recovered from 16th to fourth, then third when Irvine mysteriously developed 'braking problems' in the closing stages.

'I was told to ease off,' explained Irvine, effectively confirming what Maranello's sporting director Jean Todt had said earlier from the pit wall.

'Eddie had brake problems in the closing stages and we warned him of this,' said Todt. 'For that reason he did not take any unnecessary risks in keeping his team-mate behind him.'

A gradually drying track surface had transformed qualifying into something of a lottery with Giancarlo Fisichella's Benetton and Jean Alesi's Sauber ending up in the right places at the right time to button up the front row of the grid between them. Come the race, however, and Mika Häkkinen soon corrected that anomaly.

The McLaren driver accelerated cleanly through from the second row to take the lead going into the first corner with Michael Schumacher's Ferrari following him through. But if the two key title contenders reckoned they could get down to the serious business of the day without further ado, they were sadly mistaken.

As the McLaren and Ferrari raced for the second corner, further back on the grid Olivier Panis was left stranded with clutch problems and, going into the first turn, Toranosuke Takagi's Tyrrell managed to spin into the barrier, causing Johnny Herbert's slow-starting Sauber and both Minardis to steer into the gravel trap in avoidance.

'Panis stalled in front of me on the grid as the red lights went out,' explained Takagi, 'and, in order to get round him and avoid the other cars on the start, I moved to the right, up close to the pit wall.

'I then got good traction and caught up with a group of other cars, still on the inside line. Unfortunately the line was very dirty, and when I hit the brakes the back end snapped away from me and I spun off.'

Takagi was out on the spot, the rear wing ripped from his Tyrrell, but the other three managed to extricate themselves from the gravel trap and continue. At the second corner there was another helping of chaos as Pedro Diniz spun and collected his Arrows team-mate Mika Salo. Coulthard, who had qualified down in 14th place, spun his McLaren in avoidance only to have its nose damaged as Salo spin-turned his way back into the action.

'A car stalled on the grid, so I had to lift off and lost some places,' explained Coulthard. 'At the start I was taking the attitude that I would just try to keep out of trouble, and I had that same attitude at the second corner.

'As I went into the corner I looked in the mirror and saw a car [Trulli's] coming down the outside, so I moved right to give him room only for Diniz to come up the inside and spin me round. Then I was hit by Salo when he did a "doughnut" [spin turn] in front of me, so I had to come into the pits for a new front wing, then join at the back of the pack, although the safety car meant that I did not lose as much time as I might otherwise have done.'

With the safety car being promptly deployed in the wake of this mayhem, Häkkinen came through at reduced speed to lead the opening lap from Schumacher, Fisichella, Rubens Barrichello's Stewart-Ford, Alesi's Sauber and Irvine's Ferrari. Salo pulled in to retire with collision damage, but Coulthard was able to make his pit stop for repairs without losing a lap and joined in at the tail of the slow-moving queue before the pack was unleashed again at the end of lap three.

Schumacher, running a two-stop strategy, immediately went onto the attack in an effort to overtake Häkkinen's leading McLaren, which was only stopping once. On the next lap he tried to overtake the McLaren with an audacious lunge round the outside of an infield left-hander, but ran wide. Fisichella nipped through ahead of the Ferrari and Barrichello's Stewart pulled level.

Michael sat it out eyeball to eyeball

Villeneuve signs BAR contract

THE formal confirmation of Jacques Villeneuve's decision to join the new British American Racing team was announced on the eve of first practice for the Austrian Grand Prix.

It was being rumoured that Villeneuve had put his signature to a $25 million, two-year deal with the team, but BAR managing director Craig Pollock made it clear that a confidentiality clause prevented discussion of any aspect of the contract – even its duration.

The 27-year-old Canadian had finally decided to leave Williams after a three-year relationship which saw him win the 1997 World Championship. Instead he had opted to commit himself to Pollock's ambitious new F1 venture, set to operate out of a new factory at Brackley, near Silverstone.

'Anything can be a gamble,' said Villeneuve when asked about the possible risks involved. 'You just have to quantify the good sides about it, and there are a lot of positives [at BAR]. The people in the team are people I worked with in the past. I know that they can do a very good job, and they have showed me a lot of things that made me confident in what they could achieve in the future.'

'I was happy at Williams, although the results didn't come this year as we wanted. I expect next year to be an interim season [for them] and I just don't want to do another season like this one.'

Pollock was obviously delighted at having secured Villeneuve's services. 'For weeks everybody up and down the paddock had been saying that the deal with Jacques had been signed,' he said. 'He's been in discussion with other teams and it was only when I finally negotiated a contract to use Supertec [Renault] engines next season that I could begin to seriously negotiate with him.

'We spent right up until 2.00 a.m. this morning [the Thursday prior to the Austrian GP] fighting over details of a deal. Jacques is quite an operator when it comes to going through a contract; when he's looking after his own interests he can be a formidable partner or opponent.

'By having signed Jacques we are putting enormous pressure on ourselves to perform. We have a World Champion who knows the Renault engine, but Jacques is a risk taker and this is certainly that – a calculated risk, perhaps, but a risk for him none the less.'

ow right: When in Rome . . . Michael umacher makes himself at home.

ow: Purple haze. Jacques Villeneuve ed weeks of speculation by firming that he would be leaving iams to join the new British American ing team set up by his former nager Craig Pollock for 1999.

Sutton Motorsport Images

David Coulthard came to Austria intent on proving a point. Following his acute disappointment at Silverstone, the Scot could have been forgiven for thinking that his luck might be about to change when his McLaren MP4/13 wound up setting fastest time in Friday's free practice session.

Not that David was taking anything for granted. The Scot had become too battle-worn to count on making any major inroads into team-mate Mika Häkkinen's 26-point World Championship lead with only seven of the season's 16 races still to run.

'I think we are making progress in a good direction as far as sorting out the handling and tuning it in for the circuit is concerned,' said Coulthard. 'But as far as turning around my bid for the championship is concerned, I'm not even thinking about that.

'Now I'm taking every race weekend as it comes. I'm paid a lot of money to play in racing cars and I'm just enjoying that at the moment.'

Coulthard's cautious approach was quite understandable. After an overnight thunderstorm of Wagnerian proportions, the tarmac of the A1-Ring circuit had been washed raw and was at its most abrasively challenging as a result when the cars edged out onto the circuit for the first time on Friday morning.

Steve Etherington/EPI

Although last year's race was won by Jacques Villeneuve's Goodyear-shod Williams it was clear that the track offered a potential advantage to the Bridgestone opposition. Italian rising star Jarno Trulli had set third-fastest qualifying time in his Bridgestone-shod Prost and led for the first 37 laps of the race before hitting trouble, while the Stewart-Fords of Rubens Barrichello and Jan Magnussen had also run competitively in the top six on the Japanese rubber.

With that in mind, Coulthard could enjoy a degree of confidence, although he finished the day with only a 0.001s – one-thousandth of a second – advantage over Giancarlo Fisichella's Benetton, with Häkkinen in the other McLaren-Mercedes third fastest.

All told, it looked pretty promising for the Bridgestone squad, even though technical director Hirohide Hamashima explained that the A1-Ring rivals Budapest as the most difficult circuit on the championship schedule at which to predict tyre wear rates.

In Saturday morning's free practice session Coulthard again set the fastest time, with Häkkinen next up, both deciding to select the harder 'option' tyre compound for qualifying and the race. With high ambient temperatures expected for race day, the harder tyre option was followed by virtually the entire field – whether Goodyear or Bridgestone – with the exception of Sauber drivers Jean Alesi and Johnny Herbert, who both plumped for Goodyear's softer compound.

All this carefully judged pre-planning was then thrown straight out of the window as far as qualifying was concerned when the heavens opened and the circuit was suddenly enveloped in one of those characteristic Austrian summer monsoons. There was just nothing for it but to sit in the pits, keeping fingers firmly crossed that the downpour would eventually ease sufficiently to permit a half-way decent stab at a qualifying time.

This situation was made all the more nerve-racking by the fact that only 12 qualifying laps are permitted under current F1 rules. In these conditions, that presented all the competitors with a serious dilemma. Did one get out early in an effort to set some respectable times, but risk running out of laps before a dry line appeared? Or did one hang on until later, with the danger that the weather might deteriorate further and all chance of a decent grid position be literally washed away?

For the first half-hour of the session these were largely academic considerations. It was hosing down so heavily that one wit suggested that qualifying might have to be run behind the safety car. Finally, with only 33 minutes of the hour-long session remaining, Toranosuke Takagi's Tyrrell led Damon Hill's Jordan out onto the rain-slicked tarmac and the battle for grid positions belatedly got under way.

In the end, it was Giancarlo Fisichella's Benetton which ended up quickest in this unrepresentative session, the Italian being in the right place at the right time to claim his first-ever pole position. Jean Alesi put the Sauber C17 into second position on the grid, but the cards could just as easily have fallen as badly for him as they did for his 18th-placed team-mate Johnny Herbert.

'When I went out for my last run, I knew that Jean was already on a fast lap, so I kept looking for him in the mirrors ready to let him go by,' said Herbert. 'Eventually he came past, but by then my tyre temperatures had dropped because I was running slowly, and that made me run wide in the first corner of my flying lap.

'That in turn put me on the wet section of the track, which dropped the temperature of the intermediates [even] further, so I couldn't improve.'

As for the McLaren drivers, Mika Häkkinen was on course for pole position only to be foiled by slower traffic on his final lap. The Finn had to settle for third, a whole lot better than Coulthard's bitterly disappointing 14th.

'I didn't manage to do a [decent] time partly because initially I had difficulties getting the intermediates to come in and then I kept locking the rear end on the entry to corners,' he shrugged. 'Finally, I ran wide on my last timed lap, so that kind of performance puts me 14th on the grid.'

On the outside of the second row sat Michael Schumacher's Ferrari, fourth fastest. 'We had planned to stay on wets,' he explained, 'but then we saw the other drivers improving their times on intermediates and decided to fit the same. This took some time as we changed the settings, so I got out too late and could not get the best out of the car.'

Team-mate Eddie Irvine had to settle for eighth in the other Ferrari, admitting that the team was too indecisive and he never got a run on intermediates at the end. The two Italian cars were separated in the line-up by Rubens Barrichello's Stewart, Mika Salo's Arrows and the Williams FW20 of Heinz-Harald Frentzen.

Frentzen was among several drivers who reckoned they could have bagged pole, given one more lap in the unpredictable conditions. 'Just one more lap and my tyres would have been warm enough to go at least a second faster,' he shrugged.

In the Jordan camp Ralf Schumacher found that his best run on full wets earned him ninth on the grid, six places ahead of Damon Hill, who had run intermediates but perhaps made his bid a little too early. Midway through the session he was jousting for fastest time in the mid 1m 35s/37s bracket. Eventually, Fisichella would run a 1m 29s to clinch pole position.

For his part, Mika Salo reckoned he could have been even quicker had he not caught Herbert's Sauber on the final corner of his best lap, but Pedro Diniz was disappointed to be right down in 13th place after sliding off the track early in the session.

Olivier Panis qualified his Prost-Peugeot tenth ahead of Jacques Villeneuve, who spun off and stalled, losing much time coming back to take over the spare Williams. 'When I got into the T-car the set-up was different and I didn't know the state of the track,' he explained, 'so I didn't go out on intermediates. I went out on wets, but came in to put intermediates on for two laps, but it wasn't soon enough to improve on my time.'

Jos Verstappen took 12th place for Stewart, while Jarno Trulli wound up a disappointed 16th ahead of Alexander Wurz, the local Benetton hero never really feeling at ease with his car all weekend. One thing the rain did not do was materially upset the order at the tail of the field: the last two rows of the grid were occupied by the Tyrrells and Minardis as usual, no matter what unexpected shuffling about occurred further up the pack.

Bryn Williams

Michael Cooper/Allsport

Damon Hill was heartened by the performance of his Jordan as he climbed from 15th on the grid to seventh at the chequered flag.

Bottom far left: Esteban Tuero has Johnny Herbert for company as he seeks refuge in the gravel trap after becoming involved in Tora Takagi's first-corner accident.

Bottom left: The nose of David Coulthard's McLaren is damaged as Mika Salo attempts to spin-turn his stranded Arrows. The Scot produced one of his best drives of the season to finish second after a stop for repairs.

DIARY

McLaren's Ron Dennis says he is disappointed that Ferrari has decided to share with the media the subject of a meeting in the Italian team's motorhome when Dennis and team manager Dave Ryan indicated they believed that Ferrari was using an asymmetric braking system which did not comply with the rules.

Benetton signs deal to use Supertec (née Mecachrome) engines for the 1999 and 2000 seasons.

Heinz-Harald Frentzen opens talks with the Prost-Peugeot team.

Jörg Müller tipped for Sauber test as possible candidate to replace Johnny Herbert in 1999.

Damon Hill resigns as a director of the Grand Prix Drivers' Association.

with the Stewart driver and reclaimed the place, but he had to wait until next time round before he could repass Fisichella. By lap eight, despite slight braking problems with his McLaren, Häkkinen had eased open a 1.1s advantage over Schumacher with Fisichella a steady third and Irvine, who had by now passed Alesi's Sauber, moving up to fourth as Barrichello pulled in to retire with brake problems.

On lap 17 Schumacher ran wide at the last corner, bouncing luridly over the gravel in an unscheduled excursion which ripped off the Ferrari's nose section and damaged its barge boards. Being just beyond the pit lane entrance, the disabled Ferrari had to complete one further lap before coming in for attention. Once repairs had been carried out, Michael rejoined in 16th and last place, leaving Häkkinen leading comfortably from Fisichella, Irvine and Alesi.

On the same lap, Heinz-Harald Frentzen's Williams retired from sixth place with a major engine failure, allowing the fast-recovering Coulthard to take the position.

Four laps later, Fisichella made his first refuelling stop, dropping behind Irvine and emerging from the pits wheel to wheel with Alesi's Sauber. Side by side they raced uphill towards the Remus Kurve, prompting a sense of dark inevitability over what would occur next. Predictably enough, the two exuberant drivers collided as they went into the turn, but you wouldn't have guessed it was anybody's fault from the mutual admiration society they subsequently put on public display.

'I had a lighter fuel load and went for the outside as I braked for the corner,' explained Alesi, 'but as I turned in he slid into me and we both spun. Because of the long first gear we were using in the race, and the steep uphill gradient in that corner, the engine stalled when I tried to restart.

'I never like to have accidents, but it's even worse when you have them with somebody you like, and I really like Giancarlo!'

Fisichella charmingly responded in similar vein. 'I don't want to complain about Jean Alesi,' he said. 'Usually he is a very fair driver, but this incident could have been avoided. I had just left the pits after a tyre stop when I found myself alongside Jean.

'I overtook him, then when I braked I saw him shoot past on my left and close the door in front of me. It is a shame because the car was going really well and I was driving very carefully.'

The race now settled down with Häkkinen comfortably ahead of Irvine's Ferrari and Coulthard really slicing into the Ulsterman's advantage, the third-placed McLaren lapping steadily a second a lap faster than the Italian car. Ralf Schumacher was now up to fourth ahead of Jarno Trulli's Prost and Jacques Villeneuve's Williams FW20.

On lap 28 Irvine made his first refuelling stop (8.6s) and dropped to third behind Coulthard. Six laps later Häkkinen made his single scheduled stop (10.4s), pulling in just before he was poised to lap a group of slower cars, and returned to the race in second place behind Coulthard. This was duly corrected on lap 36 when David made a 10.6s routine stop, resuming 15.1s behind the Finn in second place.

On lap 42 Michael Schumacher's Ferrari came in for its second refuelling stop, briefly dropping from fifth to seventh. A lap later Ralf Schumacher and Villeneuve made their second and sole stops respectively, rejoining the battle in fourth and seventh places.

This now put Michael in hot pursuit of his brother and over the next ten laps the Ferrari closed inexorably on the yellow Jordan. Going into lap 53 he was right on Ralf's tail, but he almost lost control for the Remus Kurve as his sibling showed an uncompromising streak which is clearly in the family genes.

'He [Ralf] was obviously fast, and he is there to race, not to give me any presents,' said Michael. 'He works for a different team and he fought all the way to the end. He did it in a fair way. After the drivers' briefing there was an arrangement [between all the drivers] that we would change line once only when being overtaken.

'Ralf did it perfectly, he only moved over once. I had the outside free, which wasn't the nice line. But at the next corner [two laps later] I had more acceleration and caught him on the straight. It was perfect.'

So now Schumacher was fourth with only Irvine separating him from the two McLarens. Hey presto, on lap 61 Eddie began easing his pace under instructions from the pits. His lap times lengthened by around two seconds a lap into the 1m 16s bracket until Michael pulled onto his tail and, eventually, sailed past into third place on lap 68.

'We were very marginal on brakes, both of us,' said Schumacher, deadpan. 'Eddie seemed to be a bit worse than me and the team asked us to slow down. At one stage I was able to overtake Eddie then.' Shortly afterwards, the FIA clarified its attitude to team orders: it was OK to effectively nominate one driver to aim for the World Championship while the other supported him. Ganging up between teams against another competitor was not permitted. So Ferrari's self-conscious explanation had not been necessary.

Meanwhile, Häkkinen was savouring his fifth victory of the season, his satisfaction with the day's work surpassed only by Coulthard's relief that a hard-won second place had put him back on the rostrum for the first time since Barcelona, five races back down the World Championship trail.

'When you have a car as good as my car was today, it makes it quite easy to overtake,' said David modestly. 'I want to compliment all the drivers I overtook today because they were 100 per cent fair and absolutely committed in selecting the lines they wanted.'

Behind the two Ferraris, Ralf Schumacher continued the fine work he had started at Silverstone by consolidating his strong fifth place. 'The car performed well until my battle with Michael,' he said, 'after which my front tyres were not so good, so I had to back off to clean them up.'

Starting 11th on the grid didn't exactly bode well for Jacques Villeneuve, but he slogged through to sixth at the chequered flag, probably more than he could have hoped for under the circumstances. 'I spent half the race stuck behind Trulli,' he shrugged. 'His car was very slow, but there was nothing I could do.'

It was subsequently discovered that Trulli had been grappling with a broken left-rear shock absorber in the second stint, which accounted for the drop-off in his lap times and the lack of grip he had been experiencing.

Damon Hill came home just outside the points in seventh place, with Herbert's Sauber, the Benetton B198 of Alexander Wurz, Trulli's Prost, Shinji Nakano's Minardi and the Tyrrell of Ricardo Rosset completing the list of finishers.

Hill had no complaints at all about his Jordan 198. He ran a light fuel load for the first stint which meant that his was the first of the scheduled refuelling stops on lap 19, after which he ran through to lap 45 before stopping again. Overall, it never quite enabled him to overtake enough cars.

'But for a bit of traffic here and there we could have had both cars in the points,' said Damon. 'The car felt the best it has all season, so things are looking good.' Only over the next few races would the 1996 World Champion come to realise just how good that could be.

GROSSER PREIS VON ÖSTERREICH

24–26 JULY 1998

A1-RING

Race distance: 71 laps, 190.543 miles/306.649 km

Race weather: Dry, hot and sunny

ROUND 10

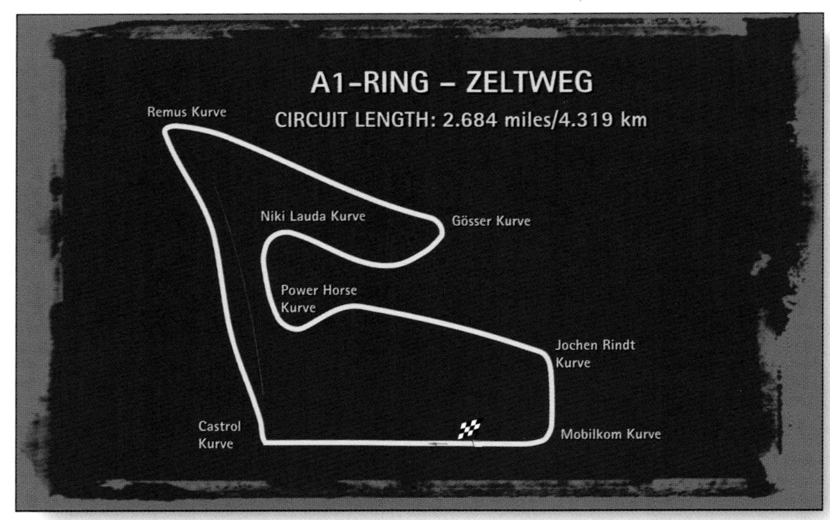

Pos.	Driver	Nat.	No.	Entrant	Car/Engine	Tyres	Laps	Time/Retirement	Speed (mph/km/h)
1	**Mika Häkkinen**	**SF**	**8**	**West McLaren Mercedes**	**McLaren MP4/13-Mercedes FO110G V10**	**B**	**71**	**1h 30m 44.086s**	**126.000/202.777**
2	**David Coulthard**	**GB**	**7**	**West McLaren Mercedes**	**McLaren MP4/13-Mercedes FO110G V10**	**B**	**71**	**1h 30m 49.375s**	**125.877/202.580**
3	**Michael Schumacher**	**D**	**3**	**Scuderia Ferrari Marlboro**	**Ferrari F300 047 V10**	**G**	**71**	**1h 31m 23.178s**	**125.101/201.331**
4	**Eddie Irvine**	**GB**	**4**	**Scuderia Ferrari Marlboro**	**Ferrari F300 047 V10**	**G**	**71**	**1h 31m 28.062s**	**124.990/201.152**
5	**Ralf Schumacher**	**D**	**10**	**B&H Jordan Mugen Honda**	**Jordan 198-Mugen Honda MF310C V10**	**G**	**71**	**1h 31m 34.740s**	**124.838/200.907**
6	**Jacques Villeneuve**	**CDN**	**1**	**Winfield Williams**	**Williams FW20-Mecachrome GC37/01 V10**	**G**	**71**	**1h 31m 37.288s**	**124.780/200.814**
7	Damon Hill	GB	9	B&H Jordan Mugen Honda	Jordan 198-Mugen Honda MF310C V10	G	71	1h 31m 57.710s	124.318/200.071
8	Johnny Herbert	GB	15	Red Bull Sauber Petronas	Sauber C17-Petronas SPE01D V10	G	70		
9	Alexander Wurz	A	6	Mild Seven Benetton Playlife	Benetton B198-Playlife V10	B	70		
10	Jarno Trulli	I	12	Gauloises Prost Peugeot	Prost AP01-Peugeot A16 V10	B	70		
11	Shinji Nakano	J	22	Fondmetal Minardi Ford	Minardi M198-Ford Zetec-R V10	B	70		
12	Ricardo Rosset	BR	20	Tyrrell Ford	Tyrrell 026-Ford Zetec-R V10	G	69		
	Jos Verstappen	NL	19	Stewart Ford	Stewart SF2-Ford Zetec-R V10	B	51	Engine	
	Esteban Tuero	RA	23	Fondmetal Minardi Ford	Minardi M198-Ford Zetec-R V10	B	30	Spun off	
	Giancarlo Fisichella	I	5	Mild Seven Benetton Playlife	Benetton B198-Playlife V10	B	21	Collision with Alesi	
	Jean Alesi	F	14	Red Bull Sauber Petronas	Sauber C17-Petronas SPE01D V10	G	21	Collision with Fisichella	
	Heinz-Harald Frentzen	D	2	Winfield Williams	Williams FW20-Mecachrome GC37/01 V10	G	16	Engine	
	Rubens Barrichello	BR	18	Stewart Ford	Stewart SF2-Ford Zetec-R V10	B	8	Brakes	
	Pedro Diniz	BR	16	Danka Zepter Arrows	Arrows A19 V10	B	3	Accident damage	
	Mika Salo	SF	17	Danka Zepter Arrows	Arrows A19 V10	B	1	Accident damage	
	Olivier Panis	F	11	Gauloises Prost Peugeot	Prost AP01-Peugeot A16 V10	B	0	Broken clutch	
	Toranosuke Takagi	J	21	Tyrrell Ford	Tyrrell 026-Ford Zetec-R V10	G	0	Accident	

Fastest lap: Coulthard, on lap 30, 1m 12.878s, 132.568 mph/213.348 km/h.

Lap record: Jacques Villeneuve (F1 Williams FW19-Renault V10), 1m 11.814s, 134.656 mph/216.709 km/h (1997).

B – Bridgestone G – Goodyear

All results and data © FIA 1998

Grid order	1	2	3	4	5	6	7	8	9	10	11	12	13	14	15	16	17	18	19	20	21	22	23	24	25	26	27
5 FISICHELLA	8	8	8	8	8	8	8	8	8	8	8	8	8	8	8	8	8	8	8	8	8	8	8	8	8	8	8
14 ALESI	3	3	3	5	3	3	3	3	3	3	3	3	3	3	3	3	5	5	5	5	5	4	4	4	4	4	4
8 HÄKKINEN	5	5	5	3	5	5	5	5	5	5	5	5	5	5	5	5	3	4	4	4	4	7	7	7	7	7	7
3 M. SCHUMACHER	18	18	18	18	18	18	18	4	4	4	4	4	4	4	4	4	4	14	7	7	7	10	10	10	10	10	10
18 BARRICHELLO	14	14	14	14	14	14	14	14	14	14	14	14	14	14	14	14	14	7	14	14	14	12	12	12	12	12	12
17 SALO	4	4	4	4	4	4	4	2	2	2	2	2	2	2	2	2	7	10	10	10	10	1	1	1	1	1	1
2 FRENTZEN	2	2	2	2	2	2	2	10	10	10	10	10	10	10	10	7	10	9	9	12	12	19	19	19	15	15	15
4 IRVINE	10	10	10	10	10	10	10	9	9	9	9	9	9	7	7	10	9	3	12	1	1	15	15	15	9	9	9
10 R. SCHUMACHER	9	9	9	9	9	9	9	18	12	7	7	7	7	9	9	9	12	12	1	19	19	9	9	9	19	3	3
11 PANIS	19	19	19	12	12	12	12	12	7	12	12	12	12	12	12	12	1	1	19	15	15	6	22	3	3	22	22
1 VILLENEUVE	6	6	6	1	1	1	1	1	1	1	1	1	1	1	1	1	19	19	15	6	6	22	3	22	22	23	19
19 VERSTAPPEN	12	12	12	19	19	19	19	7	19	19	19	19	19	19	19	19	15	15	6	9	9	23	23	23	23	19	6
16 DINIZ	1	23	1	20	20	7	7	19	20	20	20	20	20	20	20	20	6	6	20	20	20	3	6	6	6	6	20
7 COULTHARD	20	1	20	7	7	20	20	20	15	15	15	15	15	15	15	15	20	20	22	22	22	20	20	20	20	20	23
9 HILL	16	20	22	22	22	22	22	15	6	6	6	6	6	6	6	6	22	22	23	23	23						
12 TRULLI	22	16	15	15	15	15	15	22	22	22	22	22	22	22	22	22	23	23	3	3	3						
6 WURZ	7	22	7	6	6	6	6	6	23	23	23	23	23	23	23	23											
15 HERBERT	15	15	16	23	23	23	23	23																			
23 TUERO	23	7	23																								
21 TAKAGI	17																										
22 NAKANO																											
20 ROSSET																											

Grid order	28	29	30	31	32	33	34	35	36	37	38	39	40	41	42	43	44	45	46	47	48	49	50	51	52	53
5 FISICHELLA	8	8	8	8	8	8	8	7	7	8	8	8	8	8	8	8	8	8	8	8	8	8	8	8	8	8
14 ALESI	7	7	7	7	7	7	7	8	8	7	7	7	7	7	7	7	7	7	7	7	7	7	7	7	7	7
8 HÄKKINEN	4	4	4	4	4	4	4	4	4	4	4	4	4	4	4	4	4	4	4	4	4	4	4	4	4	4
3 M. SCHUMACHER	10	10	10	10	10	10	10	10	10	10	10	10	10	10	10	10	10	10	10	10	10	10	10	10	10	10
18 BARRICHELLO	12	12	12	12	12	12	12	3	3	3	3	3	3	3	3	1	9	9	3	3	3	3	3	3	3	3
17 SALO	1	1	1	1	1	1	3	1	1	1	1	1	1	1	1	9	3	3	1	1	1	1	1	1	1	1
2 FRENTZEN	15	15	15	15	3	3	1	12	12	12	9	9	9	9	9	3	1	1	6	6	6	9	9	9	9	9
4 IRVINE	9	9	3	3	15	15	15	15	15	9	12	6	6	6	6	6	6	6	9	9	9	15	15	15	15	15
10 R. SCHUMACHER	3	3	9	9	9	9	9	9	9	15	22	15	15	15	15	15	15	15	15	15	15	6	6	6	6	6
11 PANIS	22	22	22	22	22	22	22	22	22	22	6	12	12	12	12	12	12	12	12	12	12	12	12	12	12	12
1 VILLENEUVE	19	19	19	19	19	6	6	6	6	6	15	19	19	19	19	19	19	19	19	22	22	22	22	22	22	22
19 VERSTAPPEN	6	6	6	6	6	19	19	19	19	19	19	22	22	22	22	22	22	22	22	19	19	19	19	19	20	20
16 DINIZ	20	20	20	20	20	20	20	20	20	20	20	20	20	20	20	20	20	20	20	20	20	20	20	20		
7 COULTHARD	23	23	23																							
9 HILL																										
12 TRULLI																										
6 WURZ																										
15 HERBERT																										
23 TUERO																										
21 TAKAGI																										
22 NAKANO																										
20 ROSSET																										

Pit stop
One lap behind leader

STARTING GRID

5 **FISICHELLA** Benetton	14 **ALESI** Sauber
8 **HÄKKINEN** McLaren	3 **M. SCHUMACHER** Ferrari
18 **BARRICHELLO** Stewart	17 **SALO** Arrows
2 **FRENTZEN** Williams	4 **IRVINE** Ferrari
10 **R. SCHUMACHER** Jordan	11 **PANIS** Prost
1 **VILLENEUVE** Williams	19 **VERSTAPPEN** Stewart
16 **DINIZ** Arrows	7 **COULTHARD** McLaren
9 **HILL** Jordan	12 **TRULLI** Prost
6 **WURZ** Benetton	15 **HERBERT** Sauber
23 **TUERO** Minardi	21 **TAKAGI** Tyrrell
22 **NAKANO** Minardi	20 **ROSSET** Tyrrell

58	59	60	61	62	63	64	65	66	67	68	69	70	71	●
8	8	8	8	8	8	8	8	8	8	8	8	8	8	1
7	7	7	7	7	7	7	7	7	7	7	7	7	7	2
4	4	4	4	4	4	4	4	4	4	3	3	3	3	3
3	3	3	3	3	3	3	3	3	3	4	4	4	4	4
10	10	10	10	10	10	10	10	10	10	10	10	10	10	5
1	1	1	1	1	1	1	1	1	1	1	1	1	1	6
9	9	9	9	9	9	9	9	9	9	9	9	9	9	
15	15	15	15	15	15	15	15	15	15	15	15	15		
6	6	6	6	6	6	6	6	6	6	6	6	6		
12	12	12	12	12	12	12	12	12	12	12	12	12		
22	22	22	22	22	22	22	22	22	22	22	22	22		
20	20	20	20	20	20	20	20	20	20	20	20			

FOR THE RECORD

First Grand Prix pole position
Giancarlo Fisichella

TIME SHEETS

QUALIFYING

Weather: Heavy rain, then gradually drying

Pos.	Driver	Car	Laps	Time
1	Giancarlo Fisichella	Benetton-Playlife	12	1m 29.598s
2	Jean Alesi	Sauber-Petronas	12	1m 30.317s
3	Mika Häkkinen	McLaren-Mercedes	12	1m 30.517s
4	Michael Schumacher	Ferrari	10	1m 30.551s
5	Rubens Barrichello	Stewart-Ford	12	1m 31.005s
6	Mika Salo	Arrows	11	1m 31.028s
7	Heinz-Harald Frentzen	Williams-Mecachrome	11	1m 31.515s
8	Eddie Irvine	Ferrari	9	1m 31.651s
9	Ralf Schumacher	Jordan-Mugen Honda	12	1m 31.917s
10	Olivier Panis	Prost-Peugeot	12	1m 32.081s
11	Jacques Villeneuve	Williams-Mecachrome	11	1m 32.083s
12	Jos Verstappen	Stewart-Ford	12	1m 32.099s
13	Pedro Diniz	Arrows	12	1m 32.206s
14	David Coulthard	McLaren-Mercedes	12	1m 32.399s
15	Damon Hill	Jordan-Mugen Honda	11	1m 32.718s
16	Jarno Trulli	Prost-Peugeot	12	1m 32.906s
17	Alexander Wurz	Benetton-Playlife	10	1m 33.185s
18	Johnny Herbert	Sauber-Petronas	10	1m 33.205s
19	Esteban Tuero	Minardi-Ford	12	1m 33.399s
20	Toranosuke Takagi	Tyrrell-Ford	12	1m 34.090s
21	Shinji Nakano	Minardi-Ford	9	1m 34.536s
22	Ricardo Rosset	Tyrrell-Ford	11	1m 34.910s

FRIDAY FREE PRACTICE

Weather: Dry, hot and sunny

Pos.	Driver	Laps	Time
1	David Coulthard	36	1m 13.703s
2	Giancarlo Fisichella	43	1m 13.704s
3	Mika Häkkinen	30	1m 13.746s
4	Johnny Herbert	45	1m 14.103s
5	Rubens Barrichello	35	1m 14.302s
6	Alexander Wurz	34	1m 14.397s
7	Michael Schumacher	25	1m 14.411s
8	Eddie Irvine	31	1m 14.523s
9	Damon Hill	46	1m 14.535s
10	Jean Alesi	35	1m 14.627s
11	Jarno Trulli	44	1m 14.685s
12	Olivier Panis	50	1m 14.755s
13	Jacques Villeneuve	39	1m 14.820s
14	Ralf Schumacher	28	1m 15.117s
15	Toranosuke Takagi	48	1m 15.158s
16	Jos Verstappen	35	1m 15.231s
17	Heinz-Harald Frentzen	25	1m 15.345s
18	Mika Salo	31	1m 15.696s
19	Shinji Nakano	43	1m 16.171s
20	Pedro Diniz	35	1m 16.303s
21	Esteban Tuero	28	1m 16.582s
22	Ricardo Rosset	36	1m 18.469s

SATURDAY FREE PRACTICE

Weather: Dry, hot and sunny

Pos.	Driver	Laps	Time
1	David Coulthard	37	1m 11.655s
2	Mika Häkkinen	36	1m 11.819s
3	Eddie Irvine	40	1m 12.569s
4	Heinz-Harald Frentzen	33	1m 12.673s
5	Michael Schumacher	32	1m 12.690s
6	Jean Alesi	37	1m 12.789s
7	Damon Hill	35	1m 13.010s
8	Giancarlo Fisichella	37	1m 13.074s
9	Ralf Schumacher	41	1m 13.259s
10	Jacques Villeneuve	35	1m 13.354s
11	Jarno Trulli	33	1m 13.396s
12	Johnny Herbert	35	1m 13.421s
13	Alexander Wurz	27	1m 13.671s
14	Toranosuke Takagi	21	1m 13.730s
15	Mika Salo	34	1m 13.802s
16	Rubens Barrichello	22	1m 13.887s
17	Olivier Panis	33	1m 13.966s
18	Pedro Diniz	34	1m 13.999s
19	Jos Verstappen	29	1m 14.070s
20	Ricardo Rosset	36	1m 14.351s
21	Esteban Tuero	39	1m 14.738s
22	Shinji Nakano	34	1m 14.906s

WARM-UP

Weather: Dry, warm and overcast

Pos.	Driver	Laps	Time
1	Mika Häkkinen	16	1m 13.301s
2	David Coulthard	15	1m 13.602s
3	Michael Schumacher	17	1m 14.307s
4	Eddie Irvine	16	1m 14.350s
5	Jean Alesi	17	1m 14.474s
6	Toranosuke Takagi	16	1m 14.480s
7	Rubens Barrichello	17	1m 14.881s
8	Giancarlo Fisichella	14	1m 14.941s
9	Alexander Wurz	18	1m 14.942s
10	Ralf Schumacher	13	1m 15.086s
11	Jarno Trulli	17	1m 15.097s
12	Damon Hill	10	1m 15.162s
13	Johnny Herbert	15	1m 15.368s
14	Heinz-Harald Frentzen	9	1m 15.376s
15	Mika Salo	16	1m 15.574s
16	Pedro Diniz	14	1m 15.638s
17	Jos Verstappen	18	1m 15.702s
18	Esteban Tuero	17	1m 15.788s
19	Olivier Panis	19	1m 16.006s
20	Shinji Nakano	20	1m 16.142s
21	Jacques Villeneuve	12	1m 16.159s
22	Ricardo Rosset	13	1m 16.309s

RACE FASTEST LAPS

Weather: Dry, hot and sunny

Driver	Time	Lap
David Coulthard	1m 12.878s	30
Michael Schumacher	1m 13.029s	41
Mika Häkkinen	1m 13.412s	31
Jacques Villeneuve	1m 13.730s	66
Ralf Schumacher	1m 13.972s	69
Alexander Wurz	1m 14.040s	70
Giancarlo Fisichella	1m 14.044s	20
Eddie Irvine	1m 14.066s	58
Damon Hill	1m 14.135s	63
Johnny Herbert	1m 14.639s	63
Jean Alesi	1m 14.791s	21
Heinz-Harald Frentzen	1m 15.446s	16
Shinji Nakano	1m 15.575s	37
Jos Verstappen	1m 15.610s	43
Jarno Trulli	1m 15.709s	59
Esteban Tuero	1m 15.769s	19
Ricardo Rosset	1m 16.100s	28
Rubens Barrichello	1m 16.822s	5
Pedro Diniz	2m 02.090s	2

CHASSIS LOG BOOK

1	Villeneuve	Williams FW20/5
2	Frentzen	Williams FW20/4
	spare	Williams FW20/3
3	M. Schumacher	Ferrari F300/188
4	Irvine	Ferrari F300/185
	spare	Ferrari F300/181
5	Fisichella	Benetton B198/6
6	Wurz	Benetton B198/7
	spare	Benetton B198/4
7	Coulthard	McLaren MP4/13/4
8	Häkkinen	McLaren MP4/13/6
	spare	McLaren MP4/13/3
9	Hill	Jordan 198/3
10	R. Schumacher	Jordan 198/4
	spare	Jordan 198/5
11	Panis	Prost AP01/5
12	Trulli	Prost AP01/6
	spare	Prost AP01/2
14	Alesi	Sauber C17/6
15	Herbert	Sauber C17/1
	spare	Sauber C17/2
16	Diniz	Arrows A19/2
17	Salo	Arrows A19/5
	spare	Arrows A19/1
18	Barrichello	Stewart SF2/4
19	Verstappen	Stewart SF2/3
	spare	Stewart SF2/2
20	Rosset	Tyrrell 026/2
21	Takagi	Tyrrell 026/3
	spare	Tyrrell 026/4
22	Nakano	Minardi M198/4
23	Tuero	Minardi M198/5
	spare	Minardi M198/3

POINTS TABLES

Drivers

1	Mika Häkkinen	66
2	Michael Schumacher	58
3	David Coulthard	36
4	Eddie Irvine	32
5	Alexander Wurz	17
6	Giancarlo Fisichella	15
7	Jacques Villeneuve	12
8	Heinz-Harald Frentzen	8
9	Rubens Barrichello	4
10 =	Jean Alesi	3
10 =	Mika Salo	3
10 =	Ralf Schumacher	3
13 =	Johnny Herbert	1
13 =	Pedro Diniz	1
13 =	Jan Magnussen	1

Constructors

1	McLaren	102
2	Ferrari	90
3	Benetton	32
4	Williams	20
5	Stewart	5
6 =	Sauber	4
6 =	Arrows	4
8	Jordan	3

FIA WORLD CHAMPIONSHIP • ROUND 11

GERMAN
grand prix

HÄKKINEN
COULTHARD
VILLENEUVE
HILL
M. SCHUMACHER
R. SCHUMACHER

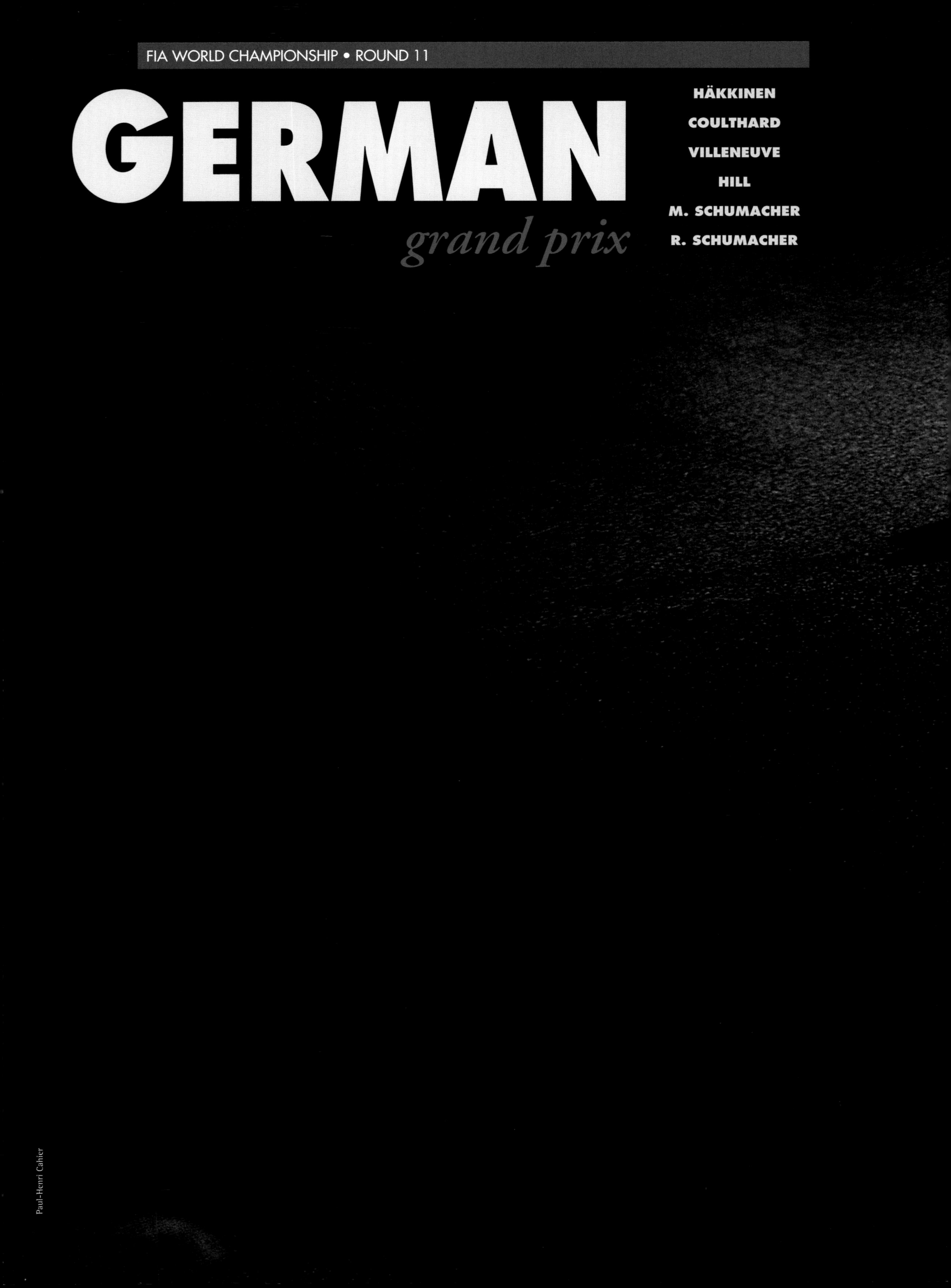

Paul-Henri Cahier

8
Mobil

Mika Häkkinen and David Coulthard sparred relentlessly for the distinction of being fastest McLaren-Mercedes driver on the German car company's home turf from the very start of Friday's free practice session. Yet it was not all plain sailing. Optimising the aerodynamic balance for the MP4/13s on this ultra-fast circuit proved to be a tricky business and during Saturday morning's session both men spun after they'd sacrificed a touch too much rear downforce as they juggled to improve front-end grip.

In low-downforce trim Coulthard turned a record 222 mph through the Hockenheim speed trap during that session, but an engine failure in qualifying on this track where the engines are on full throttle for 62 per cent of the time and 74 per cent of the lap distance prevented the Scot from mounting a late challenge to the eighth pole position of Häkkinen's career.

The qualifying session began on a track surface made damp by a recent rain shower and there were only 26 minutes remaining when the first car edged out onto the circuit.

Mika's 1m 41.838s best was also a shade inside last year's Hockenheim pole time, the first occasion this year on which cars competing under the revised F1 regulations had been quicker than at the corresponding event in 1997.

Peter Nygaard/GP Photo

The two McLaren drivers opted for Bridgestone's harder tyre choice for qualifying and the race. 'There was a small performance advantage offered by the softer choice,' explained Ron Dennis, 'but we had experienced some slight structural problems with them, so we decided to risk running the harder tyre which would offer us more flexibility as regards pit stop strategies.'

Häkkinen was well satisfied. 'The car's balance was not perfect,' he grinned, 'but we made some improvements for qualifying and it was definitely much better. One of the problems with racing drivers is that they are never happy with their cars. But I am very happy with the improvements that were made.'

After his engine failure, Coulthard came back to take the spare MP4/13 for his final run. 'It felt like there was a bit more grip on the circuit as I started that last run,' he said, 'but it was always going to be a long shot as to whether you would improve or not on your first run in a different car.'

In third place on the grid, perhaps slightly unexpectedly, was Jacques Villeneuve's Williams FW20. The Canadian really had the Mecachrome-engined car well cranked up and said, 'This was the first time I actually enjoyed a Williams in low-downforce configuration because in both 1996 and '97 the car was very difficult to drive here. But I am sure we can hold our own in the race tomorrow.'

Jacques also added that he felt he might have challenged for pole position – or at least for a place on the front row – had he not caught one of the Stewart SF2s coming through the stadium section.

In many respects, the stars of the qualifying show were the Jordan 198s, benefiting from input from new chief designer Mike Gascoyne. Running without their aerodynamic 'barge boards' for the second consecutive race, Ralf Schumacher and Damon Hill were right on the pace from the outset and with the latest development version of the Japanese V10s installed for qualifying – improving mid-range performance – it was no real surprise that they emerged in fourth and fifth places on the grid.

By contrast, Ferrari had a positively dismal time during qualifying, struggling with lack of mechanical grip through the comparatively slow stadium section. As far as Maranello was concerned, Hockenheim was bracketed with Monaco and Monza as the tracks on which Schumacher expected to have the most handling problems.

At aerodynamic extremes the F300 was very difficult to handle and Michael's problems on home ground were compounded by a time-consuming, unaccountable spin at the Ostkurve during Saturday free practice followed shortly afterwards by an engine failure. Friday's free practice session had been expended evaluating the latest longer-wheelbase version of the F300, but the cars were returned to standard-wheelbase trim for Saturday before the other problems cropped up.

The net result was that Schumacher went into the crucial hour of qualifying with only two trouble-free laps under his belt at the wheel of the standard car. Yet Michael admitted that this was only part of the difficulty.

'Even without my problems in this morning's free practice, I would have only been a couple of tenths quicker,' he said. 'As can be seen from Eddie [Irvine]'s time, our performance level was not good enough.' The two Italian cars wound up sixth and ninth, with the Ulsterman ahead on this occasion.

Separating the two Ferraris were the Benetton B198s of Alexander Wurz and Giancarlo Fisichella. 'The session didn't go too badly,' said the Austrian. 'Initially I was over-driving the car as this was my first experience of a low-downforce set-up and I pushed both cars and tyres over the limit. The third time I went out I was a lot less aggressive and it worked out well.'

Fisichella believed that he could have gone at least 0.3s quicker had it not been for a clutch failure prior to his final run which made the car difficult to drive. 'I think our race set-up is pretty good,' he conceded, 'but it will be tough starting from the fourth row.'

Joining Schumacher's Ferrari on the fifth row was Heinz-Harald Frentzen's Williams, the German driver ending the day in an extremely disappointed mood. 'We have had a big problem with the set-up which we have to solve,' he said thoughtfully. 'The balance of the car was totally wrong, which is why I was unable to improve my time at all.'

Side by side on the sixth row sat the Sauber C17s of Jean Alesi and Johnny Herbert. Both were a little dismayed that their lap times had failed to earn them a better grid position.

'I changed the set-up a little bit midway through the session to see if we would make it better,' mused Alesi, 'but it was a little bit slower. So for my last run I went back to the same downforce I started with and the car felt happier that way.'

As for Herbert, valuable time lost during the morning free practice session with a major gearbox electronics problem proved impossible to claw back. 'So I missed the majority of that session, and it's always difficult when that happens because you don't have the time in qualifying to improve the set-up,' he explained.

'The car felt bad. It was oversteering and giving me little feed-back. We never found a decent set-up in the time available.'

The best the Stewart-Ford team could manage was 13th place for Rubens Barrichello, this being the first weekend at which the latest Series 5 Zetec-R V10s would be run right through both qualifying and the race. The Brazilian was guardedly optimistic and equally certain he had lost another grid place right at the end of the session.

'Ralf Schumacher wasn't aware that I was making a fast approach at the entrance of the stadium,' he said. 'He had slowed down but his car was still on the racing line. I thought that maybe if he had a problem he should have gone off-line. It caused an unnecessary distraction because I knew I was on a quick lap and it was a disappointing end to what was a good qualifying session for me.'

Team-mate Jos Verstappen found himself unable to better 19th in the final order, struggling throughout the weekend to get the handling balance worked out to his liking.

Yet again, precious little went right in the Prost-Peugeot camp. After raising hopes on Friday when he was third-fastest Bridgestone runner after the McLarens, Jarno Trulli found his car beset by lack of grip and slipped to 14th in the final grid order. That was two places ahead of team-mate Olivier Panis, who crashed in the stadium at the start of the Saturday morning session and had to use the untried spare AP01 in qualifying.

There were mixed fortunes for the Tyrrell drivers. Toranosuke Takagi did really well to qualify 15th, even though the Japanese novice felt he could have done much better had he not spun into a tyre barrier in his race chassis after his first run, then been obliged to take the spare. Team-mate Ricardo Rosset crashed quite heavily in free practice, thereafter withdrawing from any further participation for the weekend on the advice of FIA medical delegate Professor Sid Watkins.

The Arrows team always knew that qualifying at Hockenheim would be something of a struggle, even though the latest C-specification V10 engine had shown promise the previous weekend in Austria. Mika Salo battled oversteer to line up 17th, while Pedro Diniz took the spare A19 fitted with the engine from his race car and was right behind in 18th.

Esteban Tuero may have had F3000 experience at Hockenheim, but it didn't much help his efforts for Minardi. Gearbox problems lost him time on Friday, then he spun off on Saturday morning and – just when it looked as if things couldn't get any worse – a major engine failure forced him into the spare car for qualifying; and then he got a puncture. That left him 21st and last, right behind team-mate Shinji Nakano.

Previous pages: **Mika Häkkinen overcame fuel consumption worries to give Mercedes its first win on home soil since returning to Grand Prix racing in 1994.**

Below left: **Ricardo Rosset applies an ice pack to his injured elbow after a heavy crash on Saturday morning which forced the hapless Brazilian to sit out the rest of the weekend.**

Below right: **Keep your head still, please, Sir. David Coulthard's visor is given a wipe during the course of another immaculate McLaren refuelling stop.**

MIKA Häkkinen and David Coulthard left Ferrari trailing for the second successive weekend when they delivered another decisive display of McLaren-Mercedes superiority on the German car maker's home ground.

Häkkinen's second win in eight days was also a fitting way to celebrate the announcement that the two drivers would be staying with the team through to the end of 1999. This had been revealed on the eve of the race by Mercedes board director Jürgen Hubbert, who said, 'We are happy with what they have done for us in the past and believe they are both capable of being World Champion.'

This was McLaren's sixth 1-2 success in 12 races and saw Häkkinen pull 16 points clear of his key rival Michael Schumacher in the see-sawing battle for the 1998 World Championship. The German ace could finish no better than fifth after a troubled weekend during which he battled to achieve a worthwhile handling balance at high speed.

Third place fell to Jacques Villeneuve's Williams FW20 ahead of Damon Hill, who scored his first points of the season in the Jordan-Mugen Honda.

McLaren's latest success marked the first occasion on which a Mercedes-engined F1 car had won on German soil since the legendary Juan Manuel Fangio won at the Nürburgring in 1954. It was also another giant stride by Häkkinen towards becoming only the second-ever Finnish World Champion, 16 years after his manager Keke Rosberg won the title in a Williams.

Unlike the Austrian race a week earlier, on this occasion Coulthard fought no rearguard action, battling through from the back of the field to join his team-mate on the rostrum. Instead the Scot ran steadily in Häkkinen's wheel tracks all afternoon.

After taking his place on the starting grid, Giancarlo Fisichella was advised that there was a problem with his Benetton's engine, so he immediately hopped out and ran over to the team's garage, where he was hurriedly strapped into the spare car. He just managed to make it out onto the circuit before the pit lane closed.

Once he was back on the grid, the mechanics did their best to modify the cockpit to make the Italian as comfortable as possible, but with the spare B198 initially set up for Alexander Wurz it was always going to be something of an uneasy compromise.

At the start the two McLarens got away in routine formation, Häkkinen just slotting into the first right-hander ahead of Coulthard and the Jordans of

British Grand Prix stewards to blame

THREE top international stewards returned their licences to the FIA for an unspecified period after being held responsible for the shambles at the British Grand Prix which resulted in winner Michael Schumacher having a ten-second stop-go penalty rescinded once the event was over.

Two days after the McLaren team's appeal over the Silverstone result had been rejected, at an extraordinary general meeting of the FIA World Council stewards Nazir Hoosein (India), Roger Peart (Canada) and Howard Lapsley (Britain) were found to have made three key mistakes. They returned their superlicences voluntarily as an acknowledgement of their responsibility.

The key mistakes were:

1. They treated information from the Race Director as a formal report of an incident.

2. They failed to note the time at which, and the lap on which, the alleged incident took place. As a result the wrong rule was applied and was applied outside the permitted time.

3. They failed to communicate their decision to the Race Director with the result that the information did not appear on the TV monitors as requested by the rules.

In mitigation, the FIA noted that these events took place when extreme conditions of torrential rain placed race control under considerable stress. It was also announced that steps would be taken to review procedures to prevent such events from occurring again in the future.

On a separate note, the FIA issued a clarification on F1 team orders which seemed to play straight into Ferrari's hands. It was now confirmed that it is perfectly legitimate for a team to decide that one of its drivers is its championship contender and for the other to support him.

Ralf Schumacher and Damon Hill plus Jacques Villeneuve's Williams, the Canadian outbraking his former team-mate as they went into the first chicane.

The circuit had been brushed by a light rain shower in the moments immediately before the start, but this did not develop into anything serious. Further back on the grid, Wurz had almost stalled his Benetton, giving Michael Schumacher a heart-stopping moment as he swerved his Ferrari around his near-stationary rival.

By the end of the opening lap Häkkinen led by 1.4s from Coulthard, Ralf Schumacher, Villeneuve, Hill, Eddie Irvine's Ferrari, Michael Schumacher, Fisichella, Heinz-Harald Frentzen's Williams and Jean Alesi's Sauber. Next time round the gap between the two McLarens was down to 1.2s, while on the third lap Pedro Diniz's Arrows retired from 19th place with a throttle problem.

On the same lap Olivier Panis was signalled that he had incurred a ten-second stop-go penalty for jumping the start in his Prost-Peugeot, but apart from that the race settled down into a predictable and rather processional pattern.

In third place, running on a two-stop strategy, Ralf Schumacher's Jordan began inching towards Coulthard's second-placed McLaren, but the young German's charge was blunted on lap 14 when he came in for the first of those stops. The Jordan was stationary for just 8.9s, but dropped from third to ninth and left Villeneuve with a clear run in third place.

'On reflection, I think the pit stop strategy we chose did not work out,' said Ralf later, 'although I do not think that was the main reason why I did not finish as high up as I had hoped. After the first stop the car did not feel the same as it had done all weekend. I was not able to brake as late as I had been, and was losing grip, so I was not able to keep up the same pace as I had at the beginning.'

On lap 23 Villeneuve and Hill made their refuelling stops, resuming in fifth and seventh. That left the two McLarens ahead with Michael Schumacher third until he came in next time round, allowing Villeneuve up into fourth place. On lap 25 Irvine dropped from third to eighth when he brought his Ferrari in for its stop, the Ulsterman later admitting that he had had something of a mixed day, eventually finishing the race in eighth place.

'I worked very hard for little reward,' he shrugged. 'My start was all right, but with a little too much wheelspin. Then Michael was behind me, and when I locked up the right-front wheel under braking he managed to get past.

'I could sit behind him quite comfortably, but, before the pit stop, I pushed harder and overdid it at one of the chicanes, which cost me time. I lost out to Fisichella in the pit stops, but kept pressing him as hard as I could.'

Sporting Pictures (UK) Ltd

Bryn Williams

DIARY

Jordan technical director Gary Anderson linked with possible new job at Arrows.

Malaysia emerges as the sole realistic new F1 venue for 1999.

Eddie Irvine clinches deal to stay with Ferrari for a fourth season.

Scot Peter Dumbreck clinches All-Japan Formula 3 title with three races still to go.

arno Trulli listens intently as team owner ılain Prost offers his thoughts on the roblems besetting the cars that bear his llustrious name.

Below: **Brothers and Arms. The German ans saw both Schumacher brothers finish n the points, although neither was ever n contention for victory.**

Lukas Gorys

Häkkinen made his 9.9s refuelling stop on lap 26, allowing Coulthard to trip the timing beam in the lead for two laps before coming in for his own stop at the end of lap 27. He resumed in second, Mika just squeezing back ahead as the two cars accelerated past the pit exit.

'At the pit stop I thought there might be a chance for me to get past,' reflected David afterwards. 'As Mika went into the pits, I noticed from the screen on my dashboard that we were eight-tenths slower on that lap than I had been up to that point.

'I knew if I went back to my regular lap time [before my own stop] then that could make the crucial difference. But I then got two slower cars in front of me on the "in" lap before my pit stop. That made me so frustrated that I tried to make up the lost time under braking into my refuelling area and I overshot.

'In the end, that cancelled everything out when I returned to the track and came up behind Mika again.'

On lap 29 Ralf Schumacher made his second refuelling stop from fourth place, resuming in sixth, and over the next few laps Villeneuve really started to make inroads into the McLaren advantage. On lap 33 the World Champion was 5.1s behind Häkkinen, but in another three laps he was only 2.1s behind, prompting Coulthard to start lapping slower cars in a defensive manner, subtly trying to box in the Williams each time he came up on a back-marker.

Even though the McLarens' performance may have looked like an unruffled demonstration run, the fact was that both Häkkinen and Coulthard were extremely worried about the challenge posed by Villeneuve in the closing stages of the race.

Although the leading McLaren had started trailing an ominous haze of liquid which gradually laid an opaque film across Coulthard's visor, the slight loss of performance was caused by Häkkinen leaning off the fuel mixture under instructions from the McLaren engineers.

'At one point we were slightly worried that Mika's car had not taken on its full fuel allocation at the pit stop,' said McLaren managing director Ron Dennis. 'Even though we then checked our figures and convinced ourselves that this was not in fact the case, we played safe by adjusting the mixture to run as economically as possible.'

It all worked out well enough in the end. By lap 41 Häkkinen was beginning to open out his advantage over the third-placed Williams as Villeneuve started to encounter trouble, his challenge blunted by an apparent transmission problem.

'I suddenly picked up a lot of wheelspin on the inside rear wheel,' he reported. 'The revs were rising, but the car was going no faster. It could have been something to do with the clutch or the differential.'

Nevertheless, this was the reigning World Champion's best performance of the season and his first visit to the rostrum since clinching his title with third place in the previous year's controversial European Grand Prix at Jerez, where Michael Schumacher had tried to knock him off the circuit.

In fourth place, Damon Hill was extremely satisfied that he had at last shaken the monkey off his back and managed to score his first points of the season.

'I made a really good start and got ahead of Jacques as we went out of the stadium, but he towed past me before we reached the first chicane,' he recalled with some satisfaction. 'From that point I just had to hang on, keep pushing and just punching in the laps as hard as I could.

'I got into a good rhythm and was driving to the maximum to get fourth place, which was about as good as we could hope for. I think I am probably too seasoned to become ecstatic about the fact that I've at last scored my first points of the season. I just feel that we are clawing our way back into the zone where things start to get more interesting.

'We must focus on maintaining this improvement and I will be working hard to do well in Hungary. We want the trend to continue there, even though we have not gone particularly well up to now on high-downforce circuits.'

Michael Schumacher's Ferrari F300 was next home in fifth place. On the face of it, this was a highly disappointing result on a low-downforce circuit which, in any case, had not been expected to produce a great deal for the Maranello squad. Yet it was not quite as bad as some might have wanted to paint it, the German driver ending up only 12.6s behind Häkkinen's winning McLaren at the chequered flag.

'I am sorry that I was unable to do better in front of my home crowd,' he admitted, 'but after qualifying ninth and being off the pace all weekend, there was no reason to expect a miracle during the race. My main problem was lack of grip on the infield section, where it was difficult simply to keep the car on the road.'

Behind brother Ralf's Jordan in sixth place, Giancarlo Fisichella squeezed home less than a second ahead of Irvine's Ferrari. 'In the race the set-up and the cockpit of the spare car were not exactly the same as my car,' explained Fisichella. 'I would have been pleased to gain a point, but I am happy to have finished the race.'

Behind Irvine came a frustrated Frentzen, who failed to get the best out of a chassis set-up more to Villeneuve's taste, while the top ten was completed by a philosophical Jean Alesi in the Sauber C17.

'The start was not so good for me because when Wurz nearly stalled, I had to lift off and move to the left to avoid hitting him,' said the Frenchman. 'After that I pushed hard all race. The car was fine and gave me absolutely no problem today, but I just wasn't quick enough.'

Team-mate Johnny Herbert ran in close contact with his team-mate in 11th place for much of the race until his car developed a gearbox problem and he missed a chicane as a result.

'I discovered that if I changed down quickly I could get third gear, but going into the 38th lap when I downchanged at the first corner I only got the gear momentarily,' he said. 'Then as the car went into neutral, the system cut out the engine. It was a disappointing end to a disappointing weekend for me.'

The Stewart-Ford team emerged empty-handed from another frustrating weekend. Rubens Barrichello was running in the group battling for tenth until gearbox temperatures edged out of control and he had to quit. For his part, Jos Verstappen struggled for traction in the early stages and eventually stopped with an apparent transmission breakage.

Outside the top ten Alexander Wurz's Benetton came home 11th after his clutch problem at the start. 'I didn't have any problems getting past the first back-markers,' he explained, 'but then I got stuck behind Johnny Herbert and he was losing an awful lot of oil, so it was very slippery. Once Johnny was out of the race I managed to go at least half to one second a lap quicker.'

Into 12th place came Jarno Trulli's Prost-Peugeot ahead of Toranosuke Takagi's Tyrrell, Mika Salo's Arrows, Olivier Panis – who suffered another unscheduled delay when his Prost picked up a puncture – and Esteban Tuero's Minardi.

For Mercedes-Benz, posting a 1-2 success on its home turf was like a promotional dream come true. For McLaren it was additional confirmation that they were on the road towards the World Championship. Nothing could stand in their way now. Could it?

GROSSER MOBIL 1 PREIS VON DEUTSCHLAND

31 JULY–2 AUGUST 1998

HOCKENHEIM

Race distance: 45 laps, 190.782 miles/307.035 km

Race weather: Dry, hot and sunny

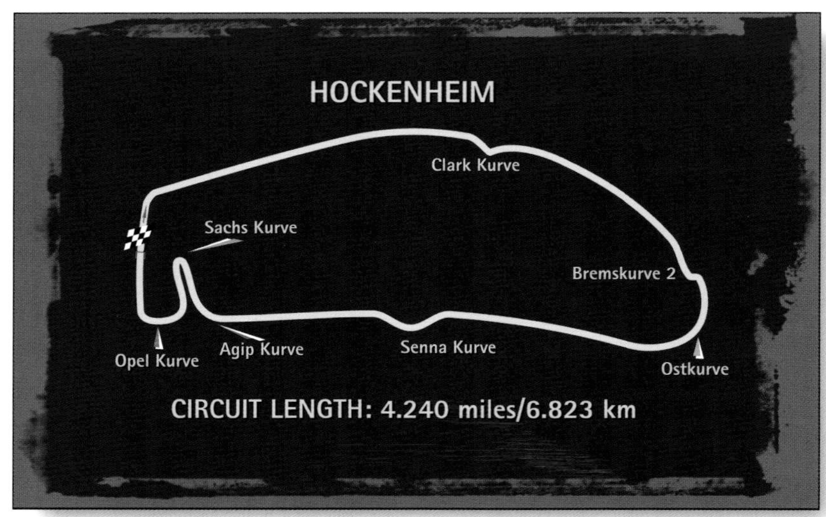

Pos.	Driver	Nat.	No.	Entrant	Car/Engine	Tyres	Laps	Time/Retirement	Speed (mph/km/h)
1	**Mika Häkkinen**	**SF**	**8**	**West McLaren Mercedes**	**McLaren MP4/13-Mercedes FO110G V10**	**B**	**45**	**1h 20m 47.984s**	**141.671/227.997**
2	**David Coulthard**	**GB**	**7**	**West McLaren Mercedes**	**McLaren MP4/13-Mercedes FO110G V10**	**B**	**45**	**1h 20m 48.410s**	**141.657/227.976**
3	**Jacques Villeneuve**	**CDN**	**1**	**Winfield Williams**	**Williams FW20-Mecachrome GC37/01 V10**	**G**	**45**	**1h 20m 50.561s**	**141.595/227.875**
4	**Damon Hill**	**GB**	**9**	**B&H Jordan Mugen Honda**	**Jordan 198-Mugen Honda MF310C V10**	**G**	**45**	**1h 20m 55.169s**	**141.461/227.659**
5	**Michael Schumacher**	**D**	**3**	**Scuderia Ferrari Marlboro**	**Ferrari F300 047 V10**	**G**	**45**	**1h 21m 00.597s**	**141.303/227.405**
6	**Ralf Schumacher**	**D**	**10**	**B&H Jordan Mugen Honda**	**Jordan 198-Mugen Honda MF310C V10**	**G**	**45**	**1h 21m 17.722s**	**140.807/226.607**
7	Giancarlo Fisichella	I	5	Mild Seven Benetton Playlife	Benetton B198-Playlife V10	B	45	1h 21m 19.010s	140.770/226.547
8	Eddie Irvine	GB	4	Scuderia Ferrari Marlboro	Ferrari F300 047 V10	G	45	1h 21m 19.633s	140.752/226.518
9	Heinz-Harald Frentzen	D	2	Winfield Williams	Williams FW20-Mecachrome GC37/01 V10	G	45	1h 21m 20.768s	140.719/226.465
10	Jean Alesi	F	14	Red Bull Sauber Petronas	Sauber C17-Petronas SPE01D V10	G	45	1h 21m 36.355s	140.271/225.744
11	Alexander Wurz	A	6	Mild Seven Benetton Playlife	Benetton B198-Playlife V10	B	45	1h 21m 45.978s	139.995/225.301
12	Jarno Trulli	I	12	Gauloises Prost Peugeot	Prost AP01-Peugeot A16 V10	B	44		
13	Toranosuke Takagi	J	21	Tyrrell Ford	Tyrrell 026-Ford Zetec-R V10	G	44		
14	Mika Salo	SF	17	Danka Zepter Arrows	Arrows A19 V10	B	44		
15	Olivier Panis	F	11	Gauloises Prost Peugeot	Prost AP01-Peugeot A16 V10	B	44		
16	Esteban Tuero	RA	23	Fondmetal Minardi Ford	Minardi M198-Ford Zetec-R V10	B	43		
	Johnny Herbert	GB	15	Red Bull Sauber Petronas	Sauber C17-Petronas SPE01D V10	G	37	Gearbox	
	Shinji Nakano	J	22	Fondmetal Minardi Ford	Minardi M198-Ford Zetec-R V10	B	36	Gearbox	
	Rubens Barrichello	BR	18	Stewart Ford	Stewart SF2-Ford Zetec-R V10	B	27	Gearbox	
	Jos Verstappen	NL	19	Stewart Ford	Stewart SF2-Ford Zetec-R V10	B	24	Transmission	
	Pedro Diniz	BR	16	Danka Zepter Arrows	Arrows A19 V10	B	2	Throttle	
DNQ	Ricardo Rosset	BR	20	Tyrrell Ford	Tyrrell 026-Ford Zetec-R V10	G			

Fastest lap: Coulthard, on lap 17, 1m 46.116s, 143.829 mph/231.471 km/h.

Lap record: Gerhard Berger (F1 Benetton B197-Renault V10), 1m 45.747s, 144.331 mph/232.278 km/h (1997).

B – Bridgestone G – Goodyear

All results and data © FIA 1998

Grid order	1	2	3	4	5	6	7	8	9	10	11	12	13	14	15	16	17	18	19	20	21	22	23	24	25	26	27	28	29	30	31	32	33	34	35	36	37	38	39	40	41	42	43	44	45	●
8 HÄKKINEN	8	8	8	8	8	8	8	8	8	8	8	8	8	8	8	8	8	8	8	8	8	8	8	8	8	7	7	8	8	8	8	8	8	8	8	8	8	8	8	8	8	8	8	8	8	1
7 COULTHARD	7	7	7	7	7	7	7	7	7	7	7	7	7	7	7	7	7	7	7	7	7	7	7	7	7	8	8	7	7	7	7	7	7	7	7	7	7	7	7	7	7	7	7	7	7	2
1 VILLENEUVE	10	10	10	10	10	10	10	10	10	10	10	10	10	1	1	1	1	1	1	1	1	1	1	3	1	1	1	1	1	1	1	1	1	1	1	1	1	1	1	1	1	1	1	1	1	3
10 R. SCHUMACHER	1	1	1	1	1	1	1	1	1	1	1	1	1	10	9	9	9	9	9	9	9	9	9	4	4	10	10	10	10	9	9	9	9	9	9	9	9	9	9	9	9	9	9	9	9	4
9 HILL	9	9	9	9	9	9	9	9	9	9	9	9	9	9	3	3	3	3	3	3	3	3	3	1	10	9	9	9	9	3	3	3	3	3	3	3	3	3	3	3	3	3	3	3	3	5
4 IRVINE	4	4	4	3	3	3	3	3	3	3	3	3	3	3	4	4	4	4	4	4	4	4	4	10	9	3	3	3	3	10	10	10	10	10	10	10	10	10	10	10	10	10	10	10	10	6
6 WURZ	3	3	3	4	4	4	4	4	4	4	4	4	4	4	5	5	5	5	5	5	5	10	10	9	3	5	5	5	5	5	5	5	5	5	5	5	5	5	5	5	5	5	5	5	5	
5 FISICHELLA	5	5	5	5	5	5	5	5	5	5	5	5	5	5	2	2	2	2	2	2	2	5	6	5	5	4	4	4	4	4	4	4	4	4	4	4	4	4	4	4	4	4	4	4	4	
3 M. SCHUMACHER	2	2	2	2	2	2	2	2	2	2	2	2	2	2	10	10	10	10	10	10	10	2	5	2	2	2	2	2	2	2	2	2	2	2	2	2	2	2	2	2	2	2	2	2	2	
2 FRENTZEN	14	14	14	14	14	14	14	14	14	14	14	14	14	14	14	14	14	14	14	14	14	6	2	14	14	14	14	14	14	14	14	14	14	14	14	14	14	14	14	14	14	14	14	14	14	
14 ALESI	15	18	18	18	18	18	18	18	18	18	18	18	18	18	15	15	15	15	15	15	15	15	14	18	18	18	15	15	15	15	15	15	15	15	15	15	15	6	6	6	6	6	6	6	6	
15 HERBERT	18	15	15	15	15	15	15	15	15	15	15	15	15	15	18	6	6	6	6	6	6	12	12	15	15	15	6	6	6	6	6	6	6	6	6	6	6	12	12	12	12	12	12	12		
18 BARRICHELLO	12	12	12	12	12	12	12	12	12	12	6	6	6	6	6	12	12	12	12	12	12	14	18	6	6	6	18	12	12	12	12	12	12	12	12	12	12	21	21	21	21	21	17	21		
12 TRULLI	11	11	11	11	11	11	6	6	6	6	12	12	12	12	12	19	18	18	18	18	18	18	15	12	12	12	12	21	21	21	21	21	21	21	21	21	21	17	17	17	17	17	21	17		
21 TAKAGI	19	19	19	19	19	6	19	19	19	19	19	19	19	19	19	18	19	19	19	19	19	19	17	17	21	21	21	17	17	17	17	17	17	17	17	17	17	11	11	11	11	11	11	11		
11 PANIS	17	17	17	6	6	19	11	17	17	17	17	17	17	17	17	17	17	17	17	17	17	17	19	22	17	17	17	22	22	22	22	22	22	22	22	22	11	23	23	23	23	23	23			
17 SALO	6	6	6	17	17	17	17	21	21	21	21	21	21	21	21	21	21	21	21	21	22	22	22	19	22	22	22	11	11	11	11	11	11	11	11	11	23									
16 DINIZ	21	21	21	21	21	21	21	22	22	22	22	22	22	22	22	22	22	22	22	22	11	11	21	21	11	11	11	23	23	23	23	23	23	23	23	23										
19 VERSTAPPEN	16	16	22	22	22	22	22	23	23	23	23	23	23	11	11	11	11	11	11	11	21	21	11	11	23	23	23																			
22 NAKANO	22	22	23	23	23	23	23	11	11	11	11	11	11	23	23	23	23	23	23	23	23	23	23	23																						
23 TUERO	23	23																																												

Pit stop

One lap behind leader

STARTING GRID

8 **HÄKKINEN** McLaren	7 **COULTHARD** McLaren
1 **VILLENEUVE** Williams	10 **R. SCHUMACHER** Jordan
9 **HILL** Jordan	4 **IRVINE** Ferrari
6 **WURZ** Benetton	5 **FISICHELLA** Benetton
3 **M. SCHUMACHER** Ferrari	2 **FRENTZEN** Williams
14 **ALESI** Sauber	15 **HERBERT** Sauber
18 **BARRICHELLO** Stewart	12 **TRULLI** Prost
21 **TAKAGI** Tyrrell	11 **PANIS** Prost
17 **SALO** Arrows	16 **DINIZ** Arrows
19 **VERSTAPPEN** Stewart	22 **NAKANO** Minardi
23 **TUERO** Minardi	

Did not qualify:

ROSSET (Tyrrell)

Lukas Gorys

TIME SHEETS

QUALIFYING

Weather: Dry, hot and sunny

Pos.	Driver	Car	Laps	Time
1	Mika Häkkinen	McLaren-Mercedes	12	1m 41.838s
2	David Coulthard	McLaren-Mercedes	9	1m 42.347s
3	Jacques Villeneuve	Williams-Mecachrome	12	1m 42.365s
4	Ralf Schumacher	Jordan-Mugen Honda	12	1m 42.994s
5	Damon Hill	Jordan-Mugen Honda	12	1m 43.183s
6	Eddie Irvine	Ferrari	11	1m 43.270s
7	Alexander Wurz	Benetton-Playlife	11	1m 43.341s
8	Giancarlo Fisichella	Benetton-Playlife	12	1m 43.369s
9	Michael Schumacher	Ferrari	12	1m 43.459s
10	Heinz-Harald Frentzen	Williams-Mecachrome	11	1m 43.467s
11	Jean Alesi	Sauber-Petronas	12	1m 43.663s
12	Johnny Herbert	Sauber-Petronas	11	1m 44.599s
13	Rubens Barrichello	Stewart-Ford	12	1m 44.776s
14	Jarno Trulli	Prost-Peugeot	12	1m 44.844s
15	Toranosuke Takagi	Tyrrell-Ford	11	1m 44.961s
16	Olivier Panis	Prost-Peugeot	12	1m 45.197s
17	Mika Salo	Arrows	12	1m 45.276s
18	Pedro Diniz	Arrows	12	1m 45.588s
19	Jos Verstappen	Stewart-Ford	11	1m 45.623s
20	Shinji Nakano	Minardi-Ford	12	1m 46.713s
21	Esteban Tuero	Minardi-Ford	12	1m 47.265s
	Ricardo Rosset	Tyrrell-Ford		no time

FRIDAY FREE PRACTICE

Weather: Bright and warm

Pos.	Driver	Laps	Time
1	Mika Häkkinen	33	1m 43.946s
2	David Coulthard	29	1m 44.138s
3	Damon Hill	31	1m 44.294s
4	Jean Alesi	34	1m 44.546s
5	Michael Schumacher	22	1m 44.757s
6	Eddie Irvine	29	1m 44.780s
7	Jacques Villeneuve	29	1m 44.928s
8	Heinz-Harald Frentzen	32	1m 45.186s
9	Johnny Herbert	35	1m 45.364s
10	Ralf Schumacher	34	1m 45.511s
11	Jarno Trulli	34	1m 45.611s
12	Alexander Wurz	32	1m 45.943s
13	Giancarlo Fisichella	31	1m 46.005s
14	Mika Salo	30	1m 46.163s
15	Rubens Barrichello	24	1m 46.257s
16	Olivier Panis	33	1m 46.484s
17	Toranosuke Takagi	21	1m 46.743s
18	Pedro Diniz	27	1m 46.903s
19	Jos Verstappen	23	1m 47.086s
20	Esteban Tuero	18	1m 48.175s
21	Shinji Nakano	25	1m 48.832s
22	Ricardo Rosset	21	1m 49.986s

SATURDAY FREE PRACTICE

Weather: Sunny and hot

Pos.	Driver	Laps	Time
1	David Coulthard		1m 43.006s
2	Mika Häkkinen		1m 43.175s
3	Jacques Villeneuve		1m 43.444s
4	Damon Hill		1m 43.746s
5	Heinz-Harald Frentzen		1m 44.084s
6	Ralf Schumacher		1m 44.114s
7	Giancarlo Fisichella		1m 44.129s
8	Jean Alesi		1m 44.399s
9	Eddie Irvine		1m 44.655s
10	Michael Schumacher		1m 45.038s
11	Alexander Wurz		1m 45.153s
12	Jarno Trulli		1m 45.343s
13	Toranosuke Takagi		1m 45.533s
14	Mika Salo		1m 45.535s
15	Rubens Barrichello		1m 45.537s
16	Jos Verstappen		1m 46.543s
17	Pedro Diniz		1m 46.677s
18	Shinji Nakano		1m 47.366s
19	Johnny Herbert		1m 48.128s
20	Esteban Tuero		1m 48.299s
21	Ricardo Rosset		1m 48.652s
	Olivier Panis		no time

WARM-UP

Weather: Sunny and hot

Pos.	Driver	Laps	Time
1	David Coulthard	10	1m 44.812s
2	Ralf Schumacher	15	1m 45.271s
3	Mika Häkkinen	11	1m 45.691s
4	Jacques Villeneuve	11	1m 45.741s
5	Michael Schumacher	12	1m 46.002s
6	Eddie Irvine	14	1m 46.035s
7	Damon Hill	11	1m 46.460s
8	Giancarlo Fisichella	13	1m 46.513s
9	Jean Alesi	13	1m 46.936s
10	Alexander Wurz	12	1m 46.988s
11	Rubens Barrichello	12	1m 47.003s
12	Heinz-Harald Frentzen	13	1m 47.188s
13	Johnny Herbert	10	1m 47.279s
14	Jos Verstappen	11	1m 47.461s
15	Olivier Panis	11	1m 47.588s
16	Mika Salo	9	1m 47.878s
17	Jarno Trulli	14	1m 48.133s
18	Pedro Diniz	11	1m 48.496s
19	Shinji Nakano	10	1m 48.572s
20	Toranosuke Takagi	11	1m 48.961s
21	Esteban Tuero	10	1m 49.001s

RACE FASTEST LAPS

Weather: Dry, hot and sunny

Driver	Time	Lap
David Coulthard	1m 46.116s	17
Mika Häkkinen	1m 46.252s	17
Jacques Villeneuve	1m 46.274s	35
Damon Hill	1m 46.317s	37
Ralf Schumacher	1m 46.350s	7
Michael Schumacher	1m 46.381s	37
Eddie Irvine	1m 46.459s	36
Giancarlo Fisichella	1m 46.831s	15
Alexander Wurz	1m 46.880s	16
Heinz-Harald Frentzen	1m 46.890s	32
Jean Alesi	1m 46.964s	43
Johnny Herbert	1m 47.345s	15
Rubens Barrichello	1m 47.544s	17
Olivier Panis	1m 47.775s	41
Jarno Trulli	1m 48.446s	27
Toranosuke Takagi	1m 48.608s	22
Mika Salo	1m 48.899s	34
Jos Verstappen	1m 49.147s	5
Shinji Nakano	1m 49.424s	17
Esteban Tuero	1m 50.314s	12
Pedro Diniz	1m 51.259s	2

CHASSIS LOG BOOK

1	Villeneuve	Williams FW20/5
2	Frentzen	Williams FW20/4
	spare	Williams FW20/3
3	M. Schumacher	Ferrari F300/186
4	Irvine	Ferrari F300/185
	spare	Ferrari F300/188
5	Fisichella	Benetton B198/6
6	Wurz	Benetton B198/7
	spare	Benetton B198/4
7	Coulthard	McLaren MP4/13/4
8	Häkkinen	McLaren MP4/13/6
	spare	McLaren MP4/13/3
9	Hill	Jordan 198/3
10	R. Schumacher	Jordan 198/4
	spare	Jordan 198/5
11	Panis	Prost AP01/2
12	Trulli	Prost AP01/6
	spare	Prost AP01/5
14	Alesi	Sauber C17/6
15	Herbert	Sauber C17/1
	spare	Sauber C17/2
16	Diniz	Arrows A19/2
17	Salo	Arrows A19/5
	spare	Arrows A19/6
18	Barrichello	Stewart SF2/4
19	Verstappen	Stewart SF2/3
	spare	Stewart SF2/2
20	Rosset	Tyrrell 026/2
21	Takagi	Tyrrell 026/3
	spare	Tyrrell 026/4
22	Nakano	Minardi M198/4
23	Tuero	Minardi M198/5
	spare	Minardi M198/3

POINTS TABLES

Drivers

1	Mika Häkkinen	76
2	Michael Schumacher	60
3	David Coulthard	42
4	Eddie Irvine	32
5	Alexander Wurz	17
6	Jacques Villeneuve	16
7	Giancarlo Fisichella	15
8	Heinz-Harald Frentzen	8
9 =	Rubens Barrichello	4
9 =	Ralf Schumacher	4
11 =	Jean Alesi	3
11 =	Mika Salo	3
11 =	Damon Hill	3
14 =	Johnny Herbert	1
14 =	Pedro Diniz	1
14 =	Jan Magnussen	1

Constructors

1	McLaren	118
2	Ferrari	92
3	Benetton	32
4	Williams	24
5	Jordan	7
6	Stewart	5
7 =	Sauber	4
7 =	Arrows	4

FIA WORLD CHAMPIONSHIP • ROUND 12

HUNGARIAN

grand prix

Sutton Motorsport Images

M. SCHUMACHER
COULTHARD
VILLENEUVE
HILL
FRENTZEN
HÄKKINEN

Although Michael Schumacher was to have the upper hand in the race, qualifying had been a very different story with Mika Häkkinen just managing to shave inside McLaren team-mate David Coulthard's best by 0.158s to snatch pole position. David had again made an unforced error when he spun over a kerb during Saturday morning's free practice session, ruining an MP4/13 undertray.

The Jerez test prior to the Hungarian race had also produced a downside for McLaren, sweltering temperatures of around 40 degrees perhaps contributing to five Mercedes engine failures, admittedly for varying reasons. Yet once at the Hungaroring, Häkkinen again stamped his mastery on the whole proceedings, Coulthard seemingly now at the stage of the season where, whatever he did, Mika could slice a tenth of a second off it.

In fact, Coulthard looked extremely confident from the outset. 'I had hoped to have a bigger margin on second place,' Häkkinen admitted, 'but David was going so fast that it was really difficult to get it any bigger.'

David admitted that his final run was spoiled by traffic. 'I was just a little late getting out of the pits and didn't have much time to play with,' he said. 'When I asked the team at the second-last corner how much time I had, they said "ten seconds". I didn't know how long it would take me to get from the second-last corner to the start/finish line, so I tried to leave a bit of a gap to the Minardi [ahead of me].

Lukas Gorys

'But one of the Jordans was going slowly in the middle of the last corner to get a good start to the lap, so the Minardi had to slow down. I ended up catching it and having to overtake it at the first corner. There is no way you can do a fast qualifying lap overtaking a car, so I backed off straight away.'

Schumacher three-wheeled his Ferrari F300 to a lurid-looking third place on the grid. From the trackside, the car seemed to be handling like a pig, bouncing nervously over every bump on the circuit. Maranello had attributed its dismal Hockenheim performance to poor ride in low-downforce configuration. But that didn't explain how awful it looked on this tight track.

Damon Hill was absolutely delighted after the Jordan-Mugen Honda had carried him to fourth place on the grid. He didn't need reminding that it was five years to the race since he had scored his maiden F1 victory in a Williams FW15C-Renault.

'That was a very different man back then,' said Damon thoughtfully, 'so different, in fact, that I sometimes don't recognise him. We have been competitive all weekend and have kept this up for qualifying, so I am very happy. But it will be a tough race.'

Hill used the softer available Goodyear compound, but Ralf Schumacher followed his brother's example and opted for the harder rubber. Even so, Ralf was disappointed to be only tenth in the final grid order.

'I still struggled with understeer for much of the time,' said Ralf, 'but I think for the race we are looking quite good. I lost over three-tenths in the last corner of my penultimate run, which probably cost me seventh place, and on the last run there was just too much traffic to make a good time.'

Eddie Irvine could manage only fifth place on the grid, a full second slower than Michael Schumacher in the other Ferrari. 'We improved the car since this morning,' he admitted, 'but it is still not perfect. We could make the car better over the bumps, but I had to make it stiffer for qualifying and I will run it that way for the race also. If it is too soft, it is too slow.'

Sixth and seventh places on the grid were bagged by the Williams FW20s of Jacques Villeneuve and Heinz-Harald Frentzen, the German driver feeling really unwell with a serious stomach bug, vomiting uncontrollably and unable to keep any food down. He did a good job in the circumstances.

Villeneuve was slightly disappointed. 'On the last run the balance of the car was pretty good,' he reported. 'I was happier with it on old, as opposed to new, tyres. We got it right for the last run, but I just didn't use the last set very well.'

In eighth and ninth places, the Benetton B198s of Giancarlo Fisichella and Alexander Wurz were similarly closely matched. All three of the team's chassis were to the revised longer-wheelbase specification for this race and featured modified rear suspension. Both drivers reckoned the longer wheelbase was an improvement, but when Fisichella flew off the road on his first qualifying lap he had to spend the rest of that crucial hour in the spare B198.

'I was frustrated and made a few small mistakes,' he admitted. 'The only crumb of comfort is that we chose the hard tyres and so we should be competitive in the race, even if it is practically impossible to overtake here.' Wurz was similarly disappointed, explaining that he had been unlucky with traffic on his last flying lap.

Jean Alesi's was the best-qualifying Sauber C17 in 11th place. 'Yesterday we had too much understeer, today too much oversteer,' he explained. 'But we left the car as it was for qualifying and I just did my best. The performance of both team and car is stable, and we seem to be in a zone where just a couple of tenths off our lap times would make a big difference to our grid positions and thus our chances of scoring points.'

By contrast, Johnny Herbert was a distant 15th. 'This morning the car was again twitchy, and I had a spin which damaged the undertray,' he explained. 'We changed things a little for qualifying, and after my first run we made another change which made the car worse.

'I spun at the second corner and lost my second run as a result, and then lost more time because of confusion over whether I had sufficient fuel to do a final two-lap stint. In the end that was academic, because I hit traffic in the second timed segment, so that chance was ruined too.'

Separating the two Saubers were the Arrows A19s of Pedro Diniz and Mika Salo plus Rubens Barrichello in the Stewart SF2-Ford. Diniz did a splendid job despite considerable pain caused by an eye problem which required treatment at the circuit medical centre and Salo also admitted that the Arrows felt 'very comfortable to drive'. It was a good day for Tom Walkinshaw's brigade.

Barrichello qualified 14th after encountering traffic on what he hoped would be his best run. Verstappen, meanwhile, had a rotten time on Saturday. The morning began with an engine failure followed by a tangle with Ricardo Rosset's Tyrrell on his first lap after an ultra-quick Ford engine change by the Stewart mechanics. He struggled for balance to qualify 17th.

The Prost-Peugeot squad, which confirmed in Hungary that Olivier Panis and Jarno Trulli would be staying on in 1999, celebrated this news with one of its worst qualifying performances of the season. Trulli spun off early on Friday afternoon, missing much dry-weather running, and ended up 16th, not helped by feeling below par. Panis found his car struggling over the bumps and could qualify no better than 20th, splitting the two Minardis.

Toranosuke Takagi's Tyrrell emerged 18th fastest, but team-mate Rosset failed to make the 107 per cent qualifying cut by a huge 0.7s margin, the fourth time he had fallen at this crucial barrier so far this season.

Ferrari and McLaren lock horns over rule eligibility

FERRARI'S technical director Ross Brawn used a press conference at the Hungaroring vigorously to reject McLaren suggestions that the Italian team had modified its F300 challenger in the light of observations made by Ron Dennis.

The McLaren boss had earlier taken the opportunity to shed some more light on what he had said to the Ferrari management at the A1-Ring on the matter of certain systems he believed the Italian cars were running.

'During the Austrian Grand Prix, I informed Jean Todt that we were considering protesting their car on the basis of having a braking system which did not comply with the regulations,' he explained.

'It is very clear, we discussed elements of the braking system. Anybody can re-run the tapes from the practice session of the Austrian GP, and if you have a fundamental understanding of car dynamics, the wrong wheels are locking up on the entrance to corners – not the unloaded wheel, it's the loaded wheel. You can see there and in tests, and at Silverstone, that the outcome of those problems sometimes saw the drivers leave the circuit.

'We believe – or we can now see – there has either been an optimisation, or something has changed. Because we now feel that the system, if there is a system, is in accordance with the regulations; and to substantiate that view we have over the last four weeks asked many questions of the FIA, sought clarifications, and now have an understanding of what is and is not permissible.'

Brawn described this as 'bullshit'. He continued: 'You can't defend yourself against an accusation like that, so it's a very nasty and malicious thing to say. If someone says you have a fantastic system that no one can detect, how can you prove them wrong?

'If we have turned the system off, where has the time come from now? Circumstances played into his hands. He had his whinge in Austria and then we had a problem in Germany.'

DIARY

The Williams team denies rumours that it might switch to Ford V10 engines for 1999 as an interim measure while waiting for development of the forthcoming BMW F1 V10 to be completed.

Indianapolis Motor Speedway President Tony George negotiates with Bernie Ecclestone about the possibility of an F1 race on a new track at the famous speedway starting in 2000.

Peugeot Sport chief Corrado Provera hints that the French company will continue in F1 beyond the end of 2000 if the Prost team manages to achieve the required results.

A track invasion by spectators after the Budapest race could result in the Hungarian GP organisers incurring substantial fines from the FIA.

Left: **Due deference. A guard of honour is provided for the drivers by the Marlboro girls. Supercool heroes Mika Häkkinen and Eddie Irvine enjoy the adulation.**

Williams had a good weekend, with Jacque Villeneuve *(below)* **on the podium for the second race in a row and Heinz-Harald Frentzen** *(right)* **defying illness to finish fift**

Winfield
WOODY WOODPECKER
SONAX
falke

Winfield
Williams
WOODY WOODPECKER
SONAX
falke

REPSOL
REPSOL

Wayne Johnson/At Speed Photographic

Michael Schumacher prepares to lap the Jordan of his younger brother Ralf. The accumulation of 'marbles' next to the racing line adds to the difficulties faced by drivers trying to overtake at this tortuous circuit.

MICHAEL Schumacher scored his fifth Ferrari victory of the season on the twisty Hungaroring circuit, where a lack of overtaking opportunities meant making the most of an astute, well-judged refuelling strategy as much as his relentless determination behind the wheel.

Ferrari switched from a two- to a three-stop strategy, concluding as the race unfolded that this would be the quickest route to complete the gruelling 77-lap race on the harder of the two available Goodyear tyre compounds.

After Michael had qualified third, he certainly needed some creative means of vaulting ahead of the fast-qualifying McLaren-Mercs and the whole game plan paid off magnificently. When he emerged from his third pit visit just five seconds ahead of David Coulthard's MP4/13, the day was complete and all he had to do was simply cruise home to victory ahead of the Scot.

'It was very much a race run at qualifying speed throughout for me,' said Schumacher, admitting the team did not make the decision to change from a two-stop to a three-stop strategy until he had refuelled for the first time on lap 25.

'We [finally] employed a three-stop strategy, which was pretty difficult, and it didn't seem to be working out at the beginning, because I fell behind Jacques Villeneuve at the first pit stop.

'Ross Brawn [the Ferrari technical director] took the decision what to do and told me what the strategy was after that first stop, but as I was sitting behind Jacques I was wondering whether it was the right thing.'

At the start Mika Häkkinen's pole-position McLaren accelerated cleanly into an immediate lead with Coulthard and Schumacher following him through the first tricky downhill right-hander. Damon Hill's Jordan held fourth place for the first few seconds of the race, but Eddie Irvine's Ferrari ran round the outside of him in the first turn, pushing him back to fifth.

Further back, Ralf Schumacher's Jordan ran wide at the same point and had dropped from tenth to 13th by the time the two McLarens confidently completed the first lap just 0.828s apart, the silver cars already edging away from the Ferrari duo.

By lap three it was clear that this was a three-horse race. Häkkinen, Coulthard and Schumacher were pulling clear, so much so that there was already a 3.0s gap between the two Ferraris. Hill was fifth ahead of the Williams FW20s of Jacques Villeneuve and Heinz-Harald Frentzen.

Häkkinen was setting a cracking

Schumi's Barmy Army. The fans who had made the trip to Budapest from Germany and Italy in the hope of seeing a Michael Schumacher win were rewarded with a mesmerising drive to victory by the brilliant German.

pace, although perhaps not pulling away from Coulthard as quickly as might have been expected. With 12 laps completed the first three were covered by 3.9s with Irvine a further 6.8s further back. In fact Eddie was in trouble. Next time round he was in the pits for good, complaining that fourth and fifth gears had packed up.

It later emerged that the cause of the problem was electrical and more esoteric. During practice and qualifying he'd suffered another burst of the backache which had troubled him intermittently for much of the season.

As a result, the Ferrari's seat had been removed and hacked about in an effort to make it more comfortable, but when it was refitted to the car it chafed through an electrical cable, which eventually caused the gearchange problem and his retirement from the race. 'I can't complain, because this is my first mechanical failure of the season,' he said.

On lap 16 Häkkinen still led from Coulthard and Schumacher, with Hill now 19.2s behind the leading McLaren in fourth place. Villeneuve and Frentzen were next, followed by the Benetton of Alexander Wurz, Jean Alesi's Sauber-Petronas, Giancarlo Fisichella in the other Benetton and the Arrows A19s of Pedro Diniz and Mika Salo. Three laps later Salo retired from 11th place with hydraulic failure, while on lap 21 Alesi's Sauber C17 briefly slid off the circuit, allowing Fisichella to slip ahead.

Hill marked the start of the first spate of refuelling stops when he brought the Jordan in at the end of lap 24, dropping from fourth to ninth. Then on the next lap Schumacher came in for his first refuelling stop, resuming in fourth behind Villeneuve's Williams. It was a temporary setback, because Jacques would duly make his first refuelling stop six laps later, but it was enough to prompt the Ferrari engineers to make a quick recalculation. And switch Michael to a three-stop strategy as a result.

On lap 26 Coulthard made his first refuelling stop, just squeezing the McLaren back into the race ahead of Villeneuve and Schumacher, his second place intact. Two laps later Häkkinen made his first stop, accelerating back into the fray a comfortable 3.1s ahead of Coulthard.

Villeneuve was doing well in third place, but two laps before he made his first refuelling stop with 31 laps completed, team-mate Frentzen dropped from fifth to seventh after a frustratingly extended 16.3s pit visit caused when he slightly over-shot his refuelling rig. In fact, Heinz-Harald was doing a really fantastic job as he was suffering badly from what turned out to be a severe intestinal bug and many people at Williams regarded it as something of a miracle that he was taking part in the race at all.

Once Villeneuve was out of the way, Schumacher had a clear run at the two McLarens. As he tripped the timing line on lap 31 he was 7.4s behind Häkkinen's leading McLaren. Over the next four laps he slashed into that advantage, reducing it to 6.1s, 4.8s, 4.3s and finally 3.6s. Now he was right on Coulthard's tail.

On lap 43 came the defining moment of the race. Schumacher dodged in from third place for his second refuelling stop. The Ferrari was stationary for just 6.8s. You didn't have to have a degree in higher mathematics to work out that he would have to stop again. But, amazingly, McLaren seemed to shadow his every move.

On lap 44 Coulthard was called in for a second refuelling stop, dropping from second to third. Now the Scot was faced with a 33-lap third stint in a 77-lap race. His McLaren rejoined the track heavy with fuel. Even heavier than he realised, as it subsequently transpired that the car had been overfuelled even by the requirements of the longer-than-expected run through to the end of the race.

On lap 46 Häkkinen, by now suffering the first signs of the dire handling problems which were to cripple his race, made his second refuelling stop. He resumed in second place, and would stay ahead of Coulthard for another six laps, battling deteriorating handling, before the Scot found a way past. It was the second vital strategic fumble of the McLaren team's race.

'After my second stop, Ross told me over the radio that I had 19 laps to pick up 25 seconds to make enough time for my third stop,' recounted Schumacher. 'I said, "Thank you, I will obviously try my best!" and it turned out to be enough.'

It was later established that Häkkinen's problem was that the front anti-roll bar had come adrift and jammed one of the suspension pushrods.

Mika never quite knew how the car was going to react to any steering input and, after a succession of lurid moments, realised there was no choice but to ease up, even cutting the revs on the straight and changing gear as cautiously as he could.

With Schumacher's Ferrari pressing hard, the German driver suffered a rare lapse at the end of lap 52 when he locked up and slid wide on the final corner. Just as it had been in Buenos Aires, where he survived a similar episode while holding the lead, the luck was with Michael and he coaxed his car back onto the track.

Equally helpful was the strategy of his brother Ralf, whose Jordan had just been lapped by the Ferrari. Schumacher Junior eased off slightly, allowing his sibling to regain the circuit still ahead of him rather than landing Michael with the challenge of lapping him all over again.

None of this took the edge off the elder Schumacher's hunger. By the time he broke the 1m 20s barrier on lap 54, the McLarens were clearly in trouble. Coulthard was running almost two seconds a lap slower, handicapped by his extra fuel weight, while Häkkinen was sometimes in the 1m 24s bracket. Meanwhile, much further back, Rubens Barrichello retired his Stewart-Ford from 13th place with gearbox overheating after a disappointing run following a poor start.

From lap 58 through to his third stop at the end of lap 62, Schumacher lapped consistently in the high 1m 19s range. It was therefore no surprise when he emerged from that stop around five seconds ahead of Coulthard and retained his lead through to the chequered flag.

Meanwhile, Häkkinen's struggle continued. On lap 67 he dropped to fourth behind Villeneuve, then four laps later he was overtaken by both Hill and Frentzen. By the time he fell victim to the German driver's Williams, the McLaren had slowed to the 1m 26s bracket and Patrick Head told Frentzen over the radio not to take any risks and wait for the straight before breezing past. Mika was a sitting duck.

Coulthard was clearly bitterly disappointed that he had not been able to get on terms with Schumacher after Häkkinen encountered his problems.

'Based on our tests last week in Jerez, we were confident that the tyre we were to use in qualifying would also be quick in the race,' he said. 'But we seemed to hit a bit of a brick wall in terms of performance when I didn't seem to be able to go as quick after my second stop as before.

'I can't say I was happy with a two-stop strategy because we didn't win. At the point where Michael wanted to build his gap in preparation for his last stop, I was losing a couple of seconds behind Mika when he had his problems, but once I got on a clear track I was not quick enough.'

Hill was delighted to have finished fourth for the second consecutive Grand Prix. 'If we keep this up, we will eventually end up on the podium,' he said. 'It would have been fantastic to have kept Villeneuve behind me, but there was not much I could do as he was on a harder [faster] tyre, and every time I pulled away he caught up with me, until eventually he was able to pass.'

Hill's was a rather better performance than that of his team-mate Ralf Schumacher, who took a long time to work through to an eventual ninth place at the chequered flag after his error at the first corner.

Frentzen completed the race a gallant fifth, almost completely dehydrated and clearly extremely unwell. On medical advice, Heinz-Harald was later flown in his own private jet from Budapest to Vienna, where he spent the next four days recuperating from his intestinal infection.

Outside the top six, neither Sauber C17 had an untroubled run, Jean Alesi failing to catch the slowing Häkkinen by 11 seconds. 'Again, I had a good start,' reported Jean, 'and all afternoon I was quicker than both Benettons. We were able to run very close together fighting initially for eighth place, but on the 21st lap the electronic blipper didn't work properly when I was changing down a gear. That caused my slight off-track moment. But the car was very, very consistent and we just needed a little more of everything to be closer to the top guys.'

Johnny Herbert wound up tenth after losing it at the hairpin while grappling with worn tyres on lap 74, a slip which allowed Ralf Schumacher to nip by for ninth. In eighth place, shadowing Alesi to the flag, was Giancarlo Fisichella, who had dropped behind the Sauber driver at the second round of pit stops. At least the Italian's Benetton had survived to the finish, in contrast to the sister car of team-mate Alexander Wurz, who had stopped with gearbox failure eight laps from the end when holding seventh place.

Pedro Diniz brought his Arrows A19 home in 11th with Olivier Panis's Prost-Peugeot, Jos Verstappen's Stewart-Ford, Tora Takagi's Tyrrell and the Minardi of Shinji Nakano the only other competitors running at the chequered flag. Jarno Trulli's Prost AP01 had retired after 28 laps with electronics problems when in 12th place.

Schumacher's win had narrowed Häkkinen's World Championship points lead from 16 to seven with only four Grands Prix remaining and 40 points to race for. This dramatic reversal in fortune came as the Finn seemingly stood poised to throw the chance of a third World Championship title beyond the reach of his German rival. Clearly, this was not over by a long chalk.

MARLBORO MAGYAR NAGYDIJ

14–16 AUGUST 1998

HUNGARORING

Race distance: 77 laps, 190.036 miles/305.844 km

Race weather: Dry, hot and sunny

ROUND 12

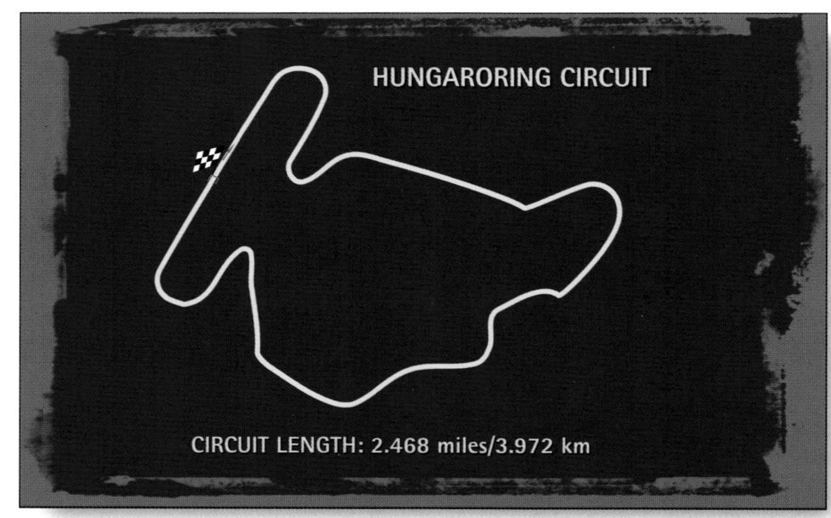

Pos.	Driver	Nat.	No.	Entrant	Car/Engine	Tyres	Laps	Time/Retirement	Speed (mph/km/h)
1	**Michael Schumacher**	**D**	**3**	**Scuderia Ferrari Marlboro**	**Ferrari F300 047 V10**	**G**	**77**	**1h 45m 25.550s**	**108.157/174.062**
2	**David Coulthard**	**GB**	**7**	**West McLaren Mercedes**	**McLaren MP4/13-Mercedes FO110G V10**	**B**	**77**	**1h 45m 34.983s**	**107.995/173.802**
3	**Jacques Villeneuve**	**CDN**	**1**	**Winfield Williams**	**Williams FW20-Mecachrome GC37/01 V10**	**G**	**77**	**1h 46m 09.994s**	**107.401/172.847**
4	**Damon Hill**	**GB**	**9**	**B&H Jordan Mugen Honda**	**Jordan 198-Mugen Honda MF310C V10**	**G**	**77**	**1h 46m 20.626s**	**107.223/172.559**
5	**Heinz-Harald Frentzen**	**D**	**2**	**Winfield Williams**	**Williams FW20-Mecachrome GC37/01 V10**	**G**	**77**	**1h 46m 22.060s**	**107.199/172.520**
6	**Mika Häkkinen**	**SF**	**8**	**West McLaren Mercedes**	**McLaren MP4/13-Mercedes FO110G V10**	**B**	**76**		
7	Jean Alesi	F	14	Red Bull Sauber Petronas	Sauber C17-Petronas SPE01D V10	G	76		
8	Giancarlo Fisichella	I	5	Mild Seven Benetton Playlife	Benetton B198-Playlife V10	B	76		
9	Ralf Schumacher	D	10	B&H Jordan Mugen Honda	Jordan 198-Mugen Honda MF310C V10	G	76		
10	Johnny Herbert	GB	15	Red Bull Sauber Petronas	Sauber C17-Petronas SPE01D V10	G	76		
11	Pedro Diniz	BR	16	Danka Zepter Arrows	Arrows A19 V10	B	74		
12	Olivier Panis	F	11	Gauloises Prost Peugeot	Prost AP01-Peugeot A16 V10	B	74		
13	Jos Verstappen	NL	19	Stewart Ford	Stewart SF2-Ford Zetec-R V10	B	74		
14	Toranosuke Takagi	J	21	Tyrrell Ford	Tyrrell 026-Ford Zetec-R V10	G	74		
15	Shinji Nakano	J	22	Fondmetal Minardi Ford	Minardi M198-Ford Zetec-R V10	B	74		
	Alexander Wurz	A	6	Mild Seven Benetton Playlife	Benetton B198-Playlife V10	B	69	Gearbox	
	Rubens Barrichello	BR	18	Stewart Ford	Stewart SF2-Ford Zetec-R V10	B	54	Gearbox	
	Jarno Trulli	I	12	Gauloises Prost Peugeot	Prost AP01-Peugeot A16 V10	B	28	Electronics	
	Mika Salo	SF	17	Danka Zepter Arrows	Arrows A19 V10	B	18	Hydraulic leak	
	Eddie Irvine	GB	4	Scuderia Ferrari Marlboro	Ferrari F300 047 V10	G	13	Gearbox	
	Esteban Tuero	RA	23	Fondmetal Minardi Ford	Minardi M198-Ford Zetec-R V10	B	13	Gearbox	
DNQ	Ricardo Rosset	BR	20	Tyrrell Ford	Tyrrell 026-Ford Zetec-R V10	G			

Fastest lap: M. Schumacher, on lap 60, 1m 19.286s, 112.064 mph/180.349 km/h.

Lap record: Nigel Mansell (F1 Williams FW14B-Renault V10), 1m 18.308s, 113.349 mph/182.418 km/h (1992).

B – Bridgestone G – Goodyear

All results and data © FIA 1998

Grid order	1	2	3	4	5	6	7	8	9	10	11	12	13	14	15	16	17	18	19	20	21	22	23	24	25	26	27	28	29
8 HÄKKINEN	8	8	8	8	8	8	8	8	8	8	8	8	8	8	8	8	8	8	8	8	8	8	8	8	8	8	8	8	8
7 COULTHARD	7	7	7	7	7	7	7	7	7	7	7	7	7	7	7	7	7	7	7	7	7	7	7	7	7	7	7	7	7
3 M. SCHUMACHER	3	3	3	3	3	3	3	3	3	3	3	3	3	3	3	3	3	3	3	3	3	3	3	3	3	1	1	1	1
9 HILL	4	4	4	4	4	4	4	4	4	4	4	4	9	9	9	9	9	9	9	9	9	9	9	1	1	3	3	3	3
4 IRVINE	9	9	9	9	9	9	9	9	9	9	9	9	4	1	1	1	1	1	1	1	1	1	1	9	2	2	2	2	2
1 VILLENEUVE	1	1	1	1	1	1	1	1	1	1	1	1	1	2	2	2	2	2	2	2	2	2	2	2	6	6	6	5	5
2 FRENTZEN	2	2	2	2	2	2	2	2	2	2	2	2	2	6	6	6	6	6	6	6	6	6	6	6	5	5	5	6	14
5 FISICHELLA	6	6	6	6	6	6	6	6	6	6	6	6	6	14	14	14	14	14	14	14	5	5	5	5	14	14	14	14	9
6 WURZ	14	14	14	14	14	14	14	14	14	14	14	14	14	5	5	5	5	5	5	5	14	14	14	14	9	9	9	9	6
10 R. SCHUMACHER	5	5	5	5	5	5	5	5	5	5	5	5	5	16	16	16	16	16	16	16	10	10	10	10	10	10	15	15	15
14 ALESI	16	16	16	16	16	16	16	16	16	16	16	16	16	17	17	17	17	17	10	10	16	16	16	15	15	15	10	10	10
16 DINIZ	17	17	17	17	17	17	17	17	17	17	17	17	17	10	10	10	10	10	15	15	15	15	15	16	16	16	12	12	16
17 SALO	10	10	10	10	10	10	10	10	10	10	10	10	10	15	15	15	15	15	12	12	12	12	12	18	19	19	16	16	18
18 BARRICHELLO	15	15	15	15	15	15	15	15	15	15	15	15	15	12	12	12	12	12	18	18	18	18	18	19	11	12	18	18	19
15 HERBERT	12	12	12	12	12	12	12	12	12	12	12	12	12	18	18	18	18	18	19	19	19	19	19	11	12	11	19	19	11
12 TRULLI	18	18	18	18	18	18	18	18	18	18	18	18	18	19	19	19	19	19	22	22	22	11	11	12	18	18	11	11	22
19 VERSTAPPEN	19	19	19	19	19	19	19	19	19	19	19	19	19	22	22	22	22	22	11	11	11	22	22	22	22	22	22	22	21
21 TAKAGI	23	23	23	23	22	22	22	22	22	22	22	22	22	21	21	21	21	11	21	21	21	21	21	21	21	21	21	21	
22 NAKANO	22	22	22	22	21	21	21	21	21	21	21	21	21	11	11	11	11	21											
11 PANIS	21	21	21	21	23	23	23	23	23	23	23	23	23																
23 TUERO	11	11	11	11	11	11	11	11	11	11	11	11	11																

Grid order	30	31	32	33	34	35	36	37	38	39	40	41	42	43	44	45	46	47	48	49	50	51	52	53	54	55	56	57	58
8 HÄKKINEN	8	8	8	8	8	8	8	8	8	8	8	8	8	8	8	8	8	3	3	3	3	3	3	3	3	3	3	3	3
7 COULTHARD	7	7	7	7	7	7	7	7	7	7	7	7	7	7	7	3	3	8	8	8	8	8	7	7	7	7	7	7	7
3 M. SCHUMACHER	1	3	3	3	3	3	3	3	3	3	3	3	3	3	3	7	7	7	7	7	7	7	8	8	8	8	8	8	8
9 HILL	3	1	9	9	9	9	9	9	9	9	9	9	9	9	9	9	9	9	9	9	9	1	1	1	1	1	1	1	1
4 IRVINE	9	9	1	1	1	1	1	1	1	1	1	1	1	1	1	1	1	1	1	1	1	9	2	2	2	9	9	9	9
1 VILLENEUVE	14	2	2	2	2	2	2	2	2	2	2	2	2	2	2	2	2	2	2	2	2	2	9	9	9	2	2	2	2
2 FRENTZEN	2	6	6	6	6	6	6	6	6	6	6	6	6	6	6	6	6	6	6	6	14	14	6	6	6	6	6	6	6
5 FISICHELLA	6	5	5	5	5	5	5	5	5	5	5	5	5	5	5	5	5	5	5	5	5	6	14	14	14	14	14	14	14
6 WURZ	5	14	14	14	14	14	14	14	14	14	14	14	14	14	14	14	14	14	14	14	6	10	5	5	5	5	5	5	5
10 R. SCHUMACHER	15	15	15	10	10	10	10	10	10	10	10	10	10	10	10	10	10	10	10	10	10	5	10	15	15	15	15	15	15
14 ALESI	10	10	10	15	15	15	15	15	15	15	15	15	15	15	15	15	15	15	15	15	15	15	15	10	10	10	10	10	10
16 DINIZ	16	16	16	16	16	16	16	16	16	16	16	16	16	16	16	16	16	18	18	19	19	11	16	16	16	16	16	16	16
17 SALO	18	18	18	18	18	18	18	18	18	18	18	18	18	18	18	18	18	16	19	11	11	16	18	18	19	19	19	19	19
18 BARRICHELLO	19	19	19	19	19	19	19	19	19	19	19	19	19	19	19	19	19	19	11	16	16	18	19	19	11	11	11	11	11
15 HERBERT	11	11	11	11	11	11	11	11	11	11	11	11	11	11	11	11	11	11	16	18	18	19	11	11	18	21	21	21	21
12 TRULLI	22	22	22	22	22	22	22	22	22	22	22	22	22	22	22	22	22	22	22	21	21	21	21	21	21	22	22	22	22
19 VERSTAPPEN	21	21	21	21	21	21	21	21	21	21	21	21	21	21	21	21	21	21	21	22	22	22	22	22	22				
21 TAKAGI																													
22 NAKANO																													
11 PANIS																													
23 TUERO																													

Pit stop

One lap behind leader

STARTING GRID

8 **HÄKKINEN** McLaren	7 **COULTHARD** McLaren
3 **M. SCHUMACHER** Ferrari	9 **HILL** Jordan
4 **IRVINE** Ferrari	1 **VILLENEUVE** Williams
2 **FRENTZEN** Williams	5 **FISICHELLA** Benetton
6 **WURZ** Benetton	10 **R. SCHUMACHER** Jordan
14 **ALESI** Sauber	16 **DINIZ** Arrows
17 **SALO** Arrows	18 **BARRICHELLO** Stewart
15 **HERBERT** Sauber	12 **TRULLI** Prost
19 **VERSTAPPEN** Stewart	21 **TAKAGI** Tyrrell
22 **NAKANO** Minardi	11 **PANIS** Prost
23 **TUERO** Minardi	

Did not qualify:

ROSSET (Tyrrell)

63	64	65	66	67	68	69	70	71	72	73	74	75	76	77	
3	3	3	3	3	3	3	3	3	3	3	3	3	3	3	1
7	7	7	7	7	7	7	7	7	7	7	7	7	7	7	2
8	8	8	8	1	1	1	1	1	1	1	1	1	1	1	3
1	1	1	1	8	8	8	8	9	9	9	9	9	9	9	4
9	9	9	9	9	9	9	9	2	2	2	2	2	2	2	5
2	2	2	2	2	2	2	2	8	8	8	8	8	8		6
6	6	6	6	6	6	6	14	14	14	14	14	14	14		
14	14	14	14	14	14	14	5	5	5	5	5	5	5		
5	5	5	5	5	5	5	15	15	15	15	10	10	10		
15	15	15	15	15	15	15	10	10	10	10	15	15	15		
10	10	10	10	10	10	10	16	16	16	16	16				
16	16	16	16	16	16	16	11	11	11	11	11				
11	11	11	11	11	11	11	19	19	19	19	19				
19	19	19	19	19	19	19	21	21	21	21	21				
21	21	21	21	21	21	21	22	22	22	22	22				
22	22	22	22	22	22	22									

TIME SHEETS

QUALIFYING

Weather: Dry, hot and sunny

Pos.	Driver	Car	Laps	Time
1	Mika Häkkinen	McLaren-Mercedes	11	1m 16.973s
2	David Coulthard	McLaren-Mercedes	11	1m 17.131s
3	Michael Schumacher	Ferrari	10	1m 17.366s
4	Damon Hill	Jordan-Mugen Honda	12	1m 18.214s
5	Eddie Irvine	Ferrari	12	1m 18.325s
6	Jacques Villeneuve	Williams-Mecachrome	12	1m 18.337s
7	Heinz-Harald Frentzen	Williams-Mecachrome	12	1m 19.029s
8	Giancarlo Fisichella	Benetton-Playlife	12	1m 19.050s
9	Alexander Wurz	Benetton-Playlife	12	1m 19.063s
10	Ralf Schumacher	Jordan-Mugen Honda	12	1m 19.171s
11	Jean Alesi	Sauber-Petronas	12	1m 19.210s
12	Pedro Diniz	Arrows	12	1m 19.706s
13	Mika Salo	Arrows	12	1m 19.712s
14	Rubens Barrichello	Stewart-Ford	11	1m 19.876s
15	Johnny Herbert	Sauber-Petronas	11	1m 19.878s
16	Jarno Trulli	Prost-Peugeot	12	1m 20.042s
17	Jos Verstappen	Stewart-Ford	12	1m 20.198s
18	Toranosuke Takagi	Tyrrell-Ford	12	1m 20.354s
19	Shinji Nakano	Minardi-Ford	12	1m 20.635s
20	Olivier Panis	Prost-Peugeot	12	1m 20.663s
21	Esteban Tuero	Minardi-Ford	12	1m 21.725s
22	Ricardo Rosset	Tyrrell-Ford	11	1m 23.140s

107 per cent time: 1m 22.361s

FRIDAY FREE PRACTICE

Weather: Windy, rain, later drying

Pos.	Driver	Laps	Time
1	David Coulthard	25	1m 19.989s
2	Mika Häkkinen	29	1m 20.186s
3	Michael Schumacher	25	1m 20.439s
4	Jacques Villeneuve	37	1m 20.441s
5	Eddie Irvine	29	1m 20.778s
6	Damon Hill	35	1m 20.779s
7	Giancarlo Fisichella	39	1m 21.110s
8	Ralf Schumacher	18	1m 21.198s
9	Heinz-Harald Frentzen	35	1m 21.218s
10	Rubens Barrichello	23	1m 21.414s
11	Johnny Herbert	27	1m 21.571s
12	Jos Verstappen	28	1m 21.903s
13	Jean Alesi	22	1m 21.990s
14	Mika Salo	28	1m 22.145s
15	Alexander Wurz	36	1m 22.297s
16	Olivier Panis	30	1m 22.442s
17	Shinji Nakano	31	1m 22.940s
18	Toranosuke Takagi	37	1m 23.261s
19	Pedro Diniz	22	1m 23.450s
20	Esteban Tuero	46	1m 23.671s
21	Ricardo Rosset	28	1m 25.611s
22	Jarno Trulli	21	1m 25.700s

SATURDAY FREE PRACTICE

Weather: Bright and sunny

Pos.	Driver	Laps	Time
1	Mika Häkkinen	25	1m 17.337s
2	David Coulthard	23	1m 17.495s
3	Michael Schumacher	22	1m 18.588s
4	Giancarlo Fisichella	23	1m 18.792s
5	Jacques Villeneuve	29	1m 19.016s
6	Damon Hill	38	1m 19.091s
7	Heinz-Harald Frentzen	24	1m 19.107s
8	Ralf Schumacher	34	1m 19.183s
9	Eddie Irvine	32	1m 19.252s
10	Alexander Wurz	32	1m 19.286s
11	Jean Alesi	26	1m 19.449s
12	Johnny Herbert	24	1m 19.800s
13	Rubens Barrichello	29	1m 19.936s
14	Mika Salo	31	1m 20.552s
15	Pedro Diniz	27	1m 20.589s
16	Jos Verstappen	8	1m 20.883s
17	Olivier Panis	31	1m 20.920s
18	Shinji Nakano	32	1m 21.373s
19	Jarno Trulli	31	1m 21.585s
20	Toranosuke Takagi	17	1m 21.634s
21	Esteban Tuero	27	1m 22.008s
22	Ricardo Rosset	30	1m 23.279s

WARM-UP

Weather: Dry and bright

Pos.	Driver	Laps	Time
1	Mika Häkkinen	14	1m 18.694s
2	David Coulthard	13	1m 19.555s
3	Heinz-Harald Frentzen	13	1m 19.967s
4	Michael Schumacher	13	1m 20.325s
5	Ralf Schumacher	15	1m 20.385s
6	Jacques Villeneuve	17	1m 20.580s
7	Damon Hill	15	1m 20.906s
8	Eddie Irvine	14	1m 20.935s
9	Giancarlo Fisichella	13	1m 21.334s
10	Johnny Herbert	16	1m 21.441s
11	Jean Alesi	15	1m 21.799s
12	Jarno Trulli	15	1m 21.920s
13	Alexander Wurz	15	1m 21.924s
14	Rubens Barrichello	14	1m 22.095s
15	Mika Salo	15	1m 22.119s
16	Olivier Panis	11	1m 22.344s
17	Toranosuke Takagi	15	1m 22.704s
18	Jos Verstappen	12	1m 22.961s
19	Shinji Nakano	16	1m 22.991s
20	Pedro Diniz	12	1m 23.231s
21	Esteban Tuero	15	1m 23.685s

RACE FASTEST LAPS

Weather: Dry, hot and sunny

Driver	Time	Lap
Michael Schumacher	1m 19.286s	60
Jacques Villeneuve	1m 20.078s	57
Heinz-Harald Frentzen	1m 20.356s	57
Mika Häkkinen	1m 20.545s	30
David Coulthard	1m 20.546s	28
Damon Hill	1m 20.680s	75
Ralf Schumacher	1m 20.875s	71
Eddie Irvine	1m 20.984s	11
Giancarlo Fisichella	1m 21.060s	48
Johnny Herbert	1m 21.329s	37
Jean Alesi	1m 21.439s	35
Alexander Wurz	1m 21.479s	48
Toranosuke Takagi	1m 22.495s	48
Olivier Panis	1m 22.538s	17
Rubens Barrichello	1m 23.294s	50
Jarno Trulli	1m 23.318s	25
Pedro Diniz	1m 23.429s	43
Shinji Nakano	1m 23.573s	50
Jos Verstappen	1m 23.644s	48
Mika Salo	1m 23.716s	18
Esteban Tuero	1m 25.450s	7

CHASSIS LOG BOOK

1	Villeneuve	Williams FW20/5
2	Frentzen	Williams FW20/4
	spare	Williams FW20/6
3	M. Schumacher	Ferrari F300/188
4	Irvine	Ferrari F300/185
	spare	Ferrari F300/186
5	Fisichella	Benetton B198/4
6	Wurz	Benetton B198/7
	spare	Benetton B198/6
7	Coulthard	McLaren MP4/13/7
8	Häkkinen	McLaren MP4/13/5
	spare	McLaren MP4/13/4
9	Hill	Jordan 198/3
10	R. Schumacher	Jordan 198/4
	spare	Jordan 198/5
11	Panis	Prost AP01/7
12	Trulli	Prost AP01/6
	spare	Prost AP01/5
14	Alesi	Sauber C17/6
15	Herbert	Sauber C17/7
	spare	Sauber C17/2
16	Diniz	Arrows A19/1
17	Salo	Arrows A19/5
	spare	Arrows A19/2
18	Barrichello	Stewart SF2/4
19	Verstappen	Stewart SF2/3
	spare	Stewart SF2/2
20	Rosset	Tyrrell 026/4
21	Takagi	Tyrrell 026/5
	spare	Tyrrell 026/2
22	Nakano	Minardi M198/4
23	Tuero	Minardi M198/5
	spare	Minardi M198/3

POINTS TABLES

Drivers

1	Mika Häkkinen	77
2	Michael Schumacher	70
3	David Coulthard	48
4	Eddie Irvine	32
5	Jacques Villeneuve	20
6	Alexander Wurz	17
7	Giancarlo Fisichella	15
8	Heinz-Harald Frentzen	10
9	Damon Hill	6
10 =	Rubens Barrichello	4
10 =	Ralf Schumacher	4
12 =	Jean Alesi	3
12 =	Mika Salo	3
14 =	Johnny Herbert	1
14 =	Pedro Diniz	1
14 =	Jan Magnussen	1

Constructors

1	McLaren	125
2	Ferrari	102
3	Benetton	32
4	Williams	30
5	Jordan	10
6	Stewart	5
7 =	Sauber	4
7 =	Arrows	4

BELGIAN grand prix

HILL
R. SCHUMACHER
ALESI
FRENTZEN
DINIZ
TRULLI

DIARY

Johnny Herbert signs to join Stewart-Ford team from 1999.

A new safety system designed to restrain wayward wheels with Kevlar rope is approved by the F1 Commission for introduction in 1999.

Former Arrows F1 driver Max Papis is chosen to drive for Bobby Rahal's CART team in 1999.

Eddie Jordan suggests that Michael Schumacher should mind his own business and not unsettle brother Ralf with suggestions that he should switch to another F1 team next season.

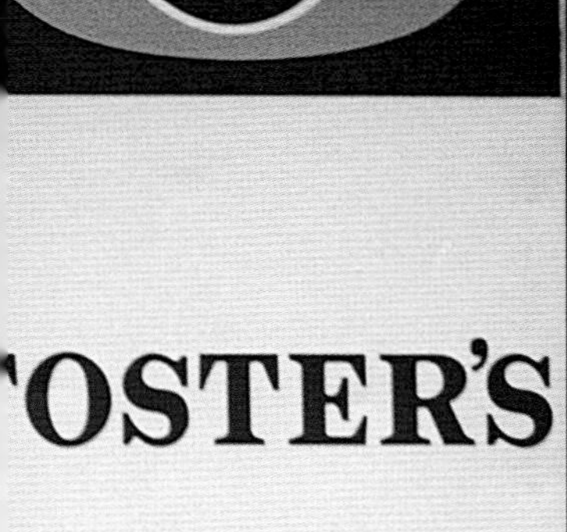

Paul-Henri Cahier

An exultant Damon Hill performs Michael Schumacher's trademark victory celebration on the podium. Nothing beats winning, and Damon had been waiting nearly two years to enjoy a moment like this once again.

ONLY the smallest helping of good luck was needed for Damon Hill to drive the Jordan F1 team into the history books in atrocious conditions of torrential rain at Spa-Francorchamps, the former World Champion heading his team-mate Ralf Schumacher across the line to complete the most unexpected grand slam of the 1998 F1 season so far.

It was the 22nd Grand Prix victory of Hill's career, coming almost two years after his last win for Williams when he clinched the 1996 title in the Japanese GP at Suzuka. It had taken Jordan 127 races over eight seasons to post its first victory, a success made all the sweeter by the chaos and mayhem around them which saw only eight of the 22 original starters making it to the chequered flag.

While Hill basked in his well-deserved restoration to F1's front line and the Jordan lads celebrated a success which had been a long time coming, the English driver's old rival Michael Schumacher was at the centre of controversy after his Ferrari crashed into the back of David Coulthard's McLaren at the height of the downpour, three-wheeling back to the pits after losing his right-front wheel against the Scot's MP4/13, which he was poised to lap at the time.

Schumacher clearly believed the incident was certainly not of his making, leaping from his damaged car in the pit lane and storming up to the McLaren pit where mechanics fought to keep him away from Coulthard, whom he accused of causing the accident.

'Are you trying to kill me?' he shouted as he was dragged away. Schumacher was called to the stewards immediately after the race to account for his unruly behaviour, while Coulthard's car – which had lost its rear wing in the impact – was repaired and resumed the race to finish a distant seventh.

The stewards duly considered the incident and eventually dismissed it as a racing accident with no action being taken against either driver.

For his part, Hill was lucky to get through a massive 12-car accident coming out of the first corner which caused the race to be stopped at the end of the opening lap. 'All I saw was what looked like a Ferrari and Coulthard's McLaren touching a bit as we came out of the La Source hairpin,' he recalled.

'Coulthard then got away slightly, there was a lot of spray, and the next thing I saw was that he'd hit the wall on the right-hand side and he's coming back across the track. I was coming at him, and I could see that he was coming across, together with a bouncing wheel, so I had to just go for it and got through without hitting a thing.'

Behind Hill, cars pinballed in all directions with wheels and debris flying dangerously close to the front row of the grandstand. After the dust and debris had settled, Coulthard, Eddie Irvine's Ferrari, Alexander Wurz's Benetton, Johnny Herbert's Sauber, the Prosts of Jarno Trulli and Olivier Panis, the Tyrrells of Toranosuke Takagi and Ricardo Rosset, the Arrows of Mika Salo and Pedro Diniz, Shinji Nakano's Minardi and Rubens Barrichello's Stewart all lay scattered across the track.

With as many spare cars pressed into action as possible, only Panis, Salo, Rosset and Barrichello – who complained of an injured elbow – failed to make the restart.

In the aftermath of this disappointment, Salo got himself into hot water when he went to the stewards' room and requested permission to leave the circuit as he could not take part in the restart. He was informed that he should wait until a further investigation had been completed, but the Finn lost his temper and became abusive. He later returned and made a formal apology, after which he was permitted to depart.

After a 53-minute delay the field lined up to take the restart with Irvine, Trulli, Takagi, Herbert, Wurz and Diniz all strapped into their teams' spare cars. Prior to the restart, McLaren took the questionable decision to switch Häkkinen's car from Bridgestone full wets to intermediates, apparently tracking Schumacher's decision to start the race on Goodyear intermediates. Unfortunately the Bridgestone intermediates were not in the same class as their rivals and it was no surprise when Mika ran wide away from the apex of La Source as the pack got under way again, allowing Hill to drive through on the inside to snatch an immediate lead.

As Häkkinen slid wide, so he found himself wheel to wheel with Schumacher's Ferrari. What happened next varied depending on which camp was offering the explanation. Ferrari's view was that Häkkinen just spun, but there was definite light contact with Michael's car, giving rise to the contrary view that the McLaren had been squeezed and assisted into a gentle spin. Having ended up facing in the direction from which he'd come, Häkkinen then found his car savaged by Johnny Herbert's Sauber, so that was the end of that.

Hill led through Eau Rouge from Irvine, but up the hill towards Les Combes Schumacher hauled past his team-mate with Jean Alesi fourth ahead of the Williams FW20s of Jacques Villeneuve and Heinz-Harald Frentzen. Further around the lap, Wurz made to overtake Coulthard and the two cars collided, the McLaren resuming at the tail of the field but the Austrian was out on the spot.

'The race should have been started behind the safety car,' said Wurz firmly. 'The first crash was really scary, but at least no one was hurt. My second start in the T-car went very well but then I came up behind Coulthard and he was sliding all over the track. I wasn't there for a Sunday drive, so I took the risk to overtake him.'

Meanwhile, as Hill led by 0.74s from Schumacher at the end of the opening lap, the safety car was deployed while Häkkinen's damaged McLaren was removed from the exit of La Source. At the end of lap two the safety car was withdrawn and over the next three laps Hill began to ease away slightly.

By the end of lap five the Jordan team leader had opened the gap over Schumacher to 1.37s, but by now the rain was intensifying and the Ferrari began to ease closer again. Villeneuve spun down from fourth to sixth but continued without any damage.

On lap eight Schumacher drew tight onto Hill's tail as the two cars slammed through the high-speed Blanchimont left-hander, then neatly outbraked the Jordan to take the lead. He immediately pulled away, extending his advantage to an amazing 5.3s next time round as the rain got even heavier.

'From the start, it looked to me as though he [Michael] had more downforce,' said Hill. 'I went for intermediates on the grid and after the restart I went for a lower-downforce setting in the assumption that it [the weather] was going to get better.

'It worked for a few laps and then it started to rain again, and it worked against me. Michael was able to close and then get past.'

On lap ten Irvine came trailing into the pits from third place after spinning at Les Combes. He resumed a disappointed ninth and would later reflect: 'I had jumped into the spare, which was originally set up for Michael, and although the mechanics did a great job to get it changed to suit me it was still far from ideal.

'I should have driven at just a comfortable level rather than trying to hang on to Michael and Damon, which I was able to do. Maybe I pushed too hard, but I went off.'

Clive Mason/Allsport

Wayne Johnson/At Speed Photographic

Above: **Viewed from the outside of La Source across the dank paddock, a giant television screen confirms that the race has been stopped.**

Far left: **Mika Häkkinen's championship hopes appeared to have suffered a devastating blow when he was eliminated from the restarted race at the first corner.**

Left: **Road rage. An irate Michael Schumacher speeds back to the pits on three wheels after his horrifying collision with David Coulthard's McLaren, determined to confront the Scot.**

Below: **The Benetton of Giancarlo Fisichella careers into the escape road at the Bus Stop after piling into the back of Shinji Nakano's Minardi in the murk.**

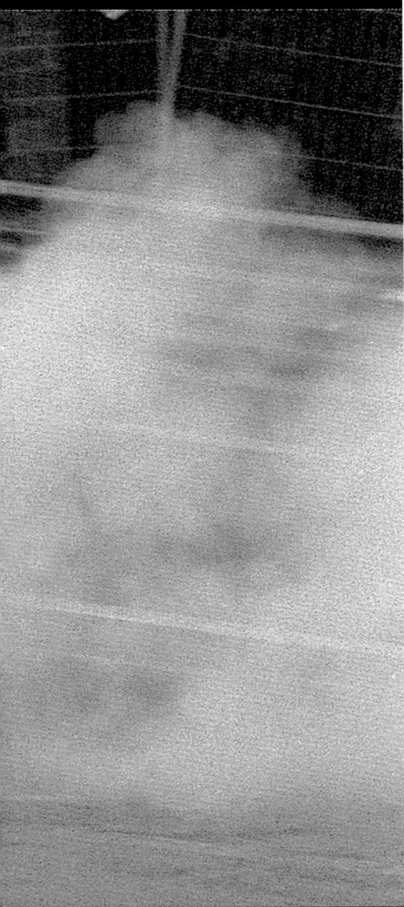

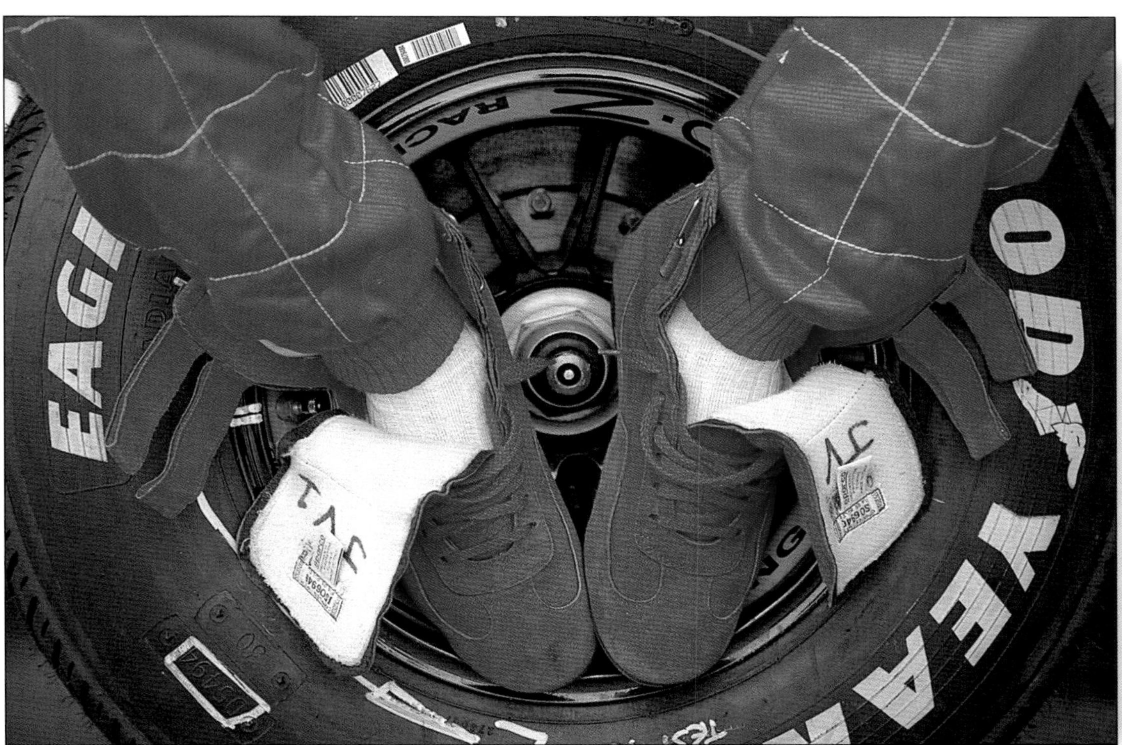

Steve Etherington/EPI

Both McLaren drivers proved strong contenders in the hour-long battle for grid positions. They'd switched from the wider front Bridgestone used in the last race to the narrower option, both drivers reporting that the cars felt better balanced in this guise. Mika Häkkinen and David Coulthard were worried that too much front-end grip from the wide Bridgestones would give them excessive oversteer on Spa's dauntingly fast swerves and their choice proved right on the button when they lined up on the front row of the grid only 0.2s apart.

Coulthard dominated much of the session only for Häkkinen to pip him right at the end. 'To have lost pole position on the final run is a bit disappointing,' said David. 'I know exactly where I lost the time. I was quicker on my final run and tried to sneak a bit more kerb going into the Bus Stop. Unfortunately, it didn't work out.'

Häkkinen had recovered well from an accident in Friday morning's free practice period. He touched a wet kerb at Stavelot in the closing moments of the session, his MP4/13 sustaining considerable damage, but the team changed the front suspension, nose and floor in time for Mika to return to action late in the second part of the session.

Damon Hill did a superb job to line up third fastest, making him the best-placed Goodyear runner of the weekend, 0.3s ahead of Michael Schumacher's Ferrari F300. The German had to be content with the outside of the second row, despite benefiting from the availability of a special qualifying engine.

Eddie Irvine was close behind in fifth place on the grid ahead of Jacques Villeneuve's Williams and Giancarlo Fisichella's Benetton B198 – the third Bridgestone runner on the grid, even though the Italian was almost two seconds slower than Häkkinen's pole time.

Neither Ferrari driver was particularly satisfied. Schumacher reckoned he might have been a bit quicker had it not been for a yellow flag at the Bus Stop, while Irvine also found himself delayed at that point by Ricardo Rosset's slow-running Tyrrell.

Villeneuve had been the centre of much attention during Friday's free practice session after he walked away from a spectacular 185 mph accident at Eau Rouge, perhaps proving that he really is a chip off his father Gilles's old block.

'I think it was my best [biggest] crash in F1 so far,' said Jacques. 'I just lost it. I was going too fast, got sideways and that was it. But I am confident we should complete all our planned laps tomorrow.

'The fast corners on this circuit suit the car's handling qualities, although we need to work to make it a little more stable. I am OK after the accident, but at the time I thought, "Oh, this one is going to hurt!" '

Villeneuve lost control as he powered through the dramatic left/right flick which sees cars bottom out in a dip before hurtling up a steep hill, over a blind brow and out onto an even faster straight.

The Williams spun broadside before skating across the gravel run-off area and slamming into a tyre barrier on the right-hand side of the circuit with a fearful impact which saw the session red-flagged to a halt in order for the wrecked car to be recovered. But Villeneuve was able to walk away without a scratch.

'The adrenalin is pumping, so I guess that hides anything from yesterday's crash,' said Jacques after qualifying. 'But I wasn't hurt at all. I've had some good training on the ovals.' The delay caused by Jacques's accident played right into McLaren's hands, giving the team extra time to rebuild Häkkinen's car for the afternoon.

The Williams team's second driver Heinz-Harald Frentzen was three places further back, disappointed over set-up mistakes and the fact that his fourth run was spoiled when he came up behind the dawdling Toranosuke Takagi's Tyrrell, which was on its slowing-down lap.

Behind Fisichella in eighth place came Ralf Schumacher's Jordan, the young German admitting that he was a little dissatisfied. 'I did not feel as comfortable with the car as I have done in recent races and struggled a little with understeer,' he admitted. 'Hopefully we will have it sorted out for the race.'

Completing the top ten was Jean Alesi's Sauber-Petronas. 'As usual in qualifying, it was very difficult to get everything done that we wanted to,' he explained, 'but in the circumstances I'm happy with my best lap. My car was a lot better than it felt yesterday and my only real mechanical problem was a leaking brake at the start of the session.'

Johnny Herbert was two places further back, the Saubers separated by the Benetton of a rather downcast Alexander Wurz. 'We changed a lot of things in the set-up,' said Herbert, 'and the car felt a lot better. While Eau Rouge was the problem initially, the focus then switched to Stavelot. I was having trouble getting out of there cleanly and that was affecting my speed all the way down to the Bus Stop. I'm beginning to think that I haven't yet got my car tuned for the latest tyres because it wallows in hard cornering.'

Jarno Trulli qualified his Prost AP01 in 13th place despite losing set-up time during the morning after his car suffered transmission trouble. 'I was only able to do two fast qualifying laps due to a braking problem,' he said. 'If we had run a little more this morning I am sure we could have gained a few tenths.' Team-mate Olivier Panis was two places further back, commenting that he felt 'the car was driving me rather than me driving it'.

The Stewart-Fords of Rubens Barrichello and Jos Verstappen lined up 14th and 17th. 'My last lap felt very good,' said Rubens. 'The adjustments we made to the front suspension have improved the car's handling quite a lot. I thought that I might have been higher on the grid, but it looks like Prost and Sauber found more than we did overnight.'

For his part, Verstappen suffered an engine failure during the morning session and then had a touch too much understeer at certain points on the circuit, although he admitted this was much reduced.

In the Arrows camp there had been a feeling of upbeat anticipation over the possible performance of the team's new D-spec V10 engine, but when both Mika Salo and Pedro Diniz suffered failures on Saturday morning C-spec engines were fitted for the second part of the session.

After a speedy engine change Salo rejoined the free practice session with only 15 minutes to go, but crashed heavily at Eau Rouge on his first lap. Thankfully he was unhurt and passed fit to take part in qualifying, but he had to drive the spare car and admitted that he was probably not performing at his best *en route* to 18th place on the grid.

Pedro Diniz was two places further up. 'During qualifying we had some problems balancing the car,' said the Brazilian. 'It was understeering a little, but in the end it wasn't so bad.'

Takagi lined up 19th ahead of his Tyrrell team-mate Rosset while Esteban Tuero's Minardi was beaten to penultimate place by team-mate Shinji Nakano, despite the Japanese driver having to run back from Blanchimont to take the spare M198 after his race car stopped on the circuit after only six laps.

Paul-Henri Cahier

BENSON

Previous pages: Damon Hill leads the Ferraris of Eddie Irvine and Michael Schumacher up the hill to Les Combes on the first lap of the restarted race. The German quickly moved to the front, but his dramatic exit allowed Hill to give the Jordan team its long-overdue maiden win.

Ralf Schumacher *(left)* made Eddie Jordan's happiness complete by following his team-mate home in second place, dutifully resisting the temptation to go for the victory himself.

Always superb in the wet, Jean Alesi finished a strong third for Sauber after making up six places on the opening lap.

Nigel Snowdon

On lap 11 Ralf Schumacher made a strategically shrewd early first stop to change from intermediates to full wet tyres, dropping from sixth to seventh. In that respect, the young German was well before the rush.

At the end of lap 16 Michael Schumacher, Hill, Alesi, Frentzen and Giancarlo Fisichella's Benetton all made their first stops, the net result being that Ralf Schumacher now found himself running in third behind his brother and Hill once the contest settled down into a pattern again. Villeneuve briefly went through into the lead as the first four stopped, but spun into the barrier on the straight approaching Les Combes, bringing to an end his eventful weekend.

When he resumed the race, Schumacher was 22 seconds ahead of Hill, but he relentlessly continued to open the gap, despite the fact that the conditions were, if anything, getting worse. It seemed on the face of it a classic example of a Senna-style need not just to win, but to utterly dominate the entire event.

On lap 24 Schumacher came up behind Coulthard with only a couple of laps left before his second refuelling stop. For almost a lap he shadowed the McLaren as Ron Dennis told David over the radio 'you must make way for Schumacher as promptly as possible,' or words to that effect.

Coulthard replied that he could see next to nothing in his mirrors, such was the intensity of the spray being thrown up by his rear wheels. 'You must tell me exactly where he is,' he replied.

On lap 25, coming down the hill to the Pouhon left-hander, Schumacher made to pass Coulthard just as David eased his rate of acceleration to help the Ferrari overtake. The Italian car's right-front wheel struck the McLaren's left-rear and was instantly ripped off. Schumacher's hopes of scoring a potentially vital victory were history.

Both cars trailed back to the pits where Coulthard refused to be intimidated by Schumacher's histrionics. 'Coming into the pits and asking me whether I was trying to kill him is totally unacceptable,' he said. 'I can't find words to describe how disappointed I am in Michael as a man that he could have still been in that state after driving back to the pits.

'It was disgusting behaviour. If he still feels the same when he has calmed down, I have no further interest in discussing the matter with him.'

Just to round off a particularly bleak day for Ferrari, Irvine spun off out of seventh place on the lap after Schumacher's departure from the fray. 'I came out of my [second] pit stop behind Fisichella,' said Eddie. 'I was quicker than him, but could not see where I was going. I clipped a kerb and spun off. It was an embarrassing race for me.'

On lap 27 Hill was lucky to escape a grassy excursion at the 'Bus Stop' but continued with his lead intact. Seconds later, Fisichella, by then up to fifth, had a simply massive accident at the same point when he slammed into the back of Shinji Nakano's Minardi. The wreckage of his Benetton came to rest, briefly aflame, on the exit of the chicane and the safety car was deployed for another five-lap stint.

'You couldn't see anything and I destroyed my car,' said the shaken Fisichella. 'I don't understand why they waited so long to bring out the safety car. Over my last ten laps the visibility was zero.'

When the cars were again unleashed, Hill completed lap 33 just 2.4s ahead of Ralf Schumacher. In the closing stages of the race, Ralf was told to forget about any ideas of challenging Hill for the win. This moment was too precious to squander and Ralf did as he was told – with questionable grace, it has to be said, since he later remarked that this best result of his career would not affect any future plans he might have to switch teams. To go to Williams, in other words.

Alesi was delighted with his strong run to third place from tenth on the grid. Yet the Frenchman was one of many drivers to express acute, continuing concern about the appalling weather conditions. 'I was surprised the safety car was pulled off towards the end,' he said, 'because there were cars parked on either side of the track and it was easy to aquaplane in many places.'

Damon Hill also hinted at similar concerns, confiding that he had clipped one of the Prosts while lapping the French car coming up towards the Blanchimont left-hander. Only later did the Jordan team discover that this brush had caused a slow puncture in one of Hill's tyres, which was replaced routinely at his first refuelling stop.

Frentzen, Pedro Diniz's Arrows and Jarno Trulli's Prost completed the list of those who'd run more or less trouble-free throughout, while Coulthard and Nakano were still circulating at the end in their repaired machines. Of the non-finishers, only Jos Verstappen and Esteban Tuero had suffered mechanical failures. As far as the World Championship was concerned, the battle had now been put on hold as neither of the two contenders had come away from Spa-Francorchamps with a single extra point.

Ferrari keeps heat on Coulthard

FERRARI raised the temperature of its rivalry with McLaren to a dangerously high level a few days after the Belgian Grand Prix by again blaming David Coulthard for the accident which cost Michael Schumacher victory at Spa-Francorchamps.

The Italian team's release seemed provocatively timed to coincide with Coulthard's appearance at Monza testing only four days after the controversial race. As the Scot accelerated out onto the circuit he was greeted with cat-calls and shouts of disapproval from the crowd.

The release from the Italian team claimed that 'after some disconcerting interpretations, Ferrari has once again examined all the various film and photographic evidence from the race, which shows unequivocally that:

'For almost an entire lap, Coulthard ignored the blue flags and never allowed Schumacher to go by, [that] on several occasions Schumacher moved off line to show Coulthard he was there and [that] Coulthard's sudden slowing down while on the racing line made the collision inevitable, given the poor visibility.'

The bulletin made no mention of Schumacher's aggressive approach to Coulthard in the pit lane after the incident, when he had to be restrained from approaching the Scottish driver.

'His [Schumacher's] actions were not those of a former champion,' said Clay Regazzoni, the former Ferrari driver who won the 1970 Italian Grand Prix. 'Michael is the best driver, but he knows it so well that he drives with arrogance and thinks he's a demi-god.'

McLaren responded to the Ferrari allegations, noting that it was 'understandable that immediately following this incident emotions were running high and incorrect conclusions reached'.

They also pointed out that the stewards had not blamed Coulthard and that examination of performance data downloaded from the McLaren's computer systems indicated that the Scot did not do anything wrong.

It was clear that there could be no reconciling these two conflicting views, but McLaren diplomatically left the door open for a truce by stating that although 'it does not wish to become involved in a protracted public discussion with Ferrari on the incident, it extends an invitation to discuss the matter further in private if there is a wish to do so'.

Race distance: 44 laps, 190.498 miles/306.577 km

Race weather: Heavy rain, cool

ROUND 13

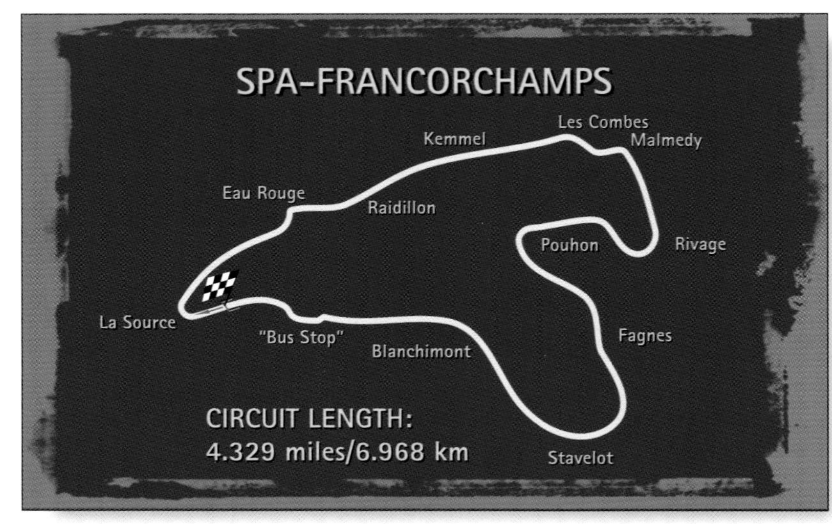

Pos.	Driver	Nat.	No.	Entrant	Car/Engine	Tyres	Laps	Time/Retirement	Speed (mph/km/h)
1	**Damon Hill**	**GB**	**9**	**B&H Jordan Mugen Honda**	**Jordan 198-Mugen Honda MF310C V10**	**G**	**44**	**1h 43m 47.407s**	**110.130/177.238**
2	**Ralf Schumacher**	**D**	**10**	**B&H Jordan Mugen Honda**	**Jordan 198-Mugen Honda MF310C V10**	**G**	**44**	**1h 43m 48.339s**	**110.113/177.210**
3	**Jean Alesi**	**F**	**14**	**Red Bull Sauber Petronas**	**Sauber C17-Petronas SPE01D V10**	**G**	**44**	**1h 43m 54.647s**	**110.002/177.031**
4	**Heinz-Harald Frentzen**	**D**	**2**	**Winfield Williams**	**Williams FW20-Mecachrome GC37/01 V10**	**G**	**44**	**1h 44m 19.650s**	**109.563/176.325**
5	**Pedro Diniz**	**BR**	**16**	**Danka Zepter Arrows**	**Arrows A19 V10**	**B**	**44**	**1h 44m 39.089s**	**109.223/175.778**
6	**Jarno Trulli**	**I**	**12**	**Gauloises Prost Peugeot**	**Prost AP01-Peugeot A16 V10**	**B**	**42**		
7	David Coulthard	GB	7	West McLaren Mercedes	McLaren MP4/13-Mercedes FO110G V10	B	39		
8	Shinji Nakano	J	22	Fondmetal Minardi Ford	Minardi M198-Ford Zetec-R V10	B	39		
	Giancarlo Fisichella	I	5	Mild Seven Benetton Playlife	Benetton B198-Playlife V10	B	26	Collision with Nakano	
	Michael Schumacher	D	3	Scuderia Ferrari Marlboro	Ferrari F300 047 V10	G	25	Collision with Coulthard	
	Eddie Irvine	GB	4	Scuderia Ferrari Marlboro	Ferrari F300 047 V10	G	25	Spun off	
	Esteban Tuero	RA	23	Fondmetal Minardi Ford	Minardi M198-Ford Zetec-R V10	B	17	Electrics	
	Jacques Villeneuve	CDN	1	Winfield Williams	Williams FW20-Mecachrome GC37/01 V10	G	16	Accident	
	Toranosuke Takagi	J	21	Tyrrell Ford	Tyrrell 026-Ford Zetec-R V10	G	10	Spun off	
	Jos Verstappen	NL	19	Stewart Ford	Stewart SF2-Ford Zetec-R V10	B	8	Engine	
	Mika Häkkinen	SF	8	West McLaren Mercedes	McLaren MP4/13-Mercedes FO110G V10	B	0	Collision with Herbert	
	Alexander Wurz	A	6	Mild Seven Benetton Playlife	Benetton B198-Playlife V10	B	0	Collision with Coulthard	
	Johnny Herbert	GB	15	Red Bull Sauber Petronas	Sauber C17-Petronas SPE01D V10	G	0	Collision with Häkkinen	
DNS	Olivier Panis	F	11	Gauloises Prost Peugeot	Prost AP01-Peugeot A16 V10	B		Accident at first start	
DNS	Rubens Barrichello	BR	18	Stewart Ford	Stewart SF2-Ford Zetec-R V10	B		Accident at first start	
DNS	Mika Salo	SF	17	Danka Zepter Arrows	Arrows A19 V10	B		Accident at first start	
DNS	Ricardo Rosset	BR	20	Tyrrell Ford	Tyrrell 026-Ford Zetec-R V10	G		Accident at first start	

Fastest lap: M. Schumacher, on lap 9, 2m 03.766s, 125.939 mph/202.679 km/h.

Lap record: Alain Prost (F1 Williams FW15C-Renault V10), 1m 51.095s, 140.424 mph/225.990 km/h (1993).

B – Bridgestone   G – Goodyear

All results and data © FIA 1998

Grid order	1	2	3	4	5	6	7	8	9	10	11	12	13	14	15	16	17	18	19	20	21	22
8 HÄKKINEN	9	9	9	9	9	9	9	3	3	3	3	3	3	3	3	3	3	3	3	3	3	3
7 COULTHARD	3	3	3	3	3	3	3	9	9	9	9	9	9	9	9	9	9	9	9	9	9	9
9 HILL	4	4	4	4	4	4	4	4	4	2	2	2	2	14	14	14	10	10	10	10	10	10
3 M. SCHUMACHER	14	14	1	1	2	2	2	2	2	14	14	14	14	2	2	1	14	14	14	14	14	14
4 IRVINE	1	1	2	2	14	14	14	14	14	1	1	1	1	1	1	2	2	2	2	2	2	2
1 VILLENEUVE	2	2	14	14	1	1	1	1	1	10	10	5	5	5	5	5	4	4	4	4	4	4
5 FISICHELLA	10	10	10	10	10	10	10	10	10	4	5	10	10	10	10	10	16	16	5	5	5	5
10 R. SCHUMACHER	5	5	5	5	5	5	5	5	5	5	16	16	16	16	16	16	5	5	16	16	16	7
2 FRENTZEN	16	16	16	16	16	16	16	16	16	16	4	4	4	4	4	4	12	12	12	12	7	16
14 ALESI	19	19	19	19	19	19	19	19	21	21	12	12	12	12	12	12	22	7	7	7	12	12
6 WURZ	21	21	21	21	21	21	21	21	22	12	22	22	22	22	22	22	7	22	22	22	22	22
15 HERBERT	22	22	22	22	22	22	22	22	12	22	7	7	7	7	7	7	23					
12 TRULLI	12	12	12	12	12	12	12	12	7	7	23	23	23	23	23	23						
18 BARRICHELLO	23	23	7	7	7	7	7	7	23	23												
11 PANIS	7	7	23	23	23	23	23	23														
16 DINIZ																						
19 VERSTAPPEN																						
17 SALO																						
21 TAKAGI																						
20 ROSSET																						
22 NAKANO																						
23 TUERO																						

Grid order	23	24	25	26	27	28	29	30	31	32	33	34	35	36	37	38	39	40	41	42	43	44	●
8 HÄKKINEN	3	3	3	9	9	9	9	9	9	9	9	9	9	9	9	9	9	9	9	9	9	9	1
7 COULTHARD	9	9	9	10	10	14	10	10	10	10	10	10	10	10	10	10	10	10	10	10	10	10	2
9 HILL	10	10	10	14	14	10	14	14	14	14	14	14	14	14	14	14	14	14	14	14	14	14	3
3 M. SCHUMACHER	14	14	14	2	2	2	2	2	2	2	2	2	2	2	2	2	2	2	2	2	2	2	4
4 IRVINE	2	2	2	5	16	16	16	16	16	16	16	16	16	16	16	16	16	16	16	16	16	16	5
1 VILLENEUVE	4	4	5	16	12	12	12	12	12	12	12	12	12	12	12	12	12	12	12	12			6
5 FISICHELLA	5	5	4	12	7	7	7	7	7	7	7	7	7	7	7	7	7						
10 R. SCHUMACHER	7	16	16	22	22	22	22	22	22	22	22	22	22	22	22	22	22						
2 FRENTZEN	16	7	12	7																			
14 ALESI	12	12	22																				
6 WURZ	22	22	7																				

Pit stop
One lap behind leader

FOR THE RECORD

First Grand Prix win

Jordan

STARTING GRID

	8 **HÄKKINEN** McLaren
7 **COULTHARD** McLaren	
	9 **HILL** Jordan
3 **M. SCHUMACHER** Ferrari	
	4 **IRVINE** Ferrari
1 **VILLENEUVE** Williams	
	5 **FISICHELLA** Benetton
10 **R. SCHUMACHER** Jordan	
	2 **FRENTZEN** Williams
14 **ALESI** Sauber	
	6 **WURZ** Benetton
15 **HERBERT** Sauber	
	12 **TRULLI** Prost
18 **BARRICHELLO*** Stewart	
	11 **PANIS*** Prost
16 **DINIZ** Arrows	
	19 **VERSTAPPEN** Stewart
17 **SALO*** Arrows	
	21 **TAKAGI** Tyrrell
20 **ROSSET*** Tyrrell	
	22 **NAKANO** Minardi
23 **TUERO** Minardi	

* did not take restart

Wayne Johnson/At Speed Photographic

TIME SHEETS

QUALIFYING

Weather: Cool, dry and overcast

Pos.	Driver	Car	Laps	Time
1	Mika Häkkinen	McLaren-Mercedes	11	1m 48.682s
2	David Coulthard	McLaren-Mercedes	12	1m 48.845s
3	Damon Hill	Jordan-Mugen Honda	11	1m 49.728s
4	Michael Schumacher	Ferrari	12	1m 50.027s
5	Eddie Irvine	Ferrari	12	1m 50.189s
6	Jacques Villeneuve	Williams-Mecachrome	12	1m 50.204s
7	Giancarlo Fisichella	Benetton-Playlife	12	1m 50.462s
8	Ralf Schumacher	Jordan-Mugen Honda	12	1m 50.501s
9	Heinz-Harald Frentzen	Williams-Mecachrome	11	1m 50.686s
10	Jean Alesi	Sauber-Petronas	11	1m 51.189s
11	Alexander Wurz	Benetton-Playlife	12	1m 51.648s
12	Johnny Herbert	Sauber-Petronas	11	1m 51.851s
13	Jarno Trulli	Prost-Peugeot	10	1m 52.572s
14	Rubens Barrichello	Stewart-Ford	12	1m 52.670s
15	Olivier Panis	Prost-Peugeot	12	1m 52.784s
16	Pedro Diniz	Arrows	12	1m 53.037s
17	Jos Verstappen	Stewart-Ford	12	1m 53.149s
18	Mika Salo	Arrows	8	1m 53.207s
19	Toranosuke Takagi	Tyrrell-Ford	12	1m 53.237s
20	Ricardo Rosset	Tyrrell-Ford	11	1m 54.850s
21	Shinji Nakano	Minardi-Ford	12	1m 55.084s
22	Esteban Tuero	Minardi-Ford	12	1m 55.520s

FRIDAY FREE PRACTICE

Weather: Dry and bright

Pos.	Driver	Laps	Time
1	Michael Schumacher	24	1m 51.895s
2	Mika Häkkinen	21	1m 51.906s
3	David Coulthard	23	1m 52.629s
4	Damon Hill	25	1m 53.100s
5	Heinz-Harald Frentzen	32	1m 53.534s
6	Jacques Villeneuve	19	1m 53.589s
7	Eddie Irvine	28	1m 53.601s
8	Jean Alesi	30	1m 53.660s
9	Ralf Schumacher	18	1m 54.116s
10	Johnny Herbert	29	1m 54.130s
11	Alexander Wurz	29	1m 54.158s
12	Giancarlo Fisichella	30	1m 54.171s
13	Rubens Barrichello	26	1m 54.433s
14	Jarno Trulli	33	1m 54.878s
15	Olivier Panis	32	1m 55.182s
16	Jos Verstappen	28	1m 55.263s
17	Mika Salo	29	1m 55.730s
18	Toranosuke Takagi	33	1m 56.080s
19	Pedro Diniz	29	1m 56.431s
20	Esteban Tuero	33	1m 57.014s
21	Shinji Nakano	30	1m 57.682s
22	Ricardo Rosset	34	1m 58.178s

SATURDAY FREE PRACTICE

Weather: Cool and dry

Pos.	Driver	Laps	Time
1	Mika Häkkinen	21	1m 50.319s
2	David Coulthard	23	1m 50.702s
3	Damon Hill	27	1m 51.368s
4	Jacques Villeneuve	23	1m 51.859s
5	Eddie Irvine	22	1m 51.972s
6	Michael Schumacher	23	1m 52.058s
7	Jean Alesi	24	1m 52.102s
8	Heinz-Harald Frentzen	22	1m 52.136s
9	Ralf Schumacher	25	1m 52.346s
10	Giancarlo Fisichella	25	1m 52.542s
11	Alexander Wurz	21	1m 53.020s
12	Johnny Herbert	28	1m 53.379s
13	Toranosuke Takagi	22	1m 53.898s
14	Olivier Panis	17	1m 53.933s
15	Rubens Barrichello	25	1m 54.071s
16	Mika Salo	9	1m 54.814s
17	Jarno Trulli	11	1m 55.049s
18	Pedro Diniz	16	1m 55.302s
19	Jos Verstappen	15	1m 55.451s
20	Shinji Nakano	22	1m 56.329s
21	Ricardo Rosset	23	1m 56.604s
22	Esteban Tuero	23	1m 57.000s

WARM-UP

Weather: Damp

Pos.	Driver	Laps	Time
1	Michael Schumacher	11	2m 07.839s
2	Eddie Irvine	12	2m 08.608s
3	Mika Häkkinen	11	2m 09.120s
4	Giancarlo Fisichella	11	2m 09.127s
5	Ralf Schumacher	12	2m 09.539s
6	Damon Hill	11	2m 10.076s
7	David Coulthard	7	2m 10.258s
8	Alexander Wurz	12	2m 10.917s
9	Rubens Barrichello	12	2m 11.374s
10	Jean Alesi	11	2m 11.546s
11	Heinz-Harald Frentzen	10	2m 11.860s
12	Jacques Villeneuve	9	2m 13.781s
13	Pedro Diniz	10	2m 13.853s
14	Toranosuke Takagi	8	2m 14.038s
15	Johnny Herbert	10	2m 14.147s
16	Jarno Trulli	9	2m 14.680s
17	Mika Salo	8	2m 16.139s
18	Ricardo Rosset	11	2m 16.174s
19	Shinji Nakano	9	2m 16.217s
20	Jos Verstappen	7	2m 17.733s
21	Esteban Tuero	5	2m 20.842s
22	Olivier Panis	4	2m 26.065s

RACE FASTEST LAPS

Weather: Heavy rain, cool

Driver	Time	Lap
Michael Schumacher	2m 03.766s	9
Damon Hill	2m 05.630s	7
Heinz-Harald Frentzen	2m 06.284s	7
Eddie Irvine	2m 06.561s	6
Jean Alesi	2m 07.597s	7
Jacques Villeneuve	2m 07.825s	8
Ralf Schumacher	2m 08.399s	7
Giancarlo Fisichella	2m 09.528s	5
David Coulthard	2m 10.950s	33
Pedro Diniz	2m 11.331s	5
Jarno Trulli	2m 11.701s	13
Toranosuke Takagi	2m 12.327s	6
Jos Verstappen	2m 12.425s	8
Shinji Nakano	2m 13.230s	12
Esteban Tuero	2m 19.996s	5

CHASSIS LOG BOOK

1	Villeneuve	Williams FW20/6
2	Frentzen	Williams FW20/4
	spare	Williams FW20/3
3	M. Schumacher	Ferrari F300/188
4	Irvine	Ferrari F300/185
	spare	Ferrari F300/186
5	Fisichella	Benetton B198/3
6	Wurz	Benetton B198/7
	spare	Benetton B198/6
7	Coulthard	McLaren MP4/13/7
8	Häkkinen	McLaren MP4/13/5
	spare	McLaren MP4/13/3
9	Hill	Jordan 198/3
10	R. Schumacher	Jordan 198/4
	spare	Jordan 198/5
11	Panis	Prost AP01/7
12	Trulli	Prost AP01/6
	spare	Prost AP01/2
14	Alesi	Sauber C17/6
15	Herbert	Sauber C17/7
	spare	Sauber C17/2
16	Diniz	Arrows A19/1
17	Salo	Arrows A19/5
	spare	Arrows A19/2
18	Barrichello	Stewart SF2/4
19	Verstappen	Stewart SF2/3
	spare	Stewart SF2/2
20	Rosset	Tyrrell 026/4
21	Takagi	Tyrrell 026/5
	spare	Tyrrell 026/2
22	Nakano	Minardi M198/4
23	Tuero	Minardi M198/5
	spare	Minardi M198/3

POINTS TABLES

Drivers

1	Mika Häkkinen	77
2	Michael Schumacher	70
3	David Coulthard	48
4	Eddie Irvine	32
5	Jacques Villeneuve	20
6	Alexander Wurz	17
7	Damon Hill	16
8	Giancarlo Fisichella	15
9	Heinz-Harald Frentzen	13
10	Ralf Schumacher	10
11	Jean Alesi	7
12	Rubens Barrichello	4
13 =	Mika Salo	3
13 =	Pedro Diniz	3
15 =	Johnny Herbert	1
15 =	Jan Magnussen	1
15 =	Jarno Trulli	1

Constructors

1	McLaren	125
2	Ferrari	102
3	Williams	33
4	Benetton	32
5	Jordan	26
6	Sauber	8
7	Arrows	6
8	Stewart	5
9	Prost	1

ITALIAN grand prix

M. SCHUMACHER
IRVINE
R. SCHUMACHER
HÄKKINEN
ALESI
HILL

The jubilant Ferrari team crowd onto the pit wall to cheer home Michael Schumacher and Eddie Irvine, who scored Maranello's first 1–2 success at Monza in a decade.

Peter Nygaard/GP Photo

DIARY

Ferrari celebrates its 600th Grand Prix, which took place in Belgium, with a huge party at Monza attended by former team drivers Phil Hill, John Surtees, René Arnoux, Michele Alboreto, Gerhard Berger and Niki Lauda.

Dario Franchitti scores first CART win at Road America in Team Green Reynard-Honda.

Toyota is again rumoured to be carrying out an evaluation of a proposed F1 programme.

Ross Brawn denies that Ferrari is contemplating development of a brand-new V12-cylinder F1 engine.

IT was the result which 125,000 madly enthusiastic Ferrari fans probably stayed awake dreaming about, yet could never quite bring themselves to believe might come to pass. Michael Schumacher and Eddie Irvine outlasted the opposition to score a historic 1-2 success for Maranello in the Italian Grand Prix at Monza, the first time for ten years that Ferrari had achieved such an overwhelming grand slam in its home race.

By any standards it was an impressive result, setting up the World Championship for a dramatic grandstand finish. Schumacher's title rival Mika Häkkinen could only struggle home fourth behind Ralf Schumacher's Jordan, the Finn's McLaren-Mercedes crippled by horrendous brake problems in the closing stages of the race.

Consequently the two contenders finished the weekend tied on 80 points with 20 still to play for over the two remaining events on the F1 calendar.

'After our poor performance at Hockenheim, which is also a low-downforce circuit, we thought that Monza would be very difficult for us,' said Schumacher. 'But all the hard work paid off today. Now I am looking forward to Nürburgring and Suzuka, as both circuits should suit our car.'

Even after Schumacher had secured his first pole position of the 1998 season here on the Prancing Horse's home turf, events seemed set to fulfil the worst fears of the crowd as the McLaren MP4/13s of Häkkinen and his team-mate David Coulthard catapulted through from the second row of the grid to take first and second places at the start.

The first few seconds of the race were lurid in the extreme. Schumacher moved to the right in a desperate attempt to head off Häkkinen after the pole-position Ferrari made a poor getaway. Mika in turn had to yank the MP4/13 even harder to the right, almost shaving the nose of Jacques Villeneuve's Williams FW20, which had shared the front row with the German driver.

Häkkinen led down to the first chicane ahead of his team-mate with Irvine, who had overtaken Schumacher on the left as they accelerated away from the line, third, Villeneuve fourth and Michael fifth. As the pack approached the braking area for the second chicane after Curva Grande, Schumacher came hurtling down the inside of Villeneuve to grab fourth place at such an unexpected speed that the Canadian was given the option of conceding or colliding. Prudently, he didn't make a dispute of it.

'My start was terrible,' said Schumacher. 'I got everything wrong which I could have got wrong. I was lucky to catch up Jacques [Villeneuve] in the second corner to get back behind Eddie and obviously he let me by, which enabled me to catch up the McLarens. I wasn't expecting that, to be honest.'

By the end of the opening lap Häkkinen was 0.58s ahead of Coulthard with Irvine and Schumacher next up. Further back, Pedro Diniz's Arrows had missed the first chicane, making a grass-cutting detour without gaining any advantage, and second time round Damon Hill's Jordan, Toranosuke Takagi's Tyrrell and Esteban Tuero's Minardi followed suit. Rightly, no penalties were incurred.

On lap three Schumacher, who had elected to use his spare Ferrari F300, which he preferred, duly went ahead of Irvine to claim third place while Häkkinen continued to lead, even though the Finn could already detect the first signs of impending trouble with his McLaren.

Mika had also started the race in the spare McLaren MP4/13 after his race chassis developed an engine problem during the warm-up. Yet almost from the word go he found himself struggling with progressively worsening oversteer.

By lap eight he was really beginning to have serious problems, so the team agreed that Coulthard, whose car was running strongly, should take the lead and attempt to go for a win. Häkkinen, meanwhile, would be left to do his best to finish ahead of Schumacher in his own private battle for the drivers' title.

Further back, on lap six Diniz had again fallen foul of the first chicane, running over the grass and gaining a place from Takagi's Tyrrell. But the Brazilian driver allowed his rival back ahead even before they reached the second chicane so again no penalty was given.

Diniz's troubled run eventually ended on lap 11 when he spun out of 18th place, the abandoned Arrows A19 being lifted away by a tractor while the experimental in-cockpit warning light system was employed to advise his rivals that a car was being recovered from the trackside.

'I had a problem with my brakes and my rear wheels were locking again and again,' explained Diniz. 'I braked into Lesmo and my wheels locked. I could not catch the car, so I spun off. I was unable to re-select a gear, so that was that.'

Two laps later Johnny Herbert spun off, ending an acutely disappointing

MONZA QUALIFYING

Prior to the start of the on-track action at Monza, Michael Schumacher and David Coulthard had a long talk about their Spa collision behind closed doors. In effect, they agreed to disagree about the subtleties of the incident. But they at least managed to bury the hatchet.

'David and I have generally got on well in the past and we can still get on well,' said Schumacher. 'It was good and necessary to have a talk between ourselves to sort out some questions. That is what we did, and there are no further problems.' Coulthard broadly agreed, but confined his comments to an amused grin and general pleasantries. Getting Michael to see other people's viewpoints has never been a simple task.

Practice and qualifying at Monza produced unpredictable and unexpected weather conditions. Friday free practice saw the second hour spoiled by intermittent rain and Eddie Irvine ending up fastest in his Ferrari. Although Michael Schumacher estimated that the F300 was still about half a second away from the McLaren MP4/13s, it was certainly a morale-boosting performance.

'Even though Friday's time is never very important it is still a nice feeling to be at the top of the page, ahead of Michael and in front of all the fans here at Monza,' said Irvine. 'I don't know if I can be quickest again tomorrow, but I feel we can really put McLaren under pressure.'

Come qualifying the track was damp but drying after a heavy shower during the morning. Nobody went out for the first half-hour and it eventually fell to Tora Takagi and Damon Hill to lead the pack out onto the circuit with just 26 minutes left. Heinz-Harald Frentzen's Williams set the initial pace on 1m 29.984s, but the ferocious contest would continue right up to the last few minutes of the session.

Just as in Austria, it was all a question of keeping one's nerve and judging the last run as finely as possible. With five minutes of the session still to go Schumacher and Irvine were 11th and 12th, but the Ferrari number one rose to the occasion superbly to clinch pole position, although his team-mate had to be content with fifth on the grid.

'By the time I went out on dry-weather tyres the circuit was only slightly damp at the Lesmos,' recalled Michael, 'and we got everything right. The car worked quite well and should be good enough to dictate the pace tomorrow.

'On my best lap I ran slightly wide at the last corner and lost a bit of time, then I went over the chicane on my next lap and that was it. We had been expecting to go better than we did in testing, but this is a great position from which to be starting such an important race.'

Irvine was moderately content with his efforts. 'Not bad,' he shrugged. 'I went out on a set-up we had not tried and it gave me a bit too much understeer, but there was no time to change it. I started my last lap – which was my quickest one – behind a slower car and as I could not pass it into the first corner, I got a bit held up.'

For his part Jacques Villeneuve was only partly satisfied with the feel of his Williams FW20 and seemed almost surprised when he emerged with second place on the grid. 'We made quite big set-up changes to the car overnight,' he explained. 'Then I came into the pits to change tyres and alter the aero balance and achieved the time. The car seems to work well in low downforce, but I couldn't brake hard and had too much understeer.'

By contrast, Heinz-Harald Frentzen was a very disappointed 12th, also finding that his car suffered from worsening understeer as the track dried out. 'I had a good wet-weather set-up,' he explained, 'but the car just didn't work in the dry.'

The McLaren MP4/13s of Mika Häkkinen and David Coulthard qualified third and fourth fastest, both drivers' efforts spoiled by traffic in the closing stages of the session. 'I was never quite confident,' said Häkkinen, 'but I think the Bridgestones were rather caught out by the cooler temperatures.

'I think we were the victim of circumstances. Although it is always easy to list the "ifs" and "buts" I have to say that things started well on my last timed lap, but I ran into traffic and had to slow down.'

Ralf Schumacher was sixth fastest for Jordan, very happy with his performance despite admitting to a mistake on his best lap, but an extremely frustrated Damon Hill could not improve on 14th. 'I got stuck behind a McLaren which was in turn stuck behind an Arrows so I had to go round the outside of them on my best lap,' explained the Englishman.

Alexander Wurz qualified seventh fastest in his Benetton B198, both he and team-mate Giancarlo Fisichella wishing that they'd been able to use the wider Bridgestone front tyre which their chassis certainly preferred. The Austrian was quite content with his performance although he lost any realistic chance of improving his time when he got caught up in traffic. Fisichella ended up a disappointed 11th for much the same reasons.

Eighth fastest was Jean Alesi's Sauber-Petronas while team-mate Johnny Herbert had a dispiriting time, spinning into a barrier and being obliged to take the spare C17, only to catch both Hill and Coulthard on what he hoped would be his best lap. He had to be content with 15th place.

In the Prost-Peugeot camp there was much optimism after both AP01s managed to qualify in the top ten, Olivier Panis just pipping Jarno Trulli for the inside of the fifth row. Both drivers were, for once, satisfied with their cars and did not have to change anything on them.

Behind Fisichella and Frentzen, Rubens Barrichello's Stewart SF2 qualified 13th, although the Brazilian had hoped to hang on to eighth place in the grid order, which he had held early in the session. 'But I developed more understeer towards the end,' he explained. 'The changes we made to the set-up had little effect and I lost too much time in the high-speed corners like Parabolica.'

Barrichello and team-mate Jos Verstappen, who struggled for handling balance and could not better 17th, used the latest Series 6 version of the Ford Zetec-R V10 in qualifying but reverted to the proven Series 5 version for the race.

Mika Salo managed to qualify his Arrows A19 16th, just ahead of Verstappen, but he too suffered from poor handling balance and some brake problems. Pedro Diniz, who had lost 45 minutes with electrical problems during the dry spell in Friday's free practice, was down in 20th, his time bettered by the Tyrrell 026s of Ricardo Rosset and Toranosuke Takagi. Sharing the back row of the grid were the two Minardi M198s of Shinji Nakano and Esteban Tuero, the team's only consolation being that it had used the occasion of its home race to announce the recruitment of Cesare Fiorio as its sporting director.

Photos: Paul-Henri Cahier

Herbert signs for Stewart, Frentzen joins Jordan

JOHNNY Herbert stood poised to bring a fund of badly needed knowledge and experience to the Stewart-Ford F1 team under the terms of a new two-year contract which would see the Englishman switch from the Sauber-Petronas squad at the start of the 1999 season.

That was the view expressed by team founder Jackie Stewart at Monza. 'I think we will benefit from a closer comparison of lap times between Rubens [Barrichello] and Johnny than we did between Rubens, Jan Magnussen and Jos Verstappen,' he said.

'I think Johnny has the speed and for a team like ours, at this stage in its growth, we need to have drivers of equal status, something which we haven't had so far.'

Paul-Henri Cahier

Meanwhile, in the Jordan camp, it was revealed that Heinz-Harald Frentzen would be taking over from Ralf Schumacher, who had confirmed after Spa that he was leaving the team, at least in part thanks to his brother Michael's intervention with what Eddie Jordan regarded as unwelcome and unsolicited advice.

Ralf was briefly embroiled in a High Court action with Jordan to establish whether he had the right to leave the team to join Williams. The young German wanted a pay rise to around a reputed $4 million next season, but Jordan claimed he was tied by the terms of an existing deal forged with his manager Willi Weber for a much lower retainer. The eventual intervention of Bernie Ecclestone resulted in the matter being resolved amicably with Ralf being released to continue negotiations with both Williams and British American Racing.

Damon Hill described Jordan's decision to sign Frentzen as 'a smart move' when asked his view at Monza. 'I was initially quite surprised, because I had expected Eddie to be looking for a younger driver, maybe someone who was new to F1,' said Hill.

'But as Eddie says, we now have two drivers who have each won Grands Prix. It is a formidable package now and Eddie has two drivers who can bring home results for the constructors' trophy.'

Following its recent upsurge of form, Jordan was also believed to be in the throes of negotiating a two-year extension to its Mugen Honda engine supply deal, which was currently due to expire at the end of 1999.

Carnival time. As the drivers are paraded round the circuit to allow the fans to see their heroes out of the cockpit, some of the F1 stars seem more interested in catching up on the gossip than in waving to the paying public.

Below: A packed crowd, most of them fervently hoping for a home win, wait expectantly for the start.

weekend for the 1995 Monza winner. 'Unbeknown to me, some pliers had been left in the footwell of my car before the race began,' he said with a calm which seemed commendable under the circumstances.

'I made a reasonable start and gained a couple of places, but from the second lap the pliers began to foul the brake pedal and twice I had to adjust the [brake] balance to compensate. The first time I lost a place to [Rubens] Barrichello and then I had a couple of other moments. I couldn't be exactly sure what was going on, only that the car suddenly felt inconsistent and difficult to drive. As I went into the second Lesmo, the pedal felt odd as the pliers interfered again, and I spun into the gravel. As you can imagine, I am not very happy.'

Next time round Damon Hill, running a two-stop strategy, made his first refuelling stop after passing a huge number of cars from 14th place on the grid. He dropped from sixth to 13th, which allowed team-mate Ralf Schumacher to take up the pursuit of Villeneuve.

Lap 15 saw Olivier Panis retire from 19th place with a worrying rear-end vibration on his Prost, while two laps later Coulthard's McLaren suffered a huge engine failure at Curva Grande and pulled off onto the grass on the right-hand side of the circuit.

'The car was very strong, the chassis set-up working well and then it tightened up as I came out of the first chicane and the engine blew,' shrugged Coulthard. 'It was very disappointing because we had such a good car and a performance advantage at this circuit.'

Häkkinen and Schumacher both arrived to find the road apparently blocked by a smokescreen from the expiring Merc V10, braking to near walking pace before Michael dodged ahead of Häkkinen as they went through the next chicane to take the lead.

'It had been Mika and myself challenging each other for a number of laps,' said Schumacher. 'Then there was this tremendous engine blow-up which made it impossible to see through the corner. We just didn't know where the car was and we both had to slow down big time.

'Mika briefly went onto the grass and then lost it slightly into the second chicane. He went wide and struggled, so I out-accelerated him out of the corner towards the first Lesmo. It was hairy: I mean, he obviously pulled over and tried to close the door, but I still went through. That decided the race for me.'

The event now settled down with Schumacher edging away from Häkkinen while Irvine was third ahead of Villeneuve, Ralf Schumacher, Jean Alesi's Sauber C17 and Alexander Wurz's Benetton, which would eventually retire on lap 25 with gearbox failure.

By that stage Michael had eked out a 3.9s advantage over Häkkinen with Irvine, Villeneuve, Ralf Schumacher and Alesi still heading the pursuit. On lap 31 Schumacher Senior came in for his sole refuelling stop, which took 9.3s, and the Ferrari resumed in second behind Häkkinen. Next time round Irvine, who had lost three seconds to the pursuing Villeneuve with a moment at the first Lesmo on lap 28, came in for his own 8.3s stop, which dropped him behind the Williams. That was corrected on the following lap when Jacques brought the FW20 in for its sole stop, resuming in fourth.

On lap 34 Häkkinen made his sole 9.7s refuelling stop, which put him back into the race in second some 5.7s behind Schumacher's Ferrari. With a differently pressured set of tyres Mika felt much more confident and could now really pile on the pressure, trimming Michael's advantage to 3.6s by lap 42 and then down to 2.6s on lap 45.

Meanwhile, Villeneuve lost fourth place after spinning into the gravel trap at the second Lesmo. 'During the whole race I was locking front wheels and in the end I locked my rears, causing me to spin,' said Jacques. 'We were running too little downforce to keep up on the straights and not enough on the corners – we were somewhere in between – and it was a hard car to drive.' In fact Jacques had dropped his left-rear wheel onto the gravel exiting the first Lesmo – a slip picked up by eagle-eyed ITV commentator Martin Brundle – and dirt on his tyres certainly contributed to his abrupt departure from the race.

Approaching the second chicane on

Heinz-Harald Frentzen clatters his Williams over the saw-tooth kerbing with Damon Hill poised to pounce on the slightest error. It had been revealed that the pair would be team-mates in 1999.

Below: The perfect team player, Eddie Irvine helped keep Ferrari in contention for the constructors' championship with another measured drive to second place.

lap 46 Häkkinen suddenly found his McLaren pitched into a terrifying 175 mph spin. The car's crazy gyrations ended in the gravel trap, but its driver certainly had his wits about him, since he didn't let the engine stall and coaxed the thankfully intact MP4/13 back onto the circuit.

The McLaren had suffered near-total front brake failure and Häkkinen could do nothing more than struggle on at reduced speed to finish fourth at the chequered flag. Ron Dennis would later describe Mika's last few laps at Monza as 'the most heroic seven laps of the entire season'. This was by no means an exaggeration.

On his final lap before he was confronted with this dramatic problem, Häkkinen went round in 1m 25.139s, the fastest lap of the race. This slumped to 1m 45.062s as he recovered from his pirouette, but on lap 47 he was back to 1m 31.575s and by lap 50 he actually went round in 1m 30.526s – only five seconds off a competitive pace with brakes on the rear wheels only. Yet this heroism was not enough to preserve his championship lead.

The pressure was now off Schumacher, who could ease off slightly and roll it home to a convincing and emotional victory. On lap 49 Irvine went past Häkkinen to take second and Ralf Schumacher finally overtook the crippled McLaren to snatch the last place on the rostrum with two of the 53 laps left to run.

A technical post-mortem by McLaren subsequently revealed that a fluid leak from a brake caliper was responsible for the disastrous situation which Häkkinen encountered. At the root of the problem was a left-front brake pad which was not perfectly bedded in. Consequently that pad suffered a higher level of wear than the other pads on that caliper, the piston came out and the brake fluid escaped.

McLaren came to Monza fully aware that the circuit was matched only by Montreal in terms of its demands on braking performance, but exhaustive tests prior to the race convinced the team that new discs would be more than adequate for the job.

'We were using a new material in the brakes,' said McLaren MD Martin Whitmarsh, 'and perhaps our lack of full knowledge about it may have resulted in a less-than-optimum bedding-in of the pad.'

Schumacher was obviously elated by his victory and Irvine similarly satisfied with second, although he reported that his F300 was very stiffly set up and difficult to drive. He eased his pace slightly after running wide at Lesmo, then piled on the pressure when he heard that Häkkinen was in trouble. 'Once I had passed him, I slowed down again,' he explained.

It was another terrific weekend for the Jordan team with Ralf Schumacher taking his second podium in as many races. 'A great day for us,' he said, 'and good to see us closing in on Benetton and Williams for third in the constructors' championship.'

Hill's two-stop strategy vaulted him to sixth at the chequered flag and he was equally satisfied. 'I think I overtook more people in today's race than I've done in the past two seasons,' he grinned. 'It was absolutely crazy at the start, passing people all the time, and in fact I couldn't believe it when I was told it was time for my first pit stop because I was so busy enjoying myself.'

Splitting the Jordans at the chequered flag were Häkkinen's McLaren and Alesi's Sauber C17, the Frenchman another to use the spare car, which he preferred after the warm-up. Heinz-Harald Frentzen finished a frustrated seventh in the sole surviving Williams FW20 after missing his pit signal and starting to run out of fuel as he exited the Variante Ascari. He managed to struggle back to the pits but lost a lot of time as a result.

Eighth fell to Giancarlo Fisichella in the only Benetton B198 to reach the finish. On a one-stop strategy, the Italian reported his car was unwieldy and difficult to drive on a heavy fuel load in the opening stages of the race. 'As the car got lighter I managed to pick up speed, but we still lacked grip,' he explained. 'At the pit stop we had a problem with a sticking wheel nut and lost a place which I was unable to recover.'

Toranosuke Takagi's Tyrrell was next up ahead of Rubens Barrichello in the Stewart-Ford, Esteban Tuero's Minardi, Ricardo Rosset's Tyrrell and the Prost of Jarno Trulli, which managed to set the fifth-fastest race lap after early handling problems were rectified at his fuel stop when a loose rear wheel was discovered.

'I have dreamed of seeing Ferrari in this situation ever since I returned to Maranello [in 1992],' said Ferrari President Luca di Montezemolo after the race. 'Today reminds me of that extraordinary occasion for me and for the *tifosi* in 1975 when we finished first and third here at Monza with Regazzoni and Lauda.'

Schumacher stayed late into the evening at Monza, mingling with the *tifosi* on the startline as he reflected on just what a memorable day it had been. Technical reliability rather than out-and-out performance had won Maranello the day. The McLaren-Mercedes was still the quickest package. But the silver cars had stumbled again.

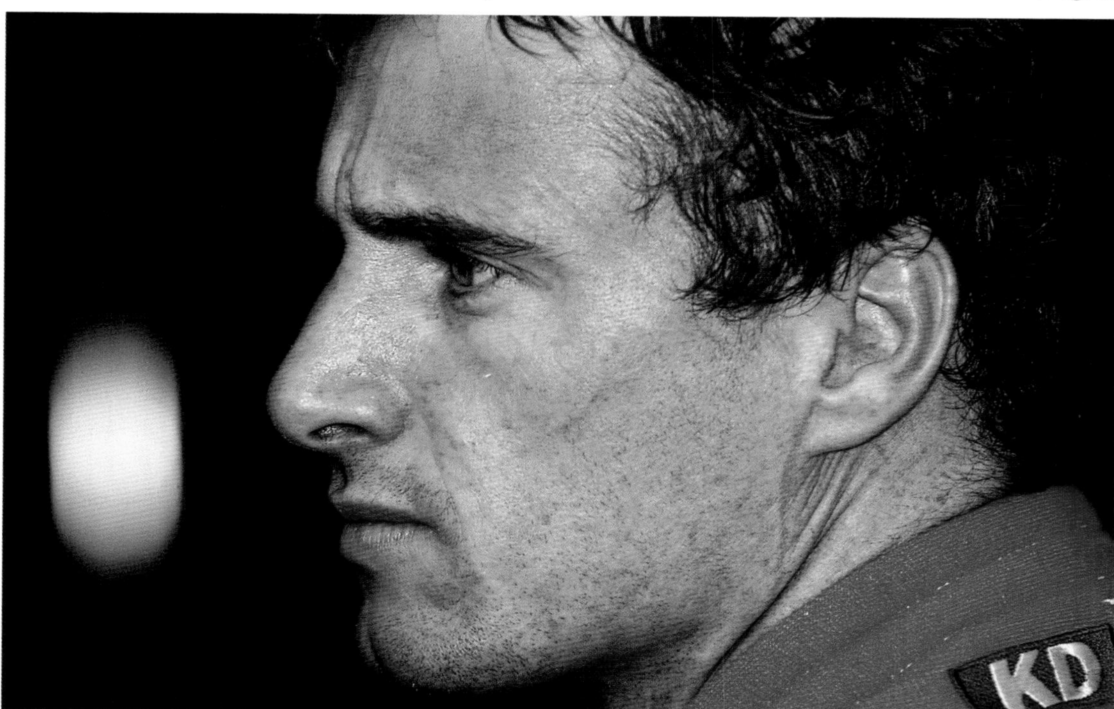

Picture left: Paul-Henri Cahier   Picture far left: Bryn Williams

Ferrari celebrated both past glories and present-day success at Monza.

To mark the team's participation in its 600th Grand Prix in Belgium, a number of legendary former Ferrari drivers were invited to demonstrate some of Maranello's most successful cars. *Top:* **John Surtees leads the pageant in a 375, followed by Phil Hill, who was reunited with his 246 Dino** *(above left).* **Il Grande John** *(above)* **remains a firm favourite with the Italian fans.**

Meanwhile the fabled Monza banking *(left)*, **long since disused, faces the threat of demolition.**

Right: **Back in the present, an overjoyed Michael Schumacher leaps higher than ever as he enjoys his latest victory. Brother Ralf can only look up at him in admiration.**

CAMPARI
PREMIO
Formula 1
FIA
FORMULA 1
WORLD
CHAMPIONSHIP
Marlboro
Shell
GOODYEAR
Asprey
OMP
M. Schumacher
MOËT
MOËT & CHANDON

69° GRAN PREMIO CAMPARI D'ITALIA

11–13 SEPTEMBER 1998

MONZA

Race distance: 53 laps, 189.858 miles/305.548 km

Race weather: Fine and dry

ROUND 14

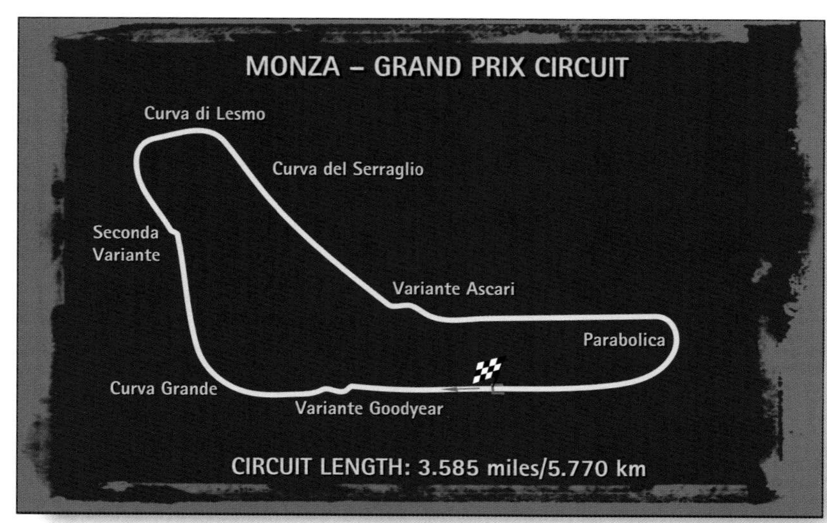

Pos.	Driver	Nat.	No.	Entrant	Car/Engine	Tyres	Laps	Time/Retirement	Speed (mph/km/h)
1	**Michael Schumacher**	**D**	**3**	**Scuderia Ferrari Marlboro**	**Ferrari F300 047 V10**	**G**	**53**	**1h 17m 09.672s**	**147.632/237.591**
2	**Eddie Irvine**	**GB**	**4**	**Scuderia Ferrari Marlboro**	**Ferrari F300 047 V10**	**G**	**53**	**1h 17m 47.649s**	**146.431/235.658**
3	**Ralf Schumacher**	**D**	**10**	**B&H Jordan Mugen Honda**	**Jordan 198-Mugen Honda MF310C V10**	**G**	**53**	**1h 17m 50.824s**	**146.331/235.498**
4	**Mika Häkkinen**	**SF**	**8**	**West McLaren Mercedes**	**McLaren MP4/13-Mercedes FO110G V10**	**B**	**53**	**1h 18m 05.343s**	**145.878/234.768**
5	**Jean Alesi**	**F**	**14**	**Red Bull Sauber Petronas**	**Sauber C17-Petronas SPE01D V10**	**G**	**53**	**1h 18m 11.544s**	**145.685/234.458**
6	**Damon Hill**	**GB**	**9**	**B&H Jordan Mugen Honda**	**Jordan 198-Mugen Honda MF310C V10**	**G**	**53**	**1h 18m 16.360s**	**145.536/234.218**
7	Heinz-Harald Frentzen	D	2	Winfield Williams	Williams FW20-Mecachrome GC37/01 V10	G	52		
8	Giancarlo Fisichella	I	5	Mild Seven Benetton Playlife	Benetton B198-Playlife V10	B	52		
9	Toranosuke Takagi	J	21	Tyrrell Ford	Tyrrell 026-Ford Zetec-R V10	G	52		
10	Rubens Barrichello	BR	18	Stewart Ford	Stewart SF2-Ford Zetec-R V10	B	52		
11	Esteban Tuero	RA	23	Fondmetal Minardi Ford	Minardi M198-Ford Zetec-R V10	B	51		
12	Ricardo Rosset	BR	20	Tyrrell Ford	Tyrrell 026-Ford Zetec-R V10	G	51		
13	Jarno Trulli	I	12	Gauloises Prost Peugeot	Prost AP01-Peugeot A16 V10	B	50		
	Jos Verstappen	NL	19	Stewart Ford	Stewart SF2-Ford Zetec-R V10	B	39	Gearbox/overheated	
	Jacques Villeneuve	CDN	1	Winfield Williams	Williams FW20-Mecachrome GC37/01 V10	G	37	Spun off	
	Mika Salo	SF	17	Danka Zepter Arrows	Arrows A19 V10	B	32	Hydraulics	
	Alexander Wurz	A	6	Mild Seven Benetton Playlife	Benetton B198-Playlife V10	B	24	Gearbox	
	David Coulthard	GB	7	West McLaren Mercedes	McLaren MP4/13-Mercedes FO110G V10	B	16	Engine	
	Olivier Panis	F	11	Gauloises Prost Peugeot	Prost AP01-Peugeot A16 V10	B	15	Rear vibration	
	Shinji Nakano	J	22	Fondmetal Minardi Ford	Minardi M198-Ford Zetec-R V10	B	13	Engine	
	Johnny Herbert	GB	15	Red Bull Sauber Petronas	Sauber C17-Petronas SPE01D V10	G	12	Spun off	
	Pedro Diniz	BR	16	Danka Zepter Arrows	Arrows A19 V10	B	10	Spun off	

All results and data © FIA 1998

Fastest lap: Häkkinen, on lap 45, 1m 25.139s, 151.560 mph/243.977 km/h.

Lap record: Mika Häkkinen (F1 McLaren MP4/12-Mercedes V10), 1m 24.808s, 152.192 mph/244.929 km/h (1997).

B – Bridgestone G – Goodyear

Grid order	1	2	3	4	5	6	7	8	9	10	11	12	13	14	15	16	17	18	19	20	21	22	23	24	25	26	27	28	29	30	31	32	33	34	35	36	37	38	39
3 M. SCHUMACHER	8	8	8	8	8	8	8	7	7	7	7	7	7	7	7	7	3	3	3	3	3	3	3	3	3	3	3	3	3	3	3	8	8	8	3	3	3	3	3
1 VILLENEUVE	7	7	7	7	7	7	7	8	8	8	8	8	8	8	8	8	8	8	8	8	8	8	8	8	8	8	8	8	8	8	8	3	3	3	8	8	8	8	8
8 HÄKKINEN	4	4	3	3	3	3	3	3	3	3	3	3	3	3	3	3	4	4	4	4	4	4	4	4	4	4	4	4	4	4	4	4	1	4	4	4	4	4	4
7 COULTHARD	3	3	4	4	4	4	4	4	4	4	4	4	4	4	4	4	1	1	1	1	1	1	1	1	1	1	1	1	1	1	1	1	4	1	1	1	1	10	10
4 IRVINE	1	1	1	1	1	1	1	1	1	1	1	1	1	1	1	1	10	10	10	10	10	10	10	10	10	10	10	10	10	10	14	14	10	10	10	10	10	14	14
10 R. SCHUMACHER	14	10	10	10	10	10	10	10	10	10	9	9	9	9	10	10	14	14	14	14	14	14	14	14	14	14	14	14	14	14	10	10	5	5	9	9	14	9	9
6 WURZ	10	14	14	14	9	9	9	9	9	9	10	10	10	10	14	14	6	6	6	6	6	6	6	6	5	5	5	5	5	5	5	5	2	2	5	14	9	2	2
14 ALESI	6	6	6	9	14	14	14	14	14	14	14	14	14	14	6	6	5	5	5	5	5	5	5	5	2	2	2	2	2	2	2	2	9	9	2	2	2	5	5
11 PANIS	5	5	9	6	6	6	6	6	6	6	6	6	6	6	5	5	2	2	2	2	2	2	2	2	9	9	9	9	9	9	9	9	14	14	14	5	5	19	19
12 TRULLI	12	12	5	5	5	5	5	5	5	5	5	5	5	5	12	2	9	9	9	9	9	9	9	9	17	17	17	17	17	17	17	17	19	19	19	19	19	21	21
5 FISICHELLA	9	9	12	12	12	12	12	12	12	12	12	12	12	12	2	18	17	17	17	17	17	17	12	17	19	19	19	19	19	19	19	19	18	18	21	21	21	18	18
2 FRENTZEN	2	2	2	2	2	2	2	2	2	2	2	2	2	2	18	9	18	12	12	12	12	12	17	19	21	21	18	18	18	18	18	18	21	21	18	18	18	23	23
18 BARRICHELLO	15	15	15	15	18	18	18	18	18	18	18	18	18	18	9	17	12	19	19	19	19	19	19	21	18	18	21	21	21	21	21	21	23	23	23	23	23	20	20
9 HILL	18	18	18	18	15	15	15	15	15	15	15	15	17	17	17	12	19	21	21	21	21	21	21	18	23	23	23	23	23	23	23	23	20	20	20	20	20	12	12
15 HERBERT	11	11	11	11	19	19	19	19	19	17	17	17	19	19	19	19	21	18	18	18	18	18	18	20	20	20	20	20	20	20	20	20	12	12	12	12	12		
17 SALO	19	19	19	19	11	11	11	17	17	19	19	19	21	20	20	21	20	20	20	20	20	20	20	23	12	12	12	12	12	12	12	12							
19 VERSTAPPEN	16	16	16	16	16	17	17	21	21	21	21	21	22	21	21	20	23	23	23	23	23	23	23	12															
20 ROSSET	23	17	17	17	17	16	21	16	16	16	22	22	20	23	23	23																							
21 TAKAGI	17	21	21	21	21	21	16	11	22	22	20	20	23	11	11																								
16 DINIZ	21	23	23	23	22	22	22	22	20	20	23	23	11																										
22 NAKANO	22	22	22	22	20	20	20	20	23	23	11	11																											
23 TUERO	20	20	20	20	23	23	23	23	11	11																													

Pit stop

One lap behind leader

STARTING GRID

3 **M. SCHUMACHER** Ferrari	1 **VILLENEUVE** Williams
8 **HÄKKINEN** McLaren	7 **COULTHARD** McLaren
4 **IRVINE** Ferrari	10 **R. SCHUMACHER** Jordan
6 **WURZ** Benetton	14 **ALESI** Sauber
11 **PANIS** Prost	12 **TRULLI** Prost
5 **FISICHELLA** Benetton	2 **FRENTZEN** Williams
18 **BARRICHELLO** Stewart	9 **HILL** Jordan
15 **HERBERT** Sauber	17 **SALO** Arrows
19 **VERSTAPPEN** Stewart	20 **ROSSET** Tyrrell
21 **TAKAGI** Tyrrell	16 **DINIZ** Arrows
22 **NAKANO** Minardi	23 **TUERO** Minardi

43	44	45	46	47	48	49	50	51	52	53	●
3	3	3	3	3	3	3	3	3	3	3	1
8	8	8	8	8	8	4	4	4	4	4	2
4	4	4	4	4	4	8	8	10	10	10	3
10	10	10	10	10	10	10	10	8	8	8	4
14	14	14	14	14	14	14	14	14	14	14	5
9	9	9	9	9	9	9	9	9	9	9	6
2	2	2	2	2	2	2	2	2	2		
5	5	5	5	5	5	5	5	5	5		
21	21	21	21	21	21	21	21	21	21		
18	18	18	18	18	18	18	18	18	18		
23	23	23	23	23	23	23	23	23			
20	20	20	20	20	20	20	20	20			
12	12	12	12	12	12	12	12				

TIME SHEETS

QUALIFYING

Weather: Damp track, drying gradually

Pos.	Driver	Car	Laps	Time
1	Michael Schumacher	Ferrari	9	1m 25.289s
2	Jacques Villeneuve	Williams-Mecachrome	12	1m 25.561s
3	Mika Häkkinen	McLaren-Mercedes	10	1m 25.679s
4	David Coulthard	McLaren-Mercedes	11	1m 25.987s
5	Eddie Irvine	Ferrari	11	1m 26.159s
6	Ralf Schumacher	Jordan-Mugen Honda	11	1m 26.309s
7	Alexander Wurz	Benetton-Playlife	10	1m 26.567s
8	Jean Alesi	Sauber-Petronas	12	1m 26.637s
9	Olivier Panis	Prost-Peugeot	11	1m 26.681s
10	Jarno Trulli	Prost-Peugeot	12	1m 26.794s
11	Giancarlo Fisichella	Benetton-Playlife	10	1m 26.817s
12	Heinz-Harald Frentzen	Williams-Mecachrome	10	1m 26.836s
13	Rubens Barrichello	Stewart-Ford	10	1m 27.247s
14	Damon Hill	Jordan-Mugen Honda	12	1m 27.362s
15	Johnny Herbert	Sauber-Petronas	9	1m 27.510s
16	Mika Salo	Arrows	9	1m 27.744s
17	Jos Verstappen	Stewart-Ford	11	1m 28.212s
18	Ricardo Rosset	Tyrrell-Ford	12	1m 28.286s
19	Toranosuke Takagi	Tyrrell-Ford	8	1m 28.346s
20	Pedro Diniz	Arrows	9	1m 28.387s
21	Shinji Nakano	Minardi-Ford	9	1m 29.101s
22	Esteban Tuero	Minardi-Ford	12	1m 29.417s

FRIDAY FREE PRACTICE

Weather: Breezy, overcast then rain

Pos.	Driver	Laps	Time
1	Eddie Irvine	23	1m 24.987s
2	Michael Schumacher	12	1m 25.246s
3	David Coulthard	26	1m 25.690s
4	Jacques Villeneuve	26	1m 26.053s
5	Mika Häkkinen	16	1m 26.159s
6	Heinz-Harald Frentzen	26	1m 26.528s
7	Jarno Trulli	25	1m 26.748s
8	Damon Hill	25	1m 26.838s
9	Giancarlo Fisichella	17	1m 26.885s
10	Alexander Wurz	18	1m 26.886s
11	Ralf Schumacher	29	1m 27.079s
12	Johnny Herbert	29	1m 27.541s
13	Olivier Panis	12	1m 27.676s
14	Rubens Barrichello	19	1m 28.066s
15	Ricardo Rosset	18	1m 28.098s
16	Toranosuke Takagi	29	1m 28.135s
17	Jos Verstappen	14	1m 28.606s
18	Esteban Tuero	30	1m 28.847s
19	Shinji Nakano	27	1m 28.849s
20	Mika Salo	11	1m 29.603s
21	Pedro Diniz	7	1m 53.671s
22	Jean Alesi	2	18m 20.632s

SATURDAY FREE PRACTICE

Weather: Heavy rain

Pos.	Driver	Laps	Time
1	Heinz-Harald Frentzen	14	1m 39.479s
2	Ralf Schumacher	12	1m 39.955s
3	Giancarlo Fisichella	11	1m 40.261s
4	David Coulthard	15	1m 40.295s
5	Mika Häkkinen	16	1m 40.321s
6	Jacques Villeneuve	11	1m 40.364s
7	Eddie Irvine	9	1m 40.608s
8	Alexander Wurz	11	1m 40.588s
9	Rubens Barrichello	17	1m 40.613s
10	Michael Schumacher	4	1m 40.656s
11	Toranosuke Takagi	12	1m 40.697s
12	Jean Alesi	9	1m 40.827s
13	Olivier Panis	6	1m 41.307s
14	Johnny Herbert	11	1m 41.372s
15	Jos Verstappen	13	1m 41.435s
16	Damon Hill	17	1m 41.437s
17	Mika Salo	10	1m 42.402s
18	Pedro Diniz	10	1m 43.515s
19	Jarno Trulli	12	1m 43.564s
20	Esteban Tuero	14	1m 44.279s
21	Shinji Nakano	12	1m 44.820s
22	Ricardo Rosset	6	1m 48.985s

WARM-UP

Weather: Bright and warm

Pos.	Driver	Laps	Time
1	David Coulthard	14	1m 25.632s
2	Mika Häkkinen	12	1m 25.965s
3	Michael Schumacher	17	1m 26.924s
4	Toranosuke Takagi	13	1m 27.021s
5	Eddie Irvine	16	1m 27.041s
6	Damon Hill	13	1m 27.052s
7	Ralf Schumacher	16	1m 27.054s
8	Jacques Villeneuve	12	1m 27.238s
9	Heinz-Harald Frentzen	14	1m 27.481s
10	Jarno Trulli	11	1m 27.485s
11	Alexander Wurz	12	1m 27.571s
12	Johnny Herbert	13	1m 27.667s
13	Jean Alesi	15	1m 27.712s
14	Giancarlo Fisichella	14	1m 27.845s
15	Rubens Barrichello	13	1m 27.974s
16	Olivier Panis	13	1m 27.975s
17	Mika Salo	14	1m 28.219s
18	Jos Verstappen	15	1m 28.523s
19	Pedro Diniz	11	1m 28.582s
20	Esteban Tuero	13	1m 29.273s
21	Shinji Nakano	14	1m 29.339s
22	Ricardo Rosset	10	1m 29.917s

RACE FASTEST LAPS

Weather: Fine and dry

Driver	Time	Lap
Mika Häkkinen	1m 25.139s	45
Michael Schumacher	1m 25.483s	26
David Coulthard	1m 25.959s	14
Ralf Schumacher	1m 26.194s	49
Jarno Trulli	1m 26.285s	50
Eddie Irvine	1m 26.359s	48
Jacques Villeneuve	1m 26.479s	29
Heinz-Harald Frentzen	1m 26.656s	40
Giancarlo Fisichella	1m 26.659s	41
Damon Hill	1m 26.730s	52
Jean Alesi	1m 26.840s	52
Alexander Wurz	1m 27.620s	24
Toranosuke Takagi	1m 27.726s	46
Rubens Barrichello	1m 27.770s	46
Mika Salo	1m 27.866s	25
Olivier Panis	1m 28.395s	10
Jos Verstappen	1m 28.583s	32
Johnny Herbert	1m 29.092s	10
Esteban Tuero	1m 29.093s	51
Pedro Diniz	1m 29.124s	9
Ricardo Rosset	1m 29.393s	50
Shinji Nakano	1m 29.853s	13

CHASSIS LOG BOOK

1	Villeneuve	Williams FW20/6
2	Frentzen	Williams FW20/7
	spare	Williams FW20/4
3	M. Schumacher	Ferrari F300/186
4	Irvine	Ferrari F300/184
	spare	Ferrari F300/185
5	Fisichella	Benetton B198/6
6	Wurz	Benetton B198/4
	spare	Benetton B198/5
7	Coulthard	McLaren MP4/13/6
8	Häkkinen	McLaren MP4/13/4
	spare	McLaren MP4/13/2
9	Hill	Jordan 198/4
10	R. Schumacher	Jordan 198/3
	spare	Jordan 198/5
11	Panis	Prost AP01/7
12	Trulli	Prost AP01/3
	spare	Prost AP01/2
14	Alesi	Sauber C17/6
15	Herbert	Sauber C17/2
	spare	Sauber C17/7
16	Diniz	Arrows A19/7
17	Salo	Arrows A19/6
	spare	Arrows A19/1
18	Barrichello	Stewart SF2/2
19	Verstappen	Stewart SF2/3
	spare	Stewart SF2/1
20	Rosset	Tyrrell 026/2
21	Takagi	Tyrrell 026/5
	spare	Tyrrell 026/1
22	Nakano	Minardi M198/3
23	Tuero	Minardi M198/5
	spare	Minardi M198/4

POINTS TABLES

Drivers

1 =	Mika Häkkinen	80
1 =	Michael Schumacher	80
3	David Coulthard	48
4	Eddie Irvine	38
5	Jacques Villeneuve	20
6 =	Damon Hill	17
6 =	Alexander Wurz	17
8	Giancarlo Fisichella	15
9	Ralf Schumacher	14
10	Heinz-Harald Frentzen	13
11	Jean Alesi	9
12	Rubens Barrichello	4
13 =	Mika Salo	3
13 =	Pedro Diniz	3
15 =	Johnny Herbert	1
15 =	Jan Magnussen	1
15 =	Jarno Trulli	1

Constructors

1	McLaren	128
2	Ferrari	118
3	Williams	33
4	Benetton	32
5	Jordan	31
6	Sauber	10
7	Arrows	6
8	Stewart	5
9	Prost	1

HÄKKINEN
M. SCHUMACHER
COULTHARD
IRVINE
FRENTZEN
FISICHELLA

FIA WORLD CHAMPIONSHIP • ROUND 15

LUXEMBOURG grand prix

Main photo: Michael Schumacher had much to reflect upon after a clear-cut defeat at the hands of Mika Häkkinen had dealt a crushing blow to his championship chances.

Right: The victorious Finn acknowledges Mercedes' contribution to his success before making his way to the rostrum.

Photo left: Bryn Williams Main photo: Paul-Henri Cahier

Paul-Henri Cahier

YET again the balance of F1 power was dramatically reversed in the Luxembourg Grand Prix at the Nürburgring as Mika Häkkinen took the McLaren MP4/13-Mercedes to a clear-cut and decisive win over Michael Schumacher's Ferrari F300 in front of a capacity crowd which had turned out to see the German ace take another giant stride towards the World Championship.

They trudged home in a mood of acute disappointment. In one of the most assured performances of his career, Häkkinen celebrated his 30th birthday a day early by delivering the eighth McLaren victory of the season against the odds after Schumacher and his team-mate Eddie Irvine had dominated the front row of the grid in the two scarlet Italian cars.

Häkkinen's win moved him four points ahead of Schumacher in the drivers' championship table with only ten points from the final round left to race for. Even second place to Schumacher at Suzuka would now be sufficient to clinch the title for Häkkinen as they would both have 96 points and seven victories but the McLaren driver would win on the strength of three second places to Schumacher's two.

Despite this, at the Nürburgring the Finn's prospects had initially looked unpromising. He spent practice and qualifying battling a frustrating handling imbalance but finally got everything right in the half-hour race morning warm-up. From then on Häkkinen knew that his McLaren was a potential winner.

At the start Irvine seized an immediate lead from Schumacher but he made a slight error negotiating the tight chicane at the end of the lap, a slip which allowed the German driver to neatly overtake on the short straight leading to the final corner.

At the end of the opening lap Schumacher led by 0.251s from Irvine, Häkkinen, David Coulthard's McLaren, the Benetton B198s of Giancarlo Fisichella and Alexander Wurz, Heinz-Harald Frentzen's Williams FW20 and the Jordan 198 of Ralf Schumacher. Trailing in slowly after the pack had disappeared round the second lap, Esteban Tuero's Minardi pitted to have a driveshaft changed, the young Argentine driver losing nine laps before resuming at the tail of the field.

By lap three Schumacher had opened his advantage to 2.02s and it began to look as though Häkkinen, apparently boxed in behind Irvine in third place, was in deep tactical trouble. Later Mika reflected: 'I wasn't too worried, I was just pushing. I think Eddie must have had a problem with his car, because when I was running behind him I could see it all over the place in the corners.'

Nevertheless, by the time the McLaren driver managed to outbrake Irvine very cleanly into the Veedol chicane on lap 14, Schumacher's Ferrari was 8.4s away up the road. On the face of it this was a decisive advantage. Further back there had already been some retirements among the also-rans, Pedro Diniz stopping his Arrows with hydraulic failure on lap seven while the same lap also claimed Jarno Trulli's Prost with gearbox problems.

For his part, Irvine was playing things absolutely straight. He had no intention whatsoever of becoming embroiled in any sort of controversy which might attach to blatantly holding up Häkkinen. When he allowed the McLaren through he did so because he knew that he was not realistically able to stay ahead any longer.

'Unfortunately, the understeer we got rid of over the course of the weekend came back this afternoon,' he explained. 'I could not have pushed harder or I would have gone off the track. My tyres were suffering because of this and that made the problem worse. Mika caught me a little by surprise when he got past. He seemed to close up very quickly in the last 150 metres before the chicane. I stayed on the right-hand side of the track but he managed to get by.'

On lap 16, Häkkinen trimmed Schumacher's advantage to 7.4s. Next time

Advantage Ferrari as Eddie Irvine leads team-mate Michael Schumacher on the opening lap. The Italian cars had monopolised the front row of the grid but were unable to reproduce that form on race day.

round Michael opened it back out to 8.3s as Mika lost time sliding wide over the chicane. By lap 19 the gap was stabilised at 8.0s, but two laps later it was down to 6.8s and then it shrank to 5.7s on lap 22. Schumacher was finding his handling balance simply wasn't up to scratch and there was nothing he could really do about the McLaren's superior speed.

On lap 22 Ralf Schumacher's arrival in the pit lane heralded the first spate of refuelling stops. The German driver's Jordan was stationary for 5.7s and dropped from eighth to 12th. Next time round Fisichella's Benetton made a 9.2s stop, dropping five places to tenth, and then Schumacher's Ferrari came in on lap 24.

Michael's machine was at rest for 8.6s and resumed in second place. Meanwhile Wurz dropped from fifth to tenth following an 11.5s stop and, on the next lap, Irvine made a 10.6s pit visit which demoted him from third to seventh.

When Schumacher came into the pits on lap 24 he tripped the timing line just 3.5s ahead of Häkkinen. For the next four laps Mika stayed out running times in the low 1m 20s bracket while Michael, his car still not handling perfectly, was hard pressed to lap in the mid-1m 21s area. This was the crucial stage of the race where the advantage changed hands.

On lap 28 Häkkinen made his first 8.7s refuelling stop and managed to accelerate out of the pits and into the first corner just as Schumacher arrived, the Ferrari weaving dramatically, right on his tail. It was quite remarkable to see the body language almost literally radiated from the Ferrari's cockpit. One could just sense that Michael simply couldn't work out how he'd been wrong-footed.

'I was a bit surprised that he had been able to get in front of me, because I had built up a lead of more than five seconds before I came into the pits,' he mused after the race. 'I don't know how many laps longer Mika stayed out than I had done [it

NÜRBURGRING QUALIFYING

Friday's free practice session at the Nürburgring left the McLaren-Mercedes team in a guardedly optimistic frame of mind. Mika Häkkinen set fastest time, but the Finn knew from long experience that this was merely the preliminary shadow boxing prior to what promised to be an unusually serious battle in qualifying the following day.

Yet whatever the outcome of the struggle for grid positions, McLaren was hoping to bury memories of the previous year's race when Häkkinen and David Coulthard had retired within a lap of each other with engine failures.

The roles of Coulthard and Ferrari number two Eddie Irvine inevitably stood to attract enormous scrutiny throughout the weekend. Neither had a chance of taking the title, but if there was any way they could subtly influence the outcome of the championship contest in favour of their respective team-mates they would miss no opportunity to do so.

This seemed particularly ironic as the season had started with doubts being cast over the validity of the team orders which saw Häkkinen finishing ahead of Coulthard in the Australian Grand Prix at Melbourne. The sport's governing body had since legitimised such tactics, leaving all bets off between McLaren and Ferrari from the moment qualifying began for this crucial penultimate race of the season.

Jacques Villeneuve's Williams FW20 led the field out onto the circuit ten minutes into the hour-long session, setting the first baseline on 1m 20.637s. Michael Schumacher kicked off his efforts with a huge spin on his first run after being 0.5s up at the first timing split, after which he retired to the pits for a short while.

Then Irvine went quickest on 1m 20.514s, followed by Heinz-Harald Frentzen on 1m 20.291s and Ralf Schumacher on 1m 20.132s. Häkkinen was the first to dip below the 1m 20s mark with a 1m 19.452s, but Michael Schumacher responded with a shattering 1m 18.561s on his third run after a wing change and that ended the argument for good.

'A fantastic result at this point in the season,' enthused Michael. But an equally impressive achievement was Irvine's second place on the grid. 'I still had too much understeer this morning,' said the Ulsterman, 'but we worked and worked on it and got rid of most of it for the afternoon. It's great to have only the back of Michael's car to look at on the grid.'

At the end of the day, Häkkinen was a rather downcast third, reporting that his MP4/13 had proved frustratingly slow on the last sector of the lap. 'I was never anything like happy with the car,' he said. 'In our experience problems in qualifying will be similar in the race, so we have to hope to sort it out in the warm-up and that the warm-up is dry.'

David Coulthard ended the session fifth fastest. 'Obviously disappointing,' he commented, 'but I did not manage to sort myself out into the perfect lap and had some inconsistencies from one set of tyres to another.'

Giancarlo Fisichella managed to split the McLarens in his Benetton B198 and might well have claimed third place on the grid had he not made a slight error on the last corner of his best lap, running wide from the tricky apex onto the start/finish straight. 'Today I was totally focused on qualifying on the second row,' said Fisichella, 'and I am just a little disappointed as I realised the front row was actually within reach.

'Today the tyres worked perfectly. We used the same compound as we had in Canada and Monaco, where we were really competitive and got results.'

Ralf Schumacher's Jordan-Mugen Honda qualified sixth fastest, the young German surviving a high-speed spin at the corner that had caught out his brother earlier in the session. 'I think we can be pleased with this performance,' said Ralf. 'It was frustrating to have spun on the last run, but in order to make up places you have to take risks. I said we would do well to qualify around fifth or sixth, so I am satisfied.'

Four places further back, his team-mate Damon Hill felt much less content with his efforts. 'I have not really been on form all weekend and am suffering from a bad cold, which does not help,' he explained. 'I have tried several set-up changes but cannot manage to find a balance to suit me. There is obviously nothing wrong with the car, but unfortunately I am not getting the best out of it.'

In seventh and ninth places on the grid were the Williams FW20s of Frentzen and Villeneuve, separated by Alexander Wurz's Benetton. Frentzen spent his time battling with understeer and oversteer while Villeneuve complained of excessive understeer and simply could not seem to cure it. For his part, Wurz felt quite happy with his Benetton.

Just outside the top ten, Jean Alesi and Johnny Herbert lined up 11th and 13th in their Sauber C17s. 'Our problem today is still too much understeer,' said Alesi. 'Since yesterday we have made some progress with the set-up, but we only achieved something in between Friday's performance and what we really hoped for. We found 50 per cent of what we needed.'

Herbert felt quite heartened to be only 0.2s away from the Frenchman. 'On my last run I had a very good first-sector time,' he reflected, 'but under braking for turn six the back stepped out as I downshifted, so I was on slightly the wrong line for the back straight. That cost me time and I couldn't quite make it all up again at the chicane.'

Despite complaining of poor grip levels, Rubens Barrichello did a good job with the Stewart SF2-Ford to line up 12th, six places ahead of team-mate Jos Verstappen. In the Prost-Peugeot camp Jarno Trulli looked confident as he edged out team-mate Olivier Panis, the two AP01s lining up 14th and 15th. Panis lost too much time during the morning's free practice session with a major transmission problem and simply couldn't make up for those crucial missing laps.

In the Arrows garage there was little positive to report. Mika Salo battled lack of grip to qualify his A19 in 16th place with Pedro Diniz one place further back, the Brazilian's race chassis suffering a hydraulic leak which obliged him to take the spare car for the second half of the session. At least the latest D-spec Arrows V10 engines had a trouble-free day to provide the team with a sliver of consolation.

Tora Takagi's Tyrrell pipped Shinji Nakano's Minardi for 19th place with Esteban Tuero's Minardi and Ricardo Rosset's Tyrrell rounding off the last row of the grid.

DIARY

Honda's forthcoming works F1 team is guaranteed the 12th – and last – position under the terms of the Concorde Agreement for the 2000 World Championship.

Former Jordan technical director Gary Anderson faces possible legal action after confusion as to whether he will join the Arrows or Stewart F1 teams.

Juan Pablo Montoya clinches F3000 title at Nürburgring after Nick Heidfeld is relegated to back of grid following fuel infringement in qualifying.

Just when it seemed as though the championship battle had swung in favour of Michael Schumacher, Mika Häkkinen regained the initiative, decisively outpacing his rival in the best performance of his career.

was four], but I was believing it would be enough.

'Even so, I knew it would be tight. Even if I had kept him behind me at the first stop, there would have been another chance for him to get by at the second. So overall, we have to accept that we weren't fast enough for this race.'

On lap 29 Coulthard brought the other McLaren in for its first refuelling stop, surrendering third place. David had struggled with poor handling balance almost from the start and, while he had edged closer to Irvine in the opening stages of the race, his lap times were such that he began to come under threat from both Benettons in the run-up to the first refuelling stops.

'I struggled all weekend with the car set-up,' he later explained. 'I think I was left behind by Mika the whole weekend. I didn't adopt the [chassis] set-up which he tried in the warm-up. I struggled in the race, especially when the first set of tyres started to wear.'

Jacques Villeneuve was up to third place when he made what was planned to be his sole refuelling stop on lap 31. He dropped to ninth, but the World Champion had more problems ahead. Somehow his full quota of fuel had not gone into the car at the first stop due to a rig problem, so he was back on lap 45 for a top-up, dropping from sixth to 11th. This setback effectively wiped out any chance of his finishing in the points.

During the second stint Häkkinen settled down to run around 0.8s ahead of Schumacher, the Finn picking his way through traffic with great confidence and good judgement. Coulthard had emerged from his first stop in fourth place, briefly running between Villeneuve and Irvine before the Williams driver made his refuelling stop.

Irvine was then left in fourth place ahead of a tight battle for fifth between Frentzen, Fisichella and Wurz. On lap 38 Fisichella managed to scramble ahead of the Williams only to drop back to seventh next time round after skidding on oil dropped a couple of laps earlier by Ricardo Rosset's expiring Tyrrell 026.

'That was a real shame,' shrugged the Italian after the race. 'I wanted to beat the Williams at all costs as they were only one point ahead of us in the constructors' championship. I can't be happy with sixth place when fourth was within my reach.'

On lap 42 Fisichella made his second stop, dropping to 11th, while next time round Frentzen and Wurz made refuelling stops from fifth and sixth places, resuming in ninth and 11th, now separated once more by Fisichella.

Zanardi tests F1 Williams

DOUBLE CART champion Alex Zanardi impressed the Williams team with his intelligent and versatile approach on his first F1 test in one of the Mecachrome-engined FW20s at Barcelona's Circuit de Catalunya during the week following the Luxembourg Grand Prix.

The 31-year-old Italian, who had signed a three-year contract to drive for Williams from the start of 1999, set a best time of 1m 24.43s, fractionally slower than regular test drivers Juan Pablo Montoya and Max Wilson.

'From a pure technical point of view, the most important thing was to adapt to a two-pedal set-up with left-foot braking,' said Zanardi. 'I never did it before. The cars also require more precision. It requires you to brake every time at the same point and to go on the power every time at the same point.'

Zanardi began testing on the Tuesday morning and finished mid-afternoon the following day in order to return to the USA for Sunday's CART race at Houston, Texas. He would not thereafter be able to test for Williams until early December, when he would be joined by his new team-mate Ralf Schumacher.

'I think we were surprised how quickly he adapted to the car,' said Patrick Head. 'He said he didn't really like the left-foot braking set-up, but it was a case of "Sorry, chap, but it's not possible to change it on this car." Perhaps we can think about it for the FW21, but our two current drivers prefer it.

'Alex was lucid and logical. It was a good test, run as usual with lots of fuel in the car and not too many new sets of tyres thrown at it. His only real problem was that his neck was aching by the end. CART ovals all involve fast left-hand corners whereas the quick turns at Barcelona are all right-handers.'

Ecclestone: his bond is the word

AS the battle for the World Championship neared its climax, Bernie Ecclestone's Formula 1 empire launched plans for a new bond issue on the London stock exchange which could raise as much as £1.2 billion to fund the expansion of the digital television technology which the FIA Vice-President's group has pioneered over the past couple of years.

Not only did this move apparently pave the way for a full stock market flotation of Bernie's business interests, shelved in 1997 but now rescheduled to take place in two or three years' time, it also fuelled continuing speculation that the multi-millionaire plans to expand into the football world if the planned European Super League comes to fruition.

The new F1 bonds were being issued by Formula 1 Finance BV, which is based outside the UK. Moneys raised from these bonds would be held by an Ecclestone family trust set up for Bernie's wife Slavicia and daughters Tamara and Petra. Bernie's solicitor Stephen Mullens said, 'The trust is not based in the UK and does not pay UK tax.'

Mullens also explained that he felt the bonds would help the City better understand the nature of F1's business in preparation for a full stock exchange listing. He described the decision to issue the bonds, which were to be secured on future revenues from pay-per-view television, as the first step towards building a firm investor base.

One of the problems facing the earlier efforts to float the F1 business was a European Commission investigation into Ecclestone's long-term control of international motor racing's broadcasting rights. However, Mullens explained that the flotation's delay did not relate to this investigation. 'We have a very good record of working with them and I don't see any problems with the EU,' he insisted.

This left the order Häkkinen, Michael Schumacher, Coulthard, Irvine, Ralf Schumacher and Villeneuve, followed by Damon Hill's Jordan and Jean Alesi's Sauber.

On lap 47 Michael made his second 7.4s refuelling stop, during which a front wing adjustment was made to help improve the handling balance. Next time round Häkkinen made his own second stop in 6.9s, slipping back into the race 2.93s ahead of the Ferrari. Ralf Schumacher and Alesi also made their second stops from fifth and seventh places, rejoining the race in sixth and 11th.

When Irvine came in on lap 49, Hill's Jordan was up to fourth, but the Englishman dropped to tenth at his second refuelling stop at the end of lap 51. That left Ralf a strong fifth ahead of the key Williams and Benetton opposition, but the young German driver's great home run ended on lap 53 when he retired with a broken disc bell.

'Very disappointing,' he admitted afterwards. 'My start was not perfect, but we managed to make up several places thanks to an excellent pit stop strategy. The brakes were quite soft for a while and I tried to save them for the last dozen or so laps, but I was not able to.'

On lap 52 Coulthard had made his second refuelling stop, retaining third place, after which the race ran through to its finish without any further drama. In the closing stages the track was brushed by a few light spots of rain, but it was nothing significant. After sustaining an advantage of around five seconds over the last few laps, Häkkinen rolled it right off to win by just 2.2s after 67 laps. It was a sweet moment indeed for the Finn, who, after all, had yet to relinquish the World Championship lead he had held since the first race of the year.

Coulthard, Irvine, Frentzen and Fisichella completed the top six points-scoring positions. In seventh place, Wurz felt extremely disappointed. 'It is not a great result,' he said. 'In my first pit stop I couldn't engage first gear. I don't know why this happened, but I lost a few seconds. Giancarlo and I had a good battle with Frentzen, but towards the end of the race I had some trouble with the brakes and couldn't push as hard as I would have liked.'

Eighth place fell to the frustrated Villeneuve while Hill trailed home ninth, unable to work out a decent handling balance all weekend. In tenth place Alesi was surprisingly sanguine about the performance of his Sauber C17. 'It's just a shame that F1 is so competitive at the moment,' he said. 'Our lap times were good, but things are so close that everything must be right in practice and qualifying, not just the race.'

Team-mate Johnny Herbert retired with a broken engine after 37 laps while the Stewart-Fords of Rubens Barrichello and Jos Verstappen sandwiched Olivier Panis's Prost in 11th and 13th places.

Both Stewart drivers suffered from a consistent lack of grip throughout the race, Rubens opting for a one-stop strategy while Verstappen made two refuelling stops. Completing the list of finishers were Mika Salo's Arrows A19, Shinji Nakano's Minardi and the Tyrrell-Ford of Toranosuke Takagi. Tuero was still running at the chequered flag, 11 laps down on the winner, but was not classified.

Back in the paddock the delighted McLaren-Mercedes team celebrated noisily. The Ferrari squad, for its part, was left quietly to reflect on a day when the cooler ambient temperature caught them and their choice of Goodyear rubber off-guard. As Michael Schumacher's facial expression on the rostrum made plain, the Nürburgring weekend was not supposed to have finished like this at all.

GROSSER WARSTEINER PREIS VON LUXEMBURG

25–27 SEPTEMBER 1998

NÜRBURGRING

Race distance: 67 laps, 189.664 miles/305.235 km

Race weather: Cool, light overcast

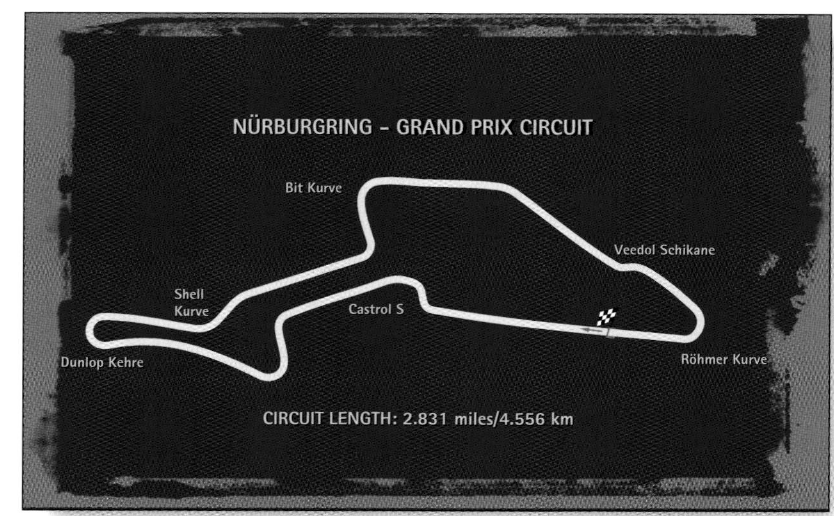

Pos.	Driver	Nat.	No.	Entrant	Car/Engine	Tyres	Laps	Time/Retirement	Speed (mph/km/h)
1	**Mika Häkkinen**	**SF**	**8**	**West McLaren Mercedes**	**McLaren MP4/13-Mercedes FO110G V10**	**B**	**67**	**1h 32m 14.789s**	**123.363/198.534**
2	**Michael Schumacher**	**D**	**3**	**Scuderia Ferrari Marlboro**	**Ferrari F300 047 V10**	**G**	**67**	**1h 32m 17.000s**	**123.314/198.455**
3	**David Coulthard**	**GB**	**7**	**West McLaren Mercedes**	**McLaren MP4/13-Mercedes FO110G V10**	**B**	**67**	**1h 32m 48.952s**	**122.606/197.316**
4	**Eddie Irvine**	**GB**	**4**	**Scuderia Ferrari Marlboro**	**Ferrari F300 047 V10**	**G**	**67**	**1h 33m 12.971s**	**122.080/196.469**
5	**Heinz-Harald Frentzen**	**D**	**2**	**Winfield Williams**	**Williams FW20-Mecachrome GC37/01 V10**	**G**	**67**	**1h 33m 15.036s**	**122.034/196.396**
6	**Giancarlo Fisichella**	**I**	**5**	**Mild Seven Benetton Playlife**	**Benetton B198-Playlife V10**	**B**	**67**	**1h 33m 16.148s**	**122.010/196.357**
7	Alexander Wurz	A	6	Mild Seven Benetton Playlife	Benetton B198-Playlife V10	B	67	1h 33m 19.578s	121.936/196.237
8	Jacques Villeneuve	CDN	1	Winfield Williams	Williams FW20-Mecachrome GC37/01 V10	G	66		
9	Damon Hill	GB	9	B&H Jordan Mugen Honda	Jordan 198-Mugen Honda MF310C V10	G	66		
10	Jean Alesi	F	14	Red Bull Sauber Petronas	Sauber C17-Petronas SPE01D V10	G	66		
11	Rubens Barrichello	BR	18	Stewart Ford	Stewart SF2-Ford Zetec-R V10	B	65		
12	Olivier Panis	F	11	Gauloises Prost Peugeot	Prost AP01-Peugeot A16 V10	B	65		
13	Jos Verstappen	NL	19	Stewart Ford	Stewart SF2-Ford Zetec-R V10	B	65		
14	Mika Salo	SF	17	Danka Zepter Arrows	Arrows A19 V10	B	65		
15	Shinji Nakano	J	22	Fondmetal Minardi Ford	Minardi M198-Ford Zetec-R V10	B	65		
16	Toranosuke Takagi	J	21	Tyrrell Ford	Tyrrell 026-Ford Zetec-R V10	G	65		
	Esteban Tuero	RA	23	Fondmetal Minardi Ford	Minardi M198-Ford Zetec-R V10	B	56		
	Ralf Schumacher	D	10	B&H Jordan Mugen Honda	Jordan 198-Mugen Honda MF310C V10	G	53	Brake disc	
	Johnny Herbert	GB	15	Red Bull Sauber Petronas	Sauber C17-Petronas SPE01D V10	G	37	Engine	
	Ricardo Rosset	BR	20	Tyrrell Ford	Tyrrell 026-Ford Zetec-R V10	G	36	Engine	
	Jarno Trulli	I	12	Gauloises Prost Peugeot	Prost AP01-Peugeot A16 V10	B	6	Gearbox	
	Pedro Diniz	BR	16	Danka Zepter Arrows	Arrows A19 V10	B	6	Hydraulics	

Fastest lap: Häkkinen, on lap 25, 1m 20.450s, 126.680 mph/203.873 km/h.

Lap record: Heinz-Harald Frentzen (F1 Williams FW19-Renault V10), 1m 18.805s, 129.324 mph/208.128 km/h (1997).

B – Bridgestone G – Goodyear

All results and data © FIA 1998

Grid order	1	2	3	4	5	6	7	8	9	10	11	12	13	14	15	16	17	18	19	20	21	22	23	24	25	26	27	28	29	30	31	32	33	34	35	36	37	38	39	40	41	42	43	44	45	46	47	48	49	50
3 M. SCHUMACHER	3	3	3	3	3	3	3	3	3	3	3	3	3	3	3	3	3	3	3	3	3	3	3	3	8	8	8	8	8	8	8	8	8	8	8	8	8	8	8	8	8	8	8	8	8	8	8	8	8	8
4 IRVINE	4	4	4	4	4	4	4	4	4	4	4	4	4	8	8	8	8	8	8	8	8	8	8	8	3	3	3	3	3	3	3	3	3	3	3	3	3	3	3	3	3	3	3	3	3	3	3	3	3	3
8 HÄKKINEN	8	8	8	8	8	8	8	8	8	8	8	8	8	4	4	4	4	4	4	4	4	4	4	4	7	7	7	7	7	1	1	7	7	7	7	7	7	7	7	7	7	7	7	7	7	7	7	7	7	7
5 FISICHELLA	7	7	7	7	7	7	7	7	7	7	7	7	7	7	7	7	7	7	7	7	7	7	7	7	4	2	1	1	1	7	7	4	4	4	4	4	4	4	4	4	4	4	4	4	4	4	4	4	4	9
7 COULTHARD	5	5	5	5	5	5	5	5	5	5	5	5	5	5	5	5	5	5	5	5	5	5	6	6	2	1	4	4	4	4	4	2	2	2	2	2	2	5	2	2	2	2	2	10	10	10	10	10	9	4
10 R. SCHUMACHER	6	6	6	6	6	6	6	6	6	6	6	6	6	6	6	6	6	6	6	6	6	6	5	2	1	9	2	2	2	2	2	5	5	5	5	5	5	2	6	6	6	6	6	1	1	9	9	9	10	10
2 FRENTZEN	2	2	2	2	2	2	2	2	2	2	2	2	2	2	2	2	2	2	2	2	2	2	2	1	9	4	5	5	5	5	5	6	6	6	6	6	6	6	5	5	5	5	10	9	9	14	14	14	2	2
6 WURZ	10	10	10	10	10	10	10	10	10	10	10	10	10	10	10	10	10	10	10	10	10	10	1	9	14	14	6	6	6	6	6	10	10	10	10	10	10	10	10	10	10	10	1	14	14	2	2	2	5	5
1 VILLENEUVE	1	1	1	1	1	1	1	1	1	1	1	1	1	1	1	1	1	1	1	1	1	1	9	14	5	5	14	10	10	10	10	1	1	1	1	1	1	1	1	1	1	1	9	2	2	5	5	5	6	6
9 HILL	9	9	9	9	9	9	9	9	9	9	9	9	9	9	9	9	9	9	9	9	9	9	14	5	6	6	10	9	9	9	9	9	9	9	9	9	9	9	9	9	9	9	14	5	5	6	6	6	1	1
14 ALESI	18	18	18	18	14	14	14	14	14	14	14	14	14	14	14	14	14	14	14	14	14	14	15	15	15	10	9	14	14	14	14	14	14	14	14	14	14	14	14	14	14	14	5	6	6	1	1	1	14	14
18 BARRICHELLO	14	14	14	14	15	15	15	15	15	15	15	15	15	15	15	15	15	15	15	15	15	15	10	10	10	15	15	15	15	15	15	15	15	15	15	15	15	18	18	18	18	18	18	18	18	18	18	18	18	18
15 HERBERT	15	15	15	15	18	18	18	18	18	18	18	18	18	18	18	18	18	18	18	18	18	18	18	18	18	18	18	18	18	18	18	18	18	18	18	18	18	22	11	11	11	11	11	21	21	11	11	11	11	11
12 TRULLI	12	12	12	12	12	12	11	11	11	11	11	11	11	11	11	11	11	11	11	11	11	11	11	11	11	22	22	22	22	22	22	22	22	22	22	22	22	11	19	19	19	19	19	11	11	19	19	19	19	19
11 PANIS	16	16	16	16	16	16	19	19	19	19	19	19	19	19	19	19	19	19	19	19	19	17	17	17	17	11	11	11	11	11	11	11	11	11	11	11	11	19	22	17	17	17	21	19	19	17	17	17	17	17
17 SALO	11	11	11	11	11	11	17	17	17	17	17	17	17	17	17	17	17	17	17	17	17	19	22	22	22	19	19	19	19	19	19	19	19	19	19	19	19	17	17	21	21	21	17	17	17	22	22	22	22	22
16 DINIZ	19	19	19	19	19	19	21	21	21	21	21	21	21	21	21	21	21	21	21	21	21	21	19	19	19	17	17	17	17	17	17	17	17	17	17	17	17	21	21	22	22	22	22	22	22	21	21	21	21	21
19 VERSTAPPEN	17	17	17	17	17	17	22	22	22	22	22	22	22	22	22	22	22	22	22	22	22	22	21	21	21	21	21	21	21	21	21	21	21	21	21	21	21	23	23	23	23	23	23	23	23	23	23	23	23	23
21 TAKAGI	21	21	21	21	21	21	20	20	20	20	20	20	20	20	20	20	20	20	20	20	20	20	20	20	20	20	20	20	20	20	20	20	20	20	20	20	23													
22 NAKANO	22	22	22	22	22	22	23	23	23	23	23	23	23	23	23	23	23	23	23	23	23	23	23	23	23	23	23	23	23	23	23	23	23	23	23	23														
23 TUERO	20	20	20	20	20	20																																												
20 ROSSET	23	23	23	23	23	23																																												

Pit stop

One lap behind leader

STARTING GRID

3 **M. SCHUMACHER** Ferrari	4 **IRVINE** Ferrari
8 **HÄKKINEN** McLaren	5 **FISICHELLA** Benetton
7 **COULTHARD** McLaren	10 **R. SCHUMACHER** Jordan
2 **FRENTZEN** Williams	6 **WURZ** Benetton
1 **VILLENEUVE** Williams	9 **HILL** Jordan
14 **ALESI** Sauber	18 **BARRICHELLO** Stewart
15 **HERBERT** Sauber	12 **TRULLI** Prost
11 **PANIS** Prost	17 **SALO** Arrows
16 **DINIZ** Arrows	19 **VERSTAPPEN** Stewart
21 **TAKAGI** Tyrrell	22 **NAKANO** Minardi
23 **TUERO** Minardi	20 **ROSSET** Tyrrell

4	55	56	57	58	59	60	61	62	63	64	65	66	67	●
8	8	8	8	8	8	8	8	8	8	8	8	8	8	1
3	3	3	3	3	3	3	3	3	3	3	3	3	3	2
7	7	7	7	7	7	7	7	7	7	7	7	7	7	3
4	4	4	4	4	4	4	4	4	4	4	4	4	4	4
2	2	2	2	2	2	2	2	2	2	2	2	2	2	5
5	5	5	5	5	5	5	5	5	5	5	5	5	5	6
6	6	6	6	6	6	6	6	6	6	6	6	6	6	
1	1	1	1	1	1	1	1	1	1	1	1	1		
9	9	9	9	9	9	9	9	9	9	9	9	9		
4	14	14	14	14	14	14	14	14	14	14	14	14		
8	18	18	18	18	18	18	18	18	18	18	18			
1	11	11	11	11	11	11	11	11	11	11	11			
9	19	19	19	19	19	19	19	19	19	19	19			
7	17	17	17	17	17	17	17	17	17	17	17			
2	22	22	22	22	22	22	22	22	22	22	22			
1	21	21	21	21	21	21	21	21	21	21	21			
3	23	23												

FOR THE RECORD

150th Grand Prix start

Jean Alesi

TIME SHEETS

QUALIFYING

Weather: Light overcast

Pos.	Driver	Car	Laps	Time
1	Michael Schumacher	Ferrari	11	1m 18.561s
2	Eddie Irvine	Ferrari	12	1m 18.907s
3	Mika Häkkinen	McLaren-Mercedes	12	1m 18.940s
4	Giancarlo Fisichella	Benetton-Playlife	12	1m 19.048s
5	David Coulthard	McLaren-Mercedes	12	1m 19.169s
6	Ralf Schumacher	Jordan-Mugen Honda	11	1m 19.455s
7	Heinz-Harald Frentzen	Williams-Mecachrome	12	1m 19.522s
8	Alexander Wurz	Benetton-Playlife	12	1m 19.569s
9	Jacques Villeneuve	Williams-Mecachrome	12	1m 19.631s
10	Damon Hill	Jordan-Mugen Honda	12	1m 19.807s
11	Jean Alesi	Sauber-Petronas	11	1m 20.493s
12	Rubens Barrichello	Stewart-Ford	12	1m 20.530s
13	Johnny Herbert	Sauber-Petronas	12	1m 20.650s
14	Jarno Trulli	Prost-Peugeot	12	1m 20.709s
15	Olivier Panis	Prost-Peugeot	12	1m 21.048s
16	Mika Salo	Arrows	12	1m 21.120s
17	Pedro Diniz	Arrows	12	1m 21.258s
18	Jos Verstappen	Stewart-Ford	12	1m 21.501s
19	Toranosuke Takagi	Tyrrell-Ford	12	1m 21.525s
20	Shinji Nakano	Minardi-Ford	12	1m 22.078s
21	Esteban Tuero	Minardi-Ford	12	1m 22.146s
22	Ricardo Rosset	Tyrrell-Ford	12	1m 22.822s

FRIDAY FREE PRACTICE

Weather: Bright and sunny

Pos.	Driver	Laps	Time
1	Mika Häkkinen	26	1m 19.689s
2	Giancarlo Fisichella	34	1m 20.325s
3	Jacques Villeneuve	35	1m 20.326s
4	Michael Schumacher	32	1m 20.461s
5	David Coulthard	28	1m 20.577s
6	Eddie Irvine	33	1m 20.841s
7	Alexander Wurz	37	1m 21.014s
8	Heinz-Harald Frentzen	35	1m 21.174s
9	Ralf Schumacher	22	1m 21.351s
10	Olivier Panis	44	1m 21.391s
11	Rubens Barrichello	28	1m 21.538s
12	Damon Hill	41	1m 21.738s
13	Jarno Trulli	47	1m 21.764s
14	Jean Alesi	38	1m 21.952s
15	Pedro Diniz	41	1m 22.485s
16	Jos Verstappen	25	1m 22.566s
17	Johnny Herbert	31	1m 22.603s
18	Toranosuke Takagi	35	1m 22.792s
19	Shinji Nakano	39	1m 22.967s
20	Esteban Tuero	43	1m 23.331s
21	Ricardo Rosset	27	1m 23.644s
22	Mika Salo	25	1m 24.004s

SATURDAY FREE PRACTICE

Weather: Wet, drying, then sunny

Pos.	Driver	Laps	Time
1	Mika Häkkinen	23	1m 19.850s
2	Michael Schumacher	11	1m 19.925s
3	Ralf Schumacher	33	1m 20.327s
4	David Coulthard	30	1m 20.388s
5	Jacques Villeneuve	27	1m 20.457s
6	Heinz-Harald Frentzen	33	1m 20.646s
7	Alexander Wurz	25	1m 20.819s
8	Giancarlo Fisichella	28	1m 20.834s
9	Jarno Trulli	33	1m 20.953s
10	Eddie Irvine	37	1m 20.982s
11	Damon Hill	37	1m 21.050s
12	Jean Alesi	32	1m 21.427s
13	Johnny Herbert	27	1m 21.649s
14	Mika Salo	28	1m 21.704s
15	Pedro Diniz	29	1m 21.781s
16	Rubens Barrichello	24	1m 22.276s
17	Jos Verstappen	21	1m 22.399s
18	Esteban Tuero	36	1m 22.893s
19	Toranosuke Takagi	32	1m 22.968s
20	Shinji Nakano	32	1m 23.019s
21	Olivier Panis	27	1m 23.928s
22	Ricardo Rosset	19	1m 25.570s

WARM-UP

Weather: Overcast and cool

Pos.	Driver	Laps	Time
1	Mika Häkkinen	15	1m 20.396s
2	David Coulthard	15	1m 20.915s
3	Giancarlo Fisichella	14	1m 21.362s
4	Michael Schumacher	15	1m 21.515s
5	Eddie Irvine	14	1m 21.636s
6	Alexander Wurz	19	1m 21.870s
7	Ralf Schumacher	13	1m 22.206s
8	Jacques Villeneuve	12	1m 22.257s
9	Jean Alesi	13	1m 22.278s
10	Heinz-Harald Frentzen	16	1m 22.352s
11	Damon Hill	16	1m 22.582s
12	Jos Verstappen	13	1m 22.698s
13	Johnny Herbert	15	1m 22.716s
14	Rubens Barrichello	15	1m 23.104s
15	Jarno Trulli	17	1m 23.112s
16	Olivier Panis	12	1m 23.248s
17	Pedro Diniz	14	1m 23.398s
18	Shinji Nakano	15	1m 23.555s
19	Mika Salo	12	1m 23.997s
20	Esteban Tuero	15	1m 24.178s
21	Toranosuke Takagi	16	1m 24.333s
22	Ricardo Rosset	13	1m 25.225s

RACE FASTEST LAPS

Weather: Cool, light overcast

Driver	Time	Lap
Mika Häkkinen	1m 20.450s	25
David Coulthard	1m 20.715s	61
Michael Schumacher	1m 21.001s	65
Heinz-Harald Frentzen	1m 21.394s	65
Giancarlo Fisichella	1m 21.506s	65
Eddie Irvine	1m 21.667s	62
Jacques Villeneuve	1m 21.701s	33
Damon Hill	1m 21.741s	66
Alexander Wurz	1m 21.778s	61
Ralf Schumacher	1m 21.881s	21
Jean Alesi	1m 21.979s	43
Johnny Herbert	1m 22.712s	23
Olivier Panis	1m 22.931s	61
Toranosuke Takagi	1m 23.392s	47
Rubens Barrichello	1m 23.412s	33
Mika Salo	1m 23.552s	23
Jos Verstappen	1m 23.944s	30
Esteban Tuero	1m 24.024s	50
Ricardo Rosset	1m 24.161s	23
Shinji Nakano	1m 24.210s	61
Pedro Diniz	1m 25.285s	5
Jarno Trulli	1m 25.328s	4

CHASSIS LOG BOOK

1	Villeneuve	Williams FW20/6
2	Frentzen	Williams FW20/7
	spare	Williams FW20/4
3	M. Schumacher	Ferrari F300/189
4	Irvine	Ferrari F300/184
	spares	Ferrari F300/187 & 186
5	Fisichella	Benetton B198/6
6	Wurz	Benetton B198/4
	spare	Benetton B198/5
7	Coulthard	McLaren MP4/13/6
8	Häkkinen	McLaren MP4/13/4
	spare	McLaren MP4/13/2
9	Hill	Jordan 198/4
10	R. Schumacher	Jordan 198/3
	spare	Jordan 198/5
11	Panis	Prost AP01/7
12	Trulli	Prost AP01/6
	spare	Prost AP01/2
14	Alesi	Sauber C17/6
15	Herbert	Sauber C17/2
	spare	Sauber C17/3
16	Diniz	Arrows A19/7
17	Salo	Arrows A19/6
	spare	Arrows A19/1
18	Barrichello	Stewart SF2/5
19	Verstappen	Stewart SF2/2
	spare	Stewart SF2/3
20	Rosset	Tyrrell 026/1
21	Takagi	Tyrrell 026/5
	spare	Tyrrell 026/4
22	Nakano	Minardi M198/3
23	Tuero	Minardi M198/5
	spare	Minardi M198/2

POINTS TABLES

Drivers

1	Mika Häkkinen	90
2	Michael Schumacher	86
3	David Coulthard	52
4	Eddie Irvine	41
5	Jacques Villeneuve	20
6 =	Damon Hill	17
6 =	Alexander Wurz	17
8	Giancarlo Fisichella	16
9	Heinz-Harald Frentzen	15
10	Ralf Schumacher	14
11	Jean Alesi	9
12	Rubens Barrichello	4
13 =	Mika Salo	3
13 =	Pedro Diniz	3
15 =	Johnny Herbert	1
15 =	Jan Magnussen	1
15 =	Jarno Trulli	1

Constructors

1	McLaren	142
2	Ferrari	127
3	Williams	35
4	Benetton	33
5	Jordan	31
6	Sauber	10
7	Arrows	6
8	Stewart	5
9	Prost	1

JAPANESE

As the field sets off on its third parade lap after two earlier attempts to start the race had been aborted, Michael Schumacher's pole-position Ferrari remains stationary, its path blocked by an official displaying a yellow flag. As a punishment for causing the second false start, the German was consigned to the back of the grid, leaving his World Championship hopes in ruins.

MIKA Häkkinen clinched the 1998 Formula 1 World Championship with a flawless flag-to-flag victory in the Japanese Grand Prix, a success which gave the McLaren team its first constructors' title since the late Ayrton Senna took his third and final championship crown in this same race seven years earlier.

For Michael Schumacher and the Ferrari team, a last-ditch bid to secure Maranello's first drivers' title since 1979 ended in abject disaster. After being obliged to start from the back of the grid after stalling his pole-position F300, Schumacher recovered to third place before suffering a high-speed tyre failure on the start/finish straight after running over debris from a collision between two slower cars.

In a lurid episode frighteningly like Nigel Mansell's escape after an outwardly similar failure during the 1986 Australian Grand Prix, Schumacher controlled his wayward three-wheeler with deft confidence and brought it safely to a halt at the side of the track.

For the second successive season his efforts to win the title for Ferrari had been thwarted. It was also an unfortunate note on which to end Goodyear's 34-year association with motor racing's most senior category as the tyre company withdrew from F1 after the race in line with a decision made almost one year earlier.

Watched approvingly by his mentor and manager, former World Champion Keke Rosberg, the only other Finn to have won the F1 title, back in 1982, 30-year-old Häkkinen dominated the race with unruffled composure.

'I don't know how to start explaining my feelings,' he confessed. 'It was easier than some of the races have been this year. I have been in much more difficult situations than at this Grand Prix, but obviously I was aware this morning of the pressure that was falling on me.

'It was disturbing my performance a little bit, which I would say is quite normal, but then I seemed to calm down quite a lot and it was quite easy to control the situation. But there is always one problem when you are leading easily like that – and it happened to me with about ten laps to go – which is the tendency for your mind to start thinking about other things. I almost started whistling inside the car . . .'

A tingling sense of anticipation could almost be felt through the track surface itself as Häkkinen's sleek grey

From the outset, qualifying at Suzuka was destined to be a no-holds-barred confrontation between McLaren-Mercedes and Ferrari with a crackling tension between the two teams almost hanging in the air like static electricity.

Friday's free practice session ended with Michael Schumacher's Ferrari F300 ahead of younger brother Ralf's Jordan, with Heinz-Harald Frentzen's Williams third ahead of Eddie Irvine in the other Ferrari. Michael opted for the harder of the two Goodyear compounds, but come Saturday's qualifying session he made a late switch to the softer rubber, knowing this was the only really feasible strategy to stay on terms with the McLarens.

Expectations ran high at the start of the hour-long battle for pole position and there was to be little in the way of disappointment. Five minutes into the session Mika Häkkinen set the ball rolling by taking his McLaren MP4/13 round in 1m 37.095s. In the media centre there were gasps of sheer disbelief. This was 1.6s quicker than he had managed during the morning's free practice session.

Hardly had the dust settled on the Finn's achievement than Ralf Schumacher popped up in contention, posting a 1m 39.053s to go second fastest, almost immediately displaced by Frentzen's Williams FW20. The Williams team had introduced a whole raft of technical changes for this race including a longer wheelbase, new diffuser and much higher barge boards. The signs were that they were an improvement and, on this occasion, Frentzen seemed to have the measure of team-mate Jacques Villeneuve.

Irvine went out for his first run when the session was 16 minutes old. He set fourth-quickest time in 1m 38.850s, but then Schumacher seemingly rewrote the terms of battle by recording a 1m 36.769s. It looked quick enough to be the final word.

Häkkinen had other ideas, however, launching a ferocious counter-attack. On his second run the Finn was 0.002s inside Schumacher's best at the second split only to lose precious fractions at the tight chicane and end up on 1m 36.855s. Michael then raised the stakes on 1m 36.293s, an absolutely sensational performance which brought him precious close to the 1997 Japanese GP pole time of 1m 36.071s.

Häkkinen responded with a 1m 36.471s – not quite good enough. Then he took a gamble. He removed a touch of front downforce in a bid to pick up a little more straightline speed. It looked as though it might pay off, but his final efforts came to grief when he understeered off the track on a tight right-hander and had to concede pole to his title rival. The Ferrari pit duly radioed to Schumacher that Mika's challenge had been blunted and he aborted his final lap as a result.

The predictions, press conferences and general pre-event hype, which had built up a ferocious head of steam during the five-week lay-off since the season's penultimate Grand Prix at the Nürburgring, were now over. All that remained to be seen was whether Häkkinen, one of the best drivers in the very best car, could beat the very best driver in not quite the best car.

Ferrari President Luca di Montezemolo had made the trip to Japan to lend added weight to Schumacher's efforts. If the German could win the first drivers' World Championship for the famous Maranello team since Jody Scheckter's title success 19 years earlier, it would represent the ultimate accolade for di Montezemolo, who took over at the company's helm in 1992.

'To be honest, if it wasn't for Michael, we wouldn't be close,' said Irvine with his customary candour. 'The McLaren is potentially a second a lap faster than our car. Häkkinen can only lose this championship while Michael can win it.'

A Ferrari World Championship would also represent a suitably high note on which for Goodyear to bow off the F1 stage after more than 30 years. From the start of 1999 Bridgestone will take over as F1 racing's sole tyre supplier with Goodyear's record of 368 Grand Prix wins at which to aim from a position some way in arrears. After Suzuka its modest tally stood at nine victories.

Schumacher was delighted with his pole-winning efforts.

'We didn't do many laps, but the session went pretty well to expectations,' he enthused. 'It is incredible we are doing the same sort of lap times which we were doing last year. It was great fun throwing the car around during this session.'

Irvine was disappointed to be so far off in fourth place, reporting that his car generally seemed to lack speed. Yet he ran new tyres for the first time that day at the start of qualifying. Conserving as many sets as possible seemed to be the number one priority.

'I wouldn't like to be Mika tomorrow,' said Irvine with a grin. 'We have lots in store, lots of little party tricks. Watch this space!'

Häkkinen and David Coulthard qualified their McLaren-Mercedes in second and third places, the Finn aborting his final run after that slide onto the grass. Coulthard explained that his car had felt much better in qualifying after he had successfully dialled out the understeer which frustrated his efforts during Friday's practice session.

'Naturally I am a little disappointed, but being second is not such a big problem,' said Häkkinen. 'My last lap was pretty quick until I went wide and I am annoyed with myself, especially as the conditions were ideal for the tyres and the car was handling really well.'

For his part Coulthard was just relieved to have won the battle of the number twos, ending up significantly quicker than Irvine's Ferrari. 'I am losing some time through the first sector, but as I only managed one proper run in qualifying there is plenty of scope for improvement,' he admitted.

Frentzen emerged 'best of the rest' to qualify fifth in his Williams FW20 despite a lurid slide onto the gravel on his final run. 'Ralf Schumacher blocked me for the second time in the session, which was very frustrating as I was one-tenth of a second quicker up to that point and had a good chance of perhaps pushing Irvine out of fourth place,' he said.

Villeneuve still did not have his car balanced out as well as he had hoped and wound up 0.2s slower than his German colleague. 'We finally got the car working for qualifying, which was a little bit late,' said the outgoing World Champion. 'I am personally not very pleased with my lap because I didn't get the best out of the car.'

The Jordan-Mugen Hondas of Ralf Schumacher and Damon Hill set seventh- and eighth-fastest times, the pair complaining that they suffered badly from a lack of mechanical grip negotiating the chicane. This was a disappointment for both drivers, who had a further-uprated-spec Mugen V10 for qualifying and the race and had hoped to be able to challenge for top positions behind the leading quartet.

'We always knew it would be very tough to get on terms with Williams and Ferrari,' said Ralf, who stood to be given his race car as a parting present by the team in the event of his winning the Grand Prix. 'Seventh place is not what we had hoped for, but I ran right at the limit and could not make any improvement on my time.'

Hill agreed: 'Everyone in the team was pushing to the absolute maximum and our car was on the limit, so I don't think there was anything more we could have done. Our biggest problem was mechanical grip, which cost us time in the slow-speed corners.'

Alexander Wurz and Giancarlo Fisichella completed the top ten in their Benetton-Playlifes. Fisichella reported that he was pushing to the absolute limit and eventually spun after wrestling with understeer in fast corners and oversteer in the slower turns in addition to a general lack of grip. Wurz also complained about being held up by traffic.

Just outside the top ten came the Sauber-Petronas duo, Johnny Herbert and Jean Alesi. The Englishman was quite happy to make the sixth row of the grid despite problems in traffic while Alesi ran out of fuel on his slowing-down lap at the end of the session.

Side by side on the seventh row were the two Prost-Peugeots, Olivier Panis in the standard AP01 just pipping his team-mate's 'B' spec development car. Panis said his car felt quite well balanced, despite a trip over the chicane kerb, and Trulli confirmed that he was making progress with the new chassis after a succession of niggling problems on Friday.

Mika Salo was the fastest Arrows driver in 15th place, struggling with grip in the slower corners, while the Stewart-Fords of Rubens Barrichello and Jos Verstappen lined up in 16th and 19th, unable to make any worthwhile progress on this demanding track. They were split by Tora Takagi, who was spearheading the Tyrrell team's very last F1 outing, and Pedro Diniz, who was suffering badly with flu as he wrestled with the second Arrows A19. Right at the back were both Minardis, with Ricardo Rosset failing to make the 107 per cent cut in his Tyrrell-Ford.

Honda F1 programme gets into gear

WHILE Ferrari and McLaren fought for the 1998 World Championship, Honda's factory-backed F1 project was getting into its stride under the guidance of former Tyrrell team manager Rupert Manwaring, who confirmed at Suzuka that the team's test chassis would be ready to run early in the New Year.

The Dallara-built car will spend most of 1999 spearheading the team's development programme. It is expected that the definitive race chassis for the 2000 season will be developed under the direction of former Tyrrell technical chief Harvey Postlethwaite.

'We have made no decision yet about test drivers,' said Manwaring. 'We will just wait for the dust to settle and see who is available at the end of the day. We don't think there will be any shortage of suitable candidates.'

Manwaring said he thought there would be no obvious problems if Mugen Honda continued to service the Jordan team in 2000. 'It might give us something to aim for, a useful yardstick,' he said. 'Either way, eventually our aim is to beat the opposition, whoever they might be.'

Honda withdrew from Grand Prix racing at the end of the 1992 season, bringing to a close a five-year partnership with McLaren. Since then the Japanese company had been involved in F1 through Hirotoshi Honda's Mugen facility.

Undaunted by the size of the task now facing him, Michael Schumacher scythed through the field until he came up to the Jordan of Damon Hill, who was engaged in a fierce battle with Jacques Villeneuve for fifth place.

Unable to find a way past, the German lost all chance of catching race leader Mika Häkkinen, and his gallant championship challenge was finally snuffed out when he suffered a catastrophic puncture *(below right)* when he was running in third place.

went, pausing in their positions to await the starting signal only for the whole procedure to be aborted after Jarno Trulli's Prost-Peugeot stalled down in 14th place.

The rules now require that anybody who stalls and causes a restart is put to the back of the grid. This was another bitterly disappointing setback for the young Italian. He'd started the weekend at the wheel of the promising new Prost AP01B test car, fitted with the latest Peugeot A18 V10 engine, and while this was clearly not yet fully sorted it felt much more promising than the original AP01.

Unfortunately Trulli badly damaged the new machine during Sunday's race morning warm-up when he slammed into a trackside barrier. It could not be repaired on the spot, so he switched to the original-spec AP01 spare. Now he had the additional challenge of starting at the back of the grid.

So off they went on their second parade lap. Back on the grid, Michael Schumacher pulled for first gear, and the car lurched forward and stalled. 'The engine stalled because the clutch did not free itself and I don't know why,' he later explained, 'All the work this weekend was then wasted as I had to start from the back.' It was later speculated by the team that the problem may have been caused by overheating hydraulics which affected the way in which the clutch mechanism engaged.

All this played perfectly into Häkkinen's hands. At the second restart the Finn accelerated confidently into a lead he was never to lose. From the outside of the second row, Eddie Irvine hurtled straight into second place while David Coulthard found himself badly wrong-footed, piling on a touch too many revs, which allowed Heinz-Harald Frentzen to slot into third as the McLaren driver was left grappling with excessive wheelspin.

At the end of the opening lap Häkkinen led by 1.5s from Irvine, Frentzen, Coulthard, Jacques Villeneuve's Williams and the Jordans of Damon Hill and Ralf Schumacher. Irvine was really determined to give his all on this occasion and, while Michael Schumacher had worked the other Ferrari up to tenth by the end of the second lap, Eddie had narrowed Häkkinen's advantage to 1.1s.

'I had a fantastic start and pushed very hard to try and put Mika under pressure,' he said. 'But towards the end of every stint, my tyres started to go off and I had to drop back a bit. It was just a race between me and Mika, but I could not push harder.'

Sportsphoto/SIPA Press

Paul-Henri Cahier

West
Mobil

Previous pages: Mika Häkkinen cuts his speed and pulls over close to the pit wall to share his moment of triumph with the McLaren team after sealing the 1998 World Championship in style with a dominant victory.

DIARY

Ford senior executive Neil Ressler is appointed Chairman of Cosworth Racing.

Benetton Chief Executive David Richards resigns after disagreement over long-term strategy for the team.

Jimmy Vasser's Reynard-Honda wins final CART round at Fontana, California.

Gary Anderson confirmed as chief designer of Stewart-Ford F1 team.

Both the Benetton and BAR teams emerge as rivals chasing F1 factory Renault engine contracts if the French company returns to Grand Prix racing.

Paul Tracy suspended from opening round of 1999 CART series after prompting another accident in 1998 Surfers Paradise event.

Mika is greeted with a warm handshake from rival Michael Schumacher and a pat on the head from second-place finisher Eddie Irvine as he arrives in *parc fermé* after his slowing-down lap. Happily, the championship battle was resolved without the acrimony that had scarred previous title showdowns.

Below right: The Finn receives a big hug from an overjoyed Ron Dennis, while his ever-supportive team-mate David Coulthard seems pleased to have contributed to the team's constructors' championship success.

On lap three Häkkinen stabilised his advantage at 1.2s as Schumacher moved up to ninth. Two laps later Mika really began to get into his stride, opening the lead first to 1.7s and then to 2.1s by the end of lap six. The remarkable Schumacher was now up to seventh, ahead of brother Ralf's Jordan but boxed in behind Hill's sister car, which, in turn, was climbing all over Villeneuve's Williams.

Lap nine saw Rubens Barrichello's Stewart-Ford make its first refuelling stop, dropping from 13th to 18th. The Brazilian would struggle on for another 16 laps before retiring with transmission failure after making no impression on the immediate opposition.

On lap 14 Ralf Schumacher's Jordan retired from eighth place, rolling to a smoking halt right in front of the pits. 'This was not a lucky day for the Schumachers,' he said. 'The two restarts meant the oil pressure in my car became very high and we were unable to do anything about that, which meant that eventually the engine failed. It was a disappointing way for me to end my two years at Jordan.'

On the same lap Hill made his first 9.4s refuelling stop from sixth place, dropping behind Schumacher, who was now just over 30 seconds adrift of Häkkinen's leading McLaren. Next time round Irvine made a 7.7s first refuelling stop, resuming in second some 22.8s behind Häkkinen, just as Salo's Arrows retired from 12th place with hydraulic failure.

On lap 16, a lap after audaciously passing Villeneuve's Williams, Schumacher brought the Ferrari in from fifth place for its first refuelling stop (6.8s). He resumed in sixth ahead of Alesi's Sauber and, more crucially, Hill's Jordan, which in turn would make a place on Villeneuve's Williams when the outgoing World Champion came in at the end of lap 18.

That lap also saw Häkkinen make his first refuelling stop. The McLaren crew worked with well-drilled precision, after 7.3s despatching him back into the chase some 2.9s ahead of Irvine.

By lap 21 Häkkinen was pulling away again, now moving to 5.8s ahead of Irvine as Coulthard made a 7.8s refuelling stop, having moved into third when Frentzen came in two laps earlier. The McLaren team got David back into the race ahead of the Williams driver, but such was the pace of Schumacher's Ferrari that he vaulted past them both during their pit stops to take third place.

This was actually now turning into quite a processional affair. Michael was half a minute behind Häkkinen's leading McLaren, so defeating the Finn was not a realistic option. Irvine made his second stop (6.5s) at the end of lap 28, squeezing back into the race just two seconds in front of his team-mate.

While the leaders were on their 31st lap, Tora Takagi had just accelerated his Tyrrell out of the pits following his second refuelling stop when he was rammed from behind by Esteban Tuero's Minardi under braking for the chicane. 'I can only think he locked up his brakes,' said Takagi. 'I turned in normally and, the next thing I knew, he crashed into me and took us both out of the race.'

Tuero broadly agreed that this was how things had happened. 'I touched Takagi, who had just come out of the pits,' he said. 'I was faster, saw a gap and tried to overtake him but my wheels locked and unluckily I went into him.'

This drama resulted in debris being scattered over the circuit and the World Championship contest came to a premature end when Schumacher's Ferrari ran over some of the wreckage, puncturing its right-rear tyre. As the Goodyear deflated, it then flew apart as Michael was approaching the first corner after the pits at around 165 mph. With great skill, the German ace coaxed and teased his crippled mount through the first right-handers before rolling to a halt on the grass. Häkkinen was now World Champion, come what may.

All that remained was for the Finn to make his second refuelling stop on lap 32, after which he accelerated straight back into the race 2.5s ahead of Irvine. Seven laps later, the Ulsterman, having dropped a further five seconds behind, made his third refuelling stop and resumed 24.6s behind the McLaren. Häkkinen confidently reeled off the remaining 12 laps to the chequered flag.

McLaren's revival, which had seriously started with the beginning of its Mercedes partnership in 1995, had finally come to fruition after four challenging seasons. Häkkinen's achievement also marked the re-emergence of Mercedes-Benz as an F1 winning force for the first time since the legendary Juan Manuel Fangio took one of the W196 Silver Arrows to the World Championship crown 43 years earlier.

It was a point not lost on Mercedes board director Jürgen Hubbert, who had made the trip to Japan. 'I think this success is very important for the Mercedes tradition,' he said. 'Motor sport is something quite special and belongs firmly to our heritage.

'When we resumed F1 racing again in the 1990s the image of the Silver Arrows was still there, even for those people who had never seen them in the 1930s and '50s. It shows how competitive and innovative the company is, which is very important in these difficult and commercially competitive times. We are all delighted that Mika has achieved this World Championship.'

For Häkkinen, this triumph represented just reward for a dogged and sometimes disheartening slog through from the ranks of the F1 also-rans, which he originally joined as a member of the Lotus team in 1991. Two years later he signed as McLaren's official test driver rather than race for the French Ligier squad and he eventually gained promotion to the full-time race team after Indy car star Michael Andretti failed to master the complexities of F1 and withdrew from the series before the end of the 1993 season.

More recently, he had also made a full recovery from those terrible injuries sustained in practice for the 1995 Australian Grand Prix. His Suzuka success brought McLaren's tally of Grand Prix victories to 116 since the team began racing in F1 in 1966, only three fewer than Ferrari, which had been competing since 1949.

At the chequered flag Irvine was just 6.4s behind, Mika having eased his pace in the closing stages to make certain of his decisive victory. Eddie admitted that Schumacher being moved to the back of the grid scuppered the Ferrari team's race tactics.

'It didn't change them, it destroyed them,' he said. 'For the past two or three days we had been discussing the possibilities if Mika had been there, or Michael here, with me or David somewhere else. There must have been at least 16 permutations to consider.

'Eventually it was a question of Michael having to get up to at least second position, which isn't exactly easy when you are starting from the back of the grid. When Mika got off into the lead, it became a straight race to see which of us was going to win.'

Coulthard was disappointed with third place. 'On my green-flag lap starts, I seemed to be a bit low on the revs,' he reflected. 'Normally that wouldn't have been a problem, but because the start was aborted my engineer was able to warn me to keep the revs up.

'That made me think before the eventual start proper, when I gave it too many revs and spun the wheels. I was so preoccupied in trying to make sure Eddie didn't get the jump on me that it allowed Heinz to go round the outside. I then spent a pretty uneventful first stint stuck behind him, and for the sake of the constructors' title I was probably not as aggressive as I could have been, so it was a pretty uneventful race to third place for me.'

Behind Coulthard, Hill's Jordan-Mugen Honda forced a path ahead of Frentzen's Williams FW20 as they braked for the final chicane on the last lap. It was a bold slice of overtaking, but quite unnecessary. Hill had it fixed in his mind that fourth place was absolutely essential to secure Jordan's fourth place in the constructors' championship. In fact, fifth would have been good enough, but Hill had seemingly ignored that instruction and muscled his way past the startled Williams driver.

That left Frentzen heading team-mate Villeneuve home in fifth and sixth places. Heinz-Harald's race had been blighted by the failure of his power steering on the opening lap. 'It was like driving a truck around the circuit,' he recounted. 'I was driving every lap as if it was qualifying. The steering was reset during the first pit stop, but it went again, so I had to drive virtually the whole race like this, fighting to keep the car on the track. I could not stop Damon from passing me on the last chicane.'

Patrick Head was less convinced. 'I think Heinz must not have looked in his mirrors,' he remarked wryly after the race. For his part, Villeneuve complained that his first set of tyres were not very good. 'The rear end was very sloppy,' he said. 'After the [first] stop the car was very strong and I could run harder than Damon and Heinz, but I was stuck behind them.'

Into seventh place came Jean Alesi's Sauber, the Frenchman admitting that he'd had a good race after he had pipped Giancarlo Fisichella's Benetton B198 on the final lap. Alexander Wurz was ninth ahead of Johnny Herbert, who stalled and was left at the final start and spent the whole afternoon catching up lost ground.

The final two classified runners were the Prosts of Olivier Panis and Jarno Trulli, the Italian's car suffering engine failure at the start of the final lap, but at least the team got some good experience with the 'Evo 4' version of the Peugeot A16 engine which was being raced for the first time. This was a whole lot better than the Stewart-Ford or Arrows teams, which failed to get either car to the finish.

For Häkkinen and the McLaren-Mercedes team, it was a joyful end to a year which had started on a victorious note in Melbourne. 'Mika deserved it,' said Michael Schumacher. 'He and his team were the best this year. But next season, I hope, it will be a different story.'

FUJI TELEVISION JAPANESE GRAND PRIX

30 OCTOBER–1 NOVEMBER 1998

SUZUKA

Race distance: 51 laps, 185.708 miles/298.868 km

Race weather: Dry, warm and sunny

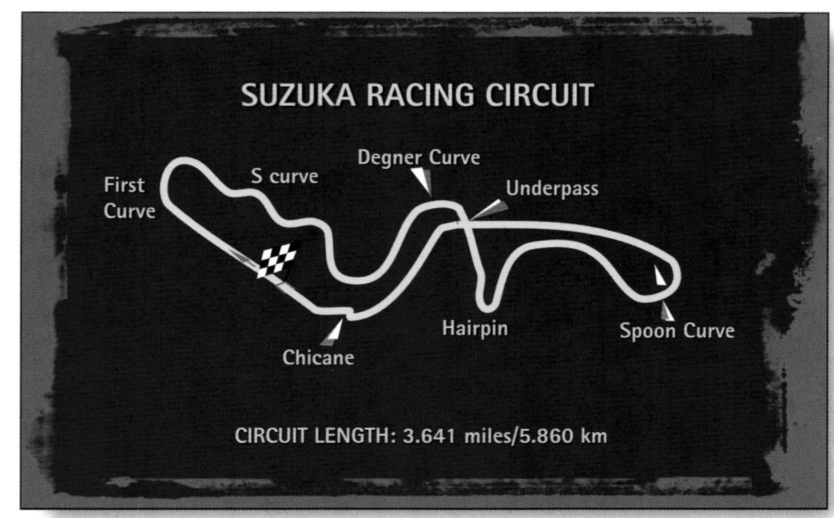

Pos.	Driver	Nat.	No.	Entrant	Car/Engine	Tyres	Laps	Time/Retirement	Speed (mph/km/h)
1	**Mika Häkkinen**	**SF**	**8**	**West McLaren Mercedes**	**McLaren MP4/13-Mercedes FO110G V10**	**B**	**51**	**1h 27m 22.535s**	**127.535/205.229**
2	**Eddie Irvine**	**GB**	**4**	**Scuderia Ferrari Marlboro**	**Ferrari F300 047 V10**	**G**	**51**	**1h 27m 29.026s**	**127.368/204.976**
3	**David Coulthard**	**GB**	**7**	**West McLaren Mercedes**	**McLaren MP4/13-Mercedes FO110G V10**	**B**	**51**	**1h 27m 50.197s**	**126.854/204.152**
4	**Damon Hill**	**GB**	**9**	**B&H Jordan Mugen Honda**	**Jordan 198-Mugen Honda MF310C V10**	**G**	**51**	**1h 28m 36.026s**	**125.760/202.392**
5	**Heinz-Harald Frentzen**	**D**	**2**	**Winfield Williams**	**Williams FW20-Mecachrome GC37/01 V10**	**G**	**51**	**1h 28m 36.392s**	**125.752/202.378**
6	**Jacques Villeneuve**	**CDN**	**1**	**Winfield Williams**	**Williams FW20-Mecachrome GC37/01 V10**	**G**	**51**	**1h 28m 38.402s**	**125.704/202.302**
7	Jean Alesi	F	14	Red Bull Sauber Petronas	Sauber C17-Petronas SPE01D V10	G	51	1h 28m 58.588s	125.229/201.537
8	Giancarlo Fisichella	I	5	Mild Seven Benetton Playlife	Benetton B198-Playlife V10	B	51	1h 29m 03.837s	125.106/201.339
9	Alexander Wurz	A	6	Mild Seven Benetton Playlife	Benetton B198-Playlife V10	B	50		
10	Johnny Herbert	GB	15	Red Bull Sauber Petronas	Sauber C17-Petronas SPE01D V10	G	50		
11	Olivier Panis	F	11	Gauloises Prost Peugeot	Prost AP01-Peugeot A16EV4 V10	B	50		
12	Jarno Trulli	I	12	Gauloises Prost Peugeot	Prost AP01-Peugeot A16EV4 V10	B	48	Engine	
	Shinji Nakano	J	22	Fondmetal Minardi Ford	Minardi M198-Ford Zetec-R V10	B	40	Throttle	
	Michael Schumacher	D	3	Scuderia Ferrari Marlboro	Ferrari F300 047 V10	G	31	Puncture	
	Toranosuke Takagi	J	21	Tyrrell Ford	Tyrrell 026-Ford Zetec-R V10	G	28	Collision with Tuero	
	Esteban Tuero	RA	23	Fondmetal Minardi Ford	Minardi M198-Ford Zetec-R V10	B	28	Collision with Takagi	
	Rubens Barrichello	BR	18	Stewart Ford	Stewart SF2-Ford Zetec-R V10	B	25	Differential	
	Jos Verstappen	NL	19	Stewart Ford	Stewart SF2-Ford Zetec-R V10	B	21	Gearbox	
	Mika Salo	SF	17	Danka Zepter Arrows	Arrows A19 V10	B	14	Hydraulics	
	Ralf Schumacher	D	10	B&H Jordan Mugen Honda	Jordan 198-Mugen Honda MF310C V10	G	13	Engine	
	Pedro Diniz	BR	16	Danka Zepter Arrows	Arrows A19 V10	B	2	Spun off	
DNQ	Ricardo Rosset	BR	20	Tyrrell Ford	Tyrrell 026-Ford Zetec-R V10	G			

All results and data © FIA 1998

Fastest lap: M. Schumacher, on lap 19, 1m 40.190s, 130.925 mph/210.703 km/h.

Lap record: Heinz-Harald Frentzen (F1 Williams FW19-Renault V10), 1m 38.942s, 132.576 mph/213.361 km/h (1997).

B – Bridgestone G – Goodyear

Grid order	1	2	3	4	5	6	7	8	9	10	11	12	13	14	15	16	17	18	19
3 M. SCHUMACHER	8	8	8	8	8	8	8	8	8	8	8	8	8	8	8	8	8	8	8
8 HÄKKINEN	4	4	4	4	4	4	4	4	4	4	4	4	4	4	4	4	4	4	4
7 COULTHARD	2	2	2	2	2	2	2	2	2	2	2	2	2	2	2	2	2	2	7
4 IRVINE	7	7	7	7	7	7	7	7	7	7	7	7	7	7	7	7	7	7	2
2 FRENTZEN	1	1	1	1	1	1	1	1	1	1	1	1	1	1	3	3	1	1	3
1 VILLENEUVE	9	9	9	9	9	9	9	9	9	9	9	9	9	3	1	1	3	3	14
10 R. SCHUMACHER	10	10	10	10	3	3	3	3	3	3	3	3	3	9	5	14	14	14	9
9 HILL	6	6	6	3	10	10	10	10	10	10	10	10	10	6	14	9	9	9	1
6 WURZ	5	5	3	6	6	6	6	6	6	6	6	6	6	5	9	11	6	6	5
5 FISICHELLA	14	3	5	5	5	5	5	5	5	5	5	5	5	14	11	6	11	5	6
15 HERBERT	11	14	14	14	14	14	14	14	14	14	14	14	14	11	6	5	5	15	15
14 ALESI	3	11	11	11	11	11	11	11	11	11	11	11	11	17	15	15	15	11	11
11 PANIS	18	18	18	18	18	18	18	18	18	17	17	17	17	15	19	21	12	12	18
12 TRULLI	17	17	17	17	17	17	17	17	17	19	19	19	19	19	21	12	21	18	19
17 SALO	16	16	19	19	19	19	19	19	19	21	21	15	15	21	12	19	18	19	12
18 BARRICHELLO	21	21	21	21	21	21	21	21	21	15	15	21	21	12	18	18	23	21	21
21 TAKAGI	19	19	12	12	12	12	12	12	12	12	12	12	12	18	22	22	19	23	22
16 DINIZ	12	12	22	22	15	15	15	15	15	18	18	18	18	22	23	23	22	22	23
19 VERSTAPPEN	22	22	23	15	22	22	22	22	22	22	22	22	22	23					
22 NAKANO	23	23	15	23	23	23	23	23	23	23	23	23	23						
23 TUERO	15	15																	

Grid order	20	21	22	23	24	25	26	27	28	29	30	31	32	33	34	35	36	37	38
3 M. SCHUMACHER	8	8	8	8	8	8	8	8	8	8	8	8	8	8	8	8	8	8	8
8 HÄKKINEN	4	4	4	4	4	4	4	4	4	4	4	4	4	4	4	4	4	4	4
7 COULTHARD	7	7	3	3	3	3	3	3	3	3	3	3	7	7	7	7	7	7	7
4 IRVINE	3	3	7	7	7	7	7	7	7	7	7	7	2	2	2	2	2	2	2
2 FRENTZEN	2	2	2	2	2	2	2	2	2	2	2	2	9	9	14	14	9	9	9
1 VILLENEUVE	9	9	9	9	9	9	9	9	9	9	9	9	1	1	9	9	1	1	1
10 R. SCHUMACHER	1	1	1	1	1	1	1	1	1	1	1	1	14	14	1	1	5	5	5
9 HILL	5	5	5	5	5	5	5	5	5	5	14	14	5	5	5	5	14	14	14
6 WURZ	6	6	6	6	6	6	6	6	6	6	6	5	6	6	6	6	6	6	6
5 FISICHELLA	14	14	14	14	14	14	14	14	14	14	5	6	15	15	15	15	15	15	15
15 HERBERT	15	11	11	11	11	11	11	11	11	15	15	15	11	11	11	11	11	11	11
14 ALESI	11	15	15	15	15	15	15	15	15	11	11	11	12	12	12	12	12	12	12
11 PANIS	18	18	18	12	12	12	12	12	12	12	12	12	22	22	22	22	22	22	22
12 TRULLI	19	12	12	21	21	21	22	22	22	22	22	22							
17 SALO	12	21	21	22	22	22	21	21	21										
18 BARRICHELLO	21	22	22	18	18	18	23	23	23										
21 TAKAGI	22	19	23	23	23	23													
16 DINIZ	23	23																	
19 VERSTAPPEN																			
22 NAKANO																			
23 TUERO																			

Pit stop

One lap behind leader

STARTING GRID

3 **M. SCHUMACHER*** Ferrari	8 **HÄKKINEN** McLaren
7 **COULTHARD** McLaren	4 **IRVINE** Ferrari
2 **FRENTZEN** Williams	1 **VILLENEUVE** Williams
10 **R. SCHUMACHER** Jordan	9 **HILL** Jordan
6 **WURZ** Benetton	5 **FISICHELLA** Benetton
15 **HERBERT** Sauber	14 **ALESI** Sauber
11 **PANIS** Prost	12 **TRULLI*** Prost
17 **SALO** Arrows	18 **BARRICHELLO** Stewart
21 **TAKAGI** Tyrrell	16 **DINIZ** Arrows
19 **VERSTAPPEN** Stewart	22 **NAKANO** Minardi
23 **TUERO** Minardi	

* started from back of grid

Did not qualify:

ROSSET (Tyrrell)

42	43	44	45	46	47	48	49	50	51	●
8	8	8	8	8	8	8	8	8	8	1
4	4	4	4	4	4	4	4	4	4	2
7	7	7	7	7	7	7	7	7	7	3
2	2	2	2	2	2	2	2	2	9	4
9	9	9	9	9	9	9	9	9	2	5
1	1	1	1	1	1	1	1	1	1	6
5	5	5	5	5	5	5	5	5	14	
14	14	14	14	14	14	14	14	14	5	
6	6	6	6	6	6	6	6	6		
15	15	15	15	15	15	15	15	15		
11	11	11	11	11	11	11	11	11		
12	12	12	12	12	12	12				

FOR THE RECORD

100th Grand Prix start

Damon Hill

TIME SHEETS

QUALIFYING

Weather: Dry, warm and sunny

Pos.	Driver	Car	Laps	Time
1	Michael Schumacher	Ferrari	8	1m 36.293s
2	Mika Häkkinen	McLaren-Mercedes	11	1m 36.471s
3	David Coulthard	McLaren-Mercedes	10	1m 37.496s
4	Eddie Irvine	Ferrari	8	1m 38.197s
5	Heinz-Harald Frentzen	Williams-Mecachrome	11	1m 38.272s
6	Jacques Villeneuve	Williams-Mecachrome	12	1m 38.448s
7	Ralf Schumacher	Jordan-Mugen Honda	12	1m 38.461s
8	Damon Hill	Jordan-Mugen Honda	12	1m 38.603s
9	Alexander Wurz	Benetton-Playlife	12	1m 38.959s
10	Giancarlo Fisichella	Benetton-Playlife	11	1m 39.080s
11	Johnny Herbert	Sauber-Petronas	12	1m 39.234s
12	Jean Alesi	Sauber-Petronas	12	1m 39.448s
13	Olivier Panis	Prost-Peugeot	12	1m 40.037s
14	Jarno Trulli	Prost-Peugeot	12	1m 40.111s
15	Mika Salo	Arrows	12	1m 40.387s
16	Rubens Barrichello	Stewart-Ford	12	1m 40.502s
17	Toranosuke Takagi	Tyrrell-Ford	11	1m 40.619s
18	Pedro Diniz	Arrows	12	1m 40.687s
19	Jos Verstappen	Stewart-Ford	11	1m 40.943s
20	Shinji Nakano	Minardi-Ford	12	1m 41.315s
21	Esteban Tuero	Minardi-Ford	12	1m 42.358s
22	Ricardo Rosset	Tyrrell-Ford	9	1m 43.259s

107 per cent time: 1m 43.033s

FRIDAY FREE PRACTICE

Weather: Sunny and bright

Pos.	Driver	Laps	Time
1	Michael Schumacher	23	1m 39.823s
2	Ralf Schumacher	34	1m 40.336s
3	Heinz-Harald Frentzen	30	1m 40.389s
4	Eddie Irvine	30	1m 40.615s
5	Mika Häkkinen	28	1m 40.644s
6	David Coulthard	28	1m 40.845s
7	Damon Hill	30	1m 41.098s
8	Jacques Villeneuve	26	1m 41.252s
9	Jos Verstappen	23	1m 42.191s
10	Giancarlo Fisichella	32	1m 42.224s
11	Alexander Wurz	33	1m 42.628s
12	Toranosuke Takagi	26	1m 42.833s
13	Jarno Trulli	38	1m 43.121s
14	Olivier Panis	25	1m 43.493s
15	Mika Salo	40	1m 43.634s
16	Jean Alesi	25	1m 43.788s
17	Rubens Barrichello	20	1m 43.854s
18	Johnny Herbert	22	1m 43.894s
19	Pedro Diniz	36	1m 44.468s
20	Shinji Nakano	29	1m 44.632s
21	Ricardo Rosset	27	1m 45.054s
22	Esteban Tuero	30	1m 46.396s

SATURDAY FREE PRACTICE

Weather: Sunny and bright

Pos.	Driver	Laps	Time
1	Michael Schumacher	17	1m 38.429s
2	David Coulthard	27	1m 38.673s
3	Mika Häkkinen	18	1m 38.752s
4	Heinz-Harald Frentzen	25	1m 38.874s
5	Jacques Villeneuve	21	1m 39.883s
6	Ralf Schumacher	21	1m 40.003s
7	Damon Hill	24	1m 40.146s
8	Giancarlo Fisichella	21	1m 40.265s
9	Eddie Irvine	15	1m 40.552s
10	Olivier Panis	18	1m 40.857s
11	Jean Alesi	22	1m 40.925s
12	Alexander Wurz	22	1m 41.002s
13	Toranosuke Takagi	18	1m 41.105s
14	Rubens Barrichello	25	1m 41.172s
15	Johnny Herbert	25	1m 41.543s
16	Mika Salo	22	1m 41.823s
17	Pedro Diniz	13	1m 41.889s
18	Jos Verstappen	20	1m 41.924s
19	Jarno Trulli	25	1m 42.786s
20	Shinji Nakano	20	1m 43.013s
21	Esteban Tuero	26	1m 43.048s
	Ricardo Rosset	0	no time

WARM-UP

Weather: Sunny and bright

Pos.	Driver	Laps	Time
1	Michael Schumacher	13	1m 40.431s
2	David Coulthard	13	1m 40.710s
3	Mika Häkkinen	12	1m 41.056s
4	Ralf Schumacher	15	1m 41.119s
5	Eddie Irvine	10	1m 41.246s
6	Heinz-Harald Frentzen	13	1m 41.452s
7	Jacques Villeneuve	13	1m 41.510s
8	Damon Hill	13	1m 41.902s
9	Giancarlo Fisichella	14	1m 42.611s
10	Mika Salo	12	1m 42.650s
11	Jean Alesi	7	1m 42.700s
12	Olivier Panis	12	1m 42.727s
13	Johnny Herbert	14	1m 42.837s
14	Alexander Wurz	12	1m 42.881s
15	Shinji Nakano	12	1m 43.593s
16	Toranosuke Takagi	12	1m 43.776s
17	Jarno Trulli	8	1m 43.834s
18	Jos Verstappen	10	1m 43.935s
19	Rubens Barrichello	12	1m 44.205s
20	Pedro Diniz	9	1m 44.273s
21	Esteban Tuero	10	1m 45.733s

RACE FASTEST LAPS

Weather: Dry, warm and sunny

Driver	Time	Lap
Michael Schumacher	1m 40.190s	19
Mika Häkkinen	1m 40.426s	35
Eddie Irvine	1m 40.870s	36
David Coulthard	1m 40.905s	42
Jacques Villeneuve	1m 42.273s	40
Damon Hill	1m 42.275s	38
Heinz-Harald Frentzen	1m 42.331s	36
Giancarlo Fisichella	1m 42.335s	20
Jean Alesi	1m 42.357s	31
Johnny Herbert	1m 42.858s	38
Ralf Schumacher	1m 42.965s	4
Olivier Panis	1m 43.073s	49
Jarno Trulli	1m 43.164s	42
Alexander Wurz	1m 43.447s	18
Shinji Nakano	1m 44.158s	37
Rubens Barrichello	1m 44.947s	8
Mika Salo	1m 45.304s	14
Toranosuke Takagi	1m 45.673s	23
Esteban Tuero	1m 45.792s	21
Jos Verstappen	1m 45.840s	19
Pedro Diniz	1m 46.099s	2

CHASSIS LOG BOOK

1	Villeneuve	Williams FW20/6
2	Frentzen	Williams FW20/7
	spare	Williams FW20/4
3	M. Schumacher	Ferrari F300/189
4	Irvine	Ferrari F300/184
	spare	Ferrari F300/186 & 188
5	Fisichella	Benetton B198/6
6	Wurz	Benetton B198/4
	spare	Benetton B198/5
7	Coulthard	McLaren MP4/13/3
8	Häkkinen	McLaren MP4/13/4
	spare	McLaren MP4/13/2 & 5
9	Hill	Jordan 198/6
10	R. Schumacher	Jordan 198/4
	spare	Jordan 198/5
11	Panis	Prost AP01/7
12	Trulli	Prost AP01B/9
	spare	Prost AP01/2 & 6
14	Alesi	Sauber C17/6
15	Herbert	Sauber C17/2
	spare	Sauber C17/5
16	Diniz	Arrows A19/7
17	Salo	Arrows A19/6
	spare	Arrows A19/5
18	Barrichello	Stewart SF2/5
19	Verstappen	Stewart SF2/2
	spare	Stewart SF2/3
20	Rosset	Tyrrell 026/1
21	Takagi	Tyrrell 026/5
	spare	Tyrrell 026/2
22	Nakano	Minardi M198/3
23	Tuero	Minardi M198/5
	spare	Minardi M198/1

POINTS TABLES

Drivers

1	Mika Häkkinen	100
2	Michael Schumacher	86
3	David Coulthard	56
4	Eddie Irvine	47
5	Jacques Villeneuve	21
6	Damon Hill	20
7 =	Heinz-Harald Frentzen	17
7 =	Alexander Wurz	17
9	Giancarlo Fisichella	16
10	Ralf Schumacher	14
11	Jean Alesi	9
12	Rubens Barrichello	4
13 =	Mika Salo	3
13 =	Pedro Diniz	3
15 =	Johnny Herbert	1
15 =	Jan Magnussen	1
15 =	Jarno Trulli	1

Constructors

1	McLaren	156
2	Ferrari	133
3	Williams	38
4	Jordan	34
5	Benetton	33
6	Sauber	10
7	Arrows	6
8	Stewart	5
9	Prost	1

Paul-Henri Cahier

DRIVERS' POINTS TABLE

Compiled by Nick Henry

Place	Driver	Nationality	Date of birth	Car	Australia	Brazil	Argentina	San Marino	Spain	Monaco	Canada	France	Britain	Austria	Germany	Hungary	Belgium	Italy	Luxembourg	Japan	Points total
1	**Mika Häkkinen**	SF	28/9/68	McLaren-Mercedes	1pf	1pf	2	R	1pf	1pf	R	3p	2p	1	1p	6p	Rp	4f	1f	1	100
2	**Michael Schumacher**	D	3/1/69	Ferrari	R	3	1	2f	3	10	1f	1	1f	3	5	1f	Rf	1p	2p	Rpf	86
3	**David Coulthard**	GB	27/3/71	McLaren-Mercedes	2	2	6p	1p	2	R	Rp	6f	R	2f	2f	2	7	R	3	3	56
4	**Eddie Irvine**	GB	10/11/65	Ferrari	4	8	3	3	R	3	3	2	3	4	8	R	R	2	4	2	47
5	**Jacques Villeneuve**	CDN	9/4/71	Williams-Mecachrome	5	7	R	4	6	5	10	4	7	6	3	3	R	R	8	6	21
6	**Damon Hill**	GB	17/9/60	Jordan-Mugen Honda	8	DQ	8	10*	R	8	R	R	R	7	4	4	1	6	9	4	20
7 =	**Heinz-Harald Frentzen**	D	18/5/67	Williams-Mecachrome	3	5	9	5	8	R	R	15*	R	R	9	5	4	7	5	5	17
7 =	**Alexander Wurz**	A	15/2/74	Benetton-Playlife	7	4	4f	R	4	R	4	5	4	9	11	R	R	R	7	9	17
9	**Giancarlo Fisichella**	I	14/1/73	Benetton-Playlife	R	6	7	R	R	2	2	9	5	Rp	7	8	R	8	6	8	16
10	**Ralf Schumacher**	D	30/6/75	Jordan-Mugen Honda	R	R	R	7	11	R	R	16	6	5	6	9	2	3	R	R	14
11	**Jean Alesi**	F	11/6/64	Sauber-Petronas	R	9	5	6	10	12*	R	7	R	R	10	7	3	5	10	7	9
12	**Rubens Barrichello**	BR	23/5/72	Stewart-Ford	R	R	10	R	5	R	5	10	R	R	R	R	DNS	10	11	R	4
13 =	**Mika Salo**	SF	30/11/66	Arrows	R	R	R	9	R	4	R	13	R	R	14	R	DNS	R	14	R	3
13 =	**Pedro Diniz**	BR	22/5/70	Arrows	R	R	R	R	R	6	9	14	R	R	R	11	5	R	R	R	3
15 =	**Johnny Herbert**	GB	25/6/64	Sauber-Petronas	6	11*	R	R	7	7	R	8	R	8	R	10	R	R	R	10	1
15 =	**Jan Magnussen**	DK	4/7/73	Stewart-Ford	R	10	R	R	12	R	6	–	–	–	–	–	–	–	–	–	1
15 =	**Jarno Trulli**	I	13/7/74	Prost-Peugeot	R	R	11	R	9	R	R	R	R	10	12	R	6	13	R	12*	1
	Shinji Nakano	J	1/4/71	Minardi-Ford	R	R	13	R	14	9	7	17*	8	11	R	15	8	R	15	R	0
	Olivier Panis	F	2/9/66	Prost-Peugeot	9	R	15*	11*	16*	R	R	11	R	R	15	12	DNS	R	12	11	0
	Ricardo Rosset	BR	27/7/68	Tyrrell-Ford	R	R	14	R	DNQ	DNQ	8	R	R	12	DNQ	DNQ	DNS	12	R	DNQ	0
	Toranosuke Takagi	J	12/2/72	Tyrrell-Ford	R	R	12	R	13	11	R	R	9	R	13	14	R	9	16	R	0
	Esteban Tuero	RA	22/4/78	Minardi-Ford	R	R	R	8	15	R	R	R	R	R	16	R	R	11	R	R	0
	Jos Verstappen	NL	4/3/72	Stewart-Ford	–	–	–	–	–	–	–	12	R	R	R	13	R	R	13	R	0

KEY

p	pole position	*	classified but not running at the finish	DNS	did not start
f	fastest lap	R	retired	DNQ	did not qualify
		DQ	disqualified		

POINTS & PERCENTAGES

Compiled by David Hayhoe

GRID POSITIONS: 1998

Pos.	Driver	Starts	Best	Worst	Average
1	**Mika Häkkinen**	16	1	3	1.69
2	**Michael Schumacher**	16	1	9	3.06
3	**David Coulthard**	16	1	14	3.13
4	**Eddie Irvine**	16	2	8	5.44
5	**Jacques Villeneuve**	16	2	13	6.69
6	**Giancarlo Fisichella**	16	1	11	7.06
7	**Heinz-Harald Frentzen**	16	3	13	7.44
8=	**Ralf Schumacher**	16	4	21	8.75
8=	**Alexander Wurz**	16	5	17	8.75
10	**Damon Hill**	16	3	15	8.94
11	**Jean Alesi**	16	2	15	10.50
12	**Johnny Herbert**	16	5	18	11.75
13	**Rubens Barrichello**	16	5	17	13.19
14	**Jarno Trulli**	16	10	16	13.87
15	**Olivier Panis**	16	9	22	14.94
16	**Mika Salo**	16	6	20	15.12
17	**Jos Verstappen**	9	12	19	16.56
18	**Pedro Diniz**	16	12	22	16.69
19	**Toranosuke Takagi**	16	13	21	17.44
20	**Jan Magnussen**	7	16	22	18.71
21	**Shinji Nakano**	16	18	22	19.94
22	**Esteban Tuero**	16	17	22	20.19
23	**Ricardo Rosset**	12	18	22	20.45

CAREER PERFORMANCES: 1998 DRIVERS

Driver	Nationality	Races	Championships	Wins	2nd places	3rd places	4th places	5th places	6th places	Pole positions	Fastest laps	Points
Jean Alesi	F	151	–	1	16	15	11	14	7	2	4	234
Rubens Barrichello	BR	97	–	–	2	1	8	6	4	1	–	56
David Coulthard	GB	74	–	4	14	6	4	4	5	8	8	173
Pedro Diniz	BR	66	–	–	–	–	–	2	3	–	–	7
Giancarlo Fisichella	I	41	–	–	3	1	3	1	3	1	1	36
Heinz-Harald Frentzen	D	81	–	1	2	6	6	8	8	1	6	88
Mika Häkkinen	SF	112	1	9	5	13	8	8	6	10	7	218
Johnny Herbert	GB	129	–	2	1	3	10	5	5	–	–	83
Damon Hill	GB	100	1	22	15	5	6	1	3	20	19	353
Eddie Irvine	GB	81	–	–	4	11	6	5	3	–	–	99
Jan Magnussen	DK	25	–	–	–	–	–	–	1	–	–	1
Shinji Nakano	J	33	–	–	–	–	–	–	2	–	–	2
Olivier Panis	F	75	–	1	3	1	3	4	5	–	–	54
Ricardo Rosset	BR	27	–	–	–	–	–	–	–	–	–	-
Mika Salo	SF	68	–	–	–	–	1	5	2	–	–	15
Michael Schumacher	D	118	2	33	19	13	6	4	4	20	34	526
Ralf Schumacher	D	33	–	–	1	2	–	5	3	–	–	27
Toranosuke Takagi	J	16	–	–	–	–	–	–	–	–	–	-
Jarno Trulli	I	30	–	–	–	–	1	–	1	–	–	4
Esteban Tuero	RA	16	–	–	–	–	–	–	–	–	–	-
Jos Verstappen	NL	57	–	–	–	2	–	1	1	–	–	11
Jacques Villeneuve	CDN	49	1	11	5	5	3	4	3	13	9	180
Alexander Wurz	A	19	–	–	–	1	5	1	–	–	1	21

Note: Drivers beginning the formation lap are deemed to have made a start

UNLAPPED: 1998

Number of cars on same lap as leader

Grand Prix	Starters	at 1/4 distance	at 1/2 distance	at 3/4 distance	at full distance
Australia	22	13	8	4	2
Brazil	22	22	10	6	4
Argentina	22	16	13	7	7
San Marino	22	17	9	6	5
Spain	21	20	9	7	4
Monaco	21	14	6	4	4
Canada	22	16	10	7	5
France	22	13	8	5	4
Britain	22	13	9	4	3
Austria	22	16	10	6	7
Germany	21	20	18	15	11
Hungary	21	14	9	6	5
Belgium	22	12	8	5	5
Italy	22	20	10	8	6
Luxembourg	22	19	13	11	7
Japan	21	20	12	8	8

LAP LEADERS: 1998

Grand Prix	Mika Häkkinen	Michael Schumacher	David Coulthard	Damon Hill	Giancarlo Fisichella	Eddie Irvine	Total
Australia	37	–	21	–	–	–	58
Brazil	72	–	–	–	–	–	72
Argentina	14	54	4	–	–	–	72
San Marino	–	–	62	–	–	–	62
Spain	63	–	2	–	–	–	65
Monaco	78	–	–	–	–	–	78
Canada	–	27	18	–	24	–	69
France	–	70	–	–	–	1	71
Britain	50	10	–	–	–	–	60
Austria	69	–	2	–	–	–	71
Germany	43	–	2	–	–	–	45
Hungary	46	31	–	–	–	–	77
Belgium	–	18	–	26	–	–	44
Italy	10	34	9	–	–	–	53
Luxembourg	43	24	–	–	–	–	67
Japan	51	–	–	–	–	–	51
Total	576	268	120	26	24	1	1015
(Per cent)	56.7	26.4	11.8	2.6	2.4	0.1	(100)

RETIREMENTS: 1998

Number of cars to have retired

Grand Prix	Starters	at 1/4 distance	at 1/2 distance	at 3/4 distance	at full distance	percentage
Australia	22	7	11	13	13	59.1
Brazil	22	4	6	8	11	50.0
Argentina	22	3	4	6	8	36.4
San Marino	22	3	8	10	13	59.1
Spain	21	–	4	5	6	28.6
Monaco	21	4	5	9	10	47.6
Canada	22	5	9	11	12	54.5
France	22	1	2	3	7	31.8
Britain	22	2	6	12	13	59.1
Austria	22	6	9	10	10	45.5
Germany	21	1	1	3	5	23.8
Hungary	21	3	4	5	6	28.6
Belgium	22	9	11	14	14	63.6
Italy	22	3	6	9	9	40.9
Luxembourg	22	2	2	4	5	22.7
Japan	21	1	5	8	9	42.9

FORMULA 3000 REVIEW

by Tom Alexander

ROOM AT THE TOP

IN some ways this was a typical year for the FIA Formula 3000 Championship.

As is customary there was some great racing behind a fierce title contest. But, once again, by the end of the season it was already clear that there was no room left in Formula 1 for a cluster of drivers who clearly have nothing more to prove at this level.

In that respect the FIA's so-called Grand Prix nursery formula remains frustratingly non-productive, which is ironic at a time when its ties with Formula 1 have never been stronger. Eight of this year's 12 races acted as Grand Prix curtain-raisers and in 1999 it will operate exclusively as an F1 support class.

It could not be a better shop window; all that remains is to find a few customers.

At least champion Juan Pablo Montoya did not go wholly unrewarded for his efforts. The 23-year-old Colombian, the pre-season favourite, was a deserving winner, though he was pushed all the way by McLaren-Mercedes protégé Nick Heidfeld.

Montoya recorded four wins, seven pole positions, five fastest laps and 65 points – a new championship record. He also became the most successful driver in FIA F3000 history, with a career total of seven wins.

The combination of Montoya and reigning champion team Super Nova looked irresistible, but it took a short while for the partnership to gel. Montoya failed to score in the first two races, once through a fluffed pit stop and once through his own impetuosity, but he was on the podium in nine of the remaining ten, a remarkable achievement in such a close formula (the top 32 cars on the grid in Barcelona were covered by less than two seconds, for instance).

He even scored a point in the odd race out, Monaco, despite completing the last couple of laps with a puncture – and minus his front wing.

Montoya was the first to admit that he changed his approach during the season. He could have won the title in 1997 but for his own determination to win every race at any price; this time he adopted a calmer approach. 'It took us a little while to retune his Latin brain,' said Super Nova boss David Sears, 'but by the middle of the season he was used to the idea of driving for points.'

After his slightly unruly Monaco weekend Montoya settled down and learned to accept that sometimes it was wise to be second – or even third – best. Mind you, that didn't stop him lapping the rest of the field as he became the first man ever to win two Pau F3000 races on what is, sadly, likely to be the formula's last appearance in the charismatic French town.

Away from the day job Montoya had a busy schedule testing for Williams, but he never allowed that to compromise his approach. He was highly impressive in the F1 car, too, and although he yearned to race with the team in 1999 his three-year deal with leading Champ Car entrant Ganassi is at least fair reward for a job well done. It is arguably the best prize ever landed by a reigning F3000 champion.

There will be no such short-term benefits for his nemesis Heidfeld. Driving for West Competition, a junior arm of McLaren headed by ex-F1 engineer David Brown and staffed by experienced F3000 personnel, the reigning German F3 champion could not have been better prepared. He

Eventual champion Juan Pablo Montoya leads his main rival for the title, Nick Heidfeld, and the rest of the closely matched field into the first corner at the start of the Barcelona race.

completed thousands of laps of testing (before 1 January, when such things become restricted) and he posed a threat at almost every race.

Less flamboyant than Montoya, 21-year-old Heidfeld was ultimately denied a straight fight for the title by a banal error on the team's part. The specification of the control fuel was changed during the season and, after he had secured provisional pole position at the Nürburgring finale (where he trailed Montoya by just three points), Heidfeld was found to have been running on a mixture of new and old. He was by no means alone in that, but the stewards were understandably focusing on the cars of Heidfeld and Montoya at the time, so he was the only one caught.

He had gained no advantage as a result, but if the contents of your fuel tank don't match the required chemical footprint, the rules are black and white. As a result he started 32nd, and last, but his recovery drive to ninth (despite a spin) showed that he is as handy a racer in adversity as he is when breezing along at the front. As Montoya was cruising to the title at the time, however, that was little consolation.

On happier days Heidfeld picked up three victories and it was a first year to be proud of. If he hangs around in 1999 (West has its fingers crossed), there is every chance that Montoya's record of seven wins will prove to be short-lived.

From mid-season it was pretty much a two-horse championship race as the pre-eminence of the top two left meagre pickings for the rest.

Jason Watt (Den Blå Avis), third last year, faded after an early-season win at Imola. The Dane's morale took a particular hammer blow in the back-to-back street races. He had dominated in Monaco and was on course to enter the record books as the first-ever F3000 race winner in the principality when he made a small, but terminal, mistake and left the door open to Heidfeld. One week later he crashed out of second place in Pau and, having thrown away 16 points, he was unable to sustain his title challenge. The bizarre statistic of the year was that both incidents occurred a) in front of a local casino and b) on the 41st lap.

He eventually slipped to fourth in the final standings – but such were his own expectations that he regarded this as a failure. By the standards of the majority, of course, it was no such thing.

The man who pipped him to third place was Gonzalo Rodriguez (Astromega), who has what it takes to become Uruguay's first serious Grand Prix driver – and the nation's first of any kind since the Fifties.

It took Rodriguez only a couple of races to appreciate that winning was a possibility, but it was a little longer before he worked out how to make the most of the opportunity. By the end of the campaign, however, his initial over-enthusiasm – which got him into several scrapes with the stewards – was but a distant memory. His victory at Spa was beautifully judged and his second, two races later at the Nürburgring, rivalled Montoya's Pau massacre as the most convincing of the year.

Leaner and fitter than he was in 1997, Rodriguez is champion material in 1999.

Highly rated Frenchman Soheil Ayari was almost left on the shelf after hanging around for winter deals that never came. Winner at Helsinki in 1997, the 28-year-old pitched in his lot with unproven Italian team Durango . . . and at the A1-Ring he gave them a first victory with a dominant display from pole.

For most of the year, however, Ayari fell foul of trying to drive around Durango's dearth of technical resources and his efforts to make the car go faster than it cared to led to a spate of accidents. And with each successive mishap the pressure on him grew. It might not be a season he will look back on with much fondness, but you could never fault him for effort.

One of the deals which bypassed Ayari was that with the Apomatox-run Prost junior team, which got off to a flying start when French F3 graduate Stéphane Sarrazin won the wet opening race at Oschersleben from 18th place on the grid. That was the product of canny racecraft and a delicate touch in awful conditions, but the promising Sarrazin showed that it was no fluke by grabbing pole in Budapest.

The team was in the throes of an overhaul, however, and with two rookie drivers on board Sarrazin was able to shine only intermittently.

The rest, largely, failed to figure on a consistent basis – and no fewer than 24 drivers registered points at some stage.

Belgian Kurt Mollekens (Arden/KTR) did lead the championship briefly after a couple of early second places, but he is unlikely to take the Watt/Ayari/Rodriguez route and pledge to a third season of F3000; he has his eyes on team management.

For all the success stories this season there were also a clutch of disappointments. The BMW Junior Team failed to live up to expectations; Max Wilson (Edenbridge), one of the finds of 1997, struggled to repeat his previous form – and his frame of mind was not helped by the positive PR heaped on his fellow Williams test driver Montoya; and it was also a dire season for the British.

Gareth Rees (Den Blå Avis) and, particularly, 1997 Enna winner Jamie Davies (DAMS) expected to be in a position to run at the front. While Rees took time to adapt to his new team's *modus operandi*, Davies was in wholly familiar surroundings. A once productive relationship fell apart as the year wore on, however, though his drive from 27th to third at Oschersleben was one of the season's highlights.

The other British drivers with a chance of making a mark all ran into financial crises: reigning national F3 champion Jonny Kane joined fellow Ulstermen Dino Morelli and Kevin McGarrity in failing to complete the season. Morelli was left with the satisfaction of racing again after the terrifying accident which left him with serious leg injuries in 1997, McGarrity with the small consolation of some points after a good drive for Nordic at Hockenheim.

Their plight – which is by no means unique to British passport holders – is a concern for teams in the short term.

There has been an explosion of interest in F3000 since it cemented its links with Formula 1 and at least 24 teams have already ordered two cars for the 1999 season. The fact remains, however, that F1 paddocks are not big enough to cope with that number and, more to the point, there simply won't be enough drivers to go round.

The FIA has already hinted that it will introduce a two-division championship in 2000, and soccer-style promotion and relegation is a real possibility. It would be good if they could sort out some form of automatic promotion for successful drivers, too.

Sutton Motorsport Images

SUPER MARIO PICK OF THE CROP

by Jim Holder

THE paradox couldn't be more extreme. In 1998 Formula 3 maintained its reputation as one of the least exciting categories in motor racing to watch, yet produced several of the most memorable championship battles in its history.

By so neatly mirroring F1, the formula continued to enhance its credentials as a stepping stone to the premier category. This was underlined by the support of McLaren to Opel Team BSR in Germany and the presence of the Stewart and Arrows Grand Prix teams in the British series.

But the category also needs to adapt if its reputation is to remain intact. Budgets continue to rise nearer the half-million-pound mark for a season, and there is no question that the ever-present problem of talent being stifled by a lack of funds is being exacerbated by the situation.

Rival categories are also vying for a share of this cash. The nascent Formula Palmer Audi – run by ex-GP driver Jonathan Palmer in Britain – overcame a stuttering start to provide fast, effective and exceedingly well promoted racing for about one-third of an F3 budget. A tangible prize for the winner in the shape of an International F3000 drive also scored points over F3.

The quality of driving, however, did not. For now, F3 continued to attract the cream of the world's junior driving talent, particularly in Britain, Germany and France.

The British series was billed as the battle of Brazil versus Britain. The pundits need not have bothered with the label, however, as the Brazilians left precious few scraps for the chasing pack to swallow.

At the start of the year, Enrique Bernoldi was untouchable. The 19-year-old had ended 1997 as the highest-placed driver continuing in the formula and, with the backing of his Promatecme team and Renault power, he quickly justified his pre-season status as championship favourite.

Five wins from seven races opened a 29-point gap over his nearest rival, Walsall's Martin O'Connell. Bernoldi wasn't just winning, but doing so with apparent ease. Talk turned to a record-breaking season – it was premature.

Paul Stewart Racing's Mario Haberfeld was 54 points behind Bernoldi at that point. In stark contrast to even O'Connell, however, Haberfeld continued to talk up his championship chances.

His justification was simple. Renault had launched a new engine for 1998, but it was proving woefully difficult for teams to harness its power. Promatecme, therefore, opted to remain with the potent 1997 version of the powerplant, which maintained its edge into the new season, but received no further development.

Haberfeld, in contrast, was hamstrung by a lacklustre start to the year from Mugen Honda. While the Japanese manufacturer developed its motor, however, Renault struggled with its 1998 engine. Only in the penultimate round of the series was the '98 engine deemed good enough to run in Bernoldi's car.

As the points advantage swung, so too did the form of Bernoldi. Too often he was left to watch from the sidelines as a result of his desire to win at all costs. Furthermore, a tendency to become caught up in other people's accidents hastened his plunge.

Haberfeld, on the other hand, shed his image from 1997 as a hot-headed racer and proved as adept at driving for points as for wins. As calculating as he was quick, rarely did he fail to get the maximum from the package he raced with. On the single occasion that he crashed, he raged at himself long enough to make sure it never happened again.

Suitably, Haberfeld's team boss Jackie Stewart took notice of his young charge's ability and let him run in the team's Grand Prix car before the season was over. Since he is blessed with abundant backing from his homeland, few doubt that these exploratory runs will turn into a full-time GP drive for Haberfeld within the next few years.

Haberfeld's team-mate and fellow Brazilian Luciano Burti did enough in his first season of F3 to suggest that he will join him. His relative lack of experience showed on occasion, but he still claimed two victories and third in the series. In doing so, the 23-year-old established himself as a name for the future.

Equally talented, but woefully underfunded, Darren Manning's career hangs in the balance. After two years running on a shoestring budget in the formula, the Yorkshireman opted to race in only selected events in 1998. That he won two of the four races he contested and claimed a second and a fourth place in the others spoke volumes. Whether anyone heard remains to be seen.

At least, however, he promoted himself to the top of a pool of exceptionally gifted but impecunious British talent. Both O'Connell and Warren Hughes demonstrated the speed and ability to win races, but were ultimately let down by the inexperience of their teams.

O'Connell signed to lead TOM'S GB

Left: Mario Haberfeld (2) lifted the British championship after an epic battle with fellow Brazilian Enrique Bernoldi *(right)*.

Below right: Darren Manning *(left)* shone in the handful of races he contested, but the honours went to Haberfeld *(right)*.

Scotland's Peter Dumbreck *(right)* made a successful switch to Japan.

The Italian championship went to Dutchman Donny Crevels *(lower right)*.

David Saelens of Belgium *(bottom)* took the French title at the last round after a dramatic counter-attack.

late in the day and was left to single-handedly guide the team's transition from its own TOM'S chassis to the Dallara. That he was able to push Bernoldi so hard early on was nothing short of incredible.

It was Hughes, however, who ended the year as top Brit. Still seeking an elusive F3000 deal, the 29-year-old opted to lead the ambitious Portman Arrows team's attack. Hampered by the recalcitrant 1998 Renault motor, he worked hard for the meagre result of fourth in the series.

Perhaps the greatest indication of the 1998 Renault motor's slow start to the year came in the French championship. Eventual champion David Saelens remained an also-ran until round nine of the series in May, when he took victory at Dijon and sparked a comeback of Haberfeld-like proportions.

A phlegmatic Belgian, Saelens drove with a quiet determination that marked him out as a talent of the future. Up until that first win, his best result of the year had been a fourth place. Once ahead, he turned on the style to claim 12 wins in a row and grab the title in the final round of the series.

It was a bitter blow for rival Franck Montagny. The Frenchman had won the first eight races of the year and held a vice-like grip on the series. His undoing was at least in part down to a temperament that demanded maximum attack, which resulted in him missing the penultimate double-header after a crash in qualifying. His ever-changing hair colours hinted at a free spirit, but it will have to be reined in if he is to find the consistency to win championships.

The intensity of the pair's battle only spilled over once the French championship had been settled and they joined the British series for its annual event at Spa-Francorchamps.

Having lost sight of the race's leaders, Montagny and Saelens began fighting over third position. They clashed on the 150 mph Kemmel straight, cannoned into the barriers and launched a furious row that could run on well beyond their F3 careers.

But perhaps the greatest indication of Saelens's ability was when he won at the Marlboro Masters event at Zandvoort. Building up momentum throughout the heats, he drove a commanding race from the front to head Bernoldi and Haberfeld.

Dumped for financial reasons from Paul Stewart Racing's British championship attack at the end of last season, Scotsman Peter Dumbreck picked up his career with the TOM'S team in Japan. His searing pace and ability to

learn both the unfamiliar circuits and culture quickly marked him out as the man to watch.

His relentless quest for victory was coupled with a mastery of knowing when not to push too hard. Consequently, he quickly amassed an unassailable title lead well before the season was over.

His main rival was team-mate Shingo Tachi, who had previously raced in the National class in Britain. The young Japanese showed considerable poise and commitment, marking himself out as one of his country's rising stars.

Another driver who learnt his trade

in the British national racing scene was eventual German Formula 3 champion Bas Leinders.

After intense pressure early in the year from Wolf Henzler, Belgian Leinders began to assert himself. However, as Henzler's form dropped away, so young Austrian Robert Lechner's improved.

Lechner proved a resilient foe, taking the championship down to the final meeting and losing out by only 21 points in the final standings.

In Christijan Albers the German series also unearthed one of the sport's rising talents. New to the formula, Albers was soon on the pace and, despite perhaps too frequent excursions from the track, claimed two wins before the end of the year.

In contrast, the Italian F3 series continued to attract only a modicum of interest from drivers looking to seriously progress their careers.

Dutchman Donny Crevels was the pace man for much of the year, but was hounded all the way to the title by the sporadically quick Michele Gasparini.

Regardless of its comparatively lowly status, however, the Italian series is still likely to promote its leading racers into F3000 next season. This is as much a testament to Italy's commitment to backing talent as anything else, but underlines that F3 continues to serve its purpose as a feeder formula.

There was enough talent on display in 1998 to suggest that this may be viewed as a vintage year for F3. Haberfeld heads the crop of F1 hopefuls, but on speed alone he may find himself facing several of his F3 adversaries in the years to come.

Photos: Sutton Motorsport Images

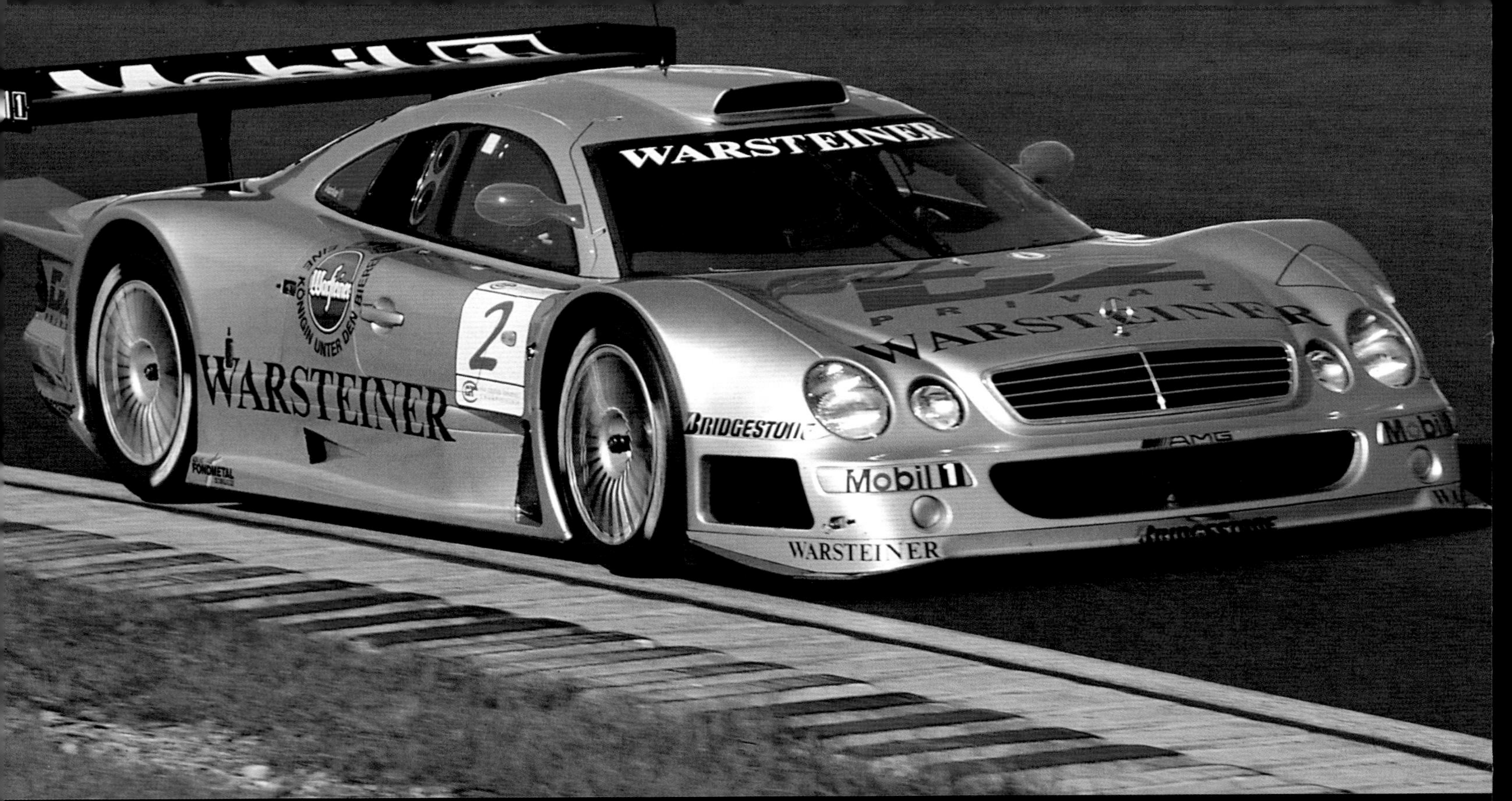

GT RACING REVIEW

by Gary Watkins

SILVERWASH

The AMG team's factory-backed Mercedes swept the board in the FIA GT Championship, winning all ten races. Veteran Klaus Ludwig and young Brazilian Ricardo Zonta won the drivers' title with their red-mirrored car *(left)*, pipping the crew of the team's other entry *(below left)*, Bernd Schneider and Mark Webber, by the narrowest of margins.

'I DON'T think we were lucky enough to win the championship.' Bernd Schneider's assessment of his and co-driver Mark Webber's failure to lift the FIA GT Championship was in no way a slight on the eventual title winners. Because all that separated the German and the Australian from 1998 champions Klaus Ludwig and Ricardo Zonta after nearly 3500 miles of racing was the slender margin of just over ten seconds – and a hefty portion of misfortune along the way.

The two AMG Mercedes team crews split the ten rounds of the second running of the FIA GT series straight down the middle, each winning five races apiece in a Three-Pointed Star whitewash. What set them apart in the final reckoning was Ludwig and Zonta's better finishing rate. The tin-top superstar, who was heading for retirement at the end of the season, and Formula 1-bound Zonta completed every race in the points. Only an engine problem in round two at Silverstone prevented the old hand and the rising star from finishing every race in the first two positions.

Reigning series champion Schneider and Webber, meanwhile, had the lion's share of the AMG team's problems. Crucially, it was two incidents that saw the number one Mercedes heading for the scenery that cost them the crown – without either they would have been champions. At Dijon in July they lost certain victory, while in the penultimate round at Homestead a clear chance of the win disappeared along with the car into the gravel. Both times British Formula 3 graduate Webber was at the wheel. In the first incident he was entirely without blame after a stone lodged in the suspension machined its way through a wheel rim. In the second, culpability for a spin and, a handful of laps later, a second off lay firmly in his court.

Schneider's comeback drive from two laps down counted as one of the performances of the season. A last-gasp fourth place set up a winner-takes-all season finale at Laguna Seca just a week later. The four-point lead Ludwig and Zonta garnered at Homestead would not be enough should they finish second to their Mercedes team-mates.

That was an outcome on which most pit lane pundits would have staked money. Instead, Ludwig's best drive of the season – combined with some clever tyre tactics – set up race victory and the title for the German veteran and the reigning Formula 3000 International Champion.

Zonta had earlier in the weekend laid the foundations with his fourth straight pole position of the season. At the end of the race, he put a seal on the victory with a new lap record. Both were proof that, by the season's end, the Brazilian had usurped 34-year-old Schneider as the fastest man at Mercedes.

There was no better way for Zonta to complete his apprenticeship – just two days after Laguna he was confirmed as a British American Racing F1 driver. For Ludwig, meanwhile, the title meant signing off a 29-season career encompassing three German touring car titles and a trio of victories in the Le Mans 24 Hours right at the top.

Ludwig's victories in the French sports car classic, it should be remembered, came with Porsche. However, the 'other' Stuttgart marque rarely looked like challenging the Three-Pointed Star's FIA GT series domination, not least after Mercedes had introduced its new CLK-LM for round three at Hockenheim. The V8-engined car, which made its debut in June's Le Mans enduro, clearly had the measure of the new 911 GT1-98 that Porsche had built in time for the start of the season.

It was difficult to pinpoint the CLK-LM's advantage. The car worked on all types of track, while the Porsche was most at home on fast, high-downforce circuits. Then there was Mercedes' significant power advantage and, perhaps most crucially, the use of Bridgestone tyres. The Japanese rubber was clearly superior in qualifying and, for the most part, more durable than Porsche's Michelin tyres. Which meant there were days when Porsche's challenge looked completely at sea, most notably around the bumpy Hungaroring in July and at the A1-Ring in Austria two months later.

Porsche had its chances to break its FIA GT series duck, particularly before the arrival of the CLK-LM. At Oschersleben, venue for the season-opener, and then again at Silverstone, a 911 GT1-98 qualified on pole and looked on course for victory before reliability problems intervened.

At the opening round, former F3000 champion Jörg Müller led for the first hour before a bodywork problem intervened shortly after fellow German Uwe Alzen took over. At round two, pole man Allan McNish disappeared into the distance until engine problems put his car out.

Porsche might still have expected to come away with that long-awaited first FIA GT victory. Alzen was lying second behind the Panoz of David Brabham when a hopeful overtaking manoeuvre went wrong. The German's misdemeanour resulted in a three-minute stop-go penalty for himself and the instant retirement of the American car.

McNish, who emerged as the fastest driver in the Porsche pack, mixed it with the silver cars on occasion later on. At Suzuka and Laguna he split the two AMG cars before ending up in the gravel both times. The first excursion came courtesy of a nudge from Zonta, the second through mechanical failure.

The Porsche factory may not have been quite in the same class as the AMG Mercedes squad, but it was still a step ahead of the rest. That was despite a 50 kg weight penalty applied to both factory teams from Stuttgart from the Donington race in an attempt to close up the gap between the factories and the pursuing pack.

The rest of the small field in the top division, GT1, never challenged the Stuttgart factories on a consistent basis. Mercedes' B-squad, Team Persson, could have come away with victory in the opening round of the season. Had Marcel Tiemann not spun at the exit of the pits at the beginning of the opening hour, he and Jean-Marc Gounon would have been well placed to take the fight to the factory car of Ludwig and Zonta.

Their eventual second place at Oschersleben represented Persson's best result of the year. The team would have to rely on the V12-engined CLK-GTR for the full season and was rarely competitive again, particularly after the AMG drivers got their hands on the new LM.

If Persson's season gradually went downhill, the second-string Porsche team's slowly improved. Ex-Formula 1 squad Zakspeed had neither the drivers nor the rubber, in the form of major sponsor Pirelli, to make best use of its two new 911 GT1-98s.

German tin-top veterans Michael Bartels and Armin Hahne notched up a lucky third at Silverstone in May, but it wasn't until the end of the season that its Italian tyres allowed the team the scent of a podium finish on merit. At the A1-Ring in September, team new boy Max Angelelli overhauled factory driver McNish for third in the closing stages, only for a last-minute splash-and-dash for fuel to drop him and Bartels back to fourth.

Zakspeed narrowly out-scored the DAMS Panoz team to take fourth in the teams' points. The solo chassis from the French team was quite often the best of the rest behind the Mercedes and Porsche works teams in the hands of Brabham and Frenchman Eric Bernard. From a surprise second on the grid, the former led at Silverstone before clashing with Alzen. Third places followed at Hockenheim and Dijon, although the team was deprived of the runner-up spot at Homestead when Bernard crashed a few laps from home.

The GT2 division was dominated by the ORECA Chrysler Viper team, which won all but one round on the way to retaining both drivers' and teams' titles. Champion drivers were ex-F1 men Olivier Beretta and Pedro Lamy with no fewer than eight wins.

Chrysler's main target was class honours in the Le Mans 24 Hours, which it duly achieved without too much drama. Drama aplenty marked the battle for overall honours in sports car racing's blue-riband event, however. High-profile assaults from Mercedes and BMW were over inside a matter of hours. Mercedes had claimed pole position with Schneider, but engine problems put both cars out of the race after two hours. BMW's pair of Williams-built contenders lasted little longer, wheel bearing failure accounting for both of its open-top sports racers. Nissan's assault looked particularly toothless, its TWR-built cars never on the pace. The Joest team, meanwhile, never truly got going with a revised version of the Porsche sports racer that had won the previous two editions of the 24 Hours.

That left the 66th running of the world's most famous motor race as a straight fight between Porsche and Toyota. The fortunes of the two marques swung back and forth through the race. Toyota led the early going, before Porsche moved to the fore as the new GT-One encountered problems. At around 6.00 a.m. on Sunday morning, the pendulum seemed as though it had swung irrevocably back the other way when the two 911 GT1-98s were wheeled into their respective garages within minutes of each other.

The car of McNish and Frenchmen Laurent Aïello and Stéphane Ortelli needed attention for a water leak. Damage to the second car driven by Müller, Alzen and veteran Bob Wollek was self-inflicted after the first-named went off at the first chicane on the Mulsanne Straight.

With 80 minutes to go, however, gearbox failure for the leading Toyota GT-One deprived Thierry Boutsen, Geoff Lees and Ralf Kelleners of a deserved victory. Waiting to pick up the pieces, as one would expect at Le Mans, was Porsche, the McNish, Aïello and Ortelli car leading home a 1-2 formation finish.

Shutterspeed Photografik

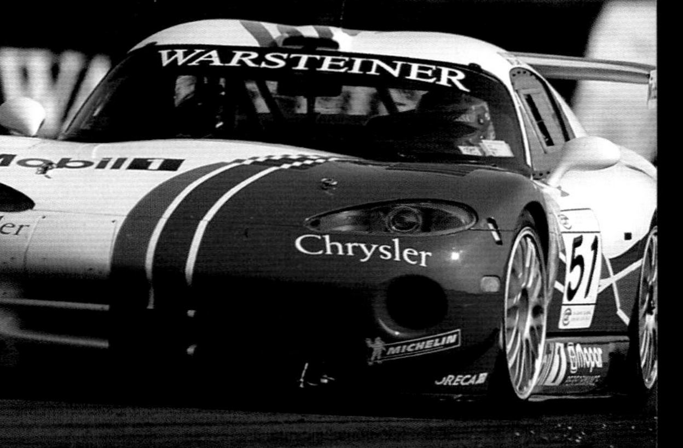

Shutterspeed Photografik

Far left: **Klaus Ludwig brought down the curtain on his illustrious career in fitting fashion by winning the drivers' title with Ricardo Zonta.**

Left: **Olivier Beretta and Pedro Lamy took the GT2 championship with their Chrysler Viper.**

There was consolation for Porsche in the form of a 1-2 finish in the Le Mans 24 Hours, the most prestigious sports car race of the year by far. The stunning Toyota GT-One set the pace on its debut, but the Boutsen/Lees/Kelleners car *(right)* **failed with victory seemingly within its grasp. Instead the win went to the Porsche of Laurent Aïello, Stéphane Ortelli and Allan McNish** *(bottom right)*, **with the sister car of Müller, Alzen and Wollek** *(below)* **in second place.**

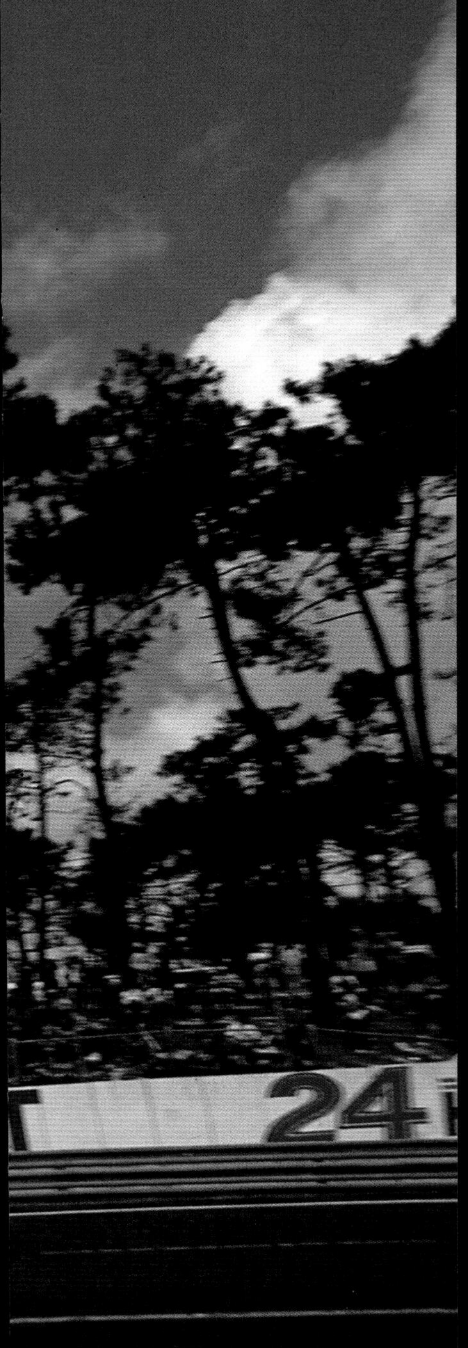

24

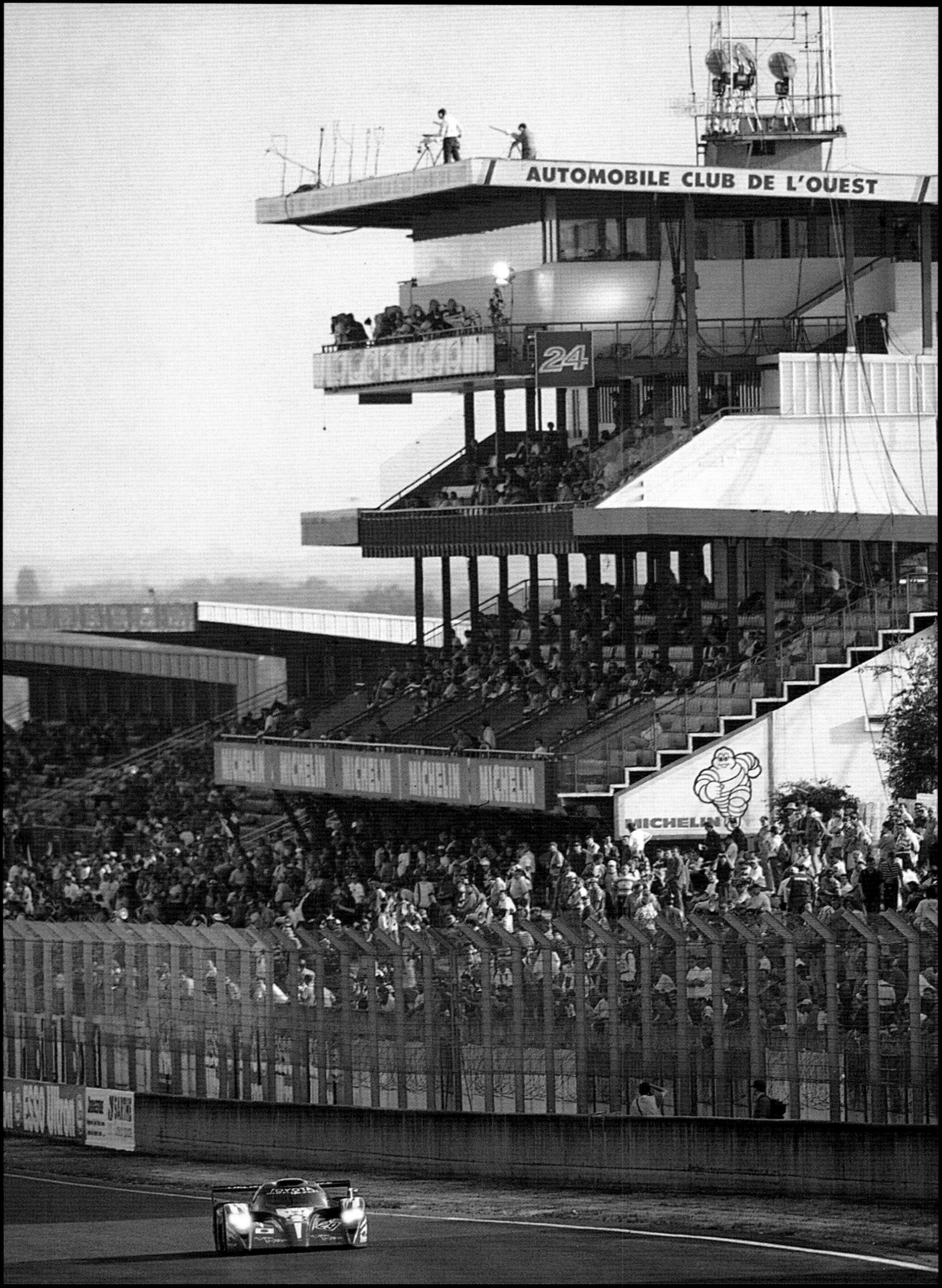
AUTOMOBILE CLUB DE L'OUEST
24
MICHELIN

Stu Forster/Allsport

Mobil
24H
A.C.O
MICHELIN

Bryn Williams

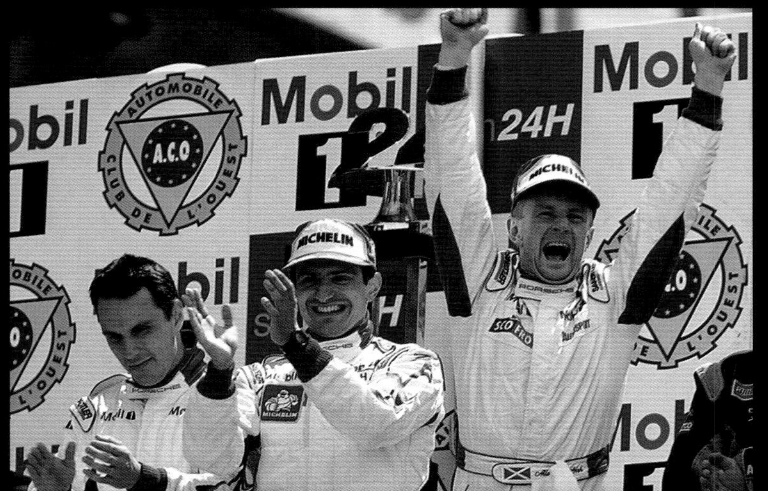

Bryn Williams

KEEPING THE CUSTOMER SATISFIED

Bryn Williams

TOURING CAR RACING REVIEW

by Marcus Simmons

Bothwell Photographic

The BTCC continued to attract big crowds and series organiser TOCA introduced a number of innovations to ensure that they were kept entertained.

Below left: The drivers' title was fought out between Anthony Reid *(left)* and Rickard Rydell. The Swede defended his lead in the points race to win the crown for Volvo *(bottom left)*, but Reid *(almost hidden)* and team-mate David Leslie (8) gave Nissan the manufacturers' title.

Right: Derek Warwick's Vauxhall Vectra and the Ford Mondeo of Will Hoy both won races but posed only an occasional threat to the front-runners.

Dave Cundy

Bothwell Photographic

THE past year has been a mixed one for touring car racing. For, behind the sheen of the discipline's most successful series, such as the British Touring Car Championship, lie worries over the future of manufacturer involvement. That's critical for this type of racing, which relies heavily on brand identity of the cars racing for its popularity.

The German Super Touring Championship, which runs to the same two-litre Super Touring rules as the BTCC, has had an equally successful season. But here the worries run deeper still – at the time of writing, only Honda and Opel could be predicted to contest the series with full manufacturer teams in 1999.

Elsewhere, the Super Touring competitions in Italy and Australia are relying on a core of just four or five importer- or manufacturer-backed cars, the French was contested almost entirely by privateers and the Japanese was finally killed off at the end of 1998.

But there have been success stories. In South America, which has formerly been separated from the rest of the world through running to its own local regulations, there is now a thriving Super Touring scene. Likewise in Sweden where, inspired by the success of home hero Rickard Rydell and Volvo in the BTCC, there were seven importer-backed teams.

There'll likely be even more in 1999, especially as Rydell delivered the result everyone in Sweden was waiting for by taking his and Volvo's first BTCC title.

This was a tough year. From the 26 races emerged nine different race winners, driving for six manufacturers. And, with just five wins to his credit – fewer than any other BTCC champion of the modern era – Rydell's accolade was down to more than just speed.

At the beginning of the season it had looked certain that he would score considerably more victories. The S40, built and run by Tom Walkinshaw's TWR operation, flew at Thruxton, and only an inspired performance from outgoing champion Alain Menu in his Williams Renault Laguna prevented the Stockholm florist from taking an opening-meeting double.

It soon became apparent, however, that the Volvo was difficult to adapt to changing weather conditions, and that's a critical handicap in any British series. TWR set to work making the car more user-friendly and less fussy – this sacrificed some of its outright speed, but ensured that Rydell would always be near the front of the pack.

The man behind the wheel did the rest. His driving style has always been aggressive yet controlled, and he added to this an ability to battle it out and indulge in the odd spot of panel-bashing without being turfed off the circuit. Once a lead of 40-odd points (just less than three wins) had been established, Rydell boxed clever until the end of the season, usually making sure he finished each meeting with just enough points on the scoreboard to not let his rivals enjoy a sniff of the title.

That was until Anthony Reid burst onto a late-season run of form with his Nissan Primera GT. The Scot, who defeated Rydell and Jacques Villeneuve to win the 1992 All-Japan Formula 3 Championship, stormed to seven wins in the Ray Mallock Limited-run car, which soon became recognised as the class act of Super Touring.

Reid's season had started slowly, due to his Nissan being unsorted and scarcely built at the first meeting. But, once early-season difficulties with engines had been remedied, he rose to prominence with a string of successes. The penultimate meeting at Oulton Park brought him to within striking distance of Rydell, but the TWR operation eked every final bit of speed out of its charge to deny Reid – who had nothing to lose and attacked at all times – at the last gasp.

Still, Nissan was happy, thanks to its victory in the manufacturers' championship. Reid combined with fellow Scot David Leslie to rack up the points for the Japanese make, which was able to celebrate one meeting early. Leslie himself had looked a threat for the drivers' title, becoming the first man to score two 1998 wins. In fact, it was the older Scot who commanded the best of the equipment at the start of the season, something which Reid was only too aware of when all was done and dusted.

Nissan's major rival Honda was up there too, with English young gun James Thompson pipping Menu for third in the points at the final meeting. This was an impressive season from the 24-year-old, who had blitzed the winter testing times but found the Prodrive-run Accord lacking when the business of racing began.

With a low-downforce aerodynamic kit, the Honda was difficult to drive and too hard on its tyres over a race distance. Thompson could often get a good qualifying position, but was struggling in the races. Mid-season Prodrive started concentrating on getting a more comfortable race set-up, and Thompson was able to take four wins, benefiting from the Neil Brown-built engine's awesome speed.

Menu was the other major player. He hadn't been publicly confident about the Renault's chances, but the Swiss must have been disappointed with a tally of only three wins. Brilliant at Thruxton – where he scored two of them – Menu battled fiercely, but allowed himself to get involved in on-track incidents more often than he would have wished. This immensely likeable man moves to the new high-profile Prodrive and Ford alliance for 1999 as team-mate to Reid, and it will be fascinating to see what he can do after ending his long and illustrious relationship with Williams and Renault.

Carrying on at Frank's team is Jason Plato, who consolidated his reputation in his second BTCC season to place fifth in the points. There was only one win, but the Englishman had a quietly impressive season in a car which was no longer the best.

Plato and Leslie certainly contributed far more to their respective teams' challenges than did Peter Kox and Gianni Morbidelli, the second drivers at Honda and Volvo. Dutchman Kox, fresh from the FIA GT Championship, was highly touted by Menu before the start of the season, but struggled to get to grips with front-wheel drive and the difficult Honda. By the end of the year he was looking better, and managed to take two front-row positions around the Knockhill assault course in Scotland.

Morbidelli, dropped by the Sauber Formula 1 team, confessed to over-driving his Volvo in the early races and found the unpredictable British weather a major obstacle in his bid to learn the rigours of tin-top racing. You can be fairly sure in saying that the Italian won't be back.

With four-wheel drive banned, Audi was forced to run with its front-wheel-drive A4 in the BTCC. Frenchman Yvan Muller, who had developed the car in the '97 German series, was drafted in in place of popular former champion Frank Biela, and duly rose to prominence as the revelation of the season.

They already knew on the Continent how good Muller is, thanks to his hat-trick of titles in the French Andros Trophy ice racing series. Sure enough, his car control was sensational. Muller's unique style meant that the Audi ran with extremely low downforce, which was a problem for team-mate John Bintcliffe, who lacked testing miles and couldn't really get to grips with the sideways technique required to drive the A4.

Audi is pulling out of the BTCC for 1999 and, while Muller is going to Vauxhall to seek his first BTCC win, Bintcliffe will likely end up in the job centre.

Muller will team up with a revitalised John Cleland who, in his tenth BTCC season with Vauxhall, delivered two early wins in his Vectra for the Triple Eight-run outfit. The team struggled to regain those heights thereafter, although Triple Eight director Derek Warwick was able to stick his oar in with a finely judged success in the wet at Knockhill which owed a lot to canny team tactics.

Similarly, Will Hoy triumphed at Silverstone in a Ford Mondeo which loved the wet but didn't much care for the dry. Works team West Surrey Racing worked hard to develop the car, but Ford had lost interest by July and instead was looking towards 1999. Hoy's regular team-mate Craig Baird had a baptism of fire in the BTCC, the highly rated New Zealander being dumped before season's end.

Bryn Williams

After a frustrating start to the season Anthony Reid and the Nissan became the BTCC's most potent combination but his brilliant charge came too late to give him the drivers' title.

Below: James Thompson took third place in the final standings after the Honda's set-up was changed to make it more effective in race trim.

Former World Champion Nigel Mansell made the occasional star appearance in Baird's Mondeo. He drove brilliantly to lead in the wet at Donington Park, then got involved in too many incidents at Brands Hatch and finished things off quietly with a circumspect day at Silverstone.

The only team even worse off was Peugeot. The Motor Sport Developments outfit just couldn't get the 406s to work, despite a mid-season change of engine supplier, and Paul Radisich and Tim Harvey were left to cast their minds back wistfully to better days. Peugeot UK then pulled the plug on its BTCC involvement at the end of the season.

The Peugeots frequently struggled to beat the independents fighting out the *Autosport* Cup. Norwegian newcomer Tommy Rustad eventually carried off the spoils, his Renault Laguna run by fellow BTCC rookies DC Cook Motorsport. With the title already wrapped up, he impressed at the final meeting on his first appearance for the factory Williams team.

Quickest independent was Matt Neal, who took an overall fastest lap at Snetterton and ran ahead of the works Nissans at Brands Hatch in his year-old Team Dynamics Primera. However, he was edged out of second in the points by the consistent Robb Gravett, who drove a two-year-old Honda Accord run by Brookes Motorsport.

Neal came closest to scooping BTCC organiser TOCA's reward of £100,000 to any independent winning a race outright. Among its other innovations were mandatory pit stops, to change two wheels, in the second race at each meeting, as well as an Indy-style one-shot showdown qualifying procedure to decide the grid for the first race. Both worked well, showing that TOCA is bristling with innovation and ideas to take touring car racing as entertainment into the 21st century.

By the time the new millennium comes around, Germany may no longer have Super Touring racing. A new 'son of Class 1' category has been mooted as the country looks to introducing a low-cost version of the lamented high-tech circus of the mid-1990s.

Nevertheless, there was a battle royal in 1998. Venezuela's Johnny Cecotto ultimately pipped French rival Laurent Aïello for the title in a BMW v. Peugeot shoot-out. BMW had scaled down its involvement for 1998, consistently complaining that the 25 kg weight penalty that its rear-wheel-drive 320i carried was unfair. But Schnitzer did a superb job with the increasingly venerable model to see off the challenge from Aïello's 406.

In Italy, Alfa's super-sexy 156 triumphed in its maiden season, Fabrizio Giovanardi at last taking his first tin-top crown after a fight with reigning champ Emanuele Naspetti's BMW.

The Swedish series went to one-time Indy car racer Fredrik Ekblom, the BMW man winning through after a tooth-and-nail battle with Volvo S40-driving double-champ Jan Nilsson. At the time of writing, former F1 racer Oscar Larrauri (BMW) was fighting out the South American crown with Peugeot driver Carlos Bueno. The Japanese series, meanwhile, looked set to go to ex-Le Mans winner Masanori Sekiya in the rear-wheel-drive Toyota Chaser.

Australia's Super Touring series was won by Brad Jones, who headed home team-mate Cameron McConville for an Audi A4 quattro 1-2. Third was veteran Jim Richards in his Volvo S40, but his season highlight was yet to come. Joined by Rydell for the Bathurst 1000, Richards won his sixth 'Great Race'. It was a thrilling contest, in which the Swedish car was chased all the way by the Nissan Primera of Steven Richards (Jim's son) and Matt Neal.

The big-banger 5-litre class Down Under went the way of TWR's sister operation, the Holden Racing Team. Returning from a season in Formula 3000, Craig Lowndes took the title at the final round in his Commodore from Perkins Holden driver Russell Ingall.

The V8-engined machines are looking likely to number more than 40 next season. Super Touring can only dream of such quantity, even though its quality is arguably better than ever. A rocky road now lies ahead as manufacturers and importers weigh up the pros and cons of the category.

Bryn Williams

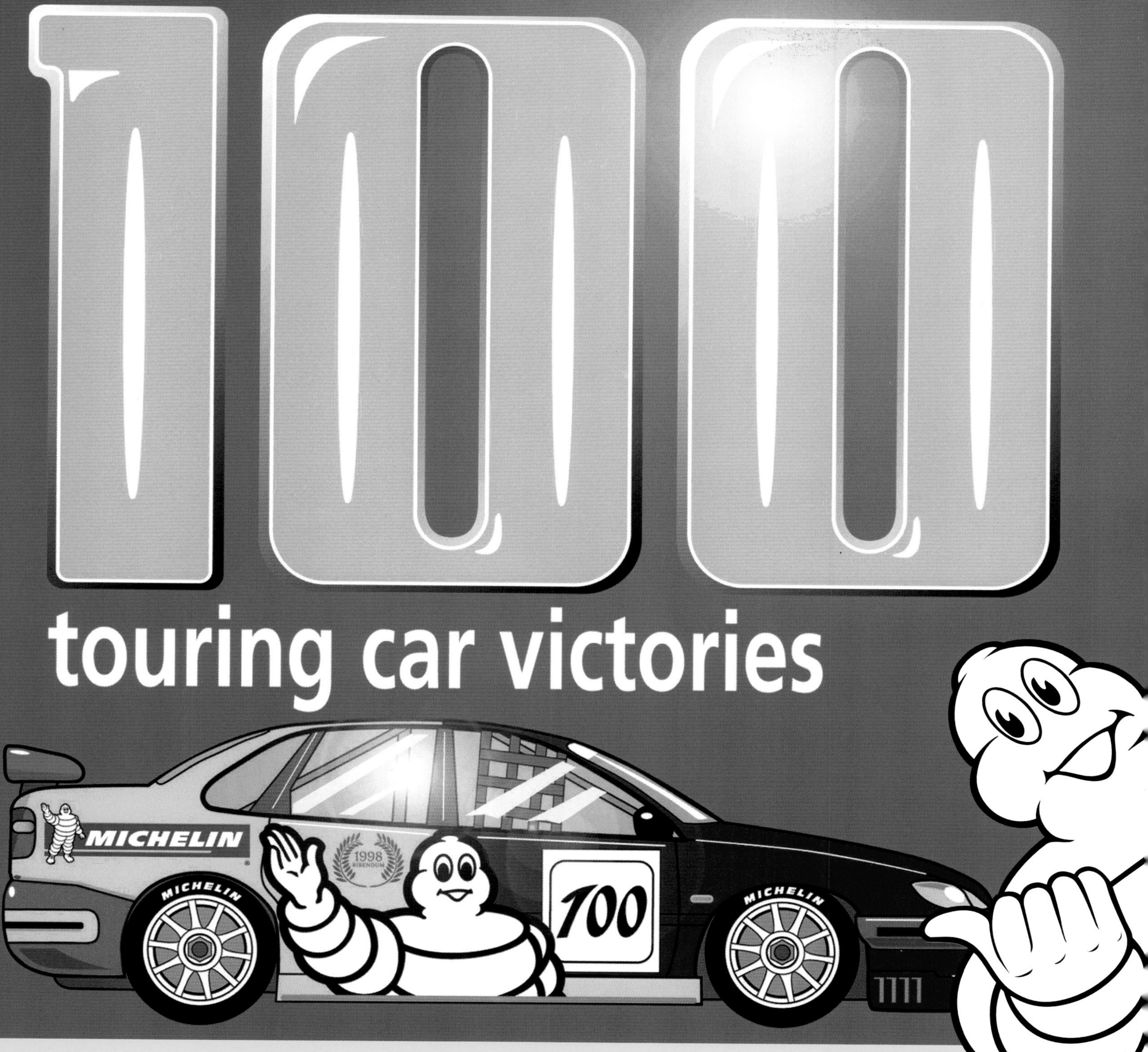

100 touring car victories

Michelin Pilots notched up 100 touring car victories by taking the 1998 BTCC title at Silverstone, which neatly coincided with the centenary of Bibendum the Michelin Man. But the ultimate winner is you the motorist. Pilots tested to the limits in the heat of competition ensure you get tyres that excel on the road. Fit the tyres fit for the British Touring Car Champions - Michelin Pilot Sport.

www.michelin.co.uk

76
TEXAS

MILESTONES

by Gordon Kirby

A COUPLE of substantial milestones were passed in American motor sporting history this year. Amid considerable ballyhoo, NASCAR celebrated its fiftieth anniversary. Much more quietly, CART turned twenty years old. NASCAR was famously born at the end of 1947 in a meeting of stock car drivers and promoters at a Daytona Beach hotel. From the beginning NASCAR has been run with an iron fist by the France family, starting with founder Bill France Sr. He handed power in 1972 to his son Bill Jr, who remains steadfastly in command. For thirty years NASCAR grew steadily, but in the last twenty years its premier, thirty-odd-race Winston Cup championship has boomed, drawing massive crowds at the track and on television to become America's most popular type of racing.

Opposite: NASCAR continued to enjoy robust health as it reached its fiftieth birthday, attracting huge crowds to venues such as Bruton Smith's imposing Texas Motor Speedway.

The fledgling Indy Racing League, presided over by Tony George *(above)*, once again proved far less popular with American race fans.

CART was created by a coalition of Indy car team owners who got together in 1978, and broke away from USAC the following year. CART recreated USAC's failing Championship or 'Champ car' series as 'Indy car' racing, bringing on board a series sponsor, PPG (where there had been none), adding street and road races to the schedule (ditto), and introducing a new, sorely needed TV package (ditto, also). These days, CART's championship is stronger than ever with FedEx taking over this year from PPG as series sponsor, twenty races on four continents in 1999, and a worldwide TV audience to rival F1, the only motor racing category to do so.

All this despite the revival of the old CART–USAC war a few years ago which resulted in young Indianapolis Motor Speedway President Tony George taking the Indy 500 out of CART's championship and forming his own, second-level, cost-controlled Indy Racing League (IRL). CART's drivers, cars and teams haven't raced at Indianapolis since 1995, and may not do so again for many years to come, and with George's struggling, ten-race IRL series (Indy 500 included) laying legal claim to the 'Indy car' name CART this past season rechristened its cars 'Champ cars'.

While initiating his split with CART, Tony George introduced NASCAR to his family's hallowed speedway in 1994 with the first running of the Brickyard 400 Winston Cup race in August. Bringing stock cars to the spiritual home of American open-wheel racing was one thing, but during the summer and autumn of 1998 Tony George was able to work out an expensive agreement with Bernie Ecclestone to bring F1 back to the United States in 2000.

George has spent a considerable portion (reliable estimates put the sum at more than US$100 million) of his family's massive fortune in launching the IRL series, and has made some profound changes to the face of American motor racing. He's banished CART from Indianapolis, turned the Indy 500 into a curious, second-level motor race, brought in NASCAR, and now hopes to bring F1 back to America and make the United States Grand Prix a fixture on a combined oval/road circuit built within the grounds of the Indianapolis Motor Speedway.

While Tony George has been exercising his wallet and playing politics at the top levels of the sport, most other important players in the vast American racing community have been paying attention to their bottom lines and acting primarily as businessmen rather than as power brokers. As George continues to spend lavishly, people like Bill France, Roger Penske, Bruton Smith and Chris Pook have taken their race-track-owning and operating companies public, trading on the New York and other stock exchanges and generating more money to further develop and expand their operations.

In London, Bernie Ecclestone tried to follow their lead, but was unable to jump through all the required EU administrative hoops, but in Detroit, where CART has its headquarters, Champ Car racing's team owners and their most recent CEO Andrew Craig were able to structure their own successful New York Stock Exchange flotation. CART went public last January and despite predictions of doom from some quarters the value of the stock held steady and even rose over the course of the year.

ancora
Barilla
TARGET
TARGET
Speed Stick
LifeSavers

Left: Alex Zanardi retained his CART championship with a string of spectacular performances in Chip Ganassi's Reynard-Honda, earning himself another chance in Formula 1 with Williams.

Jimmy Vasser *(right)* made it a 1-2 for the Ganassi team in the final points table after his rival for the runner-up spot, Dario Franchitti *(below right)*, was forced to retire from the last race of the season.

Bottom right: It was another frustrating year for Michael Andretti, who won the season-opener at Homestead for Swift but was out of luck thereafter.

Photos: Michael C. Brown

ZANARDI's SECOND CART TITLE, GANASSI's THIRD

CART's inaugural FedEx Championship Series unfolded slowly at first with five different winners in the year's first five races. It wasn't until June and July that Alessandro Zanardi was able to put his stamp on the year, winning four of five midsummer races and suddenly emerging as a runaway champion. In his second championship year, and the third in a row for Chip Ganassi's team, the 31-year-old Italian was ultimately all-dominant, a mature, confident champion. From Long Beach in April through to Toronto in July, Alessandro, or Alex as he's now known, was first or second in eight of nine races. He won six of them and carried off the PPG Cup at Vancouver in September with four races left. Not since Rick Mears back in 1981 had anyone wrapped up the championship so quickly.

Zanardi won seven of 19 races in 1998, one short of Al Unser Jr's and Michael Andretti's CART record, but set a new mark for points with 285, 51 more than Andretti's 1991 tally. Alex also got to 15 wins faster than any other driver in CART history – Mears was again the record holder. Yet he was unable to earn a single pole this year and was on the front row for only four races. As dominant as Zanardi was, no fewer than six other drivers managed to win Champ Car races this season and on different days the double champion was beaten fair and square by Jimmy Vasser, Dario Franchitti, Greg Moore, Adrian Fernandez, Michael Andretti and Bryan Herta.

Early in the year Moore looked like putting together a championship challenge, but both Greg and the Forsythe team made mistakes, and through the heart of the season their attack tailed off. Nobody else was able to match Zanardi's consistent competitiveness on all types of track, nor could any other team equal the amazing reliability record produced by Ganassi's team as neither Zanardi nor team-mate Vasser suffered a single mechanical DNF!

Near the end of the year Zanardi found a match as Dario Franchitti began to fulfil his promise with Barry Green's team. Often the man to beat in the season's closing months, Franchitti was on the front row in eight of the last eleven races and won three of the last six. Franchitti's late-season charge almost resulted in the deflation of Chip Ganassi's dream of finishing 1-2 in the championship, but a blown engine while Dario was running second between Moore and Vasser in the season-closing Marlboro 500 at the California Speedway enabled Zanardi and Vasser to take the top two places in the points table, the first time team-mates have done that since Penske swept the top three places in 1994. Nevertheless, with Zanardi off to F1, the 25-year-old Scotsman will start the 1999 Champ Car season as a title favourite in company with '96 champion Vasser and Moore.

The race of the year was the U.S. 500 at the high-banked Michigan Speedway at the end of July. The event was wreathed in tragedy when Adrian Fernandez crashed into the wall while battling for the lead and his car's right-front wheel bounced over the tall restraining fence into the grandstands, killing three spectators. The fence was immediately increased in height for the following month's NASCAR race, but most experts agreed Fernandez's accident was a freak of nature, the first time in the 31-year history of the Michigan oval track, in fact, that any fan had been killed.

The 500 carried on at a furious pace with a record-setting 62 official lead changes at the start/finish stripe, and close to two hundred passes for the lead taking place around the entire track during the 250-lap, 500-mile contest. It was a breathtaking race, the most exciting many fans say they've ever seen, but overshadowed entirely by the desperate tragedy that took place in the Turn Four grandstands that hot July afternoon.

The fierce drafting and back-and-forth racing witnessed at this year's U.S. 500 and Marlboro 500 resulted from special, identical wings fitted to all the cars. Created by CART's technical committee in partnership with the four competing Champ Car manufacturers – Reynard, Penske, Swift and Lola – the new wing was designed by Swift's chief engineer Mark Handford and became known as the 'Handford Wing'. Its goal was to reduce downforce and add drag in an effort to reduce lap speeds by 10 mph on the two fastest tracks that CART's Champ cars race on.

The goal was achieved, but an intriguing by-product was that the new wing created much closer racing than usual on a superspeedway as nobody was able to break away from the draft and a driver could move from tenth place to first in two or three laps, and be back in tenth three laps later! Some of the drivers were frustrated by the results and concerned by the possibility of a huge, multi-car accident, but the fans loved it.

A SUBLIME COMBINATION

Meanwhile, the past three years have proven not only that Zanardi is a superb driver, but also that Chip Ganassi's team is indefatigably the best in the business. This year, Target/Chip Ganassi Racing became the first team since Penske in 1981-83 to

Michael C. Brown

Michael C. Brown

Bryn Williams

Far left: Greg Moore started the year strongly but his championship challenge faded as the season unfolded.

Bobby Rahal *(left)* remained competitive in his last season as a driver before retiring from the cockpit to concentrate on his role as a team owner.

In the second half of the season Scotsman Dario Franchitti *(below left)* was right on the pace and he will start 1999 as one of the title favourites.

win the championship in three straight years, and, more than anything else, the reliability record tells the story. As noted, neither Zanardi nor Vasser suffered a single mechanical failure in a race this season, and Vasser has had only one mechanical DNF in the past three years! From time to time there have been problems in practice and qualifying, but the team's race day record is something to be marvelled at.

To Ganassi's great credit he has built the most stable and broadly experienced team at work today in CART. It starts with managing director Tom Anderson and team manager Mike Hull, a pair of unwavering Steady Eddies, both of whom have been around almost for ever, Anderson in particular. Anderson and chief engineer Mo Nunn bring something like three-quarters of a century of experience to the team and both have been with Ganassi from the start more than ten years ago when Chip purchased the assets of Pat Patrick's original CART team.

Ganassi, Anderson and Nunn have gathered around them people like team manager Hull and Julian Robertson, a very bright, ex-F1 engineer who runs Vasser's car, as well as chief mechanics Rob Hill and Grant Weaver, another pair of eminently unflappable operators. The list goes on, because there's plenty of experience all the way through the team, and many of them have been there for quite a while, something that can't be said for some of the older, more storied CART teams that have fallen behind in recent years.

Zanardi dominated the middle third of the season, winning four races in a row – at Detroit, Portland, Cleveland and Toronto – in June and July. A very aggressive driver and a tough racer, Zanardi is a civilised Italian gentleman and a reporter's delight, with long, expansive answers to most questions and amusing proto-American, or half-English, turns of phrase. His sharp intellect enables Zanardi to be a very technically minded driver, disciplined and astute in the art of testing, tuning and setting up a modern single-seater.

Alex has also shown everyone that he's a great racer, and is, of course, the 'Doughnut King', celebrating his CART victories with what has become his trademark exhibition of Latin exuberance. And, as everyone asks, if the chance comes to do it in F1, will Max and Bernie permit it? Having watched him closely for three years, I'm sure the opportunity for Zanardi to test the FIA's good humour, with 'doughnuts', and possibly in other ways, will definitely arise.

Team-mate Vasser won at Nazareth, Milwaukee and the California Speedway, and was a close second in the U.S. 500 at Michigan – ovals all. His victory in the season finale enabled Jimmy to edge Franchitti by nine points for second in the championship. Vasser recently signed a new three-year contract with Ganassi and now takes on the role of team leader, with F3000 champion Juan Pablo Montoya taking over from Zanardi. If the team continues to operate at the same impressively high level it has achieved in the past three years, Vasser stands as the man to beat in 1999, with Montoya hoping to profit from the great opportunity of replacing the reigning champion.

A highlight of the second half of the season was Franchitti's steady emergence as a regular contender for victory at tracks of every kind. Dario's move at the end of last year from Carl Hogan's single-car Mercedes team to Barry Green's expanding, two-car Honda-powered squad was derided by some, but it turned out to be exactly the right move for the young Scotsman's career.

Franchitti was a close second behind Zanardi at Long Beach early in the year and was on the pole and led in Brazil, battling wheel to wheel with Zanardi until an electronics failure stopped him. At Toronto in July he was again on the pole and ran away with the race until spinning because of a soft brake pedal, and at Mid-Ohio the next month he took his third pole but crashed with Herta and Vasser at the first turn.

A week later, at Road America, the USA's finest road circuit in Elkhart Lake, Wisconsin, Dario finally got it right. He started from the third row but was quickly into the thick of the battle and ran away after the second round of pit stops, beating Zanardi by seven seconds with the rest of the field half a minute and more behind. Franchitti won again, from the pole, in Vancouver. He finished fourth at Laguna Seca, then won his third race of the year in the rain in Houston, challenged only by team-mate Paul Tracy. Dario took his fifth pole of the year in Surfers Paradise and finished a close second to Zanardi, putting himself in a position to beat Vasser to second in the championship, but it wasn't to be.

In the final race of the season at the California Speedway Franchitti ran in the thick of the amazing 230 mph battle for the lead and at half-distance was running a strong and comfortable second, directly ahead of his rival for the runner-up spot in the championship, Vasser, when his engine suddenly blew up. Disappointing for sure, but Dario was pleased to have been so competitive on the big superspeedway and is quietly confident that he will be a competitive factor on the full range of tracks next year, and therefore capable of mounting a championship challenge.

Team-mate Tracy joined Team Green at the end of last year after being dumped unceremoniously by Penske. The season past was 29-year-old Tracy's eighth in CART and, aside from one year with Newman/Haas, it was his first as a former Penske driver. At Green's team there was plenty of support, but Paul was outpaced from the start by the brilliant Franchitti and wasn't able to qualify near the front until the end of the year. Unfortunately, Tracy's season was typified by his collision with Franchitti in Houston and his spin into the barrier while leading on a restart with just five laps to go in the season-closing 500-mile race at the California Speedway.

Paul's position with Green's set-up is solid. Everyone in the team has great respect for him as a racer, and Franchitti could not be a friendlier, more gracious team-mate. With the preferred Reynard-Honda/Firestone package and a strong working environment, Tracy must find his feet and perform in 1999, or face a tough new millennium.

Stepping forward to establish himself as one of Champ Car racing's most reliable front-runners, on the other hand, was Adrian Fernandez, who won convincingly at Motegi in the spring and at Mid-Ohio in late summer. In his first year with Pat Patrick's team, the Mexican hero finished a good fourth in the championship, beating the likes of Greg Moore and his own team-mate Scott Pruett. Fernandez emerged as a very steady performer on a variety of tracks and was the first Ford/Cosworth driver in the championship.

Prior to 1997, Pruett had been Patrick's only driver for three years, starting in 1994 when he carried out testing duties for Firestone in preparation for its re-entry into Champ Car racing. What turned out to be Pruett's final year with Patrick was much like all the rest – he was frequently competitive, threatening occasionally to win, but never able to put everything together with consistency. Pruett twice finished second and was part of a Patrick 1-2 when Fernandez triumphed at Mid-Ohio. He was sixth in the championship behind Fernandez and Greg Moore.

Fifth-placed Moore was often a pacesetter and was occasionally the

Michael C. Brown

Left: Young Brazilian Tony Kanaan was crowned CART's rookie of the year after a highly impressive first season in Champ Car racing.

Two veterans achieved long-held ambitions in 1998: former Grand Prix regular Eddie Cheever *(right)* won the Indy 500 after a well-judged drive, while seven-times Winston Cup champion Dale Earnhardt *(far right)* finally scored his first victory in the classic Daytona 500.

Below right: Jeff Gordon was once again the dominant force in NASCAR, winning the championship for the third time in four seasons.

man to beat. The young Canadian led the championship for two races after beating Zanardi in Brazil with a magnificent outside pass but Moore's championship challenge evaporated after he crashed at the first turn on the opening lap at Portland in June. Race after race he fell further and further behind, although Greg won the U.S. 500 at the end of July in style, outduelling Vasser and Zanardi, and was a strong second between the two Ganassi drivers in the other superspeedway race at the end of the season. New team-mate Patrick Carpentier had two poles at Nazareth and Milwaukee, but no results and finished a distant 19th in the points table.

Newman-Haas's pair of black Swift-Fords driven by Michael Andretti and Christian Fittipaldi were frequently among the leading bunch, but were at least as often among the disappointed. Andretti started the year with a fine win at Homestead, but despite leading almost as many laps as Zanardi he never won again. Michael crashed out of at least three races he could have won – at Nazareth, Milwaukee and the California Speedway – and wound up a distant seventh in the title chase. Team-mate Fittipaldi rarely escapes fate's most luckless twists, although when things go well he can impress, as he did when he finished third in Surfers Paradise near the end of the year. With only six finishes, however, Fittipaldi trailed home 14th in the standings.

In his third year with Bobby Rahal's team and fifth in Champ cars, Bryan Herta finally scored his first victory. Herta did it in style, fending off Zanardi at Laguna Seca, the very track where Zanardi blitzed him on the last lap two years ago. Bryan was on the pole three times and the front row for two more races, but made it to the podium just three times and had to be content with eighth in the table behind Pruett and Andretti.

In what was dubbed his 'Last Ride' as a driver, team owner Rahal was placed tenth in the championship. Bobby's final year was highlighted by finishing a very competitive third at Mid-Ohio, his home track, but his strongest race of the year came at Long Beach, where he qualified on the outside of the front row alongside team-mate Herta and led briefly before losing two laps in a multi-car incident that blocked the track. After a frustrating delay, Rahal rejoined, turning the race's fastest lap.

Rookie of the year was 23-year-old Brazilian Tony Kanaan, who had won the Indy Lights title the previous season and moved up to Champ cars with Steve Horne's Tasman Motorsports. Kanaan impressed frequently, taking back-to-back third places at Laguna Seca and Houston, and finished ninth in the championship. With enough money to do a little more testing, Kanaan is capable of winning in 1999.

Another deeply disappointing year for Roger Penske's team yielded but one podium, a third for Al Unser Jr at Milwaukee at the end of May. The all-new Penske PC27 was a very good car, designed to maximise the benefits of Mercedes-Benz's tiny new 108E engine, but reliability problems and a lack of leadership within the team meant Unser finished only half the races, ending the year in 11th place overall. Team-mate Andre Ribeiro had a dismal first year with Penske and finished 22nd in the championship. Big changes are afoot at Penske, with a new general manager expected to replace Chuck Sprague and a wholesale and much-needed shake-up possible within the race team.

Other disappointments included Gil de Ferran with Derrick Walker's team, and Mark Blundell and Mauricio Gugelmin at PacWest. De Ferran frequently ran well but always seemed to hit trouble, failing to finish the last six races. Blundell and Gugelmin struggled after being compelled to start the new year with '97 cars. It wasn't until the very end of the season that PacWest began to get a technical grip, and instead of being championship contenders as hoped they never made the podium and finished 15th (Gugelmin) and 18th (Blundell) in the points table.

After being beaten by Mercedes in 1997, Honda earned its second CART manufacturers' championship in three years. Honda-powered cars won 13 races in 1998, finished 1-2-3 in the championship and have scored 31 victories over the last four years. CART's constructors' title was taken for the fourth consecutive year by Reynard, whose cars won no fewer than 18 of the 19 races. Reynards have now recorded a total of fifty Champ Car victories since Michael Andretti's first win for the marque at the beginning of 1994. On the tyre front Firestone was equally dominant, chalking up 18 victories to Goodyear's one.

The addition of Chip Ganassi's new Chicago Motor Speedway means there will be twenty FedEx Championship Series races next year, and there are at least two or three other venues anxious to establish new Champ Car dates. With full, high-quality fields at every race, a successful early 1998 flotation on the New York Stock Exchange, and strong sponsorship from well-known rapid-freight and delivery specialists FedEx, Champ Car racing is benefiting also from a booming worldwide TV market and an exemplary safety record, with not one driver spending a night in hospital in 1998. CART has weathered its unwanted split with Indianapolis and is enjoying better racing and more youthful vitality than ever, with not a single driver in next year's field over forty, 16 of them in their twenties, and an average age of 28, equal to F1.

BRACK IS IRL CHAMPION

In his second year in the category and first with A.J. Foyt's team, Swede Kenny Brack claimed the IRL championship. Brack won three mid-season races and took the title at a canter in the end, finishing fifth and a distant tenth in the last two races of the year but handily out-pointing Davey Hamilton and Tony Stewart. Second-placed Hamilton did not win a race and was less able to rise to the end-of-year championship challenge than Brack. The IRL's poster-boy Stewart and John Menard's team once again looked good for a few laps here and there before making one blunder after another.

The IRL's keynote race, the Indy 500, was won by F1 and CART veteran Eddie Cheever, who put in a spirited performance in the final sprint to the flag to beat 1996 winner Buddy Lazier. That was Eddie's only day in the sun, however, as he finished eighth in the championship behind 1996 Indy 500 winner Arie Luyendyk. Arie is another veteran who had a miserable year, highlighted by a lone win in the season's final race at Las Vegas. There were smiles all round as well when John Paul Jr won the second-last race of the year in Texas. It was sports car stalwart Paul's first win in an Indy-type car in 15 years – he scored his only other Indy car victory in CART's Michigan 500 back in 1983.

Those moments aside there was again an unfortunate sourness around the IRL as the series continued to struggle to draw fans or much press coverage. Crowds were down everywhere over last year. There were even empty seats at the Indy 500! As few as 5000 people bought tickets for the IRL races in New Hampshire and Las Vegas, and New Hampshire promoter Bob Bahre confirmed he won't run any more IRL races.

Questions abound at most other IRL venues because of weak, dwindling crowds, and it appears that Tony George will face a serious shortage of races in 2000 if Bruton Smith pulls the plug after next year on the four races at his three tracks in Texas, Charlotte and Atlanta. All year, many IRL team owners complained vociferously to George and IRL executive director Leo Mehl about their inability to attract major sponsors, and as the IRL formula goes into its third year urgent questions are being asked about the commercial viability of the series.

There was also a running argument about cheating through much of 1998 between top team owners Foyt and Menard. Each believed the other was beating the rulebook, and in the end it was Menard who was caught and fined for running flexible tail-wings on his cars.

'The more the IRL has these rule enforcement problems,' Menard made the point, 'the less likely it is that the CART guys are going to come over here and subject themselves to this type of treatment. If they do this to me, think what they're going to do to somebody else.'

For a while Menard talked about becoming a partner with driver Robby Gordon in a new CART team. One of the IRL's biggest supporters, and certainly its richest, Menard finally decided to stick with the IRL for 1999, although with a completely revamped team and a new driver in Texan Greg Ray. Menard's former star driver Tony Stewart has moved on to NASCAR, which seems to have become the preferred destination for most IRL drivers. Is this part of Tony George's legacy, that the Indy 500 is now a round of a series that is a training ground for NASCAR? Tell me it ain't so!

AT THE TOP OF HIS GAME

As we reported last year, in NASCAR the Jeff Gordon Era has arrived with full force. Gordon won his third Winston Cup championship in four years in 1998, dominating like never before at the tender age of 27. Gordon won 13 Winston Cup races this year, equalling Richard Petty's 1973 record, and has now won a whopping 33 races in the past three years! In 1998, he set a record for points, beating Cale Yarborough's standard of 5000 from 21 years ago. Over the 33-race Winston Cup season, Gordon scored 5328 points, an amazing 88 per cent of maximum, leaving runner-up Mark Martin 364 points behind and the rest of the field 700 and more points adrift. In short, he annihilated 'em.

Gordon drives for Rick Hendrick's three-car team, which has now swept the NASCAR title four years running,

David Taylor/Allsport USA

Nigel Kinrade

Winston Cup racing provides a feast of non-stop action. Attention switches to the pits at Martinsville as the drivers take advantage of a caution period to make a routine stop for fuel and tyres.

with team-mate Terry Labonte winning the 1996 championship. Hendrick's Chevrolet team has long been considered one of the best in the business, running three cars for many years and leading Chevrolet's factory attack in NASCAR. A midget and sprint car driver as a teenager, Gordon joined Hendrick's team at the end of 1992 when he was just 21, and won his first championship at 24 in 1995, becoming the youngest champion in Winston Cup history.

Gordon is twenty years younger than many of his contemporaries, but there's no doubt that the fresh-faced Californian-by-way-of-Indiana is leading a flood of new, young drivers into NASCAR's top league. Included are Jeff and Ward Burton, Bobby Labonte and Jeremy Mayfield, as well as this year's second-division NASCAR Busch Grand National Champion, 21-year-old Dale Earnhardt Jr, and runner-up Matt Kenseth.

These days Gordon is so successful that he's become the man many fans love to hate. At the traditional, pre-race driver introductions, he gets as many boos as cheers, but Gordon sees that kind of thing as the price of fame. Indeed, in the United States, he's now as well known as any racing driver, his profile expanded by a starring role in Pepsi commercials with other American sports superstars like Michael Jordan.

Gordon regularly credits much of his on-track success to crew chief Ray Evernham, who's in charge of Gordon's cars and is a young, energetic man at the peak of his own career. Visible proof of Evernham's genius comes in many races when Gordon finds himself struggling with an ill-handling car in fifth or sixth. After a few quick, astute tweaks to chassis set-up, tyre pressures or spoiler angle, however, Gordon's car comes to life in the race's final 100 miles and he's able to race to win.

Team owner Rick Hendrick has been fighting leukaemia this year, and has not been able to attend any races. In his stead, the team has been run by his brother John, with '96 champion Labonte finishing ninth in this year's championship, winning one race, and third driver Ricky Craven being replaced by Wally Dallenbach Jr after Craven was seriously injured in a multi-car accident at Talladega.

Second to Gordon in the '98 Winston Cup title chase was the ever-stoic Mark Martin, who won seven times himself and finished in the top five in 21 races, but couldn't come close to catching Gordon. Martin will turn forty in January, and he's led Jack Roush's Ford team since 1988, regularly winning races and contending, for a portion of the season at least, for the championship. Wiry and fit, Martin is a relentless competitor who just can't seem to get his arms around the Winston Cup trophy.

Roush ran no fewer than five cars in 1998, including one for Jeff Burton, who often ran up front, won two races and finished a strong fifth in the championship. Roush's other cars were driven by Chad Little, Johnny Benson and Kevin LePage, who replaced Ted Musgrave.

Third in the championship was taken by veteran Dale Jarrett, who won three times aboard one of Robert Yates's top-rated Fords. At 41, Jarrett has led Yates's team for the past four years and is one of NASCAR's most reliable and clean drivers. Joining him in Yates's team in 1998 was young USAC midget and sprint car champion Kenny Irwin, who had a steady if slightly disappointing first season in stock cars. Irwin finished 28th in the points table with one fifth place his best result, but that was good enough to make him Winston Cup rookie of the year.

Amid the expanding trend towards multi-car teams, Roger Penske and former Ford racing boss Mike Kranefuss merged their NASCAR operations to form Penske-Kranefuss Racing. Veteran Rusty Wallace and 29-year-old newcomer Jeremy Mayfield became team-mates and for a while through the early season the pair ran at the top of the points chart, challenging Gordon. Both won at least once – Mayfield for the first time – but neither was able to sustain a championship drive. Wallace, a former champion, faded to finish fourth overall while Mayfield fell to seventh at season's end.

Sixth in the championship went to Terry Labonte's younger brother Bobby, who drives for retired NFL coach Joe Gibbs's team. Labonte won two races and often ran competitively in Gibbs's Pontiacs, finishing between Jeff Burton and Mayfield in this year's Winston Cup standings.

Seven-times Winston Cup champion Dale Earnhardt, now 47, started the year in style by scoring a long-overdue victory in the season-opening Daytona 500. Although Earnhardt has won everything else in stock car racing, he had never won the classic 500-mile race at Daytona, but this year he pulled it off in consummate form, beating Bobby Labonte and Mayfield to the chequered flag. Dale's season went downhill thereafter, however, as he rarely ran up front and didn't win again. He ended the year eighth in the points table behind Mayfield and ahead of Terry Labonte and another veteran, Bobby Hamilton.

Other previous champions still racing in NASCAR include 1988 champ Bill Elliott and 1981, '82 and '85 champion Darrell Waltrip. Elliott was 42 this year, Waltrip 51, but they're still at it, sometimes struggling, or even failing to qualify. Elliott never cracked the top five this year and finished 19th in the points table. Waltrip managed a single fifth place, and was 24th in the championship.

NEW FACES . . .

As noted, Dale Earnhardt Jr won NASCAR's second-division Busch Grand National title. Young Earnhardt won seven races in his first full season on the circuit and moves up to Winston Cup in 1999 thanks to a five-year sponsorship deal with Budweiser. Will he challenge Gordon in the years ahead?

With the proceeds from its stock market flotation, CART bought both the Indy Lights and Toyota/Atlantic championships in 1998. This means the Lights and Atlantic series, which have long run as support events at most CART races, are now formally tied to CART as official training, or driver development, categories. Brazilian Cristiano da Matta won the 1998 Indy Lights championship and moves up to Champ cars next year as Scott Pruett's team-mate at the Toyota-powered Arciero-Wells Racing CART team. Canadian Lee Bentham won the Toyota/Atlantic title, and may also move up to Champ cars next year.

. . . AND OLD

The already sadly depleted world of American sports car racing was fissured even more this year by the creation of two separate sports car sanctioning bodies. The SCCA's revived United States Road Racing Championship for CanAm cars was won by Riley & Scott-Ford driver James Weaver from team-mate Butch Leitzinger. In Professional Sports Car's World Sports Car Championship, Leitzinger turned the tables on Weaver, while Panoz drivers Andy Wallace and David Brabham were crowned GT champions. And the SCCA's only remaining 'professional' racing championship – the TransAm series – was won for the first time by veteran Paul Gentilozzi's Corvette.

THE "TEAM" IN TEAM KOOL GREEN

A walk through the paddock and infield of the FedEx Championship Series

Above: Team KOOL Green on parade. Paul Tracy and his pit crew line up behind their car on the grid at Motegi.

Below: Dario Franchitti always tries to find time to sign autographs for the fans.

SOAKING up the sights and sounds of the paddock area can quite often be one of the highlights, if not the best part of a race weekend for a fan. Pushing close to see the car, snapping photos, swapping some shop talk with a mechanic, meeting their favorite driver or, if they're lucky, even getting some autographs along the way.

Team KOOL Green drivers Paul Tracy and Dario Franchitti are favorites of fans in hot pursuit of autographs from the stars of the CART FedEx Championship Series. Tracy and Franchitti usually have some time booked on race weekends to sign posters, hero cards, shirts, hats and other racing memorabilia – like the weekend at the season finale in Fontana.

"It's one of the fun parts of the job," says Tracy of the autograph sessions. "Fans get a real kick out of meeting us and what a lot of people don't realize is that it's flattering for us as well. It's important to be accessible to the fans because without them there would be no show. I think athletes in other sports get that confused sometimes."

Franchitti adds, "It's such a small thing to do for fans, who really give so much of themselves to the sport. I'm a lot like them myself. Ayrton Senna was my racing hero and I would be thrilled to meet Sean Connery."

Tracy and Franchitti are the first points of contact for the public in its perception of Team KOOL Green. It's their image, persona and, of course, their record on the track which determines popularity for the team. However, a team is also measured by other factors away from the track such as its merchandising, hospitality, promotions, sponsorship and overall public relations.

Now...let's take a quick tour around the different parts of the track to get a better understanding of the larger "team" in Team KOOL Green!

Not far away from the autograph session another large crowd has gathered to watch and take part in the KOOL Racing Simulator Challenge. It's as close as you can get to racing without actually being strapped in and putting the helmet on yourself. Alex Gurney, who recently finished his rookie season in the Barber Dodge Pro Series, is an up-and-comer in Team Green's driver development program. Gurney faced a steep learning curve after graduating as the '97 winner of the Team Green Academy. He improved steadily throughout the season, finishing 10th in the overall standings. And, while he's not racing at Fontana, he is providing a real treat for some die-hard race fans by racing against them on the simulator.

"I haven't had a lot of practice on this machine, so I felt some pressure to win," says Gurney, who has strong racing bloodlines as the son of the legendary Dan Gurney. "But I pulled it out in the end. These fans are really good because they play so much, but the guys running the simulator are the best."

KOOL Racing Simulators travel from race to race and to bar locations across the United States. The people running the games get a lot of practice showing race fans how to blast their way around the track. It's their work on a race weekend which lends a carnival atmosphere to the track, with games and prizes to be won.

Any prizes handed out would usually come from the Team KOOL Green merchandise area right next to the simulators. It's here where race fans can load up on T-shirts with Tracy emblazoned across the back or a Team KOOL Green ball cap with Dario's #27 stitched on the side. According to merchandise manager Heather Walker, Tracy is a T-shirt kind of guy, while Franchitti's favorite piece of clothing – "the rug" – is a sweater stitched together with different fabrics.

"We have a lot of fantastic products of the highest quality," says Walker. "People looking around tend to purchase hats and T-shirts because those items can be signed easily by the drivers. High-end stuff like helmets and team jackets are things collectors and the racing fanatics buy."

When racing fanatics come to mind, the biggest ones can generally be found with a stroll over to the media center. A lot of reporters will eat, sleep and live racing. Media play an important role, keeping fans up to date with what happens in the world of Champ Cars. One of the tools media have come to rely on is the KOOL Media Korner, a 45-foot mobile media center with work stations which include basic phone, fax and copier services. The Korner is not only a supplemental work area for sports media, but also a place where lifestyle media can work to introduce new fans to the sport.

Most race weekends the KOOL Media Korner is right next door to the sponsor hospitality area, where business goes on behind the scenes. Customers can enjoy the on-track activities in air-conditioned comfort or in front of one of the big screen televisions. The finest foods and entertainment are also a part of the package. Highlights quite often include a pace car ride or an opportunity to share a conversation with Tracy or Franchitti.

Opposite page: Fun and games (top) with the KOOL Race Car Simulator, while a must visit for race fans is the merchandising stand.

Left: Team Kool Green drivers Dario Franchitti and Paul Tracy nose-to-tail at Long Beach.

Below: Kim Green (foreground) and Barry Green (background).

Bottom: Naoki Hattori - on the podium for Team KOOL Green in Indy Lights.

"Being involved in racing is important in meeting the marketing objectives of KOOL," explains sponsorship manager Bert Kremer. "Our hospitality unit also provides a relaxed atmosphere to conduct business with our customers and suppliers. The success of our sponsorship program is also helping to strengthen the sport and to create stars of the future through driver development."

While 1998 was only KOOL's third year in the sport, the sponsor has already established itself as one of the strongest supporters of North American auto racing. One of the ways the company lent its support in 1998 was as co-title sponsor in the 25th anniversary season of the KOOL/Toyota Atlantic Championship. The development series also played a role in KOOL's driver development program, as drivers benefited through a contingency awards program. KOOL also provided additional support to two drivers in the series, Matt Sielsky and Jeff Shafer.

The company entered the motorsport scene in 1996 by supporting Team KOOL Green's Indy Lights effort, a team which KOOL supported again in 1998 with Japanese driver Naoki Hattori behind the wheel. Hattori scored podium finishes in Long Beach (3rd), Toronto (2nd) and Trois-Rivières (3rd). Team KOOL Green played an integral role over two seasons in helping Hattori jump to a Champ Car in '99 with Walker Racing. But, as we move from the hospitality area to the paddock again, we can see that Hattori is racing at Fontana one final time for the team where he got his start.

Two of the principals in forwarding the career of Hattori, as well as a host of other drivers, are brothers Barry and Kim Green. Barry owns Team KOOL Green, while Kim is the general manager. Together, they have a keen eye for talent and getting the most out of everyone on their team. They have also been instrumental in assisting drivers like Shafer, Sielsky and Gurney through the Team Green Academy. However, on this day the Greens are more concerned about preparing the #26 and #27 KOOL cars for the final race of the season at the California Speedway.

"Take a good look around at how everyone is working together," says Barry Green, pointing to his crew, mechanics and engineers busy at work. "We've got over 60 people in our operation and each one of them makes a contribution in our overall success as a team. And everyone must work together as a team to be successful. The driver is nothing if he doesn't have the team behind him."

Kim Green adds, "The chemistry on this team is terrific. Paul and Dario are in the spotlight, sure, but our drivers know how important the guys in the pits can be in winning races. The pit crew reminds me a lot of the offensive line in football. They're the unsung heroes, who only get their name mentioned on TV when they make a mistake. We have suffered the agony of defeat, but fortunately for our group we've also enjoyed the sweet taste of victory."

Tracy and Franchitti have wrapped up the autograph session and have returned to the team transporters. The crew continues to work, as the drivers huddle with the engineers. It's a beehive of activity and the fans begin to crowd around again. It's almost time for the final race and to close the book on the 1998 campaign.

Once the checkered flag falls on the season, Paul and Dario will have one month of vacation before starting again with off-season testing. They'll return to Team KOOL Green in 1999 to compete in a 20-race schedule. And you can rest assured that Shafer, Sielsky and Gurney, among others, will be watched with great interest.

SNAPSHOT ON A SEASON: DARIO'S WINNING WAYS

Arm aloft, Dario crosses the finish line at Road America to signal his first Champ Car victory. His win in Vancouver (opposite page) helped him to challenge for second place in the PPG Cup behind champion Alex Zanardi.

RACING tradition and lore must start somewhere. And for Dario Franchitti, it began with a clenched fist raised out from the cockpit of his #27 KOOL Reynard-Honda as he took the checkered flag at Road America for his first Champ Car victory.

Days before that magical moment, Franchitti could be found making waves in Elkhart Lake on the back of a Sea-doo. Stunts and daredevil maneuvers were a must surrounded by fellow drivers and friends, Greg Moore, Max Papis and his teammate Paul Tracy.

"Paul and Greg were crazy out there, but I guess we all were," says Franchitti, flashing a mischievous smile. "The fun we had out on the lake really was a great release for me, putting me at ease throughout the weekend. Elkhart is a relaxing, quiet community and I guess the atmosphere was to my liking."

Team KOOL Green's crew affectionately refer to Franchitti as 'Dario Speedwagon'. Together, they had gone through a rough stretch of three disappointing races prior to the win at Road America (August 16). In Toronto (July 19), he led the first 79 laps of the Molson Indy from the pole before disaster struck. Brake problems resulted in a spin, ending his race with 16 laps remaining.

"I'd have to say that Toronto was the lowest point in the season," recalls Franchitti. "I love the city and I had won the pole there in my rookie season. Seeing me win the pole for a second consecutive year had everybody on Team KOOL Green really excited. And when we checked out on the field, we could almost taste the victory. Then to be stopped dead in the middle of the track was such a sinking feeling.

"But we never sank! We dusted ourselves off and went back to work. Unfortunately, we never did have the car working right in Michigan and eventually the engine blew. Mid-Ohio made me really angry. We were on the pole again, but I was caught in a first-corner accident and didn't even complete a lap. So we were hungry again at Road America."

Making his 30th career start, Franchitti had his work cut out starting behind Michael Andretti, Bryan Herta, Bobby Rahal, Scott Pruett and Gil de Ferran. However, he seized the lead for the first time on lap 26. Franchitti gave up the lead when he pitted two laps later, but went to the front of the pack again on lap 30. Franchitti ran away with the race after the final round of pit stops, winning by a comfortable 7.102 seconds over runner-up Alex Zanardi.

"When I saw the white flag, I thought 'Come on, win this!' and I didn't stop talking myself around the course until climbing the final hill to the finish line," explains Franchitti. "Then, when the checkered flag came out...it was just such an emotional moment. I remember pumping my fist from the car and the guys screaming on the radio.

"When I brought the car into victory circle, all the guys were there. It was a team win and the work of the Team KOOL Green guys on the pit stops helped me to run away with it."

For team owner Barry Green the victory was his first in 51 races, since Jacques Villeneuve won in Cleveland on July 23, 1995. Villeneuve won five races for Green and, like Franchitti, his first victory came at Road America (September 11, 1994). Green's team now has three CART victories on the 4.048-mile Road America course, as Villeneuve recorded a second victory there on July 9, 1995.

"Road America is a special race track," explains Green. "It was just a matter of time with Dario. And what a perfect race he drove. The pit crew was perfect and we finally got the monkey off our back."

Winning also prompted the kind of celebration by Franchitti and the crew which will not be soon forgotten. Franchitti was in the mood to party. He invited everyone at his post-race media conference to Siebkens, a tiny tavern steeped in racing tradition and memorabilia. As the evening went on, Franchitti added to the lore of the old bar.

"It's a fantastic little place with lots of old racing stickers on the walls, so we just added one more," Franchitti explains, again with the mischievous grin. "One of the guys plastered a big Team KOOL Green sticker underneath the dart board and someone else handed me a pen. The crowd in the bar started yelling at me to sign it. It was hard to write by this point, but I dated it and gave it my autograph.

"All in all it was a great night. Greg Moore treated me to dinner with a couple of friends and then we continued on into the night...and the morning. I can't say I'm used to hangovers, but I guess champagne and beer can be a pretty potent combination."

Left: Dario enjoys some Sea-doo fun with teammate Paul.
Bottom: Close friend and racing rival, Greg Moore and Dario find time to discuss proceedings during the race weekend.

With three weeks in between races, Franchitti had plenty of time to recover. He enjoyed a visit back home to Scotland and flew to Canada early for the Molson Indy Vancouver. Moore, who lives just outside the city in Maple Ridge, B.C., had invited Franchitti to spend some time in the Rocky Mountains.

"Greg and I have become really good friends, I guess because we're close in age and have similar interests," says Franchitti. "We did some mountain biking and toured his home town. He said I had to see the mountains up close and he was right – they are simply massive."

Relaxed and ready to go for the Molson Indy Vancouver, Franchitti set the pace in qualifying by winning his fourth pole position of the season. For the first 21 laps his lead went unchallenged, until varying pit-stop strategies clouded the outcome. Helio Castro-Neves, Al Unser Jr. and Alex Barron took turns leading, but with eight laps to go Franchitti was running second and closing on the leader, Andretti. On the inside of Turn 9, Franchitti passed Andretti and never looked back, enjoying a 3.437-second margin of victory.

It was a special day for Dario Franchitti and Team KOOL Green for another reason. Not only did they win back-to-back races, but Franchitti also became the first driver to win from the pole in 21 races, since Alex Zanardi won in Cleveland on July 13, 1997. By winning from the pole, Franchitti earned a bonus pole award of $330,000, as well as $100,000 for winning the race.

"I wasn't sure of the win there at the end when I was behind Michael," explains Franchitti, reliving the moment. "I was looking all the time for a way to pass. The brake pedal was going long again, like in Toronto, and that was worrying me. But then, when I passed Michael, I thought 'All right!'

"It was a great feeling. The Team KOOL Green guys kind of beat me up when I came into the victory circle. They're big guys and they were hitting me pretty hard - they were just a bit happy!"

Media asked him again about a post-race celebration and where he would go in Vancouver. Not knowing the city Franchitti left the choice up to Moore, who picked The Roxy, a favorite hangout for the local fans. Packed to the rafters, a house band was banging it out on stage and three bars kept the place buzzing all night.

"There was no hangover," cautions Franchitti. "It's not like we party every weekend. We work hard to win races and we play hard when it happens. So, with a race at Laguna Seca one week after Vancouver, I was on my best behavior."

Again, with the mischievous smile.

Franchitti was true to his word, putting in another strong performance at Laguna Seca. He finished fourth on the tight twisting road course, which did little to diminish his confidence riding into Houston next.

Houston's inaugural CART race turned out to be a wet and wild affair, which Franchitti led from start to finish for his third victory of the season. Wet conditions required a single-file start on rain tires, but Franchitti beat pole-winner pal Greg Moore to the first corner. Pit stops and team strategy were important factors on the slick street circuit, as conditions went from wet to dry to wet again. But Franchitti's Team KOOL Green crew kept him in the lead for all 70 laps. He led the field across the finish line under yellow as lightning, thunder and heavy rain shortened the race by 30 laps.

"It was like an ice rink out there at the start," recalls Franchitti. "It was a very difficult day, but I love racing in the rain. Team KOOL Green called an excellent race for me, telling me when to pit for slicks and back to rain tires. Full marks to the team. We scored the hat trick this season with three wins."

Winning in Houston also moved Franchitti up to third in the overall standings with 143 points. He had closed the gap to just five points between himself and Jimmy Vasser. Alex Zanardi had already won the championship, but $500,000 was still up for grabs to the series runner-up with two races left in the season.

Australia saw Franchitti score his sixth podium of the season by finishing second to Zanardi at the Honda Indy. Franchitti started from the pole position, his fifth of the year, and a solid start allowed him to lead Zanardi for the opening 13 laps. The leaders dove into the pits with the first full course yellow and Zanardi beat Franchitti out and led the rest of the way. Vasser did not finish, allowing Franchitti to pull ahead by 12 points.

Sadly at the season-finale in California, Franchitti's engine blew early while running second. He was forced to watch from the sidelines, as Vasser won the race to take home the $500,000 for second in the championship, as well as a $1 million race-prize.

"I don't care about the money," says Franchitti now. "One or two hundred thousand (dollars) up or down doesn't really matter. Finishing second would have been great, but third overall is still a good reflection of the kind of season we had. Team KOOL Green was the team to beat in the second half of the season."

This time, a quiet smile of confidence.

PAUL TRACY: A MAN IN MOTION

PAUL TRACY'S reputation on track is for being a hard-charging veteran, who runs on the ragged edge during a race.

Tracy has his critics and he was dinged a few times by CART officials for aggressive driving in his first year for Team KOOL Green. His fans will tell you Tracy is simply a fierce competitor – which he is – but get Tracy away from the track and he's a lot more laid back. At home, you'll find him tinkering in the garage, listening to music or just sitting back with his wife Liisa, watching a movie.

"I have a job to do and it's to win races, so I'm a different person when the helmet goes on and the visor comes down," explains Tracy. "When we're not racing, I'm just like anybody else. I'm looking to have fun or to relax with one of my hobbies."

When time permits during the off-season, Paul and Liisa can usually be found (or not found, if they prefer) piloting their powerboat on Lake Meade near their adopted home of Las Vegas, Nevada.

Tracy uses a pair of 1000-horsepower Chevrolet engines in his powerboat, a sleek catamaran-style capable of 130 mph. In fact, its awesome performance potential was a big factor in Paul and Liisa's decision to move from their former home along the relatively crowded Colorado River in Parker, Ariz., to Las Vegas, where they would have the vast expanses of Lake Meade to "open 'er up", so to speak.

Boating is not a year-round sport, even on a desert lake. The chilly (for Las Vegas) temperatures in the off-season usually turn Tracy's attention to his other hobbies, principally skiing and snowboarding.

"It gets a little cold out in Vegas in the winter," he says. "I try to go skiing twice a winter. Liisa's parents live in Denver, so we go there at Thanksgiving and Christmas and I go skiing with her brothers. If we're not skiing in Colorado, Liisa and I like to go to Deer Valley in Park City, Utah."

When he's not skiing, Tracy can be found working on the pair of one-off Harley-Davidson motorcycles he usually has in his garage. Although the lurid candy apple, starburst and metallic paint jobs are the work of custom paint artists, Tracy does much of the mechanical work himself.

"I like to build motorcycles, then sell them," he says. "I build one and ride it for four or six months, then I sell it and roll that money over and start another one. I just enjoy building them; I love to build something different."

Of course, Tracy likes to ride his motorcycles too. A regular visitor to Bike Week at Daytona International Speedway – usually conveniently scheduled the week after CART's Spring Training at nearby Miami-Dade Homestead Motorsports Complex – he has also become a fixture at the annual Harley-Davidson rally in Sturgis, South Dakota, in August.

"I go to Sturgis every year," says Paul. "It's just such beautiful country around there. We stay at a campground about thirty miles outside of town, and from there we go up to Mt. Rushmore, we go all through the winding back roads in the Black Hills...it's so nice. The first time I went there was in '93, and I put 1000 miles on my bike in five days.

"We go into Sturgis at night to look at the weirdos," he says. "I get noticed once in awhile, but mainly people are just there to have a good time and they don't make a big fuss. Really, for me it's an opportunity to get away for a few days and do something nice instead of just going home and doing laundry, packing

Left: Paul enjoys karting and touring with wife Liisa on the back of one of Paul's custom-built Harleys.

On track (far left) at a pit stop in the Team KOOL Green #26 car and (below left) chatting with team owner Barry Green between practice sessions.

Bottom: Paul and some friends test the limit in his new powerboat near his Las Vegas home on Lake Meade.

and turning around and leaving for the next race."

The 1998 season was a year of transition for Tracy, entering his eighth campaign on the CART circuit. Tracy, who had spent six years with Roger Penske and had a one-year stint with Newman/ Haas, found a new home with Barry Green's outfit – Team KOOL Green.

"Even though it wasn't one of my best seasons, Barry and the entire team were great to work with," says Tracy, reflecting on his change of scenery. "We went into the season knowing that it would be quite an adjustment for me – changing from Penske/ Mercedes/Goodyear to Reynard/ Honda/Firestone. At times, I've been guilty of trying to apply a Penske set-up on the Reynard, which has set us back in qualifying. So, every race weekend we're playing catch-up.

"To explain the difference in set-up to reporters, I ask them to imagine finding the letters on their computer keyboard rearranged. Maybe even add a few new letters to the language and put them on the keyboard. The set-up between the two chassis can be that different."

What does Tracy like so much about Team KOOL Green? He cites the atmosphere and the relationship he has with Barry Green. Tracy says the two communicate easily because Green was once a driver.

"Barry really knows the business of racing," Tracy explains. "It's not his hobby, it's his livelihood and it always has been. I have a lot of respect for what he has accomplished and I appreciate the faith he has in me. When I was on probation he backed me up all the way and I'm grateful for it.

"Even on the radio during a race, Barry is the voice of reason for me. I'm pretty intense out there and I want to get to the front as soon as I can. Barry keeps me settled and lets me know when I can make a run for it."

Green acknowledges Tracy's reputation and aggressive style of driving may have led to some of his troubles in the '98 season. However, Green says he will never ask Tracy to change the way he drives.

"Paul is always in a hurry to get to the front of the line and as a team owner that's the kind of driver you want," says Green. "CART cracked down on a lot of drivers this year. And if you look at their names, it was the big-name drivers...Zanardi, Moore, Herta. Those guys give it everything they've got and Paul is like that."

Tracy's season could not be summed up any better than by how it finished. He was leading with just four laps to go in the season-finale, a 500-mile race at California Speedway. Greg Moore, Jimmy Vasser and Alex Zanardi were chasing Tracy when a caution bunched up the pack again. Tracy needed a good re-start with the green flag, but he was perhaps too hard on the throttle and spun off the track to a stop in the infield. A chance to redeem a tough season and to win a $1 million race-prize was lost.

Finishing fifth on three separate occasions (Japan, Nazareth, Mid-Ohio) was the best result for Tracy in 1998. He was also running strong races in Milwaukee and Michigan, but problems in the pits kept him off the podium. Down the stretch though, Tracy and his crew enjoyed a pair of second row starts (Houston and Australia) and were contending in every race. They worked hard all season and will be looking for the payback in 1999.

Left: Dario Franchitti and Jack Christiansen celebrate one of five poles for Team KOOL Green in 1998.

Below: Paul Tracy burns rubber for fans at a sponsor event.

THE RHODES BACK TO THE TOP

By Paul Lawrence

Above: The Class of '98
Right: MGF Cup champion James Rhodes

FOUR years out of the cockpit is a long time in motor racing. James Rhodes, once a promising single-seater star, could easily have slipped into oblivion after such an absence. However, his career was rescued in 1998 as Team Firstair entrusted its MGF to the Northampton racer. He repaid the team's faith in style by winning the inaugural MGF title. For both Rhodes and MG, it had been a pretty good season. Big grids of hard-driven cars made the MGF Cup a roaring success.

The category was all about giving the MGF a sporting profile and used the 1800 cc model as a platform. A seam-welded shell and a dry-sumped version of the K series engine turned the F into a racer and the 190Ps sportster boasted uprated suspension, brakes, gearbox and transmission to cope with the demands of competition.

The main pre-season test day was held in mid-March and, even at that stage, the battle lines were drawn as the leading contenders started to emerge. Having run successfully in just about every one-make category, Alastair Lyall was one of the pre-season favourites in his Trinity Motors-backed entry.

However, Lyall's campaign hardly got off to a good start when he upended his car in a Silverstone gravel trap during the test day. Damage was not extensive but it was a salutary lesson that, if a driver of Lyall's calibre could be caught out, the rear-wheel drive MGF needed treating with respect.

When the championship opened back at Silverstone in early April, first blood went to Rhodes. Having messed up qualifying, he started mid-grid but scythed through the field with a consummate display of his talents. He won convincingly to hammer home a message. Rhodes was back! But even while swigging the champagne, James knew that he was now a marked man.

'I've made a rod for my own back. Now I've got to do it all again next time,' said the Epsom Rover-backed driver. Onto the podium with him that day came Brian Heerey and Suzi Hart-Banks. Heerey, showing one of his flashes of blinding pace, was bouncing back from an 18-month break from racing, but it would be nine races before the Foxfield Garage MGF was back in a podium position.

Alongside Rhodes, Hart-Banks was the big star of the opening race. Showing no signs of being daunted by her surroundings, Suzi proved that she could run with the best of them.

Rhodes demonstrated that Silverstone was no fluke when the series resumed at Brands three weeks later. However, a second victory was denied when Matthew Kelly brushed the back of Rhodes's car at Clearways and tipped it into a spin. This duo was so far clear of the rest that Rhodes was able to continue in second as Kelly took the big prize. Sidelined by gearbox gremlins at Silverstone, Kelly now proved that, at this stage of the season, he alone could match Rhodes.

That fact was emphasised a week later at Oulton Park as Rhodes and Kelly left the rest of the pack for dead. However, more gearbox maladies put Kelly out in Cheshire and Rhodes made it two from three. With every one of the 12 rounds counting towards the end-of-season score, Kelly was already in big trouble with the Clive Sutton Group-entered car.

Rhodes completed his hat-trick on the Silverstone Grand Prix circuit in mid-May when he had to fend off an early challenge from Hart-Banks. Suzi then showed her determination by battling mightily with Lyall for second and Alastair needed all his experience and pace to grab the place. Lyall had been quietly gathering points through the early races and was shaping up to be the biggest threat to Rhodes for the overall title.

Knowing that, over the opening races, he could not match the pace set by Rhodes, Alastair simply got on with the job of stacking up points while he and the team worked to develop the car. It was a gambit that came close to earning them the title.

However, the Rhodes express came temporarily off the rails in round five at Croft at the end of May. James clashed with Lyall and ended his race embedded in the gravel trap at Clervaux. Kelly had already stamped his authority on the race and clinched his second victory as Hart-Banks got ahead of Lyall for the runner-up position.

In a summer of dire weather, changing conditions were to feature in two of three races through June and July. At Snetterton in mid-June Kelly won for the third time as seasoned veterans Dave Loudoun and Nick Carr made the podium with the pair of Edwards of Stratford-backed cars. While Hart-Banks and Lyall also made the top six, Rhodes was back in sev-

Wet weather merely enhanced the excitement of the MGF Cup. Bill Sollis (left) splashes around Silverstone ahead of Barry Benham (9) and Vince Martin (8).

Bottom: Fun and games at Paddock Hill Bend. As a few competitors find themselves facing the wrong way at the back of the pack, Mark Jones (10), Nigel Reuben (12) and Piers Johnson power towards Druids.

enth and his early-season advantage was starting to look just a little shaky.

Two weeks later, Lyall drove a tenacious race at Knockhill to score what would be his only win of the season. At a circuit where overtaking is very difficult, Lyall knew that if he could get to the front he would almost certainly be able to stay there. He duly did, and despite having Rhodes and Kelly large in his mirrors for nearly 25 laps, Lyall was unshakeable.

Rhodes knew that to take a risk trying to pass Lyall could prove disastrous and Kelly found that out the hard way when an unsuccessful move on Rhodes dropped him to tenth. After seven of the 12 races, Lyall sat just five points behind Rhodes as the teams headed home from Scotland.

The highlight of the season came next with a race on the British Grand Prix support programme. The race ran in soaking conditions, but that made little difference to Rhodes who splashed to his fourth win of the season. He also extended his lead over Lyall who was back in fourth behind Piers Johnson and Kelly.

The GP race was also significant for Hart-Banks, who T-boned the spinning car of Heerey heavily, causing a red flag while she was removed from the wrecked vehicle. Suzi would be back for the next race but Heerey was forced to sit out round nine at Donington.

Buoyed by his second place at Silverstone, Johnson went one better at Donington to win in the Priest of Chesham car. It was a stylish drive as Lyall and Loudoun chased him home. In yet another twist in his season, Rhodes had a torrid time and ran at the tail of a pack squabbling for top-six placings. Then, on the final corner, he was comprehensively mugged and plummeted to ninth for his lowest finish of the season. He and Lyall were now dead level on points.

After an agonising four-week break, the Cup resumed at Castle Combe for what proved to be a rather bizarre race. Lyall and Rhodes shared the front row and got away first, only to be penalised for false starts by the eager Castle Combe judges.

Unaware of the penalties they faced, Lyall and Rhodes battled furiously for the lead with Lyall winning on the road. However, with a ten-second penalty applied they fell to fifth and sixth. 'I can't believe they took it off us,' said Lyall, after discovering that his attacking performance counted for so little.

Realising the significance and ferocity of the battle for the lead, Hart-Banks was content to run third but was jubilant to be declared winner when the results were amended. Behind Suzi, Heerey and a troubled Kelly moved up to claim podium positions. Although devastated to have his victory taken away, Lyall could at last take some consolation from the day as he now led the title for the first time, just two points up on Rhodes.

Even better news for Lyall was the fact that the eleventh and penultimate race of the season was at his favourite track, around the high-speed sweeps of Thruxton. His spirits were high and Alastair sensed that the title was well within his reach. But he was to be proved spectacularly wrong in the Hampshire race.

With Kelly and Rhodes setting the pace, Lyall attacked into the Complex and spun. He tried to charge back up the field but another spin later in the

1st JAMES RHODES

2nd ALASTAIR LYALL

3rd MATTHEW KELLY

4th SUZI HART-BANKS

5th DAVE LOUDON

6th PIERS JOHNSON

7th NIGEL REUBEN

8th ROB MEARS

9th MARK HAZELL

10th STEPHEN WARBURTON

James Rhodes – the comeback man

FOR James Rhodes, 1998 was an all or nothing year. Despite four years out of racing, he still felt he had much to offer. But James is not a driver to slope up and down pit-lanes hoping to gather a few crumbs in the way of drives. If a team wanted him for the right reasons, he would give his all. If not, then the sport would lose this undoubted talent. 'I never doubted my ability but I'd been out of racing for a long time,' said Rhodes.

At the start of the season a saviour came along in the shape of Ian Barnwell, boss of Team Firstair. In much the way that Barnwell had given Richard Dean the chance to win the '96 Rover Turbo Cup, so he now threw a lifeline to Rhodes.

James grabbed it with both hands and, bar a couple of low-key weekends, was the man to beat in MGFs. His name was back in the frame and he will surely look back on 1998 and the MGF campaign as the year that changed his life. Now he wants to make it in touring cars and is planning to use the Vauxhall Vectra Challenge as the next step towards his goal.

Below: Alastair Lyall is put under extreme pressure by fellow championship contender Matt Kelly. Brian Heerey, Suzi Hart-Banks and eventual champion, James Rhodes, lead the pursuing pack.

race effectively crushed his title hopes. Rhodes was content to follow Kelly to the flag and, at a stroke, regained his title lead by a massive 23 points. Just one race remained, and Rhodes needed only a few points at Silverstone to clinch the title.

Lyall had no choice but to go all out for victory, but an inspired Loudoun and Kelly kept him back in third. Fifth was more than enough to make Rhodes champion after a season that put his name firmly back in the racing spotlight.

Lyall scored well in every race except Thruxton and, had he settled for third place that day, could have been champion. But hindsight is a wonderful thing, and Alastair lost the title simply by trying to win it. Kelly proved much in '98 and benefited enormously from concentrating on a single race programme with a sensible budget.

Hart-Banks, meanwhile, demonstrated a fine talent matched by a willingness to mix it with the toughest of opponents. GT racing beckons for this highly promotable young lady.

The rest of the top ten was packed by Rover Turbo old-boys Loudoun, Johnson, Rob Mears, Mark Hazell and Stephen Warburton who surrounded eighth-placed Nigel Reuben. When not racing his own car in the colours of Premier Motors (Romford), Reuben also prepared Hart-Banks's car. Finishing on the podium at Thruxton topped Nigel's season.

With backing from G. Kingsbury & Son Ltd, Mears had a great start to the season. However, his modest budget was overstretched and a lean patch of results mid-season took the edge off his bid. However, the highly experienced former Formula 3 racer was back in the top six by the end of the season.

Showing newly found consistency, Hazell was invariably in the points with the Loughborough Rover entry and twice reached the top five in his best season for some time. Equally, young Warburton showed flashes of front-running pace and second at Oulton was the highlight of his season with backing from MGF dealers Seward. However, a couple of incidents, including a scary shunt into the pit wall at Brands, held his season back.

Mini champion Bill Sollis ran strongly in the colours of The Chequered Flag until his budget ran out and Carr did well despite missing a number of races for business and health reasons.

Among the others to chalk up top-six finishes in a supremely competitive season were former touring car racer Ray Armes (Trident Garages), Vince Martin (Diamond Rover) and Andy Ackerley (Beadles (Dartford) Ltd).

With nearly every car carrying the support of an MGF dealer, the competition for the dealers' championship was almost as intense as that for the drivers' title. Having joined forces with Rhodes three races into the season, Epsom Rover just missed out on the Dealer Award – the honours for which went to Lyall's supporters, Trinity Motors of Hinckley.

Overall champions

1	James Rhodes	249
2	Alastair Lyall	230
3	Matthew Kelly	217
4	Suzi Hart-Banks	153
5	Dave Loudoun	151
6	Piers Johnson	149
7	Nigel Reuben	121
8	Rob Mears	107
9	Mark Hazell	105
10	Stephen Warburton	97

OTHER MAJOR RESULTS

Compiled by David Hayhoe

International Formula 3000 Championship

All cars are Lola T96/50-Zytek Judd V8.

FIA INTERNATIONAL FORMULA 3000 CHAMPIONSHIP, Oschersleben Circuit, Germany, 11 April. Round 1. 56 laps of the 2.279-mile/3.667-km circuit, 127.600 miles/205.352 km.

1 Stéphane Sarrazin, F, 1h 24m 52.384s, 90.205 mph/145.171 km/h.

2 Nick Heidfeld, D, 1h 25m 03.667s; **3** Jamie Davies, GB, 1h 25m 29.870s; **4** Thomas Biagi, I, 1h 25m 32.885s; **5** Cyrille Sauvage, F, 1h 25m 42.857s; **6** Gaston Mazzacane, RA, 1h 25m 45.684s; **7** Jason Watt, DK, 1h 26m 12.806s; **8** Bertrand Godin, CDN, 1h 26m 14.742s; **9** Rui Aguas, P, 55 laps; **10** Brian Smith, RA, 55; **11** Boris Derichebourg, F, 55; **12** Jonny Kane, GB, 55; **13** Fabrice Walfisch, F, 55; **14** Dominik Schwager, D, 55; **15** Juan Pablo Montoya, CO, 55; **16** Oliver Martini, I, 54; **17** Max Wilson, BR, 47 (DNF – spin); **18** Nicolas Minassian, F, 44 (DNF – accident); **19** Christian Horner, GB, 29 (DNF – accident); **20** Mark Shaw, GB, 28 (DNF – spin); **21** Gonzalo Rodriguez, U, 19 (DNF – spin); **22** Werner Lupberger, ZA, 19 (DNF – spin); **23** Alex Müller, D, 12 (DNF – steering); **24** Gareth Rees, GB, 11 (DNF – accident); **25** Soheil Ayari, F, 11 (DNF – handling); **26** Kurt Mollekens, B, 3 (DNF – spin); **27** André Couto, MAC, 2 (DNF – accident); **28** Bruno Junqueira, BR, 2 (DNF – accident); **29** Giovanni Montanari, I, 0 (DNF – accident).

Paolo Ruberti, I, finished 3rd in 1h 25m 25.602s but was disqualified due to a bodywork infringement.

Fastest race lap: Montoya, 1m 20.387s, 102.042 mph/164.221 km/h.

Fastest qualifying lap: Montoya, 1m 18.475s, 104.528 mph/168.222 km/h.

Did not qualify: Kevin McGarrity, GB; Grégoire de Galzain, F; Giorgio Vinella, I; Marcelo Battistuzzi, BR; Fabrizio Gollin, I; Leopoldo 'Polo' Perez de Villaamil, E.

Championship points: 1 Sarrazin, 10; **2** Heidfeld, 6; **3** Davies, 4; **4** Biagi, 3; **5** Sauvage, 2; **6** Mazzacane, 1.

FIA INTERNATIONAL FORMULA 3000 CHAMPIONSHIP, Autodromo Enzo e Dino Ferrari, Imola, Italy, 26 April. Round 2. 42 laps of the 3.063-mile/4.930-km circuit, 128.526 miles/206.843 km.

1 Jason Watt, DK, 1h 16m 38.513s, 100.618 mph/161.929 km/h.

2 Kurt Mollekens, B, 1h 16m 39.081s; **3** Gonzalo Rodriguez, U, 1h 16m 39.517s; **4** Nick Heidfeld, D, 1h 16m 41.324s; **5** André Couto, MAC, 1h 16m 47.626s; **6** Boris Derichebourg, F, 1h 16m 48.900s; **7** Gaston Mazzacane, RA, 1h 16m 50.135s; **8** Jamie Davies, GB, 1h 16m 50.558s; **9** Oliver Martini, I, 1h 16m 51.532s; **10** Thomas Biagi, I, 1h 16m 52.608s; **11** Dominik Schwager, D, 1h 16m 55.346s; **12** Christian Horner, GB, 1h 16m 57.086s; **13** Werner Lupberger, ZA, 1h 16m 57.417s; **14** Kevin McGarrity, GB, 1h 17m 00.788s; **15** Giovanni Montanari, I, 1h 17m 01.692s; **16** Bruno Junqueira, BR, 1h 17m 02.602s; **17** Fabrizio Gollin, I, 1h 17m 02.989s; **18** Fabrice Walfisch, F, 1h 17m 03.559s; **19** Nicolas Minassian, F, 1h 17m 48.258s; **20** Mark Shaw, GB, 1h 17m 51.225s; **21** Jonny Kane, GB, 41 laps; **22** Marcelo Battistuzzi, BR, 41; **23** Soheil Ayari, F, 38 (DNF – spin); **24** Stéphane Sarrazin, F, 38; **25** Giorgio Vinella, I, 33 (DNF – accident); **26** Bertrand Godin, CDN, 32 (DNF – puncture); **27** Max Wilson, BR, 25 (DNF – accident); **28** Cyrille Sauvage, F, 25 (DNF – accident); **29** Juan Pablo Montoya, CO, 14 (DNF – accident); **30** Grégoire de Galzain, F, 14 (DNF – spin); **31** Brian Smith, RA, 12 (DNF – spin); **32** Alex Müller, D, 1 (DNF – gearbox); **33** Gareth Rees, GB, 1 (DNF – accident damage); **34** Dino Morelli, GB, 0 (DNF – accident); **35** Paolo Ruberti, I, 0 (DNF – accident).

Fastest race lap: Rodriguez, 1m 41.814s, 108.316 mph/174.318 km/h.

Fastest qualifying lap: Montoya, 1m 40.695s, 109.520 mph/176.255 km/h.

Championship points: 1= Sarrazin, 10; **1=** Watt, 10; **3** Heidfeld, 9; **4** Mollekens, 6; **5=** Davies, 4; **5=** Rodriguez, 4.

FIA INTERNATIONAL FORMULA 3000 CHAMPIONSHIP, Circuit de Catalunya, Montmeló, Barcelona, Spain, 9 May. Round 3. 44 laps of the 2.938-mile/4.728-km circuit, 129.188 miles/207.908 km.

1 Juan Pablo Montoya, CO, 1h 12m 50.057s, 106.424 mph/171.272 km/h.

2 Kurt Mollekens, B, 1h 12m 57.817s; **3** Boris Derichebourg, F, 1h 12m 59.450s; **4** Dominik Schwager, D, 1h 13m 00.281s; **5** Soheil Ayari, F, 1h 13m 00.814s; **6** Max Wilson, BR, 1h 13m 19.340s; **7** Jason Watt, DK, 1h 13m 30.008s; **8** Giovanni Montanari, I, 1h 13m 30.402s; **9** Oliver Martini, I, 1h 13m 30.901; **10** Alex Müller, D, 1h 13m 31.388s; **11** Cyrille Sauvage, F, 1h 13m 32.016s; **12** Werner Lupberger, ZA, 1h 13m 34.124s; **13** Jamie Davies, GB, 1h 13m 37.551s; **14** André Couto, MAC, 1h 13m 38.290s; **15** Stéphane Sarrazin, F, 1h 13m 39.109s; **16** Bruno Junqueira, BR, 1h 13m 43.211s; **17** Rui Aguas, P, 1h 13m 49.830s; **18** Grégoire de Galzain, F, 1h 13m 51.807s; **19** Dino Morelli, GB, 1h 13m 52.353s; **20** Fabrice Walfisch, F, 1h 13m 53.125s; **21** Gonzalo Rodriguez, U, 1h 13m 53.687s; **22** Bertrand Godin, CDN, 1h 14m 11.566s; **23** Paolo Ruberti, I, 1h 14m 35.998s; **24** Leopoldo 'Polo' Perez de Villaamil, E, 43 laps; **25** Giorgio Vinella, I, 43; **26** Nick Heidfeld, D, 43; **27** Kevin McGarrity, GB, 43; **28** Gaston Mazzacane, RA, 40 (DNF – accident); **29** Jonny Kane, GB, 40 (DNF – accident); **30** Gareth Rees, GB, 39 (DNF – fuel system); **31** Brian Smith, RA, 39 (DNF – clutch); **32** Nicolas Minassian, F, 38 (DNF – brakes); **33** Marcelo Battistuzzi, BR, 38 (DNF – brakes); **34** Mark Shaw, GB, 26 (DNF – spin); **35** Christian Horner, GB, 13 (DNF – accident damage).

Fastest race lap: Heidfeld, 1m 37.267s, 108.734 mph/174.990 km/h.

Fastest qualifying lap: Montoya, 1m 35.289s, 110.991 mph/178.623 km/h.

Did not qualify: Fabrizio Gollin, I.

Championship points: 1 Mollekens, 12; **2=** Sarrazin, 10; **2=** Watt, 10; **2=** Montoya, 10; **5** Heidfeld, 9; **6** Derichebourg, 5.

AUTOSPORT INTERNATIONAL TROPHY, Silverstone Grand Prix Circuit, Towcester, Northamptonshire, Great Britain, 16 May. Round 4. 40 laps of the 3.194-mile/5.140-km circuit, 127.754 miles/205.600 km.

1 Juan Pablo Montoya, CO, 1h 10m 08.886s, 109.272 mph/175.857 km/h.

2 Nick Heidfeld, D, 1h 10m 21.792s; **3** Jason Watt, DK, 1h 10m 34.186s; **4** Gareth Rees, GB, 1h 10m 35.162s; **5** Max Wilson, BR, 1h 10m 35.499s; **6** Gaston Mazzacane, RA, 1h 10m 39.644s; **7** Nicolas Minassian, F, 1h 10m 44.018s; **8** Kurt Mollekens, B, 1h 10m 44.348s; **9** Bruno Junqueira, BR, 1h 10m 44.699s; **10** Dino Morelli, GB, 1h 10m 56.222s; **11** Alex Müller, D, 1h 10m 56.785s; **12** Boris Derichebourg, F, 1h 10m 57.212s; **13** Giovanni Montanari, I, 1h 10m 58.090s; **14** Dominik Schwager, D, 1h 10m 58.644s; **15** Brian Smith, RA, 1h 11m 07.470s; **16** Jamie Davies, GB, 1h 11m 08.878s; **17** Rui Aguas, P, 1h 11m 10.184s; **18** Werner Lupberger, ZA, 1h 11m 10.646s; **19** Bertrand Godin, CDN, 1h 11m 11.839s; **20** Jonny Kane, GB, 1h 11m 24.405s; **21** Paolo Ruberti, I, 1h 11m 38.298s; **22** Giorgio Vinella, I, 1h 11m 49.778s; **23** Grégoire de Galzain, F, 1h 11m 50.027s; **24** Stéphane Sarrazin, F, 39 laps; **25** Fabrice Walfisch, F, 35 (DNF – spin); **26** Gonzalo Rodriguez, U, 35 (DNF – handling); **27** Oliver Martini, I, 32 (DNF – spin); **28** André Couto, MAC, 25 (DNF – spin); **29** Fabrizio Gollin, I, 25 (DNF – handling); **30** Christian Horner, GB, 15 (DNF – accident); **31** Kevin McGarrity, GB, 8 (DNF – accident); **32** Mark Shaw, GB, 8 (DNF – accident); **33** Soheil Ayari, F, 6 (DNF – accident damage); **34** Marcelo Battistuzzi, BR, 5 (DNF – accident); **35** Cyrille Sauvage, F, 5 (DNF – accident).

Fastest race lap: Montoya, 1m 41.366s, 113.429 mph/182.546 km/h.

Fastest qualifying lap: Montoya, 1m 38.602s, 116.609 mph/187.664 km/h.

Championship points: 1 Montoya, 20; **2** Heidfeld, 15; **3** Watt, 14; **4** Mollekens, 12; **5** Sarrazin, 10; **6** Derichebourg, 5.

FIA INTERNATIONAL FORMULA 3000 CHAMPIONSHIP, Monte Carlo Street Circuit, Monaco, 23 May. Round 5. 50 laps of the 2.092-mile/3.367-km circuit, 104.608 miles/168.350 km.

1 Nick Heidfeld, D, 1h 18m 04.955s, 80.382 mph/129.363 km/h.

2 Gonzalo Rodriguez, U, 1h 18m 08.817s; **3** Jamie Davies, GB, 1h 18m 24.466s; **4** Stéphane Sarrazin, F, 1h 18m 31.562s; **5** Kurt Mollekens, B, 1h 18m 53.173s; **6** Juan Pablo Montoya, CO, 1h 19m 16.516s; **7** Rui Aguas, P, 1h 19m 16.879s; **8** Dino Morelli, GB, 1h 19m 17.520s; **9** Nicolas Minassian, F, 1h 19m 32.485s; **10** Dominik Schwager, D, 1h 19m 40.176s; **11** Brian Smith, RA, 49 laps; **12** Gaston Mazzacane, RA, 49; **13** Giovanni Montanari, I, 49; **14** Werner Lupberger, ZA, 49; **15** Cyrille Sauvage, F, 49; **16** Christian Horner, GB, 49; **17** Gareth Rees, GB, 48 (DNF – accident); **18** Paolo Ruberti, I, 48; **19** Fabrizio Gollin, I, 44 (DNF – accident); **20** Marcelo Battistuzzi, BR, 43 (DNF – gearbox); **21** Jason Watt, DK, 40 (DNF – accident); **22** Bruno Junqueira, BR, 29 (DNF – accident); **23** Bertrand Godin, CDN, 20 (DNF – gearbox); **24** Alex Müller, D, 18 (DNF – spin); **25** Boris Derichebourg, F, 17 (DNF – spin); **26** André Couto, MAC, 16 (DNF – accident).

Fastest race lap: Montoya, 1m 31.602s, 82.223 mph/132.325 km/h.

Fastest qualifying lap: Watt, 1m 30.925s, 82.835 mph/133.310 km/h.

Did not qualify: Kevin McGarrity, GB; Fabrice Walfisch, F; Giorgio Vinella, I; Soheil Ayari, F.

Did not pre-qualify: Mark Shaw, GB; Grégoire de Galzain, F; Max Wilson, BR; Oliver Martini, I.

Championship points: 1 Heidfeld, 25; **2** Montoya, 21; **3=** Watt, 14; **3=** Mollekens, 14; **5** Sarrazin, 13; **6** Rodriguez, 10.

58th GRAND PRIX AUTOMOBILE DE PAU, Circuit de Pau, France, 1 June. Round 6. 75 laps of the 1.715-mile/2.760-km circuit, 128.624 miles/207.000 km.

1 Juan Pablo Montoya, CO, 1h 33m 10.179s, 82.832 mph/133.305 km/h.

2 Max Wilson, BR, 74 laps; **3** Nick Heidfeld, D, 74; **4** Gareth Rees, GB, 74; **5** Kurt Mollekens, B, 74; **6** André Couto, MAC, 74; **7** Nicolas Minassian, F, 74; **8** Brian Smith, RA, 73; **9** Gaston Mazzacane, RA, 73; **10** Oliver Martini, I, 73; **11** Alex Müller, D, 61 (DNF – fuel pump); **12** Paolo Ruberti, I, 59 (DNF – spin); **13** Jason Watt, DK, 41 (DNF – accident damage); **14** Werner Lupberger, ZA, 24 (DNF – accident); **15** Soheil Ayari, F, 17 (DNF – accident); **16** Bruno Junqueira, BR, 10 (DNF – accident); **17** Stéphane Sarrazin, F, 10 (DNF – accident); **18** Jamie Davies, GB, 3 (DNF – gearbox); **19** Rui Aguas, P, 3 (DNF – spin/stall); **20** Giovanni Montanari, I, 3 (DNF – spin/stall); **21** Gonzalo Rodriguez, U, 1 (DNF – accident damage); **22** Cyrille Sauvage, F, 1 (DNF – clutch); **23** Boris Derichebourg, F, 0 (DNF – accident damage).

Fastest race lap: Montoya, 1m 12.953s, 84.629 mph/136.197 km/h.

Fastest qualifying lap: Montoya, 1m 12.086s, 85.647 mph/137.835 km/h.

Did not qualify: Bertrand Godin, CDN; Mark Shaw, GB; Grégoire de Galzain, F; Fabrizio Gollin, I; Christian Horner, GB; Dominik Schwager, D; Fabrice Walfisch, F; Marcelo Battistuzzi, BR; Giorgio Vinella, I.

Championship points: 1 Montoya, 31; **2** Heidfeld, 29; **3** Mollekens, 16; **4** Watt, 14; **5** Sarrazin, 13; **6** Rodriguez, 10.

FIA INTERNATIONAL FORMULA 3000 CHAMPIONSHIP, A1-Ring, Knittelfeld, Austria, 25 July. Round 7. 48 laps of the 2.684-mile/4.319-km circuit, 128.818 miles/207.312 km.

1 Soheil Ayari, F, 1h 11m 04.222s, 108.752 mph/175.020 km/h.

2 Juan Pablo Montoya, CO, 1h 11m 25.272s; **3** Jason Watt, DK, 1h 11m 31.832s; **4** Gonzalo Rodriguez, U, 1h 11m 32.593s; **5** Nicolas Minassian, F, 1h 11m 35.195s; **6** Bruno Junqueira, BR, 1h 11m 37.352s; **7** Nick Heidfeld, D, 1h 11m 42.055s; **8** Stéphane Sarrazin, F, 1h 11m 42.282s; **9** Oliver Martini, I, 1h 11m 43.193s; **10** Kurt Mollekens, B, 1h 11m 49.298s; **11** Alex Müller, D, 1h 11m 49.785s; **12** Thomas Biagi, I, 1h 11m 51.949s; **13** Cyrille Sauvage, F, 1h 12m 05.400s; **14** Giovanni Montanari, I, 1h 12m 08.719s; **15** Boris Derichebourg, F, 1h 12m 09.883s; **16** Werner Lupberger, ZA, 1h 12m 17.414s; **17** Christian Horner, GB, 1h 12m 29.787s; **18** Marcelo Battistuzzi, BR, 47 laps; **19** Bertrand Godin, CDN, 47; **20** Mark Shaw, GB, 47; **21** Fabrizio Gollin, I, 47; **22** Oliver Tichy, A, 46; **23** David Cook, GB, 36 (DNF – spin); **24** Dominik Schwager, D, 36 (DNF – faulty gauge); **25** Max Wilson, BR, 27 (DNF – accident); **26** André Couto, MAC, 20 (DNF – spin); **27** Jamie Davies, GB, 19 (DNF – spin); **28** Gareth Rees, GB, 10 (DNF – accident damage); **29** Grégoire de Galzain, F, 10 (DNF – accident damage); **30** Giorgio Vinella, I, 1 (DNF – spin); **31** Gaston Mazzacane, RA, 0 (DNF – accident); **32** Fabrice Walfisch, F, 0 (DNF – accident); **33** Kevin McGarrity, GB, 0 (DNF – accident).

Fastest race lap: Ayari, 1m 24.139s, 114.826 mph/184.794 km/h.

Fastest qualifying lap: Ayari, 1m 23.948s, 115.087 mph/185.215 km/h.

Championship points: 1 Montoya, 37; **2** Heidfeld, 29; **3** Watt, 18; **4** Mollekens, 16; **5=** Sarrazin, 13; **5=** Rodriguez, 13.

FIA INTERNATIONAL FORMULA 3000 CHAMPIONSHIP, Hockenheimring, Heidelberg, Germany, 1 August. Round 8. 31 laps of the 4.240-mile/6.823-km circuit, 131.428 miles/211.513 km.

1 Nick Heidfeld, D, 1h 12m 57.599s, 108.082 mph/173.942 km/h.

2 Jason Watt, DK, 1h 13m 27.801s; **3** Juan Pablo Montoya, CO, 1h 13m 43.345s; **4** Kevin McGarrity, GB, 1h 14m 04.219s; **5** Bruno Junqueira, BR, 1h 14m 16.979s; **6** Gareth Rees, GB, 1h 14m 18.696s; **7** Boris Derichebourg, F, 1h 14m 21.855s; **8** Werner Lupberger, ZA, 1h 14m 22.300s; **9** Oliver Tichy, A, 1h 14m 22.979s; **10** Thomas Biagi, I, 1h 14m 30.122s; **11** Gonzalo Rodriguez, U, 1h 14m 34.797s; **12** Bertrand Godin, CDN, 1h 14m 53.501s; **13** Oliver Martini, I, 1h 15m 00.989s; **14** Dominik Schwager, D, 1h 15m 02.458s; **15** Tomas Enge, CZ, 1h 15m 13.540s; **16** Jamie Davies, GB, 30 laps; **17** Grégoire de Galzain, F, 30; **18** Christian Horner, GB, 30; **19** Mark Shaw, GB, 30; **20** Alex Müller, D, 29 (DNF – accident); **21** Nicolas Minassian, F, 29 (DNF – accident); **22** Max Wilson, BR, 4 (DNF – accident); **23** Soheil Ayari, F, 4 (DNF – accident); **24** Stéphane Sarrazin, F, 0 (DNF – accident after first start); **25** Kurt Mollekens, B, 0 (DNF – accident after first start); **26** Cyrille Sauvage, F, 0 (DNF – accident after first start); **27** Marcelo Battistuzzi, BR, 0 (DNF – accident after first start); **28** Giovanni Montanari, I, 0 (DNF – accident after first start); **29** André Couto, MAC, 0 (DNF – accident after first start); **30** Gaston Mazzacane, RA, 0 (DNF – accident after first start); **31** Fabrice Walfisch, F, 0 (DNF – accident after first start); **32** Rui Aguas, P, 0 (DNF – accident after first start).

Fastest race lap: Heidfeld, 2m 01.464s, 125.655 mph/202.223 km/h.

Fastest qualifying lap: Heidfeld, 1m 59.620s, 127.593 mph/205.340 km/h.

Did not qualify: Fabrizio Gollin, I; David Cook, GB.

Championship points: 1 Montoya, 41; **2** Heidfeld, 39; **3** Watt, 24; **4** Mollekens, 16; **5=** Sarrazin, 13; **5=** Rodriguez, 13.

FIA INTERNATIONAL FORMULA 3000 CHAMPIONSHIP, Hungaroring, Mogyorod, Budapest, Hungary, 15 August. Round 9. 52 laps of the 2.468-mile/3.972-km circuit, 128.340 miles/206.544 km.

1 Nick Heidfeld, D, 1h 20m 14.689s, 95.962 mph/154.435 km/h.

2 Stéphane Sarrazin, F, 1h 20m 17.407s; **3** Juan Pablo Montoya, CO, 1h 20m 43.145s; **4** Nicolas Minassian, F, 1h 20m 52.686s; **5** André Couto, MAC, 1h 20m 58.174s; **6** Oliver Martini, I, 1h 21m 01.147s; **7** Gonzalo Rodriguez, U, 1h 21m 02.822s; **8** Cyrille Sauvage, F, 1h 21m 19.507s; **9** Oliver Tichy, A, 1h 21m 27.460s; **10** Jason Watt, DK, 1h 21m 29.824s; **11** Marcelo Battistuzzi, BR, 1h 21m 30.775s; **12** Tomas Enge, CZ, 1h 21m 30.976s; **13** Thomas Biagi, I, 1h 21m 35.457s; **14** Bertrand Godin, CDN, 1h 21m 35.783s; **15** Jamie Davies, GB, 51 laps; **16** Mark Shaw, GB, 51; **17** Werner Lupberger, ZA, 51; **18** Dominik Schwager, D, 51; **19** Giovanni Montanari, I, 51; **20** Alex Müller, D, 51; **21** Giorgio Vinella, I, 50; **22** Kevin McGarrity, GB, 48 (DNF – spin); **23** Gaston Mazzacane, RA, 42 (DNF – brakes); **24** Grégoire de Galzain, F, 38 (DNF – spin); **25** Fabrizio Gollin, I, 34 (DNF – spin); **26** Fabrice Walfisch, F, 30 (DNF – accident); **27** Christian Horner, GB, 27 (DNF – spin); **28** Boris Derichebourg, F, 20 (DNF – accident); **29** Bruno Junqueira, BR, 19 (DNF – accident); **30** Max Wilson, BR, 9 (DNF – accident); **31** Soheil Ayari, F, 9 (DNF – accident).

Fastest race lap: Heidfeld, 1m 31.174s, 97.452 mph/156.834 km/h.

Fastest qualifying lap: Sarrazin, 1m 29.471s, 99.307 mph/159.819 km/h.

Did not start: Gareth Rees, GB (oil leak); David Cook, GB (accident in practice).

Championship points: 1 Heidfeld, 49; **2** Montoya, 45; **3** Watt, 24; **4** Sarrazin, 19; **5** Mollekens, 16; **6** Rodriguez, 13.

FIA INTERNATIONAL FORMULA 3000 CHAMPIONSHIP, Circuit de Spa-Francorchamps, Stavelot, Belgium, 29 August. Round 10. 29 laps of the 4.330-mile/6.968-km circuit, 125.562 miles/202.072 km.

1 Gonzalo Rodriguez, U, 1h 03m 10.530s, 119.250 mph/191.915 km/h.

2 Juan Pablo Montoya, CO, 1h 03m 10.565s; **3** Soheil Ayari, F, 1h 03m 14.885s; **4** Nick Heidfeld, D, 1h 03m 24.026s; **5** Alex Müller, D, 1h 03m 31.761s; **6** Marcelo Battistuzzi, BR, 1h 03m 46.427s; **7** Tomas Enge, CZ, 1h 03m 46.992s; **8** Jason Watt, DK, 1h 03m 54.827s; **9** Oliver Martini, I, 1h 04m 00.762s; **10** Thomas Biagi, I, 1h 04m 05.561s; **11** Werner Lupberger, ZA, 1h 04m 07.449s; **12** Gareth Rees, GB, 1h 04m 09.728s; **13** Max Wilson, BR, 1h 04m 10.171s; **14** André Couto, MAC, 1h 04m 11.163s; **15** Jamie Davies, GB, 1h 04m 11.758s; **16** Giovanni Montanari, I, 1h 04m 14.286s; **17** Boris Derichebourg, F, 1h 04m 15.457s; **18** Oliver Tichy, A, 1h 04m 20.222s; **19** Nicolas Minassian, F, 1h 04m 23.542s; **20** Cyrille Sauvage, F, 1h 04m 27.114s; **21** Bertrand Godin, CDN, 1h 04m 27.913s; **22** Fabrice Walfisch, F, 1h 04m 30.274s; **23** Hidetoshi Mitsusada, J, 1h 05m 06.909s; **24** Mark Shaw, GB, 1h 05m 07.248s; **25** Grégoire de Galzain, F, 1h 05m 14.840s; **26** Bruno Junqueira, BR, 22 laps (DNF – fuel pressure); **27** Dominik Schwager, D, 20 (DNF – spin); **28** Stéphane Sarrazin, F, 6 (DNF).

Fastest race lap: Ayari, 2m 09.792s, 120.092 mph/193.269 km/h.

Fastest qualifying lap: Montoya, 2m 07.690s, 122.069 mph/196.451 km/h.

Did not qualify: Giorgio Vinella, I; Christian Horner, GB; Kurt Mollekens, B; Fabrizio Gollin, I; Gaston Mazzacane, RA.

Championship points: 1 Heidfeld, 52; **2** Montoya, 51; **3** Watt, 24; **4** Rodriguez, 23; **5** Sarrazin, 19; **6=** Mollekens, 16; **6=** Ayari, 16.

36th GRAN PREMIO del MEDITERRANEO, Ente Autodromo di Pergusa, Enna-Pergusa, Sicily, Italy, 6 September. Round 11. 41 laps of the 3.076-mile/4.950-km circuit, 126.107 miles/202.950 km.

1 Juan Pablo Montoya, CO, 1h 04m 29.540s, 117.323 mph/188.813 km/h.

2 Nick Heidfeld, D, 1h 04m 34.990s; **3** Soheil Ayari, F, 1h 04m 39.897s; **4** Gareth Rees, GB, 1h 04m 41.186s; **5** Oliver Martini, I, 1h 04m 41.726s; **6** Werner Lupberger, ZA, 1h 04m 52.169s; **7** Jamie Davies, GB, 1h 04m 53.442s; **8** Kurt Mollekens, B, 1h 04m 59.598s; **9** André Couto, MAC, 1h 05m 21.969s; **10** Grégoire de Galzain, F, 1h 05m 43.346s; **11** Boris Derichebourg, F, 1h 05m 47.226s; **12** Bertrand Godin, CDN, 1h 06m 01.325s; **13** Gaston Mazzacane, RA, 1h 06m

03.479s*; **14** Fabrizio Gollin, I, 1h 06m 05.831s; **15** Giorgio Vinella, I, 40 laps; **16** Mark Shaw, GB, 40; **17** Christian Horner, GB, 40; **18** Bruno Junqueira, BR, 40**; **19** Nicolas Minassian, F, 40; **20** Alex Müller, D, 40; **21** James Taylor, GB, 38; **22** Gonzalo Rodriguez, U, 37 (DNF – fuel pump); **23** Fabrice Walfisch, F, 30 (DNF – spin); **24** Jason Watt, DK, 20 (DNF – accident); **25** Tomas Enge, CZ, 18 (DNF – accident); **26** Hidetoshi Mitsusada, J, 15 (DNF – accident); **27** Max Wilson, BR, 10 (DNF – accident damage); **28** Stéphane Sarrazin, F, 9 (DNF – engine); **29** Oliver Tichy, A, 4 (DNF – accident); **30** Marcelo Battistuzzi, BR, 1 (DNF – accident); **31** Giovanni Montanari, I, 1 (DNF – accident); **32** Dominik Schwager, D, 0 (DNF – accident); **33** Thomas Biagi, I, 0 (DNF – gearbox).
** includes 10s penalty and ** includes 30s penalty for chicane jumping.*
Fastest race lap: Montoya, 1m 33.212s, 118.792 mph/191.177 km/h.
Fastest qualifying lap: Heidfeld, 1m 32.127s, 120.191 mph/193.429 km/h.
Championship points: **1** Montoya, 61; **2** Heidfeld, 58; **3** Watt, 24; **4** Rodriguez, 23; **5** Ayari, 20; **6** Sarrazin, 19.

FIA INTERNATIONAL FORMULA 3000 CHAMPIONSHIP, Nürburgring, Nürburg/Eifel, Germany, 26 September. Round 12. 45 laps of the 2.831-mile/4.556-km circuit, 127.394 miles/205.020 km.
1 Gonzalo Rodriguez, U, 1h 12m 37.085s, 105.258 mph/169.396 km/h.
2 Jason Watt, DK, 1h 13m 02.665s; **3** Juan Pablo Montoya, CO, 1h 13m 07.378s; **4** Kurt Mollekens, B, 1h 13m 15.870s; **5** André Couto, MAC, 1h 13m 16.797s; **6** Tomas Enge, CZ, 1h 13m 19.408s; **7** Dominik Schwager, D, 1h 13m 30.733s; **8** Fabrice Walfisch, F, 1h 13m 34.789s; **9** Nick Heidfeld, D, 1h 13m 39.117s; **10** Giovanni Montanari, I, 1h 13m 43.899s; **11** Bertrand Godin, CDN, 1h 13m 54.114s; **12** Thomas Biagi, I, 1h 13m 55.238s; **13** Alex Müller, D, 1h 14m 00.598s; **14** Jamie Davies, GB, 1h 14m 01.866s; **15** Hidetoshi Mitsusada, J, 1h 14m 03.298s; **16** Grégoire de Galzain, F, 1h 14m 08.706s; **17** Christian Horner, GB, 44 laps; **18** Mark Shaw, GB, 44; **19** Stéphane Sarrazin, F, 44; **20** Gareth Rees, GB, 43 (DNF – spin); **21** James Taylor, GB, 43; **22** Giorgio Vinella, I, 43; **23** Max Wilson, BR, 42 (DNF – spin); **24** Oliver Martini, I, 33 (DNF – brakes); **25** Gaston Mazzacane, RA, 30 (DNF – brakes); **26** Marcelo Battistuzzi, BR, 19 (DNF – accident); **27** Oliver Tichy, A, 14 (DNF – misfire); **28** Fabrizio Gollin, I, 11 (DNF – spin); **29** Boris Derichebourg, F, 7 (DNF – spin); **30** Werner Lupberger, ZA, 1 (DNF – accident); **31** Soheil Ayari, F, 1 (DNF – accident damage); **32** Bruno Junqueira, BR, 1 (DNF – accident damage).
Fastest race lap: Rodriguez, 1m 32.857s, 109.755 mph/176.633 km/h.
Fastest qualifying lap: Montoya, 1m 31.973s, 110.809 mph/178.331 km/h.
Did not start: Bas Leinders, B.

Final championship points
1 Juan Pablo Montoya, CO, 65; **2** Nick Heidfeld, D, 58; **3** Gonzalo Rodriguez, U, 33; **4** Jason Watt, DK, 30; **5** Soheil Ayari, F, 20; **6=** Kurt Mollekens, B, 19; **6=** Stéphane Sarrazin, F, 19; **8** Gareth Rees, GB, 10; **9** Max Wilson, BR, 9; **10** Jamie Davies, GB, 8; **11** André Couto, MAC, 7; **12=** Boris Derichebourg, F, 5; **12=** Nicolas Minassian, F, 5; **14=** Thomas Biagi, I, 3; **14=** Bruno Junqueira, BR, 3; **14=** Oliver Martini, I, 3; **14=** Kevin McGarrity, GB, 3; **14=** Dominik Schwager, D, 3; **19=** Gaston Mazzacane, RA, 2; **19=** Alex Müller, D, 2; **19=** Cyrille Sauvage, F, 2; **22=** Marcelo Battistuzzi, BR, 1; **22=** Tomas Enge, CZ, 1; **22=** Werner Lupberger, ZA, 1.

British Formula 3 Championship

AUTOSPORT BRITISH FORMULA 3 CHAMPIONSHIP, Donington Park Grand Prix Circuit, Derbyshire, Great Britain, 22 March. Round 1. 20 laps of the 2.500-mile/4.023-km circuit, 50.000 miles/80.467 km.
1 Enrique Bernoldi, BR (Dallara F398-Renault), 29m 48.530s, 100.641 mph/161.966 km/h.
2 Martin O'Connell, GB (Dallara F398-TOM'S Toyota), 29m 54.405s; **3** Luciano Burti, BR (Dallara F398-Mugen Honda), 29m 58.745s; **4** Mario Haberfeld, BR (Dallara F398-Mugen Honda), 30m 00.260s; **5** Marc Hynes, GB (Dallara F398-Renault), 30m 08.397s; **6** Jamie Spence, GB (Dallara F398-Renault), 30m 09.400s; **7** Ricardo Mauricio, BR (Dallara F398-Mugen Honda), 30m 18.089s; **8** David Cook, GB (Dallara F398-Opel), 30m 20.763s; **9** Narain Karthikeyan, IND (Dallara F398-Opel), 30m 22.977s; **10** Yudai Igarashi, J (Dallara F398-Mugen Honda), 30m 25.794s.
Fastest race lap: Bernoldi, 1m 28.530s, 101.660 mph/163.607 km/h.
National Class winner: Phillip Scifleet, AUS (Dallara F396-TOM'S Toyota), 30m 57.338s (15th).
Fastest qualifying lap: Bernoldi, 1m 27.476s, 102.885 mph/165.578 km/h.
Championship points. **1** Bernoldi, 21; **2** O'Connell, 15; **3** Burti, 12; **4** Haberfeld, 10; **5** Hynes, 8; **6** Spence, 6. **National Class:** **1** Scifleet, 21.

AUTOSPORT BRITISH FORMULA 3 CHAMPIONSHIP, Thruxton Circuit, Andover, Hampshire, Great Britain, 29 March. Round 2. 19 laps of the 2.356-mile/3.792-km circuit, 44.764 miles/72.041 km.
1 Enrique Bernoldi, BR (Dallara F398-Renault), 22m 08.552s, 121.298 mph/195.210 km/h.
2 Martin O'Connell, GB (Dallara F398-TOM'S Toyota), 22m 09.501s; **3** Warren Hughes, GB (Dallara F398-Renault), 22m 12.968s; **4** Mario Haberfeld, BR (Dallara F398-Mugen Honda), 22m 18.161s; **5** Luciano Burti, BR (Dallara F398-Mugen Honda), 22m 22.499s; **6** Jamie Spence, GB (Dallara F398-Renault), 22m 23.975s; **7** Kristian Kolby, DK (Dallara F398-Mugen Honda), 22m 27.960s; **8** Alexander Yoong, MAL (Dallara F398-Renault), 22m 33.017s; **9** Narain Karthikeyan, IND (Dallara F398-Opel), 22m 41.848s; **10** Ben Collins, GB (Dallara F398-Opel), 22m 42.522s.
Fastest race lap: Bernoldi, 1m 09.133s, 122.685 mph/197.443 km/h.
National Class winner: Phillip Scifleet, AUS (Dallara F396-TOM'S Toyota), 22m 54.680s (18th).
Fastest qualifying lap: O'Connell, 1m 08.593s, 123.651 mph/198.997 km/h.
Championship points. **1** Bernoldi, 42; **2** O'Connell, 30; **3=** Burti, 20; **3=** Haberfeld, 20; **5=** Spence, 12; **5=** Hughes, 12. **National Class:** **1** Scifleet, 42; **2** Carway, 15.

AUTOSPORT BRITISH FORMULA 3 CHAMPIONSHIP, Silverstone International Circuit, Towcester, Northamptonshire, Great Britain, 5 April. Round 3. 20 laps of the 2.252-mile/3.624-km circuit, 45.088 miles/72.562 km.
1 Mario Haberfeld, BR (Dallara F398-Mugen Honda), 25m 40.878s, 105.340 mph/169.528 km/h.
2 Enrique Bernoldi, BR (Dallara F398-Renault), 25m 41.317s; **3** Marc Hynes, GB (Dallara F398-Renault), 25m 52.109s; **4** Warren Hughes, GB (Dallara F398-Renault), 25m 54.396s; **5** Ricardo Mauricio, BR (Dallara F398-Mugen Honda), 25m 59.126s; **6** Alexander Yoong, MAL (Dallara F398-Renault), 25m 59.636s; **7** Yudai Igarashi, J (Dallara F398-Mugen Honda), 26m 10.785s; **8** Paula Cook, GB (Dallara F398-Opel), 26m 15.543s; **9** Adam Wilcox, GB (Dallara F398-Mugen Honda), 26m 22.673s; **10** Andrej Pavicevic, AUS (Dallara F398-Mugen Honda), 26m 25.862s.
Fastest race lap: Haberfeld, 1m 16.146s, 106.469 mph/171.345 km/h.
National Class winner: Phillip Scifleet, AUS (Dallara F396-TOM'S Toyota), 26m 31.903s (12th).
Fastest qualifying lap: Haberfeld, 1m 25.924s, 94.353 mph/151.847 km/h.
Championship points. **1** Bernoldi, 57; **2** Haberfeld, 41; **3** O'Connell, 30; **4** Hughes, 22; **5=** Burti, 20; **5=** Hynes, 20. **National Class:** **1** Scifleet, 63; **2** Carway, 30.

AUTOSPORT BRITISH FORMULA 3 CHAMPIONSHIP, Brands Hatch short Circuit, Dartford, Kent, Great Britain, 26 April. 23 and 30 laps of the 1.2036-mile/1.937-km circuit.
Round 4 (27.683 miles/44.551 km)
1 Enrique Bernoldi, BR (Dallara F398-Renault), 15m 51.320s, 104.758 mph/168.592 km/h.
2 Martin O'Connell, GB (Dallara F398-TOM'S Toyota), 15m 51.821s; **3** Mario Haberfeld, BR (Dallara F398-Mugen Honda), 15m 54.302s; **4** Ben Collins, GB (Dallara F398-Opel), 15m 56.221s; **5** Warren Hughes, GB (Dallara F398-Renault), 15m 56.652s; **6** Kristian Kolby, DK (Dallara F398-Mugen Honda), 15m 57.753s; **7** Marc Hynes, GB (Dallara F398-Renault), 15m 58.341s; **8** Alexander Yoong, MAL (Dallara F398-Renault), 15m 59.531s; **9** Jamie Spence, GB (Dallara F398-Renault), 16m 01.698s; **10** Luciano Burti, BR (Dallara F398-Mugen Honda), 16m 04.232s.
Fastest race lap: Hynes, 40.763s, 106.296 mph/171.067 km/h.
National Class winner: Phillip Scifleet, AUS (Dallara F396-TOM'S Toyota), 16m 36.236s (19th).
Fastest qualifying lap: Haberfeld, 41.395s, 104.674 mph/168.456 km/h.

Round 5 (36.108 miles/58.110 km)
1 Luciano Burti, BR (Dallara F398-Mugen Honda), 20m 52.548s, 103.779 mph/167.017 km/h.
2 Warren Hughes, GB (Dallara F398-Renault), 20m 53.328s; **3** Martin O'Connell, GB (Dallara F398-TOM'S Toyota), 20m 53.585s; **4** Jamie Spence, GB (Dallara F398-Renault), 20m 54.052s; **5** Ricardo Mauricio, BR (Dallara F398-Mugen Honda), 20m 55.320s; **6** Ben Collins, GB (Dallara F398-Opel), 20m 55.703s; **7** David Cook, GB (Dallara F398-Opel), 21m 01.664s; **8** Alexander Yoong, MAL (Dallara F398-Renault), 21m 02.465s; **9** Paula Cook, GB (Dallara F398-Opel), 21m 03.115s; **10** Andrej Pavicevic, AUS (Dallara F398-Mugen Honda), 21m 09.047s.
Fastest race lap: Burti, 41.116s, 105.383 mph/169.599 km/h.
National Class winner: Warren Carway, IRL (Dallara F396-TOM'S Toyota), 21m 25.459s (13th).
Fastest qualifying lap: Haberfeld, 40.711s, 106.432 mph/171.286 km/h.
Championship points. **1** Bernoldi, 77; **2** O'Connell, 57; **3** Haberfeld, 53; **4** Hughes, 45; **5** Burti, 42; **6** Hynes, 25. **National Class:** **1** Scifleet, 100; **2** Carway, 50; **3** White, 12.

AUTOSPORT BRITISH FORMULA 3 CHAMPIONSHIP, Oulton Park International Circuit, Tarporley, Cheshire, Great Britain, 4 May. Round 6. 13 laps of the 2.776-mile/4.468-km circuit, 36.088 miles/58.078 km.
Race stopped after 7 laps and restarted for a further 6.
1 Enrique Bernoldi, BR (Dallara F398-Renault), 19m 59.895s, 108.273 mph/174.249 km/h.
2 Martin O'Connell, GB (Dallara F398-TOM'S Toyota), 20m 03.952s; **3** Luciano Burti, BR (Dallara F398-Mugen Honda), 20m 12.909s; **4** Jamie Spence, GB (Dallara F398-Renault), 20m 13.817s; **5** Kristian Kolby, DK (Dallara F398-Mugen Honda), 20m 17.489s; **6** Warren Hughes, GB (Dallara F398-Renault), 20m 18.332s; **7** Ricardo Mauricio, BR (Dallara F398-Mugen Honda), 20m 18.701s; **8** Andrej Pavicevic, AUS (Dallara F398-Mugen Honda), 20m 31.237s; **9** Alexander Yoong, MAL (Dallara F398-Renault), 20m 38.846s; **10** Paula Cook, GB (Dallara F398-Opel), 20m 50.566s.
Fastest race lap: Bernoldi, 1m 30.894s, 109.948 mph/176.944 km/h.
National Class winner: Phillip Scifleet, AUS (Dallara F396-TOM'S Toyota), 20m 52.399s (12th).
Fastest qualifying lap: Bernoldi, 1m 29.944s, 111.109 mph/178.813 km/h.
Championship points. **1** Bernoldi, 98; **2** O'Connell, 72; **3** Burti, 54; **4** Haberfeld, 53; **5** Hughes, 51; **6** Spence, 34. **National Class:** **1** Scifleet, 121; **2** Carway, 50; **3** White, 12.

AUTOSPORT BRITISH FORMULA 3 CHAMPIONSHIP, Silverstone Grand Prix Circuit, Towcester, Northamptonshire, Great Britain, 17 May. Round 7. 15 laps of the 3.194-mile/5.140-km circuit, 47.955 miles/77.176 km.
1 Enrique Bernoldi, BR (Dallara F398-Renault), 26m 16.170s, 109.530 mph/176.272 km/h.
2 Luciano Burti, BR (Dallara F398-Mugen Honda), 26m 19.286s; **3** Mario Haberfeld, BR (Dallara F398-Mugen Honda), 26m 20.520s; **4** Kristian Kolby, DK (Dallara F398-Mugen Honda), 26m 21.468s; **5** Martin O'Connell, GB (Dallara F398-TOM'S Toyota), 26m 25.675s; **6** Ricardo Mauricio, BR (Dallara F398-Mugen Honda), 26m 26.124s; **7** Warren Hughes, GB (Dallara F398-Renault), 26m 30.461s; **8** Marc Hynes, GB (Dallara F398-Renault), 26m 32.034s; **9** Jamie Spence, GB (Dallara F398-Mugen Honda), 26m 35.533s; **10** Miku Santarvirta, SF (Dallara F398-Mugen Honda), 26m 36.660s.
Fastest race lap: Bernoldi, 1m 43.873s, 110.697 mph/178.149 km/h.
National Class winner: Phillip Scifleet, AUS (Dallara F396-TOM'S Toyota), 27m 01.375s (16th).
Fastest qualifying lap: Bernoldi, 1m 43.669s, 110.915 mph/178.500 km/h.
Championship points. **1** Bernoldi, 119; **2** O'Connell, 80; **3** Burti, 69; **4** Haberfeld, 65; **5** Hughes, 55; **6** Spence, 36. **National Class:** **1** Scifleet, 142; **2** Carway, 65; **3** White, 12.

AUTOSPORT BRITISH FORMULA 3 CHAMPIONSHIP, Croft Circuit, Croft-on-Tees, North Yorkshire, Great Britain, 24 May. Round 8. 25 laps of the 2.127-mile/3.423-km circuit, 53.175 miles/85.577 km.
1 Mario Haberfeld, BR (Dallara F398-Mugen Honda), 31m 32.734s, 101.139 mph/162.768 km/h.
2 Martin O'Connell, GB (Dallara F398-TOM'S Toyota), 31m 37.685s; **3** Luciano Burti, BR (Dallara F398-Mugen Honda), 31m 42.153s; **4** Warren Hughes, GB (Dallara F398-Renault), 31m 48.724s; **5** Darren Manning, GB (Dallara F398-Mugen Honda), 31m 53.907s; **6** Ben Collins, GB (Dallara F398-Opel), 31m 54.218s; **7** Marc Hynes, GB (Dallara F398-Renault), 31m 55.471s; **8** David Cook, GB (Dallara F398-Opel), 31m 57.672s; **9** Ricardo Mauricio, BR (Dallara F398-Mugen Honda), 32m 01.426s; **10** Yudai Igarashi, J (Dallara F398-Mugen Honda), 32m 11.094s.
Fastest race lap: Haberfeld, 1m 14.800s, 102.369 mph/164.747 km/h.
National Class winner: Phillip Scifleet, AUS (Dallara F396-TOM'S Toyota), 32m 28.758s (16th).
Fastest qualifying lap: Haberfeld, 1m 13.588s, 104.055 mph/167.460 km/h.
Championship points. **1** Bernoldi, 119; **2** O'Connell, 95; **3** Haberfeld, 86; **4** Burti, 81; **5** Hughes, 65; **6** Spence, 36. **National Class:** **1** Scifleet, 162; **2** Carway, 81; **3** White, 12.

AUTOSPORT BRITISH FORMULA 3 CHAMPIONSHIP, Snetterton Circuit, Norfolk, Great Britain, 14 June. Round 9. 25 laps of the 1.952-mile/3.141-km circuit, 48.800 miles/78.536 km.
1 Darren Manning, GB (Dallara F398-Mugen Honda), 29m 32.239s, 99.129 mph/159.532 km/h.
2 Mario Haberfeld, BR (Dallara F398-Mugen Honda), 29m 35.188s; **3** Warren Hughes, GB (Dallara F398-Renault), 29m 35.596s; **4** Ricardo Mauricio, BR (Dallara F398-Mugen Honda), 29m 36.144s; **5** Adam Wilcox, GB (Dallara F398-TOM'S Toyota), 29m 40.325s; **6** Ben Collins, GB (Dallara F398-Opel), 29m 41.995s; **7** Alexander Yoong, MAL (Dallara F398-Renault), 29m 42.402s; **8** Tim Spouge, GB (Dallara F398-Mugen Honda), 29m 47.814s; **9** Yudai Igarashi, J (Dallara F398-Mugen Honda), 29m 58.713s; **10** Kristian Kolby, DK (Dallara F398-Mugen Honda), 29m 59.296s.
Fastest race lap: Manning, 1m 03.285s, 111.041 mph/178.702 km/h.
National Class winner: Phillip Scifleet, AUS (Dallara F396-TOM'S Toyota), 30m 18.018s (14th).
Fastest qualifying lap: Luciano Burti, BR (Dallara F398-Mugen Honda), 1m 02.667s, 112.136 mph/180.465 km/h.
Championship points. **1** Bernoldi, 119; **2** Haberfeld, 101; **3** O'Connell, 95; **4** Burti, 81; **5** Hughes, 77; **6** Mauricio, 42. **National Class:** **1** Scifleet, 183; **2** Carway, 96; **3=** White, 12; **3=** Hayr, 12.

AUTOSPORT BRITISH FORMULA 3 CHAMPIONSHIP, Silverstone Grand Prix Circuit, Towcester, Northamptonshire, Great Britain, 11 July. Round 10. 12 laps of the 3.194-mile/5.140-km circuit, 38.622 miles/62.156 km.
Race staged in two parts of 10 and 2 laps.
1 Darren Manning, GB (Dallara F398-Mugen Honda), 23m 21.312s, 99.221 mph/159.680 km/h.
2 Warren Hughes, GB (Dallara F398-Renault), 23m 27.347s; **3** Ricardo Mauricio, BR (Dallara F398-Mugen Honda), 23m 30.461s; **4** Kristian Kolby, DK (Dallara F398-Mugen Honda), 23m 33.998s; **5** Mario Haberfeld, BR (Dallara F398-Mugen Honda), 23m 34.586s; **6** Alexander Yoong, MAL (Dallara F398-Renault), 23m 35.565s; **7** Adam Wilcox, GB (Dallara F398-TOM'S Toyota), 23m 39.548s; **8** Tim Spouge, GB (Dallara F398-Mugen Honda), 23m 49.026s; **9** Andrej Pavicevic, AUS (Dallara F398-Mugen Honda), 23m 53.726s; **10** Yudai Igarashi, J (Dallara F398-Mugen Honda), 23m 57.102s.
Fastest race lap: Martin O'Connell, GB (Dallara F398-TOM'S Toyota), 1m 47.273s, 107.188 mph/172.503 km/h.
National Class winner: Phillip Scifleet, AUS (Dallara F396-TOM'S Toyota), 24m 12.259s (11th).
Fastest qualifying lap: Manning, 1m 43.045s, 111.586 mph/179.581 km/h.
Championship points. **1** Bernoldi, 119; **2** Haberfeld, 109; **3** O'Connell, 96; **4** Hughes, 92; **5** Burti, 81; **6** Mauricio, 54. **National Class:** **1** Scifleet, 203; **2** Carway, 97; **3** Hayr, 27.

AUTOSPORT BRITISH FORMULA 3 CHAMPIONSHIP, Pembrey Circuit, Llanelli, Dyfed, Great Britain, 16 August. 20 and 15 laps of the 1.456-mile/2.343-km circuit.
Round 11 (29.120 miles/46.864 km)
1 Mario Haberfeld, BR (Dallara F398-Mugen Honda), 20m 27.416s, 85.409 mph/137.452 km/h.
2 Warren Hughes, GB (Dallara F398-Renault), 20m 29.471s; **3** Jamie Spence, GB (Dallara F398-Mugen Honda), 20m 33.151s; **4** Enrique Bernoldi, BR (Dallara F398-Renault), 20m 33.430s; **5** Luciano Burti, BR (Dallara F398-Mugen Honda), 20m 35.760s; **6** Narain Karthikeyan, IND (Dallara F398-Mugen Honda), 20m 36.021s; **7** Ben Collins, GB (Dallara F398-Opel), 20m 37.011s; **8** Marc Hynes, GB (Dallara F398-Renault), 20m 37.459s; **9** Kristian Kolby, DK (Dallara F398-Mugen Honda), 20m 38.158s; **10** Ricardo Mauricio, BR (Dallara F398-Mugen Honda), 20m 38.559s.
Fastest race lap: Haberfeld, 50.696s, 103.393 mph/166.395 km/h.
National Class winner: Phillip Scifleet, AUS (Dallara F396-TOM'S Toyota), 20m 47.771s (12th).
Fastest qualifying lap: Haberfeld, 50.287s, 104.234 mph/167.748 km/h.

Round 12 (21.840 miles/35.148 km)
1 Luciano Burti, BR (Dallara F398-Mugen Honda), 13m 00.777s, 100.700 mph/162.060 km/h.
2 Mario Haberfeld, BR (Dallara F398-Mugen Honda), 13m 01.179s; **3** Marc Hynes, GB (Dallara F398-Renault), 13m 03.328s; **4** Narain Karthikeyan, IND (Dallara F398-Mugen Honda), 13m 04.191s; **5** Ricardo Mauricio, BR (Dallara F398-Mugen Honda), 13m 04.534s; **6** Jamie Spence, GB (Dallara F398-Mugen Honda), 13m 06.458s; **7** Enrique Bernoldi, BR (Dallara F398-Renault), 13m 08.680s; **8** Martin O'Connell, GB (Dallara F398-TOM'S Toyota), 13m 09.989s; **9** Ben Collins, GB (Dallara F398-Opel), 13m 10.918s; **10** Andrej Pavicevic, AUS (Dallara F398-Mugen Honda), 13m 11.360s.
Fastest race lap: Haberfeld, 51.181s, 102.413 mph/164.818 km/h.
National Class winner: John Ingram, GB (Dallara F396-HKS Mitsubishi), 13m 50.130s (19th).
Fastest qualifying lap: Burti, 50.727s, 103.330 mph/166.293 km/h.
Championship points. **1** Haberfeld, 146; **2** Bernoldi, 133; **3** Burti, 109; **4** Hughes, 107; **5** O'Connell, 99; **6** Mauricio, 63. **National Class:** **1** Scifleet, 237; **2** Carway, 97; **3** Hayr, 54.

AUTOSPORT BRITISH FORMULA 3 CHAMPIONSHIP, Donington Park Club Circuit, Derbyshire, Great Britain, 30 August. Round 13. 20 laps of the 1.957-mile/3.149-km circuit, 39.140 miles/62.990 km.
1 Enrique Bernoldi, BR (Dallara F398-Renault), 22m 47.041s, 103.072 mph/165.879 km/h.
2 Ricardo Mauricio, BR (Dallara F398-Mugen Honda), 22m 49.872s; **3** Mario Haberfeld, BR (Dallara F398-Mugen Honda), 22m 50.280s; **4** Luciano Burti, BR (Dallara F398-Mugen Honda), 22m 50.692s; **5** Warren Hughes, GB (Dallara F398-Renault), 22m 51.337s; **6** Kristian Kolby, DK (Dallara F398-Mugen Honda), 22m 51.794s; **7** Marc Hynes, GB (Dallara F398-Renault), 22m 52.522s; **8** Andrej Pavicevic, AUS (Dallara F398-Mugen Honda), 23m 01.079s; **9** Michael Bentwood, GB (Dallara F398-Mugen Honda), 23m 02.104s; **10** Ben Collins, GB (Dallara F398-Opel), 23m 04.154s.
Fastest race lap: Kolby, 1m 05.226s, 108.012 mph/173.829 km/h.
National Class winner: Mike Kirkham, GB (Dallara F396-HKS Mitsubishi), 23m 36.301s (16th).
Fastest qualifying lap: Haberfeld, 1m 03.918s, 110.222 mph/177.386 km/h.
Championship points. **1** Haberfeld, 158; **2** Bernoldi, 153; **3** Burti, 119; **4** Hughes, 115; **5** O'Connell, 99; **6** Mauricio, 78. **National Class:** **1** Scifleet, 237; **2** Carway, 97; **3** Hayr, 69.

AUTOSPORT BRITISH FORMULA 3 CHAMPIONSHIP, Thruxton Circuit, Andover, Hampshire, Great Britain, 13 September. Round 14. 19 laps of the 2.356-mile/3.792-km circuit, 44.764 miles/72.041 km.
1 Mario Haberfeld, BR (Dallara F398-Mugen Honda), 24m 17.050s, 110.600 mph/177.994 km/h.
2 Martin O'Connell, GB (Dallara F398-TOM'S Toyota), 24m 22.337s; **3** Luciano Burti, BR (Dallara F398-Mugen Honda), 24m 23.105s; **4** Kristian Kolby, DK (Dallara F398-Mugen Honda), 24m 23.592s; **5** Andrej Pavicevic, AUS (Dallara F398-Mugen Honda), 24m 36.665s; **6** Marc Hynes, GB (Dallara F398-Renault), 24m 37.713s; **7** Warren Hughes, GB (Dallara F398-Renault), 24m 50.967s; **8** Ben Collins, GB (Dallara F398-Opel), 25m 08.422s; **9** Alexander Yoong, MAL (Dallara F398-Mugen Honda), 25m 09.095s; **10** Adam Wilcox, GB (Dallara F398-Opel), 25m 17.625s.
Fastest race lap: Kolby, 1m 10.948s, 119.547 mph/192.392 km/h.
National Class winner: no entries.
Fastest qualifying lap: Jamie Spence, GB (Dallara F398-Mugen Honda), 1m 08.478s, 123.859 mph/199.331 km/h.
Championship points. **1** Haberfeld, 178; **2** Bernoldi, 153; **3** Burti, 131; **4** Hughes, 119; **5** O'Connell, 114; **6** Mauricio, 78. **National Class:** **1** Scifleet, 237; **2** Carway, 97; **3** Hayr, 69.

FINA F3 MASTERS, Circuit de Spa-Francorchamps, Stavelot, Belgium, 27 September. Round 15. 14 laps of the 4.330-mile/6.968-km circuit, 60.616 miles/97.552 km.
1 Mario Haberfeld, BR (Dallara F398-Mugen Honda), 32m 11.900s, 112.955 mph/181.783 km/h.
2 Darren Manning, GB (Dallara F398-Mugen Honda), 32m 19.808s; **3** Narain Karthikeyan, IND (Dallara F398-Mugen Honda), 32m 23.702s; **4** Enrique Bernoldi, BR (Dallara F398-Renault), 32m 24.514s; **5** Kristian Kolby, DK (Dallara F398-Mugen Honda), 32m 25.688s; **6** Alexander Yoong, MAL (Dallara F398-Mugen Honda), 32m 28.427s; **7** Marcel Fässler, CH (Martini MK73-Opel), 32m 28.869s; **8** Ben Collins, GB (Dallara F398-Opel), 32m 31.578s; **9** Warren Hughes, GB (Dallara F398-Renault), 32m 33.407s; **10** Michael Bentwood, GB (Dallara F398-Mugen Honda), 32m 39.855s.
Fastest race lap: Manning, 2m 17.039s, 113.741 mph/183.049 km/h.
National Class winner: no entries.
Fastest qualifying lap: Luciano Burti, BR (Dallara F398-Mugen Honda), 2m 15.448s, 115.077 mph/185.199 km/h.
Championship points. **1** Haberfeld, 198; **2** Bernoldi, 163; **3** Burti, 131; **4** Hughes, 121; **5** O'Connell, 114; **6** Mauricio, 78. **National Class:** **1** Scifleet, 237; **2** Carway, 97; **3** Hayr, 69.

AUTUMN GOLD CUP, Silverstone International Circuit, Towcester, Northamptonshire, Great Britain, 4 October. Round 16. 22 laps of the 2.252-mile/3.624-km circuit, 49.591 miles/79.809 km.
1 Mario Haberfeld, BR (Dallara F398-Mugen Honda), 30m 49.251s, 96.540 mph/155.367 km/h.
2 Kristian Kolby, DK (Dallara F398-Mugen Honda), 30m 54.966s; **3** Narain Karthikeyan, IND (Dallara F398-Mugen Honda), 30m 58.034s; **4** Warren Hughes, GB (Dallara F398-Renault), 31m 01.578s; **5** Michael Bentwood, GB (Dallara F398-Mugen Honda), 31m 05.316s; **6** Luciano Burti, BR (Dallara F398-Mugen Honda), 31m 08.180s; **7** Yudai Igarashi, J (Dallara F398-Mugen Honda), 31m 12.231s; **8** Ben Collins, GB (Dallara F398-Opel), 31m 15.930s; **9** Tim Spouge, GB (Dallara F398-Mugen Honda), 31m 33.119s; **10** Adam Wilcox, GB (Dallara F398-Opel), 31m 40.756s.
Fastest race lap: Hughes, 1m 17.454s, 104.671 mph/168.452 km/h.
National Class winner: John Ingram, GB (Dallara F396-HKS Mitsubishi), 32m 02.532s (13th).
Fastest qualifying lap: Enrique Bernoldi, BR (Dallara F398-Renault), 1m 15.465s, 107.430 mph/172.892 km/h.

Final championship points
1 Mario Haberfeld, BR, 218; **2** Enrique Bernoldi, BR, 163; **3** Luciano Burti, BR, 137; **4** Warren Hughes, GB, 132; **5** Martin O'Connell, GB, 114; **6** Kristian Kolby, DK, 82; **7** Ricardo Mauricio, BR, 78; **8** Darren Manning, GB, 65; **9** Marc Hynes, GB, 57; **10** Jamie Spence, GB, 54; **11** Ben Collins, GB, 45; **12** Narain Karthikeyan, IND, 44; **13** Alexander Yoong, MAL, 35; **14** Andrej Pavicevic, AUS, 19; **15** Adam Wilcox, GB, 16; **16** Yudai Igarashi, J, 15; **17** Michael Bentwood, GB, 11; **18** David Cook, GB, 10; **19** Tim Spouge, GB, 8; **20** Paula Cook, GB, 7; **21** Marcel Fässler, CH, 4; **22** Miku Santarvirta, SF, 1.

National Class
1 Phillip Scifleet, AUS, 237; **2** Warren Carway, IRL, 97; **3** Steven Hayr, NZ, 69; **4** John Ingram, GB, 56; **5** Mike Kirkham, GB, 21; **6** Stephen White, GB, 12.

French Formula 3 Championship

GRAND PRIX DE LA VILLE DE NIMES, Circuit de Lédenon, Remoulins, Nimes, France, 29 March. Round 1. 2 x 14 laps of the 1.957-mile/3.150-km circuit.
Race 1 (27.402 miles/44.100 km/h)
1 Franck Montagny, F (Martini MK73-Opel), 18m 56.278s, 86.818 mph/139.719 km/h.
2 David Terrien, F (Dallara F396-Opel), 18m 58.565s; 3 Marcel Fässler, CH (Martini MK73-Opel), 19m 04.395s; 4 Steeve Hiesse, F (Dallara F396-Opel), 19m 11.822s; 5 Jonathan Cochet, F (Martini MK73-Opel), 19m 14.633s; 6 Stéphane Sallaz, F (Dallara F396-Opel), 19m 15.128s; 7 Sébastien Bourdain, F (Martini MK73-Opel), 19m 15.898s; 8 David Saelens, B (Dallara F396-Renault), 19m 17.251s; 9 Romain Dumas, F (Dallara F396-Opel), 19m 17.769s; 10 Benoit Tréluyer, F (Dallara F396-Fiat), 19m 19.154s.
Fastest race lap: Terrien, 1m 20.248s, 87.807 mph/141.312 km/h.
Fastest qualifying lap: Montagny, 1m 18.587s, 89.663 mph/144.299 km/h.

Race 2 (27.402 miles/44.100 km/h)
1 Franck Montagny, F (Martini MK73-Opel), 18m 53.409s, 87.037 mph/140.073 km/h.
2 David Terrien, F (Dallara F396-Opel), 18m 54.855s; 3 Stéphane Sallaz, F (Dallara F396-Opel), 19m 00.081s; 4 Marcel Fässler, CH (Martini MK73-Opel), 19m 00.390s; 5 Steeve Hiesse, F (Dallara F396-Opel), 19m 12.965s; 6 David Saelens, B (Dallara F396-Renault), 19m 14.530s; 7 David Loger, F (Dallara F396-Fiat), 19m 18.907s; 8 Sébastien Bourdain, F (Martini MK73-Opel), 19m 19.686s; 9 Jonathan Cochet, F (Martini MK73-Opel), 19m 24.420s; 10 Sébastien Dumez, F (Dallara F396-Renault), 19m 24.871s.
Fastest race lap: Sallaz, 1m 20.430s, 87.608 mph/140.992 km/h.

COUPES DE PAQUES DE NOGARO, Circuit Automobile Paul Armagnac, Nogaro, France, 12/13 April. Rounds 2 and 3. 3 x 7 laps and 1 x 9 laps of the 2.259-mile/3.636-km circuit.
Round 2, Race 1 (15.815 miles/25.452 km)
1 Franck Montagny, F (Martini MK73-Opel), 12m 49.025s, 74.035 mph/119.147 km/h.
2 David Terrien, F (Dallara F396-Opel), 12m 58.995s; 3 Steeve Hiesse, F (Dallara F396-Opel), 13m 01.615s; 4 Damien Bianchi, F (Dallara F396-Fiat), 13m 15.368s; 5 Sébastien Bourdais, F (Martini MK73-Opel), 13m 17.099s; 6 Jonathan Cochet, F (Martini MK73-Opel), 13m 25.227s; 7 Benoit Tréluyer, F (Dallara F396-Fiat), 13m 25.539s; 8 Sébastien Dumez, F (Dallara F396-Renault), 13m 33.266s; 9 Stéphane Sallaz, F (Dallara F396-Opel), 13m 38.634s; 10 David Loger, F (Dallara F396-Fiat), 13m 39.213s.
Fastest race lap: Romain Dumas, F (Dallara F396-Opel), 1m 47.442s, 75.701 mph/121.829 km/h.
Fastest qualifying lap: Montagny, 1m 22.770s, 98.266 mph/158.144 km/h.

Round 2, Race 2 (15.815 miles/25.452 km)
1 Franck Montagny, F (Martini MK73-Opel), 12m 20.546s, 76.882 mph/123.729 km/h.
2 David Terrien, F (Dallara F396-Opel), 12m 21.420s; 3 Steeve Hiesse, F (Dallara F396-Opel), 12m 30.599s; 4 Damien Bianchi, F (Dallara F396-Fiat), 12m 34.150s; 5 Stéphane Sallaz, F (Dallara F396-Opel), 12m 37.313s; 6 Sébastien Bourdais, F (Martini MK73-Opel), 12m 38.389s; 7 David Loger, F (Dallara F396-Fiat), 12m 52.613s; 8 Marcel Fässler, CH (Martini MK73-Opel), 12m 54.416s; 9 Jonathan Cochet, F (Martini MK73-Opel), 12m 54.758s; 10 Sébastien Philippe, F (Elise 395-Renault), 13m 01.415s.
Fastest race lap: Terrien, 1m 44.614s, 77.748 mph/125.123 km/h.

Round 3, Race 1 (15.815 miles/25.452 km)
1 Franck Montagny, F (Martini MK73-Opel), 9m 58.826s, 95.077 mph/153.011 km/h.
2 David Terrien, F (Dallara F396-Opel), 10m 04.442s; 3 Sébastien Bourdais, F (Martini MK73-Opel), 10m 05.779s; 4 Benoit Tréluyer, F (Dallara F396-Fiat), 10m 07.308s; 5 David Saelens, B (Dallara F396-Renault), 10m 08.502s; 6 Steeve Hiesse, F (Dallara F396-Opel), 10m 12.956s; 7 Sébastien Dumez, F (Dallara F396-Renault), 10m 16.697s; 8 Sébastien Philippe, F (Elise 395-Renault), 10m 24.513s; 9 Jonathan Cochet, F (Martini MK73-Opel), 10m 24.856s; 10 Iradj Alexander David, F (Dallara F396-Fiat), 10m 27.108s.
Fastest race lap: Montagny, 1m 23.341s, 97.593 mph/157.061 km/h.
Fastest qualifying lap: Treluyer, 1m 47.551s, 75.625 mph/121.706 km/h.

Round 3, Race 2 (20.334 miles/32.724 km)
1 Franck Montagny, F (Martini MK73-Opel), 12m 34.110s, 97.070 mph/156.219 km/h.
2 David Terrien, F (Dallara F396-Opel), 12m 34.663s; 3 Sébastien Bourdais, F (Martini MK73-Opel), 12m 45.792s; 4 Benoit Tréluyer, F (Dallara F396-Fiat), 12m 47.432s; 5 David Saelens, B (Dallara F396-Renault), 12m 48.496s; 6 Steeve Hiesse, F (Dallara F396-Opel), 12m 48.833s; 7 Sébastien Dumez, F (Dallara F396-Renault), 12m 55.788s; 8 Marcel Fässler, CH (Martini MK73-Opel), 12m 56.076s; 9 Jonathan Cochet, F (Martini MK73-Opel), 12m 58.597s; 10 Iradj Alexander David, F (Dallara F396-Fiat), 13m 00.864s.
Fastest race lap: Terrien, 1m 23.192s, 97.768 mph/157.342 km/h.

TROPHÉES JEAN BERNIGNAUD, Circuit de Nevers, Magny-Cours, France, 3 May. Round 4. 15 and 14 laps of the 2.641-mile/4.250-km circuit.
Race 1 (39.612 miles/63.750 km)
1 Franck Montagny, F (Martini MK73-Opel), 24m 20.373s, 97.649 mph/157.152 km/h.
2 David Terrien, F (Dallara F396-Opel), 24m 21.200s; 3 Steeve Hiesse, F (Dallara F396-Opel), 24m 21.696s; 4 Sébastien Bourdais, F (Martini MK73-Opel), 24m 22.359s; 5 David Saelens, B (Dallara F396-Renault), 24m 22.989s; 6 Marcel Fässler, CH (Martini MK73-Opel), 24m 23.907s; 7 Benoit Tréluyer, F (Dallara F396-Fiat), 14 laps; 8 Sébastien Dumez, F (Dallara F396-Renault), 14; 9 Romain Dumas, F (Dallara F396-Opel), 14; 10 Iradj Alexander David, F (Dallara F396-Fiat), 14.
Fastest race lap: Montagny, 1m 32.527s, 102.748 mph/165.357 km/h.
Fastest qualifying lap: Terrien, 1m 31.593s, 103.791 mph/167.036 km/h.

Race 2 (36.972 miles/59.500 km)
1 Franck Montagny, F (Martini MK73-Opel), 21m 48.656s, 101.706 mph/163.679 km/h.
2 David Terrien, F (Dallara F396-Opel), 21m 50.556s; 3 Steeve Hiesse, F (Dallara F396-Opel), 21m 53.192s; 4 David Saelens, B (Dallara F396-Renault), 21m 57.823s; 5 Sébastien Bourdais, F (Martini MK73-Opel), 21m 58.199s; 6 Benoit Tréluyer, F (Dallara F396-Fiat), 22m 03.060s; 7 Stéphane Sallaz, F (Dallara F396-Opel), 22m 05.561s; 8 Marcel Fässler, CH (Martini MK73-Opel), 22m 05.743s; 9 Iradj Alexander David, F (Dallara F396-Fiat), 22m 11.327s; 10 Sébastien Dumez, F (Dallara F396-Renault), 22m 11.861s.
Fastest race lap: Terrien, 1m 32.632s, 102.632 mph/165.170 km/h.

GRAND PRIX DIJON-BOURGOGNE, Circuit de Dijon-Prenois, Fontaine-les-Dijon, France, 17 May. Round 5. 2 x 14 laps of the 2.361-mile/3.800-km circuit.
Race 1 (33.057 miles/53.200 km)
1 David Saelens, B (Dallara F396-Renault), 17m 29.649s, 113.376 mph/182.461 km/h.
2 Marcel Fässler, CH (Martini MK73-Opel), 17m 31.508s; 3 Franck Montagny, F (Martini MK73-Opel), 17m 31.995s; 4 David Terrien, F (Dallara F396-Opel), 17m 37.817s; 5 Benoit Tréluyer, F (Dallara F396-Fiat), 17m 41.438s; 6 Sébastien Dumez, F (Dallara F396-Renault), 17m 41.966s; 7 Sébastien Bourdais, F (Martini MK73-Opel), 17m 44.064s; 8 Romain Dumas, F (Dallara F396-Opel), 17m 44.881s; 9 Steeve Hiesse, F (Dallara F396-Opel), 17m 46.222s; 10 Damien Bianchi, F (Dallara F396-Fiat), 17m 48.827s.
Fastest race lap: Saelens, 1m 14.212s, 114.542 mph/184.337 km/h.
Fastest qualifying lap: Saelens, 1m 12.929s, 116.557 mph/187.580 km/h.

Race 2 (33.057 miles/53.200 km)
1 David Saelens, B (Dallara F396-Renault), 17m 28.006s, 113.554 mph/182.747 km/h.
2 Franck Montagny, F (Martini MK73-Opel), 17m 28.550s; 3 Marcel Fässler, CH (Martini MK73-Opel), 17m 33.456s; 4 David Terrien, F (Dallara F396-Opel), 17m 35.472s; 5 Sébastien Dumez, F (Dallara F396-Renault), 17m 37.601s; 6 Sébastien Bourdais, F (Martini MK73-Opel), 17m 43.488s; 7 Romain Dumas, F (Dallara F396-Opel), 17m 44.498s; 8 Damien Bianchi, F (Dallara F396-Fiat), 17m 46.671s; 9 Tiago Monteiro, P (Dallara F396-Fiat), 17m 51.180s; 10 Yann Goudy, F (Dallara F394-Fiat), 17m 54.611s.
Fastest race lap: Saelens, 1m 14.360s, 114.314 mph/183.970 km/h.

FRENCH FORMULA 3 CHAMPIONSHIP, Circuit de Pau Ville, France, 31 May. Round 6. 2 x 14 laps of the 1.715-mile/2.760-km circuit.
Race 1 (24.010 miles/38.640 km)
1 David Saelens, B (Dallara F396-Renault), 17m 46.659s, 81.034 mph/130.411 km/h.
2 Damien Bianchi, F (Dallara F396-Fiat), 17m 50.561s; 3 Marcel Fässler, CH (Martini MK73-Opel), 17m 53.696s; 4 David Terrien, F (Dallara F396-Opel), 17m 56.363s; 5 Franck Montagny, F (Martini MK73-Opel), 17m 57.238s; 6 Steeve Hiesse, F (Dallara F396-Opel), 17m 58.854s; 7 Sébastien Dumez, F (Dallara F396-Renault), 17m 59.299s; 8 Sébastien Philippe, F (Elise 395-Renault), 18m 06.186s; 9 Yann Goudy, F (Dallara F394-Fiat), 18m 20.270s; 10 Pascal Hernandez, F (Dallara F396-Fiat), 18m 21.681s.
Fastest race lap: Montagny, 1m 14.389s, 82.995 mph/133.568 km/h.
Fastest qualifying lap: Saelens, 1m 28.536s, 69.734 mph/112.226 km/h.

Race 2 (24.010 miles/38.640 km)
1 David Saelens, B (Dallara F396-Renault), 17m 35.901s, 81.859 mph/131.740 km/h.
2 Marcel Fässler, CH (Martini MK73-Opel), 17m 38.560s; 3 Sébastien Dumez, F (Dallara F396-Renault), 17m 45.113s; 4 Damien Bianchi, F (Dallara F396-Fiat), 17m 46.429s; 5 Sébastien Bourdais, F (Martini MK73-Opel), 17m 48.621s; 6 Franck Montagny, F (Martini MK73-Opel), 17m 58.152s; 7 Yann Goudy, F (Dallara F394-Fiat), 18m 00.574s; 8 Pascal Hernandez, F (Dallara F396-Fiat), 18m 02.353s; 9 Jonathan Cochet, F (Martini MK73-Opel), 18m 03.702s; 10 Benjamin Alvaro, F (Dallara F394-Fiat), 18m 17.881s.
Fastest race lap: Saelens, 1m 14.162s, 83.249 mph/133.977 km/h.

38th TROPHÉES D'AUVERGNE, Circuit de Charade, Clermont-Ferrand, France, 14 June. Round 7. 2 x 12 laps of the 2.470-mile/3.975-km circuit.
Race 1 (29.639 miles/47.700 km)
1 David Saelens, B (Dallara F396-Renault), 21m 31.208s, 82.637 mph/132.992 km/h.
2 Franck Montagny, F (Martini MK73-Opel), 21m 31.435s; 3 Steeve Hiesse, F (Dallara F396-Opel), 21m 36.114s; 4 Sébastien Dumez, F (Dallara F396-Renault), 21m 49.879s; 5 Benoit Tréluyer, F (Dallara F396-Fiat), 21m 58.832s; 6 Sébastien Bourdais, F (Martini MK73-Opel), 22m 03.265s; 7 Sébastien Philippe, F (Elise 395-Renault), 22m 05.918s; 8 David Terrien, F (Dallara F396-Opel), 22m 06.120s; 9 Jonathan Cochet, F (Martini MK73-Opel), 22m 08.287s; 10 Iradj Alexander David, F (Dallara F396-Fiat), 22m 11.458s.
Fastest race lap: Montagny, 1m 44.761s, 84.877 mph/136.597 km/h.
Fastest qualifying lap: Saelens, 1m 42.722s, 86.562 mph/139.308 km/h.

Race 2 (29.639 miles/47.700 km)
1 David Saelens, B (Dallara F396-Renault), 21m 03.811s, 84.429 mph/135.875 km/h.
2 Franck Montagny, F (Martini MK73-Opel), 21m 04.170s; 3 Steeve Hiesse, F (Dallara F396-Opel), 21m 12.057s; 4 Sébastien Dumez, F (Dallara F396-Renault), 21m 13.276s; 5 Benoit Tréluyer, F (Dallara F396-Fiat), 21m 14.236s; 6 David Terrien, F (Dallara F396-Opel), 21m 20.473s; 7 Sébastien Philippe, F (Elise 395-Renault), 21m 28.963s; 8 Jonathan Cochet, F (Martini MK73-Opel), 21m 29.109s; 9 Tiago Monteiro, P (Dallara F396-Fiat), 21m 30.774s; 10 Stéphane Sallaz, F (Dallara F396-Opel), 21m 32.854s.
Fastest race lap: Montagny, 1m 44.600s, 85.008 mph/136.807 km/h.

7th COUPE DU VAL DE VIENNE, Circuit du Val de Vienne, Le Vigeant, France, 5 July. Round 8. 2 x 14 laps of the 2.334-mile/3.757-km circuit.
Race 1 (32.683 miles/52.598 km)
1 David Saelens, B (Dallara F396-Renault), 22m 12.300s, 88.312 mph/142.125 km/h.
2 Stéphane Sallaz, F (Dallara F396-Opel), 22m 17.249s; 3 David Terrien, F (Dallara F396-Opel), 22m 17.811s; 4 Marcel Fässler, CH (Martini MK73-Opel), 22m 21.435s; 5 Sébastien Dumez, F (Dallara F396-Renault), 22m 22.978s; 6 Benoit Tréluyer, F (Dallara F396-Fiat), 22m 25.581s; 7 Sébastien Bourdais, F (Martini MK73-Opel), 22m 26.141s; 8 Jonathan Cochet, F (Martini MK73-Opel), 22m 33.801s; 9 Tiago Monteiro, P (Dallara F396-Fiat), 22m 34.346s; 10 Steeve Hiesse, F (Dallara F396-Opel), 22m 35.332s.
Fastest race lap: Saelens, 1m 34.333s, 89.090 mph/143.377 km/h.
Fastest qualifying lap: Saelens, 1m 33.698s, 89.694 mph/144.349 km/h.

Race 2 (32.683 miles/52.598 km)
1 David Saelens, B (Dallara F396-Renault), 22m 17.697s, 87.956 mph/141.551 km/h.
2 Stéphane Sallaz, F (Dallara F396-Opel), 22m 21.225s; 3 David Terrien, F (Dallara F396-Opel), 22m 21.556s; 4 Marcel Fässler, CH (Martini MK73-Opel), 22m 24.198s; 5 Sébastien Dumez, F (Dallara F396-Renault), 22m 24.890s; 6 Sébastien Bourdais, F (Martini MK73-Opel), 22m 25.232s; 7 Steeve Hiesse, F (Dallara F396-Opel), 22m 33.979s; 8 Jonathan Cochet, F (Martini MK73-Opel), 22m 35.904s; 9 Tiago Monteiro, P (Dallara F396-Fiat), 22m 36.298s; 10 David Loger, F (Dallara F396-Fiat), 22m 40.434s.
Fastest race lap: Saelens, 1m 34.670s, 88.773 mph/142.867 km/h.

CIRCUIT PAUL RICARD, Circuit ASA Paul Ricard, Le Beausset, France, 19 July. Round 9. 2 x 12 laps of the 2.369-mile/3.813-km circuit.
Race 1 (28.431 miles/45.756 km)
1 David Saelens, B (Dallara F396-Renault), 16m 04.334s, 106.139 mph/170.814 km/h.
2 Franck Montagny, F (Martini MK73-Opel), 16m 05.481s; 3 Marcel Fässler, CH (Martini MK73-Opel), 16m 13.802s; 4 Tiago Monteiro, P (Dallara F396-Fiat), 16m 16.103s; 5 Steeve Hiesse, F (Dallara F396-Opel), 16m 16.165s; 6 Benoit Tréluyer, F (Dallara F396-Fiat), 16m 17.931s; 7 Sébastien Bourdais, F (Martini MK73-Opel), 16m 19.826s; 8 Damien Bianchi, F (Dallara F396-Fiat), 16m 21.457s; 9 David Terrien, F (Dallara F396-Opel), 16m 22.431s; 10 Stéphane Sallaz, F (Dallara F396-Opel), 16m 23.418s.
Fastest race lap: Saelens, 1m 19.791s, 106.897 mph/172.034 km/h.
Fastest qualifying lap: Saelens, 1m 18.652s, 108.445 mph/174.526 km/h.

Race 2 (28.431 miles/45.756 km)
1 David Saelens, B (Dallara F396-Renault), 16m 12.302s, 105.269 mph/169.414 km/h.
2 Franck Montagny, F (Martini MK73-Opel), 16m 12.950s; 3 Marcel Fässler, CH (Martini MK73-Opel), 16m 19.987s; 4 Stéphane Sallaz, F (Dallara F396-Opel), 16m 24.920s; 5 David Terrien, F (Dallara F396-Opel), 16m 25.942s; 6 Sébastien Bourdais, F (Martini MK73-Opel), 16m 26.719s; 7 Tiago Monteiro, P (Dallara F396-Fiat), 16m 27.772s; 8 Damien Bianchi, F (Dallara F396-Fiat), 16m 28.434s; 9 Jonathan Cochet, F (Martini MK73-Opel), 16m 29.309s; 10 Sébastien Philippe, F (Elise 395-Fiat), 16m 30.879s.
Fastest race lap: Montagny, 1m 20.395s, 106.094 mph/170.742 km/h.

56th GRAND PRIX D'ALBI, Circuit d'Albi, France, 6 September. Round 10. 2 x 13 laps of the 2.206-mile/3.551-km circuit.
Race 1 (28.684 miles/42.163 km)
1 David Saelens, B (Dallara F396-Renault), 15m 34.384s, 110.515 mph/177.857 km/h.
2 Marcel Fässler, CH (Martini MK73-Opel), 15m 37.734s; 3 Sébastien Dumez, F (Dallara F396-Renault), 15m 42.856s; 4 Benoit Tréluyer, F (Dallara F396-Fiat), 15m 43.539s; 5 Stéphane Sallaz, F (Dallara F396-Opel), 15m 44.061s; 6 Damien Bianchi, F (Dallara F396-Fiat), 15m 50.947s; 7 Sébastien Bourdais, F (Martini MK73-Opel), 15m 51.471s; 8 Tiago Monteiro, P (Dallara F396-Fiat), 15m 52.087s; 9 David Terrien, F (Dallara F396-Opel), 15m 53.559s; 10 Sébastien Philippe, F (Elise 395-Renault), 15m 54.686s.
Fastest race lap: Saelens, 1m 10.375s, 112.872 mph/181.650 km/h.
Fastest qualifying lap: Saelens, 1m 08.436s, 116.070 mph/186.796 km/h.

Race 2 (28.684 miles/42.163 km)
1 David Saelens, B (Dallara F396-Renault), 15m 31.726s, 110.831 mph/178.364 km/h.
2 Sébastien Dumez, F (Dallara F396-Renault), 15m 32.651s; 3 Damien Bianchi, F (Dallara F396-Fiat), 15m 38.144s; 4 Tiago Monteiro, P (Dallara F396-Fiat), 15m 38.315s; 5 Sébastien Bourdais, F (Martini MK73-Opel), 15m 44.646s; 6 Jonathan Cochet, F (Martini MK73-Opel), 15m 45.747s; 7 Sébastien Philippe, F (Elise 395-Renault), 15m 51.921s; 8 Yann Goudy, F (Dallara F394-Fiat), 15m 52.790s; 9 Patrick d'Aubreby, F (Dallara F394-Fiat), 15m 53.844s; 10 Stéphane Sallaz, F (Dallara F396-Opel), 15m 54.782s.
Fastest race lap: Saelens, 1m 10.434s, 112.777 mph/181.498 km/h.

COUPES D'AUTOMNE, Circuit Le Mans-Bugatti, France, 20 September. Round 11. 2 x 10 laps of the 2.756-mile/4.435-km circuit.
Race 1 (27.558 miles/44.350 km)
1 Franck Montagny, F (Martini MK73-Opel), 16m 50.087s, 98.217 mph/158.066 km/h.
2 David Saelens, B (Dallara F396-Renault), 16m 55.088s; 3 Marcel Fässler, CH (Martini MK73-Opel), 16m 56.309s; 4 Sébastien Bourdais, F (Martini MK73-Opel), 16m 57.103s; 5 Steeve Hiesse, F (Dallara F396-Opel), 16m 59.467s; 6 David Terrien, F (Dallara F396-Opel), 16m 59.912s; 7 Sébastien Dumez, F (Dallara F396-Renault), 17m 02.090s; 8 Benoit Tréluyer, F (Dallara F396-Fiat), 17m 02.580s; 9 Stéphane Sallaz, F (Dallara F396-Opel), 17m 02.909s; 10 Jonathan Cochet, F (Martini MK73-Opel), 17m 03.364s.
Fastest race lap: Montagny, 1m 39.732s, 99.475 mph/160.089 km/h.
Fastest qualifying lap: Montagny, 1m 38.513s, 100.706 mph/162.070 km/h.

Race 2 (27.558 miles/44.350 km)
1 Franck Montagny, F (Martini MK73-Opel), 16m 42.674s, 98.944 mph/159.234 km/h.
2 David Saelens, B (Dallara F396-Renault), 16m 52.759s; 3 Marcel Fässler, CH (Martini MK73-Opel), 16m 53.986s; 4 Sébastien Bourdais, F (Martini MK73-Opel), 16m 54.568s; 5 Steeve Hiesse, F (Dallara F396-Opel), 16m 54.993s; 6 David Terrien, F (Dallara F396-Opel), 16m 55.618s; 7 Sébastien Dumez, F (Dallara F396-Renault), 16m 59.508s; 8 Stéphane Sallaz, F (Dallara F396-Opel), 17m 00.407s; 9 Jonathan Cochet, F (Martini MK73-Opel), 17m 00.933s; 10 Benoit Tréluyer, F (Dallara F396-Fiat), 17m 01.319s.
Fastest race lap: Montagny, 1m 39.798s, 99.409 mph/159.983 km/h.

Final championship points
Class A
1 David Saelens, B, 229; 2 Franck Montagny, F, 226; 3 David Terrien, F, 154; 4 Marcel Fässler, CH, 138; 5 Steeve Hiesse, F, 107; 6 Sébastien Bourdais, F, 98; 7 Sébastien Dumez, F, 95; 8 Stéphane Sallaz, F, 73; 9 Benoit Tréluyer, F, 66; 10 Damien Bianchi, F, 61; 11 Jonathan Cochet, F, 40; 12 Tiago Monteiro, P, 31; 13 Sébastien Philippe, F, 21; 14 Romain Dumas, F, 11; 15= David Loger, F, 10; 15= Yann Goudy, F, 10; 17 Iradj Alexander David, F, 6; 18 Pascal Hernandez, F, 4; 19 Patrick d'Aubreby, F, 2; 20 Benjamin Alvaro, F, 1.

Class B
1 Yann Goudy, F, 252; 2 Patrick d'Aubreby, F, 210; 3 Bernard Cognet, F, 162; 4 Benjamin Alvaro, B, 91; 5 Didier Sirgue, F, 76; 6 Wolfgang Payr, 24; 7 Sylvain Jot, F, 6.

Trophée Sebastien Enjolras
(Best rookies of the year)
1 Sébastien Bourdais, F; 2 Sébastien Dumez, F; 3 Benoit Tréluyer, F; 4 Jonathan Cochet, F; 5 Tiago Monteiro, P; 6 Romain Dumas, F; 7 David Loger, F; 8 Iradj Alexander David, F.

German Formula 3 Championship

ADAC-PREIS-HOCKENHEIM – F3, Hockenheimring short circuit, Heidelberg, Germany, 18/19 April. 2 x 32 laps of the 1.639-mile/2.638-km circuit.
Round 1 (52.454 miles/84.416 km)
1 Bas Leinders, B (Dallara F397-Opel), 37m 33.182s, 83.807 mph/134.875 km/h.
2 Pierre Kaffer, D (Martini MK73-Opel), 38m 00.445s; 3 Christijan Albers, NL (Dallara F398-Opel), 38m 01.280s; 4 Yves Olivier, B (Dallara F398-Opel), 38m 01.907s; 5 Wolf Henzler, D (Martini MK73-Opel), 38m 02.230s; 6 Jeffrey van Hooydonk, B (Dallara F398-Opel), 38m 02.616s; 7 Thomas Jäger, D (Martini MK73-Opel), 38m 15.598s; 8 Robert Lechner, A (Dallara F397-Opel), 38m 24.921s; 9 Jaroslav Wierczuk, PL (Dallara F398-Opel), 38m 25.870s; 10 Lasse Jakobsen, DK (Dallara F396-Opel), 38m 26.224s.
Fastest race lap: Henzler, 1m 03.734s, 92.589 mph/149.007 km/h.
Fastest qualifying lap: Lechner, 58.884s, 100.215 mph/161.280 km/h.

Round 2 (52.454 miles/84.416 km)
1 Bas Leinders, B (Dallara F397-Opel), 42m 19.332s, 74.363 mph/119.676 km/h.
2 Wolf Henzler, D (Martini MK73-Opel), 42m 23.146s; 3 Thomas Jäger, D (Martini MK73-Opel), 42m 35.851s; 4 Robert Lechner, A (Dallara F397-Opel), 42m 36.217s; 5 Yves Olivier, B (Dallara F398-Opel), 42m 38.146s; 6 Jeffrey van Hooydonk, B (Dallara F398-Opel), 42m 39.140s; 7 Lasse Jakobsen, DK (Dallara F396-Opel), 42m 50.371s; 8 Johan Stureson, S (Dallara F397-Opel), 42m 51.161s; 9 Lucas Luhr, D (Dallara F397-Opel), 43m 36.309s; 10 Thomas Braumüller, D (Dallara F396-Opel), 43m 40.380s.
Fastest race lap: van Hooydonk, 1m 17.227s, 76.412 mph/122.973 km/h.

ADAC-EIFELRENNEN – F3, Nürburgring, Nürburg/Eifel, Germany, 9/10 May. 2 x 18 laps of the 2.831-mile/4.556-km circuit.
Round 3 (50.957 miles/82.008 km)
1 Wolf Henzler, D (Martini MK73-Opel), 28m 56.974s, 105.613 mph/169.967 km/h.
2 Yves Olivier, B (Dallara F398-Opel), 28m 58.115s; 3 Thomas Jäger, D (Martini MK73-Opel), 29m 04.749s; 4 Jeffrey van Hooydonk, B (Dallara F398-Opel), 29m 07.567s; 5 Thomas Mutsch, D (Dallara F397-Opel), 29m 11.323s; 6 Christijan Albers, NL (Dallara F398-Opel), 29m 18.462s; 7 Norman Simon, D (Dallara F397-Opel), 29m 18.955s; 8 Lucas Luhr, D (Dallara F397-Opel), 29m 19.114s; 9 Wouter van Eeuwijk, NL (Dallara F397-Opel), 29m 22.848s; 10 Johnny Mislijevic, S (Dallara F397-Opel), 29m 23.733s.
Fastest race lap: Henzler, 1m 35.595s, 106.611 mph/171.574 km/h.
Fastest qualifying lap: Leinders, 1m 35.348s, 106.887 mph/172.018 km/h.

Round 4 (50.957 miles/82.008 km)
1 Wolf Henzler, D (Martini MK73-Opel), 29m 03.789s, 105.200 mph/169.303 km/h.
2 Jeffrey van Hooydonk, B (Dallara F398-Opel), 29m 04.826s; 3 Yves Olivier, B (Dallara F398-Opel), 29m 05.415s; 4 Norman Simon, D (Dallara F397-Opel), 29m 07.918s; 5 Lucas Luhr, D (Dallara F397-Opel), 29m 09.932s; 6 Thomas Jäger, D (Martini MK73-Opel), 29m 11.870s; 7 Bas Leinders, B (Dallara F397-Opel), 29m 12.174s; 8 Thomas Mutsch, D (Dallara F397-Opel), 29m 13.570s; 9 Tomas Enge, CZ (Martini MK73-Opel), 29m 15.604s; 10 Christijan Albers, NL (Dallara F398-Opel), 29m 15.604s.
Fastest race lap: Leinders, 1m 35.719s, 106.473 mph/171.352 km/h.

ADAC SACHSENRING RENNEN – F3, Sachsenring, Germany, 23/24 May. 2 x 24 laps of the 2.139-mile/3.442-km circuit.
Round 5 (51.330 miles/82.608 km)
1 Bas Leinders, B (Dallara F397-Opel), 32m 24.818s, 95.016 mph/152.913 km/h.
2 Norman Simon, D (Dallara F397-Opel), 32m 36.224s; 3 Jeffrey van Hooydonk, B (Dallara F398-Opel), 32m 38.159s; 4 Thomas Mutsch, D (Dallara F397-Opel), 32m 39.018s; 5

Robert Lechner, A (Dallara F397-Opel), 32m 49.382s; **6** Johan Stureson, S (Dallara F397-Opel), 32m 50.243s; **7** Johnny Mislijevic, S (Dallara F397-Opel), 32m 50.857s; **8** Lucas Luhr, D (Dallara F397-Opel), 32m 51.941s; **9** Timo Scheider, D (Martini MK73-Opel), 32m 54.325s; **10** Tim Bergmeister, D (Dallara F397-Opel), 32m 56.192s.
Fastest race lap: Leinders, 1m 20.078s, 96.150 mph/154.739 km/h.
Fastest qualifying lap: Leinders, 1m 20.049s, 96.185 mph/154.795 km/h.

Round 6 (51.330 miles/82.608 km)
1 Bas Leinders, B (Dallara F397-Opel), 32m 32.892s, 94.623 mph/152.281 km/h.
2 Jeffrey van Hooydonk, B (Dallara F398-Opel), 32m 37.937s; **3** Timo Scheider, D (Martini MK73-Opel), 32m 39.965s; **4** Johan Stureson, S (Dallara F397-Opel), 32m 45.675s; **5** Johnny Mislijevic, S (Dallara F397-Opel), 32m 45.861s; **6** Lucas Luhr, D (Dallara F397-Opel), 32m 46.021s; **7** Norman Simon, D (Dallara F397-Opel), 32m 47.879s; **8** Thomas Jäger, D (Martini MK73-Opel), 32m 50.758s; **9** Wolf Henzler, D (Martini MK73-Opel), 32m 51.086s; **10** Christijan Albers, NL (Dallara F398-Opel), 32m 57.111s.
Fastest race lap: Albers, 1m 20.276s, 95.913 mph/154.357 km/h.

ADAC NORISRING RENNEN – F3, Norisring, Nürnberg, Germany, 4/5 July. 35 and 33 laps of the 1.429-mile/2.300-km circuit.
Round 7 (50.020 miles/80.500 km)
1 Christijan Albers, NL (Dallara F398-Opel), 29m 50.484s, 100.572 mph/161.856 km/h.
2 Bas Leinders, B (Dallara F397-Opel), 29m 52.859s; **3** Robert Lechner, A (Dallara F397-Opel), 29m 54.119s; **4** Pierre Kaffer, D (Martini MK73-Opel), 30m 03.073s; **5** Tim Bergmeister, D (Dallara F397-Opel), 30m 12.207s; **6** Timo Scheider, D (Martini MK73-Opel), 30m 14.355s; **7** Norman Simon, D (Dallara F397-Opel), 30m 16.339s; **8** Steffen Widmann, D (Dallara F397-Opel), 30m 17.323s; **9** Lucas Luhr, D (Dallara F397-Opel), 30m 18.185s; **10** Thomas Mutsch, D (Dallara F397-Opel), 30m 23.788s.
Fastest race lap: Yves Olivier, B (Dallara F398-Opel), 50.446s, 101.989 mph/164.136 km/h.
Fastest qualifying lap: Kaffer, 50.526s, 101.828 mph/163.876 km/h.

Round 8 (47.162 miles/75.900 km)
1 Christijan Albers, NL (Dallara F398-Opel), 37m 31.069s, 75.423 mph/121.382 km/h.
2 Pierre Kaffer, D (Martini MK73-Opel), 37m 41.299s; **3** Robert Lechner, A (Dallara F397-Opel), 37m 41.748s; **4** Tim Bergmeister, D (Dallara F397-Opel), 37m 41.960s; **5** Steffen Widmann, D (Dallara F397-Opel), 37m 42.358s; **6** Bas Leinders, B (Dallara F397-Opel), 37m 43.239s; **7** Lucas Luhr, D (Dallara F397-Opel), 37m 44.768s; **8** Johan Stureson, S (Dallara F397-Opel), 37m 47.896s; **9** Jeffrey van Hooydonk, B (Dallara F398-Opel), 37m 48.641s; **10** Norman Simon, D (Dallara F397-Opel), 37m 50.808s.
Fastest race lap: Lechner, 1m 00.114s, 85.587 mph/137.738 km/h.

ADAC PREIS REGIO RING LAHR – F3, Lahr Circuit, Germany, 18/19 July. 2 x 25 laps of the 2.013-mile/3.240-km circuit.
Round 9 (50.331 miles/81.000 km)
1 Timo Scheider, D (Martini MK73-Opel), 29m 03.424s, 103.929 mph/167.257 km/h.
2 Robert Lechner, A (Dallara F397-Opel), 29m 04.960s; **3** Lucas Luhr, D (Dallara F397-Opel), 29m 07.845s; **4** Tim Bergmeister, D (Dallara F397-Opel), 29m 16.868s; **5** Wolf Henzler, D (Martini MK73-Opel), 29m 20.053s; **6** Steffen Widmann, D (Dallara F397-Opel), 29m 22.649s; **7** Bas Leinders, B (Dallara F397-Opel), 29m 24.257s; **8** Pierre Kaffer, D (Martini MK73-Opel), 29m 27.773s; **9** Norman Simon, D (Dallara F397-Opel), 29m 28.440s; **10** Tomas Enge, CZ (Martini MK73-Opel), 29m 30.144s.
Fastest race lap: Scheider, 1m 09.041s, 104.976 mph/168.943 km/h.
Fastest qualifying lap: Thomas Mutsch, D (Dallara F397-Opel), 1m 09.090s, 104.902 mph/168.823 km/h.

Round 10 (50.331 miles/81.000 km)
1 Timo Scheider, D (Martini MK73-Opel), 29m 13.609s, 103.325 mph/166.286 km/h.
2 Robert Lechner, A (Dallara F397-Opel), 29m 14.535s; **3** Lucas Luhr, D (Dallara F397-Opel), 29m 14.809s; **4** Tim Bergmeister, D (Dallara F397-Opel), 29m 22.395s; **5** Wolf Henzler, D (Martini MK73-Opel), 29m 24.211s; **6** Norman Simon, D (Dallara F397-Opel), 29m 25.164s; **7** Bas Leinders, B (Dallara F397-Opel), 29m 28.514s; **8** Yves Olivier, B (Dallara F398-Opel), 29m 29.759s; **9** Steffen Widmann, D (Dallara F397-Opel), 29m 31.782s; **10** Michael Becker, D (Dallara F398-Opel), 29m 34.144s.
Fastest race lap: Kaffer, 1m 08.901s, 105.190 mph/169.286 km/h.

ADAC FLUGPLATZRENNEN WUNSTORF – F3, Wunstorf Airfield Circuit, Germany, 1/2 August. 2 x 16 laps of the 3.138-mile/5.050-km circuit.
Round 11 (50.207 miles/80.800 km)
1 Thomas Jäger, D (Martini MK73-Opel), 26m 53.921s, 111.991 mph/180.232 km/h.
2 Wolf Henzler, D (Martini MK73-Opel), 26m 54.600s; **3** Steffen Widmann, D (Dallara F397-Opel), 26m 55.888s; **4** Robert Lechner, A (Dallara F397-Opel), 26m 59.244s; **5** Lucas Luhr, D (Dallara F397-Opel), 27m 05.007s; **6** Timo Scheider, D (Martini MK73-Opel), 27m 05.009s; **7** Pierre Kaffer, D (Martini MK73-Opel), 27m 06.506s; **8** Jeffrey van Hooydonk, B (Dallara F398-Opel), 27m 06.623s; **9** Christijan Albers, NL (Dallara F398-Opel), 27m 14.640s; **10** Johnny Mislijevic, S (Dallara F397-Opel), 27m 15.122s.
Fastest race lap: Widmann, 1m 38.494s, 114.693 mph/184.580 km/h.
Fastest qualifying lap: Jäger, 1m 39.070s, 114.026 mph/183.507 km/h.

Round 12 (50.207 miles/80.800 km)
1 Pierre Kaffer, D (Martini MK73-Opel), 26m 47.692s, 112.425 mph/180.930 km/h.
2 Wolf Henzler, D (Martini MK73-Opel), 26m 50.891s; **3** Steffen Widmann, D (Dallara F397-Opel), 26m 52.473s; **4** Robert Lechner, A (Dallara F397-Opel), 26m 53.872s; **5** Christijan Albers, NL (Dallara F398-Opel), 26m 54.074s; **6** Timo Scheider, D (Martini MK73-Opel), 27m 08.891s; **7** Yves Olivier, B (Dallara F398-Opel), 27m 10.619s; **8** Johan Stureson, S (Dallara F397-Opel), 27m 12.921s; **9** Jeffrey van Hooydonk, B (Dallara F398-Opel), 27m 13.977s; **10** Jaroslav Wierczuk, PL (Dallara F398-Opel), 27m 23.519s.
Fastest race lap: Henzler, 1m 39.257s, 113.811 mph/183.161 km/h.

ADAC PREIS ZWEIBRÜCKEN – F3, Zweibrücken Circuit, Germany, 16 August. 2 x 29 laps of the 1.734-mile/2.790-km circuit.
Round 13 (50.275 miles/80.910 km)
1 Bas Leinders, B (Dallara F398-Opel), 30m 19.735s, 99.460 mph/160.065 km/h.
2 Pierre Kaffer, D (Martini MK73-Opel), 30m 23.257s; **3** Timo Scheider, D (Martini MK73-Opel), 30m 24.327s; **4** Wolf Henzler, D (Martini MK73-Opel), 30m 25.380s; **5** Yves Olivier, B (Dallara F398-Opel), 30m 32.021s; **6** Robert Lechner, A (Dallara F397-Opel), 30m 34.243s; **7** Johan Stureson, S (Dallara F397-Opel), 30m 34.545s; **8** Christijan Albers, NL (Dallara F398-Opel), 30m 35.633s; **9** Lucas Luhr, D (Dallara F397-Opel), 30m 40.047s; **10** Tim Bergmeister, D (Dallara F397-Opel), 30m 48.820s.
Fastest race lap: Leinders, 1m 02.062s, 100.562 mph/161.838 km/h.
Fastest qualifying lap: Leinders, 1m 01.594s, 101.326 mph/163.068 km/h.

Round 14 (50.275 miles/80.910 km)
1 Pierre Kaffer, D (Martini MK73-Opel), 30m 20.227s, 99.433 mph/160.022 km/h.
2 Bas Leinders, B (Dallara F398-Opel), 30m 20.470s; **3** Wolf Henzler, D (Martini MK73-Opel), 30m 25.003s; **4** Robert Lechner, A (Dallara F397-Opel), 30m 30.098s; **5** Yves Olivier, B (Dallara F398-Opel), 30m 31.267s; **6** Christijan Albers, NL (Dallara F398-Opel), 30m 31.796s; **7** Lucas Luhr, D (Dallara F397-Opel), 30m 35.403s; **8** Johan Stureson, S (Dallara F397-Opel), 30m 37.066s; **9** Steffen Widmann, D (Dallara F397-Opel), 30m 44.624s; **10** Jeffrey van Hooydonk, B (Dallara F398-Opel), 30m 47.116s.
Fastest race lap: Lechner, 1m 01.451s, 101.561 mph/163.447 km/h.

ADAC PREIS SALZBURG – F3, Salzburgring, Salzburg, Austria, 30 August. 2 x 19 laps of the 2.644-mile/4.255-km circuit.
Round 15 (50.235 miles/80.845 km)
1 Robert Lechner, A (Dallara F397-Opel), 25m 42.601s, 117.234 mph/188.670 km/h.
2 Wolf Henzler, D (Martini MK73-Opel), 25m 43.961s; **3** Pierre Kaffer, D (Martini MK73-Opel), 25m 44.758s; **4** Timo Scheider, D (Martini MK73-Opel), 25m 45.417s; **5** Steffen Widmann, D (Dallara F397-Opel), 25m 46.420s; **6** Johan Stureson, S (Dallara F397-Opel), 25m 48.546s; **7** Christijan Albers, NL (Dallara F398-Opel), 25m 48.949s; **8** Tim Bergmeister, D (Dallara F397-Opel), 25m 49.047s; **9** Wouter van Eeuwijk, NL (Dallara F397-Opel), 25m 49.514s; **10** Jeffrey van Hooydonk, B (Dallara F398-Opel), 25m 50.039s.
Fastest race lap: Bas Leinders, B (Dallara F398-Opel), 1m 19.415s, 119.853 mph/192.885 km/h.
Fastest qualifying lap: Lechner, 1m 19.490s, 119.740 mph/192.703 km/h.

Round 16 (50.235 miles/80.845 km)
1 Robert Lechner, A (Dallara F397-Opel), 25m 25.056s, 118.583 mph/190.840 km/h.
2 Pierre Kaffer, D (Martini MK73-Opel), 25m 28.540s; **3** Bas Leinders, B (Dallara F398-Opel), 25m 37.758s; **4** Christijan Albers, NL (Dallara F398-Opel), 25m 38.067s; **5** Norman Simon, D (Dallara F397-Opel), 25m 42.248s; **6** Lucas Luhr, D (Dallara F397-Opel), 25m 42.553s; **7** Wolf Henzler, D (Martini MK73-Opel), 25m 46.321s; **8** Jeffrey van Hooydonk, B (Dallara F398-Opel), 25m 46.595s; **9** Wouter van Eeuwijk, NL (Dallara F397-Opel), 25m 49.598s; **10** Petr Krizan, CZ (Dallara F396-Opel), 25m 51.218s.
Fastest race lap: Kaffer, 1m 19.128s, 120.288 mph/193.585 km/h.

ADAC PREIS 'SACHSEN-ANHALT' – F3, Oschersleben Circuit, Germany, 12/13 September. 2 x 22 laps of the 2.279-mile/3.667-km circuit.
Round 17 (50.128 miles/80.674 km)
1 Bas Leinders, B (Dallara F398-Opel), 35m 45.763s, 84.102 mph/135.349 km/h.
2 Christijan Albers, NL (Dallara F398-Opel), 35m 48.901s; **3** Jeffrey van Hooydonk, B (Dallara F398-Opel), 35m 50.452s; **4** Robert Lechner, A (Dallara F397-Opel), 36m 02.928s; **5** Lucas Luhr, D (Dallara F397-Opel), 36m 03.239s; **6** Johan Stureson, S (Dallara F397-Opel), 36m 12.748s; **7** Thomas Mutsch, D (Dallara F397-Opel), 36m 19.348s; **8** Wolf Henzler, D (Martini MK73-Opel), 36m 28.467s; **9** Yves Olivier, B (Dallara F398-Opel), 36m 29.621s; **10** Thomas Jäger, D (Martini MK73-Opel), 36m 43.464s.
Fastest race lap: Luhr, 1m 36.342s, 85.143 mph/137.024 km/h.
Fastest qualifying lap: Leinders, 1m 38.500s, 83.278 mph/134.022 km/h.

Round 18 (50.128 miles/80.674 km)
1 Bas Leinders, B (Dallara F398-Opel), 30m 27.598s, 98.743 mph/158.912 km/h.
2 Jeffrey van Hooydonk, B (Dallara F398-Opel), 30m 29.069s; **3** Christijan Albers, NL (Dallara F398-Opel), 30m 29.719s; **4** Robert Lechner, A (Dallara F397-Opel), 30m 32.959s; **5** Johan Stureson, S (Dallara F397-Opel), 30m 41.036s; **6** Lucas Luhr, D (Dallara F397-Opel), 30m 42.000s; **7** Thomas Mutsch, D (Dallara F397-Opel), 30m 42.329s; **8** Wolf Henzler, D (Martini MK73-Opel), 30m 42.687s; **9** Norman Simon, D (Dallara F397-Opel), 30m 51.075s; **10** Pierre Kaffer, D (Martini MK73-Opel), 30m 52.143s.
Fastest race lap: van Hooydonk, 1m 22.295s, 99.676 mph/160.413 km/h.

ADAC BILSTEIN SUPERSPRINT – F3, Nürburgring short circuit, Nürburg/Eifel, Germany, 3/4 October. 2 and 27 laps of the 1.888-mile/3.038-km circuit.
Round 19 (3.775 miles/6.076 km)
Race scheduled for 27 laps but stopped early due to bad weather.
1 Thomas Mutsch, D (Dallara F397-Opel), 3m 28.523s, 65.180 mph/104.898 km/h.
2 Bas Leinders, B (Dallara F398-Opel), 3m 29.267s; **3** Christijan Albers, NL (Dallara F398-Opel), 3m 30.311s; **5** Jeffrey van Hooydonk, B (Dallara F398-Opel), 3m 32.676s; **6** Yves Olivier, B (Dallara F398-Opel), 3m 34.751s; **7** Timo Scheider, D (Martini MK73-Opel), 3m 36.132s; **8** Lucas Luhr, D (Dallara F397-Opel), 3m 36.974s; **9** Alex Müller, D (Dallara F397-Opel), 3m 38.419s; **10** Wolf Henzler, D (Martini MK73-Opel), 3m 39.299s.
Fastest race lap: Mutsch, 1m 25.557s, 79.430 mph/127.831 km/h.
Fastest qualifying lap: Leinders, 1m 17.501s, 87.687 mph/141.118 km/h.

Round 20 (50.969 miles/82.026 km)
1 Timo Scheider, D (Martini MK73-Opel), 29m 51.956s, 102.395 mph/164.788 km/h.
2 Steffen Widmann, D (Dallara F397-Opel), 29m 52.915s; **3** Jeffrey van Hooydonk, B (Dallara F398-Opel), 29m 53.293s; **4** Wolf Henzler, D (Martini MK73-Opel), 29m 54.639s; **5** Robert Lechner, A (Dallara F397-Opel), 29m 55.004s; **6** Yves Olivier, B (Dallara F398-Opel), 29m 59.723s; **7** Lucas Luhr, D (Dallara F397-Opel), 30m 00.471s; **8** Wouter van Eeuwijk, NL (Dallara F397-Opel), 30m 02.176s; **9** Pierre Kaffer, D (Martini MK73-Opel), 30m 03.146s; **10** Alex Müller, D (Dallara F397-Opel), 30m 04.164s.
Fastest race lap: Müller, 1m 03.896s, 106.357 mph/171.166 km/h.

Final championship points
1 Bas Leinders, B, 200; **2** Robert Lechner, A, 179; **3** Wolf Henzler, D, 168; **4** Pierre Kaffer, D, 132; **5** Christijan Albers, NL, 120; **6** Jeffrey van Hooydonk, B, 115; **7** Timo Scheider, D, 114; **8** Lucas Luhr, D, 90; **9** Yves Olivier, B, 76; **10** Steffen Widmann, D, 68; **11** Thomas Jäger, D, 58; **12** Norman Simon, D, 56; **13** Johan Stureson, S, 52; **14** Tim Bergmeister, D, 43; **15** Thomas Mutsch, D, 30; **16** Johnny Mislijevic, S, 14; **17** Wouter van Eeuwijk, NL, 9; **18** Lasse Jakobsen, DK, 5; **19=** Tomas Enge, CZ, 3; **19=** Jaroslav Wierczuk, PL, 3; **21=** Michael Becker, D, 1; **21=** Thomas Braumüller, D, 1; **21=** Petr Krizan, CZ, 1; **21=** Alex Müller, D, 1.

Italian Formula 3 Championship

GRAN PREMIO CAMPAGNANO – TROFEO IGNAZIO GIUNTI, Autodromo di Vallelunga, Campagnano di Roma, Italy, 29 March. Round 1. 38 laps of the 1.988-mile/3.200-km circuit, 75.559 miles/121.600 km.
1 Michele Gasparini, I (Dallara F396-Fiat), 43m 45.183s, 103.616 mph/166.754 km/h.
2 Maurizio Mediani, I (Dallara F396-Fiat), 43m 55.441s; **3** Paolo Montin, I (Dallara F398-Fiat), 43m 57.108s; **4** Peter Sundberg, S (Dallara F396-Fiat), 44m 04.476s; **5** Donny Crevels, NL (Dallara F398-Opel), 44m 11.187s; **6** Nikolaos 'Nico' Stremmenos, GR (Dallara F398-Opel), 44m 13.271s; **7** Ananda Mikola, RI (Dallara F398-Opel), 44m 38.567s; **8** Alberto Pedemonte, I (Dallara F398-Fiat), 44m 41.263s; **9** Nicola 'Niki' Cadei, I (Dallara F398-Fiat), 44m 45.109s; **10** Gabriele Lancieri, I (Dallara F397-Opel), 37 laps.
Fastest race lap: Gasparini, 1m 08.545s, 104.431 mph/168.065 km/h.

ITALIAN FORMULA 3 CHAMPIONSHIP, Autodromo Internazionale del Mugello, Scarperia, Firenze (Florence), Italy, 19 April. Round 2. 23 laps of the 3.259-mile/5.245-km circuit, 74.959 miles/120.635 km.
1 Michele Gasparini, I (Dallara F396-Fiat), 40m 43.140s, 110.453 mph/177.757 km/h.
2 Donny Crevels, NL (Dallara F397-Opel), 40m 43.553s; **3** Gianluca Calgagni, I (Dallara F397-Opel), 40m 50.999s; **4** Paolo Montin, I (Dallara F398-Fiat), 40m 51.111s; **5** Nicola 'Niki' Cadei, I (Dallara F398-Opel), 41m 03.952s; **6** Ananda Mikola, RI (Dallara F397-Opel), 41m 09.390s; **7** Maurizio Mediani, I (Dallara F396-Alfa Romeo), 41m 12.690s; **8** Peter Sundberg, S (Dallara F397-Fiat), 41m 13.086s; **9** Massimiliano 'Max' Busnelli, I (Dallara F397-Fiat), 41m 23.679s; **10** Nikolaos 'Nico' Stremmenos, GR (Dallara F398-Opel), 41m 27.985s.
Fastest race lap: Calcagni, 1m 45.240s, 111.485 mph/179.418 km/h.

37th TROFEO AUTOMOBILE CLUB PARMA, Autodromo Riccardo Paletti, Varano, Parma, Italy, 17 May. Round 3. 56 laps of the 1.118-mile/1.800-km circuit, 62.634 miles/100.800 km.
1 Nicola 'Niki' Cadei, I (Dallara F398-Opel), 41m 35.557s, 90.354 mph/145.410 km/h.
2 Maurizio Mediani, I (Dallara F396-Alfa Romeo), 41m 37.504s; **3** Michele Gasparini, I (Dallara F396-Fiat), 41m 40.696s; **4** Paolo Montin, I (Dallara F398-Fiat), 41m 41.026s; **5** Ananda Mikola, RI (Dallara F397-Opel), 41m 44.791s; **6** Donny Crevels, NL (Dallara F397-Opel), 41m 54.965s; **7** Nikolaos 'Nico' Stremmenos, GR (Dallara F398-Opel), 42m 03.621s; **8** Enrico Toccacelo, I (Dallara F397-Fiat), 42m 05.039s; **9** Marco Barindelli, I (Dallara F397-Fiat), 42m 05.526s; **10** Gabriele Gardel, I (Dallara F398-Fiat), 42m 06.886s.
Fastest race lap: Montin, 43.855s, 91.814 mph/147.760 km/h.

39th GRAN PREMIO LOTTERIA DI MONZA, Autodromo Nazionale di Monza, Milan, Italy, 28 June. Round 4. 21 laps of the 3.585-mile/5.770-km circuit, 75.292 miles/121.170 km.
1 Maurizio Mediani, I (Dallara F396-Alfa Romeo), 37m 25.346s, 120.716 mph/194.274 km/h.
2 Nicola 'Niki' Cadei, I (Dallara F398-Opel), 37m 26.116s; **3** Donny Crevels, NL (Dallara F397-Opel), 37m 26.309s; **4** Gianluca Calgagni, I (Dallara F397-Opel), 37m 29.962s; **5** Ananda Mikola, RI (Dallara F397-Opel), 37m 30.835s; **6** Paolo Montin, I (Dallara F398-Fiat), 37m 32.236s; **7** Alberto Pedemonte, I (Dallara F398-Renault), 37m 38.554s; **8** Michele Gasparini, I (Dallara F396-Fiat), 37m 43.969s; **9** Gabriele Lancieri, I (Dallara F397-Opel), 37m 46.213s; **10** Peter Sundberg, S (Dallara F397-Fiat), 37m 54.821s.
Fastest race lap: Montin, 1m 45.62s, 122.203 mph/196.667 km/h.

ITALIAN FORMULA 3 CHAMPIONSHIP, Autodromo Enzo e Dino Ferrari, Imola, Italy, 5 July. Round 5. 25 laps of the 3.063-mile/4.930-km circuit, 76.584 miles/123.250 km.
1 Donny Crevels, NL (Dallara F397-Opel), 45m 09.007s, 101.772 mph/163.787 km/h.
2 Ananda Mikola, RI (Dallara F397-Opel), 45m 21.505s; **3** Michele Gasparini, I (Dallara F397-Fiat), 45m 25.790s; **4** Paolo Montin, I (Dallara F398-Fiat), 45m 32.037s; **5** Massimiliano 'Max' Busnelli, I (Dallara F396-Fiat), 45m 32.809s; **6** Gabriele Lancieri, I (Dallara F397-Opel), 45m 33.731s; **7** Maurizio Mediani, I (Dallara F396-Alfa Romeo), 45m 35.852s; **8** Davide Uboldi, I (Dallara F396-Fiat), 45m 42.370s; **9** Peter Sundberg, S (Dallara F396-Fiat), 45m 42.647s; **10** Alberto Pedemonte, I (Dallara F398-Renault), 45m 43.057s.
Fastest race lap: Lancieri, 1m 47.309s, 102.770 mph/165.392 km/h.

ITALIAN FORMULA 3 CHAMPIONSHIP, Autodromo Santamonica, Misano Adriatico, Rimini, Italy, 19 July. Round 6. 29 laps of the 2.523-mile/4.060-km circuit, 73.160 miles/117.740 km.
1 Donny Crevels, NL (Dallara F397-Opel), 42m 35.816s, 103.050 mph/165.843 km/h.
2 Paolo Montin, I (Dallara F398-Fiat), 42m 44.098s; **3** Maurizio Mediani, I (Dallara F396-Alfa Romeo), 42m 59.763s; **4** Ananda Mikola, RI (Dallara F397-Opel), 43m 00.773s; **5** Peter Sundberg, S (Dallara F396-Fiat), 43m 03.246s; **6** Michele Gasparini, I (Dallara F396-Fiat), 43m 07.472s; **7** Gabriele Gardel, I (Dallara F398-Fiat), 43m 08.224s; **8** Nicola 'Niki' Cadei, I (Dallara F398-Opel), 43m 08.422s; **9** Massimiliano 'Max' Busnelli, I (Dallara F396-Fiat), 43m 15.374s; **10** Nikolaos 'Nico' Stremmenos, GR (Dallara F398-Opel), 43m 33.075s.
Fastest race lap: Montin, 1m 27.396s, 103.917 mph/167.239 km/h.

42nd GRAN PREMIO PERGUSA, Ente Autodromo di Pergusa, Enna-Pergusa, Sicily, 6 September. Round 7. 21 laps of the 3.076-mile/4.950-km circuit, 64.592 miles/103.950 km.
1 Michele Gasparini, I (Dallara F396-Fiat), 35m 00.551s, 110.699 mph/178.153 km/h.
2 Paolo Montin, I (Dallara F397-Fiat), 35m 03.103s; **3** Donny Crevels, NL (Dallara F397-Opel), 35m 04.144s; **4** Gabriele Lancieri, I (Dallara F397-Opel), 35m 08.962s; **5** Ananda Mikola, RI (Dallara F397-Opel), 35m 10.016s; **6** Alberto Pedemonte, I (Dallara F398-Renault), 35m 31.505s; **7** Peter Sundberg, S (Dallara F397-Fiat), 35m 33.909s; **8** Gabriele Gardel, I (Dallara F397-Fiat), 35m 41.523s; **9** Riccardo Ronchi, I (Dallara F398-Fiat), 35m 45.041s; **10** Enrico Toccacelo, I (Dallara F397-Fiat), 35m 51.177s.
Fastest race lap: Crevels, 1m 38.849s, 112.017 mph/180.274 km/h.

9th GRAN PREMIO DEL LEVANTE, Autodromo del Levante, Binetto, Italy, 20 September. Round 8. 63 laps of the 0.980-mile/1.577-km circuit, 61.734 miles/99.351 km.
1 Maurizio Mediani, I (Dallara F396-Alfa Romeo), 46m 29.219s, 79.679 mph/128.231 km/h.
2 Paolo Montin, I (Dallara F398-Fiat), 46m 29.487s; **3** Donny Crevels, NL (Dallara F398-Opel), 46m 29.872s; **4** Nicola 'Niki' Cadei, I (Dallara F398-Opel), 46m 30.158s; **5** Ananda Mikola, RI (Dallara F398-Opel), 46m 30.383s; **6** Alberto Pedemonte, I (Dallara F398-Renault), 46m 30.669s; **7** Peter Sundberg, S (Dallara F396-Fiat), 46m 39.893s; **8** Enrico Toccacelo, I (Dallara F397-Fiat), 46m 40.355s; **9** Michele Gasparini, I (Dallara F396-Fiat), 46m 55.343s; **10** Riccardo Ronchi, I (Dallara F398-Fiat), 46m 55.777s.
Fastest race lap: Mikola, 43.260s, 81.545 mph/131.234 km/h.

ITALIAN FORMULA 3 CHAMPIONSHIP, Autodromo di Magione, Perugia, Italy, 25 October. 2 x 39 laps of the 1.616-mile/2.600-km circuit.
Round 9 (63.007 miles/101.400 km)
1 Paolo Montin, I (Dallara F398-Fiat), 51m 14.218s, 73.783 mph/118.742 km/h.
2 Ananda Mikola, RI (Dallara F397-Opel), 51m 22.477s; **3** Maurizio Mediani, I (Dallara F396-Alfa Romeo), 51m 26.052s; **4** Alberto Pedemonte, I (Dallara F398-Renault), 51m 26.265s; **5** Michele Gasparini, I (Dallara F396-Fiat), 51m 26.936s; **6** Gianluca Calgagni, I (Dallara F397-Opel), 51m 33.789s; **7** Gabriele Gardel, I (Dallara F398-Fiat), 51m 54.347s; **8** Michele Rangoni, I (Dallara F397-Fiat), 52m 09.214s; **9** Nikolaos 'Nico' Stremmenos, GR (Dallara F398-Opel), 52m 32.229s; **10** Fabrizio de Pace, I (Dallara F397-Opel), 38 laps.
Fastest race lap: Gasparini, 1m 14.196s, 78.387 mph/126.152 km/h.

Round 10 (63.007 miles/101.400 km)
1 Donny Crevels, NL (Dallara F397-Opel), 45m 33.232s, 82.988 mph/133.556 km/h.
2 Alessandro Manetti, I (Dallara F397-Opel), 45m 33.721s; **3** Ananda Mikola, RI (Dallara F397-Opel), 45m 38.975s; **4** Maurizio Mediani, I (Dallara F396-Alfa Romeo), 45m 41.810s; **5** Enrico Toccacelo, I (Dallara F396-Fiat), 45m 53.698s; **6** Gabriele Lancieri, I (Dallara F396-Fiat), 46m 10.819s; **7** Alberto Pedemonte, I (Dallara F398-Renault), 46m 13.217s; **8** Davide Uboldi, I (Dallara F396-Fiat), 46m 14.162s; **9** Maurizio Spoldi, I (Dallara F396-Fiat), 46m 14.421s; **10** Riccardo Ronchi, I (Dallara F398-Fiat), 46m 24.301s.
Fastest race lap: Manetti, 1m 07.934s, 85.613 mph/137.781 km/h.

Final championship points
1 Donny Crevels, NL, 125; **2** Paolo Montin, I, 113; **3** Michele Gasparini, I, 103; **4** Maurizio Mediani, I, 100; **5** Ananda Mikola, RI, 94; **6** Nicola 'Niki' Cadei, I, 58; **7** Peter Sundberg, S, 32; **8** Gianluca Calgagni, I, 28; **9** Gabriele Lancieri, I, 25; **10** Alberto Pedemonte, I, 24; **11=** Enrico Toccacelo, I, 15; **11=** Andrea Manetti, I, 15; **13** Nikolaos 'Nico' Stremmenos, GR, 14; **14=** Massimiliano 'Max' Busnelli, I, 12; **14=** Gabriele Gardel, I, 12; **16** Davide Uboldi, I, 6; **17** Riccardo Ronchi, I, 3; **18** Marco Barindelli, I, 2.

Major Non-Championship Formula 3

1997 Result

The Macau Formula 3 race was run after Autocourse 1997/98 *went to press.*

FIA F3 WORLD CUP, 44th MACAU GP, Circuito Da Guia, Macau, 16 November. 27 laps of the 3.801-mile/6.117-km circuit, 102.625 miles/165.159 km.
1 Soheil Ayari, F (Dallara F396-Opel), 1h 09m 22.240s, 88.762 mph/142.849 km/h.
2 Patrice Gay, F (Dallara F396-Opel), 1h 09m 33.791s; **3** Enrique Bernoldi, BR (Dallara F397-Renault), 1h 09m 36.228s; **4**

Mark Webber, AUS (Dallara F397-Mugen Honda), 1h 09m 48.891s; 5 André Couto, MAC (Dallara F397-Opel), 1h 09m 50.697s; 6 Oriol Servia, E (Martini MK73-Opel), 1h 10m 09.294s; 7 Stéphane Sarrazin, F (Dallara F396-Fiat), 1h 10m 20.994s; 8 Ben Collins, GB (Dallara F397-HKS Mitsubishi), 1h 10m 24.482s; 9 Donny Crevels, NL (Dallara F396-Fiat), 1h 10m 26.290s; 10 Sebastien Martino, RA (Dallara F397-Opel), 1h 10m 34.100s.
Fastest race lap: Tom Coronel, NL (Dallara F397-TOM'S-Toyota), 2m 15.950s, 100.650 mph/161.980 km/h.
Fastest qualifying lap: Ayari, 2m 15.692s, 100.841 mph/162.288 km/h.

1998 Results

8th MARLBORO MASTERS OF FORMULA 3, Circuit Park Zandvoort, Holland, 9 August. 31 laps of the 1.565-mile/2.519-km circuit, 48.522 miles/78.089 km.
1 David Saelens, B (Dallara F396-Renault), 33m 21.247s, 87.286 mph/140.473 km/h.
2 Enrique Bernoldi, BR (Dallara F398-Renault), 33m 21.581s; 3 Mario Haberfeld, BR (Dallara F398-Mugen Honda), 33m 22.364s; 4 Paolo Montin, I (Dallara F398-Fiat), 33m 23.736s; 5 Sébastien Dumez, F (Dallara F398-Renault), 33m 28.914s; 6 Franck Montagny, F (Martini MK73-Opel), 33m 31.439s; 7 Jeffrey van Hooydonk, B (Dallara F398-Opel), 33m 39.615s; 8 Timo Scheider, D (Martini MK73-Opel), 33m 39.967s; 9 Luciano Burti, BR (Dallara F398-Mugen Honda), 33m 41.996s; 10 Lucas Luhr, D (Dallara F398-Opel), 33m 42.426s.
Fastest race lap: David Terrien, F (Dallara F396-Opel), 1m 03.589s, 88.613 mph/142.610 km/h.
Fastest qualifying lap: Saelens.

Result of Macau Formula 3 race will be given in Autocourse 1999/2000.

FIA Grand Touring Car Championship

FIA GT CHAMPIONSHIP, Oschersleben Circuit, Germany, 12 April. Round 1. 137 laps of the 2.279-mile/3.667-km circuit, 312.164 miles/502.379 km.
1 Ricardo Zonta/Klaus Ludwig, BR/D (Mercedes Benz CLK-GTR), 3h 14m 21.274s, 96.369 mph/155.091 km/h.
2 Marcel Tiemann/Jean-Marc Gounon, D/F (Mercedes Benz CLK-GTR), 3h 15m 11.220s; 3 Bernd Schneider/Mark Webber, D/AUS (Mercedes Benz CLK-GTR), 135 laps; 4 Alexander 'Sandy' Grau/Andreas Scheld, D/D (Porsche 911 GT1-98), 134; 5 David Brabham/Eric Bernard, AUS/F (Panoz GTR-1), 130; 6 Olivier Beretta/Pedro Lamy, MC/P (Chrysler Viper GTS-R), 126 (1st GT2 class); 7 Karl Wendlinger/David Donohue, A/USA (Chrysler Viper GTS-R), 125; 8 Franz Konrad/Nick Ham, A/GB (Porsche 911 GT2), 122; 9 Martin Stretton/Tony Seiler, GB/CH (Porsche 911 GT2), 122; 10 Michael Trunk/Bernhard Müller, D/D (Porsche 911 GT2), 122.
Bruno Eichmann/Saascha Maassen, CH/D (Porsche 911 GT2), finished 8th but were excluded.
Fastest race lap: Uwe Alzen, D (Porsche 911 GT1-98), 1m 20.206s, 102.272 mph/164.591 km/h.
Fastest qualifying lap: Alzen, 1m 19.335s, 103.395 mph/166.398 km/h.

BRITISH EMPIRE TROPHY, Silverstone Grand Prix Circuit, Towcester, Northamptonshire, Great Britain, 17 May. Round 2. 98 laps of the 3.194-mile/5.140-km circuit, 312.997 miles/503.720 km.
1 Bernd Schneider/Mark Webber, D/AUS (Mercedes Benz CLK-GTR), 2h 54m 27.912s, 107.642 mph/173.233 km/h.
2 Uwe Alzen/Jörg Müller, D/D (Porsche 911 GT1-98), 2h 54m 35.921s; 3 Michael Bartels/Armin Hahne, D/D (Porsche 911 GT1-98), 97 laps; 4 Ricardo Zonta/Klaus Ludwig, BR/D (Mercedes Benz CLK-GTR), 97; 5 Alexander 'Sandy' Grau/Andreas Scheld, D/D (Porsche 911 GT1-98), 96; 6 Thomas Bscher/Geoff Lees, D/GB (McLaren F1 GTR), 94; 7 Christophe Bouchut/Bernd Mayländer, F/D (Mercedes Benz CLK-GTR), 94; 8 David Brabham/Eric Bernard, AUS/F (Panoz GTR-1), 93; 9 Olivier Beretta/Pedro Lamy, MC/P (Chrysler Viper GTS-R), 88 (1st GT2 class); 10 Michel Neugarten/Gerd Ruch/Marco Spinelli, B/D/I (Porsche 911 GT2), 86.
Fastest race lap: Alzen, 1m 42.719s, 111.935 mph/180.142 km/h.
Fastest qualifying lap: Allan McNish, GB (Porsche 911 GT1-98), 1m 39.703s, 115.321 mph/185.591 km/h.

FIA GT CHAMPIONSHIP, Hockenheimring, Heidelberg, Germany, 28 June. Round 3. 74 laps of the 4.240-mile/6.823-km circuit, 313.732 miles/504.902 km.
1 Bernd Schneider/Mark Webber, D/AUS (Mercedes Benz CLK-LM), 2h 33m 12.100s, 122.870 mph/197.740 km/h.
2 Ricardo Zonta/Klaus Ludwig, BR/D (Mercedes Benz CLK-LM), 2h 34m 24.558s; 3 David Brabham/Eric Bernard, AUS/F (Panoz GTR-1), 73 laps; 4 Marcel Tiemann/Jean-Marc Gounon, D/F (Mercedes Benz CLK-LM), 73; 5 Thomas Bscher/Geoff Lees, D/GB (McLaren F1 GTR), 73; 6 Yannick Dalmas/Allan McNish, F/GB (Porsche 911 GT1-98), 72; 7 Michael Bartels/Armin Hahne, D/D (Porsche 911 GT1-98), 72; 8 Olivier Beretta/Pedro Lamy, MC/P (Chrysler Viper GTS-R), 69 (1st GT2 class); 9 Karl Wendlinger/David Donohue, A/USA (Chrysler Viper GTS-R), 68; 10 Uwe Alzen/Jörg Müller, D/D (Porsche 911 GT1-98), 67.
Fastest race lap: Schneider, 2m 00.333s, 126.836 mph/204.124 km/h.
Fastest qualifying lap: Schneider, 1m 57.571s, 129.816 mph/208.919 km/h.

FIA GT CHAMPIONSHIP, Circuit de Dijon-Prenois, Fontaine-les-Dijon, France, 12 July. Round 4. 132 laps of the 2.361-mile/3.800-km circuit, 311.680 miles/501.600 km.
1 Ricardo Zonta/Klaus Ludwig, BR/D (Mercedes Benz CLK-LM), 2h 46m 17.188s, 112.461 mph/180.989 km/h.
2 Yannick Dalmas/Allan McNish, F/GB (Porsche 911 GT1-98), 2h 47m 19.223s; 3 David Brabham/Eric Bernard, AUS/F (Panoz GTR-1), 130 laps; 4 Christophe Bouchut/Bernd Mayländer, F/D (Mercedes Benz CLK-GTR), 130; 5 Marcel Tiemann/Jean-Marc Gounon, D/F (Mercedes Benz CLK-GTR), 129; 6 Michael Bartels/Armin Hahne, D/D (Porsche 911 GT1-98), 129; 7 Alexander 'Sandy' Grau/Andreas Scheld, D/D (Porsche 911 GT1-98), 128; 8 Patrice Goueslard/Bob Wollek/Carl Rosenblad, F/F/S (Porsche 911 GT1-97), 124; 9 Olivier Beretta/Pedro Lamy, MC/P (Chrysler Viper GTS-R), 120 (1st GT2 class); 10 Karl Wendlinger/David Donohue, A/USA (Chrysler Viper GTS-R), 119.
Fastest race lap: Schneider, D (Mercedes Benz CLK-LM), 1m 10.861s, 119.958 mph/193.054 km/h.
Fastest qualifying lap: Schneider, 1m 08.672s, 123.782 mph/199.208 km/h.

FIA GT CHAMPIONSHIP, Hungaroring, Mogyorod, Budapest, Hungary, 19 July. Round 5. 126 laps of the 2.468-mile/3.972-km circuit, 310.979 miles/500.472 km.
1 Bernd Schneider/Mark Webber, D/AUS (Mercedes Benz CLK-LM), 3h 21m 14.739s, 92.716 mph/149.212 km/h.
2 Ricardo Zonta/Klaus Ludwig, BR/D (Mercedes Benz CLK-LM), 3h 21m 29.839s; 3 Yannick Dalmas/Allan McNish, F/GB (Porsche 911 GT1-98), 3h 22m 09.111s; 4 Bob Wollek/Jörg Müller, F/D (Porsche 911 GT1-98), 125 laps; 5 Michael Bartels/Armin Hahne, D/D (Porsche 911 GT1-98), 121; 6 Bruno Eichmann/Saascha Maassen, CH/D (Porsche 911 GT2), 113 (1st GT2 class); 7 Olivier Beretta/Pedro Lamy, MC/P (Chrysler Viper GTS-R), 113; 8 Cor Euser/Harald Becker, NL/D (Marcos LM600), 113; 9 Marco Spinelli/Michel Neugarten/Gerd Ruch, I/B/D (Porsche 911 GT2), 109; 10 Michael Trunk/Bernhard Müller, D/D (Porsche 911 GT2), 109.
Fastest race lap: Ludwig, 1m 32.300s, 96.263 mph/154.921 km/h.
Fastest qualifying lap: Schneider, 1m 28.662s, 100.213 mph/161.278 km/h.

SUZUKA 1000 KM, Suzuka International Racing Course, Suzuka-City, Mie-Ken, Japan, 23 August. Round 6. 171 laps of the 3.644-mile/5.864-km circuit, 623.076 miles/1002.744 km.
1 Bernd Schneider/Mark Webber, D/AUS (Mercedes Benz CLK-LM), 5h 46m 58.452s, 107.745 mph/173.398 km/h.
2 Ricardo Zonta/Klaus Ludwig, BR/D (Mercedes Benz CLK-LM), 169 laps; 3 Yannick Dalmas/Allan McNish/Stéphane Ortelli, F/GB/F (Porsche 911 GT1-98), 168; 4 Christophe Bouchut/Bernd Mayländer, F/D (Mercedes Benz CLK-GTR), 167; 5 Franck Lagorce/Christophe Tinseau/Johnny O'Connell, F/F/USA (Panoz GTR-1), 165; 6 Michael Bartels/Alexander 'Sandy' Grau/Andreas Scheld, D/D/D (Porsche 911 GT1-98), 165; 7 Marcel Tiemann/Jean-Marc Gounon, D/F (Mercedes Benz CLK-GTR), 163; 8 Fabien Giroix/Armin Hahne/Jean-Denis Deletraz, F/D/CH (Porsche 911 GT1-98), 163; 9 Olivier Beretta/Pedro Lamy/Dominique Dupuy, MC/P/F (Chrysler Viper GTS-R), 155 (1st GT2 class); 10 Karl Wendlinger/Justin Bell/Hideshi Matsuda, A/GB/J (Chrysler Viper GTS-R), 155.
Fastest race lap: McNish, 1m 56.416s, 112.677 mph/181.336 km/h.
Fastest qualifying lap: Schneider, 1m 52.580s, 116.516 mph/187.515 km/h.

FIA GT DONINGTON 500, Donington Park Grand Prix Circuit, Derbyshire, Great Britain, 6 September. Round 7. 125 laps of the 2.500-mile/4.023-km circuit, 312.472 miles/502.875 km.
1 Bernd Schneider/Mark Webber, D/AUS (Mercedes Benz CLK-LM), 3h 05m 00.731s, 101.336 mph/163.084 km/h.
2 Ricardo Zonta/Klaus Ludwig, BR/D (Mercedes Benz CLK-LM), 3h 05m 46.061s; 3 Yannick Dalmas/Allan McNish, F/GB (Porsche 911 GT1-98), 124 laps; 4 Uwe Alzen/Jörg Müller, D/D (Porsche 911 GT1-98), 123; 5 Marcel Tiemann/Jean-Marc Gounon, D/F (Mercedes Benz CLK-GTR), 123; 6 Armin Hahne/Andreas Scheld, D/D (Porsche 911 GT1-98), 121; 7 Thomas Bscher/Geoff Lees, D/GB (McLaren F1 GTR), 120; 8 Olivier Beretta/Pedro Lamy, MC/P (Chrysler Viper GTS-R), 114 (1st GT2 class); 9 Cor Euser/Harald Becker/Christian Vann, NL/D/GB (Marcos LM600), 112; 10 Altfrid Heger/Franz Konrad, D/A (Porsche 911 GT2), 112.
Fastest race lap: Schneider, 1m 25.550s, 105.192 mph/169.290 km/h.
Fastest qualifying lap: Ludwig, 1m 22.870s, 108.594 mph/174.765 km/h.

FIA GT CHAMPIONSHIP, A1-Ring, Knittelfeld, Austria, 20 September. Round 8. 116 laps of the 2.684-mile/4.319-km circuit, 311.309 miles/501.004 km.
1 Ricardo Zonta/Klaus Ludwig, BR/D (Mercedes Benz CLK-LM), 2h 47m 34.975s, 111.459 mph/179.375 km/h.
2 Bernd Schneider/Mark Webber, D/AUS (Mercedes Benz CLK-LM), 2h 48m 07.029s; 3 Yannick Dalmas/Allan McNish, F/GB (Porsche 911 GT1-98), 115 laps; 4 Michael Bartels/Massimiliano 'Max' Angelelli, D/I (Porsche 911 GT1-98), 115; 5 Marcel Tiemann/Jean-Marc Gounon, D/F (Mercedes Benz CLK-GTR), 115; 6 Thomas Bscher/Geoff Lees, D/GB (McLaren F1 GTR), 112; 7 Christophe Tinseau/Franck Lagorce, F/F (Panoz GTR-1), 109 (DNF – engine); 8 Karl Wendlinger/Justin Bell, A/GB (Chrysler Viper GTS-R), 106 (1st GT2 class); 9 Olivier Beretta/Pedro Lamy, MC/P (Chrysler Viper GTS-R), 106; 10 Altfrid Heger/Franz Konrad, D/A (Porsche 911 GT2), 105.
Fastest race lap: Schneider, 1m 23.802s, 115.288 mph/185.537 km/h.
Fastest qualifying lap: Zonta, 1m 22.166s, 117.583 mph/189.232 km/h.

FIA GT CHAMPIONSHIP, Miami-Dade Homestead Motorsports Complex, Florida, USA, 18 October. Round 9. 141 laps of the 2.210-mile/3.556-km circuit, 311.553 miles/501.396 km.
1 Ricardo Zonta/Klaus Ludwig, BR/D (Mercedes Benz CLK-LM), 3h 18m 51.145s, 94.005 mph/151.287 km/h.
2 Uwe Alzen/Jörg Müller, D/D (Porsche 911 GT1-98), 3h 19m 54.379s; 3 Yannick Dalmas/Allan McNish, F/GB (Porsche 911 GT1-98), 140 laps; 4 Bernd Schneider/Mark Webber, D/AUS (Mercedes Benz CLK-LM), 140; 5 Marcel Tiemann/Jean-Marc Gounon, D/F (Mercedes Benz CLK-GTR), 140; 6 David Brabham/Eric Bernard, AUS/F (Panoz GTR-1), 139; 7 Michael Bartels/Massimiliano 'Max' Angelelli/Andreas Scheld, D/I/D (Porsche 911 GT1-98), 138; 8 Olivier Beretta/Pedro Lamy, MC/P (Chrysler Viper GTS-R), 130 (1st GT2 class); 9 Stéphane Ortelli/Claudia Hurtgen, F/D (Porsche 911 GT2), 129; 10 Cor Euser/Harald Becker/Christian Vann, NL/D/GB (Marcos LM600), 128.
Fastest race lap: Schneider, 1m 16.495s, 103.988 mph/167.352 km/h.
Fastest qualifying lap: Zonta, 1m 14.298s, 107.063 mph/172.301 km/h.

FIA GT CHAMPIONSHIP, Laguna Seca Raceway, Monterey, California, USA, 25 October. Round 10. 139 laps of the 2.238-mile/3.602-km circuit, 311.107 miles/500.678 km.
1 Ricardo Zonta/Klaus Ludwig, BR/D (Mercedes Benz CLK-LM), 3h 09m 08.458s, 98.690 mph/158.827 km/h.
2 Bernd Schneider/Mark Webber, D/AUS (Mercedes Benz CLK-LM), 3h 09m 19.348s; 3 Uwe Alzen/Jörg Müller, D/D (Porsche 911 GT1-98), 138 laps; 4 David Brabham/Eric Bernard, AUS/F (Panoz GTR-1), 137; 5 Michael Bartels/Massimiliano 'Max' Angelelli, D/I (Porsche 911 GT1-98), 137; 6 Christophe Bouchut/Bernd Mayländer, F/D (Mercedes Benz CLK-GTR), 135; 7 Olivier Beretta/Pedro Lamy, MC/P (Chrysler Viper GTS-R), 127 (1st GT2 class); 8 Bruno Eichmann/Mike Hezemans, CH/NL (Porsche 911 GT2), 126; 9 Michael Trunk/Bernhard Müller, D/D (Porsche 911 GT2), 123; 10 André Ahrlé/Dirk Layer/Rob Schirle, D/USA/USA (Porsche 911 GT2), 122.
Fastest race lap: Zonta, 1m 19.094s, 101.872 mph/163.947 km/h.
Fastest qualifying lap: Zonta, 1m 16.154s, 105.805 mph/170.276 km/h.

Final championship points
GT1 Drivers
1= Klaus Ludwig, D, 77; 1= Ricardo Zonta, BR, 77; 3= Bernd Schneider, D, 69; 3= Mark Webber, AUS, 69; 5= Yannick Dalmas, F, 27; 5= Allan McNish, GB, 27; 7 Jörg Müller, D, 21; 8 Uwe Alzen, D, 19; 9= Jean-Marc Gounon, F, 17; 9= Marcel Tiemann, D, 17; 11= Eric Bernard, F, 15; 11= David Brabham, AUS, 15; 13 Michael Bartels, D, 14; 14 Armin Hahne, D, 9; 15= Christophe Bouchut, F, 7; 15= Bernd Mayländer, D, 7; 15= Andreas Scheld, D, 7; 18 Alexander 'Sandy' Grau, D, 6; 19 Massimiliano 'Max' Angelelli, I, 5; 20= Thomas Bscher, D, 4; 20= Geoff Lees, GB, 4; 20= Stéphane Ortelli, F, 4; 23 Bob Wollek, F, 3; 24= Franck Lagorce, F, 2; 24= Johnny O'Connell, USA, 2; 24= Christophe Tinseau, F, 2.

GT1 Teams
1 AMG-Mercedes, 146; 2 Porsche AG, 49; 3 Team Persson Motorsport, 24; 4 Zakspeed Racing, 20; 5 DAMS, 17; 6 Davidoff Classic, 4.

GT2 Drivers
1= Olivier Beretta, MC, 92; 1= Pedro Lamy, P, 92; 3 Karl Wendlinger, A, 38; 4 Bruno Eichmann, CH, 22; 5= Justin Bell, GB, 20; 5= Franz Konrad, A, 20; 7 David Donohue, USA, 18; 8 Saascha Maassen, D, 17; 9= Michel Neugarten, B, 15; 9= Gerd Ruch, D, 15; 11= Bernhard Müller, D, 14; 11= Michael Trunk, D, 14; 13= Harald Becker, D, 13; 13= Cor Euser, NL, 13; 13= Altfrid Heger, D, 13; 16 Marco Spinelli, I, 11; 17 Dominique Dupuy, F, 10; 18= Michel Ligonnet, F, 9; 18= Claudia Hurtgen, D, 9; 18= Stéphane Ortelli, F, 9; 21 Christian Vann, GB, 8; 22= Wolfgang Kaufmann, D, 7; 22= André Ahrlé, D, 7.

GT2 Teams
1 Viper Team ORECA, 130; 2 Roock Racing, 31; 3 Konrad Motorsport, 25; 4 Elf Haberthur Racing, 15; 5 Krauss Motorsport, 14; 6 Marcos Racing International, 13; 7= Freisinger Motorsport, 7; 7= Roock Sportsystem, 7; 9= Chamberlain Engineering, 5; 9= Stadler Motorsport, 5.

Other Sports Car Races

66th 24 HEURES DU MANS, Circuit de la Sarthe, Le Mans, France, 6-7 June. 351 laps of the 8.451-mile/13.600-km circuit, 2972.502 miles/4783.781 km.
1 Allan McNish/Laurent Aïello/Stéphane Ortelli, GB/F/F (Porsche 911 GT1-98), 24h 00m 00.000s, 123.854 mph/199.324 km/h (1st GT1 class).
2 Jörg Müller/Uwe Alzen/Bob Wollek, D/D/F (Porsche 911 GT1-98), 350 laps; 3 Kazuyoshi Hoshino/Aguri Suzuki/Masahiko Kageyama, J/J/J (Nissan R390), 347; 4 Steve O'Rourke/Tim Sugden/Bill Auberlen, GB/GB/USA (McLaren F1 GTR-BMW), 343; 5 John Nielsen/Franck Lagorce/Michael Krumm, DK/F/D (Nissan R390), 342; 6 Erik Comas/Jan Lammers/Andrea Montermini, F/NL/I (Nissan R390), 342; 7 David Brabham/Andy Wallace/Jamie Davies, AUS/GB/GB (Panoz GTR-1-Ford), 335; 8 Wayne Taylor/Eric Van de Poele/Fermin Velez, ZA/B/E (Ferrari 333SP), 332 (1st LM Prototype 1 class); 9 Ukyo Katayama/Toshio Suzuki/Keiichi Tsuchiya, J/J/J (Toyota GT-One), 326; 10 Takuya Kurosawa/Satoshi Motoyama/Masami Kageyama, J/J/J (Nissan R390), 319; 11 Justin Bell/David Donohue/Luca Drudi, GB/USA/GB (Chrysler Viper GTS-R), 317 (1st GT2 class); 12 Rocky Agusta/Almo Coppelli/Xavier Pompidou, USA/I/F (Kremer K9-Porsche), 314; 13 Olivier Beretta/Pedro Lamy/Tommy Archer, MC/P/USA (Chrysler Viper GTS-R), 312; 14 Giampiero Moretti/Didier Theys/Mauro Baldi, I/B/I (Ferrari 333SP), 311; 15 Yojiro Terada/Franck Fréon/Olivier Thévenin, J/F/F (Courage C41-Porsche), 304; 16 Henri Pescarolo/Olivier Grouillard/Franck Montagny, F/F/F (Courage C36-Porsche), 300; 17 Claudia Hurtgen/Michel Ligonnet/Robert Nearn, D/F/GB (Porsche 911 GT2), 285; 18 Michel Nourry/Thierry Perrier/Jean-Louis Ricci, F/F/F (Porsche 911 GT2), 276; 19 Matt Turner/Gary Ayles/Hans Hugenholtz, USA/GB/NL (Chrysler Viper GTS-R), 270; 20 Eric Graham/Hervé Poulain/Jean-Luc Maury-Laribière, F/F/F (Porsche 911 GT2), 268; 21 Ni Amorim/Goncalo Gomes/Manuel Mello-Breyner, P/P/P (Chrysler Viper GTS-R), 264; 22 Rob Schirle/André Ahrlé/David Warnock, GB/D/GB (Porsche 911 GT2), 247; 23 Patrice Goueslard/Jean-Luc Chereau/Pierre Yver, F/F/F (Porsche 911 GT2), 240; 24 Thierry Boutsen/Ralf Kelleners/Geoff Lees, B/D/GB (Toyota GT-One), 330 (DNF – gearbox); 25 Manuel Monteiro/Michel Monteiro/Michel Maissonneuve, P/P/F (Porsche 911 GT2), 277 (DNF – engine); 26 Eric Bernard/Christophe Tinseau/Johnny O'Connell, F/F/USA (Panoz GTR-1-Ford), 236 (DNF – gearbox); 27 Didier Cottaz/Marc Goossens/Jean-Philippe Belloc, F/B/F (Courage C51-Nissan), 232 (DNF – gearbox); 28 Thomas Bscher/Emanuele Pirro/Rinaldo Capello, D/I/I (McLaren F1 GTR-BMW), 228 (DNF – accident damage); 29 Pierre-Henri Raphanel/David Murry/James Weaver, F/USA/GB (Porsche LMP-98), 218 (DNF – accident damage); 30 Michel Ferté/Pascal Fabre/François Migault, F/F/F (Ferrari 333SP), 203 (DNF – gearbox); 31 Michel Neugarten/Jean-Claude Lagniez/David Smadja, F/F/F (Porsche 911 GT2), 198 (DNF – transmission); 32 Martin Brundle/Emmanuel Collard/Eric Helary, GB/F/F (Toyota GT-One), 191 (DNF – accident); 33 Vincenzo Sospiri/Jean-Christophe Boullion/Jérôme Policand, I/F/F (Ferrari 333SP), 187 (DNF – transmission); 34 Jean-Pierre Jarier/Robin Donovan/Carl Rosenblad, F/GB/S (Porsche 911 GT2), 164 (DNF – transmission); 35 John Morton/Harald Grohs/John Graham, USA/D/CDN (Porsche 911 GT2), 164 (DNF – accident); 36 Philippe Gache/Didier de Radiguès/Wayne Gardner, F/B/AUS (Riley & Scott Mk III-Ford), 155 (DNF – engine); 37 Fredrik Ekblom/Patrice Gay/Tetsuya Tsuchiya, S/F/J (Courage C51-Nissan), 126 (DNF – engine); 38 Michele Alboreto/Stefan Johansson/Yannick Dalmas, I/S/F (Porsche LMP-98), 107 (DNF – electrics); 39 Lionel Robert/Edouard Sezionale/Pierre Bruneau, F/F/F (Debora LMP2-BMW), 106 (DNF – gearbox); 40 Bernhard Müller/Michael Trunk/Ernest Palmberger, D/D/D (Porsche 911 GT2), 71 (DNF – engine); 41 Tom Kristensen/Hans Joachim Stuck/Steve Soper, DK/D/GB (BMW V12 Le Mans), 60 (DNF – wheel bearing); 42 Pierluigi Martini/Joachim Winkelhock/Johnny Cecotto, I/D/YV (BMW V12 Le Mans), 43 (DNF – wheel bearing); 43 Jean-Marc Gounon/Christophe Bouchut/Ricardo Zonta, F/F/BR (Mercedes Benz CLK-LM), 31 (DNF – engine); 44 Karl Wendlinger/Marc Duez/Patrick Huisman, A/B/NL (Chrysler Viper GTS-R), 28 (DNF – electrics); 45 Franz Konrad/Nick Ham/Larry Schumacher, A/GB/USA (Porsche 911 GT2), 24 (DNF – accident); 46 Bernd Schneider/Klaus Ludwig/Mark Webber, D/D/AUS (Mercedes Benz CLK-LM), 19 (DNF – engine); 47 Toni Reiler/Peter Kitchak/Angelo Zadra, GB/USA/I (Porsche 911 GT2), 2 (DNF – engine).
Fastest race lap: Brundle, 3m 41.809s, 137.206 mph/220.812 km/h.
Fastest qualifying lap: Schneider, 3m 35.544s, 141.194 mph/227.230 km/h.

PETIT LE MANS, Road Atlanta Circuit, Braselton, Georgia, USA, 10 October. 391 laps of the 2.560-mile/4.120-km circuit, 1000.960 miles/1610.889 km.
1 Eric van de Poele/Wayne Taylor/Emmanuel Collard, B/ZA/F (Ferrari 333SP), 9h 48m 36.0s, 102.035 mph/164.209 km/h (1st LMP1 class).
2 Michael Alboreto/Stefan Johansson/Jörg Müller, I/S/D (Porsche LMP1-98), 391 laps; 3 Thierry Boutsen/Ralph Kellenérs/Bob Wollek, B/D/F (Porsche GT1-97), 381 (1st GT1 class); 4 Butch Leitzinger/Scott Schubot/Henry Camferdam, USA/USA/USA (Riley & Scott Mk III), 378 (1st WSC class); 5 Anthony Lazzard/Bill Dollahite/Mike Davies, USA/USA/USA (Ferrari 333SP), 365; 6 Howard Katz/Jim Downing/Yojiro Terada, USA/USA/J (Kudzu-Mazda DLY), 349; 7 Michel Ligonnet/Lance Stewart, F/USA (Porsche 911 GT2), 337 (1st GT2 class); 8 Scott Pruett/David Brabham/Andy Wallace/Eric Bernard, USA/AUS/GB/F (Panoz GTR-1), 335; 9 Peter Argetsinger/Richard Polidori/Angelo Cilli, USA/USA/USA (Porsche 911 RSR), 335 (1st GT3 class); 10 Ross Bentley/David Besnard/Jeff Shafer/Darren Law USA/AUS/USA/USA (BMW M3), 328.
Fastest race lap: Allan McNish, GB (Porsche 911 GT1-98), 1m 15.239s, 122.490 mph/197.128 km/h.
Fastest qualifying lap: McNish, 1m 13.754s, 124.956 mph/201.097 km/h.

FedEx Championship Series

MARLBORO GRAND PRIX OF MIAMI PRESENTED BY TOYOTA, Miami-Dade Homestead Motorsports Complex, Florida, USA, 15 March. Round 1. 150 laps of the 1.502-mile/2.417-km circuit, 225.300 miles/362.585 km.
1 Michael Andretti, USA (Swift 009.c-Ford Cosworth XD), 1h 33m 39.268s, 144.339 mph/232.291 km/h.
2 Greg Moore, CDN (Reynard 98I-Mercedes Benz IC 108E), 1h 33m 39.343s; 3 Alessandro 'Alex' Zanardi, I (Reynard 98I-Honda Turbo V8), 1h 33m 40.186s; 4 Christian Fittipaldi, BR (Swift 009.c-Ford Cosworth XD), 1h 33m 42.627s; 5 Scott Pruett, USA (Reynard 98I-Ford Cosworth XD), 1h 33m 44.525s; 6 Adrian Fernandez, MEX (Reynard 98I-Ford Cosworth XD), 1h 33m 45.194s; 7 Gil de Ferran, BR (Reynard 98I-Honda Turbo V8), 1h 33m 46.078s; 8 Bryan Herta, USA (Reynard 98I-Ford Cosworth XD), 1h 33m 49.134s; 9 Dario Franchitti, GB (Reynard 98I-Honda Turbo V8), 1h 33m 49.543s; 10 Mauricio Gugelmin, BR (Reynard 98I-Mercedes Benz IC 108E), 1h 33m 50.123s.
Most laps led: Andretti, 62.
Fastest qualifying lap: Moore, 24.856s, 217.541 mph/350.098 km/h.
Championship points: 1 Andretti, 21; 2 Moore, 17; 3 Zanardi, 14; 4 Fittipaldi, 12; 5 Pruett, 10; 6 Fernandez, 8.

BUDWEISER 500, Twin Ring Motegi, Haga gun, Japan, 28 March. Round 2. 201 laps of the 1.549-mile/2.493-km circuit, 311.349 miles/501.068 km.
1 Adrian Fernandez, MEX (Reynard 98I-Ford Cosworth XD), 1h 57m 12.016s, 159.393 mph/256.519 km/h.
2 Al Unser Jr, USA (Penske PC27-Mercedes Benz IC 108E), 1h 57m 13.102s; 3 Gil de Ferran, BR (Reynard 98I-Honda Turbo V8), 1h 57m 17.404s; 4 Greg Moore, CDN (Reynard 98I-Mercedes Benz IC 108E), 1h 57m 19.939s; 5 Paul Tracy, CDN (Reynard 98I-Honda Turbo V8), 1h 57m 20.166s; 6 Tony Kanaan, BR (Reynard 98I-Honda Turbo V8), 200 laps; 7 Jimmy Vasser, USA (Reynard 98I-Honda Turbo V8), 200; 8 Dario Franchitti, GB (Reynard 98I-Honda Turbo V8), 200; 9 Andre Ribeiro, BR (Penske PC27-Mercedes Benz IC 108E), 199; 10 Mark Blundell, GB (Reynard 98I-Mercedes Benz IC 108E), 199.
Most laps led: Fernandez, 102.
Pole Position: Vasser, 25.584s, 217.964 mph/350.780 km/h (based on combined practice times. Friday qualifying cancelled due to rain).
Championship points: 1= Fernandez, 29; 1= Moore, 29; 3 Andretti, 21; 4 de Ferran, 20; 5 Unser Jr, 16; 6 Zanardi, 14.

TOYOTA GRAND PRIX OF LONG BEACH, Long Beach Street Circuit, California, USA, 5 April. Round 3. 105 laps of the 1.574-mile/2.533-km circuit, 165.270 miles/265.976 km.
1 Alessandro 'Alex' Zanardi, I (Reynard 98I-Honda Turbo V8), 1h 51m 29.113s, 88.946 mph/143.145 km/h.
2 Dario Franchitti, GB (Reynard 98I-Honda Turbo V8), 1h 51m 32.030s; 3 Bryan Herta, USA (Reynard 98I-Ford Cosworth XD), 1h 51m 33.449s; 4 Adrian Fernandez, MEX (Reynard 98I-Ford Cosworth XD), 1h 51m 34.998s; 5 Tony Kanaan, BR (Reynard 98I-Honda Turbo V8), 1h 51m 45.018s; 6 Greg Moore, CDN (Reynard 98I-Mercedes Benz IC 108E), 1h 51m 48.470s; 7 Mark Blundell, GB (Reynard 98I-Mercedes Benz IC 108E), 1h 51m 50.271s; 8 Jimmy Vasser, USA (Reynard 98I-Honda Turbo V8), 1h 51m 53.715s; 9 Helio Castro-Neves, BR (Reynard 98I-Mercedes Benz IC 108E), 1h 52m 06.487s; 10 Mauricio Gugelmin, BR (Reynard 98I-Mercedes Benz IC 108E), 1h 52m 20.565s.
Most laps led: Gil de Ferran, BR (Reynard 98I-Honda Turbo V8), 51.

Fastest qualifying lap: Herta, 50.945s, 111.226 mph/179.001 km/h.
Championship points: **1** Fernandez, 41; **2** Moore, 37; **3** Zanardi, 34; **4** Franchitti, 25; **5=** Andretti, 21; **5=** de Ferran, 21.

BOSCH SPARK PLUG GRAND PRIX PRESENTED BY TOYOTA, Nazareth Speedway, Pennsylvania, USA, 27 April. Round 4. 225 laps of the 0.946-mile/1.522-km circuit, 212.850 miles/342.549 km.
Scheduled for 26 April but postponed by a day due to rain.
1 Jimmy Vasser, USA (Reynard 98I-Honda Turbo V8), 1h 57m 20.307s, 108.839 mph/175.159 km/h.
2 Alessandro 'Alex' Zanardi, I (Reynard 98I-Honda Turbo V8), 1h 57m 21.707s; **3** Greg Moore, CDN (Reynard 98I-Mercedes Benz IC 108E), 1h 57m 23.917s; **4** Gil de Ferran, BR (Reynard 98I-Honda Turbo V8), 1h 57m 28.323s; **5** Paul Tracy, CDN (Reynard 98I-Honda Turbo V8), 1h 57m 28.605s; **6** Bobby Rahal, USA (Reynard 98I-Ford Cosworth XD), 1h 57m 29.925s; **7** Robby Gordon, USA (Reynard 98I-Toyota), 1h 57m 30.474s; **8** Bryan Herta, USA (Reynard 98I-Ford Cosworth XD), 224 laps; **9** Tony Kanaan, BR (Reynard 98I-Honda Turbo V8), 224; **10** Richie Hearn, USA (Swift 009.c-Ford Cosworth XD), 224.
Most laps led: Michael Andretti, USA (Swift 009.c-Ford Cosworth XD), 102.
Fastest qualifying lap: Patrick Carpentier, CDN (Reynard 98I-Mercedes Benz IC 108E), 18.419s, 184.896 mph/297.561 km/h.
Championship points: **1** Moore, 51; **2** Zanardi, 50; **3** Fernandez, 41; **4** de Ferran, 33; **5** Vasser, 31; **6=** Franchitti, 25; **6=** Herta, 25.

HOLLYWOOD RIO 400, Emerson Fittipaldi Speedway at Nelson Piquet International Raceway, Jacarepagua, Rio de Janeiro, Brazil, 10 May. Round 5. 133 laps of the 1.864-mile/3.000-km circuit, 247.912 miles/398.976 km.
1 Greg Moore, CDN (Reynard 98I-Mercedes Benz IC 108E), 1h 52m 14.135s, 132.531 mph/213.288 km/h.
2 Alessandro 'Alex' Zanardi, I (Reynard 98I-Honda Turbo V8), 1h 52m 14.562s; **3** Adrian Fernandez, MEX (Reynard 98I-Ford Cosworth XD), 1h 52m 18.974s; **4** Bryan Herta, USA (Reynard 98I-Ford Cosworth XD), 1h 52m 27.086s; **5** Michael Andretti, USA (Swift 009.c-Ford Cosworth XD), 1h 52m 28.459s; **6** Jimmy Vasser, USA (Reynard 98I-Honda Turbo V8), 1h 52m 29.386s; **7** Richie Hearn, USA (Swift 009.c-Ford Cosworth XD), 1h 52m 29.934s; **8** Bobby Rahal, USA (Reynard 98I-Ford Cosworth XD), 1h 52m 42.784s; **9** Mauricio Gugelmin, BR (Reynard 98I-Mercedes Benz IC 108E), 132 laps; **10** JJ Lehto, SF (Reynard 98I-Mercedes Benz IC 108E), 132.
Most laps led: Zanardi, 117.
Fastest qualifying lap: Dario Franchitti, GB (Reynard 98I-Honda Turbo V8), 39.005s, 172.039 mph/276.871 km/h.
Championship points: **1** Moore, 71; **2** Zanardi, 67; **3** Fernandez, 55; **4** Vasser, 39; **5** Herta, 37; **6** de Ferran, 33.

MOTOROLA 300, Gateway International Raceway, Madison, Illinois, USA, 23 May. Round 6. 236 laps of the 1.270-mile/2.044-km circuit, 299.720 miles/482.353 km.
1 Alessandro 'Alex' Zanardi, I (Reynard 98I-Honda Turbo V8), 2h 23m 02.140s, 125.725 mph/202.335 km/h.
2 Michael Andretti, USA (Swift 009.c-Ford Cosworth XD), 2h 23m 02.713s; **3** Greg Moore, CDN (Reynard 98I-Mercedes Benz IC 108E), 2h 23m 03.666s; **4** Jimmy Vasser, USA (Reynard 98I-Honda Turbo V8), 2h 23m 20.014s; **5** Scott Pruett, USA (Reynard 98I-Ford Cosworth XD), 2h 23m 20.451s; **6** Gil de Ferran, BR (Reynard 98I-Honda Turbo V8), 2h 23m 20.863s; **7** Helio Castro-Neves, BR (Reynard 98I-Mercedes Benz IC 108E), 2h 23m 21.102s; **8** Bobby Rahal, USA (Reynard 98I-Ford Cosworth XD), 235 laps; **9** JJ Lehto, SF (Reynard 98I-Mercedes Benz IC 108E), 235; **10** Mark Blundell, GB (Reynard 98I-Mercedes Benz IC 108E), 233.
Most laps led: Andretti, 133.
Fastest qualifying lap: Moore, 25.757s, 177.505 mph/285.667 km/h.
Championship points: **1** Zanardi, 87; **2** Moore, 85; **3** Fernandez, 55; **4** Vasser, 51; **5** Andretti, 49; **6** de Ferran, 41.

MILLER LITE 200, The Milwaukee Mile, Wisconsin State Fair Park, West Allis, Milwaukee, Wisconsin, USA, 31 May. Round 7. 200 laps of the 1.032-mile/1.661-km circuit, 206.400 miles/332.169 km.
1 Jimmy Vasser, USA (Reynard 98I-Honda Turbo V8), 1h 34m 17.011s, 131.349 mph/211.385 km/h.
2 Helio Castro-Neves, BR (Reynard 98I-Mercedes Benz IC 108E), 1h 34m 24.684s; **3** Al Unser Jr, USA (Penske PC27-Mercedes Benz IC 108E), 1h 34m 24.717s; **4** Dario Franchitti, GB (Reynard 98I-Honda Turbo V8), 1h 34m 28.302s; **5** Bobby Rahal, USA (Reynard 98I-Ford Cosworth XD), 1h 34m 42.190s; **6** Richie Hearn, USA (Swift 009.c-Ford Cosworth XD), 199 laps; **7** Paul Tracy, CDN (Reynard 98I-Honda Turbo V8), 199; **8** Adrian Fernandez, MEX (Reynard 98I-Ford Cosworth XD), 199; **9** Alessandro 'Alex' Zanardi, I (Reynard 98I-Honda Turbo V8), 199; **10** Scott Pruett, USA (Reynard 98I-Ford Cosworth XD), 199.
Most laps led: Vasser, 77.
Fastest qualifying lap: Patrick Carpentier, CDN (Reynard 98I-Mercedes Benz IC 108E), 20.028s, 185.500 mph/298.534 km/h.
Championship points: **1** Zanardi, 92; **2** Moore, 85; **3** Vasser, 72; **4** Fernandez, 59; **5** Andretti, 49; **6** de Ferran, 41.

ITT AUTOMOTIVE DETROIT GRAND PRIX, The Raceway on Belle Isle, Detroit, Michigan, USA, 7 June. Round 8. 72 laps of the 2.346-mile/3.776-km circuit, 168.912 miles/271.838 km.
1 Alessandro 'Alex' Zanardi, I (Reynard 98I-Honda Turbo V8), 1h 41m 17.673s, 100.052 mph/161.018 km/h.
2 Adrian Fernandez, MEX (Reynard 98I-Ford Cosworth XD), 1h 41m 24.297s; **3** Gil de Ferran, BR (Reynard 98I-Honda Turbo V8), 1h 41m 25.184s; **4** Dario Franchitti, GB (Reynard 98I-Honda Turbo V8), 1h 41m 26.020s; **5** Greg Moore, CDN (Reynard 98I-Mercedes Benz IC 108E), 1h 41m 27.457s; **6** Jimmy Vasser, USA (Reynard 98I-Honda Turbo V8), 1h 41m 28.081s; **7** Paul Tracy, CDN (Reynard 98I-Honda Turbo V8), 1h 41m 29.814s; **8** Tony Kanaan, BR (Reynard 98I-Honda Turbo V8), 1h 41m 34.858s; **9** Scott Pruett, USA (Reynard 98I-Ford Cosworth XD), 1h 41m 38.964s; **10** Michael Andretti, USA (Swift 009.c-Ford Cosworth XD), 1h 41m 40.071s.
Most laps led: Zanardi, 50.
Fastest qualifying lap: Moore, 1m 13.530s, 114.859 mph/184.848 km/h.
Championship points: **1** Zanardi, 113; **2** Moore, 96; **3** Vasser, 80; **4** Fernandez, 75; **5** de Ferran, 55; **6** Andretti, 52.

BUDWEISER/G.I.JOE'S 200 PRESENTED BY TEXACO/HAVOLINE, Portland International Raceway, Oregon, USA, 21 June. Round 9. 98 laps of the 1.967-mile/3.166-km circuit, 192.766 miles/310.227 km.
1 Alessandro 'Alex' Zanardi, I (Reynard 98I-Honda Turbo V8), 1h 54m 06.822s, 101.355 mph/163.115 km/h.
2 Scott Pruett, USA (Reynard 98I-Ford Cosworth XD), 1h 54m 13.661s; **3** Bryan Herta, USA (Reynard 98I-Ford Cosworth XD), 1h 54m 13.931s; **4** Tony Kanaan, BR (Reynard 98I-Honda Turbo V8), 1h 54m 19.730s; **5** Al Unser Jr, USA (Penske PC27-Mercedes Benz IC 108E), 1h 54m 20.998s; **6** Bobby Rahal, USA (Reynard 98I-Ford Cosworth XD), 1h 54m 25.212s; **7** Mauricio Gugelmin, BR (Reynard 98I-Mercedes Benz IC 108E), 1h 54m 32.398s; **8** Jimmy Vasser, USA (Reynard 98I-Honda Turbo V8), 1h 54m 33.848s; **9** Patrick Carpentier, CDN (Reynard 98I-Mercedes Benz IC 108E), 1h 54m 34.399s; **10** Richie Hearn, USA (Swift 009.c-Ford Cosworth XD), 97 laps.
Most laps led: Zanardi, 47.
Fastest qualifying lap: Herta, 58.358s, 121.341 mph/195.279 km/h.
Championship points: **1** Zanardi, 134; **2** Moore, 96; **3** Vasser, 85; **4** Fernandez, 75; **5** de Ferran, 55; **6** Herta, 54.

MEDIC DRUG GRAND PRIX OF CLEVELAND PRESENTED BY DAIRY MART, Burke Lakefront Airport Circuit, Cleveland, Ohio, USA, 12 July. Round 10. 100 laps of the 2.106-mile/3.389-km circuit, 210.600 miles/338.928 km.
1 Alessandro 'Alex' Zanardi, I (Reynard 98I-Honda Turbo V8), 1h 52m 22.282s, 112.449 mph/180.968 km/h.
2 Michael Andretti, USA (Swift 009.c-Ford Cosworth XD), 1h 52m 30.704s; **3** Dario Franchitti, GB (Reynard 98I-Honda Turbo V8), 1h 52m 31.183s; **4** Scott Pruett, USA (Reynard 98I-Ford Cosworth XD), 1h 52m 40.666s; **5** Adrian Fernandez, MEX (Reynard 98I-Ford Cosworth XD), 1h 52m 50.351s; **6** Gil de Ferran, BR (Reynard 98I-Honda Turbo V8), 1h 52m 50.890s; **7** Jimmy Vasser, USA (Reynard 98I-Honda Turbo V8), 1h 52m 51.402s; **8** Bobby Rahal, USA (Reynard 98I-Ford Cosworth XD), 1h 52m 53.547s; **9** Patrick Carpentier, CDN (Reynard 98I-Mercedes Benz IC 108E), 1h 52m 58.516s; **10** Mark Blundell, GB (Reynard 98I-Mercedes Benz IC 108E), 1h 53m 00.616s.
Most laps led: Zanardi, 68.
Fastest qualifying lap: Vasser, 56.417s, 134.385 mph/216.272 km/h.
Championship points: **1** Zanardi, 155; **2** Moore, 96; **3** Vasser, 92; **4** Fernandez, 85; **5** Andretti, 68; **6** Franchitti, 64.

MOLSON INDY TORONTO, Exhibition Place Circuit, Toronto, Ontario, Canada, 19 July. Round 11. 95 laps of the 1.721-mile/2.770-km circuit, 163.495 miles/263.120 km.
1 Alessandro 'Alex' Zanardi, I (Reynard 98I-Honda Turbo V8), 1h 52m 24.080s, 87.274 mph/140.454 km/h.
2 Michael Andretti, USA (Swift 009.c-Ford Cosworth XD), 1h 52m 26.001s; **3** Jimmy Vasser, USA (Reynard 98I-Honda Turbo V8), 1h 52m 30.782s; **4** Bobby Rahal, USA (Reynard 98I-Ford Cosworth XD), 1h 52m 32.158s; **5** Bryan Herta, USA (Reynard 98I-Ford Cosworth XD), 1h 52m 37.064s; **6** Scott Pruett, USA (Reynard 98I-Ford Cosworth XD), 1h 52m 38.687s; **7** Richie Hearn, USA (Swift 009.c-Ford Cosworth XD), 1h 52m 39.385s; **8** Massimiliano 'Max' Papis, I (Reynard 98I-Toyota), 1h 52m 48.756s; **9** Adrian Fernandez, MEX (Reynard 98I-Ford Cosworth XD), 1h 52m 56.003s; **10** Helio Castro-Neves, BR (Reynard 98I-Mercedes Benz IC 108E), 1h 52m 56.773s.
Most laps led: Franchitti, 76.
Fastest qualifying lap: Dario Franchitti, GB (Reynard 98I-Honda Turbo V8), 58.694s, 105.558 mph/169.879 km/h.
Championship points: **1** Zanardi, 175; **2** Vasser, 106; **3** Moore, 98; **4** Fernandez, 89; **5** Andretti, 84; **6** Franchitti, 66.

U.S. 500 PRESENTED BY TOYOTA, Michigan Speedway, Brooklyn, Michigan, USA, 26 July. Round 12. 250 laps of the 2.000-mile/3.219-km circuit, 500.000 miles/804.672 km.
1 Greg Moore, CDN (Reynard 98I-Mercedes Benz IC 108E), 3h 00m 48.785s, 165.917 mph/267.018 km/h.
2 Jimmy Vasser, USA (Reynard 98I-Honda Turbo V8), 3h 00m 48.786s; **3** Alessandro 'Alex' Zanardi, I (Reynard 98I-Honda Turbo V8), 3h 00m 48.793s; **4** Scott Pruett, USA (Reynard 98I-Ford Cosworth XD), 3h 00m 49.044s; **5** Richie Hearn, USA (Swift 009.c-Ford Cosworth XD), 3h 00m 49.882s; **6** Michael Andretti, USA (Swift 009.c-Ford Cosworth XD), 3h 00m 50.093s; **7** Bobby Rahal, USA (Reynard 98I-Ford Cosworth XD), 3h 00m 51.175s; **8** Patrick Carpentier, CDN (Reynard 98I-Mercedes Benz IC 108E), 3h 00m 51.954s; **9** Paul Tracy, CDN (Reynard 98I-Honda Turbo V8), 3h 00m 52.844s; **10** Bryan Herta, USA (Reynard 98I-Ford Cosworth XD), 3h 01m 14.796s.
Most laps led: Zanardi, 63.
Fastest qualifying lap: Adrian Fernandez, MEX (Reynard 98I-Ford Cosworth XD), 31.370s, 229.519 mph/369.374 km/h.
Championship points: **1** Zanardi, 190; **2** Vasser, 122; **3** Moore, 118; **4** Andretti, 92; **5** Fernandez, 90; **6** Pruett, 76.

MILLER LITE 200, Mid-Ohio Sports Car Course, Lexington, Ohio, USA, 9 August. Round 13. 83 laps of the 2.258-mile/3.634-km circuit, 186.446 miles/300.056 km.
1 Adrian Fernandez, MEX (Reynard 98I-Ford Cosworth XD), 1h 53m 39.270s, 98.428 mph/158.404 km/h.
2 Scott Pruett, USA (Reynard 98I-Ford Cosworth XD), 1h 53m 39.517s; **3** Bobby Rahal, USA (Reynard 98I-Ford Cosworth XD), 1h 53m 41.687s; **4** Mauricio Gugelmin, BR (Reynard 98I-Mercedes Benz IC 108E), 1h 53m 48.076s; **5** Paul Tracy, CDN (Reynard 98I-Honda Turbo V8), 1h 53m 49.253s; **6** Al Unser Jr, USA (Penske PC27-Mercedes Benz IC 108E), 1h 53m 52.561s; **7** Patrick Carpentier, CDN (Reynard 98I-Mercedes Benz IC 108E), 1h 53m 53.060s; **8** Tony Kanaan, BR (Reynard 98I-Honda Turbo V8), 1h 53m 53.924s; **9** Gil de Ferran, BR (Reynard 98I-Honda Turbo V8), 1h 53m 58.478s; **10** Andre Ribeiro, BR (Penske PC27-Mercedes Benz IC 108E), 1h 54m 00.055s.
Most laps led: Gugelmin, 29.
Fastest qualifying lap: Dario Franchitti, GB (Reynard 98I-Honda Turbo V8), 1m 05.679s, 123.766 mph/199.181 km/h.
Championship points: **1** Zanardi, 191; **2** Vasser, 122; **3** Moore, 118; **4** Fernandez, 110; **5=** Andretti, 92; **5=** Pruett, 92.

TEXACO/HAVOLINE 200, Road America Circuit, Elkhart Lake, Wisconsin, USA, 16 August. Round 14. 50 laps of the 4.048-mile/6.515-km circuit, 202.400 miles/325.731 km.
1 Dario Franchitti, GB (Reynard 98I-Honda Turbo V8), 1h 35m 30.767s, 127.145 mph/204.621 km/h.
2 Alessandro 'Alex' Zanardi, I (Reynard 98I-Honda Turbo V8), 1h 35m 37.869s; **3** Christian Fittipaldi, BR (Swift 009.c-Ford Cosworth XD), 1h 36m 14.689s; **4** Tony Kanaan, BR (Reynard 98I-Honda Turbo V8), 1h 36m 16.901s; **5** Adrian Fernandez, MEX (Reynard 98I-Ford Cosworth XD), 1h 36m 17.864s; **6** Paul Tracy, CDN (Reynard 98I-Honda Turbo V8), 1h 36m 22.770s; **7** Mark Blundell, GB (Reynard 98I-Mercedes Benz IC 108E), 1h 36m 22.934s; **8** Bobby Rahal, USA (Reynard 98I-Ford Cosworth XD), 1h 36m 37.139s; **9** Jimmy Vasser, USA (Reynard 98I-Honda Turbo V8), 1h 36m 37.851s; **10** Arnd Meier, D (Lola T98/00-Ford Cosworth XD), 1h 36m 38.365s.
Most laps led: Franchitti, 23.
Fastest qualifying lap: Michael Andretti, USA (Swift 009.c-Ford Cosworth XD), 1m 39.988s, 145.745 mph/234.555 km/h.
Championship points: **1** Zanardi, 206; **2** Vasser, 126; **3** Fernandez, 120; **4** Moore, 118; **5** Andretti, 93; **6** Pruett, 92.

MOLSON INDY VANCOUVER, Vancouver Street Circuit, Concord Pacific Place, Vancouver, British Columbia, Canada, 6 September. Round 15. 86 laps of the 1.802-mile/2.900-km circuit, 154.972 miles/249.403 km.
1 Dario Franchitti, GB (Reynard 98I-Honda Turbo V8), 2h 00m 37.871s, 77.081 mph/124.049 km/h.
2 Michael Andretti, USA (Swift 009.c-Ford Cosworth XD), 2h 00m 41.308s; **3** Scott Pruett, USA (Reynard 98I-Ford Cosworth XD), 2h 00m 42.616s; **4** Alessandro 'Alex' Zanardi, I (Reynard 98I-Honda Turbo V8), 2h 00m 42.873s; **5** Al Unser Jr, USA (Penske PC27-Mercedes Benz IC 108E), 2h 00m 51.703s; **6** Mauricio Gugelmin, BR (Reynard 98I-Mercedes Benz IC 108E), 2h 00m 52.804s; **7** Andre Ribeiro, BR (Penske PC27-Mercedes Benz IC 108E), 2h 00m 54.117s; **8** JJ Lehto, SF (Reynard 98I-Mercedes Benz IC 108E), 2h 00m 55.436s; **9** Massimiliano 'Max' Papis, I (Reynard 98I-Toyota), 2h 00m 57.077s; **10** Michel Jourdain Jr, MEX (Reynard 98I-Ford Cosworth XD), 2h 00m 57.486s.
Most laps led: Franchitti, 28.
Fastest qualifying lap: Franchitti, 1m 04.130s, 101.157 mph/162.796 km/h.
Championship points: **1** Zanardi, 218; **2** Vasser, 126; **3** Fernandez, 120; **4** Moore, 118; **5** Franchitti, 110; **6** Andretti, 109.

HONDA GRAND PRIX OF MONTEREY FEATURING THE TEXACO/HAVOLINE 300, Laguna Seca Raceway, Monterey, California, USA, 13 September. Round 16. 83 laps of the 2.238-mile/3.602-km circuit, 185.754 miles/298.942 km.
1 Bryan Herta, USA (Reynard 98I-Ford Cosworth XD), 1h 55m 13.472s, 96.726 mph/155.666 km/h.
2 Alessandro 'Alex' Zanardi, I (Reynard 98I-Honda Turbo V8), 1h 55m 16.815s; **3** Tony Kanaan, BR (Reynard 98I-Honda Turbo V8), 1h 55m 17.251s; **4** Dario Franchitti, GB (Reynard 98I-Honda Turbo V8), 1h 55m 17.874s; **5** Jimmy Vasser, USA (Reynard 98I-Honda Turbo V8), 1h 55m 20.646s; **6** Al Unser Jr, USA (Penske PC27-Mercedes Benz IC 108E), 1h 55m 21.35s; **7** Adrian Fernandez, MEX (Reynard 98I-Ford Cosworth XD), 1h 55m 22.601s; **8** Paul Tracy, CDN (Reynard 98I-Honda Turbo V8), 1h 55m 22.750s; **9** Christian Fittipaldi, BR (Swift 009.c-Ford Cosworth XD), 1h 55m 23.138s; **10** Michael Andretti, USA (Swift 009.c-Ford Cosworth XD), 1h 55m 23.665s.
Most laps led: Herta, 81.
Fastest qualifying lap: Herta, 1m 08.146s, 118.229 mph/190.270 km/h.
Championship points: **1** Zanardi, 234; **2** Vasser, 136; **3** Fernandez, 126; **4** Franchitti, 122; **5** Moore, 118; **6** Andretti, 112.

TEXACO GRAND PRIX OF HOUSTON, Houston Street Circuit, Texas, USA, 4 October. Round 17. 70 laps of the 1.527-mile/2.443-km circuit, 106.250 miles/170.993 km.
1 Dario Franchitti, GB (Reynard 98I-Honda Turbo V8), 1h 36m 30.979s, 66.051 mph/106.299 km/h.
2 Alessandro 'Alex' Zanardi, I (Reynard 98I-Honda Turbo V8), 1h 36m 31.625s; **3** Tony Kanaan, BR (Reynard 98I-Honda Turbo V8), 1h 36m 36.771s; **4** Jimmy Vasser, USA (Reynard 98I-Honda Turbo V8), 1h 36m 39.321s; **5** Massimiliano 'Max' Papis, I (Reynard 98I-Toyota), 1h 36m 42.149s; **6** Adrian Fernandez, MEX (Reynard 98I-Ford Cosworth XD), 1h 36m 44.404s; **7** Al Unser Jr, USA (Penske PC27-Mercedes Benz IC 108E), 1h 36m 48.704s; **8** Bryan Herta, USA (Reynard 98I-Ford Cosworth XD), 1h 36m 57.885s; **9** Richie Hearn, USA (Swift 009.c-Ford Cosworth XD), 1h 36m 58.791s; **10** JJ Lehto, SF (Reynard 98I-Mercedes Benz IC 108E), 1h 37m 06.068s.
Most laps led: Franchitti, 70.
Fastest qualifying lap: Greg Moore, CDN (Reynard 98I-Mercedes Benz IC 108E), 59.508s, 92.377 mph/148.667 km/h.
Championship points: **1** Zanardi, 250; **2** Vasser, 148; **3** Franchitti, 143; **4** Fernandez, 134; **5** Moore, 119; **6** Andretti, 112.

HONDA INDY, Surfers Paradise Street Circuit, Gold Coast, Queensland, Australia, 18 October. Round 18. 62 laps of the 2.795-mile/4.498-km circuit, 173.290 miles/278.883 km.
1 Alessandro 'Alex' Zanardi, I (Reynard 98I-Honda Turbo V8), 2h 01m 51.170s, 85.328 mph/137.321 km/h.
2 Dario Franchitti, GB (Reynard 98I-Honda Turbo V8), 2h 01m 51.492s; **3** Christian Fittipaldi, BR (Swift 009.c-Ford Cosworth XD), 2h 01m 52.199s; **4** Scott Pruett, USA (Reynard 98I-Ford Cosworth XD), 2h 01m 57.558s; **5** JJ Lehto, SF (Reynard 98I-Mercedes Benz IC 108E), 2h 02m 01.962s; **6** Adrian Fernandez, MEX (Reynard 98I-Ford Cosworth XD), 2h 02m 02.323s; **7** Tony Kanaan, BR (Reynard 98I-Honda Turbo V8), 2h 02m 02.850s; **8** Greg Moore, CDN (Reynard 98I-Mercedes Benz IC 108E), 2h 02m 04.962s; **9** Patrick Carpentier, CDN (Reynard 98I-Mercedes Benz IC 108E), 2h 02m 06.991s; **10** Bryan Herta, USA (Reynard 98I-Ford Cosworth XD), 2h 02m 07.190s.
Most laps led: Zanardi, 49.
Fastest qualifying lap: Franchitti, 1m 32.288s, 109.028 mph/175.464 km/h.
Championship points: **1** Zanardi, 271; **2** Franchitti, 160; **3** Vasser, 148; **4** Fernandez, 142; **5** Moore, 124; **6** Pruett, 120.

MARLBORO 500 PRESENTED BY TOYOTA, California Speedway, Fontana, California, USA, 1 November. Round 19. 250 laps of the 2.029-mile/3.265-km circuit, 507.250 miles/816.340 km.
1 Jimmy Vasser, USA (Reynard 98I-Honda Turbo V8), 3h 17m 54.369s, 153.785 mph/247.493 km/h.
2 Greg Moore, CDN (Reynard 98I-Mercedes Benz IC 108E), 3h 17m 54.729s; **3** Alessandro 'Alex' Zanardi, I (Reynard 98I-Honda Turbo V8), 3h 17m 55.486s; **4** Adrian Fernandez, MEX (Reynard 98I-Ford Cosworth XD), 3h 17m 55.506s; **5** Mauricio Gugelmin, BR (Reynard 98I-Mercedes Benz IC 108E), 3h 17m 55.533s; **6** Mark Blundell, GB (Reynard 98I-Mercedes Benz IC 108E), 3h 17m 55.832s; **7** Christian Fittipaldi, BR (Swift 009.c-Ford Cosworth XD), 3h 17m 56.855s; **8** Richie Hearn, USA (Swift 009.c-Ford Cosworth XD), 3h 18m 05.953s; **9** Robby Gordon, USA (Reynard 98I-Toyota), 249 laps; **10** Helio Castro-Neves, BR (Reynard 98I-Mercedes Benz IC 108E), 249.
Most laps led: Vasser, 63.
Fastest qualifying lap: Scott Pruett, USA (Reynard 98I-Ford Cosworth XD), 31.249s, 233.748 mph/376.181 km/h.

Final championship points
1 Alessandro 'Alex' Zanardi, I, 285; **2** Jimmy Vasser, USA, 169; **3** Dario Franchitti, GB, 160; **4** Adrian Fernandez, MEX, 154; **5** Greg Moore, CDN, 140; **6** Scott Pruett, USA, 121; **7** Michael Andretti, USA, 112; **8** Bryan Herta, USA, 97; **9** Tony Kanaan, BR, 92; **10** Bobby Rahal, USA, 82; **11** Al Unser Jr, USA, 72; **12** Gil de Ferran, BR, 67; **13** Paul Tracy, CDN, 61; **14** Christian Fittipaldi, BR, 56; **15** Mauricio Gugelmin, BR, 49; **16** Richie Hearn, USA, 47; **17=** Mark Blundell, GB, 36; **17=** Helio Castro-Neves, BR, 36; **19** Patrick Carpentier, CDN, 27; **20=** JJ Lehto, SF, 25; **20=** Massimiliano 'Max' Papis, I, 25; **22=** Robby Gordon, USA, 13; **22=** Andre Ribeiro, BR, 13; **24** Michel Jourdain Jr, MEX, 5; **25** Arnd Meier, D, 4; **26** P.J. Jones, USA, 3; **27** Alex Barron, USA, 2; **28** Gualter Salles, BR, 1.

Nations' Cup
1 United States, 303; **2** Italy, 285; **3** Brazil, 203; **4** Canada, 181; **5** Scotland, 160; **6** Mexico, 158; **7** England, 36; **8** Finland, 25; **9** Germany, 4; **10** Japan, 0.

Manufacturers' Championship (engines)
1 Honda, 365; **2** Ford Cosworth, 293; **3** Mercedes Benz, 225; **4** Toyota, 41.

Constructors' Championship
1 Reynard, 408; **2** Swift, 167; **3** Penske, 72; **4** Lola, 4; **5** Eagle, 1.

Rookie of the Year
1 Tony Kanaan, BR, 92; **2** Helio Castro-Neves, BR, 36; **3** JJ Lehto, SF, 25; **4** Alex Barron, USA, 2; **5** Vincenzo Sospiri, I, 0.

Marlboro Pole Award
1 Dario Franchitti, GB, 5; **2** Greg Moore, CDN, 4; **3** Bryan Herta, USA, 3; **4=** Jimmy Vasser, USA, 2; **4=** Patrick Carpentier, CDN, 2; **6=** Michael Andretti, USA, 1; **6=** Scott Pruett, USA, 1; **6=** Adrian Fernandez, MEX, 1.

Indy Car race

82nd INDIANAPOLIS 500, Indianapolis Motor Speedway, Speedway, Indiana, USA, 24 May. 200 laps of the 2.500-mile/4.023-km circuit, 500.000 miles/804.672 km.
1 Eddie Cheever Jr, USA (Dallara-Aurora), 3h 26m 40.524s, 145.155 mph/233.605 km/h.
2 Buddy Lazier, USA (Dallara-Aurora), 3h 26m 43.715s; **3** Steve Knapp, USA (G-Force-Aurora), 200 laps; **4** Davey Hamilton, USA (G-Force-Aurora), 199; **5** Robby Unser, USA (Dallara-Aurora), 198; **6** Kenny Bräck, S (Dallara-Aurora), 198; **7** John Paul Jr, USA (Dallara-Aurora), 197; **8** Andy Michner, USA (Dallara-Aurora), 197; **9** J.J. Yeley, USA (Dallara-Aurora), 197; **10** Buzz Calkins, USA (G-Force-Aurora), 195; **11** Jimmy Kite, USA (Dallara-Aurora), 195; **12** Jack Hewitt, USA (G-Force-Aurora), 195; **13** Jeff Ward, USA (G-Force-Aurora), 194; **14** Marco Greco, BR (G-Force-Aurora), 183 (DNF – engine); **15** Mike Groff, USA (G-Force-Infiniti), 183; **16** Scott Sharp, USA (Dallara-Aurora), 181 (DNF – gearbox); **17** Stéphan Grégoire, F (G-Force-Aurora), 172; **18** Greg Ray, USA (Dallara-Aurora), 167 (DNF – gearbox); **19** Raul Boesel, BR (G-Force-Aurora), 164; **20** Arie Luyendyk, NL (G-Force-Aurora), 151 (DNF – gearbox); **21** Dr Jack Miller, USA (Dallara-Infiniti), 128; **22** Roberto Guerrero, USA (Dallara-Aurora), 125; **23** Billy Boat, USA (Dallara-Aurora), 111 (DNF – drive line); **24** Scott Goodyear, CDN (G-Force-Aurora), 100 (DNF – clutch); **25** Johnny Unser, USA (Dallara-Aurora), 98 (DNF – engine); **26** Sam Schmidt, USA (Dallara-Aurora), 48 (DNF – accident); **27** Mark Dismore, USA (Dallara-Aurora), 48 (DNF – accident); **28** Stan Wattles, USA (Riley & Scott-Aurora), 48 (DNF – accident); **29** Jim Guthrie, USA (G-Force-Aurora), 48 (DNF – accident); **30** Billy Roe, USA (Dallara-Aurora), 48 (DNF – accident); **31** Robbie Buhl, USA (Dallara-Aurora), 44 (DNF – engine); **32** Donnie Beechler, USA (G-Force-Aurora), 34 (DNF – engine); **33** Tony Stewart, USA (Dallara-Aurora), 22 (DNF – engine).
(Engines: Aurora = Oldsmobile; Infiniti = Nissan)
Most laps led: Cheever, 76.
Fastest race lap: Stewart, 41.91s, 214.746 mph/345.600 km/h.
Fastest leading lap: Cheever, 42.075s, 213.904 mph/344.245 km/h.
Pole position/Fastest qualifying lap: Boat, 2m 41.072s, 223.503 mph/359.695 km/h (over four laps).
Rookie of the Year: Steve Knapp.

NASCAR Winston Cup

1997 Results

The Phoenix and Atlanta races were run after Autocourse 1997/98 *went to press.*

DURA LUBE 500 PRESENTED BY K MART, Phoenix International Raceway, Arizona, USA, 2 November. Round 31. 312 laps of the 1.000-mile/1.609-km circuit, 312.000 miles/502.115 km.
1 Dale Jarrett, USA (Ford Thunderbird), 2h 48m 55.0s, 110.824 mph/178.354 km/h.
2 Rusty Wallace, USA (Ford Thunderbird), 2h 48m 57.105s; **3** Bobby Hamilton, USA (Pontiac Grand Prix), 312 laps; **4** Ken Schrader, USA (Chevrolet Monte Carlo), 312; **5** Dale Earnhardt, USA (Chevrolet Monte Carlo), 312; **6** Mark Martin, USA (Ford Thunderbird), 312; **7** Johnny Benson Jr, USA (Pontiac Grand Prix), 312; **8** Steve Grissom, USA (Chevrolet Monte Carlo), 311; **9** Kyle Petty, USA (Pontiac Grand Prix), 311; **10** Geoff Bodine, USA (Ford Thunderbird), 311.
Fastest qualifying lap: Jimmy Spencer, USA (Ford Thunderbird), 27.495s, 130.933 mph/210.716 km/h.
Drivers' championship points: **1** Gordon, 4598; **2** Jarrett, 4521; **3** Martin, 4511; **4** Burton (Jeff), 4224; **5** Earnhardt, 4096; **6** Labonte (Terry), 4077.

NAPA 500, Atlanta Motor Speedway, Hampton, Georgia, USA, 16 November. Round 32. 325 laps of the 1.540-mile/2.478-km circuit, 500.500 miles/805.477 km.
1 Bobby Labonte, USA (Pontiac Grand Prix), 3h 07m 48.0s, 159.904 mph/257.341 km/h.
2 Dale Jarrett, USA (Ford Thunderbird), 3h 07m 51.801s; **3** Mark Martin, USA (Ford Thunderbird), 325 laps; **4** Jeff Green, USA (Chevrolet Monte Carlo), 325; **5** Derrike Cope, USA (Pontiac Grand Prix), 325; **6** Kyle Petty, USA (Pontiac Grand Prix), 324; **7** Bobby Hamilton, USA (Pontiac Grand Prix), 324; **8** Joe Nemechek, USA (Chevrolet Monte Carlo), 324; **9** Ward Burton, USA (Pontiac Grand Prix), 323; **10** Johnny Benson Jr, USA (Pontiac Grand Prix), 323.
Fastest qualifying lap: Geoff Bodine, USA (Ford Thunderbird), 28.074s, 197.478 mph/317.810 km/h.

Final championship points
Drivers
1 Jeff Gordon, USA, 4710; **2** Dale Jarrett, USA, 4696; **3** Mark Martin, USA, 4681; **4** Jeff Burton, USA, 4285; **5** Dale Earnhardt, USA, 4216; **6** Terry Labonte, USA, 4177; **7** Bobby Labonte, USA, 4101; **8** Bill Elliott, USA, 3836; **9** Rusty Wallace, USA, 3598; **10** Ken Schrader, USA, 3576; **11** Johnny Benson Jr, USA, 3575; **12** Ted Musgrave, USA, 3556; **13** Jeremy Mayfield, USA, 3547; **14** Ernie Irvan, USA, 3534; **15** Kyle Petty, USA, 3455; **16** Bobby Hamilton, USA, 3450; **17** Ricky Rudd, USA, 3330; **18** Michael Waltrip, USA, 3173; **19** Ricky Craven, USA, 3108; **20** Jimmy Spencer, USA, 3079; **21** Steve Grissom, USA, 3061; **22** Geoff Bodine, USA, 3046; **23** John Andretti, USA, 3019; **24** Ward Burton, USA, 2987; **25** Sterling Marlin, USA, 2954; **26** Darrell Waltrip, USA, 2942; **27** Derrike Cope, USA, 2901; **28** Joe Nemechek, USA, 2754; **29** Brett Bodine, USA, 2716; **30** Mike Skinner, USA, 2669.

Manufacturers
1 Ford; **2** Chevrolet; **3** Pontiac.

Rookie of The Year: Mike Skinner.
Busch Pole Award Winner: Mark Martin.

1998 Results

DAYTONA 500, Daytona International Speedway, Daytona Beach, Florida, USA, 15 February. Round 1. 200 laps of the 2.500-mile/4.023-km circuit, 500.000 miles/804.672 km.
1 Dale Earnhardt, USA (Chevrolet Monte Carlo), 2h 53m 42.0s, 172.712 mph/277.952 km/h.
2 Bobby Labonte, USA (Pontiac Grand Prix), 200 laps (under caution); **3** Jeremy Mayfield, USA (Ford Taurus), 200; **4** Ken Schrader, USA (Chevrolet Monte Carlo), 200; **5** Rusty Wallace, USA (Ford Taurus), 200; **6** Ernie Irvan, USA (Pontiac Grand Prix), 200; **7** Chad Little, USA (Ford Taurus), 200; **8** Mike Skinner, USA (Chevrolet Monte Carlo), 200; **9** Michael Waltrip, USA (Ford Taurus), 200; **10** Bill Elliott, USA (Ford Taurus), 200.
Fastest qualifying lap: Labonte (Bobby), 46.774s, 192.415 mph/309.661 km/h.
Drivers' championship points: 1 Earnhardt, 185; **2** Labonte (Bobby), 175; **3** Mayfield, 165; **4** Schrader, 160; **5** Wallace (Rusty), 160; **6** Irvan, 150.

GM GOODWRENCH SERVICE PLUS 400, North Carolina Motor Speedway, Rockingham, North Carolina, USA, 22 February. Round 2. 393 laps of the 1.017-mile/1.637-km circuit, 399.681 miles/643.224 km.
1 Jeff Gordon, USA (Chevrolet Monte Carlo), 3h 24m 51.0s, 117.065 mph/188.399 km/h.
2 Rusty Wallace, USA (Ford Taurus), 3h 24m 52.281s; **3** Mark Martin, USA (Ford Taurus), 393 laps; **4** Jimmy Spencer, USA (Ford Taurus), 393; **5** Geoff Bodine, USA (Ford Taurus), 393; **6** Bill Elliott, USA (Ford Taurus), 393; **7** Dale Jarrett, USA (Ford Taurus), 393; **8** Terry Labonte, USA (Chevrolet Monte Carlo), 393; **9** Bobby Hamilton, USA (Chevrolet Monte Carlo), 393; **10** Ricky Craven, USA (Chevrolet Monte Carlo), 393.
Fastest qualifying lap: Rick Mast, USA (Ford Taurus), 23.415s, 156.361 mph/251.639 km/h.
Drivers' championship points: 1 Wallace (Rusty), 335; **2** Earnhardt, 302; **3** Gordon, 300; **4** Mayfield, 291; **5** Elliott, 289; **6** Spencer, 278.

LAS VEGAS 400, Las Vegas Motor Speedway, Nevada, USA, 1 March. Round 3. 267 laps of the 1.500-mile/2.414-km circuit, 400.500 miles/644.542 km.
1 Mark Martin, USA (Ford Taurus), 2h 43m 58.0s, 146.554 mph/235.856 km/h.
2 Jeff Burton, USA (Ford Taurus), 2h 43m 59.605s; **3** Rusty Wallace, USA (Ford Taurus), 267 laps; **4** Johnny Benson Jr, USA (Ford Taurus), 267; **5** Jeremy Mayfield, USA (Ford Taurus), 267; **6** Ted Musgrave, USA (Ford Taurus), 267; **7** Jimmy Spencer, USA (Ford Taurus), 267; **8** Dale Earnhardt, USA (Chevrolet Monte Carlo), 267; **9** Bill Elliott, USA (Ford Taurus), 267; **10** Chad Little, USA (Ford Taurus), 267.
Fastest qualifying lap: Jarrett, 32.100s, 168.224 mph/270.731 km/h.
Drivers' championship points: 1 Wallace (Rusty), 505; **2** Earnhardt, 449; **3** Mayfield, 446; **4** Spencer, 429; **5** Elliott, 427; **6** Gordon, 412.

PRIMESTAR 500, Atlanta Motor Speedway, Hampton, Georgia, USA, 9 March. Round 4. 325 laps of the 1.540-mile/2.478-km circuit, 500.500 miles/805.477 km.
Scheduled for 8 March but postponed by a day due to rain.
1 Bobby Labonte, USA (Pontiac Grand Prix), 3h 35m 16s, 139.501 mph/224.506 km/h.
2 Dale Jarrett, USA (Ford Taurus), 325 laps (under caution); **3** Jeremy Mayfield, USA (Ford Taurus), 325; **4** Rusty Wallace, USA (Ford Taurus), 325; **5** Kenny Irwin Jr, USA (Ford Taurus), 325; **6** Dick Trickle, USA (Ford Taurus), 325; **7** Kenny Wallace, USA (Ford Taurus), 325; **8** Jeff Burton, USA (Ford Taurus), 325; **9** Johnny Benson Jr, USA (Ford Taurus), 324; **10** Todd Bodine, USA (Pontiac Grand Prix), 324.
Fastest qualifying lap: Bodine (Todd), 28.749s, 192.841 mph/310.348 km/h.
Drivers' championship points: 1 Wallace (Rusty), 665; **2** Mayfield, 616; **3** Earnhardt, 578; **4** Elliott, 557; **5** Labonte (Terry), 526; **6** Labonte (Bobby), 525.

TRANSOUTH FINANCIAL 400, Darlington Raceway, South Carolina, USA, 22 March. Round 5. 293 laps of the 1.366-mile/2.198-km circuit, 400.238 miles/644.121 km.
1 Dale Jarrett, USA (Ford Taurus), 3h 07m 40s, 127.962 mph/205.936 km/h.
2 Jeff Gordon, USA (Chevrolet Monte Carlo), 3h 07m 40.228s; **3** Rusty Wallace, USA (Ford Taurus), 293 laps; **4** Jeremy Mayfield, USA (Ford Taurus), 293; **5** Jeff Burton, USA (Ford Taurus), 293; **6** Terry Labonte, USA (Chevrolet Monte Carlo), 293; **7** Mark Martin, USA (Ford Taurus), 293; **8** Johnny Benson Jr, USA (Ford Taurus), 293; **9** Kenny Wallace, USA (Ford Taurus), 293; **10** Ted Musgrave, USA (Ford Taurus), 292.
Fastest qualifying lap: Martin, 29.156s, 168.665 mph/271.440 km/h.
Drivers' championship points: 1 Wallace (Rusty), 835, **2** Mayfield, 781; **3** Earnhardt, 705; **4** Gordon, 688; **5** Elliott, 680; **6** Labonte (Terry), 676.

FOOD CITY 500, Bristol Motor Speedway, Tennessee, USA, 29 March. Round 6. 500 laps of the 0.533-mile/0.858-km circuit, 266.500 miles/428.890 km.
1 Jeff Gordon, USA (Chevrolet Monte Carlo), 3h 13m 00.0s, 82.850 mph/133.334 km/h.
2 Terry Labonte, USA (Chevrolet Monte Carlo), 3h 13m 00.583s; **3** Dale Jarrett, USA (Ford Taurus), 500 laps; **4** Jeff Burton, USA (Ford Taurus), 500; **5** Johnny Benson Jr, USA (Ford Taurus), 500; **6** Ken Schrader, USA (Chevrolet Monte Carlo), 500; **7** Mark Martin, USA (Ford Taurus), 500; **8** Ted Musgrave, USA (Ford Taurus), 500; **9** Michael Waltrip, USA (Ford Taurus), 500; **10** Randy Lajoie, USA (Chevrolet Monte Carlo), 499.
Fastest qualifying lap: Rusty Wallace, USA (Ford Taurus), 15.440s, 124.275 mph/200.001 km/h.
Drivers' championship points: 1 Wallace (Rusty), 909; **2** Mayfield, 908; **3** Gordon, 868; **4** Labonte (Terry), 851; **5** Elliott, 803; **6** Earnhardt, 802.

TEXAS 500, Texas Motor Speedway, Fort Worth, Texas, USA, 5 April. Round 7. 334 laps of the 1.500-mile/2.414-km circuit, 501.000 miles/806.281 km.
1 Mark Martin, USA (Ford Taurus), 3h 39m 47.0s, 136.771 mph/220.112 km/h.
2 Chad Little, USA (Ford Taurus), 3h 39m 47.573s; **3** Robert Pressley, USA (Ford Taurus), 334 laps; **4** Joe Nemechek, USA (Chevrolet Monte Carlo), 334; **5** Johnny Benson Jr, USA (Ford Taurus), 334; **6** Terry Labonte, USA (Chevrolet Monte Carlo), 334; **7** Jimmy Spencer, USA (Ford Taurus), 334; **8** Bobby Labonte, USA (Pontiac Grand Prix), 334; **9** Michael Waltrip, USA (Ford Taurus), 334; **10** Steve Grissom, USA (Chevrolet Monte Carlo), 334.
Fastest qualifying lap: Mayfield, 29.047s, 185.906 mph/299.186 km/h.
Drivers' championship points: 1 Wallace (Rusty), 1036; **2** Mayfield, 1012; **3** Labonte (Terry), 1001; **4** Martin, 979; **5** Gordon, 938; **6** Elliott, 927.

GOODY'S HEADACHE POWDER 500, Martinsville Speedway, Virginia, USA, 20 April. Round 8. 500 laps of the 0.526-mile/0.847-km circuit, 263.000 miles/423.257 km.
Scheduled for 19 April but postponed by a day due to rain.
1 Bobby Hamilton, USA (Chevrolet Monte Carlo), 3h 43m 10.0s, 70.709 mph/113.796 km/h.
2 Ted Musgrave, USA (Ford Taurus), 3h 43m 16.376s; **3** Dale Jarrett, USA (Ford Taurus), 500 laps; **4** Dale Earnhardt, USA (Chevrolet Monte Carlo), 500; **5** Randy Lajoie, USA (Chevrolet Monte Carlo), 500; **6** Rusty Wallace, USA (Ford Taurus), 500; **7** Jeremy Mayfield, USA (Ford Taurus), 499; **8** Jeff Gordon, USA (Chevrolet Monte Carlo), 499; **9** Ernie Irvan, USA (Pontiac Grand Prix), 499; **10** Ken Schrader, USA (Chevrolet Monte Carlo), 499.
Fastest qualifying lap: Hamilton, 20.323s, 93.175 mph/149.951 km/h.
Drivers' championship points: 1 Wallace (Rusty), 1191; **2** Mayfield, 1158; **3** Labonte (Terry), 1086; **4=** Gordon, 1085; **4=** Jarrett, 1085; **6** Martin, 1055.

DIEHARD 500, Talladega Superspeedway, Alabama, USA, 25 April. Round 9. 188 laps of the 2.660-mile/4.281-km circuit, 500.080 miles/804.801 km.
1 Bobby Labonte, USA (Pontiac Grand Prix), 3h 30m 40.0s, 142.428 mph/229.215 km/h.
2 Jimmy Spencer, USA (Ford Taurus), 3h 30m 40.167s; **3** Dale Jarrett, USA (Ford Taurus), 188 laps; **4** Terry Labonte, USA (Chevrolet Monte Carlo), 188; **5** Jeff Gordon, USA (Chevrolet Monte Carlo), 188; **6** Ernie Irvan, USA (Pontiac Grand Prix), 188; **7** Kenny Wallace, USA (Ford Taurus), 188; **8** Ward Burton, USA (Pontiac Grand Prix), 188; **9** Sterling Marlin, USA (Chevrolet Monte Carlo), 188; **10** Randy Lajoie, USA (Chevrolet Monte Carlo), 188.
Fastest qualifying lap: Labonte (Bobby), 48.925s, 195.728 mph/314.994 km/h.
Drivers' championship points: 1 Wallace (Rusty), 1318; **2** Mayfield, 1282; **3** Labonte (Terry), 1256; **4** Jarrett, 1255; **5** Gordon, 1245; **6** Martin, 1149.

CALIFORNIA 500 PRESENTED BY NAPA, California Speedway, Fontana, California, USA, 3 May. Round 10. 250 laps of the 2.000-mile/3.219-km circuit, 500.000 miles/804.672 km.
1 Mark Martin, USA (Ford Taurus), 3h 33m 57.0s, 140.220 mph/225.662 km/h.
2 Jeremy Mayfield, USA (Ford Taurus), 3h 33m 58.287s; **3** Terry Labonte, USA (Chevrolet Monte Carlo), 250 laps; **4** Jeff Gordon, USA (Chevrolet Monte Carlo), 250; **5** Darrell Waltrip, USA (Chevrolet Monte Carlo), 250; **6** Chad Little, USA (Ford Taurus), 250; **7** Geoff Bodine, USA (Ford Taurus), 250; **8** Johnny Benson Jr, USA (Ford Taurus), 250; **9** Dale Earnhardt, USA (Chevrolet Monte Carlo), 250; **10** Jeff Burton, USA (Ford Taurus), 250.
Fastest qualifying lap: Gordon, 39.610s, 181.772 mph/292.534 km/h.
Drivers' championship points: 1 Mayfield, 1457; **2** Labonte (Terry), 1421; **3** Gordon, 1410; **4** Wallace (Rusty), 1384; **5** Martin, 1334; **6** Jarrett, 1295.

COCA-COLA 600, Charlotte Motor Speedway, Concord, North Carolina, USA, 24 May. Round 11. 400 laps of the 1.500-mile/2.414-km circuit, 600.000 miles/965.606 km.
1 Jeff Gordon, USA (Chevrolet Monte Carlo), 4h 23m 53.0s, 136.424 mph/219.553 km/h.
2 Rusty Wallace, USA (Ford Taurus), 4h 23m 53.410s; **3** Bobby Labonte, USA (Pontiac Grand Prix), 400 laps; **4** Mark Martin, USA (Ford Taurus), 400; **5** Dale Jarrett, USA (Ford Taurus), 400; **6** Joe Nemechek, USA (Chevrolet Monte Carlo), 400; **7** John Andretti, USA (Pontiac Grand Prix), 400; **8** Jeff Burton, USA (Ford Taurus), 400; **9** Johnny Benson Jr, USA (Ford Taurus), 400; **10** Ken Schrader, USA (Chevrolet Monte Carlo), 400.
Fastest qualifying lap: Gordon, 29.512s, 182.976 mph/294.472 km/h.
Drivers' championship points: 1 Gordon, 1590; **2** Mayfield, 1563; **3** Wallace (Rusty), 1559; **4** Martin, 1504; **5** Labonte (Terry), 1461; **6** Jarrett, 1455.

MBNA PLATINUM 400, Dover Downs International Speedway, Dover, Delaware, USA, 31 May. Round 12. 400 laps of the 1.000-mile/1.609-km circuit, 400.000 miles/643.738 km.
1 Dale Jarrett, USA (Ford Taurus), 3h 20m 48.0s, 119.522 mph/192.352 km/h.
2 Jeff Burton, USA (Ford Taurus), 3h 21m 01.117s; **3** Jeff Gordon, USA (Chevrolet Monte Carlo), 400 laps; **4** Bobby Labonte, USA (Pontiac Grand Prix), 400; **5** Jeremy Mayfield, USA (Ford Taurus), 400; **6** Ricky Rudd, USA (Ford Taurus), 400; **7** Mark Martin, USA (Ford Taurus), 400; **8** Buckshot Jones, USA (Chevrolet Monte Carlo), 400; **9** Ernie Irvan, USA (Pontiac Grand Prix), 400; **10** Terry Labonte, USA (Chevrolet Monte Carlo), 400.
Fastest qualifying lap: Wallace (Rusty), 23.092s, 155.898 mph/250.894 km/h.
Drivers' championship points: 1 Gordon, 1765; **2** Mayfield, 1718; **3** Wallace (Rusty), 1673; **4** Martin, 1655; **5** Jarrett, 1635; **6** Labonte (Terry), 1595.

PONTIAC EXCITEMENT 400, Richmond International Raceway, Virginia, USA, 6 June. Round 13. 400 laps of the 0.750-mile/1.207-km circuit, 300.000 miles/482.803 km.
1 Terry Labonte, USA (Chevrolet Monte Carlo), 3h 05m 29.0s, 97.044 mph/156.177 km/h.
2 Dale Jarrett, USA (Ford Taurus), 3h 05m 29.1s (under caution); **3** Rusty Wallace, USA (Ford Taurus), 400 laps; **4** Ken Schrader, USA (Chevrolet Monte Carlo), 400; **5** Mark Martin, USA (Ford Taurus), 400; **6** Jeremy Mayfield, USA (Ford Taurus), 400; **7** Jeff Burton, USA (Ford Taurus), 400; **8** Bobby Labonte, USA (Pontiac Grand Prix), 400; **9** Kenny Irwin Jr, USA (Ford Taurus), 400; **10** Sterling Marlin, USA (Chevrolet Monte Carlo), 400.
Fastest qualifying lap: Gordon, 21.504s, 125.558 mph/202.066 km/h.
Drivers' championship points: 1 Mayfield, 1868; **2** Wallace (Rusty), 1843; **3** Gordon, 1822; **4=** Jarrett, 1815; **4=** Martin, 1815; **6** Labonte (Terry), 1775.

MILLER LITE 400, Michigan Speedway, Brooklyn, Michigan, USA, 14 June. Round 14. 200 laps of the 2.000-mile/3.219-km circuit, 400.000 miles/643.738 km.
1 Mark Martin, USA (Ford Taurus), 2h 31m 14.0s, 158.695 mph/255.395 km/h.
2 Dale Jarrett, USA (Ford Taurus), 2h 31m 16.30s; **3** Jeff Gordon, USA (Chevrolet Monte Carlo), 200 laps; **4** Jeff Burton, USA (Ford Taurus), 200; **5** Jeremy Mayfield, USA (Ford Taurus), 200; **6** Bill Elliott, USA (Ford Taurus), 200; **7** Bobby Labonte, USA (Pontiac Grand Prix), 200; **8** Ward Burton, USA (Pontiac Grand Prix), 200; **9** Joe Nemechek, USA (Chevrolet Monte Carlo), 200; **10** Wally Dallenbach Jr, USA (Chevrolet Monte Carlo), 200.
Fastest qualifying lap: Burton (Ward), 39.656s, 181.561 mph/292.195 km/h.
Drivers' championship points: 1 Mayfield, 2023; **2** Gordon, 1997; **3** Martin, 1995; **4** Jarrett, 1990; **5** Wallace (Rusty), 1955; **6** Labonte (Terry), 1881.

POCONO 500, Pocono Raceway, Long Pond, Pennsylvania, USA, 21 June. Round 15. 200 laps of the 2.500-mile/4.023-km circuit, 500.000 miles/804.672 km.
1 Jeremy Mayfield, USA (Ford Taurus), 4h 14m 39.0s, 117.809 mph/189.595 km/h.
2 Jeff Gordon, USA (Chevrolet Monte Carlo), 4h 14m 39.34s; **3** Dale Jarrett, USA (Ford Taurus), 200 laps; **4** Jeff Burton, USA (Ford Taurus), 200; **5** Mark Martin, USA (Ford Taurus), 200; **6** Darrell Waltrip, USA (Chevrolet Monte Carlo), 200; **7** Wally Dallenbach Jr, USA (Chevrolet Monte Carlo), 200; **8** Dale Earnhardt, USA (Chevrolet Monte Carlo), 200; **9** Sterling Marlin, USA (Chevrolet Monte Carlo), 200; **10** Jimmy Spencer, USA (Ford Taurus), 200.
Fastest qualifying lap: Gordon, 53.558s, 168.042 mph/270.438 km/h.
Drivers' championship points: 1 Mayfield, 2208; **2** Gordon, 2172; **3** Jarrett, 2160; **4** Martin, 2155; **5** Labonte (Terry), 2008; **6** Wallace (Rusty), 1992.

SAVE MART/KRAGEN 350, Sears Point Raceway, Sonoma, California, USA, 28 June. Round 16. 112 laps of the 1.949-mile/3.137-km circuit, 218.288 miles/351.300 km.
1 Jeff Gordon, USA (Chevrolet Monte Carlo), 3h 00m 56.0s, 72.387 mph/116.496 km/h.
2 Bobby Hamilton, USA (Chevrolet Monte Carlo), 3h 00m 58.748s; **3** John Andretti, USA (Pontiac Grand Prix), 112 laps; **4** Bobby Labonte, USA (Pontiac Grand Prix), 112; **5** Rusty Wallace, USA (Ford Taurus), 112; **6** Mark Martin, USA (Ford Taurus), 112; **7** Sterling Marlin, USA (Chevrolet Monte Carlo), 112; **8** Rick Mast, USA (Ford Taurus), 112; **9** Kenny Irwin Jr, USA (Ford Taurus), 112; **10** Steve Grissom, USA (Chevrolet Monte Carlo), 112.
Fastest qualifying lap: Gordon, 1m 11.080s, 98.711 mph/158.860 km/h.
Drivers' championship points: 1 Gordon, 2357; **2** Mayfield, 2317; **3** Martin, 2305; **4** Jarrett, 2283; **5** Wallace (Rusty), 2147; **6** Labonte (Bobby), 2070.

JIFFY LUBE 300, New Hampshire International Speedway, Loudon, New Hampshire, USA, 12 July. Round 17. 300 laps of the 1.058-mile/1.703-km circuit, 317.400 miles/510.806 km.
1 Jeff Burton, USA (Ford Taurus), 3h 04m 54.0s, 102.996 mph/165.756 km/h.
2 Mark Martin, USA (Ford Taurus), 3h 05m 01.439s; **3** Jeff Gordon, USA (Chevrolet Monte Carlo), 300 laps; **4** Rusty Wallace, USA (Ford Taurus), 300; **5** Mike Skinner, USA (Chevrolet Monte Carlo), 300; **6** John Andretti, USA (Pontiac Grand Prix), 300; **7** Dale Jarrett, USA (Ford Taurus), 300; **8** Kyle Petty, USA (Pontiac Grand Prix), 300; **9** Ken Schrader, USA (Chevrolet Monte Carlo), 300; **10** Kenny Wallace, USA (Ford Taurus), 300.
Fastest qualifying lap: Ricky Craven, USA (Chevrolet Monte Carlo), 29.665s, 128.394 mph/206.630 km/h.
Drivers' championship points: 1 Gordon, 2527; **2** Martin, 2475; **3** Jarrett, 2429; **4** Mayfield, 2390; **5** Wallace (Rusty), 2307; **6** Labonte (Bobby), 2205.

PENNSYLVANIA 500, Pocono Raceway, Long Pond, Pennsylvania, USA, 26 July. Round 18. 200 laps of the 2.500-mile/4.023-km circuit, 500.000 miles/804.672 km.
1 Jeff Gordon, USA (Chevrolet Monte Carlo), 3h 42m 47.0s, 134.660 mph/216.714 km/h.
2 Mark Martin, USA (Ford Taurus), 3h 42m 48.153s; **3** Jeff Burton, USA (Ford Taurus), 200 laps; **4** Bobby Labonte, USA (Pontiac Grand Prix), 200; **5** Dale Jarrett, USA (Ford Taurus), 200; **6** Rusty Wallace, USA (Ford Taurus), 200; **7** Dale Earnhardt, USA (Chevrolet Monte Carlo), 200; **8** Ken Schrader, USA (Chevrolet Monte Carlo), 200; **9** Ernie Irvan, USA (Pontiac Grand Prix), 200; **10** Michael Waltrip, USA (Ford Taurus), 200.
Fastest qualifying lap: Ward Burton, USA (Pontiac Grand Prix), 53.316s, 168.805 mph/271.665 km/h.
Drivers' championship points: 1 Gordon, 2712; **2** Martin, 2650; **3** Jarrett, 2584; **4** Mayfield, 2499; **5** Wallace (Rusty), 2462; **6** Labonte (Bobby), 2365.

BRICKYARD 400, Indianapolis Motor Speedway, Speedway, Indiana, USA, 1 August. Round 19. 160 laps of the 2.500-mile/4.023-km circuit, 400.000 miles/643.738 km.
1 Jeff Gordon, USA (Chevrolet Monte Carlo), 3h 09m 19.0s, 126.772 mph/204.019 km/h.
2 Mark Martin, USA (Ford Taurus), 160 laps (under caution); **3** Bobby Labonte, USA (Pontiac Grand Prix), 160; **4** Mike Skinner, USA (Chevrolet Monte Carlo), 160; **5** Dale Earnhardt, USA (Chevrolet Monte Carlo), 160; **6** Ernie Irvan, USA (Pontiac Grand Prix), 160; **7** John Andretti, USA (Pontiac Grand Prix), 160; **8** Rusty Wallace, USA (Ford Taurus), 160; **9** Terry Labonte, USA (Chevrolet Monte Carlo), 160; **10** Ken Schrader, USA (Chevrolet Monte Carlo), 160.
Fastest qualifying lap: Irvan, 50.169s, 179.394 mph/288.706 km/h.
Drivers' championship points: 1 Gordon, 2897; **2** Martin, 2825; **3** Jarrett, 2704; **4** Wallace (Rusty), 2604; **5** Mayfield, 2536; **6** Labonte (Bobby), 2530.

THE BUD AT THE GLEN, Watkins Glen International, New York, USA, 9 August. Round 20. 90 laps of the 2.450-mile/3.943-km circuit, 220.500 miles/354.860 km.
1 Jeff Gordon, USA (Chevrolet Monte Carlo), 2h 20m 03.0s, 94.466 mph/152.029 km/h.
2 Mark Martin, USA (Ford Taurus), 2h 20m 06.437s; **3** Mike Skinner, USA (Chevrolet Monte Carlo), 90 laps; **4** Rusty Wallace, USA (Ford Taurus), 90; **5** Dale Jarrett, USA (Ford Taurus), 90; **6** Kyle Petty, USA (Pontiac Grand Prix), 90; **7** Sterling Marlin, USA (Chevrolet Monte Carlo), 90; **8** John Andretti, USA (Pontiac Grand Prix), 90; **9** Johnny Benson Jr, USA (Ford Taurus), 90; **10** Bobby Labonte, USA (Pontiac Grand Prix), 90.
Fastest qualifying lap: Gordon, 1m 13.298s, 120.331 mph/193.653 km/h.
Drivers' championship points: 1 Gordon, 3082; **2** Martin, 3000; **3** Jarrett, 2859; **4** Wallace (Rusty), 2769; **5** Labonte (Bobby), 2664; **6** Mayfield, 2606.

PEPSI 400 PRESENTED BY DEVILBISS, Michigan Speedway, Brooklyn, Michigan, USA, 16 August. Round 21. 200 laps of the 2.000-mile/3.219-km circuit, 400.000 miles/643.738 km.
1 Jeff Gordon, USA (Chevrolet Monte Carlo), 2h 37m 54.0s, 151.995 mph/244.612 km/h.
2 Bobby Labonte, USA (Pontiac Grand Prix), 2h 37m 55.826s; **3** Dale Jarrett, USA (Ford Taurus), 200 laps; **4** Mark Martin, USA (Ford Taurus), 200; **5** Jeff Burton, USA (Ford Taurus), 200; **6** Ernie Irvan, USA (Pontiac Grand Prix), 200; **7** Jeremy Mayfield, USA (Ford Taurus), 200; **8** Wally Dallenbach Jr, USA (Chevrolet Monte Carlo), 200; **9** John Andretti, USA (Pontiac Grand Prix), 200; **10** Chad Little, USA (Ford Taurus), 200.
Fastest qualifying lap: Irvan, 39.255s, 183.416 mph/295.180 km/h.
Drivers' championship points: 1 Gordon, 3262; **2** Martin, 3165; **3** Jarrett, 3029; **4** Wallace (Rusty), 2863; **5** Labonte (Bobby), 2839; **6** Mayfield, 2752.

GOODY'S HEADACHE POWDER 500, Bristol Motor Speedway, Tennessee, USA, 22 August. Round 22. 500 laps of the 0.533-mile/0.858-km circuit, 266.500 miles/428.890 km.
1 Mark Martin, USA (Ford Taurus), 3h 03m 54.0s, 86.949 mph/139.932 km/h.
2 Jeff Burton, USA (Ford Taurus), 3h 03m 56.185s; **3** Rusty Wallace, USA (Ford Taurus), 500 laps; **4** Dale Jarrett, USA (Ford Taurus), 500; **5** Jeff Gordon, USA (Chevrolet Monte Carlo), 500; **6** Dale Earnhardt, USA (Chevrolet Monte Carlo), 500; **7** Mike Skinner, USA (Chevrolet Monte Carlo), 500; **8** Jeremy Mayfield, USA (Ford Taurus), 500; **9** Ricky Rudd, USA (Ford Taurus), 500; **10** Kevin Lepage, USA (Ford Taurus), 500.
Fastest qualifying lap: Wallace, 15.530s, 123.554 mph/198.842 km/h.
Drivers' championship points: 1 Gordon, 3417; **2** Martin, 3350; **3** Jarrett, 3194; **4** Wallace (Rusty), 3033; **5** Labonte (Bobby), 2932; **6** Mayfield, 2899.

FARM AID ON CMT 300, New Hampshire International Speedway, Loudon, New Hampshire, USA, 30 August. Round 23. 300 laps of the 1.058-mile/1.703-km circuit, 317.400 miles/510.806 km.
1 Jeff Gordon, USA (Chevrolet Monte Carlo), 2h 49m 55.0s, 112.078 mph/180.373 km/h.
2 Mark Martin, USA (Ford Taurus), 2h 49m 55.664s; **3** John Andretti, USA (Pontiac Grand Prix), 300 laps; **4** Dale Jarrett, USA (Ford Taurus), 300; **5** Jeff Burton, USA (Ford Taurus), 300; **6** Kenny Wallace, USA (Ford Taurus), 300; **7** Bobby Labonte, USA (Pontiac Grand Prix), 300; **8** Rusty Wallace, USA (Ford Taurus), 300; **9** Dale Earnhardt, USA (Chevrolet Monte Carlo), 300; **10** Ricky Rudd, USA (Ford Taurus), 300.
Fastest qualifying lap: Gordon, 29.518s, 129.033 mph/207.659 km/h.
Drivers' championship points: 1 Gordon, 3597; **2** Martin, 3530; **3** Jarrett, 3359; **4** Wallace (Rusty), 3175; **5** Labonte (Bobby), 3083; **6** Mayfield, 3002.

PEPSI SOUTHERN 500, Darlington Raceway, South Carolina, USA, 6 September. Round 24. 367 laps of the 1.366-mile/2.198-km circuit, 501.322 miles/806.800 km.
1 Jeff Gordon, USA (Chevrolet Monte Carlo), 3h 36m 21.0s, 139.031 mph/223.748 km/h.
2 Jeff Burton, USA (Ford Taurus), 3h 36m 24.631s; **3** Dale Jarrett, USA (Ford Taurus), 367 laps; **4** Dale Earnhardt, USA (Chevrolet Monte Carlo), 367; **5** Jeremy Mayfield, USA (Ford Taurus), 366; **6** Ernie Irvan, USA (Pontiac Grand Prix), 365; **7** Rusty Wallace, USA (Ford Taurus), 365; **8** Sterling Marlin, USA (Chevrolet Monte Carlo), 365; **9** Geoff Bodine, USA (Ford Taurus), 364; **10** Kenny Wallace, USA (Ford Taurus), 364.
Fastest qualifying lap: Jarrett, 29.119s, 168.879 mph/271.785 km/h.
Drivers' championship points: 1 Gordon, 3777; **2** Martin, 3578; **3** Jarrett, 3529; **4** Wallace (Rusty), 3326; **5** Labonte (Bobby), 3201; **6** Mayfield, 3157.

EXIDE NASCAR SELECT BATTERIES 400, Richmond International Raceway, Virginia, USA, 12 September. Round 25. 400 laps of the 0.750-mile/1.207-km circuit, 300.000 miles/482.803 km.
1 Jeff Burton, USA (Ford Taurus), 3h 15m 41.0s, 91.985 mph/148.036 km/h.
2 Jeff Gordon, USA (Chevrolet Monte Carlo), 3h 15m 41.051s; **3** Mark Martin, USA (Ford Taurus), 400 laps; **4** Ken Schrader, USA (Chevrolet Monte Carlo), 400; **5** John Andretti, USA (Pontiac Grand Prix), 400; **6** Bobby Hamilton, USA (Chevrolet Monte Carlo), 400; **7** Rusty Wallace, USA (Ford Taurus), 400; **8** Mike Skinner, USA (Chevrolet Monte Carlo), 400; **9** Jimmy Spencer, USA (Ford Taurus), 400; **10** Kenny Irwin Jr, USA (Ford Taurus), 400.
Fastest qualifying lap: Wallace, 21.535s, 125.377 mph/201.775 km/h.
Drivers' championship points: 1 Gordon, 3952; **2** Martin, 3748; **3** Jarrett, 3644; **4** Wallace (Rusty), 3477; **5** Burton (Jeff), 3298; **6** Labonte (Bobby), 3259.

MBNA GOLD 400, Dover Downs International Speedway, Dover, Delaware, USA, 20 September. Round 26. 400 laps of the 1.000-mile/1.609-km circuit, 400.000 miles/643.738 km.
1 Mark Martin, USA (Ford Taurus), 3h 30m 50.0s, 113.834 mph/183.198 km/h.
2 Jeff Gordon, USA (Chevrolet Monte Carlo), 3h 30m 52.036s; **3** Jeremy Mayfield, USA (Ford Taurus), 400 laps; **4** Bobby Labonte, USA (Pontiac Grand Prix), 400; **5** Rusty Wallace, USA (Ford Taurus), 400; **6** Matt Kenseth, USA (Ford Taurus), 400; **7** Dale Jarrett, USA (Ford Taurus), 400; **8** Ernie Irvan, USA (Pontiac Grand Prix), 400; **9** John Andretti, USA (Pontiac Grand Prix), 400; **10** Bobby Hamilton, USA (Chevrolet Monte Carlo), 399.
Fastest qualifying lap: Martin, 23.002s, 156.508 mph/251.875 km/h.
Drivers' championship points: 1 Gordon, 4127; **2** Martin, 3933; **3** Jarrett, 3790; **4** Wallace (Rusty), 3637; **5=** Labonte (Bobby), 3419; **5=** Mayfield, 3419.

NAPA AUTOCARE 500, Martinsville Speedway, Virginia, USA, 27 September. Round 27. 500 laps of the 0.526-mile/0.847-km circuit, 263.000 miles/423.257 km.
1 Ricky Rudd, USA (Ford Taurus), 3h 35m 08.0s, 73.350 mph/118.045 km/h.
2 Jeff Gordon, USA (Chevrolet Monte Carlo), 3h 35m 08.533s; **3** Mark Martin, USA (Ford Taurus), 500 laps; **4** Rich Bickle, USA (Ford Taurus), 500; **5** Jeff Burton, USA (Ford Taurus), 500; **6** Terry Labonte, USA (Chevrolet Monte Carlo), 500; **7** Bill Elliott, USA (Ford Taurus), 500; **8** Ernie Irvan, USA (Pontiac Grand Prix), 499; **9** Johnny Benson Jr, USA (Ford Taurus), 499; **10** Bobby Labonte, USA (Pontiac Grand Prix), 499.
Fastest qualifying lap: Irvan, 20.229s, 93.608 mph/150.648 km/h.
Drivers' championship points: 1 Gordon, 4297; **2** Martin, 4098; **3** Jarrett, 3827; **4** Wallace (Rusty), 3716; **5** Labonte (Bobby), 3553; **6** Mayfield, 3513.

UAW-GM QUALITY 500, Charlotte Motor Speedway, Concord, North Carolina, USA, 4 October. Round 28. 334 laps of the 1.500-mile/2.414-km circuit, 501.000 miles/806.281 km.
1 Mark Martin, USA (Ford Taurus), 4h 04m 01.0s, 123.188 mph/198.252 km/h.
2 Ward Burton, USA (Pontiac Grand Prix), 4h 04m 02.110s; **3** Jeff Burton, USA (Ford Taurus), 334 laps; **4** Bobby Hamilton, USA (Chevrolet Monte Carlo), 334; **5** Jeff Gordon, USA (Chevrolet Monte Carlo), 334; **6** Kevin Lepage, USA (Ford Taurus), 334; **7** Joe Nemechek, USA (Chevrolet Monte Carlo), 334; **8** Chad Little, USA (Ford Taurus), 334; **9** Geoff Bodine, USA (Ford Taurus), 334; **10** Jimmy Spencer, USA (Ford Taurus), 334.
Fastest qualifying lap: Derrike Cope, USA (Pontiac Grand Prix), 29.721s, 181.690 mph/292.401 km/h.
Drivers' championship points: 1 Gordon, 4457; **2** Martin, 4283; **3** Jarrett, 3918; **4** Wallace (Rusty), 3801; **5** Burton (Jeff), 3672; **6** Labonte (Bobby), 3604.

WINSTON 500, Talladega Superspeedway, Alabama, USA, 11 October. Round 29. 188 laps of the 2.660-mile/4.281-km circuit, 500.080 miles/804.801 km.
1 Dale Jarrett, USA (Ford Taurus), 3h 08m 20.0s, 159.318 mph/256.397 km/h.
2 Jeff Gordon, USA (Chevrolet Monte Carlo), 3h 08m 20.140s; **3** Terry Labonte, USA (Chevrolet Monte Carlo), 188 laps; **4** Jimmy Spencer, USA (Ford Taurus), 188; **5** Jeremy Mayfield, USA (Ford Taurus), 188; **6** Bobby Labonte, USA (Pontiac Grand Prix), 188; **7** Mike Skinner, USA (Chevrolet Monte Carlo), 188; **8** Chad Little, USA (Ford Taurus), 188; **9** Michael Waltrip, USA (Ford Taurus), 188; **10** Jeff Burton, USA (Ford Taurus), 188.
Fastest qualifying lap: Ken Schrader, USA (Chevrolet Monte Carlo), 48.819s, 196.153 mph/315.678 km/h.
Drivers' championship points: 1 Gordon, 4632; **2** Martin, 4349; **3** Jarrett, 4098; **4** Wallace (Rusty), 3883; **5** Burton (Jeff), 3806; **6** Mayfield, 3761.

PEPSI 400, Daytona International Speedway, Daytona Beach, Florida, USA, 17 October. Round 30. 160 laps of the 2.500-mile/4.023-km circuit, 400.000 miles/643.738 km.
1 Jeff Gordon, USA (Chevrolet Monte Carlo), 2h 46m 02.0s, 144.549 mph/232.630 km/h.
2 Bobby Labonte, USA (Pontiac Grand Prix), 2h 46m 02.176s; **3** Mike Skinner, USA (Chevrolet Monte Carlo), 160 laps; **4** Jeremy Mayfield, USA (Ford Taurus), 160; **5** Rusty Wallace, USA (Ford Taurus), 160; **6** Terry Labonte, USA (Chevrolet Monte Carlo), 160; **7** Ward Burton, USA (Pontiac Grand Prix), 160; **8** Ernie Irvan, USA (Pontiac Grand Prix), 160; **9** Ken Schrader, USA (Chevrolet Monte Carlo), 160; **10** Dale Earnhardt, USA (Chevrolet Monte Carlo), 160.
Fastest qualifying lap: Labonte (Bobby), 46.485s, 193.611 mph/311.586 km/h.
Drivers' championship points: 1 Gordon, 4817; **2** Martin, 4459; **3** Jarrett, 4197; **4** Wallace (Rusty), 4043; **5** Labonte (Bobby), 3934; **6** Burton (Jeff), 3930.

DURA LUBE 500 PRESENTED BY K MART, Phoenix International Raceway, Arizona, USA, 25 October. Round 31. 257 laps of the 1.000-mile/1.609-km circuit, 257.000 miles/413.601 km.
Race stopped early due to rain.
1 Rusty Wallace, USA (Ford Taurus), 2h 22m 30.0s, 108.211 mph/174.149 km/h.
2 Mark Martin, USA (Ford Taurus), 257 laps (under caution); **3** Dale Earnhardt, USA (Chevrolet Monte Carlo), 257; **4** Jeff Burton, USA (Ford Taurus), 257; **5** Ted Musgrave, USA (Ford Taurus), 257; **6** John Andretti, USA (Pontiac Grand Prix), 257; **7** Jeff Gordon, USA (Chevrolet Monte Carlo), 257; **8** Kenny Wallace, USA (Ford Taurus), 257; **9** Johnny Benson Jr, USA (Ford Taurus), 257; **10** Terry Labonte, USA (Chevrolet Monte Carlo), 257.
Fastest qualifying lap: Ken Schrader, USA (Chevrolet Monte Carlo), 27.432s, 131.234 mph/211.201 km/h.
Drivers' championship points: 1 Gordon, 4963; **2** Martin, 4634; **3** Jarrett, 4264; **4** Wallace (Rusty), 4228; **5** Burton (Jeff), 4095; **6** Labonte (Bobby), 4028.

AC-DELCO 400, North Carolina Motor Speedway, Rockingham, North Carolina, USA, 1 November. Round 32. 393 laps of the 1.017-mile/1.637-km circuit, 399.681 miles/643.224 km.
1 Jeff Gordon, USA (Chevrolet Monte Carlo), 3h 06m 44.0s, 128.423 mph/206.677 km/h.
2 Dale Jarrett, USA (Ford Taurus), 3h 06m 44.520s; **3** Rusty Wallace, USA (Ford Taurus), 393 laps; **4** Mark Martin, USA (Ford Taurus), 393; **5** Jeff Burton, USA (Ford Taurus), 393; **6** Bobby Hamilton, USA (Chevrolet Monte Carlo), 393; **7** Ward Burton, USA (Pontiac Grand Prix), 393; **8** Terry Labonte, USA (Chevrolet Monte Carlo), 393; **9** Dale Earnhardt, USA (Chevrolet Monte Carlo), 393; **10** Ricky Rudd, USA (Ford Taurus), 393.
Fastest qualifying lap: Martin, 23.394s, 156.502 mph/251.865 km/h.

NAPA 500, Atlanta Motor Speedway, Hampton, Georgia, USA, 8 November. Round 33. 221 laps of the 1.522-mile/2.449-km circuit, 336.362 miles/541.229 km.
Race shortened due to rain.
1 Jeff Gordon, USA (Chevrolet Monte Carlo), 2h 57m 42.0s, 114.915 mph/184.938 km/h.
2 Dale Jarrett, USA (Ford Taurus), 2h 57m 42.739s; **3** Mark Martin, USA (Ford Taurus), 221; **4** Jeff Burton, USA (Ford Taurus), 221; **5** Todd Bodine, USA (Chevrolet Monte Carlo), 221; **6** Bobby Hamilton, USA (Chevrolet Monte Carlo), 221; **7** Ken Schrader, USA (Chevrolet Monte Carlo), 221; **8** Terry Labonte, USA (Chevrolet Monte Carlo), 221; **9** Mike Skinner, USA (Chevrolet Monte Carlo), 221; **10** Geoff Bodine, USA (Ford Taurus), 221.
Fastest qualifying lap: Kenny Irwin Jr, USA (Ford Taurus), 28.657s, 193.461 mph/311.345 km/h.

Final championship points
Drivers
1 Jeff Gordon, USA, 5328; **2** Mark Martin, USA, 4964; **3** Dale Jarrett, USA, 4619; **4** Rusty Wallace, USA, 4501; **5** Jeff Burton, USA, 4415; **6** Bobby Labonte, USA, 4180; **7** Jeremy Mayfield, USA, 4157; **8** Dale Earnhardt, USA, 3928; **9** Terry Labonte, USA, 3901; **10** Bobby Hamilton, USA, 3786; **11** John Andretti, USA, 3682; **12** Ken Schrader, USA, 3675; **13** Sterling Marlin, USA, 3530; **14** Jimmy Spencer, USA, 3464; **15** Chad Little, USA, 3423; **16** Ward Burton, USA, 3352; **17** Michael Waltrip, USA, 3340; **18** Bill Elliott, USA, 3305; **19** Ernie Irvan, USA, 3262; **20** Johnny Benson Jr, USA, 3160; **21** Mike Skinner, USA, 3153; **22** Ricky Rudd, USA, 3131; **23** Ted Musgrave, USA, 3124; **24** Darrell Waltrip, USA, 2957; **25** Brett Bodine, USA, 2907; **26** Joe Nemechek, USA, 2897; **27** Geoff Bodine, USA, 2864; **28** Kenny Irwin Jr, USA, 2760; **29** Dick Trickle, USA, 2678; **30** Kyle Petty, USA, 2675.

Manufacturers
1 Chevrolet, 240; **2** Ford, 235; **3** Pontiac, 152.

Raybestos Rookie of The Year: Kenny Irwin
Bud Pole Award Winner: Jeff Gordon
MCI Fast Pace Award (fastest lap): Jeff Gordon

Other NASCAR Results

The Suzuka race was run after Autocourse 1997/98 *went to press.*

1997 Result

NASCAR SUZUKA THUNDER SPECIAL 100, Suzuka Circuitland, Suzuka City, Mie-Ken, Japan, 23 November. 125 laps of the 1.395-mile/2.245-km circuit, 174.375 miles/280.629 km.
1 Mike Skinner, USA (Chevrolet Monte Carlo), 2h 20m 22.0s, 74.537 mph/119.956 km/h.
2 Mark Martin, USA (Ford Thunderbird), 125 laps; **3** Randy Lajoie, USA (Chevrolet Monte Carlo), 125; **4** David Green, USA (Chevrolet Monte Carlo), 125; **5** Michael Waltrip, USA (Ford Thunderbird), 125; **6** Jim Richards, USA (Pontiac Grand Prix), 125; **7** Kenny Wallace, USA (Chevrolet Monte Carlo), 124; **8** Jack Sprague, USA (Chevrolet Monte Carlo), 123; **9** Butch Gilliland, USA (Ford Thunderbird), 123; **10** Geoff Bodine, USA (Ford Thunderbird), 123.
Fastest qualifying lap: Martin, 1m 02.279s, 80.637 mph/129.773 km/h.

1998 Results

THE BUD SHOOTOUT AT DAYTONA, Daytona International Speedway, Daytona Beach, Florida, USA, 8 February, 25 laps of the 2.500-mile/4.023-km circuit, 62.500 miles/100.584 km.
1 Rusty Wallace, USA (Ford Taurus), 20m 57.0s, 178.998 mph/288.069 km/h.
2 Kenny Wallace, USA (Ford Taurus), 25 laps; **3** Bill Elliott, USA (Ford Taurus), 25; **4** Jimmy Spencer, USA (Ford Taurus), 25; **5** Ken Schrader, USA (Chevrolet Monte Carlo), 25; **6** Geoff Bodine, USA (Ford Taurus), 25; **7** Ernie Irvan, USA (Pontiac Grand Prix), 25; **8** Mark Martin, USA (Ford Taurus), 25; **9** John Andretti, USA (Chevrolet Monte Carlo), 25; **10** Todd Bodine, USA (Pontiac Grand Prix), 25.

THE WINSTON, Charlotte Motor Speedway, Concord, North Carolina, USA, 16 May. 70 laps of the 1.500-mile/2.414-km circuit, 105.000 miles/168.981 km.
Run over three segments (30, 30 and 10 laps). Aggregate results given.
1 Mark Martin, USA (Ford Taurus), 36m 34.0s, 172.288 mph/277.271 km/h.
2 Bobby Labonte, USA (Pontiac Grand Prix) 36m 34.424s; **3** Dale Jarrett, USA (Ford Taurus), 70 laps; **4** Jeff Burton, USA (Ford Taurus), 70; **5** Rusty Wallace, USA (Ford Taurus), 70; **6** Sterling Marlin, USA (Chevrolet Monte Carlo), 70; **7** Bill Elliott, USA (Ford Taurus), 70; **8** Geoff Bodine, USA (Ford Taurus), 70; **9** Bobby Hamilton, USA (Chevrolet Monte Carlo), 70; **10** Rich Bickle, USA (Ford Taurus), 70.

Result of the Motegi race will be given in Autocourse 1999/2000.

PPG-Dayton Indy Lights Championship

All cars are Lola T98/20 GS-Buick.

HOMESTEAD INDY LIGHTS RACE, Metro-Dade Homestead Motorsports Complex, Florida, USA, 15 March. Round 1. 67 laps of the 1.502-mile/2.417-km circuit, 100.634 miles/161.955 km.
1 Shigeaki Hattori, J, 52m 35.077s, 114.825 mph/184.793 km/h.
2 Cristiano da Matta, BR, 52m 35.545s; **3** Guy Smith, GB, 52m 36.497s; **4** Oriol Servia, E, 36m 40.611s; **5** Chris Simmons, USA, 36m 40.930s; **6** Paul Morris, AUS, 36m 41.107s; **7** Derek Higgins, IRL, 36m 45.233s; **8** Rodolfo Lavin, MEX, 36m 45.813s; **9** Geoff Boss, USA, 36m 47.337s; **10** Casey Mears, USA, 36m 56.644s.
Most laps led: Hattori (Shigeaki), 64.
Fastest qualifying lap: Sergio Paese, BR, 30.098s, 179.653 mph/289.124 km/h.

LONG BEACH INDY LIGHTS RACE, Long Beach Street Circuit, California, USA, 4 April. Round 2. 47 laps of the 1.574-mile/2.533-km circuit, 73.978 miles/119.056 km.
1 Cristiano da Matta, BR, 49m 20.748s, 89.951 mph/144.761 km/h.
2 Geoff Boss, USA, 49m 21.207s; **3** Naoki Hattori, J, 49m 21.831s; **4** Philipp Peter, A, 49m 24.126s; **5** Didier Andre, F, 49m 28.065s; **6** Sergio Paese, BR, 49m 29.260s; **7** Mattias Andersson, S, 49m 30.148s; **8** Guy Smith, GB, 49m 30.528s; **9** Airton Dare, BR, 49m 32.963s; **10** Luiz Garcia Jr, BR, 49m 33.303s.
Most laps led: da Matta, 47.
Fastest qualifying lap: Andre, 57.108s, 99.223 mph/159.683 km/h.

NAZARETH INDY LIGHTS RACE, Nazareth Speedway, Pennsylvania, USA, 27 April. Round 3. 100 laps of the 0.946-mile/1.522-km circuit, 94.600 miles/152.244 km.
Scheduled for 26 April but postponed by a day due to rain.
1 Cristiano da Matta, BR, 55m 56.268s, 101.470 mph/163.300 km/h.
2 Didier Andre, F, 56m 10.442s; **3** Casey Mears, USA, 56m 11.013s; **4** Brian Cunningham, USA, 56m 14.182s; **5** Airton Dare, BR, 56m 14.993s; **6** Andy Boss, USA, 56m 15.551s; **7** Naoki Hattori, J, 56m 18.102s; **8** Felipe Giaffone, BR, 56m 18.606s; **9** Mark Hotchkis, USA, 56m 20.256s; **10** Tony Renna, USA, 99 laps.
Most laps led: da Matta, 100.
Fastest qualifying lap: da Matta, 22.408s, 151.981 mph/244.590 km/h.

GATEWAY INDY LIGHTS RACE, Gateway International Raceway, Madison, Illinois, USA, 23 May. Round 4. 79 laps of the 1.270-mile/2.044-km circuit, 100.330 mph/161.465 km/h.
1 Shigeaki Hattori, J, 55m 21.083s, 108.756 mph/175.026 km/h.
2 Philipp Peter, A, 55m 21.709s; **3** Cristiano da Matta, BR, 55m 22.711s; **4** Felipe Giaffone, BR, 55m 22.978s; **5** Jorge Goeters, MEX, 55m 23.278s; **6** Derek Higgins, IRL, 55m 23.510s; **7** Casey Mears, USA, 55m 24.801s; **8** Naoki Hattori, J, 55m 25.735s; **9** Airton Dare, BR, 55m 26.225s; **10** Sergio Paese, BR, 55m 26.544s.
Most laps led: Hattori (Shigeaki), 44.
Fastest qualifying lap: Goeters, 28.982s, 157.753 mph/253.879 km/h.

MILWAUKEE INDY LIGHTS RACE, The Milwaukee Mile, Wisconsin State Fair Park, West Allis, Milwaukee, Wisconsin, USA, 31 May. Round 5. 97 laps of the 1.032-mile/1.661-km circuit, 100.104 miles/161.102 km.
1 Derek Higgins, IRL, 51m 59.624s, 115.519 mph/185.909 km/h.
2 Felipe Giaffone, BR, 52m 05.865s; **3** Sergio Paese, BR, 52m 07.175s; **4** Geoff Boss, USA, 52m 07.430s; **5** Tony Renna, USA, 52m 07.463s; **6** Jorge Goeters, MEX, 52m 16.767s; **7** Mark Hotchkis, USA, 52m 17.350s; **8** Airton Dare, BR, 52m 21.827s; **9** Philipp Peter, A, 96 laps; **10** Cristiano da Matta, BR, 96.
Most laps led: Higgins, 45.
Fastest qualifying lap: Paese, 24.597s, 151.043 mph/243.080 km/h.

DETROIT INDY LIGHTS RACE, The Raceway at Belle Isle Park, Detroit, Michigan, USA, 7 June. Round 6. 32 laps of the 2.346-mile/3.776-km circuit, 75.072 miles/120.817 km.
1 Airton Dare, BR, 50m 29.610s, 89.206 mph/143.563 km/h.
2 Cristiano da Matta, BR, 50m 30.466s; **3** Geoff Boss, USA, 50m 35.931s; **4** Mark Hotchkis, USA, 50m 36.655s; **5** Didier Andre, F, 50m 45.565s; **6** Oriol Servia, E, 50m 50.559s; **7** Brian Cunningham, USA, 50m 55.460s; **8** Guy Smith, GB, 50m 55.713s; **9** Felipe Giaffone, BR, 51m 00.139s; **10** Philipp Peter, A, 51m 00.334s.
Most laps led: Dare, 32.
Fastest qualifying lap: Dare, 1m 22.525s, 102.340 mph/164.700 km/h.

PORTLAND INDY LIGHTS RACE, Portland International Raceway, Oregon, USA, 21 June. Round 7. 38 laps of the 1.967-mile/3.166-km circuit, 74.746 miles/120.292 km.
1 Guy Smith, GB, 56m 53.931s, 78.820 mph/126.848 km/h.
2 Felipe Giaffone, BR, 56m 54.428s; **3** Luiz Garcia Jr, BR, 56m 55.809s; **4** Airton Dare, BR, 56m 56.124s; **5** Brian Cunningham, USA, 56m 57.013s; **6** Sergio Paese, BR, 56m 57.706s; **7** Paul Morris, AUS, 56m 58.541s; **8** Didier Andre, F, 56m 59.121s; **9** Jorge Goeters, MEX, 56m 59.299s; **10** Derek Higgins, IRL, 57m 00.135s.
Most laps led: Smith, 38.
Fastest qualifying lap: Smith, 1m 06.117s, 107.101 mph/172.362 km/h.

CLEVELAND INDY LIGHTS RACE, Burke Lakefront Airport Circuit, Cleveland, Ohio, USA, 12 July. Round 8. 36 laps of the 2.106-mile/3.389-km circuit, 75.816 miles/122.014 km.
1 Luiz Garcia Jr, BR, 44m 36.384s, 101.980 mph/164.121 km/h.
2 Derek Higgins, IRL, 44m 38.204s; **3** Didier Andre, F, 44m 39.961s; **4** Guy Smith, GB, 44m 40.775s; **5** Tony Renna, USA, 44m 42.709s; **6** Oriol Servia, E, 44m 43.801s; **7** Philipp Peter, A, 44m 43.867s; **8** Felipe Giaffone, BR, 44m 44.567s; **9** Jorge Goeters, MEX, 44m 44.881s; **10** Casey Mears, USA, 44m 47.527s.
Most laps led: Garcia Jr, 36.
Fastest qualifying lap: Garcia Jr, 1m 05.010s, 116.622 mph/187.685 km/h.

TORONTO INDY LIGHTS RACE, Exposition Place Circuit, Toronto, Ontario, Canada, 19 July. Round 9. 43 laps of the 1.721-mile/2.770-km circuit, 74.003 miles/119.096 km.
1 Guy Smith, GB, 47m 59.761s, 92.511 mph/148.883 km/h.
2 Naoki Hattori, J, 48m 01.172s; **3** Chris Simmons, USA, 48m 07.780s; **4** Philipp Peter, A, 48m 18.858s; **5** Didier Andre, F, 48m 20.514s; **6** Felipe Giaffone, BR, 48m 21.816s; **7** Jorge Goeters, MEX, 48m 23.525s; **8** Airton Dare, BR, 48m 24.879s; **9** Sergio Paese, BR, 48m 33.466s; **10** Oriol Servia, E, 48m 34.524s.
Most laps led: Smith, 43.
Fastest qualifying lap: Smith, 1m 05.162s, 95.080 mph/153.016 km/h.

BROOKLYN INDY LIGHTS RACE, Michigan Speedway, Brooklyn, Michigan, USA, 25 July. Round 10. 50 laps of the 2.000-mile/3.219-km circuit, 100.000 miles/160.934 km.
1 Tony Renna, USA, 45m 34.943s, 131.630 mph/211.838 km/h.
2 Cristiano da Matta, BR, 45m 35.535s; **3** Sergio Paese, BR, 45m 36.644s; **4** Andy Boss, USA, 45m 37.457s; **5** Oriol Servia, E, 45m 38.150s; **6** Guy Smith, GB, 45m 38.971s; **7** Didier Andre, F, 45m 40.045s; **8** Clint Mears, USA, 45m 41.116s; **9** Felipe Giaffone, BR, 45m 41.933s; **10** Chris Simmons, USA, 45m 42.623s.
Most laps led: Renna, 43.
Fastest qualifying lap: Renna, 39.119s, 184.054 mph/296.206 km/h.

LE GRAND PRIX PLAYER'S DE TROIS-RIVIÈRES, Trois-Rivières, Quebec, Canada, 2 August. Round 11. 50 laps of the 1.521-mile/2.448-km circuit, 76.050 miles/122.391 km.
1 Cristiano da Matta, BR, 58m 16.612s, 78.299 mph/126.009 km/h.
2 Oriol Servia, E, 58m 17.922s; **3** Naoki Hattori, J, 50 laps; **4** Guy Smith, GB, 50; **5** Didier Andre, F, 50; **6** Felipe Giaffone, BR, 50; **7** Mark Hotchkis, USA, 50; **8** Chris Simmons, USA, 50; **9** Paul Morris, AUS, 50; **10** Derek Higgins, IRL, 50.
Most laps led: da Matta, 50.
Fastest qualifying lap: da Matta, 58.716s, 93.256 mph/150.080 km/h.

VANCOUVER INDY LIGHTS RACE, Vancouver Street Circuit, Concord Pacific Place, Vancouver, British Columbia, Canada, 6 September. Round 12. 42 laps of the 1.802 mile/2.900-km circuit, 75.684 miles/121.802 km.
1 Cristiano da Matta, BR, 59m 26.074s, 76.404 mph/122.960 km/h.
2 Derek Higgins, IRL, 59m 29.530s; **3** Airton Dare, BR, 59m 29.837s; **4** Mike Borkowski, USA, 59m 31.119s; **5** Felipe Giaffone, BR, 59m 31.900s; **6** Didier Andre, F, 59m 32.007s; **7** Geoff Boss, USA, 59m 32.225s; **8** Guy Smith, GB, 59m 33.818s; **9** Philipp Peter, A, 59m 34.302s; **10** Brian Cunningham, USA, 59m 34.783s.
Most laps led: da Matta, 42.
Fastest qualifying lap: da Matta, 1m 10.441s, 92.094 mph/148.211 km/h.

MONTEREY INDY LIGHTS RACE, Laguna Seca Raceway, Monterey, California, USA, 13 September. Round 13. 34 laps of the 2.238-mile/3.602-km circuit, 76.092 miles/122.458 km.
1 Didier Andre, F, 49m 53.011s, 91.524 mph/147.293 km/h.
2 Oriol Servia, E, 49m 55.729s; **3** Derek Higgins, IRL, 49m 56.101s; **4** Geoff Boss, USA, 49m 57.444s; **5** Naoki Hattori, J, 49m 58.313s; **6** Luiz Garcia Jr, BR, 49m 59.031s; **7** Mario Dominguez, MEX, 49m 59.394s; **8** Tony Renna, USA, 50m 00.635s; **9** Shigeaki Hattori, J, 50m 01.545s; **10** Clint Mears, USA, 50m 02.336s.
Most laps led: Andre, 34.
Fastest qualifying lap: Andre, 1m 15.747s, 106.365 mph/171.177 km/h.

FONTANA INDY LIGHTS RACE, California Speedway, Fontana, California, USA, 31 October. Round 14. 50 laps of the 2.029-mile/3.265-km circuit, 101.450 miles/163.268 km.
1 Mark Hotchkis, USA, 39m 40.916s, 153.395 mph/246.865 km/h.
2 Felipe Giaffone, BR, 39m 41.289s; **3** Tony Renna, USA, 39m 41.668s; **4** Cory Witherill, USA, 39m 41.772s; **5** Didier Andre, F, 39m 41.782s; **6** Luiz Garcia Jr, BR, 39m 41.828s; **7** Derek Higgins, IRL, 39m 41.873s; **8** Casey Mears, USA, 39m 41.955s; **9** Shigeaki Hattori, J, 39m 41.993s; **10** Guy Smith, GB, 39m 42.013s.
Most laps led: Renna, 31.
Fastest qualifying lap: Renna, 38.922s, 187.668 mph/302.022 km/h.

Final championship points
1 Cristiano da Matta, BR, 154; **2** Didier Andre, F, 123; **3** Guy Smith, GB, 110; **4** Felipe Giaffone, BR, 104; **5** Derek Higgins, IRL, 94; **6** Airton Dare, BR, 78; **7** Oriol Servia, E, 73; **8** Tony Renna, USA, 68; **9** Geoff Boss, USA, 67; **10** Naoki Hattori, J, 66; **11** Philipp Peter, A, 62; **12** Luiz Garcia Jr, BR, 60; **13** Sergio Paese, BR, 53; **14** Shigeaki Hattori, J, 52; **15** Mark Hotchkis, USA, 50; **16** Jorge Goeters, MEX, 34; **17=** Brian Cunningham, USA, 33; **17=** Casey Mears, USA, 33; **19** Chris Simmons, USA, 32; **20** Andy Boss, USA, 22; **21** Paul Morris, AUS, 18; **22** Mike Borkowski, USA, 15; **23** Cory Witherill, USA, 13; **24** Clint Mears, USA, 8; **25=** Mattias Andersson, S, 6; **25=** Mario Dominguez, MEX, 6; **27** Rodolfo Lavin, MEX, 5; **28=** Bud Kaeding, USA, 1; **28=** Wim Eyckmans, B, 1.

Elf Nations Cup
1 Brazil, 243; **2** United States, 180; **3** France, 123; **4** England, 110; **5** Japan, 107; **6** Ireland, 94; **7** Spain, 73; **8** Austria, 62; **9** Mexico, 45; **10** Australia, 15; **11** Sweden, 6; **12** Belgium, 1.

Rookie of the year
1 Guy Smith; **2** Derek Higgins; **3** Oriol Servia; **4** Tony Renna; **5** Philipp Peter.